The HP-GL/2 and HP RTL Reference Guide
Third Edition

A Handbook for Program Developers

HEWLETT ®
PACKARD

ADDISON-WESLEY

An imprint of Addison Wesley Longman, Inc.

Reading, Massachusetts · Harlow, England · Menlo Park, California
Berkeley, California · Don Mills, Ontario · Sydney
Bonn · Amsterdam · Tokyo · Mexico City

Notices

First edition, April 1990
(published as *The HP-GL/2 Reference Guide*)
Second edition, November 1993
(*The HP-GL/2 and HP RTL Reference Guide*)
both editions with HP part number 5959–9733
Third edition, July 1997
with HP part number 5961–3526.

Library of Congress Cataloging-in-Publication Data

The HP-GL/2 and HP RTL reference guide :
a handbook for program developers /
Hewlett-Packard -- 3rd ed.
p. cm.
Includes index.
ISBN 0–201–31014–7
1. HP-GL/2 (Computer program language)
2. RTL (Computer program language)
3. Computer graphics. I. Hewlett-Packard.
QA76.73.H6H6 1997
006.6'6--dc21   97–25185
                                  CIP

1 2 3 4 5 6 7 8 9 –MA– 0100999897
First printing, July 1997

Trademarks

The information in this book was prepared by:
Hewlett-Packard Company
Barcelona Division
Attn: Learning Products Dept.
Avda. Graells, 501
08190 Sant Cugat del Vallès
Barcelona
Spain

Technical comments on the content are welcomed; please use the comment form at the back of the book.

The publisher offers discounts on this book when ordered in quantity for special sales.

For more information please contact:
Corporate & Professional Publishing Group
Addison Wesley Longman
One Jacob Way
Reading, Massachusetts 01867
U.S.A.

Contents

List of Figures

Preface

This is a generic guide to HP-GL/2 (Hewlett-Packard's standardized Graphics Language) and HP RTL (Hewlett-Packard's Raster Transfer Language) supported by many HP graphics peripherals. This manual describes each of the instructions of HP-GL/2 and each of the commands of HP RTL, without relying on a specific device or technology.

You must use a programming language in addition to HP-GL/2 or HP RTL. However, this book will not teach you how to program your computer. Your method of programming will depend on your computer system, the programming language you use, and your level of expertise. This book, though, does give recommendations on getting the most from your device.

Organization of this Book

This book describes how to write programs using HP-GL/2 and HP RTL.

PART 1 deals with general concepts and principles.

— **Chapter 1** on page 3 describes the concepts needed to create programs that use HP-GL/2 and HP RTL, including plotting concepts, vector and raster images, defining the limits of your picture, the coordinate system used, units of measure, and switching from one plotting context to another.

PART 2 describes HP-GL/2.

— **Chapter 2** on page 17 describes the groups of instructions that make up HP-GL/2, the status of the pen and its location, how to scale pictures, and the notation used to define HP-GL/2 instructions.

— **Chapter 3** on page 29 describes the HP-GL/2 kernel, that is, the core set of instructions supported by all HP-GL/2 devices. Each group is explained in detail, with examples. The HP-GL/2 print model is also described.

— **Chapter 4** on page 77 describes the groups of extension instructions, that are provided for specific types of peripheral devices.

— **Chapter 5** on page 95 starts with a reference summary of all the HP-GL/2 instructions, in alphabetical order of their names, and is followed by a complete description of all the HP-GL/2 instructions, in alphabetical order of their two-letter acronyms.

— **Chapter 6** on page 331 summarizes the elements of HP-GL/2 that are dependent on the device in use.

PART 3 describes HP RTL.

— **Chapter 7** on page 337 describes the concepts needed to create HP RTL raster programs. It includes a description of the notation used to define HP RTL commands.

— **Chapter 8** on page 341 explains how to set the limits of your images, how to set the image resolution, how to scale images, and also describes the coordinate system used for placing images on the page.

— **Chapter 9** on page 351 describes how to define colors, the use of color modes and palettes, and how to use indexes to select colors. It also explains how to use patterns.

- **Chapter 10** on page 365 describes the interactions between picture elements. It explains how patterns and texture relate to raster images through logical operations, the default print model, and image and pattern transparency.

- **Chapter 11** on page 373 describes how to transfer raster data to the device. It includes a description of what happens when overflow occurs, and the various supported methods of compressing data.

- **Chapter 12** on page 389 describes the interactions between HP RTL and physical device settings, HP-GL/2, and PJL.

- **Chapter 13** on page 395 contains some examples of HP RTL raster programs.

- **Chapter 14** on page 401 lists, in alphabetical order of their names, the HP RTL commands used in raster programs.

- **Chapter 15** on page 453 contains a summary of the features of HP RTL that may vary from device to device.

PART 4 consists of some general appendixes.

- **Appendix A** on page 459 has some programming hints on getting the best from your system.

- **Appendix B** on page 473 lists the logical operations used in HP-GL/2 and HP RTL.

- **Appendix C** on page 475 lists the font *kind* and *value* parameters used in the HP-GL/2 AD (Alternate Font Definition) and SD (Standard Font Definition) instructions.

A **Glossary** of terms and abbreviations and an **Index** follow at the end of the book.

Terms and Conventions Used in this Book

In this book, numbers are expressed using SI (International System of Units) standards. Numbers with more than four digits are placed in groups of three, separated by a space instead of a comma, counting to both sides of the decimal point (for example, 54 321.123 45).

All references to the RS-232-C interface apply equally to the CCITT V.24 interface.

BOLDFACE type denotes an ASCII control character, such as **ESC** (escape), **CR** (carriage return), **LF** (line feed), or **ETX** (end-of-text). See page 67.

See page 26 (for HP-GL/2) and page 338 (for HP RTL) for descriptions of other notational conventions used in this book. The term *instruction* refers to the interface with HP-GL/2; the term *command* is used consistently to refer to the interface with HP RTL or PCL. See the *Glossary* on page 483 for explanations of other terms used.

Additional Documentation

The *PCL 5 Printer Language Technical Reference Manual*, HP part number 5961–0509, describes the commands of PCL 5.

The *PCL 5 Comparison Guide*, HP part number 5961–0602, describes which HP-GL/2 instructions are supported on HP LaserJet series printers.

The Product Comparison Guide for HP Languages on HP Plotters and Large-Format Printers, HP part number 5959–9734, shows the differences between the implementations of HP-GL/2 and HP RTL on various HP devices.

The *PJL Technical Reference Manual*, HP part number 5010–3999, describes the Printer Job Language.

PART 1: Introduction to Plotting and Printing Using HP-GL/2 and HP RTL

This Part contains the following sections:

Chapter 1: Plotting and Printing

There are three types of object that you may want to print or plot on your HP device: vectors, images, and characters.

Vector objects are composed of straight lines, and are normally defined using the instructions of HP-GL/2. Combinations of straight lines can be used to form rectangles and other polygons. They can also be used to create curves—HP-GL/2 contains instructions that let you create arcs, circles, ellipses, and more complex curves. You can also use HP-GL/2 instructions to fill areas with patterns of various types. HP-GL/2 is also used to define the *logical page*, *picture frame*, or *window*, which is that part of the physical page on which objects are placed.

Characters are normally printed using the commands of the PCL Printer Language, which give you access to a wide range of character sets (*fonts*). PCL also allows you to define graphics limits. See the *PCL 5 Printer Language Technical Reference Manual* for more information about these commands. HP-GL/2 can also be used to create character labels (text) that appear on drawings.

Image objects, such as scanned photographs or other objects, are normally placed on the page using the commands of Hewlett-Packard's Raster Transfer Language, HP RTL. You can also use HP RTL to shade areas. HP RTL is essentially a subset of PCL.

A fundamental difference between HP-GL/2 and HP RTL is that the former is normally used to create the data as well as control its positioning, whereas the latter never creates data. HP RTL's data normally comes from sources like scanned images.

You can use HP-GL/2 in conjunction with either PCL or HP RTL to create different parts of a single drawing or picture, or to create consecutive pages in different environments. There are commands and instructions that allow you to switch from one environment to another. Plotters and printers that support both HP-GL/2 and HP RTL or PCL are described as *dual-context* devices.

Printing with HP-GL/2 requires leaving the PCL or HP RTL mode and entering HP-GL/2 mode. Switching between modes involves only a few commands or instructions, and software applications may easily switch between the modes as needed.

HP-GL/2 graphics may be created within application software, or imported from existing applications. For various types of images (many technical drawings and business graphics, for example), it is advantageous to use vector graphics instead of raster graphics. The advantages include faster I/O transfer of large objects and smaller disk storage requirements.

As a guideline, use raster graphics for small, complex images, or those images that cannot be accomplished with HP-GL/2 (such as scanned photographs). Use HP-GL/2 for images that would involve a large amount of I/O data transfer if printed using raster graphics, or for drawings that are already in HP-GL/2 format. If the image is easier to describe using vectors instead of raster lines, it usually prints faster using HP-GL/2.

Further detailed discussion of PCL is beyond the scope of this book, except where it directly interacts with HP-GL/2 and HP RTL; for more information about PCL, refer to the books listed in the *Preface* on page xviii.

Vectors and Raster Images

Your plotter or printer produces output from two types of data: vector or raster. ***Vector data*** defines the data as a series of straight lines, or vectors; ***raster data*** defines it in terms of the ***pixels***, or dots, that make up the image. As you can see in the following example, even straight lines are composed of a series of dots in raster images.

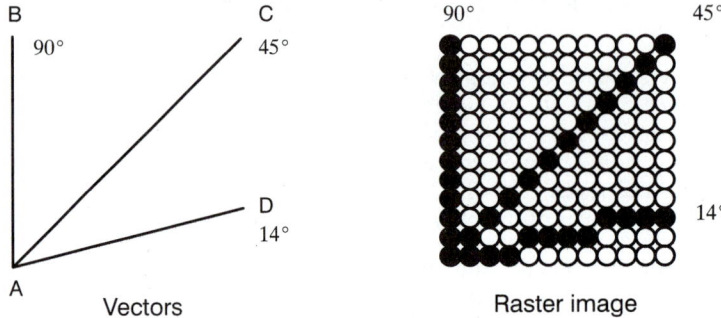

Figure 1. Vectors and Raster Images

Pen plotters are vector devices; that is, they receive vector data and produce vector output. Printers, both ink-jet and laser, and ink-jet and electrostatic plotters are raster devices. However, not all raster devices accept and handle data the same way. For example, your raster device may be able to accept vector data, which it then converts into raster data before printing or plotting. Additionally, your raster device *may* be able to accept raster data directly, thereby saving the processing time of vector-to-raster conversion, which may be significant.

Graphics Limits

The ***physical page*** is the actual piece (sheet or roll) of media, the paper or other substance on which the device is to print or plot its output. The term is also used to refer to the size of the media.

The area available for printing or plotting usually does not extend to the limits of your paper or other media. There is a physical limit beyond which your device cannot draw. This limit provides a neat margin for holding the media, and prevents the smearing of ink by pen-plotter pinch rollers and the loss of vacuum on electrostatic plotters and printers.

The device recognizes two types of graphics limits:

- Hard-clip limits
- Soft-clip limits.

Hard-clip limit refers to a physical boundary beyond which, for example, a pen cannot move. ***Soft-clip limit*** refers to a boundary set by a program, and allows pen movement only within its borders. Similarly, ink-jet and other plotters and printers have physical limits and program-set limits beyond which no plotting or printing occurs. You can set soft-clip limits at any time in your program. When you switch on or initialize the device, the hard-clip and soft-clip limits are the same.

Hard-Clip Limits

The hard-clip limits represent the physical boundary beyond which the device cannot plot or print data. These are device-dependent boundaries. Some devices can automatically sense the media size and set the hard-clip limits inside the media edges. One margin is often larger than the others; refer to the documentation for your device for details of page sizes. The hard-clip limits are also referred to as the *logical page*.

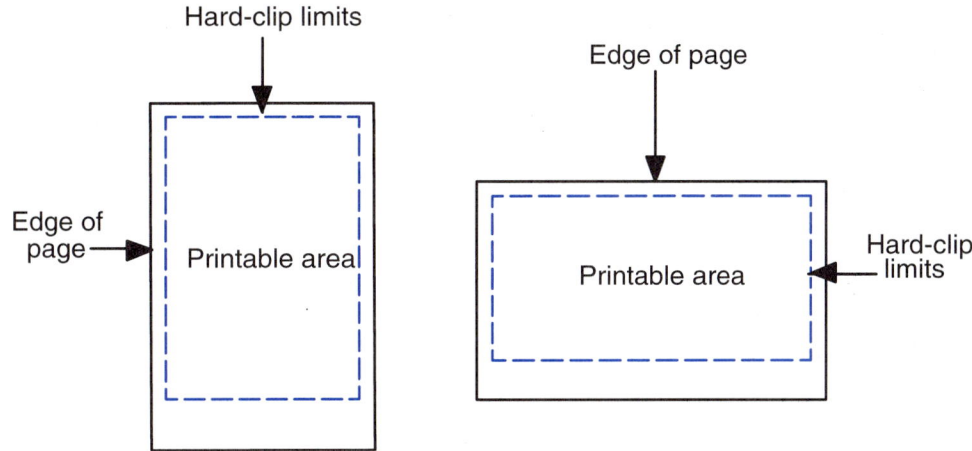

Figure 2. Hard-Clip Limits

Soft-Clip Limits

Soft-clip limits temporarily restrict the positioning of data to a specified area of the page. These limits let you draw attention to a particular set of data and they are often called *windows*. Usually soft-clip limits ensure that nothing is drawn beyond a particular portion of the page.

For example, look at the following sketch of a public library:

Figure 3. Image Before Applying Soft-Clip Limits

After printing the full picture, suppose that you decide to draw a new picture showing only the entrance area, using the space around it for text. To create the new image, just add soft-clip limits to temporarily restrict printing to the part that you want. Then add instructions to your program to extend the soft-clip limits and add the text. Refer to Figure 4:

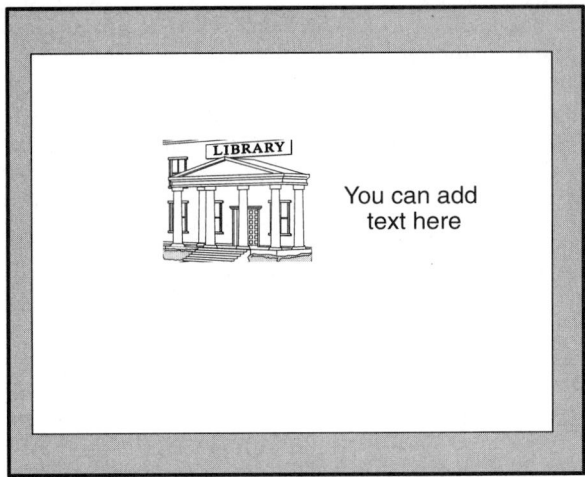

Figure 4. Image After Applying Soft-Clip Limits

Effective Window

The effective window is the area where the hard- and soft-clip limits overlap.

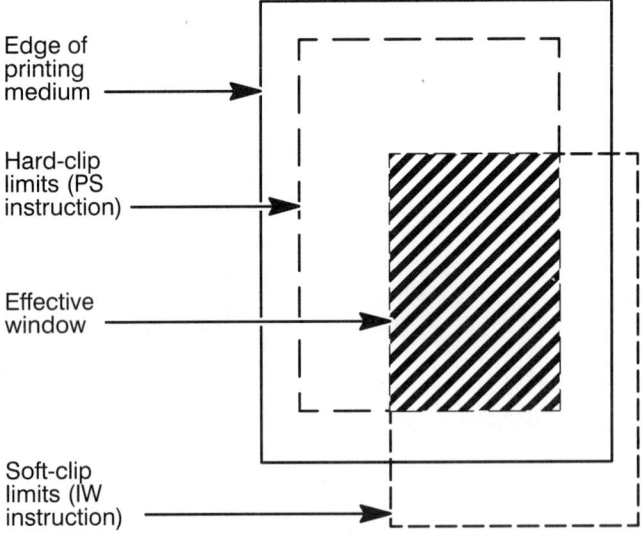

Figure 5. Hard-Clip and Soft-Clip Limits and the Effective Window

The Coordinate System

HP-GL/2, PCL, and HP RTL all use a Cartesian Coordinate System, which is a grid formed by two perpendicular axes, usually called the X-axis and Y-axis (refer to Figure 6). The intersection of the axes is called the origin of the system and has a location of (0,0).

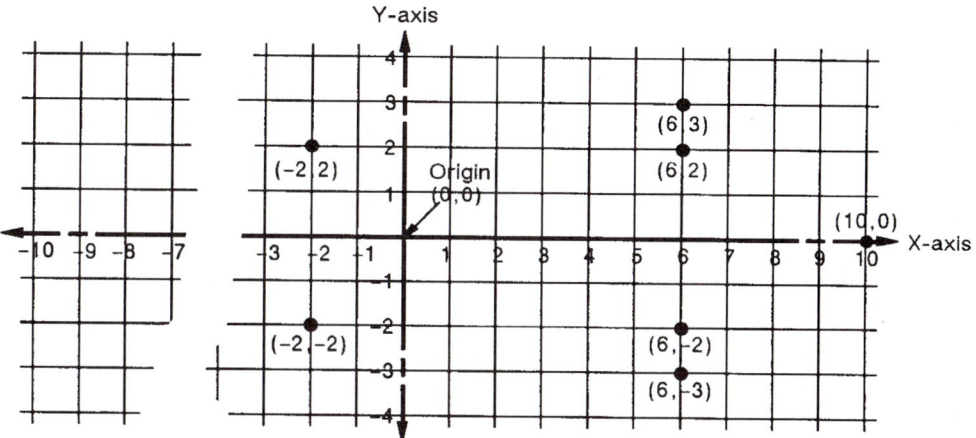

Figure 6. Coordinate System

To locate any point on the grid, move from the origin a number of units along the X-axis, then move a number of units parallel to the Y-axis. The number of units you move matches a coordinate location. Each point is designated by the combination of its X-coordinate and Y-coordinate, known as an X,Y coordinate pair. In the figure above, positive X values are plotted to the right of the origin, and positive Y values are plotted above the origin.

Study the figure above to locate these points: (0,0); (−2,2); (6,2); (6,3); (10,0); (6,−3); (6,−2); (−2,−2); (0,0). Draw a straight line between each point in the order listed; you should have drawn an arrow pointing right. This is a simple demonstration of how to define a vector picture in HP-GL/2 mode.

Note: To specify a point when programming an application, you must always give a complete X,Y coordinate pair; the X coordinate is first and the Y coordinate second. This book shows coordinate pairs in parentheses (X,Y) for clarity. **Do not use parentheses in your instruction sequence**.

Printers and Plotters

Originally there was a clear distinction between "printers"—devices on which text could be drawn—and "plotters"—devices for producing principally line drawings. Today the distinction is much more blurred, and devices that are functionally very similar can carry either name.

In the context of HP-GL/2, there are two families of devices that behave somewhat differently, and in this book we use the terms "printers" and "plotters" to distinguish them. Briefly, *plotters* are devices that support the Technical Graphics Extension of HP-GL/2, while *printers* are devices that do not. One of these differences is the orientation of the X and Y axes of their default coordinate systems. This is more fully described in the next section.

Using the default HP-GL/2 coordinate system, the origin for "printers" is in the *lower-left* corner of the window, as shown in the figure below. Using the IP or IR instruction, you can move the origin to other locations. Then, using the SC instruction, you can define practically any units for your coordinate system. See *Using Scaling Effectively* on page 33.

In HP-GL/2 for "plotters" using portrait orientation, the origin is in the *upper-left* corner, and increasing Y-values go *across* the page. In HP-GL/2 for "plotters" using landscape orientation, the origin is in the *upper-right* corner, and increasing Y-values go *down* the page. See Figure 8.

In HP RTL and PCL, the origin is in the *upper-left* corner, and increasing Y-values go *down* the page. The HP RTL coordinate system is described in *The Current Active Position (CAP)* on page 347, and interactions between different coordinate systems are explained below. Adapting the HP-GL/2 system to match PCL and HP RTL is described on pages 37 and 38.

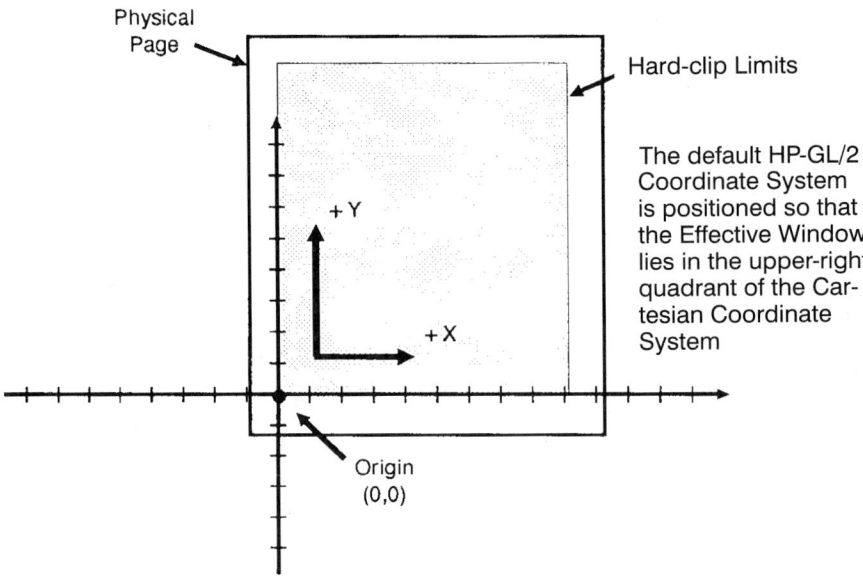

Figure 7. Origin of Coordinates for Printers

Interactions between Different Coordinate Systems

The default PCL and HP RTL coordinate systems are different from the default HP-GL/2 coordinate system; furthermore, the default system in HP-GL/2 differs for devices that support the HP-GL/2 Technical Graphics Extension (see page 77; devices termed "*plotters*" in Figure 8) and those that do not ("*printers*" in Figure 8).

For devices that support the Technical Graphics Extension, the page size is determined by the PS (Plot Size) instruction; for other devices, the page size is the picture frame size imported from PCL. In addition, the default origin is at different places, depending on the context (PCL, HP RTL, or HP-GL/2), the device type ("plotter" or "printer"), and the orientation (portrait or landscape) of the paper feed. The directions of +X and +Y also differ.

The HP-GL/2 coordinate system can be set up to match the PCL and HP RTL coordinate systems; see the examples on pages 37 and 38.

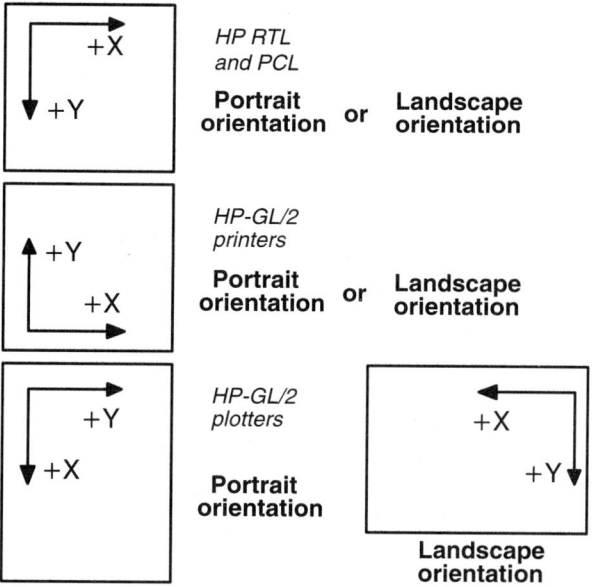

Figure 8. HP RTL, PCL, and HP-GL/2 Coordinate Systems; the "orientation" refers to the paper-feed direction

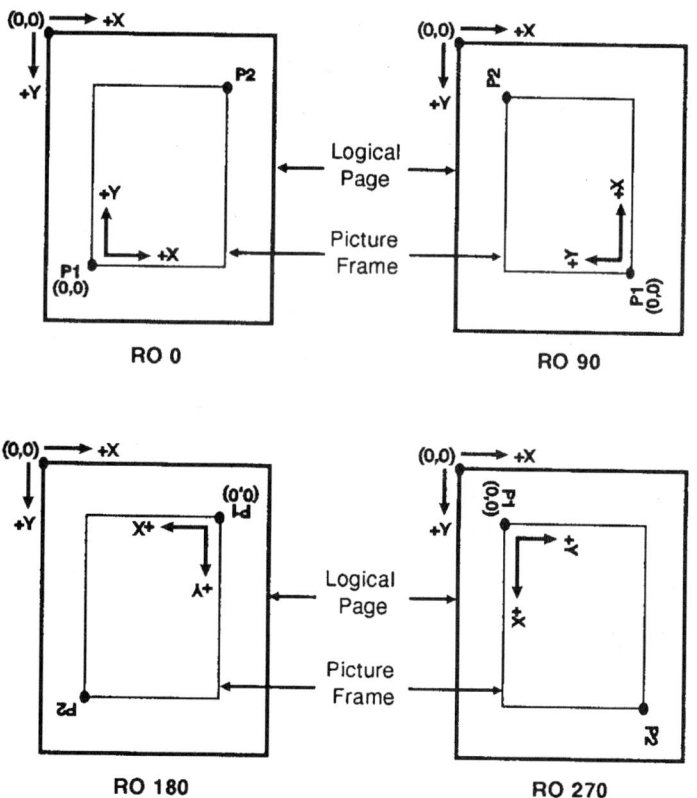

Figure 9. Effects of Rotation on the Coordinate System

The relationship between the orientation of the HP-GL/2 coordinate system and the PCL or HP RTL coordinate system is important if you are using PCL or HP RTL with HP-GL/2. Figure 9 illustrates this relationship for the default HP-GL/2 orientation for "printers" and the PCL logical page orientation. As shown in the illustration, in this HP-GL/2 orientation, the origin of the HP-GL/2 coordinate system defaults to the lower-left corner of the PCL picture frame. (The HP-GL/2 and PCL X-coordinates increase in the same direction, but the Y-coordinates increase in opposite directions.) Notice that a change in the PCL logical page orientation changes the orientation of the PCL coordinate system and the HP-GL/2 coordinate system.

The relationship between the coordinate systems can be changed using the HP-GL/2 RO (Rotate) instruction. Rotations specified by the RO instruction are relative to the default HP-GL/2 orientation (which matches the PCL orientation). Figure 9 shows how the RO instruction modifies the HP-GL/2 orientation relative to the logical page; the outer rectangles represent the PCL coordinates, the inner ones those of HP-GL/2; P1 and P2 are defined on page 31.

Note: A change in PCL print direction has no effect on the HP-GL/2 orientation, the physical position of the picture frame, or the picture frame anchor point.

Absolute and Relative Movement

HP-GL/2, PCL, and HP RTL all have the concept of a current position; in HP-GL/2, this is called the ***current pen location***; in PCL and HP RTL, it is the ***current active position***.

The PA (Plot Absolute) and PR (Plot Relative) instructions of HP-GL/2 allow you to specify whether you want to draw using absolute or relative "pen" moves. ***Absolute*** movement uses X,Y coordinates to specify an exact, fixed point relative to the origin (0,0). In Figure 10, the coordinates (3,8), (5,4), and (8,1) are always in the same place with respect to the origin, no matter where the pen is when the coordinates are issued.

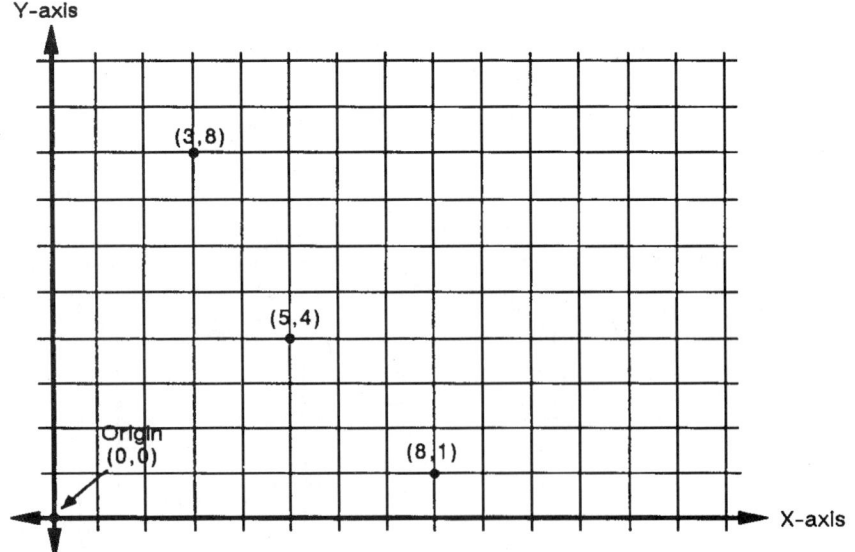

Figure 10. Absolute Movement

Relative movement uses X,Y increments to specify the number of units that the pen moves from its current pen location. All HP-GL/2 instructions that use relative increments include "relative" in their name, except the PE (Polyline Encoded) instruction. An example is the ER (Edge Rectangle Relative) instruction.

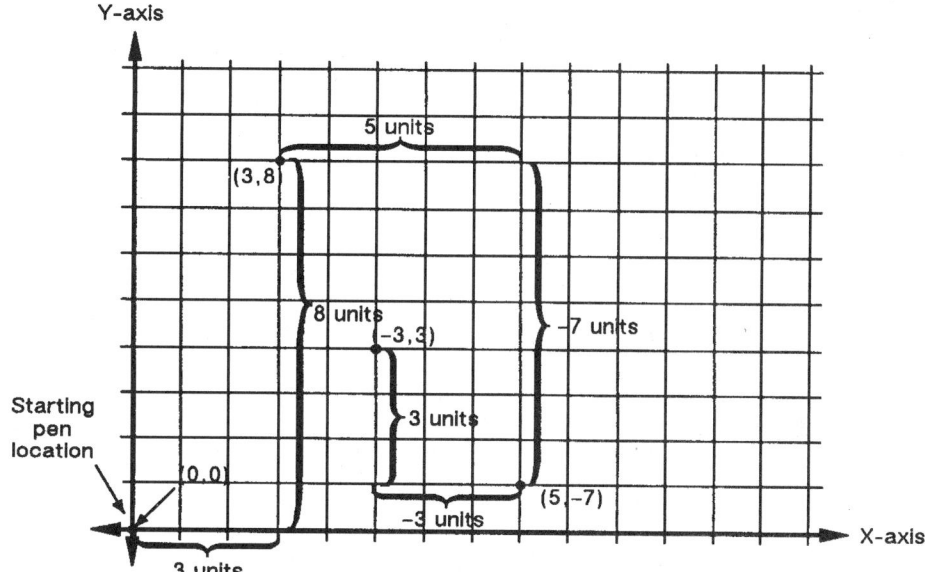

Figure 11. Relative Movement

In Figure 11, for example, assume that the pen is currently at the origin (0,0). To move to the absolute points shown in the previous figure using relative coordinates, count 3 units to the right and 8 units up from the current pen location; these are both positive directions with respect to the origin. This is the relative location (3,8). Now move 5 positive X-units and 7 negative Y-units from this location to the lower point; this is the relative location (5,–7). From this location, move to the last point by moving 3 negative X-units and 3 positive Y-units: (–3,3).

Relative movement is useful in many applications where you know the dimensions of the shape you want, but do not want to calculate the absolute coordinates. For example, if you want a box 4 X-units by 8 Y-units, you can use the ER (Edge Rectangle Relative) instruction to draw the box without having to calculate the absolute coordinates of the opposite corner. (The ER instruction draws a rectangle using the current pen location as one corner, and the specified relative coordinates as the opposite corner.)

Absolute pen movement is the default mode; coordinates received within a PU (Pen Up) or PD (Pen Down) instruction are interpreted as absolute plotter-units unless a PR (Plot Relative) instruction has established relative mode. As with absolute coordinates, the relative units can be either user-units or plotter-units (see page 12), depending on whether the SC (Scale) instruction is in effect.

Note: Relative increments are added to the current pen location. The device automatically converts the new relative location to absolute coordinates and updates the current pen location. Therefore, since relative movement can cause some rounding if scaled coordinates are not integers, absolute movement or integers should be used to guarantee end-points. Using relative coordinates can be faster in cases where the I/O speed limits your print speed, since relative coordinates are generally smaller numbers and therefore need less data to be transmitted over the I/O interface.

Units of Measure

HP-GL/2, PCL, and HP RTL use different systems for measuring units. See the *PCL 5 Printer Language Technical Reference Manual* for information on PCL units of measure.

HP-GL/2 Units of Measure

In HP-GL/2 you can measure along the X,Y axes and express coordinates using two types of units: *plotter-units* and *user-units*.

One *plotter-unit* equals 0.025 mm. When you specify distances in plotter-units, the device converts the number of plotter-units to equivalent coordinate points before printing. Under default conditions, the device uses plotter-units.

The following table lists equivalent measurements for plotter-units.

Plotter-units	Equivalent Value
1 plotter-unit =	0.025 mm ($\approx$ 0.00098 inch)
40 plotter-units =	1 mm
1016 plotter-units =	1 inch
3.39 plotter-units =	1 dot at 300 dots per inch

User-units: The size of units along the X and Y axes may be redefined using the SC (Scale) instruction; see *Scaling* on page 24 and the description of the SC instruction on page 290. User-units allow you to customize the coordinate system to represent any value. For example, you could plot the moon cycle for the year by dividing the X-axis into 31 units for days of the month and the Y-axis into 12 units for months of the year. To mark a point on December 25, you would give the coordinate (25,12) rather than calculating the exact location in plotter-units.

Before printing, the device internally converts user-units to coordinate points.

Internally, the device uses a different unit of measure. It maps HP-GL/2, HP RTL, and PCL units to this unit of measure. This internal unit is device-dependent, typically 1/7200 inch. All positioning is kept in internal units and rounded to physical dot positions when data is printed.

HP RTL Units of Measure

In HP RTL (and also PCL), coordinates are normally specified in terms of the *native resolution* of the device. You can also specify the dimensions of HP RTL images in *decipoints* (1/720-inch). See *Setting the Width and Height in HP RTL* on page 342.

Isotropic and Anisotropic Scaling

When you alter the scale of an image, you can indicate whether units are of equal size on the X- and Y-axes (*isotropic* scaling) or unequal (*anisotropic* scaling). Isotropic scaling preserves the shapes of things like circles and squares; anisotropic scaling distorts circles into ellipses and squares into rectangles. In the following diagram, the X-axis is assumed to be horizontal, and the Y-axis vertical.

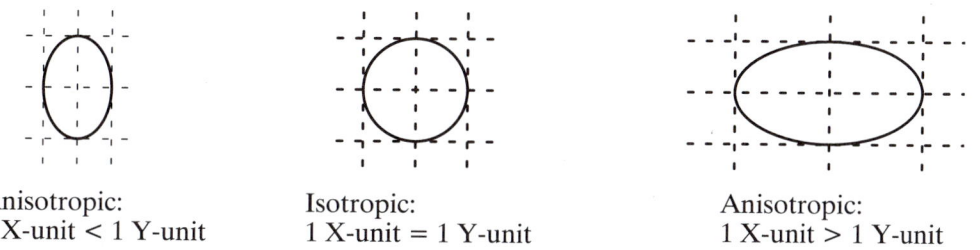

Anisotropic:
1 X-unit < 1 Y-unit

Isotropic:
1 X-unit = 1 Y-unit

Anisotropic:
1 X-unit > 1 Y-unit

Figure 12. Isotropic and Anisotropic Scaling

HP Printer Job Language (PJL)

Printers and plotters that use HP RTL also recognize some of the commands of HP's Printer Job Language (PJL). These commands allow you to control the device and its operating environment independently of the program that generates the plotted or printed image. The relevant commands are summarized on page 392.

Context Switching

There are a number of commands that are recognized by a range of plotters and printers, for switching between HP RTL, PCL, HP-GL/2, and PJL:

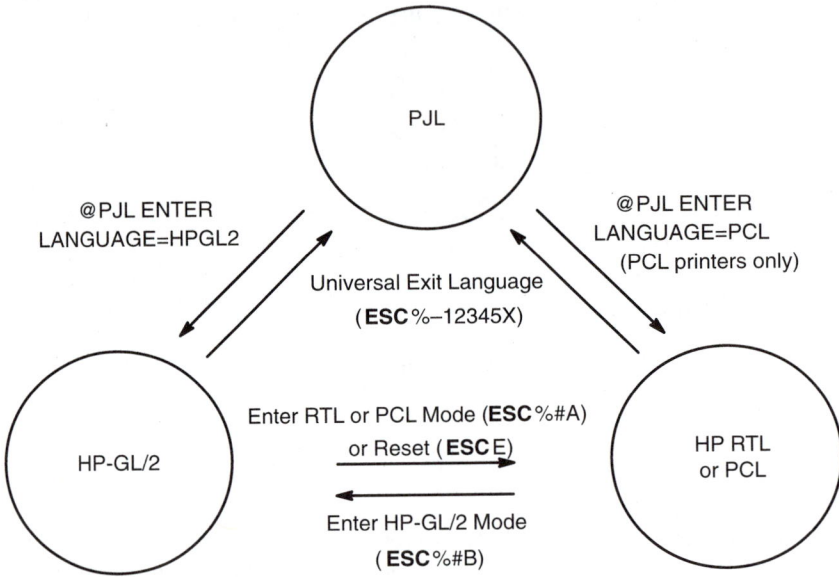

Figure 13. Switching from One Context to Another

You can find more details in the descriptions of the HP RTL commands (those beginning **ESC**), starting on page 401. The @PJL commands are described on page 392.

HP-GL/2 instructions and HP RTL commands interact with each other. There is a detailed description of the effects of each environment on the other on page 389.

PART 2: HP-GL/2

This Part contains the following sections:

Chapter 2: Introduction to HP-GL/2

HP-GL/2 is the standardized version of the Hewlett-Packard Graphics Language. It is designed to provide a set of consistent functions across a wide range of peripheral devices, both plotters and printers. Its aim is therefore to reduce programming effort and the future compatibility of your programs, while allowing great flexibility in creating images.

This chapter describes the principles of HP-GL/2 and introduces the following topics:

- The Instructions—the Kernel Groups and the Extensions.

- Pen Status and Location.

- Scaling.

- HP-GL/2 Instructions and Syntax.

HP-GL/2 consists of a kernel set of instructions that are supported on all HP-GL/2 devices. In addition, there are sets of extensions that allow you to make full use of the functions of particular types of device. These extension instructions are not supported on all HP-GL/2 devices. Details of the devices supporting each extension and instructions within groups can be found in the appropriate *Comparison Guides* (see page xviii).

In addition to using the instructions of HP-GL/2, you may also want to use the commands of the PCL Printer Language or of the HP Raster Transfer Language (HP RTL).

The Instruction Groups

HP-GL/2 is made up of a core set of instructions (called the HP-GL/2 *kernel*) and several *extensions*. All HP-GL/2 devices support the kernel instructions. The extensions (see page 20) help you to make use of special technologies or device capabilities. Many plotters support the Technical Graphics Extension; many devices also support the Palette Extension. The remaining extensions make use of specific technologies and are, therefore, device-specific.

The Kernel

The *kernel* is the foundation of HP-GL/2 and contains most of the instructions. All HP-GL/2 devices support the kernel instructions. The kernel consists of five functional groups:

- Configuration and Status.

- Vector.

- Polygon.

- Line and Fill Attributes.

- Character.

Each of these groups is explained below. Guidance on how to use the instructions of each group is given in *Chapter 3: The HP-GL/2 Kernel* on page 29.

The Configuration and Status Group

The instructions in this group help you set up the environment for your plot, by establishing default conditions and scaling and manipulating the plotting area. There is more information starting on page 29.

CO*["c...c"]*	Comment
DF	Default Values
IN*[n]*	Initialize
IP*[p1x,p1y[,p2x,p2y]]*	Input P1 and P2
IR*[p1x,p1y[,p2x,p2y]]*	Input Relative P1 and P2
IW*[xll,yll,xur,yur]*	Input Window
PG*[n]*	Advance Full Page
RO*[angle]*	Rotate Coordinate System
RP*[n]*	Replot
SC*[xmin,xmax,ymin,ymax[,type[,left,bottom]]]*	Scale
or SC*xmin,xfactor,ymin,yfactor,2*	

The Vector Group

The instructions in this group enable you to draw vector graphics, that is, lines and arcs. You can use either absolute coordinates or relative coordinates for your data. There is more information starting on page 41.

AA*xcenter,ycenter,sweep_angle[,chord_angle]*	Arc Absolute
AR*xincr,yincr,sweep_angle[,chord_angle]*	Arc Relative
AT*xinter,yinter,xend,yend[,chord_angle]*	Absolute Arc Three Point
CI*radius[,chord_angle]*	Circle
PA*[x,y[,...]]*	Plot Absolute
PD*[x,y[,...]]*	Pen Down
PE*[flag][value/x,y]...[flag][value/x,y]*	Polyline Encoded
PR*[x,y[,...]]*	Plot Relative
PU*[x,y[,...]]*	Pen Up
RT*xincrinter,yincrinter,xincrend,yincrend[,chord_angle]*	Relative Arc Three Point

The Polygon Group

The instructions in this group use the polygon buffer in your peripheral device. Some of the instructions draw shapes, while others control the filling and edges of these shapes. There is more information starting on page 44.

EA*x,y*	Edge Rectangle Absolute
EP	Edge Polygon
ER*x,y*	Edge Rectangle Relative
EW*radius,start_angle,sweep_angle[,chord_angle]*	Edge Wedge
FP*[fill_method]*	Fill Polygon
PM*[polygon_definition]*	Polygon Mode
RA*x,y*	Fill Rectangle Absolute
RR*x,y*	Fill Rectangle Relative
WG*radius,start_angle,sweep_angle[,chord_angle]*	Fill Wedge

The Line and Fill Attributes Group

The instructions in this group give you access to different line types and fill types. They also let you manipulate fill patterns and use different pen widths. There is more information starting on page 53.

AC*[x,y]*	Anchor Corner
FT*[fill_type[,option1[,option2]]]*	Fill Type
LA*[kind,value[,kind,value[,kind,value]]]*	Line Attributes
LT*line_type[,pattern_length[,mode]]*	Line Type
PW*[width[,pen]]*	Pen Width
RF*[index[,width,height,pen_number[,pen_number...]]]*	Raster Fill Definition
SM*[character[character2]]*	Symbol Mode
SP*[pen_number]*	Select Pen
UL*[index[,gap1,...gapn]]*	User-Defined Line Type
WU*[type]*	Pen Width Unit Selection

The Character Group

The instructions in this group let you use different fonts or character sets, and manipulate their direction, size, and appearance. There is more information starting on page 57.

AD*[kind,value...[,kind,value]]*	Alternate Font Definition
CF*[fill_mode[,edge_pen]]*	Character Fill Mode
CP*[spaces,lines]*	Character Plot
DI*[run,rise]*	Absolute Direction
DR*[run,rise]*	Relative Direction
DT*[label_terminator[,mode]];*	Define Label Terminator
DV*[path[,line]]*	Define Variable Text Path
ES*[width[,height]]*	Extra Space
LB*text...text label_terminator*	Label
LO*[position]*	Label Origin
SA	Select Alternate Font
SD*[kind,value...[,kind,value]]*	Standard Font Definition
SI*[width,height]*	Absolute Character Size
SL*[tangent_of_angle]*	Character Slant
SR*[width,height]*	Relative Character Size
SS	Select Standard Font
TD*[mode]*	Transparent Data

The Extensions

The *extension* instructions of HP-GL/2 let you exploit more fully the capabilities of your peripheral device. Many HP-GL/2 devices, especially plotters, support the Technical Graphics extension, and many devices also support the Palette extension. The remaining groups make use of specific technologies, and are therefore more device-specific. For example, because you cannot digitize on raster devices, those devices do not support the Digitizing extension. The extensions are:

- Technical Graphics.

- Palette.

- Dual-Context.

- Digitizing.

- Advanced Drawing.

- Advanced Text.

Each of these groups is explained below. Guidance on how to use the instructions of each group is given in *Chapter 4: The HP-GL/2 Extensions* on page 77.

The Technical Graphics Extension

The instructions in this group add flexibility that is often required in technical fields, such as computer-aided design, architectural rendering, integrated circuit layout, and so on. There is more information starting on page 77.

BP*[kind,value...[,kind,value]]*	Begin Plot
CT*[mode]*	Chord Tolerance Mode
DL*[character_number[character_number2]*	Download Character
[[,up]x,y...[,up],x,y]	
EC*[n]*	Enable Cutter
FR	Frame Advance
MC*[mode[,opcode]]*	Merge Control (also in the Advanced Drawing Extension)
MG*[message]*	Message
MT*[type]*	Media Type
NR*[timeout]*	Not Ready
OE;	Output Error
OH;	Output Hard-Clip Limits
OI;	Output Identification
OP;	Output P1 and P2
OS;	Output Status
PS*[length[,width]]*	Plot Size
QL*[quality_level]*	Quality Level
ST*[switches]*	Sort
VS*[pen_velocity[,pen_number]]*	Velocity Select

The Palette Extension

The instructions in this group help you integrate raster technology with the vector capabilities of your peripheral device; the instructions are not, however, restricted to raster devices, and pen plotters may support this extension, defaulting some instructions in accordance with their technology. There is more information starting on page 82.

CR*[black-ref_p1,white-ref_p1,black-ref_p2,*   Set Color Range for
   white-ref_p2,black-ref_p3,white-ref_p3]   Relative Color Data
NP*[n]*   Number of Pens
PC*[pen[,primary1,primary2,primary3]]*   Pen Color Assignment
SV*[screen_type[,option1[,option2]]]*   Screened Vectors
TR*[n]*   Transparency Mode

The Dual-Context Extension

The instructions in this group are useful when you want to integrate word-processed text and raster graphics images with vector graphics for desktop presentations. There is more information starting on page 83.

FI*font_id*   Primary Font Selection by ID
FN*font_id*   Secondary Font Selection by ID
SB*[n]*   Scalable or Bitmap Fonts (also in the
       Advanced Text Extension)

and the following commands of PCL and HP RTL:

ESC%#A   Enter PCL Mode/Enter HP RTL Mode
ESCE   Reset

The Digitizing Extension

The instructions in this group are used only with pen plotters, and are used for digitizing coordinates. There is more information starting on page 89.

DC   Digitize Clear
DP   Digitize Point
OD*;*   Output Digitized Point and Pen Status

The Advanced Drawing Extension

The instructions in this group allow you to draw Bezier curves, and to specify how raster devices are to place picture elements (pixels) on the page. There is more information starting on page 92.

BR*x1,y1,x2,y2,x3,y3[,...x1,y1,x2,y2,x3,y3]*   Bezier Relative
BZ*x1,y1,x2,y2,x3,y3[,...x1,y1,x2,y2,x3,y3]*   Bezier Absolute
MC*[mode[,opcode]]*   Merge Control (also in the Technical
       Graphics Extension)

PP*[mode]*   Pixel Placement

The Advanced Text Extension

The instructions that form this group allow you to use either 8-bit or 16-bit character sets and to specify the type of fonts to be used for subsequent labels. There is more information starting on page 94.

LM*[mode[,row_number]]*	Label Mode
SB*[n]*	Scalable or Bitmap Fonts (also in the Dual-Context Extension)

Pen Status and Location

Because printing vector graphics has traditionally been performed with pen plotters, the terms ***pen*** and ***pen location*** (or ***pen position***) are used to described the cursor in HP-GL/2 mode, and the current active position (CAP) in HP RTL or PCL mode. Whether the pen is logical (for raster devices) or physical (for pen plotters), it must be *selected* in order to print. Instructions such as PU (Pen Up) or PD (Pen Down), and phrases such as "current pen position" or "moving the pen" apply to the imaginary pen just as they do a physical pen on a pen plotter.

Pen Status

Pen status refers to whether the "pen" is up or down. Use the PU (Pen Up) instruction with X,Y coordinates to move the pen to the desired printing location without drawing a line. Use the PD (Pen Down) instruction with X,Y coordinates to lower the pen and begin drawing from the current location to the first specified X,Y coordinate. Some instructions automatically lower the pen.

When you enter HP-GL/2 mode for the first time following a Reset (**ESCE**) command, no pen has been selected and the pen is up. *This means that no lines are drawn when HP-GL/2 instructions are given until a pen is selected.* This can be done using the SP (Select Pen) instruction.

Most drawing instructions require that the pen be lowered to produce marks on the page. Once lowered with a PD instruction, the pen remains down for subsequent HP-GL/2 printing instructions until a PU or IN (Initialize) instruction is issued. The pen remains selected until a new SP instruction is received. You must be aware of the pen's up/down status to avoid drawing stray lines between parts of your picture.

Note: Upon entry into HP-GL/2 mode, a good programming practice is to select a pen and issue a pen-up move to the initial starting position. This ensures that a pen is selected and is in the proper position to begin drawing.

- Whenever the device receives a PD instruction, it produces a dot at the current pen location. If the pen is already down when the device receives an instruction with an automatic pen down, the unnecessary dot can mar your final output. For best results, include a PU instruction before any instruction with an automatic pen down.

- Only the portion of the pen falling within the effective window is printed. The pen is centered on a line between the beginning and end points, with half of the pen width falling on either side of this line.

- The definition of each instruction tells you whether it has an automatic pen down. If you find that part of your image is not drawn, make sure your instruction sequence uses the PD instruction before the affected instructions.

Instructions that Include an Automatic Pen-Down Movement

Every time you use a PU or PD instruction, the device updates the pen up/down status. The following instructions include an automatic PD instruction as part of their function. After performing their complete function, they return the pen to its previous up/down state.

CI	Circle
EA	Edge Rectangle Absolute
EP	Edge Polygon
ER	Edge Rectangle Relative
EW	Edge Wedge
FP	Fill Polygon
LB	Label
PE	Polyline Encoded (using a flag)
RA	Fill Rectangle Absolute
RR	Fill Rectangle Relative
SM	Symbol Mode
WG	Fill Wedge

Pen Location

Pen location refers to the X,Y coordinates of the pen. Most instructions, when completed, update the pen location. The next instruction then begins at that location. Some instructions do not update the current pen location. The definition of each instruction tells you whether the current pen location is updated or restored. Use the PU (Pen Up) instruction with the desired X,Y coordinates to lift the pen and move it to a new location.

The DF (Default Values) instruction does not reset the current pen location; the IN (Initialize) instruction moves it to the origin of the hard-clip limits. You should specify your beginning pen location for each HP-GL/2 drawing.

"Lost" Mode

Parameter values less than the range maximum are passed by the parser; these values may subsequently be unscaled into device-dependent internal resolution units (for example, 7 200 or 9 600 units-per-inch) that exceed the device-dependent internally representable number range. If this occurs, the device enters a "lost" mode; all relative drawing instructions are ignored until a instruction is received which specifies an absolute move to a point within the internally representable number range.

When "lost" mode is entered, the pen is raised and the following instructions are ignored: AA, AR, AT, CI, CP, EA, ER, EW, LB, PE, PM, PR, RA, RR, RT, and WG.

The instructions allowed in "lost" mode are: AC, AD, CF, CO, DF, DI, DR, DT, DV, ES, FT, IN, IP, IR, IW, LA, LO, LT, PA, PD, PG, PU, PW, RF, RO, RP, SA, SB, SC, SD, SI, SL, SM, SP, SR, SS, TD, UL, WU, and the PM1/PM2 forms of PM.

The instructions IN, PG, RP, and PA, with in-range parameters, clear "lost" mode; PD and PU in absolute plotting mode, with in-range parameters, also clear "lost" mode. When PD clears "lost" mode, a line is drawn from the last valid current position to the first point in the PD parameter sequence. If PA clears "lost" mode, the pen will not go down until a PD instruction is received.

When "lost" in polygon mode, "PM2" clears "lost" mode, closes the current polygon using the current pen state, and restores the original pen position and up/down state. "PM1" does not clear "lost" mode, but it does close the current subpolygon using the current pen up/down state if the starting vertex is valid. The buffer then contains:

- the valid points up to, but not including the point that set "lost" mode;

- the points after "lost" mode is cleared;

- and the closure point.

Points stored after "lost" mode is cleared are stored as pen-up points until a PD instruction is received.

When "lost" mode is entered while drawing an arc or a wedge, only the valid arc segments that were generated before the arc segment that caused the device to be "lost" are drawn. If a rectangle instruction (EA, ER, RA, or RR) contains parameters that would make the device enter "lost" mode, error 3 (invalid parameter) is set and the instruction is ignored.

Scaling

When you *scale* a drawing, you define your own units of measurement instead of using plotter-units; the device converts your units (*user-units*) to coordinate positions for placing the image on the page. *Scaling* allows control of the device using units that are easy for you to work with.

For example, you can scale your drawing to divide the drawing area into 100 squares. As you plan the drawing, you can think in terms of 100 squares rather than plotter-units. Another example of scaling is that since 400 plotter-units equals 1 centimeter, you can establish this scale to print in user-units equal to 1 centimeter each.

Scaling begins with the scaling points, P1 and P2 (see *The Scaling Points, P1 and P2* on page 31). P1 and P2 act as two points marking opposite corners of a rectangle. You can make this rectangle any size and place it anywhere in relation to the origin, depending on the plotter-unit coordinates you specify for P1 and P2. (P1 and P2 default to opposite corners of the hard-clip limits, but you can change their locations using the IP [Input P1 and P2] or IR [Input Relative P1 and P2] instructions). P1 is also the default origin (0,0) for the coordinate system.

After you have defined the positions for P1 and P2, or have accepted the default, use this imaginary rectangle to set up scaling for your drawing. With the SC (Scale) instruction you specify how many sections the rectangle divides into horizontally (the X-axis) and how many sections the rectangle divides into vertically (the Y-axis). In this way you create your user-units.

Scaling also allows you to enlarge or reduce your image by changing the locations of P1 and P2. P1 and P2 represent physical locations in relation to the hard-clip limits. When the imaginary rectangle formed by P1 and P2 is enlarged or reduced with the IP or IR instructions, the HP-GL/2 image is also enlarged or reduced to fit the new P1/P2 rectangle. (For a more detailed explanation of scaling and the SC (Scale) instruction, see page 290.)

For importing existing HP-GL/2 images, another method of enlarging or reducing drawings exists. It involves varying the size of the hard-clip limits and is described in *Absolute and Relative Pen Movement* on page 10. This method allows you to scale an image while maintaining the aspect ratio of all elements (including fonts). The Scale instruction does not affect the size of fonts.

HP-GL/2 Syntax

The following illustration shows a typical HP-GL/2 instruction and the description of its components.

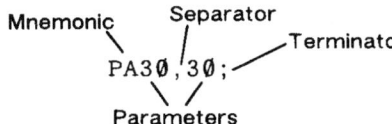

Each HP-GL/2 instruction consists of up to four parts:

- A two-character **_mnemonic_** which defines the function of the instruction. It can be uppercase or lowercase. For example, IN is the Initialize instruction, SP is the Select Pen instruction, and CI is the Circle instruction.

- **_Parameters_** are used with certain HP-GL/2 instructions to tell the device to complete the instruction in a particular way. Some instructions have no parameters, some have required parameters, and some have optional parameters. Some instructions have additional parameters that further qualify other parameters.

- **_Separators_** which separate one parameter from the next. You are recommended to use a comma as a separator, though you can use spaces. However, in some computer systems, spaces are automatically removed before being sent to the peripheral device. If the second of a pair of parameters starts with a plus or minus sign, this is also interpreted as a separator for numeric parameters. Separators are not used with the DT, LB, PE, and SM instructions.

- A **_terminator_** which separates one instruction from the next. The recommended way of separating instructions is by using no explicit terminator, that is, the mnemonic for the next instruction constitutes the separator from the previous. Most instructions can also be terminated with a semicolon, though dropping the semicolon will reduce the amount of data transmitted to the device by about 10%. Some instructions (for example, PG, PE, and all output instructions) *must* be terminated with a semicolon. The LB instruction, described on page 206, requires a special terminator set by the DT (Define Label Terminator) instruction (see page 154). We recommend you place a semicolon at the end of the last instruction in your program to terminate the instruction and ensure the proper completion of your program.

In the example above, "PA" is the mnemonic, "30" and "30" are its two parameters, "," is a separator, and ";" is the terminator.

The following illustration shows the flexibility of the syntax. Each variation of the two-instruction sequence is permissible; however, the first method is recommended—using the first letter of the next mnemonic to terminate instructions, using no spaces between parameters, and separating parameters with a comma. This method sends fewer bytes to the device, thereby reducing transmission times.

          PDPU1Ø,2Ø   PD;PU1Ø,2Ø;   PD PU 1Ø 2Ø;
              /
         Recommended

The program examples used in this book are spaced out so that the function of each instruction can be clearly seen. It is *not* recommended to arrange your instructions in this manner. In particular, do *not* leave any spaces between the DT and LB instructions and their parameters.

Notation Used in this Book to Present Instruction Syntax

The following notation is used in the descriptions of instruction syntax in this book:

MN	Instruction mnemonic, always two uppercase characters.
parameters	All parameters are shown in *italics*. A comma is always shown as the separator between parameters. A space, "+", or "–" is also valid, although not preferred. (A "+" or "–" is a valid separator only for numeric parameters.)
[ ]	Parameters in square brackets are optional; you must have an even number of X,Y coordinates.
[,...]	Any number of the previous parameter; you must have an even number of X,Y coordinates.
;	Instruction terminator. A semicolon is normally optional and is shown in square brackets in most instruction syntaxes. Although a semicolon is always shown in instruction syntaxes, any non-numeric character is also valid.
	Exceptions to the optional use of the semicolon as an instruction terminator occur in the following instructions: PE (Polyline Encoded), PG (Advance Full Page), LB (Label), and CO (Comment). PE and PG must be terminated by a semicolon. LB is terminated by the non-printing end-of-text character (**ETX**—decimal 3), or a user-defined character. The comment string of the CO instruction must be delimited by double quotes.
	A semicolon terminator is *always required* following the last instruction prior to leaving HP-GL/2 mode.
ETX	Labels require a special terminator, usually the ASCII end-of-text (**ETX**) character (decimal code 3). See the descriptions of the LB and DT instructions.

Note that although X,Y coordinates are normally shown in parentheses in text—for example, (3,4) or (0,0)—the parentheses are *not* part of the syntax and *must not* be entered in your instructions.

Omitting Optional Parameters

Some instructions have optional parameters that take on default values if they are omitted. When you omit a parameter, you must omit all subsequent parameters in the same instruction—the DT (Define Label Terminator) instruction is an exception.

For example, the LT (Line Type) instruction has three optional parameters: *line_type*, *pattern_length*, and *mode*. The following instruction shows all three being used (*line_type* = 6, *pattern_length* = 25, *mode* = 1).

    LT 6,25,1;

If you omit the second parameter you must also omit the third parameter, as shown below:

    LT 6;

The device uses the most recently specified *pattern_length* and *mode*. If you have not specified a *pattern_length* or *mode* since sending a DF (Default Values) or IN (Initialize) instruction, the device uses the parameter's defaults.

For example, if you send the following instructions (intending to omit the second parameter), the device interprets the "1" as the second parameter, not the third:

LT 6,1;   or   LT 6,,1;

Parameter Formats

You must give parameters in the format (type of units) required by each HP-GL/2 instruction. The required format is stated in the parameter table of each instruction's description, and is described below.

Numbers within the defined ranges do not cause errors; however, the range may exceed the device's physical printing area. Numbers that move the pen position outside the *effective window* result in image clipping. The ranges specified are minimums; your device may support a greater range of values than those shown in this book.

Integer

An integer from $-8\,388\,608$ (-2^{23}) to $8\,388\,607$ ($2^{23} - 1$). The device automatically rounds fractional parameters to the nearest integer within the range. Sending a number outside the parameter range may produce unexpected results.

Clamped Integer

An integer from $-32\,768$ (-2^{15}) to $32\,767$ ($2^{15} - 1$). The device automatically rounds fractional parameters to the nearest integer. Sending a number outside this range does not cause an error, but the number is "clamped" to the limits of the range. For example, when parsing a clamped integer, the device treats all numbers above $32\,767$ as $32\,767$. Certain instructions have parameters which are restricted to a smaller range. These ranges are listed in the parameter tables for each instruction. Sending a number outside the reduced parameter range may produce unexpected results.

Real

A number between $-8\,388\,608.000\,0$ (-2^{23}) and $8\,388\,607.999\,9$ ($2^{23} - 1$). You are assured of at least six significant digits (including integer and fractional portion). You may omit the decimal point when no decimal fraction is specified. Sending a number outside the parameter range may produce unexpected results. The device cannot use exponential format numbers (for example, 6.03E8). If you are using a computer or language that uses the exponential format, you must use integer variables or a formatting technique to output fixed-point real numbers.

Clamped Real

A number between $-32\,768.000\,0$ (-2^{15}) and $32\,767.999\,9$ ($2^{15} - 1$); you are assured of at least six significant digits (including integer and fractional portion). You may omit the decimal point when no decimal fraction is specified. Sending a number outside this range does not cause an error, but the number is "clamped" to the limits of the range. For example, the device treats all numbers above $32\,767.999\,9$ as $32\,767.999\,9$. Certain instructions have parameters which are restricted to a smaller range. These ranges are listed in the parameter tables for each instruction. Sending a number outside the reduced parameter range may produce unexpected results.

Label or Character

Any character or sequence of characters. In the HP-GL/2 language, text is described using the term "label". Refer to the LB (Label) instruction on page 206 for a complete description.

Current Unit

When you see the term "current units" in a parameter table, the unit system of that parameter depends on whether scaling is on or off. When scaling is on, the units are user-units; when scaling is off, the units are plotter-units (described under *Units of Measure* on page 12).

Quoted String

A character or sequence of characters enclosed in double quotes. It is used primarily in the MG (Message), BP (Begin Plot), and CO (Comment) instructions. Two consecutive double quotes form one double quote in the string.

Chapter 3: The HP-GL/2 Kernel

The Kernel instructions form a base set of instructions that are normally supported on all HP-GL/2 devices. They are grouped as follows:

This chapter also contains a description of HP-GL/2 Printing; see page 73.

The Configuration and Status Group

The Configuration and Status Group instructions help you:

- Establish default conditions and values for HP-GL/2 features.

- Scale images in the dimensional units you want to use.

- Enlarge or reduce images for different media sizes.

- Draw equal-sized and mirror-imaged drawings.

- Adapt the coordinate system to match PCL and HP RTL.

- Establish a window (soft-clip limits).

- Rotate the HP-GL/2 coordinate system.

- Add comments to your HP-GL/2 instruction sequence.

These instructions make no mark on the media; they establish default conditions, perform scaling, and manipulate the plotting area.

The following instructions form the Configuration and Status Group:

CO	Comment	Allows comments to be included in an HP-GL/2 instruction sequence.
DF	Default Values	Sets most programmable features to their default conditions.
IN	Initialize	Sets all programmable features to their default conditions.
IP	Input P1 and P2	Establishes new or default locations for the scaling points P1 and P2.

HP-GL/2 KERNEL

IR	Input Relative P1 and P2	Establishes P1 and P2 locations with respect to the hard-clip limits.
IW	Input Window	Sets up a window (soft-clip limits).
PG	Advance Full Page	Terminates the plot and advances the page (see note).
RO	Rotate Coordinate System	Rotates the HP-GL/2 coordinate system.
RP	Replot	Plots multiple copies of a stored plot (see note).
SC	Scale	Establishes a user-unit coordinate system.

Note: The PG and RP instructions are device-dependent; they are useful in plotter applications and some printer applications, but are not the optimal solution for PCL printers. Other PCL commands, for example, the Number of Copies (**ESC&l#X**) command or the Form Feed (**FF**) control code, perform similar functions.

The factory environment defaults are:

- Scale mode is off (current units are plotter-units).

- The soft-clip limits default to the hard-clip limits (in PCL dual-context mode, the window is the default picture frame).

- The default origin (0,0) depends on the type of device, and is shown on page 9. (PCL dual-context uses the PCL default logical page coordinate system).

- P1 and P2 are in opposite corners according to the viewing perspective, as shown on page 9 (in PCL dual-context mode, the lower-left and upper-right corners of the picture frame).

Establishing Default Conditions

Whether you are using HP-GL/2 mode, PCL printer language mode, or HP Raster Transfer Language (HP RTL) mode, you should establish default conditions at the beginning of each print job to prevent unexpected results due to "leftover" instruction parameters from a previous job. From within HP-GL/2 mode there are two ways to establish default conditions: using the IN (Initialize) instruction or using the DF (Default Values) instruction. You can also power the device off and then on, or use the control-panel reset function (if available) to reset the device.

Using the IN instruction sets the device to its user-selected defaults. This process is called initialization. The Reset command (**ESCE**) of PCL and HP RTL executes an IN instruction automatically, so if a reset was sent at the beginning of your print job, HP-GL/2 instruction parameters are at their user-selected default state when HP-GL/2 mode is first entered. (On devices that support the Technical Graphics Extension [see page 77] the Reset command executes a BP [Begin Plot] instruction, which includes the functions of IN.)

Note: HP-GL/2 instruction parameters are set to their default values the first time HP-GL/2 mode is entered during a print job (assuming that an **ESCE** reset is sent at the beginning of the job). After instructions have been sent to modify the current print environment, the instruction parameters are no longer set to their defaults. When you re-enter HP-GL/2 mode, immediately sending an IN instruction ensures that HP-GL/2 features are set to their default conditions (if that is what you want).

The DF instruction is not as powerful as the IN instruction. The conditions set by the DF and IN instructions are described on pages 136 and 189 respectively.

The Scaling Points, P1 and P2

When you scale a drawing, you define your own units of measurement, which the device then converts to plotter-units. Scaling relies on the relationship between two points P1 and P2. These two points are called the *scaling points* because they take on the user-unit values that you specify with the SC (Scale) instruction. You can change the locations of P1 and P2 using either the IP (Input P1 and P2), or IR (Input Relative P1 and P2) instruction.

P1 and P2 always represent an absolute location, defined in plotter-units. They designate opposite corners of a rectangular printing area. The P1/P2 rectangular area is not a graphics limit; plotting is not restricted to the P1/P2 area. You can change the size of the rectangular printing area and move it anywhere within the hard-clip limits, or even outside these limits, depending on the plotter-unit coordinates you specify using the IP or IR instructions. The biggest benefit of scaling is that your plot will normally retain the same relative proportions on any size of media, except when you use IP with parameters or IR.

If the SC (Scale) instruction is not used, that is scale mode is "off", all HP-GL/2 measurements are in fixed plotter-units (0.025 mm).

Using the Scale Instruction

Scaling allows you to establish units of measure with which you are familiar, or which are more logical to your drawing. The SC (Scale) instruction determines the number of user-units along the X- and Y-axes between P1 and P2. The actual size of the units depends on the locations of P1 and P2 and the range of user-units set up by the SC instruction.

There are three types of scaling:

- *Anisotropic scaling* indicates that the size of the units along the X-axis may be different from the size of the units on the Y-axis.

- *Isotropic scaling* indicates that the units are the same size on both axes.

- *Point-factor scaling* sets up a ratio of plotter-units to user-units.

The Scale instruction does not change the locations of P1 and P2, only their coordinate values. Also, scaling is not limited to the rectangular area defined by P1 and P2, but extends across the entire plotting range.

For example, to divide the X-axis into 12 units representing months, and the Y-axis into 10 units representing currency values, specify the X-axis to scale from 0 to 12, and the Y-axis to scale from 0 to 10. P1 becomes the origin with user-unit coordinate (0,0) and P2 becomes (12,10). The entire plotting area is now divided into the desired units. Subsequent plotting instructions use these units. If you tell the device to move to the point (3,4), it moves to the location equivalent to (3,4) user-units, *not* (3,4) plotter-units.

If you move the locations of P1 and P2, the size of the user-units changes. Assume that the previous illustration showed P1 and P2 in their default locations (the lower-left and upper-right corners, respectively, of the hard-clip limits for PCL printers). In Figure 15, P1 and P2 have the same user-unit *values* (set with the Scale instruction, SC), but their physical *locations* have been changed, using the IP (Input P1 and P2) instruction. Note that the size of the user-units has decreased.

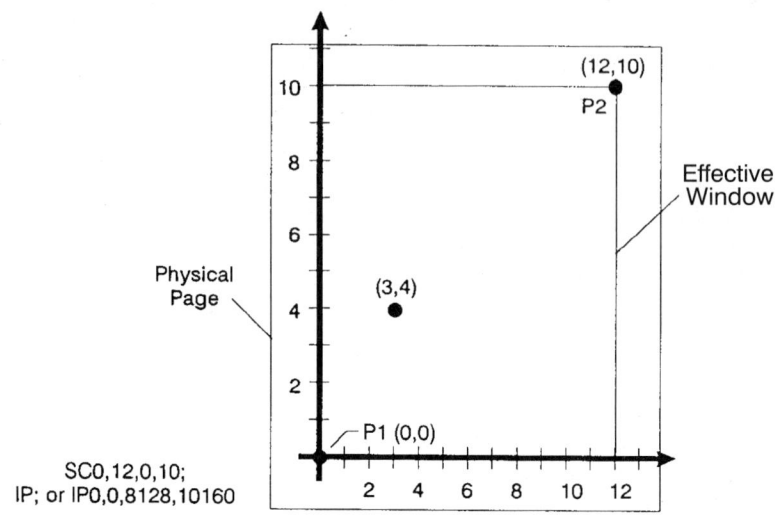

SC0,12,0,10;
IP; or IP0,0,8128,10160

Figure 14. User-Unit Scaling with Default P1 and P2

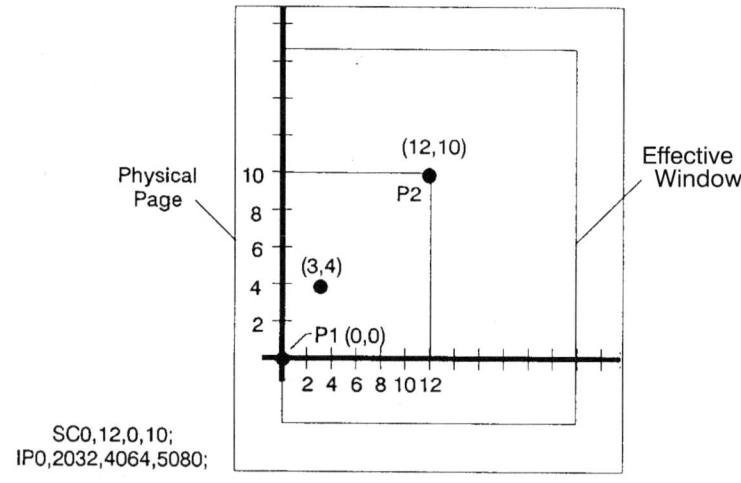

SC0,12,0,10;
IP0,2032,4064,5080;

Figure 15. Same User-Unit Scaling with New P1 and P2

To further illustrate the flexibility of user-unit scaling, Figure 16 shows the P1 and P2 locations with negative user-unit values.

Note that the framework set by the scaling points P1 and P2 is *not* a graphics limit. The user-unit coordinate system extends across the entire plotting area. You can print to a point beyond P1 or P2 as long as you are within the hard-clip limits. In this example, P1 is in the –X and –Y quadrant.

Note: You can use coordinate points that are outside of the hard-clip limits or even off the page, but only that portion of the vector graphics image that falls within the effective window is printed. For example, you can draw a small portion of the circumference of a circle with a

5-foot radius by moving the pen 5 feet from the page and issuing a CI instruction specifying a 5-foot radius; only the portion of the arc that falls within the effective window is printed.

Refer to the SC (Scale) instruction on page 290 for more information on scaling drawings.

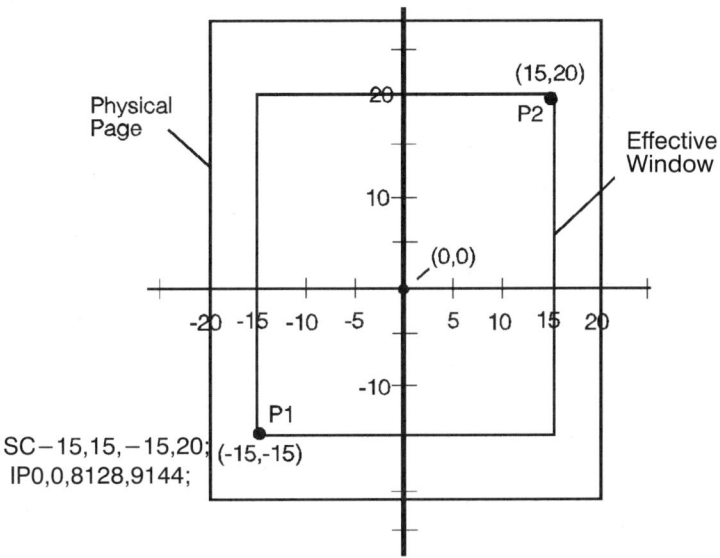

Figure 16. New P1 and P2 User-Unit Scaling with Negative Values

Using Scaling Effectively

The following sections describe how to combine scaling and P1/P2 concepts to do the following.

- Enlarge or reduce the size of a drawing.

- Draw equal-sized pictures on the same page.

- Create mirror-imaged pictures.

Enlarging or Reducing a Picture

The basic technique for changing a picture's size is to scale the printing area defined by P1 and P2, and then move the locations of P1 and P2 to define a smaller or larger area. This is especially useful when you want to print the picture on any portion of the page.

Note: Only scaled drawings (those using the SC instruction) are enlarged or reduced when the P1/P2 locations change. Use PCL picture frame scaling when you import into PCL HP-GL/2 images created without the SC instruction.

To maintain the proportions of scaled plots, set P1 and P2 to define an area with the same aspect ratio as the original scaling rectangle. For example, if the area defined by P1 and P2 is 3000 x 2000 plotter-units, its aspect ratio is 3:2. To enlarge the plot, set P1 and P2 to define a larger area that maintains a 3:2 ratio.

The following example illustrates this technique using a square (isotropic) P1/P2 scaling rectangle with a scale of 0 to 10 for both axes. After drawing a circle within the scaled area, the locations of P1 and P2 move to form a new square area that maintains the 1:1 ratio. Note that the circle printed in the new area is smaller but is still a circle, not an ellipse.

IP	0,0,2000,2000;	Set P1 to be (0,0) and P2 to be (2000,2000) plotter-units.
SC	0,10,0,10;	Set up user-unit scaling to range from (0,0) to (10,10).
SP	1;	Select pen number 1. Even though there may be no physical pen, the SP instruction must be used to enable printing.
PA	5,5;	Begin absolute plotting from the center of the square (5,5).
CI	3;	Print a circle with a radius of 3 user-units.
IP	2500,500,3500,1500;	Input a new P1 and P2 position for printing the smaller circle.
PA	5,5;	Begin absolute plotting from the center of the new square (5,5).
CI	3;	Print the second circle with a radius of 3 user-units.

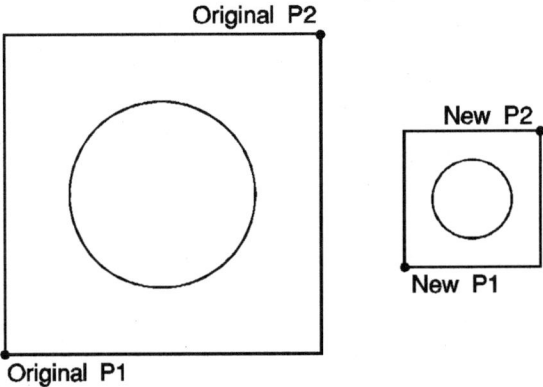

Figure 17. Changing the Size of a Drawing

Drawing Equal-Sized Pictures on a Page

You may occasionally want to print more than one drawing on the same page for a side-by-side comparison. This can be useful for comparing parts, assemblies, layouts, or other similar information. The easiest way to draw equal-sized pictures on one piece of paper is to take advantage of the fact that P2 follows P1 whenever you change the location of P1.

The following example locates P1 and P2 on the left side of the paper and scales the area for the first image. Then, for the second image, only the P1 location is moved to the right side of the paper; P2 automatically tracks P1, so the printing area retains the same dimensions as the first drawing. The printed rectangle around the second area shows P2 in its new location.

IP	500,500,5450,7500;	Set P1 to be (500,500) and P2 to be (5450,7500).
SC	0,10,0,15;	Set up user-unit scaling to range from (0,0) to (10,15).
SP	1;	Select pen number 1.
PA	0,0;	Begin absolute plotting from the origin (0,0).
PD	10,0, 10,15, 0,15, 0,0;	Pen down and print from (0,0) to (10,0) to (10,15) to (0,15) to (0,0)
PU	;	Pen up.
IP	5550,500;	Input a new P1 and allow P2 to automatically track it.
PA	0,0;	Begin absolute plotting from the new origin.
PD	10,0, 10,15, 0,15, 0,0;	Pen down and print from (0,0) to (10,0) to (10,15) to (0,15) to (0,0)
PU	;	Pen up.

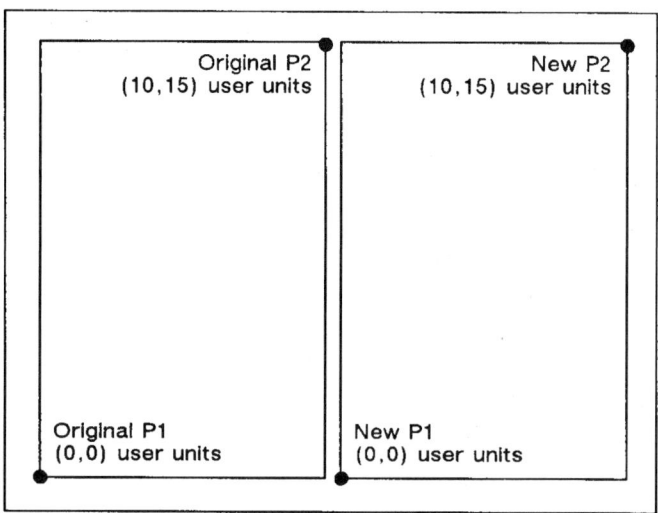

Figure 18. Drawing Pictures Side-by-Side

Note: The P1/P2 frames are not windows or graphics limits; the pen can print HP-GL/2 images anywhere within the hard-clip limits. The new P1 and P2 retain their scaled values. This allows you to use the same coordinates on both halves of the page. In contrast, if you do not assign a scale to P1 and P2, you must calculate the new plotter-unit coordinates for the drawing on the second half of the page.

Creating Mirror-Images

For most drawings, you will probably set P1 and P2 so that P1 is at the origin of the coordinate system and P2 is in the opposite corner of the scaling area. However, you can change the relationship of P1 and P2 to produce a mirror-image effect.

You can "mirror-image" any *scaled* drawing (those drawings using the SC instruction) by changing the relative locations of P1 and P2, or changing the coordinate system by using SC. You can mirror-image labels using the DI (Absolute Direction) and DR (Relative Direction) instructions, the SR (Relative Character Size) instruction, or using the SI (Absolute Character Size) instruction.

The following example uses a subroutine to generate the arrows shown in Figure 19. Because the program changes the relative locations of P1 and P2, the direction of the arrow is different in each of the four drawings. The program sets P1 and P2, draws the plot, then returns to reset P1 and P2 (using the IP instruction). This continues until all four possible mirror-images are plotted. (The original drawing is shown in each picture so you can compare the orientation of the mirror-image.)

IP	1500,3600,3000,5100;	Specify the P1/P2 locations for the first arrow figure.
SC	−15,15,−10,10;	Set up user scaling: (−15,−10) to (15,10).
(Run subroutine)		Run the subroutine (below) that prints the arrow image.
IP	3000,3600,1500,5100;	Change the physical locations of P1 and P2 to flip the image to the left.
(Run subroutine)		Print the second image.
IP	1500,5100,3000,3600;	Change the physical locations of P1 and P2 to flip the image down.

HP-GL/2
KERNEL

(Run subroutine)   Print the third image.
IP   3000,5100,1500,3600;   Change P1/P2 locations to flip the image to the left and down.
(Run subroutine)   Print the fourth image.

Subroutine that prints the arrow figure:

PA   1,2;
PD   1,4, 3,4, 3,7, 2,7, 4,9, 6,7, 5,7, 5,4, 12,4, 12,5, 14,3, 12,1, 12,2, 1,2;
PU   ;   End of subroutine.

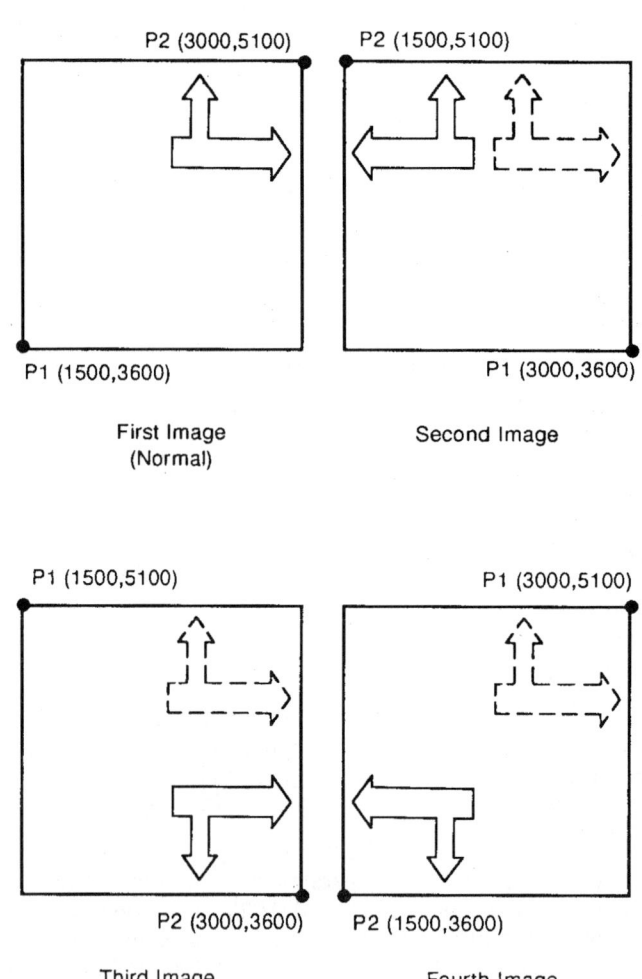

Figure 19. Creating Mirror Images

Adapting the HP-GL/2 Coordinate System for Printers to Match the PCL System

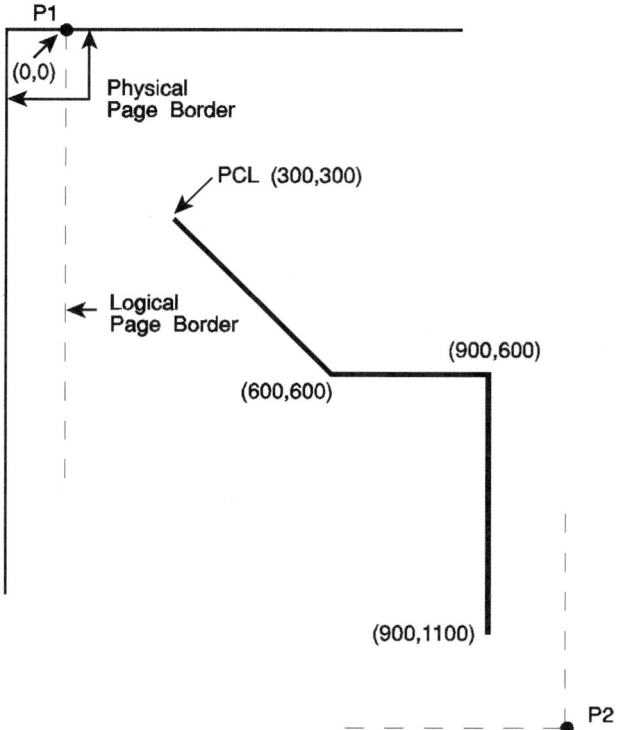

Figure 20. Matching the HP-GL/2 and PCL Coordinate Systems

The example illustrated in Figure 20 uses the IR and SC instructions to change HP-GL/2 coordinate system for "printers" (see Figure 8 on page 9) to match the default PCL coordinate system. The IR instruction is used to invert the Y-axis so that the Y values increase as the pen moves down the page. The SC instruction equates user-units to dot positions (300 dots-per-inch). The example draws a few lines in both PCL and HP-GL/2 modes to demonstrate that the coordinate systems are lined up correctly (the end points of the lines intersect).

ESCE	Reset the device.
ESC&l2A	Set the page size to letter (8.5 by 11 inches).
ESC&l0O	Specify portrait orientation.
ESC&l0E	Set top margin to 0.
ESC*p0x0Y	Move to position (0,0).
ESC*c5760x7920Y	Set PCL picture frame to 8 inches x 11 inches (size of logical page) in portrait orientation; units are decipoints (1/720-inch).
ESC*c0T	Set picture frame anchor point to current PCL cursor position (0,0).
ESC%1B	Enter HP-GL/2 mode with the HP-GL/2 cursor or pen at the PCL cursor position.
IN ;	Initialize HP-GL/2 instruction values. (The IN instruction moves the pen position from the anchor point to the HP-GL/2 origin, the lower-left corner of the PCL picture frame.) Note that on color devices, this instruction destroys the PCL color environment.

SP	1;	Select pen number 1.
SC	0,3.3867,0,–3.3867,2;	Set up a user scale with a user-unit equal to 1/300 inch. Scale instruction type 2, the scale is the ratio of plotter-units/user-units (1016 plotter-units-per-inch/300 dots-per-inch = 3.3867). The negative Y-value changes the HP-GL/2 Y direction to match that of the PCL coordinate system.
IR	0,100;	Place P1—point (0,0)—at the top of the PCL picture frame.
PU	0,0;	Lift the pen and move to (0,0), the upper left corner—since the HP-GL/2 coordinate system now matches the PCL coordinate system. Every subsequent pen move can be specified using the same coordinate numbers in either mode.
		The following instructions demonstrate that the grids are synchronized.
PU	300,300;	Lift the pen and move it to (300,300).
PD	600,600;	Draw a line to (600,600). This draws a line at a 45° angle down from the starting point.
ESC%1A		Enter PCL mode with HP-GL/2's pen position (600,600) being inherited as PCL's current active position (CAP).
ESC*c300a4b0P		Draw a horizontal line (rule) that is 300 PCL units wide by 4 PCL units. Note that the cursor position after a rule is printed is at the beginning of the rule—in this case (600,600).
ESC%1B		Enter HP-GL/2 mode (inheriting PCL's CAP).
PU	;	Lift the pen.
PR	300,0;	Move to a point 300 user-units (dots) to the right.
PD	;	Place the pen down.
PR	0,500;	Print a line 500 user-units down.
ESC%1A		Enter PCL mode with the CAP at the current HP-GL/2 pen position.
ESCE		Reset the device to end the job and eject a page.

Notes:

- Sending an IN (Initialize) or DF (Default Values) instruction causes the coordinate system to revert to the HP-GL/2 default.

- Since this example is based on the default top margin and text length, changing the top margin or the text length would move the two coordinate systems out of alignment.

- The commands starting with the Escape character (**ESC**) are PCL commands.

Adapting the HP-GL/2 Coordinate System for Plotters to Match the HP RTL System

If you place the following instructions at the head of your HP-GL/2 file (after any BP, IN, PS, QL, and MT instructions), the coordinate systems of HP-GL/2 for "plotters" (see Figure 8 on page 9) and HP RTL will be the same, in terms of their orientation and their axes (see Figure 21), and will use 300 dots per inch (dpi) as user-units instead of device units:

RO	90; (portrait layout)	or RO180; (landscape layout). This rotates the coordinate system so that the origin is in the lower-left corner with the +X-axis to the right and the +Y-axis upwards.
IP	0,0,1016,–1016;	Set the P1/P2 interval to be 1 inch (1016 plotter-units).
IR	0,100;	Move P1 and P2 so that P1 is at the HP RTL origin and P2 is 1 inch away.
SC	0,300,0,300;	Value depends on resolution; this is for 300 dpi.

| AC | 0,0; | Default the anchor corner to HP RTL (0,0). |
| PU | 0,0; | Raise the pen and move it to (0,0). |

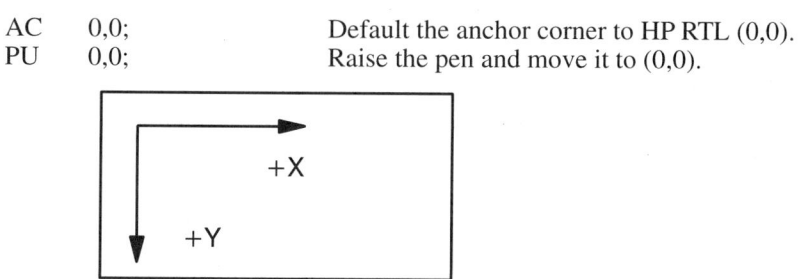

Figure 21. Coincident Coordinate Systems

Windowing: Setting up Soft-Clip Limits

Soft-clip limits temporarily restrict pen movement to a rectangular area, or **window**. When you initialize or set the device to default conditions, the soft-clip limits are the same as the hard-clip limits. To create a window, you use the IW (Input Window) instruction. The device does not draw outside the window.

Figure 22 shows the four types of line segments you can specify from one point to another.

Type	From Last Point	To New Point
1	Inside window area	Inside window area
2	Inside window area	Outside window area
3	Outside window area	Inside window area
4	Outside window area	Outside window area

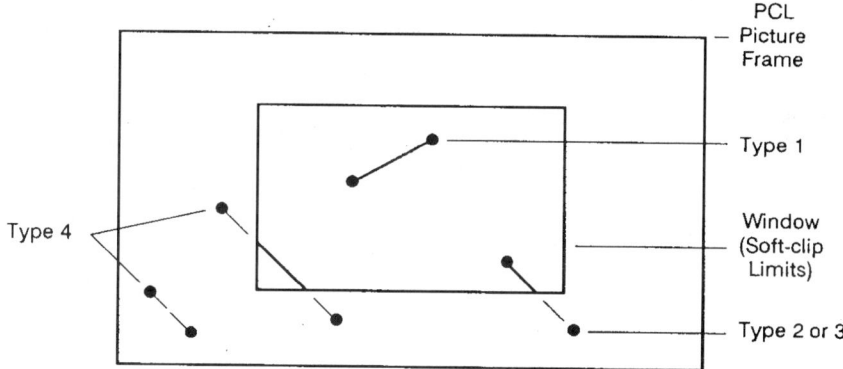

Figure 22. Line Segments and Windows

The IW instruction lets you control the size of the HP-GL/2 printing area so that you can draw a particular portion of a drawing. You can leave the rest as white space, or use the remaining area for labels, or another drawing. Refer to *Graphic Limits* on page 4, and the IW instruction description on page 197.

Rotating a Picture

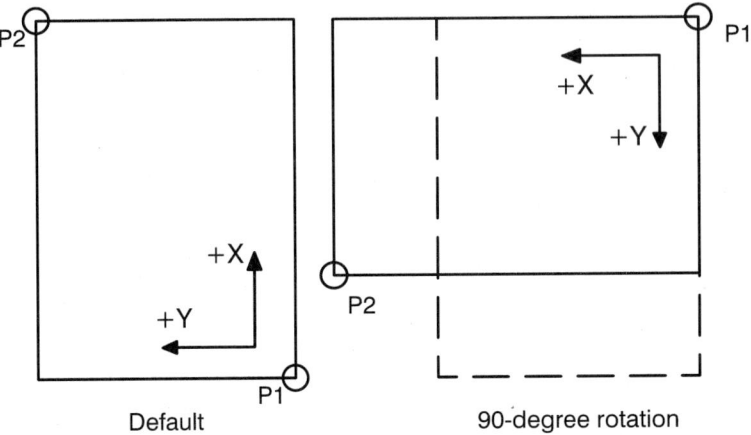

Figure 23. Rotating a Picture

Plotters always set the X-axis parallel to the longest edge of your plot; small-format printers set the Y-axis parallel to the longest edge. However, you can change this orientation using the RO (Rotate Coordinate System) instruction to rotate the coordinate system counterclockwise 90°, 180°, or 270°. Figure 23 shows the default, for most HP-GL/2 devices, and rotated orientation of the axes and locations of P1 and P2.

Note that P2 is now off the page. This occurs because the X, Y coordinates of P1 and P2 do not change. To set P1 and P2 at the hard-clip limits, use either the IP or IR instruction after the RO instruction; see page 275 for more information. If you reset your coordinate system to its default orientation, remember to reset P1 and P2, using either the IP or IR instruction again.

Ending Your Program and Advancing the Page

When using a raster device, you must indicate the end of your plot before the device will rasterize and draw it. For printers with PCL capability, this may require you to exit from HP-GL/2 mode and send a Form Feed (**FF**) control character in the PCL context. The PG (Advance Full Page) instruction automatically signals the end of incoming data for the device and starts the rasterization process. You may be able to use a control-panel function to achieve the same result, but the PG instruction is more efficient. Using PG can save you time since, for this function, you will not have to interact with the device. *In multi-user environments, PG is a necessary plot separator.*

PG advances the roll-feed paper (on pen and raster devices) the length set by the PS (Plot Size) instruction, or the default page size if there is no PS instruction. The PS instruction is described on page 259.

If your device supports it, you can make additional copies of a plot by following the PG instruction with the RP (Replot) instruction. Generally, your device must have an area, such as disk space or a memory buffer, to support this feature. Since the plot is already stored in the device, using RP frees the computer while the copies are drawn.

The Vector Group

The Vector Group instructions enable you to achieve the following results in your programs:

- Use absolute and relative coordinates when plotting.
- Draw lines, arcs, and circles.
- Encode coordinates to increase your device's throughput.

The following instructions form the Vector Group:

AA	Arc Absolute	Draws an arc using absolute coordinates.
AR	Arc Relative	Draws an arc using relative coordinates.
AT	Absolute Arc Three Point	Draws an arc from the current pen location through two absolute points.
CI	Circle	Draws a circle with a specified radius.
PA	Plot Absolute	Enables movement to absolute coordinate locations, with respect to the origin (0,0).
PD	Pen Down	Lowers the "pen" to the page.
PE	Polyline Encoded	Increases throughput by encrypting common HP-GL/2 instructions.
PR	Plot Relative	Enables movement relative to the current pen location.
PU	Pen Up	Lifts the pen from the page.
RT	Relative Arc Three Point	Draws an arc from the current pen location through two relative points.

The factory environment defaults are:

- The plotting mode is absolute (the PA instruction).
- The pen state is up (PU).

Pen Up or Down

Most HP-GL/2 instructions perform their functions with the pen either up or down. Specifying the pen's up/down state is necessary to avoid drawing unwanted lines between figures. The PU (Pen Up) instruction raises the pen and can also move to a desired plotting location before drawing. The PD (Pen Down) instruction lowers the pen and can draw from the current location to a specified location. Turning on the device or sending an IN (Initialize) instruction raises the pen. Some instructions automatically cause the pen to be down (see page 23).

Drawing Lines

You can draw lines between two points (X,Y coordinate pairs) using the PD (Pen Down) instruction and a series of absolute or relative coordinate pairs. The device draws only the portion of the line that falls within the *effective window*.

Note: When using HP-GL/2 to draw lines, you can increase your device's throughput by using the PE (Polyline Encoded) instruction to send coordinates. The PE instruction requires that you convert coordinates from decimal to base 64 or 32. This conversion is especially useful for increasing throughput when you use a serial interface. The PE instruction, with its parameters, is used in place of the PA, PD, PR, PU, and SP instructions.

In the following example, note that the PA (Plot Absolute) instruction specifies absolute plotting, and the coordinate pair (0,0) sets the beginning pen location.

PA   0,0;   Begin absolute plotting from coordinate (0,0).
PD   2500,0, 0,1500, 0,0;   Specify Pen Down and draw lines between the points.

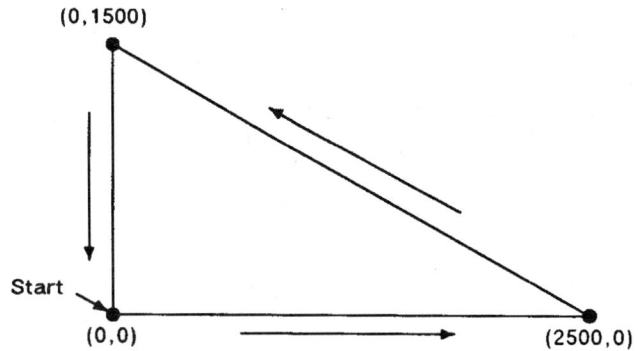

Figure 24. Drawing Lines

Note: Any line drawn along the border of the effective window causes the line to be clipped, producing a line width of one-half of what it should be. For example, in the above plot, the lines from (0,0) to (0,1500), and (0,0) to (2500,0) are clipped if the origin (0,0) is one corner of the effective window.

Drawing Circles

The CI (Circle) instruction uses your current pen position as the center of the circle; you specify the radius of the circle.

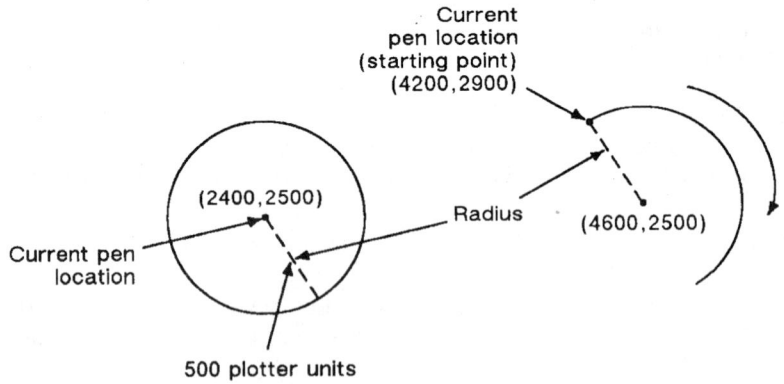

Figure 25. Drawing Circles and Arcs

The following example shows a simple instruction sequence using CI to draw a circle with a radius of 500 plotter-units. The circle is shown on the left of Figure 25.

PA   2400,2500;   Specify absolute plotting and move to position (2400,2500).
CI   500;   Draw a circle with a radius of 500 plotter-units; the center of the circle is the current pen location (2400,2500). The CI instruction automatically causes the pen to be lowered.

Drawing Arcs

The AA (Arc Absolute) and AR (Arc Relative) instructions use the following method for drawing arcs. Your current pen location becomes one end of the arc; you specify the center point with one parameter (setting the radius), and set another parameter to specify the number of degrees through which you want the arc drawn.

You can also draw arcs using the AT (Absolute Arc Three Point) and RT (Relative Arc Three Point) instructions. These instructions use three known points (your current pen location plus two points you specify) to calculate a circle and draw the appropriate arc segment of its circumference. The arc is drawn from the starting point so that it passes through the intermediate point before the end point, using clockwise or counter-clockwise drawing as required. Refer to Figure 26.

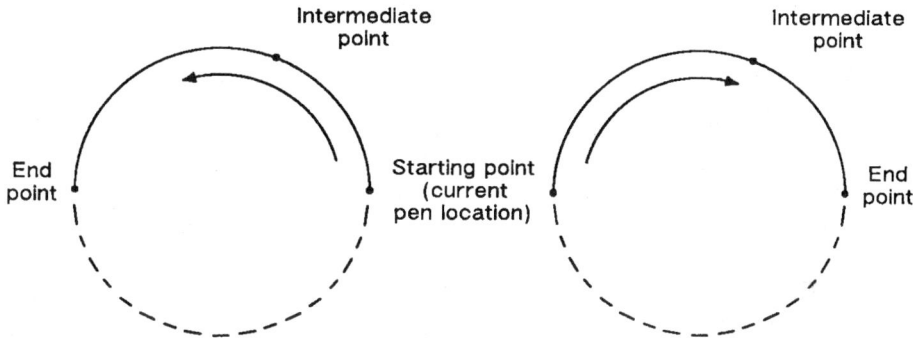

Figure 26. Arcs through Three Given Points

The following example shows a simple instruction sequence using AA to draw an arc. The arc is shown on the right of Figure 25.

PA   4200,2900;   Set starting point to (4200,2900).
PD   ;   Set pen down.
AA   4600,2500,–180;   Using the Arc Absolute instruction, specify the pivot point of the arc, thereby setting the radius; draw the arc for 180° with a *negative* angle of rotation.

Angle of Rotation

A *positive angle* of rotation is in the direction of the +X-axis to the +Y-axis as shown below. A *negative angle* of rotation is in the direction of the +X-axis to the −Y-axis.

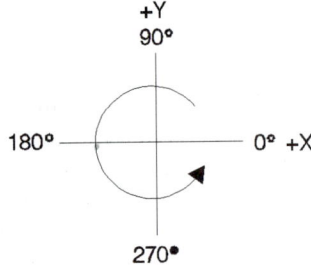

Figure 27. Angle of Rotation

The relationship of the +X-axis to +Y-axis (and −Y-axis) can change as a result of the scaling point or scaling factor changes, thus, changing the direction of a positive (or negative) angle of rotation.

The Polygon Group

All of the instructions in the Polygon Group use the *polygon buffer*, a temporary data storage area in your device. Using the polygon buffer is an integral part of drawing wedges, rectangles, and other types of polygons. Some of the instructions in this group define and draw complete shapes while others act only on the contents of the polygon buffer. The information in this section enables you to achieve the following results in your programs:

- Draw circles, wedges, and rectangles.

- Use polygon mode for drawing polygons, subpolygons, and circles.

The following instructions form the Polygon Group:

EA Edge Rectangle Absolute	Outlines a rectangle defined with absolute coordinates.
EP Edge Polygon	Outlines the contents of the polygon buffer.
ER Edge Rectangle Relative	Outlines a rectangle defined with relative coordinates.
EW Edge Wedge	Defines and outlines a wedge-shaped polygon.
FP Fill Polygon	Fills the polygon shape specified in the polygon buffer.
PM Polygon Mode	Allows you to create user-defined polygons in the polygon buffer.
RA Fill Rectangle Absolute	Fills a rectangle specified with absolute coordinates.
RR Fill Rectangle Relative	Fills a rectangle specified with relative coordinates.
WG Fill Wedge	Defines and fills a wedge-shaped polygon.

The factory environment defaults for the polygon group are:

- Polygon buffer cleared ("PM0").

- Polygon mode off ("PM2").

Filling then Edging Compared with Edging then Filling

When the transparency mode is opaque (specified by "TR0;"), filling then edging an object may produce different results from edging and then filling. This is especially true when large pen widths are used. The following example illustrates this:

TR	0;	Set transparency mode off (opaque)
PU	4000,6000;	Position pen.
PW	5;	Select pen width of 5 units.
PM	0;	Enter polygon mode.
CI	1000;	Draw a circle with a radius of 1000 units.
PM	2;	Close polygon and exit polygon mode.
FT	10,30;	Select 30% shading fill type.
FP	;	Fill...
EP	;	... then Edge polygon.
PU	4000,3000;	Select pen position (4000, 3000) for second circle.
PM	0;	Enter polygon mode.
CI	1000;	Draw another circle with a radius of 1000 units.
PM	2;	Close polygon and exit polygon mode.
EP	;	Edge...
FP	;	... then Fill polygon (circle).

The center of the left circle is located at (4000,3000). The center of the right circle is located at (4000,6000).

You should normally fill an area first and then edge it.

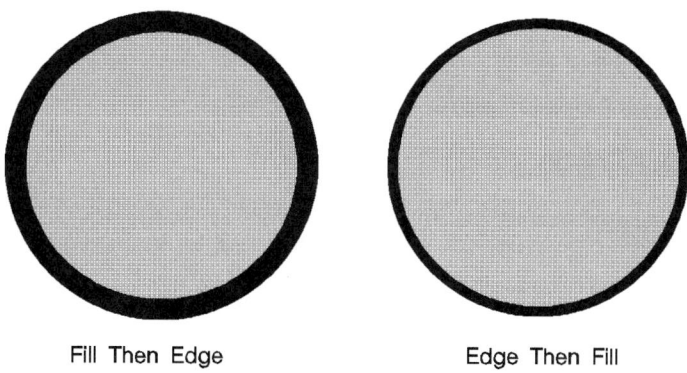

Fill Then Edge   Edge Then Fill

Figure 28. Filling and Edging Charts

Using the Polygon Buffer

The *polygon buffer* is a temporary storage area for information. In it the device collects the instructions and coordinates that define a polygon you want to print. This polygon remains in the buffer until replaced by another polygon, or until the buffer is cleared by initializing the device. Some instructions use the polygon buffer automatically, while other instructions require that you enter the polygon mode. The following instructions use the polygon buffer, but do not allow you to enter polygon mode first:

EA	Edge Rectangle Absolute
ER	Edge Rectangle Relative
EW	Edge Wedge
RA	Fill Rectangle Absolute
RR	Fill Rectangle Relative
WG	Fill Wedge

Drawing Rectangles

You can draw a rectangle by outlining (edging) the defined area using the EA (Edge Rectangle Absolute) or ER (Edge Rectangle Relative) instructions, or by filling (RA or RR), or a combination. To draw a rectangle, the device uses the current pen location for one corner; you give the coordinates for the diagonally opposite corner. The device draws the rectangle defined by these two points.

The following simple instruction sequence uses EA to draw a rectangle:

PA	10,10;	Specify absolute plotting and move to (10,10).
EA	2500,1500;	Draw the outline of a rectangle, with the lower left corner being the current pen location (10,10) and the upper right corner being (2500,1500).

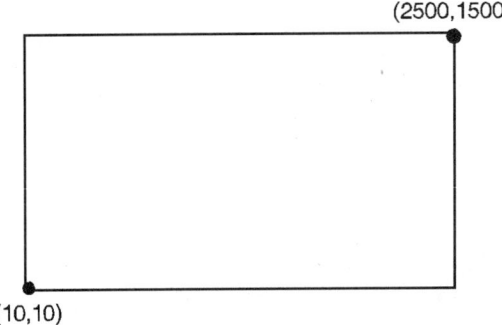

(2500,1500)

(10,10)

Figure 29. Drawing a Rectangle

The RA (Fill Rectangle Absolute) and RR (Fill Rectangle Relative) instructions fill their rectangles with the default or current fill pattern. You may also want to edge (or outline) the rectangle for better image definition with some fill types.

The following instruction sequence draws two filled rectangles, one edged and one not:

PA	0,0;	Specify absolute plotting and move to location (0,0).
FT	3;	Specify fill type 3 (hatching—parallel lines).
RR	1500,1000;	Fill a rectangular shape with the currently active fill pattern. The lower left corner of the rectangle is the current location (0,0), and the upper right corner is 1500 plotter-units in the X direction and 1000 plotter-units in the Y direction from the starting location.
EP	;	Draw an edge around the rectangle that was just drawn. Since the previous RR instruction leaves its definition in the polygon buffer (1500,1000), you do not need to specify the coordinates again.
PR	2000,0;	Specify relative plotting and move the cursor 2000 plotter-units in the X direction from the current pen location.

FT	4,100,45;	Specify fill type number 4 (cross-hatching), set the spacing to 100 plotter-units between fill lines, and set the fill line angle to 45°.
RR	1500,1000;	Fill a rectangle with the currently specified fill type. Use the current pen location (0,0) as the lower left corner of the rectangle and a point (1500,1000) relative plotter-units away for the upper right corner.

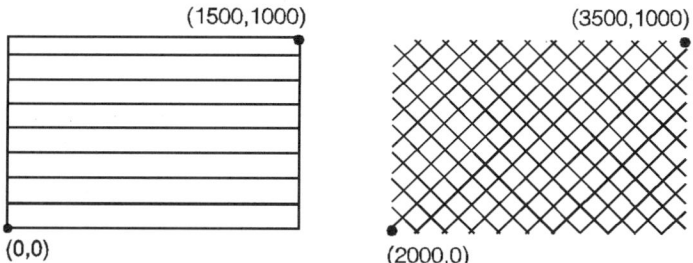

Figure 30. Filled Rectangles, with and without Edges

Drawing Wedges

A *wedge* is a section of a circle. Wedges are commonly used to draw *pie charts*. You can draw a wedge by outlining (edging) the defined area using the EW (Edge Wedge) instruction, or you can create filled wedges using the WG (Fill Wedge) instruction.

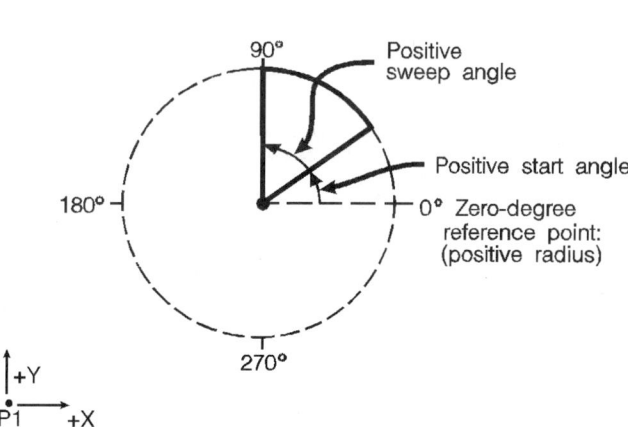

Figure 31. How Wedges are Drawn

The wedge instructions use your current pen location as the center point; you specify the radius, the start angle, and the sweep angle. The *radius* determines the length of the two sides of the wedge. The sign (positive or negative) of the radius determines the location of a *zero-degree reference point*. The *start angle* is the number of degrees from the zero-degree reference point at which you want to draw the first radius. The *sweep angle* is the number of degrees through which you want to draw the arc. To draw or fill a circle, simply specify a 360° sweep angle. Figure 31 shows the different parameters of a wedge with a positive radius.

A positive angle of rotation is in the direction of the +X-axis to the +Y-axis as shown in Figure 27 on page 44. A negative angle of rotation is in the direction of the +X-axis to the −Y-axis.

The following example draws a wedge using the EW instruction. The radius of the wedge is 600 plotter-units, the wedge begins 90° from the zero-degree reference point, and the wedge "sweeps" for 60°.

PA	2500,3500;	Specify absolute plotting and move to location (2500,3500).
EW	600,90,60;	Draw the outline of a wedge, using the current pen location (2500,3500) as the point of the wedge. The wedge has a radius of 600 plotter-units, begins at 90° from the default zero-degree reference point, and "sweeps" for 60°.

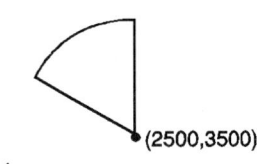

Figure 32. Simple Wedge

The following example (shown in Figure 33) uses different fill types with wedges and circles:

PA	1400,2500;	Select absolute plotting mode and move to (1400,2500).
WG	600,150,120;	Fill a wedge with radius 600 plotter-units, a start angle of 150°, and a sweep angle of 120°. Since no fill type was specified, the wedge is black (solid black is the default fill type).
PA	2300,2500;	Specify absolute plotting and move to (2300,2500).
FT	3,75,45;	Select fill type number 3 (hatching—parallel lines), with 75 plotter-units between hatching lines, and hatching lines tilted at 45°.
WG	600,90,180;	Fill a wedge with the current fill type; use a radius of 600 plotter-units, a start angle of 90°, and a sweep angle of 180°.
FT	1,0,0;	Specify a fill type of solid black.
WG	600,270,60;	Fill a wedge using the same center and radius as the previous wedge. Start the wedge at 270° with a sweep of 60°.
FT	4,60,45;	Specify fill type number 4 (cross-hatching) with 60 plotter-units between lines and the lines tilted at 45°.
WG	600,330,120;	Fill a wedge using the same center and radius as the previous two wedges. Start the wedge at 330° with a sweep of 120°.
PA	3500,2500;	Select absolute plotting and move to (3500,2500).
WG	400,0,360;	Create a filled circle using the current fill type (cross-hatching), specifying a start angle of 0° and a 360° sweep.
PA	4500,2500;	Move to (4500,2500).
FT	;	Select a solid fill.
WG	400,0,360;	Fill a 360° wedge (circle).

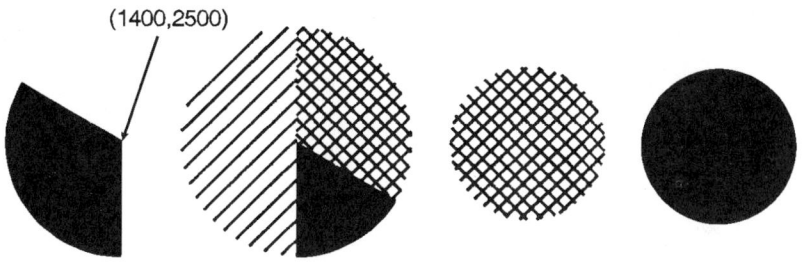

(1400,2500)

Figure 33. Filled Wedges and Circles

Drawing Polygons

A polygon consists of one or more closed sequences of connected line segments (which may cross each other). Drawing polygons requires the use of the *polygon mode*. The PM (Polygon Mode) instruction tells the device to store subsequent instructions and coordinates in the polygon buffer before printing the shape. (Rectangles and wedges are polygons which have their own drawing instructions; the device automatically generates and stores the coordinates in the polygon buffer.)

Polygon Definition Instructions

You can use the following instructions in polygon mode to create polygons. These instructions are stored in the polygon buffer until they are replaced with another polygon or the device is initialized.

AA	Arc Absolute
AR	Arc Relative
AT	Absolute Arc Three Point
BP	Begin Plot
BR	Bezier Relative
BZ	Bezier Absolute
CI	Circle
PA	Plot Absolute
PD	Pen Down
PE	Polyline Encoded
PM1/PM2	Polygon Mode
PR	Plot Relative
PU	Pen Up
RT	Relative Arc Three Point

Drawing Subpolygons

While in polygon mode, you can define either one polygon or a series of *subpolygons*. Like a polygon, a subpolygon is a closed sequence of connected line segments. For example, the block letter C in Figure 34 is one complete polygon. However, the block letter D is actually two subpolygons: the outline and the "hole".

To create one polygon, for example, the letter C, move the pen to the starting location for the polygon, then use the PM (Polygon Mode) instruction to enter polygon mode. Define the shape of the C using the appropriate instructions and coordinates, then exit polygon mode ("PM1"). Now draw the polygon using either the EP (Edge Polygon) or FP (Fill Polygon) instruction.

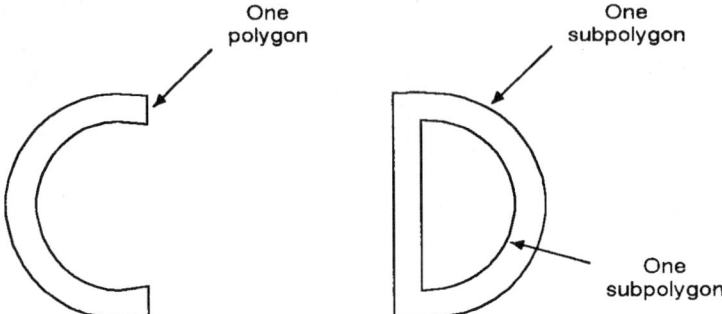

Figure 34. Drawing Subpolygons

To create a series of subpolygons, for example, the letter D, move the pen to the starting location of the first subpolygon, then enter polygon mode. Define the outer shape of the letter D using the appropriate instructions and coordinates, then close the subpolygon ("PM1"), staying in polygon mode. Define the inner shape of the D, then exit polygon mode ("PM2"). Now draw the subpolygons using either the EP or FP instruction. For more information on entering and exiting polygon mode, refer to the PM instruction discussed on page 251.

In polygon mode, you can define points with the pen up or down. However, the EP instruction only draws between points defined when the pen was down. In contrast, the FP instruction fills between all points, regardless of whether they were defined when the pen was up or down. An exception is that the line connecting two subpolygons is never drawn, and is not a fill boundary.

Filling Polygons

There are two methods which can be selected for filling polygons: the ***even/odd*** fill method (which is the default) and the ***non-zero winding*** fill method.

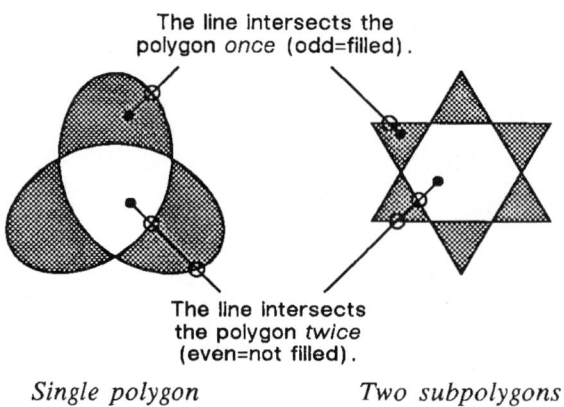

Figure 35. Filling Polygons: Even/Odd Fill Method

Even/Odd Fill Method

There is a simple way to determine which portions of a single polygon or series of subpolygons is filled when you send a FP (Fill Polygon) instruction using method 0 (fill using even/odd rule): Draw a straight line extending from any point within an enclosed area of the polygon to a point outside the polygon. FP fills the enclosed area in question only if the line you have drawn intersects the edges of the polygon an odd number of times. Figure 35 illustrates this "even/odd" rule.

Non-Zero Winding Fill Method

The **non-zero winding** fill algorithm (fill method 1) determines whether a point is inside a region enclosed by a line path using the following steps:

1. Draw a ray from the point across the path segment.

2. Add 1 every time the line segment, as drawn, crosses the ray from left to right or bottom to top.

3. Subtract 1 every time the line segment, as drawn, crosses the ray from right to left or top to bottom.

4. FP fills the enclosed area in question if the sum of steps 2 and 3 is non-zero.

Figure 36 illustrates the non-zero winding fill concept. Note the importance of the direction in which the lines are drawn.

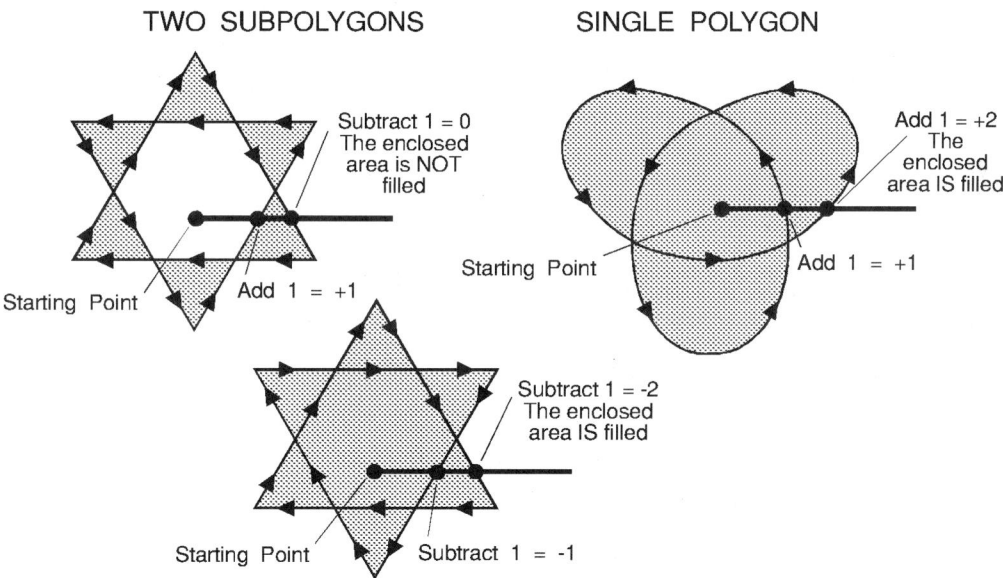

Figure 36. Filling Polygons: Non-Zero Winding Fill Method

Drawing Circles in Polygon Mode

Polygon mode interprets the CI (Circle) instruction differently from the other HP-GL/2 instructions. The device treats a circle as a complete subpolygon. The device automatically closes the first polygon (if any) before starting the circle, and uses the first coordinates (if any) after the circle is drawn to start a new subpolygon.

If you did not close your first polygon completely before sending the CI instruction, the device automatically closes the polygon by adding a point (at the starting point of the previous subpolygon). This can change your current pen location and the placement of the circle in your polygon, resulting in an inaccurate polygon.

A circle (360° arc) specified by AA, AR, AT, or RT is not treated as if it was preceded and followed by "PM1".

CI with a zero radius is a syntactically correct but geometrically degenerate subpolygon that produces a dot. The following example shows how CI can produce syntactically incomplete subpolygons:

PU	;	Pen Up.
PA	1000,1000;	Move to (1000,1000).
PM	0;	Enter polygon mode with the point (1000,1000) in the buffer.
CI	200:	The subpolygon consisting of the single point (1000,1000) is implicitly closed; it has fewer than three points, and effectively disappears. After this CI instruction, the pen-up state and the location (1000,1000) are restored, but this point is not put into the polygon buffer.
CI	500;	This CI instruction again forces closure, and the restored position point is discarded.
PM	2;	Close polygon mode.
FP	;	Fill polygon. The result is a torus *without* a center dot.

Calculating How Much of the Polygon Buffer is Used

You can use the following formula to estimate how much buffer space a polygon consumes. Each point in a polygon uses 9 bytes. The minimum number of points the device will hold is 512; if you multiply 512 points by 9 bytes per point, the result is 4608 bytes (4.5 Kbytes). That means the minimum your device can store in the polygon buffer is 4.5 Kbytes. That is the worst case, however; unless the device has a substantial amount of fonts, macros, or graphics already downloaded into user memory, you can put much more into the polygon buffer. As we just calculated, for every 4.5 Kbytes of extra unused user memory, the polygon buffer can store 512 more points. You can see how in most cases there is little chance of a polygon buffer overflow, especially with the addition of optional device memory.

The following formula explains how to calculate the buffer space used by a polygon:

number of points in polygon $\times$ 9 = buffer space consumed by polygon

Counting the Points in a Polygon

The starting pen location and each subsequent point define a polygon. As shown in the following illustration, a rectangle is defined by five points, not four. This is because the starting location is counted again as the ending location. The second shape has seven points.

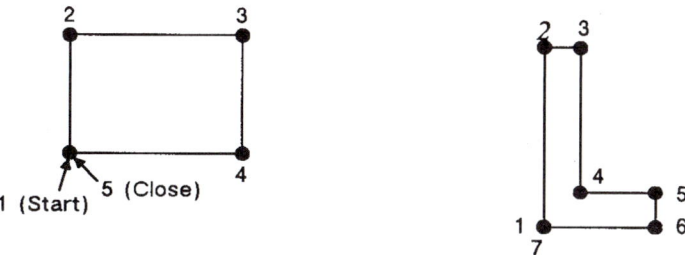

Figure 37. Counting Points in a Polygon

Counting the Points in a Circle or Arc

When a circle or arc defines a polygon, the number of points depends on the number of chords in the arc. There is always one more point than the number of chords, because the starting location is counted again as the ending location. Use the following formula to determine the number of points used to draw a circle or arc:

$$\# \text{ of Points} = \frac{\text{Arc Angle (degrees)}}{\text{Chord Angle (degrees)}} + 1$$

Using this formula, a full circle with the default chord angle of 5° consists of 73 points (360/5 + 1 = 73), and a 45° arc with a chord angle of 3° consists of 16 points (45/3 + 1 = 16).

- If the chord angle does not divide evenly into the arc, round up to the next integer before adding one: 45/2 + 1 = 23 + 1 = 24.

- In polygon mode, the smaller a circle's chord angle, the more chords will be stored in the polygon buffer to draw it.

The Line and Fill Attributes Group

The Line and Fill Attributes Group instructions enable you to achieve the following results in your HP-GL/2 applications:

- Select a pen for plotting or printing.

- Enhance your drawings with various line types (repeated patterns of dots and dashes).

- Enhance your drawings with different fill types (shading patterns).

- Position fill-type patterns.

The following instructions form the Line and Fill Attributes Group:

AC	Anchor Corner	Specifies the starting point for fill patterns.
FT	Fill Type	Selects the pattern to use when filling polygons.
LA	Line Attributes	Specifies how line ends and joins are shaped.
LT	Line Type	Selects the line pattern to use for drawing lines.
PW	Pen Width	Specifies a new pen width.
RF	Raster Fill Definition	Defines a pattern for use as area fill.
SM	Symbol Mode	Draws a symbol at each coordinate location.
SP	Select Pen	Selects a pen for plotting.
UL	User-Defined Line Type	Defines a line pattern.
WU	Pen Width Unit Selection	Specifies whether the pen width is defined in millimeters or as a percentage of the P1/P2 distance.

The factory environment defaults are:

- The line type is solid, and the line-type repeat length is 4% of the diagonal distance from P1 to P2.

- The line cap is butt, the line join is mitered, and the miter limit is 5.

- The pen color is the default HP-GL/2 palette, the pen widths are 0.35 mm, and the pen width selection mode is metric.

- The selected pen is 0 (no pen).

- Symbol mode is off.

- The fill type is solid bidirectional.

- The user-defined line types are the eight standard types as defined by the LT instruction.

- The area fill anchor corner is (0,0) plotter-units.

- The user-defined fill types are solid fill.

Using Line Attributes and Types

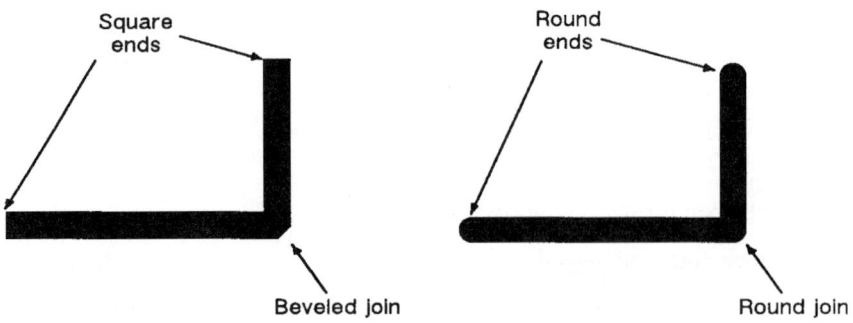

Figure 38. Line Ends Attribute

You can change the appearance of the lines you draw by using the LA (Line Attribute) and LT (Line Type) instructions. The LA instruction lets you specify whether the ends of lines and corners of joined lines should appear as square, triangular, round, or beveled.

Line types are repeated patterns of dots and/or dashes (including solid lines). The following shows some examples of line types. You can also vary the width of the lines and line types you draw by using the PW (Pen Width) instruction. Note that the pen widths used in labels are determined by the stroke weight, specified in the AD and SD instructions.

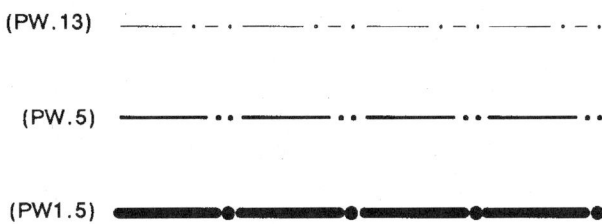

Figure 39. Different Pen Widths and Line Types

Once you specify a line type and line attributes, all lines created by the following instructions are drawn using the new line type and attributes. Line types and their interactions with fill patterns are discussed on page 56.

Instructions Affected by Line Types

AA	Arc Absolute
AR	Arc Relative
AT	Absolute Arc Three Point
BR	Bezier Relative
BZ	Bezier Absolute
CI	Circle
EA	Edge Rectangle Absolute
EP	Edge Polygon
ER	Edge Rectangle Relative
EW	Edge Wedge
FP	Fill Polygon
PA	Plot Absolute
PD	Pen Down
PE	Polyline Encoded
PR	Plot Relative
RA	Fill Rectangle Absolute
RR	Fill Rectangle Relative
RT	Relative Arc Three Point
WG	Fill Wedge

Using Fill Types

Using the FT (Fill Type) instruction adds detail to your drawings and increases their visual effectiveness. The fill type affects the following instructions:

CF   Character Fill
FP   Fill Polygon
RA   Fill Rectangle Absolute
RR   Fill Rectangle Relative
WG   Fill Wedge

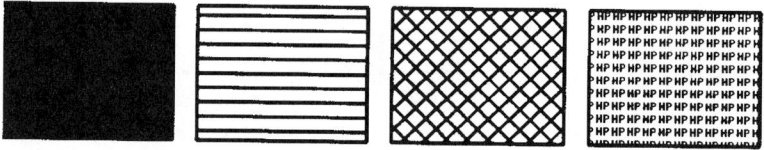

Figure 40. Fill Types

There are several different types of fill that can be used, including solid, hatch, cross-hatch, and raster. The range is device-dependent. Figure 40 shows some commonly used types. You may also be able to define your own types of fill.

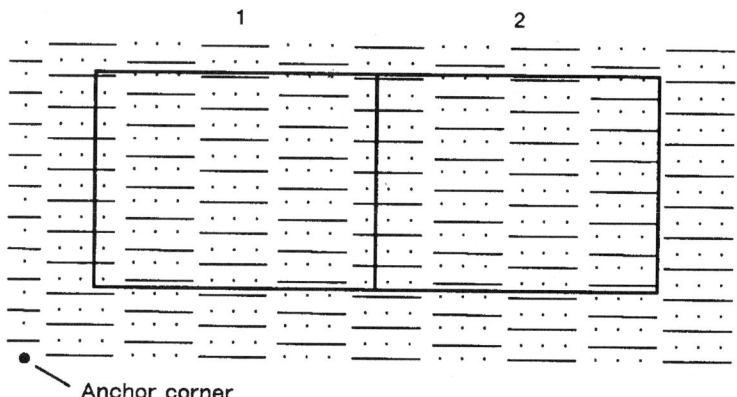

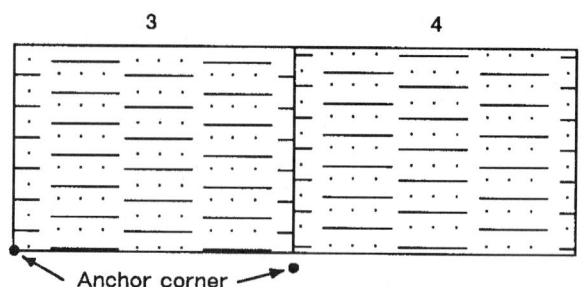

Figure 41. Fill Area Anchor Corner

When you use HP-GL/2 hatching or cross-hatch fill types, the lines are drawn using the currently selected line width, line type, and line attributes. For example, if you have selected a dashed line type and a hatched fill type, your figure is filled with dashed, parallel lines.

All fill types have an ***anchor corner***, the starting point of the fill pattern. Its default location is the current-unit origin (0,0). Conceptually, the fill type replicates out from the anchor corner in the +X-directions and +Y-directions, as shown in Figure 41. Areas are filled by that portion of the fill type resident to the area (refer to rectangles 1 and 2).

Use the AC (Anchor Corner) instruction to position the fill type in relation to the area. Rectangle 3 has an anchor corner set in its the lower-left corner. Rectangle 4 has an anchor corner set below the lower-left corner to alter the pattern's position and give contrast to the adjacent area.

Selecting a "Pen" and Changing Line Width

Even though a printer and some types of plotter do not print with a physical pen as a pen plotter does, they nevertheless use a "logical pen" which emulates the action of a physical pen. You must use the SP (Select Pen) or PE (Polyline Encoded) instruction to draw.

You can change the width of the logical pen using the PW (Pen Width) instruction. Subsequent lines are drawn using the new width. Use PW to vary the line thickness and enhance your plots. You may change widths as often as you like, without sending an SP instruction again.

For pen plotters, the PW instruction causes the plotter to behave as if a wider or narrower pen is being used, whether or not you have switched to a pen with a different width. The plotter compensates by restroking lines to the approximate width specified.

Pen (line) widths can be specified either in millimeters or as a percentage of the diagonal distance from P1 to P2. Use the WU (Pen Width Unit Selection) instruction to select how the pen width is specified. Since using the WU instruction defaults the width of all pens, send WU *before* a PW instruction.

The Character Group

When you create an HP-GL/2 graphic and want to add text, you can either enter PCL mode to add text to your image or you can print text from within HP-GL/2 mode. (There is no support for text in HP RTL mode.) If this is your first experience with HP-GL/2, you should know that the term "label" is used to indicate the printing of text. This section discusses the various ways you can "label" your images using the device's vector graphics instructions.

The Character Group instructions enable you to do the following things:

- Work with the character cell.

- Use different fonts.

- Print or plot with proportionally-spaced and fixed-spaced fonts.

- Designate and select standard and alternate fonts.

- Position and print labels using any supported font.

- Change label size, slant, and direction.

- Use variables in labels.

The following instructions form the Character Group:

AD	Alternate Font Definition	Specifies an alternate font for labeling.
CF	Character Fill Mode	Specifies how outline fonts are rendered.
CP	Character Plot	Moves the pen the specified number of character cells from the current pen location.
DI	Absolute Direction	Specifies the slope of labels independent of P1 and P2 locations.
DR	Relative Direction	Specifies the slope of labels relative to P1 and P2 locations.
DT	Define Label Terminator	Defines the character or code that "turns off" labeling.
DV	Define Variable Text Path	Specifies the label path as right, left, up, or down.
ES	Extra Space	Increases or reduces space between label characters and lines.
LB	Label	Prints text using the currently selected font.
LO	Label Origin	Positions labels relative to the current pen location.
SA	Select Alternate Font	Selects the font designated by AD for labeling.
SD	Standard Font Definition	Specifies the standard font for labeling.
SI	Absolute Character Size	Specifies an absolute character size (in centimeters).
SL	Character Slant	Specifies the slant at which labels are printed.
SR	Relative Character Size	Specifies the size of characters as a percentage of the P1/P2 distance.
SS	Select Standard Font	Selects the font designated by SD for labeling.
TD	Transparent Data	Specifies whether control characters perform their normal function or are printed as characters when printing text.

Working with the Character Cell

In each font, the basis for each character or space is the character cell. Think of the character cell as a rectangular area around a character that includes blank areas above and to the right of the character. Refer to Figure 42 and the following explanations of some terms.

Baseline—The imaginary line on which a line of text rests. A character's descender (such as the bottom of a lowercase "g") extends below the baseline.

Line Feed—The distance from the baseline of a line of text to the baseline of the next character line above or below. For most fonts, the linefeed is about 1.2 times the point size (1.33 times the point size for stick fonts).

Point Size—Traditional character measure roughly equivalent to the height of a capital letter M plus the depth of a descender. Point size is usually measured in units of 1/72-inch.

Delta-X—The implied pen movement that occurs after a character is printed. It includes the space taken up by the character as well as the white space between the characters set by the ES (Extra Space) instruction. In a *fixed-spaced* font, delta-X is the same for every character. In a *proportionally-spaced* font, delta-X varies from one character to another.

Pitch—The number of characters per inch. It is the inverse of delta-X. A pitch of 10 means that the delta-X is one-tenth of an inch; ten characters will fit into a one-inch space. Pitch is only used to measure fixed-space fonts, because proportionally-spaced fonts include characters with different delta-X values.

Cap Height—The distance from the baseline to the top of a capital letter. For most fonts, the cap height is approximately 0.7 times the point size (0.67 times the point size for the stick font).

Character Origin—The point at which the baseline meets the left edge of the character cell.

Character Width—The lateral area allocated for character rendering. This is the horizontal distance occupied by a printed character if intercharacter spacing is eliminated. Wide characters (such as "W") may span the entire character width area, while narrow characters (such as a period) include white space on both sides. For calculation purposes, nominal character width is approximately 0.5 delta-X (or 0.67 delta-X for the stick font).

Character Plot (CP) Cell—A rectangular area with the height of a linefeed and a width extending from the beginning of one character to the beginning of the next (delta-X).

Character Plot (CP) Cell Width—The distance from the left edge of one character to the beginning of the next character.

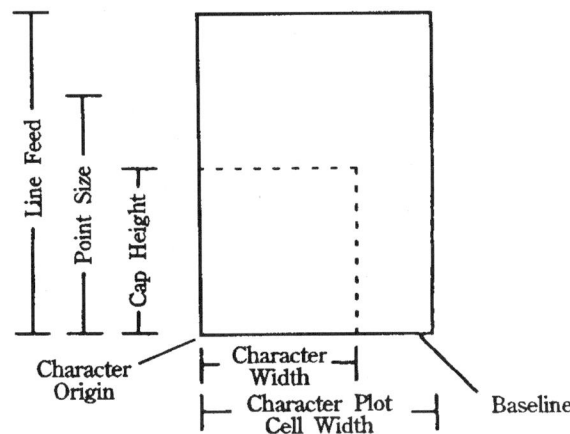

Figure 42. Character Cell and HP-GL/2

Types of Fonts

In HP-GL/2 mode, the device uses at least one of three different types of fonts:

- ***Scalable Outline Fonts***—Characters can be displayed at any size. The characters are defined as a set of points on the outline of a character and corresponding mathematical relationships describing the interaction between these outline points. A scalable outline character can be resized (using SI and SR), rotated (using DI, DR, and RO), and distorted (using SL).

- ***Bitmap Fonts***—Characters defined as an array of dots in a raster pattern. Bitmap characters cannot be transformed using DI, DR, SI, SR, or SL, but they can be used with all of the other instructions in this section—see the SB (Scalable or Bitmap Fonts) instruction, which is in the Dual-Context Extension, on page 288. Bitmap characters are always placed in an orthogonal direction to the page, closest to the print direction established using the DI and DR instructions (see Figure 73 on page 140).

Bitmap fonts affect labels as follows:

- Bitmap characters can only be printed horizontally or vertically. If the print direction (DI or DR) is not orthogonal, the offset between characters follows the print direction, but the characters themselves are rotated to the nearest 90°.

- Bitmap characters cannot be stretched. A size instruction (SI or SR) renders labels in the closest available size. The SI or SR *height* parameter determines the best-fit size for proportionally-spaced fonts, the *width* parameter for fixed-space fonts.

- Bitmap fonts cannot be slanted or edged; SL and CF have no effect on them.

- ***Stick and Arc Fonts***—Characters are drawn as a series of vectors. The characters are defined as a set of end-points. You can resize (using SI or SR), rotate (using RO, DI, and DR), and distort (using SL) stick fonts. Stick fonts are defined on a dimensionless grid. The main body of each character fits within a 32-by-32-unit box, with descenders extending beneath. The stick font is fixed-spaced, and the arc font is proportionally-spaced. All HP-GL/2 devices support stick fonts.

  Stick fonts (typefaces 48, 49, and 50) are a series of vectors whose width depends on the character size and the stroke weight parameter in the AD or SD instruction. The formula used is device-dependent, but is typically:

$$\text{line width} = 0.1 \times \min(\text{height}, 1.5 \times \text{character width}) \times 1.13^{\text{stroke weight}}$$

  where **stroke weight** is an integer in the range –7 to +7. An AD or SD with a stroke weight of 9999 renders the stick font in the current pen width.

The figures below show each type of font in relation to its character cell.

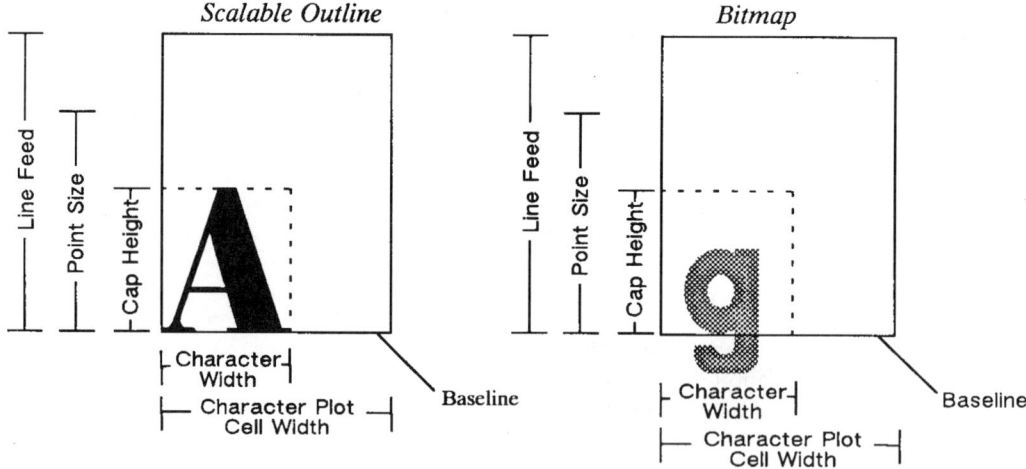

Figure 43. Scalable and Bitmap Character Cell

Note: Proportionally-spaced fonts do not actually have a fixed character "cell". The width occupied by each character depends on the character's shape.

- ***Fixed-Vector Font***—The horizontal space for all characters is the same, and each character is always drawn using a fixed number of vectors, regardless of its size or direction.

- **Variable-Arc Font**—Characters are proportionally spaced, that is, the amount of horizontal space occupied by each character varies from one character to another. Characters are drawn using arcs, so that they have smoother contours.

- **Fixed-Arc Font**—The horizontal space for all characters is the same. Characters are drawn using arcs for greater smoothness.

- **Drafting Font**—Characters are designed to provide reliable character recognition in situations where photo reduction may cause image degradation and loss of resolution. The characters are drawn in such a way as to avoid confusion between lines and figures. Thus the letter "B" and the digit "8" have a wider bottom than top part, but the "8" has a full, round shape to avoid blur. The digits "6" and "9" have large bodies, but with open stems. The set also includes symbols used in drafting, such as ∞ and △. The HP Drafting font is a fixed-space vector font.

When you use the SI (Absolute Character Size) or SR (Relative Character Size) instructions to change the size of the characters, or use the ES (Extra Space) instruction to add extra space around them, you alter the size of the CP (Character Plot) cell.

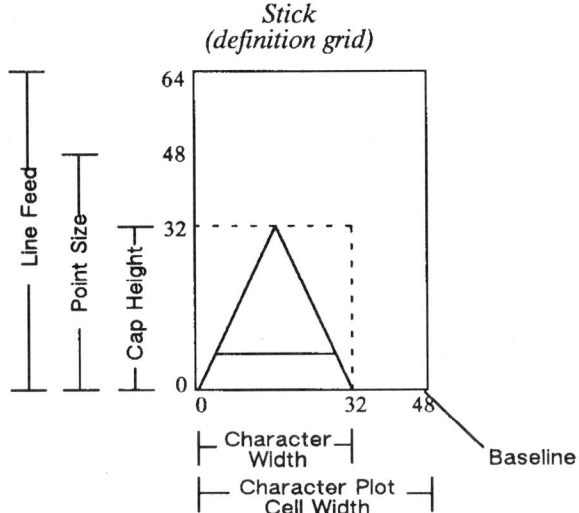

Figure 44. Stick Font Character Cell

Printing or Plotting with Fixed-Spaced and Proportionally-Spaced Fonts

Figures 45 and 46 show the difference between fixed-spaced and proportionally-spaced fonts.

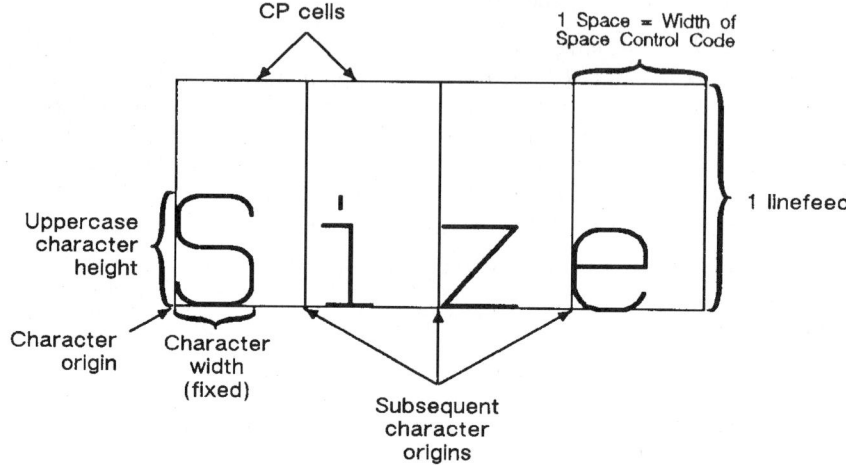

Figure 45. Fixed-Spaced Font

Proportionally-spaced (variable-space) fonts, by definition, use different amounts of horizontal space for each letter. This variation produces some differences in the definition of the character cell, and in the way some of the labeling instructions work with these fonts. These differences are described in this section.

With proportionally-spaced fonts, the actual space occupied by each character varies according to the character's width (see Figure 46).

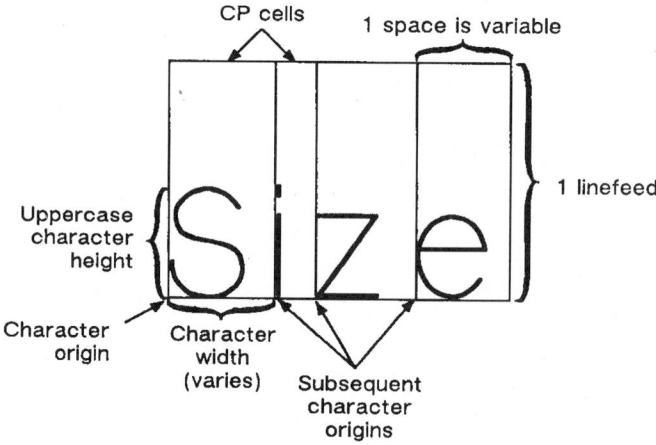

Figure 46. Proportionally-Spaced Font

When printing proportionally-spaced fonts, the CP (Character Plot) instruction uses the width of the Space (**SP**) control code to determine horizontal spaces and the Line Feed height for determining vertical spacing. The ES (Extra Space) instruction (see page 169) uses the horizontal escapement distance (a font metric) to compute horizontal spaces and the Line Feed height for determining vertical spacing. Both of the character size instructions (SI and SR) use cap height and average character width in calculating character size. Otherwise, these instructions behave the same as they do with fixed-spaced fonts.

Designating and Selecting Fonts

If you intend to label with the default fixed-spaced (stick) font, you do not need to use the SD or AD instructions for designating standard and alternate fonts. However, if you intend to use a different font (for example, to match accompanying PCL text), you must use the SD or AD instructions to designate fonts before you can select those fonts for labeling (using either SA or SS).

Standard and Alternate Fonts

The following outlines some of the principles to use when labeling with different fonts:

- Designate the standard and alternate fonts using the SD or AD instruction *before* labeling. If you are using the stick font (the default) as your standard font, you need specify only your alternate font.

- Select either the standard or alternate font, using either the SS or SA instruction before labeling.

  Note that labeling always begins with the standard font, unless you use the SA instruction before you begin your label (or finish the previous label in the alternate font).

- Switch from the standard font to the alternate font, either using SS and SA or the Shift In/Shift Out method. If you are changing fonts within a text string, the Shift In/Shift Out method is usually more efficient. Switch from the standard font to the alternate font using the ASCII Shift Out control character (**SO**, decimal code 14). Switch from the alternate font to the standard font using the ASCII Shift In control character (**SI**, decimal code 15). (Note that a Shift In [**SI**] or Shift Out [**SO**] outside of the label instruction string is ignored.) See *Accessing Special Characters* on page 72.

How Your Device Selects Fonts

The following summarizes the procedure that your device follows to select a font. The criteria are based on the parameters of the AD and SD instructions. The procedure is necessary because fixed-space and variable-space fonts use different criteria to determine text size. For fixed-space fonts, the pitch determines the size. The height parameter of the AD and SD instructions is only used to distinguish between fonts with equal pitch. For variable-space fonts, the height parameter of the AD and SD instructions determines the text size; the pitch parameter is ignored. Your HP-GL/2 device performs the following steps in order:

1. If the specified *character set* does not exist, the device uses the user default set (set from the control panel, if there is one) or the factory default set.

2. If the specified *font spacing* (fixed or variable) is available, it is used; otherwise the device uses the remaining space option.

3. If the remaining fonts are proportionally spaced, the *pitch* is ignored. For fixed-space fonts, if the specified pitch is not available, the device selects the next greater pitch. If no greater pitch is available, the device selects the closest available smaller pitch. (A pitch of

12 characters per inch [cpi] is greater than one of 10 cpi; greater pitch means smaller characters.) Note that any specified pitch is available for scalable fonts.

4. The device selects the closest available height to the *height* parameter. The closest available height is in terms of absolute difference. For example, if the device has 6-, 8-, and 12-point fonts and the specified height is 10, both 8- and 12-point fonts are selected for the next selection criterion. All fonts with heights within a quarter-point of the specified height are considered to satisfy the height criteria. Note that any specified height is available for scalable fonts. Height is ignored for fixed-space fonts.

5. If the specified *posture* (upright or italic) is available in the remaining fonts, the device selects that posture; otherwise, this attribute is ignored.

6. If the specified *stroke weight* is available in the remaining fonts, the device selects that stroke weight. Note that any stroke weight is available for stick fonts.

   If the specified stroke weight is greater than or equal to zero and is not available, the device selects the next thicker stroke weight. If no thicker stroke weight is available, the device selects the next thinner stroke weight.

   If the specified stroke weight is less than zero and is not available, the device selects the next thinner stroke weight. If no thinner stroke weight is available, the device selects the next thicker stroke weight.

7. If the specified *typeface* is available, the device selects that typeface; otherwise, the device ignores this attribute. The stick fonts are typefaces 48, 49, and 50. The character set and posture selections must match an available stick font.

8. If more than one font emerges after this procedure, the location of fonts provides the following order of priority:

   Downloaded bitmap soft fonts in ascending font ID order.

   Downloaded scalable soft fonts in ascending font ID order.

   Bitmap external cartridge fonts.

   Scalable external cartridge fonts.

   Bitmap internal fonts.

   Scalable internal fonts.

9. If multiple fonts remain, a font in the specified *orientation* (the result of the DI or DR instruction) is selected. If none of the fonts is defined in the specified orientation, automatic rotation is applied to one of the remaining fonts.

Using Labels

Use the LB (Label) instruction to add text to plots, to create text charts, or to emphasize areas of a diagram or graph that need special attention or explanation. You can control almost all aspects of the label's appearance: its position, size, slant, spacing, and direction. All labels are drawn using the font currently designated (refer to the SD or AD instructions) and selected for use (refer to the SS or SA instructions).

If you are using a font other than the default, use SD (Standard Font Definition) or AD (Alternate Font Definition) instructions to *designate* a font. Then, use the SS (Select Standard Font) or SA (Select Alternate Font) instructions to *select* the designated font for use. You can follow the LB (Label) instruction with virtually any characters, including non-printing control codes, such as a Line Feed (**LF**) or Carriage Return (**CR**).

At the end of a label, you must use a special label terminator to signify the end of text. The default terminator is the ASCII end-of-text character **ETX** (decimal code 3), or you can define a terminator using the DT instruction. Without the label terminator in place, your device continues to label your picture with all subsequent HP-GL/2 instructions and parameters.

Note: Symbol mode, set by the SM instruction, is a special case of a Label.

The following example demonstrates printing a simple label using the SD instruction to designate a font, the SS instruction to select that font, the DT instruction to define a label terminator, and the LB instruction to print the label, including Carriage Returns and Line Feeds.

Note: In the examples, if a Carriage Return-Line Feed pair is required in the example, it is indicated as **CR LF**.

PA	1500,2500;	Specify absolute plotting and move to (1500,2500).
SD	1,21,2,1,4,25,5,1,6,0,7,52;	Designate the 25-point Univers Italic font as the standard font.
DT*,1;		Define the asterisk character as the label terminator (the "1" indicates that the terminator—the asterisk—shouldn't be printed). (Don't leave any spaces before the asterisk.)
SA	;	Select the alternate font for printing. Since an alternate font hasn't been designated, the default (say, 11.5-point) stick font is selected.
LBThis is the Stick Font	(Default)**CR LF CR LF***;	Print the first line of text, followed by two Carriage Returns and two Line Feed control codes. Notice how the asterisk terminates the label. Note also that if you include any spaces between the "LB" and "This", they will cause spaces to appear on the plotted page.
SS	;	Select the standard font.
LBThis is Univers Italic*;		Print the line of text in the newly specified font.

This is the Stick Font   (Default)
(1500,2500)

This is Univers Italic

Figure 47. Printing Labels

Default Label Conditions

The following label default conditions are established when the device is initialized, or set to default conditions. To change these settings, refer to the appropriate section or instruction.

- **Symbol set (character set)**—HP Roman-8.

- **Font spacing**—Device-dependent.

- **Pitch**—Device-dependent; normally 9 characters per inch. (Refer to your device's HP-GL/2 option documentation for any of the following instructions: AD, SD, SI, SR.)

- **Height**—Device-dependent; normally 11.5 point.

- **Posture**—Device-dependent.

- **Stroke weight**—Device-dependent.

- **Typeface**—HP-GL/2 stick.

  (For each of the above settings, refer to the AD and SD [Alternate and Standard Font Definition] instructions.)

- **Label terminator**—ASCII end-of-text character **ETX** (decimal code 3). Refer to the DT (Define Label Terminator) instruction.

- **Label starting point**—Current pen location (LO1). Refer to the LO (Label Origin) instruction.

- **Label direction**—Horizontal (the positive X-direction; it may be vertical on the paper). Refer to the DI, DR, and DV instructions.

- **Label direction mode**—Absolute. Refer to the DI instruction.

- **Label size mode**—Absolute. Refer to the SI instruction.

- **Character width and height**—Device-dependent. Refer to the SI instruction.

- **Space between characters and lines**—Normal (no extra space). Refer to the ES (Extra Space) instruction.

- **Character slant**—None (vertical). Refer to the SL (Character Slant) instruction.

- **Character fill mode**—Solid fill, no edging. Refer to the CF (Character Fill Mode) instruction.

- **Transparent data mode**—Off. Refer to the TD instruction.

Character Positioning

LB uses the current pen position as the reference for the label position. LO (Label Origin) can left-align, center, right-align, and adjust the vertical position about the current pen position.

The default label starting point is approximately at the intersection of the left edge of the character and the baseline. After printing a character, the pen position is updated by that character's delta-X distance to the starting point of the next character (unless modified by ES). This continues until the end of the label string (unless an embedded control character such as a carriage return or line feed is encountered). When printing the label, the pen position is updated according to the current path (DV) and label origin (LO). DV operates during the label, determining the character-to-character direction.

LB updates the pen position, but not the carriage-return point. **LF** characters move the carriage-return point down; DV changes this direction. The carriage-return point is maintained in physical units, not user units.

Moving to the Carriage-Return Point

When you begin labeling, the current pen location is the ***carriage-return point*** (the beginning of your line of text is the point to which the pen is "returned" when a carriage return (**CR**) control code is sent to the device). When the device encounters a CP (Character Plot) instruction, or a carriage return control code within a Label instruction, the pen moves to the carriage-return point, adjusted up or down by any line feeds.

The following instructions update the carriage-return point to the current location:

AA	Arc Absolute
AR	Arc Relative
AT	Absolute Arc Three Point
BR	Bezier Relative
BZ	Bezier Absolute
CP	Character Plot (see note)
DF	Default Values
DI	Absolute Direction
DR	Relative Direction
DV	Define Variable Text Path
IN	Initialize
LO	Label Origin
PA	Plot Absolute
PD	Pen Down (see note)
PE	Polyline Encoded
PR	Plot Relative
PU	Pen Up (see note)
RO	Rotate Coordinate System
RT	Relative Arc Three Point

Note: A PD or PU instruction *with parameters* also updates the carriage-return point. The CP instruction with a non-zero *lines* parameter updates the carriage-return point's vertical location.

The LB (Label) instruction does not update the carriage-return point to the current pen location, but continues labeling from the current pen location. This feature allows you to issue several label instructions that write one long label and still use a **CR** to get to the beginning of the entire label.

Control Characters

There are two modes of operation for printing HP-GL/2 labels: *normal* and *transparent data*.

Normal mode is the default; all character codes within a label are printed using the currently selected font, undefined character codes produce a space, and all control codes are ignored unless they perform a function, as follows (these are the codes in the PC-8 compatible symbol sets):

Control Code	Decimal code	Description
Null (**NUL**)	0	No Operation (NOP).
End-of-text (**ETX**)	3	An indication of the end of a label. If an alternative label terminator has been defined (using the DT instruction), this code performs no operation (NOP).
Bell(**BEL**)	7	No Operation (NOP).
Backspace (**BS**)	8	The pen moves to the position before the last printed character. For proportionally-spaced fonts, a backspace centers the overstriking character on the overstruck character; the pen position should end up at the same position as before the backspace. A backspace as the first character of a label is ignored.

Control Code	Decimal code	Description
Horizontal Tab (**HT**)	9	The pen moves to the next tab stop. Stops are located at the carriage-return point and at every eighth column between that point and the edge of the current window. A column is equal to the width of a Space character in the current font; it may be modified by the ES instruction.
Line Feed (**LF**)	10	The pen position and carriage-return point advance one line from their current positions. For HP-GL/2 labels, a line is the character-cell height.
Vertical Tab (**VT**)	11	No Operation (NOP).
Form Feed (**FF**)	12	No Operation (NOP).
Carriage Return (**CR**)	13	The pen position is updated to the carriage-return point (usually the pen position when the LB instruction was executed, adjusted by any line feeds).
Shift Out (**SO**)	14	Invoke the Alternate Font (equivalent to the SA instruction).
Shift In (**SI**)	15	Invoke the Standard Font (equivalent to the SS instruction).
Escape (**ESC**)	27	No Operation (NOP).
Space (**SP**)	32	The pen position moves one column to the right. If the current font contains a character definition for the space code, it is printed; otherwise it is a non-printing space. The space width may be modified by the ES instruction.

Transparent data mode, enabled by the TD instruction, prints all character codes in the current font; a space is printed for undefined character codes. The only functionality of a character code (*including control codes*) is the printing of a graphic image or a space. The only exception is the currently defined label terminator which prints an image or a space (if DT mode is 0) and also terminates the label.

For example, in the PC-8 symbol set, the eighth note musical symbol is identified by a character code of 13. In transparent data mode, a code of 13 produces the eighth note; in normal mode it produces a carriage return.

In the 8-bit compatible symbol sets, character codes 0 through 31 and 128 through 159 are control codes. The 7-bit compatible sets are treated in the same way, except that codes 128 through 255 are undefined (128 through 159 are NOPs and 160 through 255 are spaces). Values 32 and 255 are not considered control codes because they produce a space in any mode.

Adding Carriage Returns and Line Feeds to Labels

Carriage returns and line feeds are non-printing ASCII control characters. You can insert these formatting characters using a character-string function like CHR$ in BASIC, or by producing them directly from the keyboard. Most of the examples in this book represent these characters in bold uppercase letters such as **CR** and **LF**.

When you use a string function such as CHR$, you must separate it from the label in a suitable manner, using a concatenation symbol such as "+", ";", or ",". For example, in BASIC you use the "+" symbol between the label (which is enclosed in quotation marks, and the CHR$ function, like these:

"LBThis is a label"+CHR$(3)
"LBThis is another label"+CHR(13)+CHR$(10)+"on two lines"+CHR$(3)

If you can enter control characters from the keyboard, the same two labels would be:

"LBThis is a label**ETX**"
"LBThis is another label**CRLF**on two lines**ETX**"

Both pairs of examples produce the following labels:

This is a label
This is another label
on two lines

Enhancing Labels

You can enhance your labels by changing such aspects as the character size and slant, the space between characters and lines, and the orientation or placement of the label on the page. To effectively use these enhancements you should understand the properties of the character cell. Refer to *Working with the Character Cell* on page 58.

Character Size and Slant

Two mechanisms control the character size:

- The AD and SD (font definition) instructions allow the specification of the point size or pitch. The character size of proportionally-spaced fonts depends on the point size; pitch is ignored. The size of fixed-space fonts depends on pitch. AD and SD preserve a character's design aspect and cannot by themselves create tall skinny characters or short fat ones.

- The SI and SR (character size) instructions perform graphic transformations on characters in order to produce a certain size. These instructions can vary a character's cap height and width independently, allowing tall skinny or short fat characters.

To obtain the most typographically correct characters, use "SI;" to disable graphic transformations so that characters will be as close as possible to what the font designer intended. Size will be based solely on parameters last specified by AD or SD. If special graphic effects are required (such as rubbering or mirroring of characters), enable them with SI or SR.

You can change the size of the characters using the SI (Absolute Character Size) and SR (Relative Character Size) instructions. The SI instruction establishes the character width and height in centimeters of the uppercase "A" and maintains this character size independent of the location of P1 and P2 or the page size. The SR instruction establishes the character width and height of the uppercase "A" as a percentage of the distance between P1 and P2. Subsequent changes in the location of P1 and P2 cause the character size to change with the SR instruction. Changing the character size changes the size of the CP (Character Plot) cell and proportionally changes the line width used in labels (refer to AD and SD).

Note: When the Shift In (**SI**) or Shift Out (**SO**) control codes are used to select a font, the font size reverts to that font specified using the AD or SD instructions.

You can use the SL (Character Slant) instruction to slant the characters at a specified angle in either direction from the left vertical side of the CP (Character Plot) cell. The CP cell is not altered.

Character Spaces and Text Lines

You can use the ES (Extra Space) instruction to automatically increase or decrease spaces between all characters or lines. For example, ES can be used to increase space between every character in a label (such as "M E M O R A N D U M"), or to increase or decrease space between every line of text (such as double-spacing).

You can use the CP (Character Plot) instruction to move the pen a specific number of lines or spaces (character cells) from the current pen location. Use the CP instruction, for example, to indent a label a certain number of spaces.

Label Orientation and Placement

You can place your labels anywhere on the page in any orientation. The DI (Absolute Direction) instruction specifies the angle at which you want to print the characters, independent of the location of P1 and P2. The DR (Relative Direction) instruction specifies the angle at which you want to print the characters as a function of the P1 and P2 distance; thus when you change P1 and P2, the label angle changes to maintain the same orientation.

The DI and DR instructions allow you to print text at any angle with the letters in their normal side-by-side orientation.

Figure 48. Label Orientation and Direction

Note: Bitmap characters are always printed orthogonally to the page (refer to Figure 73 on page 140). Scalable characters print in the direction specified.

The DV (Define Variable Text Path) instruction allows you to specify the text path (right, left, up, or down) and the direction of Line Feeds with respect to the text path.

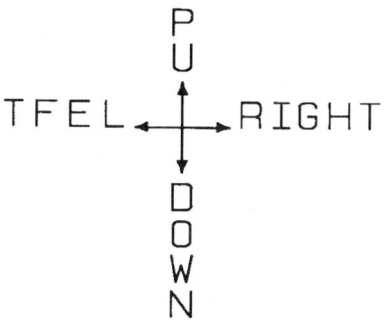

Figure 49. DV Instruction with +X to the Right and +Y Upwards

The LO (Label Origin) instruction simplifies placing labels on a drawing. Normally, the first character origin is the current pen location when the Label instruction is issued. The LO instruction allows you to specify that the label be centered or right- or left-justified from a point. For example, the following illustration shows four centered lines of text.

Lines of any length
can easily be
centered
without cumbersome calculations.

Figure 50. Label Origin Instruction to Center Text

These lines use one (X,Y) coordinate pair, one LO instruction to center labels, and a Carriage Return and Line Feed after each line. Without this instruction, an alternative method would involve calculating the length of the line in CP (Character Plot) cells, dividing by two, and using the CP instruction to backspace the required number of cells. The LO instruction saves calculation, decreases the number of characters sent to the device, and allows you to take advantage of proportionally-spaced fonts when the character widths are not known to the software.

Terminating Labels

LB tells the device to print every character following the instruction, rather than interpreting the characters as graphics instructions. In order to allow the normal terminator, the semicolon (;), to be used in text, the instruction is defined so that you must use the special label terminator to tell the device to once again interpret characters as graphics instructions. (If the instruction had been defined otherwise, you wouldn't be able to print semicolons in your text.)

The default label terminator is the non-printing ASCII end-of-text character **ETX**—decimal code 3, and denoted in BASIC by CHR$(3). You must use the label terminator, or the device prints the rest of your file as text instead of executing the instructions. You can change the label terminator using the DT (Define Label Terminator) instruction.

Accessing Special Characters

There are several ways of accessing special characters (those not normally available on your keyboard):

- Use a function defined for your programming language, such as CHR$ in BASIC to enter the decimal code, for example, CHR$(120) to draw the character "½" in symbol set 5 (Roman Extensions).

- On some computers, you can produce ASCII control characters from the keyboard by pressing two keys simultaneously. Check your computer documentation for the availability of this option and for the appropriate combination of keys on your system. Here are some common control characters and their equivalents for some computer systems:

Control Character	ASCII code (decimal)	Keyboard equivalent
ETX (end-of-text)	3	**CONTROL** and **C**
BS (backspace)	8	**CONTROL** and **H**
LF (line feed)	10	**CONTROL** and **J**
CR (carriage return)	13	**CONTROL** and **M**

- Use the SS (Select Standard Font) and SA (Select Alternate Font) instructions to switch between character sets, as in the following example.

SD	1,21,2,0,7,48;	Define the US ASCII (1,21) stick font (7,48) with fixed spacing (2,0) as the standard font.
AD	1,83,2,1,7,50;	Define the Spanish (1,83) HP-GL fixed arc font (7,50) with variable spacing (2,1) as the alternate font.
SS	;	Select the standard font.
LBUS ASCII, fixed-vector font**ETX**;		Print the first label.
CP	−22,−2;	Reposition 22 spaces left and two down for the second label.
SA	;	Select the alternate font.
LBSPANISH SET, variable-arc font**ETX**;		Print the first part of the second label.
CP	−17,−2;	Reposition the cursor.
LB]sus se<u>CHR$(124)</u>as?**ETX**;		Print the remainder of the Spanish label. Here, the keyboard "]" character (ASCII 93) corresponds to the "¿" in the Spanish character set, and "<u>CHR$(124)</u>" is whatever produces ASCII character number 124 ("ñ") from that character set (use for the latter whatever means is available with your programming language).

This generates:

```
US ASCII, fixed-vector font
```

SPANISH SET, variable-arc font

¿sus señas?

- Use the equivalent ASCII character on your keyboard in the label string. For example, in symbol set 5 (Roman Extensions), the character "½" is ASCII code 120, which is the character "x" on an English keyboard.

- If you need to use a special character from another set in the middle of a label, using the SS and SA instructions to toggle between sets can be inefficient. Instead, it might be easier to use the control characters shift-in (**SI**, decimal code 15) and shift-out (**SO**, 14) to toggle between the sets. For example:

SD	1,115,3,3,4,30;	Define a standard font
AD	1,5,3,3,4,30;	and an alternate font containing the symbol "½" (accessed from the keyboard as "x")
LB3**SO**x**SI**–5**ETX**;		Create the label, producing:

3½–5

HP-GL/2 Printing

The HP-GL/2 print model specifies how images are constructed and combined when rendering a page in HP-GL/2. The following terms are used:

Primitive—Any graphic item that marks the page (characters, vectors, polygons, and so on).

Destination—A composite of all primitives previously placed on the page.

Source—A solid black primitive possibly with added attributes such as current color and area fill. HP-GL/2 source data does not have transparent bits.

Pattern—An area fill attribute for a graphic object like a polygon, for example, solid fills, hatched fills, shaded fills, and user-defined raster patterns. (User-defined raster patterns can be either color or monochrome; all other fills are monochrome.)

Current Color—The color of the currently selected pen.

Texture—Monochrome pattern plus current color. See page 366.

Transparency mode—Determines how the pattern's white pixels affect the destination. In transparent mode (1), white pixels have no effect on the destination. In opaque mode (2), white pixels block out corresponding destination areas.

Area Fills

The Line and Fill Attributes group contains instructions for filling primitives: FT (Fill Type) and RF (Raster Fill Definition). The Palette extension contains instructions that determine pen colors (PC) and the number of pens (NP).

The following table shows which graphic images may have color or area fill applied:

Graphic Image	Color	Area Fill
Vectors	Yes	No
Arcs, circles	Yes	No
Polygons*	Yes	Yes
Characters:		
Vector	Yes	Yes
Scalable	Yes	Yes
Bitmapped	Yes	Yes

*	"Polygons" refers to objects filled with the FP instruction that were created with the polygon, wedge, and rectangle instructions (EA, ER, EW, PM, RA, RR, and WG).

The current color can be applied to any area except user-defined fills having color information (defined by RF and accessed by "FT11"). Area fills cannot be combined; for example, you cannot obtain a "shaded hatch" except by defining a user-defined pattern or screened vectors (using SV).

The Kernel Print Model

In the HP-GL/2 kernel print model, non-white source pixels, to which current color and pattern have been added, replace destination pixels. White pixels imposed on the source by a pattern are transparent and have no effect.

Extended Print Model

More options are allowed when the Technical Graphics and Palette extensions are added to the kernel. Two instructions then determine the state of the HP-GL/2 print model: TR (Transparency Mode) and MC (Merge Control).

- MC can perform logical operations (AND, OR, exclusive-OR, and NOT) on non-white source, texture, and destination pixels.

- TR determines whether white source pixels affect the destination.

The kernel print model is equivalent to "TR1" (transparent), "MC0" (replacement) in the extended print model.

HP-GL/2, HP RTL, and PCL Print Models

Although the HP-GL/2 and the HP RTL and PCL print models are slightly different (notably in their treatment of whites), logical raster operations ("ROPs") using TR and MC are similar. Dual-context applications may prefer to remain in HP-GL/2 for efficiency and use the HP-GL/2 print model. The complete set of 256 logical operations is listed on page 473.

	HP RTL and PCL Print Model	HP-GL/2 Print Model
Default Print Model	The non-white source and pattern pixels are OR'd with each other and replace destination pixels.	The non-white source and pattern pixels are OR'd with each other and replace destination pixels.
Transparency Modes	HP RTL and PCL have both source and pattern transparency modes, which determine whether white source and pattern pixels are applied to the destination.	HP-GL/2 has pattern transparency mode, but not source transparency mode, since there is no bounding box as in raster mode or character cells.
	"White" is defined by the white reference in the color space.	The CR instruction defines "white" by setting a white reference.
	Default transparency: white source and pattern pixels are transparent.	Default transparency: white pattern pixels are transparent.
Current Color	The current color is selected from the palette by the Foreground Color (**ESC***v#S) command. The default is black.	The current color is selected from the palette by the SP instruction. The default is pen number 0 (normally white).
	HP RTL and PCL cannot import HP-GL/2 patterns.	HP-GL/2 can import HP RTL and PCL patterns.

	HP RTL and PCL Print Model	HP-GL/2 Print Model
Area Fill	Area fill is selected by pre-defined (**ESC***c#G) and downloadable (**ESC***c#W) patterns.	Area fill is selected by pre-defined (FT) and downloadable (RF) patterns.
Logical Operations	**ESC***l#O determines the interaction between source, texture, and destination.	"MC1" determines the interaction between source, texture, and destination.

HP-GL/2
KERNEL

Chapter 4: The HP-GL/2 Extensions

This chapter describes the Extension instructions that rely on specific technologies or functionality. The Extensions are:

- The Technical Graphics Extension   page 77.

- The Palette Extension   page 82.

- The Dual-Context Extension   page 83.

- The Digitizing Extension   page 89.

- The Advanced Drawing Extension   page 92.

- The Advanced Text Extension   page 94.

The Technical Graphics Extension

Many HP-GL/2 devices, in particular pen plotters, support the Technical Graphics Extension, though most of these instructions are not available on PCL devices. These instructions give added flexibility when your applications require more technical functions, such as computer-aided design and drawing, architectural rendering, integrated circuit layout, and so on. The instructions in the Technical Graphics Extension let you achieve the following results:

- Specify chord tolerances for arcs, circles, and wedges.

- Design and download user-defined characters.

- Turn on and off the device's automatic cutter.

- Advance the media for long-axis plotting.

- Write a message to the device's control panel.

- Ask the device to output information to the computer.

- Specify a user-defined page size.

- Set the quality level of output.

- Sort your plot data for faster throughput on pen plotters.

- Set the pen speed on pen plotters.

These instructions form the Technical Graphics Extension (those marked * are device-specific):

BP	Begin Plot	Indicates the beginning of a plot.
CT	Chord Tolerance Mode	Allows you to adjust the number of chords in an arc or circle by indicating how chords are to be specified.

DL	Download Character	Allows you to store user-defined characters a buffer.*
EC	Enable Cutter	Turns a device's automatic cutter on or off.*
FR	Frame Advance	Advances the media to the next frame for long-axis plotting.
MC	Merge Control	Controls the pixel color when two or more graphics elements intersect. (This instruction is also part of the Advanced Drawing Extension.)
MG	Message	Writes a message to the device's front-panel display.*
MT	Media Type	Indicates the type of media loaded in the device.
NR	Not Ready	Takes the device off-line.*
OE	Output Error	Outputs any program errors (for debugging).
OH	Output Hard-Clip Limits	Outputs the hard-clip limit coordinates.
OI	Output Identification	Outputs a device identification string.
OP	Output P1 and P2	Outputs the P1 and P2 coordinate locations.
OS	Output Status	Outputs device status information.
PS	Plot Size	Sets the hard-clip limits to a given size.
QL	Quality Level	Indicates the level of quality for plotting.
ST	Sort	Indicates the types of sorting the device can use.
VS	Velocity Select	Sets the pen speed for all or for selected pens.*

Defining a Picture

A picture begins with a BP instruction and is terminated by a PG, RP, or another BP instruction. The picture is divided into the ***picture header*** and the ***picture body***. The picture header contains the instructions that set up the picture to be plotted. The picture body contains the instructions that actually cause the device to mark the paper.

The Picture Header State

The BP, PG, or RP instructions or power-up start the picture header state. The following instructions, if used, must be issued in the picture header:

MT	Media Type
PS	Plot Size
QL	Quality Level.

Each of these instructions affects the entire picture.

Note that the following instructions are permitted in the picture header; however, the PS (Plot Size) instruction defaults their settings and therefore should precede them:

AC	Anchor Corner
IP	Input P1 and P2
IR	Input Relative P1 and P2
IW	Input Window.

The Picture Body State

Any instruction that could result in marks being made on the page or edges added to the polygon-fill buffer terminates the picture header and starts the picture body. The following instructions start the picture body (if it is in picture header state) and are allowed in picture body state:

AA	Arc Absolute
AR	Arc Relative
AT	Absolute Arc Three Point
BR	Bezier Relative
BZ	Bezier Absolute
CI	Circle
CP	Character Plot
EA	Edge Rectangle Absolute
EP	Edge Polygon
ER	Edge Rectangle Relative
EW	Edge Wedge
FP	Fill Polygon
LB	Label
PA	Plot Absolute
PD	Pen Down
PE	Polyline Encoded
PM	Polygon Mode
PR	Plot Relative
PU	Pen Up (with parameters)
RA	Fill Rectangle Absolute
RR	Fill Rectangle Relative
RT	Relative Arc Three Point
WG	Fill Wedge.

Replotting and the Picture Header

RP (Replot) should be placed immediately following the picture, with no intervening instructions other than output requests. The currently stored plot referenced by RP will disappear upon the next BP instruction, and also upon the next transition into the picture body. If a picture does not start with a BP (that is, it began after the last PG or RP), and an RP is issued while still in the picture header, it is device-dependent whether the previous picture is replotted.

Chords and Chord Tolerance

To draw curves, the device draws a series of straight lines, called *chords*, for each arc segment. The smoothness of the curve depends on the number of chords used to draw it—the more chords, the smoother the shape appears. Figure 65 on page 125 shows circles drawn with different numbers of chords.

The number of chords in any curved shape is determined by the *chord tolerance*—the allowable deviation from a smooth curve. Many instructions let you set the chord tolerance you want. Chord tolerance can be specified as either an angle in degrees, or as the maximum distance the arc drawn may deviate from the true arc. These two methods are called *chord angle* and *deviation distance*. The chord angle is the default method. The CT (Chord Tolerance Mode) instruction selects the method.

Note: Do not use an "adaptive" line type (see the description of the LT instruction on page 215) when you draw circles, arcs, wedges, or polygons. The device will attempt to draw the complete pattern in every chord; there are 72 chords in a circle using the default chord angle.

The Downloadable Set and User-Defined Characters

If you need special label characters or symbols that are not included in any of the supplied character sets, you can design your own characters or symbols, or even an entire character set. The DL (Download Character) instruction allows you to download these characters. The DL instruction can define up to 94 characters to be stored in a buffer for repeated use during a plot. The character plot cell used by the DL instruction is always a fixed-space character cell, regardless of the spacing in the current font.

Merging Pixels

The MC (Merge Control) instruction controls the color of pixels where two or more page marking primitives intersect on the page. This instruction, like the Logical Operation (**ESC***l#O) command of HP RTL, supports all 256 Microsoft Windows ternary (ROP3) raster operation codes—see page 473. Raster operations specify how source, destination, and pattern data are combined to produce final images. A common application of the MC instruction is the rendering of complex polygon fill patterns. You can find a more detailed explanation of how raster operations work in *Chapter 10: Interactions between Picture Elements* on page 365.

Obtaining Device Output

When the device receives an output instruction, it responds by making the information available in the form of an output response that can be read by a computer with an input statement. Most programming languages use an input statement such as ENTER, INPUT, READ, READLN, FSCANF, or GET to read the response from the device. When you read the output response, be sure to specify the correct number and type of variables that are to receive the data. For example, BASIC requires that a character string variable should be in the form A\$, and a numeric variable is in the form A. Refer to your programming language documentation for the correct input statement to use and the correct format for numeric and character-string variables. Output responses containing more than one piece of information should be read completely to clear the output buffer, with a separate variable for each piece of information. For example, the OH (Output Hard-Clip Limits) instruction outputs four integers; an input statement might be:

```
fscanf (device, "%d,%d,%d,%d\n", &x1, &y1, &x2, &y2);
```

or:

```
INPUT #1, A,B,Y,Z
```

Note that the output instructions *must* be terminated with a semicolon.

Output instructions should not be used on networks or unidirectional interfaces.

For Centronics Users

The Centronics interface supports data transmission in one direction only. The output instructions do not return information to the computer. However, they will perform other expected operations, such as setting or clearing status bits in the device's memory.

For HP-IB Users

A device signals the end of its output response with an output response terminator. For HP-IB users, the default output response terminator is a carriage return followed by a line feed (**CR LF**).

Be sure that your device is *not* set to LISTEN ONLY. If it is, the device will not send an output response and your program will halt. Refer to your product documentation for more information about HP-IB addressing.

For RS-232-C, IEEE-1284-compatible interface, and MIO Users

The device outputs information according to the handshake protocol. Your computer documentation should specify whether or not delays are required.

A device signals the end of its output response with an output response terminator. For the RS-232-C, IEEE-1284-compatible, and MIO interfaces, the default output response terminator is a carriage return (**CR**).

Using Output Instructions

Use the following procedures for sending output instructions to your device:

1. Send the output instruction to the device as you do other HP-GL/2 instructions. Note that all the output instructions use terminators, normally a semicolon, and have no parameters.

2. Read the device's output response immediately, using an input statement appropriate to your computer language, keeping in mind the number and type of variables.

Do not send multiple output instructions and then try to read all the responses sequentially. This can lead to intermittent timing problems, depending on what the computer and the device are currently doing.

Identifying the Device and its Functions

When you have more than one peripheral (for example, several plotters and printers) connected to a computer, it may be necessary to have the device output its identification so that you can be sure it is on-line. The OI (Output Identification) instruction can output the device ID to the computer.

Obtaining Error Information

Use the OE (Output Error) instruction for error retrieval. The OE instruction outputs the error number that corresponds to the first HP-GL/2 error the device receives. Use this instruction to identify errors by number when debugging a program. In addition, these errors set the error bit of the status byte in the response to OS (Output Status) instruction.

Obtaining Status Byte Information

The eight-bit status byte stores information about device operating conditions. Use the OS (Output Status) instruction to learn the status of the device's current operating conditions. Each condition is assigned a bit number (from 0 to 7) and a corresponding decimal value. (The conditions, bit numbers, and corresponding decimal values are shown in the description of the

OS instruction.) You can obtain the value of the status byte by reading the response to the OS instruction or executing an HP-IB serial poll of the device.

Summary of Output Responses

The following table lists output responses generated by HP-GL/2 output instructions. Note that numeric ranges do not include the sign of the response. For example, if a five-digit response is a negative value, a minus sign precedes the five digits; the minus sign does not replace a digit. In addition to these parameters, the output terminator is always sent at the end of output, and commas are sent to separate parameters.

Instruction	Parameters Returned	Type	Range
OE	Error number	Integer	1 digit
OH	X_{LL}, Y_{LL}, X_{UR}, Y_{UR}	Integers	up to 6 digits each (plotter-units)
OI	Model number	String	up to 30 characters
OP	$P1_X$, $P1_Y$, $P2_X$, $P2_Y$	Integers	up to 8 digits each
OS	Status number	Integer	up to 3 digits

The Palette Extension

This Extension contains instructions that satisfy the functionality of devices, such as raster devices, with special palette features. If you have access to a pen plotter and a raster device, you will want to define a palette to get the most from your HP-GL/2 program on the raster device, while maintaining pen plotter functionality. Pen plotters may support this extension, defaulting some instructions in accordance with pen plotter technology.

The following instructions form the Palette Extension:

CR	Set Color Range for Relative Color Data	Sets the color range for red-green-blue (RGB) data.
NP	Number of Pens	Sets the size of the HP-GL/2 palette.
PC	Pen Color Assignment	Assigns colors to specific pens.
SV	Screened Vectors	Selects the type of screening (fill) to apply to vectors and areas.
TR	Transparency Mode	Designates an overlaying white area of pattern or area fill as transparent or opaque.

Defining Your Palette

The palette is an array of virtual pens, each having an associated color value and an associated width (pen-width is strictly an HP-GL/2 concept, not a PCL or HP RTL concept). The PC instruction defines pen colors in terms of red-green-blue (RGB) components. The PW and WU instructions (of the Line and Fill Attributes Group in the HP-GL/2 Kernel) set pen widths. The SP instruction selects a pen. A palette should be defined just after initialization and before sending graphics data. Defining a palette includes the following:

1. Indicating the size of the palette (NP). On dual-context color printers, the palette should be created in PCL and then used within HP-GL/2.

2. Assigning a color to each pen in the palette (PC).

3. Specifying the width for each pen in the palette (PW—part of the Line and Fill Attributes Group).

For maximum flexibility, you may want to allow the user to specify values for these items.

For pen plotters it is the responsibility of the user to ensure that the correct pens (color and width) have been loaded into the appropriate carousel stall.

Devices may support logical pens beyond the number of physical pens. Devices perform a modulo function on any logical pen number beyond the physical number so the device can select the appropriate physical pen.

Dual-Context Operation

HP-GL/2, PCL, and HP RTL create different default palettes at reset or power-up. However, only one palette can be active at a time. Therefore, when switching from one context to another, the active palette is always transferred and becomes the active palette in the other contexts. PCL, HP RTL, or HP-GL/2 can all modify the active palette.

Effect of a Color Palette on Monochrome Devices

Most large-format monochrome devices produce varying levels of gray-scale when you request area fills and lines for pens other than black and white in the color palette. However, the gray scale is unpredictable when drawing a raster pattern with a colored pen. For example, yellow may be converted to a light shade of gray, and red to a darker shade of gray. A red pen used in a 10% raster fill pattern may produce an area fill more dense than expected.

Small-format monochrome devices may not have gray-scale capability. All lines produced will be 100% black.

The Dual-Context Extension

The Dual-Context Extension is implemented by devices that support both HP-GL/2 and Hewlett-Packard's PCL Printer Language or Raster Transfer Language (HP RTL), allowing both raster and vector images on the same page. Apart from some minor differences, HP RTL is a subset of PCL. This extension gives you the flexibility to switch modes on devices that support both vector and text or raster facilities, typically for desk-top presentations, where you may want to merge word-processed text and graphics images with vector graphics images.

The Dual-Context Extension contains the following commands and instructions:

ESC%#A	Enter PCL Mode or Enter HP RTL Mode	Instructs the device to interpret subsequent instructions as PCL or HP RTL commands.
ESC%#B	Enter HP-GL/2 Mode	Instructs the device to interpret subsequent instructions as HP-GL/2 instructions.
ESCE	Reset	Restores certain device defaults.
FI	Primary Font Selection by ID	Designates a font as the primary font.
FN	Secondary Font Selection by ID	Designates a font as the secondary font.
SB	Scalable or Bitmap Fonts	Specifies the type of font to be used in labels. (This instruction is also part of the Advanced Text Extension.)

The Dual-Context Extension includes three additional HP-GL/2 instructions and three PCL or HP RTL escape sequences that are recognized in the HP-GL/2 context. See *Part 3* of this book for a description of the HP RTL commands.

HP RTL does not have a "picture frame" into which HP-GL/2 pictures are fitted; it uses the whole of the logical page.

The following terms are used in describing PCL devices:

Picture presentation directives—PCL commands that enter and leave the HP-GL/2 context, define a delimiting rectangle (the picture frame) for the HP-GL/2 plot, and specify a scaling factor.

Picture frame—The destination rectangle when transferring an HP-GL/2 plot to the PCL logical page. PCL picture frame size commands specify its size.

Picture frame scaling factor—The ratio of the size of the picture frame to the size of the HP-GL/2 plot. There may be two scaling factors for the X and Y directions.

Picture frame anchor point—The upper left corner of the picture frame, which is set to the current active position (CAP) in the PCL environment when the picture frame anchor point command is executed.

Refer to the *PCL5 Printer Language Technical Reference Manual* or *Part 3* of this book (for HP RTL) for a complete description of the dual-context environment.

Using Dual-Context PCL or HP RTL Commands

The three commands listed above that begin with an escape character (**ESC**), are recognized by some devices to switch between modes or to reset a device. The escape control code is decimal 27. The character "#" in these commands must be replaced by a numeric value, to further describe the function of the command. Full details of all PCL commands can be found in the PCL documentation. HP RTL commands are in *Part 3* of this book, starting on page 335.

The **ESC%−1B** command, which if you use it must be at the start of your HP-GL/2 programs, is a PCL and HP RTL command which puts your device into HP-GL/2 mode. Subsequent data is interpreted as HP-GL/2 data. Merging with PCL or HP-RTL images is disabled. Not all devices support this stand-alone mode.

The **ESC%#A** command, besides entering PCL or HP RTL mode, controls the translation of the pen location to PCL or HP RTL equivalents, called the *current active position* (CAP). The CAP can be moved explicitly anywhere within the PCL or HP RTL logical page.

In PCL devices, after an **ESCE** command, the CAP is "floating" until printable data or a command affecting the CAP is received. This means that it moves in accordance with PCL orientation, margin, and spacing commands. Once printable data or an instruction or command affecting the CAP is received, the CAP becomes "fixed", that is, it is no longer affected by changes to orientation, margins, or spacing.

Switching Contexts

Two commands, **ESC%#A** and **ESC%#B** are used to switch between HP-GL/2 and PCL or HP RTL contexts. **ESC%2B** or **ESC%3B** can also transfer the PCL coordinate system and measurement unit. The active palette is always transferred and remains active in either context. **ESCE**, which resets the device in HP-GL/2, PCL, and HP RTL modes and has the same functionality as IN, always returns the device to PCL or HP RTL parsing mode.

HP-GL/2 may be integrated with PCL in two ways:

- Using the PCL picture frame (**ESC%0B** or **ESC%1B**).

- Using the PCL coordinate system and measurement unit (**ESC**%2B or **ESC**%3B).

HP-GL/2 may be integrated with HP RTL in one way:

- Using the HP RTL logical page (**ESC**%0B or **ESC**%1B).

Defining the PCL Picture Frame

HP-GL/2 plots may be placed on the PCL logical page by specifying the size and location of a destination rectangle or ***picture frame***. To use this method, specify the size and location of the picture frame using PCL picture presentation commands before entering HP-GL/2. A plot created using the SC (Scale) instruction (scaling on) is automatically scaled to fit the picture frame. A plot created in absolute plotter-units with scaling off may be explicitly scaled by other PCL picture presentation commands before the transfer. The data flow for this method looks like this:

PCL commands

...
Specify the PCL picture frame dimensions and anchor point
Explicitly scale the HP-GL/2 plot if it was originally drawn in plotter-units
Enter HP-GL/2 with **ESC**%0B or **ESC**%1B
HP-GL/2 instructions

...
Exit HP-GL/2 with **ESC**%#A
PCL commands

Note that if no picture frame is defined, the PCL logical page is used as the default.

Transferring the PCL Coordinate System

By transferring the PCL coordinate system and measurement unit into HP-GL/2, vector and raster objects can be intermixed on the logical page as necessary. To use this method of integrating HP-GL/2 and PCL, use a value of 2 or 3 with **ESC**%#B; note that values of 2 and 3 are not supported on all devices. The PCL current active position (CAP) may also be transferred. The data stream then looks like this:

PCL commands

...
Enter HP-GL/2 with **ESC**%2B or **ESC**%3B
HP-GL/2 instructions

...
Exit HP-GL/2 with **ESC**%#A
PCL commands

When you enter HP-GL/2 using **ESC**%2B or **ESC**%3B, the PCL origin, axes, and print direction transfer into HP-GL/2. Imported PCL graphics are rotated because the Y-axes of PCL and HP-GL/2 increase in opposite directions. RO moves the HP-GL/2 origin to where the PCL origin would be if it were rotated by the PCL Print Direction command (**ESC**&a#P). HP-GL/2 instructions that use current units use PCL dot units.

A SC (Scale) instruction with parameters switches back to the HP-GL/2 coordinate system: defaults are set, SC is executed, and picture-frame scaling is applied. An "IN", "BP", or "SC;" instruction restores the PCL dot coordinate system.

Exiting HP-GL/2 after **ESC**%2B performs an "RO0" and turns off user-defined scaling; then plotter-units are used.

Merging with HP RTL

Many HP RTL devices support HP-GL/2 with the Technical Graphics Extension. For such devices, always start in HP-GL/2 with the picture header. The data stream looks like this:

HP-GL/2 instructions

...
Exit HP-GL/2 and enter HP RTL with **ESC**%#A
HP RTL commands

...
Enter HP-GL/2 with **ESC**%0B or **ESC**%1B
HP-GL/2 instructions

Note that the HP-GL/2 origin and orientation are not modified by HP RTL.

Palettes

HP-GL/2 and HP RTL or PCL create different default palettes at reset or power-up. Both contexts allow the active palette to be modified. In dual-context operations, only one palette can be active at a time. Therefore, when switching from one context to another, the active palette is always transferred and becomes the active palette in both contexts. In HP-GL/2, the relevant palette instructions are:

IN, Initialize	Defaults the palette size to two pens for monochrome raster devices and eight pens for color raster devices. The 8-pen default HP-GL/2 palette is different from the default RGB 8-pen PCL and HP RTL palette.
PC, Pen Color Assignment	Modifies palette colors. HP RTL and PCL use the palette programming commands **ESC***v#A, **ESC***v#B, **ESC***v#C, and **ESC***v#I.
CR, Set Color Range for Relative Color Data	Sets the range for specifying relative color data. HP RTL and PCL use the Configure Image Data (**ESC***v#W) command.
SP, Select Pen	Selects a "current" color. HP RTL and PCL use the Foreground Color (**ESC***v#S) command.

PCL Fonts

Fonts are not transferred between contexts, but HP-GL/2 complies with PCL font specifications. The AD and SD instructions use the same font selection algorithm as PCL, based on font attribute priority to find the closest match to the user's request. See *How Your Device Selects Fonts* on page 63. The SB instruction, in the Dual-Context extension, may specify either scalable or bitmap fonts.

PCL Macros

PCL macros can include HP-GL/2 instructions. The HP-GL/2 instructions in the macro must be contained within a shell of PCL macro commands, the **ESC**%#B command for entering HP-GL/2, and the **ESC**%#A command to re-enter PCL.

Modifications to HP-GL/2 Instructions in Dual-Context Mode

The following HP-GL/2 instructions are modified in Dual-Context Mode as summarized below. Functional differences are also described in the individual instruction descriptions. Those marked with an asterisk (*) are for PCL only.

AC, Anchor Corner (*)	IN, DF, or **ESCE** place the anchor point at the lower-left corner of the picture frame relative to the current coordinate system.
BP, Begin Plot (*) (Technical Extension)	In PCL devices, the PG portion of BP is ignored and BP is mapped to IN regardless of the *kind* and *value* parameters. Data previously formatted for the current page is not cleared. (In HP RTL devices, BP performs the PG and IN functions.)
DF, Default Values (*)	"AC;" places the anchor point at the lower-left corner of the picture frame relative to the current coordinate system. "IW;" sets the user window equal to PCL picture frame window.
FT, Fill Type	Additional fill types (21 and 22) are imported from PCL or HP RTL. Fill type 21 selects a PCL or HP RTL predefined patterned fill. Option 1 specifies a pattern type from 1 to 6 (see the FT instruction description). Option 2 is ignored. Fill type 22 uses the PCL or HP RTL user-defined fill specified by **ESC***c#W. Option 1 is the PCL or HP RTL ID of the user-defined fill. Option 2 is ignored. An invalid option 1 (for example, the pattern has been deleted), prints a solid fill in the current color.
IP, Input P1 and P2 (*)	"IP;" sets P1 to the lower-left corner of the PCL picture frame (viewed from the current HP-GL/2 orientation) and P2 to the opposite corner. Parameters are scaled by the picture frame scaling factor.
IR, Input Relative P1 and P2 (*)	The references to the hard-clip limits are replaced by the PCL picture frame. The default positions for P1 and P2 are the lower-left and upper-right corners of the picture frame, as viewed from the current orientation.
IW, Input Window (*)	"IW;" defaults the window to the PCL picture frame. The maximum printable area is the intersection of the user-defined window, the PCL picture frame, the PCL logical page, and the hard-clip limits. Parameters specified in plotter-units are scaled by the picture frame scaling factor.
PG, Advance Full Page	PG is ignored in PCL. A page eject can only be accomplished by the form feed (**FF**) character. In PCL, a form feed causes an unconditional page eject and advances the current active position to the same horizontal position at the top of the next form (top margin). A PCL reset, page length, page size, orientation, or input cassette control instruction causes a conditional page eject. When a page is ejected, the PCL or HP RTL cursor is set to the "home position" (at the left and top margin) on the new page. A page eject caused by a PCL command does not effect the HP-GL/2 cursor position.

PM, Polygon Mode	**ESC**E is also recognized in polygon mode.
PS, Plot Size (*) (Technical Extension)	In PCL devices, PS is ignored when HP-GL/2 is entered by **ESC**%#B with 0 or a positive value; the plot size is set by the PCL picture frame. (In HP RTL devices, PS operates as defined while the device is in picture-header state.)
PW, Pen Width (*)	Metric widths are scaled by the ratio of the size of the PCL picture frame to the HP-GL/2 plot size. For example, if HP-GL/2 plot size is twice as large as the PCL picture frame, *"WUPW.3"* sets the vector width to 0.15 mm.
RO, Rotate Coordinate System (*)	Rotations are relative to the default HP-GL/2 coordinate system, as defined for PCL or HP RTL. P1 or P2 may be rotated outside the current picture frame; they can be repositioned to the rotated lower-left and upper-right corners of the picture frame by issuing an "IP;" or an "IR;" instruction. The user-defined window is rotated, and any portion that is rotated outside the picture frame is clipped to the picture frame. The window can be set equal to the picture frame by an "IW;" instruction.
RP, Replot (*)	This instruction is ignored in PCL; a page eject can only be accomplished from the PCL context by sending a form feed (**FF**) control character.
SC, Scale (*)	When user-scaling mode is off, current units are: (plotter-units * (PCL picture-frame-size ÷ HP-GL/2 plot-size)) Left and bottom parameters are relative to the PCL picture frame, viewed from the current orientation. The directional implications of left and bottom assume the default P1/P2 orientation.
SI, Absolute Character Size (*)	The *width* and *height* parameters, in centimeters, are adjusted by the picture frame scaling factor.
SV, Screened Vectors (Palette Extension)	Additional screen types (21 and 22) are imported from PCL or HP RTL. Screen type 21 selects PCL or HP RTL predefined patterned fill. Option 1 specifies a pattern fill type between 1 and 6 (see the SV instruction description). Option 2 is ignored. Screen type 22 selects the PCL or HP RTL user-defined fill specified by **ESC***c#W. Option 1 is the PCL or HP RTL ID of the fill. Option 2 is ignored. An invalid option 1 (for example, a deleted pattern), prints a solid fill in the current color.
TD, Transparent Data	**ESC**E is a special case. In normal mode, **ESC**E within a label string will cause a device reset and transition to the PCL or HP RTL environment. In transparent mode, **ESC**E within a label string is printed rather than performing a device reset.

| WU,
Pen Width Unit
Selection (*) | If an HP-GL/2 plot size is specified, metric units are adjusted by the current PCL picture frame scaling factor. |

The Digitizing Extension

This section defines a block of instructions that satisfy the digitizing requirements of pen plotters. This Extension is available on pen plotters only; raster devices are incapable of digitizing an image. Check your product's documentation to determine whether this extension is supported. The information in this section discusses the instructions used in digitizing, together with the methods and procedures for digitizing and verifying the entry of a point.

"Digitizing" is moving the pen or a digitizing sight to a point on the plotting surface, registering the point, and sending the X,Y coordinates of that point to the computer. This lets you recreate a drawing from hard-copy, instead of redesigning it from scratch or scanning the entire drawing into your computer.

Devices that implement this extension include front-panel controls for moving the pen or digitizing sight and for entering and storing the X,Y coordinates and pen status of the digitized point.

The Digitizing Extension instructions are:

DC	Digitize Clear	Clears and exits digitize mode
DP	Digitize Point	Enters digitize mode
OD	Output Digitize Point and Pen Status	Outputs the coordinate location of the digitized point

The Digitizing Procedure

Although you can use a pen for digitizing, we recommend you use a digitizing sight. Refer to your product's documentation for information on using a digitizing sight. Digitize with the sight in the pen-down position for the highest accuracy.

Note: To avoid smearing ink on the tip of the digitizing sight or damaging the sight, do not load the digitizing sight directly into the pen carousel.

When you are ready to digitize your plot, use the DP (Digitize Point) instruction to enter digitize mode. Refer to your pen plotter's documentation to enter the digitized point from the plotter's control panel. After entering the point, use the OD (Output Digitized Point and Pen Status) instruction to send the X,Y coordinates of the point and the pen status (up or down) to your computer. The DC (Digitize Clear) instruction clears and exits digitize mode.

Digitizing with the Plotter

Familiarize yourself with the Digitizing Extension instructions listed above before reviewing the digitizing methods here. When digitizing, you must make sure that a point has been entered before attempting to retrieve that point. The following sections show you the methods for digitizing and retrieving points.

Manual Digitizing

The manual method is the easiest digitizing method to understand. However, it is not efficient when you want to enter many points, or when user interaction during program execution is not possible. The following steps detail a typical program using the manual method:

1. Put the plotter into digitizing mode by sending a DP instruction to the device.

2. Have the program display or print a message on the computer screen prompting you to enter a point.

3. Cause the program to pause until instructed to continue. Using the BASIC INPUT statement and entering an empty string when the user is ready to continue will work on some systems. Some versions of BASIC use statements such as STOP, WAIT, or PAUSE.

4. Move the digitizing sight (or pen) to the desired point using the control-panel cursor-control buttons. Complete final positioning with the sight or pen down. Press the appropriate button on your pen plotter's control panel (refer to your plotter's documentation).

5. Cause the program to resume. The way you resume program execution depends on the statement you used to halt the program. If you used an input statement in step 3, press the Return key on the computer.

6. Output he digitized information to the computer using the OD (Output Digitized Point and Pen Status) instruction. Have your computer read the information (X,Y coordinates and the pen state). Then take the necessary steps to process the digitized data.

Using this method, you do not need to monitor the status byte because the program does not proceed to the OD instruction until you enter a point and cause the program to resume.

The following program digitizes a single point and displays the coordinates and pen status:

Send to the device:	"DP;"
Prompt the user:	"Press plotter's Enter button to digitize the point."
Prompt the user:	"Press computer's Return key to continue."
Wait for the Return key.	
Send to the device:	"OD;"
Read from the device:	X,Y,P
Print out:	X,Y,P

Monitoring the Status Byte

The second digitizing method monitors bit position 2 of the plotter's status byte, which is set when a digitized point is available. Refer to the OS (Output Status) instruction for details of the contents of the status byte.

There are a variety of ways to monitor bit position 2, depending on the instructions available in your computer. If there are instructions in your programming language to check bits directly, the third least significant bit should be checked for the occurrence of a 1.

If no bit operations are available, the status byte can be operated on arithmetically to check for the availability of a digitized point. Executing successive divisions by a power of 2 and checking the answer for an odd or even integer is a common way of monitoring bits without converting the number to binary form. The following steps detail a program using this method:

1. Send a DP instruction to the plotter.

2. Have the program display or print a message on the computer screen prompting you to enter a point.

3. Send an OS instruction followed by a loop dividing the status value and checking for a final odd or even value.

   When you press the control-panel button to enter a digitized point, the X,Y coordinates and the pen status information are stored and bit position 2 is set. The status value increments by the value of bit 2; your division yields the odd integer, allowing the program to continue.

4. Send an OD instruction. Read and display the X,Y coordinates and pen status. Then take the necessary steps to process the digitized data.

Example: Digitizing by Monitoring the Status Byte

The following program checks the proper bit of the status byte. The program uses an integer statement (INT) that truncates, not rounds—refer to your programming language documentation.

Send to the device:	"DP;"
Prompt the user:	"Press plotter's Enter button to digitize the point."
Send to the device:	"OS;"
Read from the device:	STATUS

```
STATUS = INT(STATUS/4)
If STATUS = INT(STATUS/2)*2 then loop to the "send OS;" statement above
```

Send to the device:	"OD;"
Read from the device:	X,Y,P
Print out:	X,Y,P

Example: Digitizing Many Points

When the computer is used to monitor bit position 2, it may not process the data points immediately. Allocate space for the total number of points to be digitized. Then establish a loop to process the total number of points and call a subroutine each time to check that a point has been entered.

When you are prompted to enter a point in the following example, use the cursor keys to move the digitizing sight to each location, then press the appropriate control-panel button that enters digitized points. After digitizing the program's 25 points, all coordinates are displayed on the computer's screen.

```
For C = 1 to 25
     Send to the device:   "DP;"
     Prompt the user:      "Enter point number" C
     Execute subroutine (see below)
     Send to the device:   "OD;"
     Read from the device: X(C),Y(C),P(C)
Next C
For C = 1 to 25
     Print out: X(C),Y(C),P(C)
Next C

Subroutine to check status bit 2:
     Send to the device:   "OS;"
     Read from the device: STATUS
     STATUS=INT(STATUS/4)
     If STATUS = INT(STATUS/2)*2  then loop in subroutine
     Return from subroutine.
```

The Advanced Drawing Extension

The Advanced Drawing Extension groups four instructions that are of use in advanced drawing environments. The following instructions make up the Advanced Drawing Extension:

BR	Bezier Relative	Draws Bezier curves using relative coordinates.
BZ	Bezier Absolute	Draws Bezier curves using absolute coordinates.
MC	Merge Control	Controls the pixel color when two or more graphics elements intersect. (This instruction is also part of the Technical Graphics Extension.)
PP	Pixel Placement	Determines how pixels are placed on a grid during polygon fills on raster devices.

Drawing Bezier Curves

The BZ (Bezier Absolute) and BR (Bezier Relative) instructions use your current pen position as the first control point in the Bezier curve. You specify the second, third, and fourth control points. If you are drawing more than one curve, the fourth control point of the first curve (X_3, Y_3) becomes the first control point of the next curve. The following example shows a simple instruction sequence using BZ to draw a Bezier curve in the shape of a sine wave (shown in the figure following the example).

PA	1000,5000;	Specify absolute plotting and move to position (1000,5000).
PD	;	Pen down.
BZ	2000,8000, 4000,2000, 5000,5000;	Draw a Bezier curve with (1000,5000) as the starting point (first control point). Specify (2000,8000), (4000,2000), and (5000,5000) as the second, third, and fourth control points.

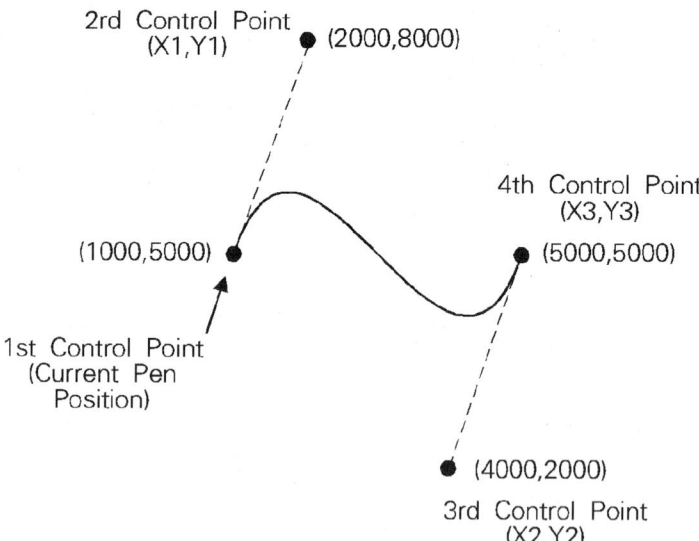

Figure 51. Bezier Curve

Merging and Placing Pixels

The MC (Merge Control) instruction controls the color of pixels where two or more page marking primitives intersect on the page. This instruction, like the Logical Operation (**ESC*l#O**) command of HP RTL, supports all 256 Microsoft Windows ternary (ROP3) raster operation codes—see page 473. Raster operations specify how source, destination, and pattern data are combined to produce final images. A common application of the MC instruction is the rendering of complex polygon fill patterns. You can find a more detailed explanation of how raster operations work in *Chapter 10: Interactions between Picture Elements* on page 365.

When it is printing or plotting, the device places pixels on a theoretical grid covering the printable area of a page. When the sides of two polygons touch each other, the pixels along the border may be printed twice or not at all, depending on the logical operation in effect (see the left side of Figure 52). For example, if a source rectangle consisting of all 1's is exclusive-ORed with a destination that also consists of all 1's, a white rectangle (all 0's) is printed. If another source rectangle is placed on the page touching the first rectangle, the two rectangles are white-filled except at their common border; that is because (1 xor 1) xor 1 = 1, black.

To correct this situation, two models of pixel placement are used: grid intersection and grid centered. The grid intersection model is the default; pixels are rendered on the intersections of the grid. In the grid-centered model, the number of rows and columns are each reduced by one, and pixels are placed at the centers of the squares, rather than at the intersections.

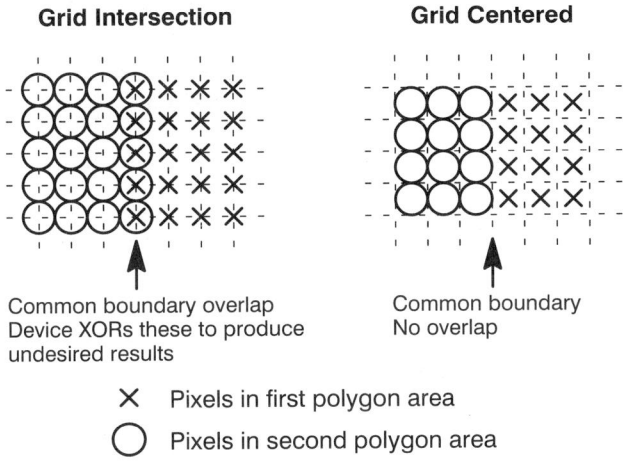

Figure 52. Pixel Placement Variations

Figure 53 shows the concepts of the two models. Assume a rectangle extends from coordinate position (1,1) to position (3,4), with the origin of coordinates at the top left, and the X-axis horizontal. The grid-centered model produces a rectangle that is one dot row thinner and one dot row shorter than the grid intersection model. Thus when two or more polygons on a page share a common border, grid centering can be turned on.

Microsoft Windows fills polygons based on the grid-centered method.

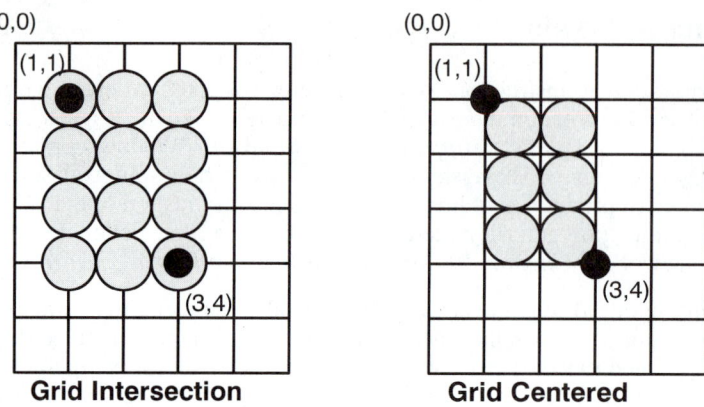

Figure 53. Pixel Placement

The Advanced Text Extension

The Advanced Text Extension contains two instructions that are of use if you use two-byte character sets, such as Kanji, and if you want to access bitmap fonts from within the HP-GL/2 environment. The following instructions make up the Advanced Text Extension:

LM	Label Mode	Determines how LB and SM interpret two-byte characters.
SB	Scalable or Bitmap Fonts	Specifies the type of font to be used in labels. (This instruction is also part of the Dual-Context Extension.)

Chapter 5:
HP-GL/2 Instruction Reference

In the following table, the instructions of HP-GL/2 are listed in order of their **names**. On the reference pages that follow the table, the instructions are listed in order of their two-character **mnemonics**; that order is also used in the summary table that starts on page 97. For **groupings** of the instructions (the Kernel groups and the Extensions), see pages 17 through 22. Note that not all devices support all instructions; see the appropriate *Comparison Guide* for details.

Instruction name	Instruction syntax	Page
Absolute Arc Three Point	AT*xinter,yinter,xend,yend[,chord_angle]*	110
Absolute Character Size	SI*[width,height]*	298
Absolute Direction	DI*[run,rise]*	139
Advance Full Page	PG*[n]*	249
Alternate Font Definition	AD*[kind,value...[,kind,value]]*	106
Anchor Corner	AC*[x,y]*	103
Arc Absolute	AA*xcenter,ycenter,sweepangle[,chord_angle]*	100
Arc Relative	AR*xincr,yincr,sweep_angle[,chord_angle]*	108
Begin Plot	BP*[kind,value...[,kind,value]]*	113
Bezier Absolute	BZ*x1,y1,x2,y2,x3,y3[,...x1,y1,x2,y2,x3,y3]*	118
Bezier Relative	BR*x1,y1,x2,y2,x3,y3[,...x1,y1,x2,y2,x3,y3]*	116
Character Fill Mode	CF*[fill_mode[,edge_pen]]*	120
Character Plot	CP*[spaces,lines]*	128
Character Slant	SL*[tangent_of_angle]*	301
Chord Tolerance Mode	CT*[mode]*	133
Circle	CI*radius[,chord_angle]*	123
Comment	CO*["c...c"]*	127
Default Values	DF	136
Define Label Terminator	DT*[label_terminator[,mode]];*	154
Define Variable Text Path	DV*[path[,line]]*	156
Digitize Clear	DC	135
Digitize Point	DP	148
Download Character	DL*[character_number[character_number2]* *[[,up]x,y...[,up],x,y]*	144
Edge Polygon	EP	164
Edge Rectangle Absolute	EA*x,y*	160
Edge Rectangle Relative	ER*x,y*	166
Edge Wedge	EW*radius,start_angle,* *sweep_angle[,chord_angle]*	171
Enable Cutter	EC*[n]*	163
Extra Space	ES*[width[,height]]*	169
Fill Polygon	FP*[fill_method]*	179

Instruction name	Instruction syntax	Page
Fill Rectangle Absolute	RA*x,y*	269
Fill Rectangle Relative	RR*x,y*	281
Fill Type	FT*[fill_type[,option1[,option2]]]*	183
Fill Wedge	WG*radius,start_angle,* *sweep_angle[,chord_angle]*	324
Frame Advance	FR	181
Initialize	IN*[n]*	189
Input P1 and P2	IP*[p1x,p1y[,p2x,p2y]]*	191
Input Relative P1 and P2	IR*[p1x,p1y[,p2x,p2y]]*	194
Input Window	IW*[xll,yll,xur,yur]*	197
Label	LB*text...text label_terminator*	206
Label Mode	LM*[mode[,row_number]]*	208
Label Origin	LO*[position]*	211
Line Attributes	LA*[kind,value[,kind,value[,kind,value]]]*	200
Line Type	LT*line_type[,pattern_length[,mode]]*	215
Media Type	MT*[type]*	223
Merge Control	MC*[mode[,opcode]]*	220
Message	MG*[message]*	222
Not Ready	NR*[timeout]*	227
Number of Pens	NP*[n]*	225
Output Digitized Point and Pen Status	OD*;*	228
Output Error	OE*;*	229
Output Hard-Clip Limits	OH*;*	231
Output Identification	OI*;*	232
Output P1 and P2	OP*;*	233
Output Status	OS*;*	235
Pen Color Assignment	PC*[pen[,primary1,primary2,primary3]]*	239
Pen Down	PD*[x,y[,...]]*	241
Pen Up	PU*[x,y[,...]]*	262
Pen Width	PW*[width[,pen]]*	264
Pen Width Unit Selection	WU*[type]*	328
Pixel Placement	PP*[mode]*	255
Plot Absolute	PA*[x,y[,...]]*	237
Plot Relative	PR*[x,y[,...]]*	257
Plot Size	PS*[length[,width]]*	259
Polygon Mode	PM*[polygon_definition]*	251
Polyline Encoded	PE*[flag][value/x,y]...[flag][value/x,y]*	243
Primary Font Selection by ID	FI*font_id*	175
Quality Level	QL*[quality_level]*	267
Raster Fill Definition	RF*[index[,width,height,* *pen_number[,pen_number...]]]*	272
Relative Arc Three Point	RT*xincrinter,yincrinter,* *xincrend,yincrend[,chord_angle]*	284

Instruction name	Instruction syntax	Page
Relative Character Size	SR*[width,height]*	308
Relative Direction	DR*[run,rise]*	149
Replot	RP*[n]*	279
Rotate Coordinate System	RO*[angle]*	275
Scalable or Bitmap Fonts	SB*[n]*	288
Scale	SC*[xmin,xmax,ymin,ymax[,type[,left, bottom]]]*	290
Screened Vectors	SV*[screen_type[,option1[,option2]]]*	313
Secondary Font Selection by ID	FN*font_id*	177
Select Alternate Font	SA	287
Select Pen	SP*[pen_number]*	306
Select Standard Font	SS	311
Set Color Range for Relative Color Data	CR*[black-ref_p1,white-ref_p1, black-ref_p2,white-ref_p2, black-ref_p3,white-ref_p3]*	131
Sort	ST*[switches]*	312
Standard Font Definition	SD*[kind,value...[,kind,value]]*	296
Symbol Mode	SM*[character[character2]]*	303
Transparency Mode	TR*[n]*	318
Transparent Data	TD*[mode]*	316
User-Defined Line Type	UL*[index[,gap1,...gapn]]*	320
Velocity Select	VS*[pen_velocity[,pen_number]]*	322

In addition, the following commands of PCL and HP RTL may be available to you:

Command name	Command syntax	Page
Enter PCL Mode	**ESC%#A**	420
Enter RTL Mode	**ESC%#A**	420
Enter HP-GL/2 Mode	**ESC%#B**	418
Escape	**ESCE**	435

HP-GL/2
INSTRUCTIONS

The following table lists the HP-GL/2 instructions in order of their mnemonics:

Instruction syntax	Instruction name	Page
AA*xcenter,ycenter,sweepangle[,chord_angle]*	Arc Absolute	100
AC*[x,y]*	Anchor Corner	103
AD*[kind,value...[,kind,value]]*	Alternate Font Definition	106
AR*xincr,yincr,sweep_angle[,chord_angle]*	Arc Relative	108
AT*xinter,yinter,xend,yend[,chord_angle]*	Absolute Arc Three Point	110
BP*[kind,value...[,kind,value]]*	Begin Plot	113
BR*x1,y1,x2,y2,x3,y3[,...x1,y1,x2,y2,x3,y3]*	Bezier Relative	116
BZ*x1,y1,x2,y2,x3,y3[,...x1,y1,x2,y2,x3,y3]*	Bezier Absolute	118

Instruction syntax	Instruction name	Page
OD;	Output Digitized Point and Pen Status	228
OE;	Output Error	229
OH;	Output Hard-Clip Limits	231
OI;	Output Identification	232
OP;	Output P1 and P2	233
OS;	Output Status	235
PA[x,y[,...]]	Plot Absolute	237
PC[pen[,primary1,primary2,primary3]]	Pen Color Assignment	239
PD[x,y[,...]]	Pen Down	241
PE[flag][value/x,y]...[flag][value/x,y]	Polyline Encoded	243
PG[n]	Advance Full Page	249
PM[polygon_definition]	Polygon Mode	251
PP[mode]	Pixel Placement	255
PR[x,y[,...]]	Plot Relative	257
PS[length[,width]]	Plot Size	259
PU[x,y[,...]]	Pen Up	262
PW[width[,pen]]	Pen Width	264
QL[quality_level]	Quality Level	267
RAx,y	Fill Rectangle Absolute	269
RF[index[,width,height, pen_number[,pen_number...]]]	Raster Fill Definition	272
RO[angle]	Rotate Coordinate System	275
RP[n]	Replot	279
RRx,y	Fill Rectangle Relative	281
RTxincrinter,yincrinter, xincrend,yincrend[,chord_angle]	Relative Arc Three Point	284
SA	Select Alternate Font	287
SB[n]	Scalable or Bitmap Fonts	288
SC[xmin,xmax,ymin,ymax[,type[,left, bottom]]]	Scale	290
SD[kind,value...[,kind,value]]	Standard Font Definition	296
SI[width,height]	Absolute Character Size	298
SL[tangent_of_angle]	Character Slant	301
SM[character[character2]]	Symbol Mode	303
SP[pen_number]	Select Pen	306
SR[width,height]	Relative Character Size	308
SS	Select Standard Font	311
ST[switches]	Sort	312
SV[screen_type[,option1[,option2]]]	Screened Vectors	313
TD[mode]	Transparent Data	316
TR[n]	Transparency Mode	318
UL[index[,gap1,...gapn]]	User-Defined Line Type	320
VS[pen_velocity[,pen_number]]	Velocity Select	322
WGradius,start_angle, sweep_angle[,chord_angle]	Fill Wedge	324
WU[type]	Pen Width Unit Selection	328

HP-GL/2
INSTRUCTIONS

AA, Arc Absolute

Purpose

To draw an arc, using absolute coordinates, which starts at the current pen location and pivots around the specified center point.

Syntax

AA X_{center}, Y_{center}, sweep_angle[,chord_angle][;]

Parameter	Format	Functional Range	Parameter Default
X_{center}, Y_{center}	current units	*device-dependent* (at least -2^{23} to $2^{23} - 1$)	no default
sweep_angle	clamped real	$-32\ 768$ to $32\ 767$	no default
chord_angle*	clamped real	*device-dependent* (at least $0°$ to $180°$)	*device-dependent* (usually $5°$)

*   If you have used the "CT1" instruction, the *chord_angle* is interpreted as a *deviation distance* in current units; see the CT instruction on page 133.

Group

This instruction is in the Vector Group.

Use

The AA instruction draws an arc starting at the current pen location using the current pen up/down status and line type and attributes. After drawing the arc, the pen location is updated to the end of the arc; the carriage-return point (see page 66) is moved to the end of the arc.

Note: Do *not* use an adaptive line type when drawing arcs with small chord angles. The device attempts to draw the complete pattern in every chord (there are 72 chords in a circle using the default chord angle).

- **X_{center}, Y_{center}:** Specify the absolute location of the center of the arc. (The center of the arc is the center of the circle that would be drawn if the arc was $360°$.) Coordinates are interpreted in current units: as user-units when scaling is on; as plotter-units when scaling is off. If current scaling is not isotropic, the arc drawn is elliptical rather than circular.

- **sweep_angle:** Specifies in degrees the angle through which the arc is drawn. A positive angle draws an arc in the positive direction (counter-clockwise rotation); a negative angle draws the arc in the negative direction (clockwise rotation). All values outside the range $-360°$ to $+360°$ are converted modulo 360.

- **chord_angle:** Specifies, in degrees, the chord angle used to draw the arc. The default is a device-dependent angle, normally $5°$. The *chord_angle* specifies the maximum angle created when lines from each end of the chord intersect the center point of the circle (see Figure 54). The smaller the chord angle, the smoother the curve. The useful range is from $0.0°$ to $180.0°$. A chord angle less than $0.5°$ is clamped to $0.5°$. The specified value is interpreted modulo 360°; if the result is greater than 180°, 360° *minus the modulo result* is used.

The number of chords used is the absolute value of *sweep_angle* ÷ *chord_angle*; a non-integer quotient is rounded up.

The chord angle used to draw the arc is set to *sweep_angle* ÷ number of chords. If the sweep angle is less than 0.5°, the chord angle is set to the sweep angle.

If either the sweep angle or the calculated radius is zero and the pen is down, a dot (zero-length vector) is drawn at the current pen position.

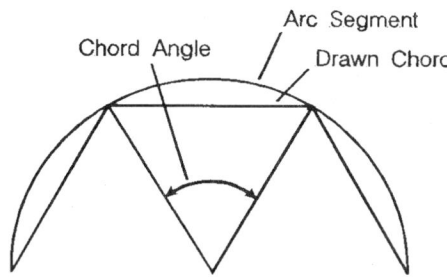

Figure 54. Chord Angle

For a specific chord angle, a circle or arc always has the same number of chords, regardless of its size. For example, for the usual default chord angle, a circle is always composed of 72 chords (360°/5° per chord = 72 chords). This results in larger circles appearing less smooth than smaller circles with the same chord angle; setting the chord angle to a smaller number will help large circles or arcs appear more smooth (see Figure 55).

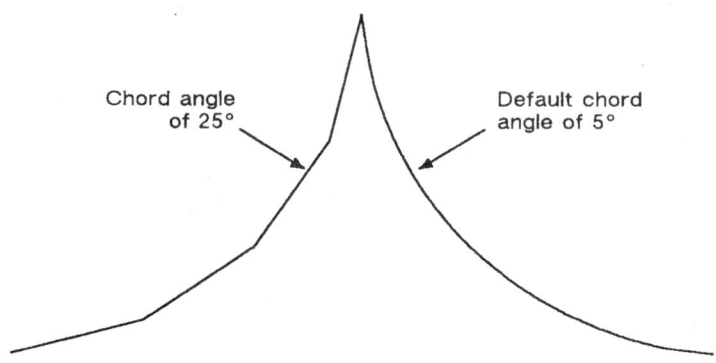

Figure 55. Changing Arc Smoothness with the Chord Angle

Note that the CT (Chord Tolerance Mode) instruction in the Technical Graphics extension changes the above computation.

Related Instructions

AR	Arc Relative
AT	Absolute Arc Three Point
BR	Bezier Relative
BZ	Bezier Absolute
CI	Circle
CT	Chord Tolerance Mode
LA	Line Attributes
LT	Line Type
PW	Pen Width
RT	Relative Arc Three Point

Example

PA	2000,0;	Specify (2000,0) as the starting point.
PD	;	Pen down.
AA	0,0,45,25;	Draw a 45° arc (positive angle) with center coordinates of (0,0) and a chord angle of 25°.
PU	1050,1060;	Lift the pen and move to (1050,1060).
PD	;	Pen down.
AA	0,0,–45,10;	Draw a 45° arc (negative angle) using the same center point as the first arc, but with a 10° chord angle.
PU	1000,0;	Lift the pen and move to (1000,0).
PD	;	Pen down.
AA	0,0,45;	Draw another 45° arc (positive angle) with the same center point, but with the default chord angle (usually 5°).

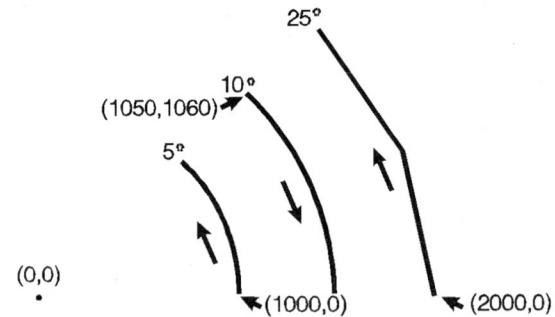

Figure 56. Varying the Chord Angle

AC, Anchor Corner

Purpose

To position the starting point of any fill pattern. Use AC to ensure that the selected fill pattern is positioned as expected within the figure.

Syntax

AC *X,Y[;]*

or

AC *[;]*

Parameter	Format	Functional Range	Parameter Default
X, Y coordinates	current units	*device-dependent* (at least -2^{23} to $2^{23} - 1$)	no default

Group

This instruction is in the Line and Fill Attributes Group.

Use

The ***anchor corner*** is the point at which any fill pattern starts. Setting the anchor corner guarantees that a corner point of the selected fill pattern is at the specified coordinate, aligned vertically and horizontally.

- **No parameters:** Defaults the anchor corner to the origin of the hard-clip limits (or plotting area). This is not necessarily equivalent to "AC0,0", which starts the fill pattern at the current-unit origin.

- **X, Y coordinates:** Define the position of the starting point for any fill pattern.

If the X,Y location is defined in plotter-units, turning scaling on or changing the locations of P1 and P2 has no effect on the anchor corner location. If, however, the X,Y location is defined in user-units, the physical location of the anchor corner moves with changes in scaling or to P1 and P2. For example, assume the scaling is from 0 to 10 in both axes and the anchor corner is specified as the point (2,3). If the scaling is changed to 0 to 5 in both axes, the anchor corner is still (2,3) but it is in a different physical location now that the user-units are a different size (the user-units have become twice as large). Turning off scaling causes the anchor corner to be frozen in the plotter-unit equivalent of its current user-unit value.

IN and DF default the anchor corner to the origin of the hard-clip limits relative to the current coordinate system.

A more detailed description of the use of the anchor corner is in *Using Fill Types* on page 56.

Using AC in a Dual-Context Environment

IN (Initialize), DF (Default Values), or **ESCE** (Reset) place the anchor point at the origin of the hard-clip limits relative to the current coordinate system. The equivalent, though not identical, HP RTL and PCL command is Pattern Reference Point (**ESC***p#R).

Example

The following example first prints three adjacent squares with fill patterns anchored at the origin of the hard-clip limits. The fill pattern is continuous across each of the squares. In the set of squares below that, each square has an anchor corner set at its own origin. Notice how this helps distinguish between the adjacent figures. The orientation shown is for a PCL printer; for a plotter, the orientation is rotated –90° or –180°.

PA	3000,3000;	Specify absolute plotting and move to location (3000,3000).
FT	3,400,45;	Specify fill type number 3 (parallel lines), with each line 400 plotter-units apart and set at a 45° angle.
RR	1000,1000;	Fill a rectangle using the current pen location as one corner, and a point 1000 plotter-units in the +X-direction and 1000 plotter-units in the +Y-direction as the opposite corner.
ER	1000,1000;	Edge the outline of the rectangle just filled.
PR	1000,0;	Move 1000 plotter-units in the +X-direction.
FT	4,400,45;	Select fill type number 4 (cross-hatch).
RR	1000,1000;	Create a rectangle the same size as the first one, and fill it with cross-hatch.
ER	1000,1000;	Edge its outline.
PR	1000,0;	Move to the right another 1000 plotter-units.
FT	3,400,45;	Create another rectangle of the same size, this time filled with pattern number 3 again.
RR	1000,1000;	
ER	1000,1000;	
PA	3000,1500;	Move to absolute location (3000,1500).
AC	3000,1500;	Move the anchor corner to location (3000,1500).
RR	1000,1000;	Fill a rectangle with the same dimensions as the previous three rectangles and edge its outline.
ER	1000,1000;	
PA	4000,1500;	Move to location (4000,1500).
AC	4000,1500;	Specify that location as the anchor corner.
FT	4,400,45;	Select fill type number 4 (cross-hatch).
RR	1000,1000;	Fill and edge another rectangle.
ER	1000,1000;	
PA	5000,1500;	Move to absolute location (5000,1500).
AC	5000,1500;	Specify that location as the anchor corner.
FT	3,400,45;	Select fill type number 3; fill and edge another rectangle.
RR	1000,1000;	
ER	1000,1000;	

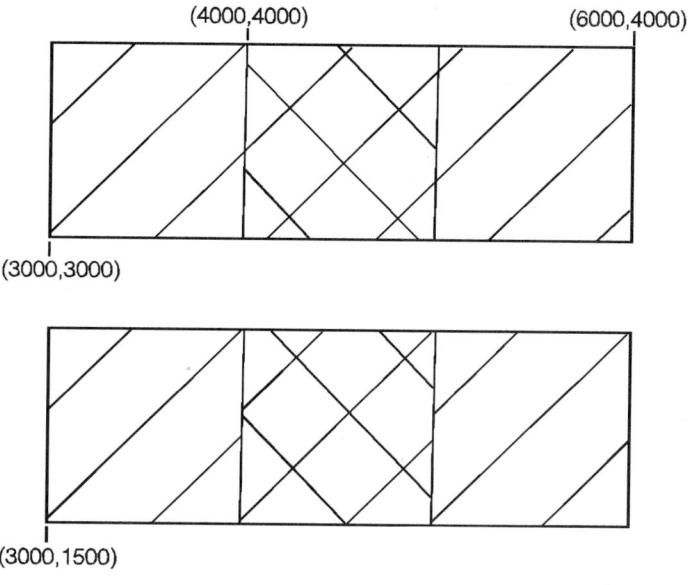

Figure 57. Using the AC (Anchor Corner) Instruction

Related Instructions and Commands

FP	Fill Polygon
FT	Fill Type
RA	Fill Rectangle Absolute
RF	Raster Fill Definition
RR	Fill Rectangle Relative
SV	Screened Vectors
WG	Fill Wedge
ESC*p#R	Pattern Reference Point

Possible Error Conditions

Error Condition	Error Number	Printer or Plotter Response
Position overflow	3	Ignores instruction

AD, Alternate Font Definition

Purpose

To define an alternative character set (font) and its characteristics: symbol set identification, font spacing, pitch, height, posture, stroke weight, and typeface. To define a standard font, use the SD instruction.

Syntax

AD *kind,value...[,kind,value][;]*
    or
AD *[;]*

Parameter	Format	Functional Range	Parameter Default
kind	clamped integer	1 to 7	no default
value	clamped real	*kind*-dependent*	*kind*-dependent*

* Refer to the table following the parameter descriptions.

Group

This instruction is in the Character Group.

Use

This instruction is similar to the SD (Standard Font Definition) instruction (see page 296) that defines the primary HP-GL/2 font. The AD instruction defines an alternate HP-GL/2 font and its characteristics: font spacing, pitch, height, posture, stroke weight, and typeface. It allows the font characteristics to be assigned to the secondary (alternate) font definition. Use AD to set up an alternate font that you can easily access when labeling.

- **No parameters:** Defaults the alternate font characteristics to that of the device-dependent default scalable font, not a bitmap font.

- **kind:** Specifies the characteristic for which you are setting a *value* (see the following table).

- **value:** Defines the properties of the characteristic specified by the *kind* parameter.

Note: When selecting fonts, the different characteristics (symbol set, spacing, pitch, and so on) are prioritized as shown in the table, with character set being the highest priority and typeface being the lowest. The font selection priority is the same for HP-GL/2 as for PCL font selection. For more information about the priority of font characteristics, see *How Your Device Selects Fonts* on page 63.

The tables in *Appendix C: Font Definitions* on page 475 list the *kind* parameters with their associated *values* (note that these tables are also valid for the SD [Standard Font Definition] instruction). For *kinds* 1 and 7, your device may support values other than those listed there. Refer to your *User's Guide* or HP-GL/2 option manual for more information about the attributes and values supported.

Any combination of *kind, value* parameters is allowed; the last *value* specified for a given *kind* prevails.

Kind	Attribute	Range of Values	Default Value	Description
1	Character set	*device-dependent*	277	Roman-8
2	Font Spacing	0 (fixed), 1 (proportional)	*device-dependent*	fixed spacing
3	Pitch	>0 to 32 767 (valid to 2 decimal places)	*device-dependent*	characters per inch
4	Height	0 to 32 767	*device-dependent*	font point size
5	Posture	0 to 32 767	*device-dependent*	upright or italic
6	Stroke Weight	−7 to 7, 9999	0	normal
7	Typeface	*device-dependent*	*device-dependent*	scalable font

The IN (Initialize) and DF (Default Values) instructions restore default alternate font attributes.

Related Instructions

DT   Define Label Terminator
FI   Select Primary Font
FN   Select Secondary Font
LB   Label
SA   Select Alternate Font
SB   Scalable or Bitmap Fonts
SD   Standard Font Definition
SI   Absolute Character Size
SR   Relative Character Size
SS   Select Standard Font
TD   Transparent Data

Example

The instruction "AD1,21,2,1,4,30,5,1,6,3,7,5;" designates a 30-point *Times Roman Bold Italic* font in the ASCII symbol set (use the SA [Select Alternate Font] instruction to select this font after it is designated):

AD	1,21	Symbol set—US ASCII
	2,1	Spacing—proportional
	4,30	Height—30-point
	5,1	Posture—italic
	6,3	Stroke weight—bold
	7,5;	Typeface—Times Roman

Note that the *pitch* parameter is missing in this instruction because the designated font is proportionally spaced.

AR, Arc Relative

Purpose

To draw an arc, using relative coordinates, which starts at the current pen location and pivots around the specified center point.

Syntax

AR X_{incr}, Y_{incr}, sweep_angle[, chord_angle][;]

Parameter	Format	Functional Range	Parameter Default
X,Y increments	current units	*device-dependent* (at least -2^{23} to $2^{23}-1$)	no default
sweep_angle	clamped real	$-32\ 768$ to $32\ 767$	no default
*chord_angle****	clamped real	$0.0°$ to $360°$	*device-dependent* (usually $5°$)

* If you have used the "CT1" instruction, the *chord_angle* is interpreted as a *deviation distance* in current units; see the CT instruction on page 133.

Group

This instruction is in the Vector Group.

Use

The AR instruction draws the arc starting at the current pen location using the current pen up/down status, line type, and attributes. After drawing the arc, the pen location remains at the end of the arc; the carriage-return point (see page 66) is moved to the end of the arc.

Note: Do *not* use an adaptive line type when drawing arcs with small chord angles. The device attempts to draw the complete pattern in every chord (there are 72 chords in a circle using the default chord angle).

- **X, Y increments:** Specify the center of the arc relative to the current location. (The center of the arc is the center of the circle that would be drawn if the arc was 360°.) Coordinates are interpreted in current units: as user-units when scaling is on; as plotter-units when scaling is off. If current scaling is not isotropic, the arc drawn is elliptical rather than circular.

- **sweep_angle:** Specifies (in degrees) the angle through which the arc is drawn. A positive angle draws an arc in the positive direction (counter-clockwise rotation); a negative angle draws the arc in the negative direction (clockwise rotation). All values outside the range $-360°$ to $+360°$ are converted modulo 360.

  If either the sweep angle or the calculated radius is zero and the pen is down, a dot (zero-length vector) is drawn at the current pen position.

- **chord_angle:** Specifies the chord angle used to draw the arc. The default is a device-dependent angle, normally 5°. Refer to the AA (Arc Absolute) instruction discussion on page 100 for information on setting and determining the chord angle.

  Note that the CT (Chord Tolerance Mode) instruction in the Technical Graphics extension changes the computation.

Related Instructions

AA	Arc Absolute
AT	Absolute Arc Three Point
BR	Bezier Relative
BZ	Bezier Absolute
CI	Circle
CT	Chord Tolerance Mode
LA	Line Attributes
LT	Line Type
PW	Pen Width
RT	Relative Arc Three Point

Example

PA	1500,1500;	Specify the starting position as (1500,1500).
PD	;	Put the pen down.
AR	0,2000,80,25;	Draw an arc with a center point 0 plotter-units in the X direction and 2000 plotter-units in the Y direction from (1500,1500). Specify the arc section to be 80° (positive angle), with a chord angle of 25°.
AR	2000,0,80;	Draw an arc with a center point 2000 plotter-units in the X direction and 0 plotter-units in the Y direction from the current pen position. Specify the arc section to be 80° (positive angle), with a default chord angle (usually 5°).

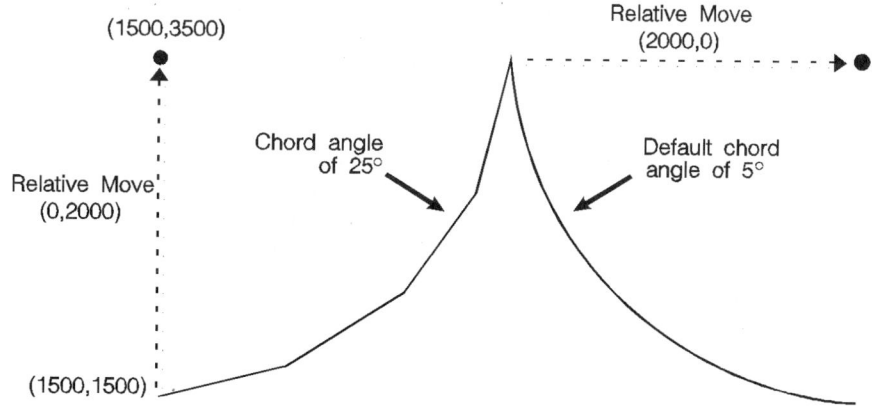

Figure 58. Using the AR (Arc Relative) Instruction to Draw Arcs

AT, Absolute Arc Three Point

Purpose

To draw an arc segment, using absolute coordinates, from a starting point, through an intermediate point, to an end point. Use AT when you know these three points of an arc.

Syntax

AT $X_{inter}, Y_{inter}, X_{end}, Y_{end}[,chord\_angle][;]$

Parameter	Format	Functional Range	Parameter Default
X, Y intermediate and end points	current units	*device-dependent* (at least -2^{23} to $2^{23} - 1$)	no defaults
chord_angle*	clamped real	$0°$ to $360°$	*device-dependent* (usually $5°$)

* If you have used the "CT1" instruction, the *chord_angle* is interpreted as a *deviation distance* in current units; see the CT instruction on page 133.

Group

This instruction is in the Vector Group.

Use

The AT instruction uses the current pen location and two specified points to calculate a circle and draw the appropriate arc segment of its circumference. The arc starts at the current pen location, using the current pen, line type, line attributes and pen up/down status. You specify the intermediate and end points. After drawing the arc, the pen location remains at the end of the arc; the carriage-return point (see page 66) is moved to the end of the arc.

- **X_{inter}, Y_{inter}:** Specify the absolute location of an intermediate point of the arc. The arc is drawn in a positive or negative angle of rotation, as necessary, so that it passes through the intermediate point before the end point.

- **X_{end}, Y_{end}:** Specify the absolute location of the end point of the arc.

- **chord_angle:** Specifies the chord angle used to draw the arc. The default is a device-dependent angle, normally $5°$. (The AA [Arc Absolute] instruction description on page 100 contains more information on chords and chord angles.)

Intermediate and end point coordinates are interpreted in current units: as user-units when scaling is on; as plotter-units when scaling is off. If current scaling is not isotropic, the arc drawn is elliptical rather than circular. Note the following about locating the intermediate and end points:

- If the intermediate point and end point are the same as the current pen location, the instruction draws a dot.

- If the intermediate point is the same as either the current pen location or the end point, a line is drawn between the current pen location and the end point.

- If the end point is the same as the current pen location, a circle is drawn, with its diameter being the line from the current pen position to the intermediate point.

- If the current pen position, intermediate point, and end point are collinear, a straight line is drawn.

- If the intermediate point does not lie between the current pen location and the end point, and the three points are collinear, two lines are drawn; one from the current pen location and the other from the end point, leaving a gap between them. Refer to the following illustration. Both lines extend to the hard-clip limits or current window.

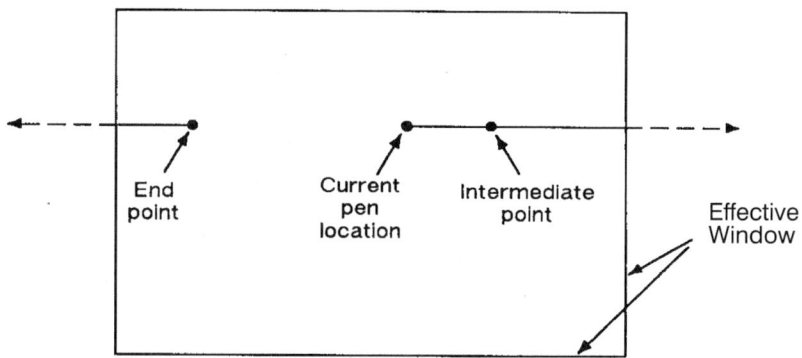

Figure 59. Collinear Points with the Intermediate Point outside the End Points

Note that the CT (Chord Tolerance Mode) instruction in the Technical Graphics extension changes the computation.

Related Instructions

AA	Arc Absolute
AR	Arc Relative
BR	Bezier Relative
BZ	Bezier Absolute
CI	Circle
CT	Chord Tolerance Mode
LA	Line Attributes
LT	Line Type
PW	Pen Width
RT	Relative Arc Three Point

Example

PA	1000,100;	Specify (1000,100) as the starting location.
PD	2500,100;	Place the pen down, and draw a line to (2500,100).
PU	650,1150;	Lift the pen, and move to (650,1150).
PD	1000,1150;	Place the pen down, and draw a line to (1000,1150).
PU	650,450;	Lift the pen, and move to (650,450).
PD	1000,450;	Place the pen down, and draw a line to (1000,450).
PU	1000,100;	Lift the pen, and move to (1000,100).
PD	1000,1500,2500,1500;	Place the pen down, draw a line to (1000,1500), then to (2500,1500).
AT	3200,800,2500,100;	Print an arc, starting at current pen position (2500,1500), passing through (3200,800) and ending at (2500,100).
PU	3200,900;	Lift the pen, and move to (3200,900).
PD	;	Set the pen down.
AT	3300,800,3200,700;	Print an arc, starting at the current pen position, passing through (3300,800) and ending at (3200,700).
PU	3300,800;	Lift the pen, and move to (3300,800).
PD	3500,800;	Pen down, and draw a line to (3500,800).

Figure 60. Drawing Arcs through Three Points

BP, Begin Plot

Purpose

To place the device into the picture header state and indicate the beginning of a new plot.

Syntax

BP *kind,value...[,kind,value][;]*
            or
BP*[;]*

Parameter	Format	Functional Range	Parameter Default
kind	clamped integer	1 to 5	no default
value	*kind*-dependent	*kind*-dependent	*kind*-dependent

Group

This instruction is in the Technical Graphics Extension.

Use

BP produces the equivalent of PG (Advance Full Page) and IN (Initialize). It begins a new plot regardless of whether the previous plot was terminated. It makes the previous plot unavailable, that is, BP followed by RP (Replot) produces nothing.

- **No parameters**: all *value*s are defaulted.

- **kind** and **value** parameters: The *kind* parameter is a clamped integer between 1 and 5; the *value* parameter is *kind*-dependent. These parameters must be specified in pairs, as shown in the table on the next page.

For a buffered raster device, the default behavior of BP is to discard the previous plot if it has not yet been printed with either PG or RP. The instruction "BP4,1" allows overriding the default behavior by generating a PG. For a plotter or other "plot as you parse" device, a "4,1" pair is always NOP'd and a BP instruction always results in a conditional page advance. For spooled plotters, the previous plot may or may not be discarded before printing if it was not properly terminated.

BP starts a new plot and guarantees that it starts on a clean page. It performs an IN to ensure that the plot starts in a known state, and puts the device into picture header state.

BP starts a new plot regardless of whether the last plot was terminated properly, even when one or more of its parameters are in error. This provides a measure of error recovery, in case that the previous user's application did not complete plotting properly. The parameters specified in the BP instruction apply only to the plot started by the current BP.

BP is recognized in polygon mode (the polygon buffer is cleared), but not in label mode.

Kind	Format	Meaning and Value
1	quoted string (see page 28)	**Picture name**: The default is a device-dependent name, such as a sequence number or the time of day if a clock is available. The parameter value can be used by devices that implement control-panel spool-queue manipulation to identify the plot for the user. The value parameter is assumed to be in the same language as for the control-panel when it was powered on; that is, if you power up the machine in Spanish, the device assumes that the picture name is encoded in the Spanish character set.
2	clamped integer	**Number of copies**: The default is 1. When the device receives an RP (Replot) instruction, only the additional number of copies specified by RP are made; this is regardless of the number of copies specified (and already printed) by BP. For example, "BP2,3; *plot data* RP2" results in a total of five copies of the plot, not nine.
3	clamped integer	**File-disposition code**: Controls replot capability. **0** Enables replot; saves the file if room exists (the default). **1** Destroys the file after printing. The file is not saved in memory or on disk. This value prevents retrieval of the file through the RP instruction or the device's control panel. Note that "BP2,n,3,1" still produces n copies of the plot.
4	clamped integer	**Render last plot if unfinished**: **0** No (the default). **1** Yes.
5	clamped integer	**Autorotation**: A device may choose to rotate the hard-clip limits 90° to save paper. This option can disable such autorotation, giving the computer complete control over where the plot is placed. Support of autorotation is device-dependent. **0** Enable (the default). **1** Disable.

If the same *kind* parameter is used more than once, the last one prevails. For example, "BP4,0,4,1;" does render the previous plot.

Pen plotters do not recognize *kind* = 4 or 5.

Using BP in a Dual-Context PCL Environment

If you entered HP-GL/2 mode with **ESC**%#B (where # is 0 or positive), the device ignores the PG functionality of the BP instruction. Data previously formatted for the current page is not cleared.

When you enter HP-GL/2 mode with **ESC**%−1B, the behavior of the BP instruction is dependent on the device technology, as follows:

• If the device is a buffered raster device, the default behavior of BP discards the previous plot if it has not yet been printed with either PG or RP. The instruction "BP4,1" allows overriding the default behavior by generating a PG.

- For a pen plotter or any device that plots data as it is received, a "BP4,1" is always ignored and a BP instruction always results in a conditional page advance (if the page has been plotted on, the page is advanced). **ESC**%#B is ignored.

Using BP in a Dual-Context HP RTL Environment

If you use the BP instruction in a dual-context HP RTL device, the device performs only the PG function of the instruction.

Related Instructions and Commands

IN   Initialize
PG   Advance Full Page
RP   Replot
ESC%#B Enter HP-GL/2 mode command from PCL or HP RTL

BR, Bezier Relative

Purpose

To draw a series of Bezier curves using relative coordinates.

Syntax

BR *X1,Y1,X2,Y2,X3,Y3,...[X1,Y1,X2,Y2,X3,Y3][;]*

Parameter	Format	Functional Range	Parameter Default
X, Y increments	current units	*device-dependent* (at least -2^{23} to $2^{23}-1$)	no default

Group

This instruction is in the Advanced Drawing Extension.

Use

BR draws a Bezier curve using the present pen position as the first control point, and the defined control points as increments. All curve control points are relative to the first control point of that curve.

- **X,Y coordinates:** Specify the location of the second (X1,Y1), third (X2,Y2), and fourth (X3,Y3) control points in relative increments, that is, all of these values are relative to the current pen location at the start of the Bezier curve.

The curves are drawn with the current pen, line type, line attributes, and pen state (up or down); and they are clipped to the hard-clip limits and the soft-clip window. The current pen location is updated to the end point of the curve at the termination of each Bezier curve defined by the instruction. After each new Bezier curve, the last control point is used by the next Bezier curve as its first control point. The carriage-return point (see page 66) is moved to the last X,Y.

After the first four control points are defined (one present-position control point and three control points) the optional parameters define subsequent Bezier curves by adding three additional control points.

BR is allowed in Polygon Mode. The first chord after "PM1" is not treated as a pen-up move.

Related Instructions

AA	Arc Absolute
AR	Arc Relative
AT	Absolute Arc Three Point
BZ	Bezier Absolute
CI	Circle
LA	Line Attributes
LT	Line Type
PW	Pen Width
RT	Relative Arc Three Point

Example

PS	5000,7000;	Plot Size 5000 by 7000 units.
SP	1;	Select Pen number 1.
PA	1016,5080;	Plot Absolute to the location (1016,5080), the first control point.
PD	;	Pen Down.
BR	0,3048, 4572,0, 3556,2032, –508,1016, 2540,508, 2540,–5080;	Points 1, 2, and 3 (the control points of the first Bezier curve) are relative to (1016,5080). Point 3 becomes the first control point for the second Bezier curve—the new current position is updated to (4572,7112). Points 4, 5, and 6 are relative to (4572,7112). Point 6 becomes the final current position (7112,2032).

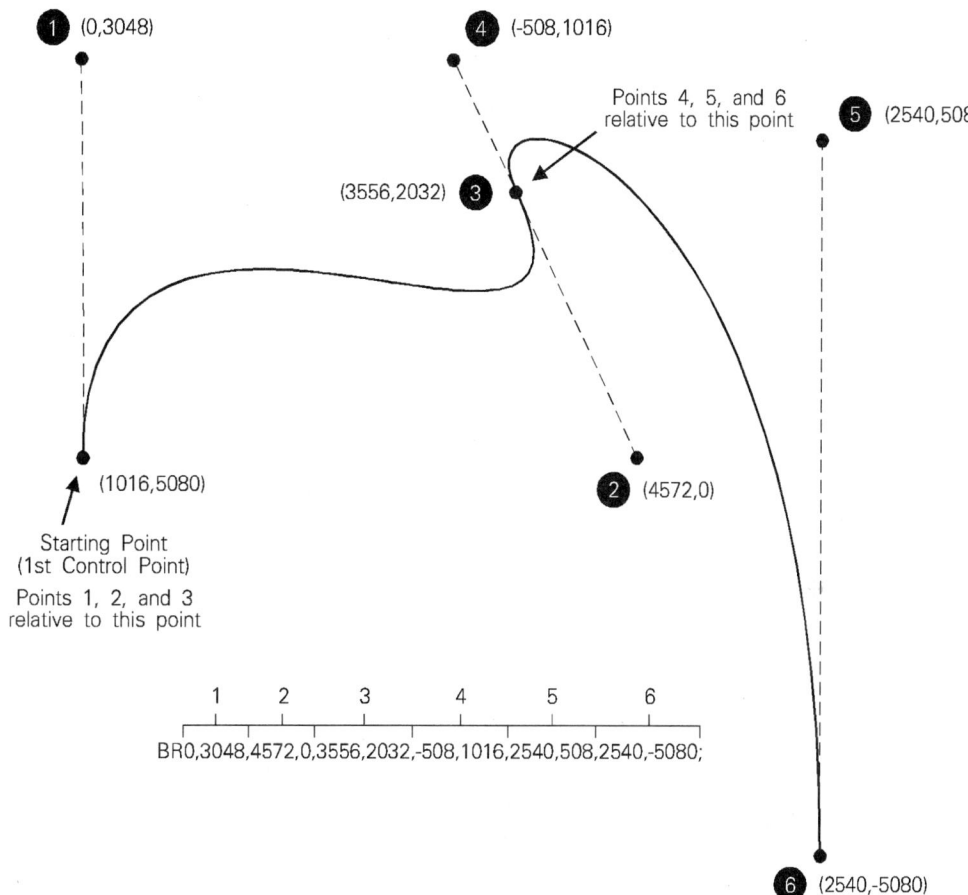

Figure 61. Bezier Curves Using Relative Coordinates

Possible Error Conditions

Error Condition	Error Number	Printer or Plotter Response
Invalid number of control points	2	The Bezier segment is discarded

BZ, Bezier Absolute

Purpose

To draw a series of Bezier curves using absolute coordinates.

Syntax

BZ *X1,Y1,X2,Y2,X3,Y3,...[X1,Y1,X2,Y2,X3,Y3][;]*

Parameter	Format	Functional Range	Parameter Default
X, Y coordinates	current units	*device-dependent*	no default

Group

This instruction is in the Advanced Drawing Extension.

Use

BZ draws a Bezier curve using the present pen position as the first control point, and the defined points as further control points. All curve control points are in absolute coordinates.

- **X, Y coordinates:** Specify the location of the second (X1,Y1), third (X2,Y2), and fourth (X3,Y3) control points in absolute coordinates.

The curves are drawn with the current pen, line type, line attributes, and pen state (up or down); and they are clipped to the hard-clip limits and the soft-clip window. The current pen location is updated to the end point of the curve at the termination of each Bezier curve defined by the instruction. After each new Bezier curve, the last control point is used by the next Bezier curve as the first control point. The carriage-return point (see page 66) is moved to the last X,Y.

After the first four control points are defined (one present-position control point and three control points) the optional parameters define subsequent Bezier curves by adding three additional control points.

BZ is allowed in Polygon Mode. The first chord after "PM1" is not treated as a pen-up move.

Related Instructions

AA	Arc Absolute
AR	Arc Relative
AT	Absolute Arc Three Point
BR	Bezier Relative
CI	Circle
LA	Line Attributes
LT	Line Type
PW	Pen Width
RT	Relative Arc Three Point

Example

PS	5000,7000;	Plot Size 5000 by 7000 units.
SP	1;	Select Pen number 1.
PA	1016,5080;	Plot Absolute to the location (1016,5080), the first control point.
PD	;	Pen Down.
BZ	1016,8128, 5588,5080, 4572,7112, 4064,8128, 7112,7620, 7112,2032;	

Points 1, 2, and 3 (the second, third, and fourth control points of the first Bezier curve; point 3 becomes the first control point for the second Bezier curve) followed by points 4, 5, and 6 (the second, third, and fourth control points of the second Bezier curve; point 6 becomes the final current position).

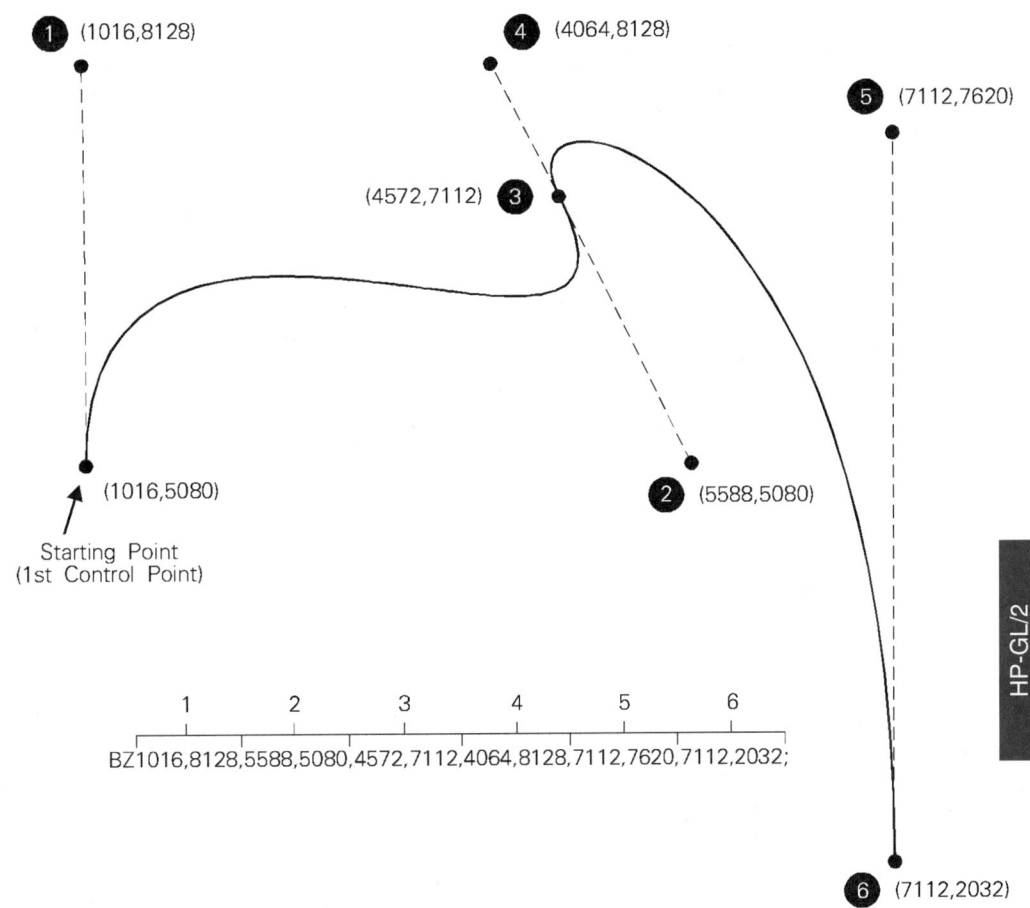

Figure 62. Bezier Curves Using Absolute Coordinates

Possible Error Conditions

Error Condition	Error Number	Printer or Plotter Response
Invalid number of control points	2	The Bezier segment is discarded

CF, Character Fill Mode

Purpose

To specify the way scalable outline fonts are filled and edged; bitmap and stick fonts cannot be edged and can be filled only with raster fill, shading, or PCL and HP RTL cross-hatch patterns. Scalable characters may be filled with any of the fill patterns specified by the FT instruction (shading, hatching, cross-hatch, and user-defined raster fill patterns). If your device does not support outline fonts, this instruction may perform no operation (a NOP); pen plotters generally do not support outline fonts.

Syntax

CF *fill_mode[,edge_pen][;]*
    or
CF *[;]*

Parameter	Format	Functional Range	Parameter Default
fill_mode	clamped integer	0, 1, 2, or 3	0 (solid fill, no edging)
edge_pen	integer	*device-dependent* (at least -2^{23} to $2^{23}-1$)	current pen

Group

This instruction is in the Character Group.

Use

- **No parameters:** Defaults characters to solid fill with no edging. Equivalent to "CF0,0".

- **fill_mode:** Specifies how the device renders filled characters according to the following parameter values:

  0   Specifies solid fill using the current pen and edging with the specified pen (or current pen if the *edge_pen* parameter is not specified).

  1   Specifies edging with the specified pen (or current pen if the *edge_pen* parameter is not specified). Characters are filled only if they cannot be edged (bitmap or stick characters), using the edge pen.

  2   Specifies filled characters using the current fill type (refer to the FT instruction on page 183). If the fill pattern does not incorporate color information, the currently selected pen is used. Characters are not edged; if the *edge_pen* parameter is specified, it is ignored.

  3   Specifies filled characters using the current fill type (refer to the FT instruction). If the fill pattern does not incorporate color information, the currently selected pen is used. Characters are edged with the specified pen (or current pen if the *edge_pen* parameter is not specified).

- **edge_pen:** For characters that are to be edged, this parameter indicates the pen that is used to edge the character. Edging width is device-dependent and varies with the character size; it is not determined by the width of the pen specified as the edge pen. If *edge_pen* is greater than the maximum number of pens in the device, the modulo function is applied, as described for the SP instruction on page 306. Specifying pen 0 for the edge pen does not necessarily mean that no edging will take place; it indicates that edging will be done by pen 0. (However, on monochrome devices, 0 *does* mean no edging, and 1 means black edging.)

The following table summarizes the functions of this instruction:

Fill	No edging	Edge using current pen	Edge using pen 0
Solid	CF;	CF0;	CF0,0;
None	—	CF1;	CF1,0;
Current fill type	CF2;	CF3;	CF3,0;

Note that the DI (Absolute Direction) and DR (Relative Direction) instructions do not cause rotation of fill patterns. Fill patterns remain fixed with respect to the current coordinate system. The CF instruction remains in effect until another CF instruction is executed, or the device is initialized or set to default conditions.

The effect of CF on the three font types is device-dependent. At least the following minimum implementation is supported:

- For bitmap fonts, filling is limited (at least shading, user-defined RF, and PCL or HP RTL patterns are supported) and edging may not be supported.

- For stick fonts, filling is limited and edging may not be supported.

- For scalable outline fonts, both filling and edging are supported.

Note also that the edge pen width is not specifiable; its thickness automatically increases with the point size.

The thickness of fill lines for hatching and cross hatch is selected using the PW (Pen Width) instruction. Due to the way hatching and cross-hatch lines are drawn, they may extend beyond the character outline by up to 1/2 of the current pen width. When using a small pen width and specifying a black edge pen, the edging covers up hatching lines that extend outside the character outline. However, as the pen width increases, the edge pen may not be wide enough to compensate for this, resulting in a fill that overlaps the character edges. To ensure that the character fill looks correct when using hatching patterns, use a narrow pen width, especially for small point sizes (see Figure 63).

Figure 63. Character Fill Overflow

Related Instructions

DI   Absolute Direction
DR   Relative Direction
SB   Scalable or Bitmap Fonts
FT   Fill Type

Example

The following series of instructions produce the result shown below:

SD	1,21,2,1,4,140,5,0,6,3,7,52;	Specify a 140-point Univers Bold font.
SS	;	Select it for printing.
PA	1000,3000;	Specify absolute plotting and move to (1000,3000).
DT*;		Specify an asterisk (*) as the label terminator (non-printing).
FT	3,50,45;	Specify a hatching fill type with 50 plotter-units between each line, with the lines set at a 45° angle.
CF	1,1;	Select character fill mode 1 (edge) and edge with pen number 1 (black on a monochrome device).
LBA*;		Print the letter "A".
PR	127,0;	Move the pen position 127 plotter-units to the right.
PW	.1;	Set the pen width to 0.1 mm.
CF	3,1;	Select character fill mode 3 (fill and edge) and edge with pen number 1.
LBB*;		Print the letter "B".
PW	.5;	Set the pen width to 0.5 mm to change the thickness of the fill lines.
LBC*;		Print the letter "C".

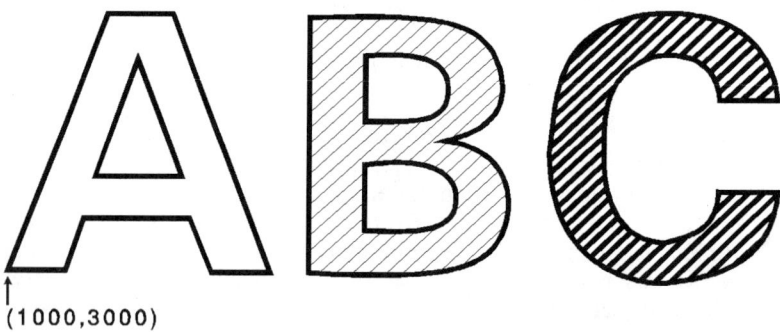

(1000,3000)

Figure 64. Using the CF (Character Fill) Instruction

CI, Circle

Purpose

To draw the circumference of a circle using the specified radius and chord angle. If you want a filled circle, refer to the WG (Fill Wedge) instruction on page 324 or *Drawing Circles in Polygon Mode* on page 52.

Syntax

CI *radius[,chord_angle][;]*

Parameter	Format	Functional Range	Parameter Default
radius	current units	*device-dependent* (at least -2^{23} to $2^{23}-1$)	no default
chord_angle*	clamped real	$0.0°$ to $360°$	*device-dependent* (usually $5°$)

* If you have used the "CT1" instruction, the *chord_angle* is interpreted as a *deviation distance* in current units; see the CT instruction on page 133.

Group

This instruction is in the Vector Group.

Use

The CI instruction includes an automatic pen down. When a CI instruction is received, the pen lifts, moves from the center of the circle (the current pen location) to the starting point on the circumference, lowers the pen, draws the circle, then returns with the pen up to the center of the circle. After the circle is drawn, the previous pen up/down status is restored. To avoid leaving a dot at the center of the circle, move to and from the circle's center with the pen up.

- **radius:** Measured from the current pen location. Coordinates are interpreted in current units: as user-units when scaling is on; as plotter-units when scaling is off. If you specify a negative radius, the circle begins and ends at the $180°$ reference point (see Figure 27 on page 44). A zero *radius* produces a dot.

- **chord_angle:** Specifies the chord angle used to draw the arc. The default is a device-dependent angle, normally $5°$. Refer to the AA (Arc Absolute) instruction discussion for an explanation of the chord angle. If you use the CT (Chord Tolerance Mode) instruction described on page 133 and begin specifying chords in terms of deviation distance, this parameter is that distance in current units.

Each chord of the circle is drawn using the currently defined line type, width, and attributes. (Refer to *The Line and Fill Attributes Group* on page 53 for more information.) Do *not* use an adaptive (negative) line type to draw a circle, as the device attempts to draw a complete pattern for *every* chord (normally 72 with the default chord angle). Always use isotropic scaling in drawings that contain circles, unless you want your circles to "stretch" with aspect ratio changes of the drawing (anisotropic scaling may produce an ellipse—see Figure 12 on page 13). There is more information in *Scaling* on page 24.

Note that the CT (Chord Tolerance Mode) instruction in the Technical Graphics extension changes the computation.

Related Instructions

AA	Arc Absolute
AR	Arc Relative
AT	Absolute Arc Three Point
CT	Chord Tolerance Mode
EW	Edge Wedge
LA	Line Attributes
LT	Line Type
PW	Pen Width
RT	Relative Arc Three Point
SC	Scale
WG	Fill Wedge

Example: Effects of Chord Angle on Circle Smoothness

SP	1;	Select pen number 1 (black).
SC	−3000,3000,−2000,2000,1;	Specify scaling mode, making P1 equal to (−3000,−2000) user-units and P2 equal to (3000,2000) user-units. Isotropic scaling is specified.
PA	−1700,2000;	Specify absolute plotting and move to (−1700,2000), the center of the circle to be drawn.
CI	750,45;	Draw a circle with a radius of 750 user-units and a chord angle of 45° (8 chords).
PA	300,2000;	Specify absolute plotting and move to (300,2000) to draw another circle.
CI	750,30;	Draw this circle with a radius of 750 user-units and a chord angle of 30° (12 chords).
PA	−1700,−200;	Specify absolute plotting and move to (−1700,−200), the center point of a third circle.
CI	750,15;	Draw this circle with a radius of 750 user-units and a chord angle of 15° (24 chords).
PA	300,−200;	Specify absolute plotting and move to (300,−200), the center of the fourth circle.
CI	750;	Draw this circle with a radius of 750 user-units and a chord angle defaulted, normally to 5° (72 chords).

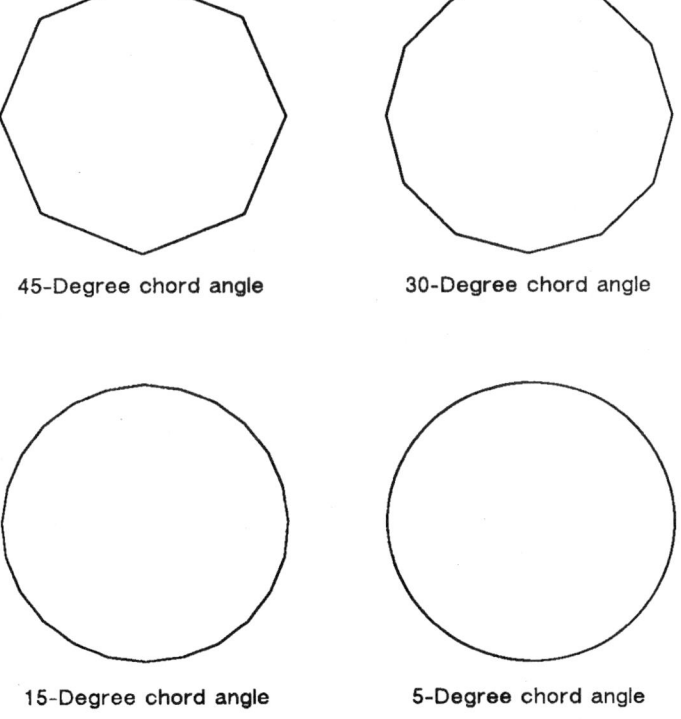

Figure 65. Effects of Chord Angle on Circle Smoothness

Example: Circles with Different Radii and Line Types

SC	–75,75,–75,75,1;	Set up user scaling with (–75,–75) as P1 and (75,75) as P2; the "1" parameter specifies isotropic scaling.
PA	0,0;	Specify absolute plotting and move to user-unit location (0,0).
LT	;	Specify a default line type (solid).
CI	5;	Draw a circle with a radius of 5 user-units.
LT	0;	Select line type 0 (dotted).
CI	–12;	Draw a circle with a radius of 12 user-units (the minus sign indicates starting at the 180° point).
LT	1;	Select line type 1.
CI	19;	Draw a circle with a radius of 19 user-units.
LT	2;	Then select line type 2.
CI	–26;	Draw a circle with a radius of 26 user-units.
LT	3;	Select line type 3.
CI	33;	Draw a circle with a radius of 33 user-units.
LT	4;	Then select line type 4.
CI	–40;	Draw a circle with radius of 40 user-units.
LT	5;	Draw the outer two circles; the first with a line type of 5
CI	47;	and a radius of 47 user-units.
LT	6;	Draw the second with a line type of 6
CI	54;	and a radius of 54 user-units.

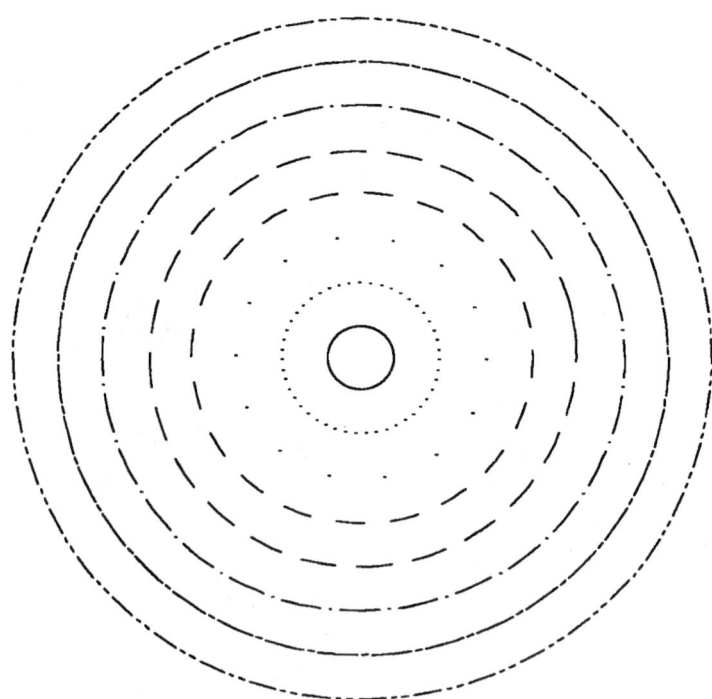

Figure 66. Drawing Circles with Different Radii and Line Types

CO, Comment

Purpose

To allow comments to be inserted within an HP-GL/2 instruction sequence. The comment string of the CO instruction must be delimited by double quotes. HP-GL/2 comments are ignored by the device.

Syntax

CO *["c...c"][;]*

Parameter	Format	Functional Range	Parameter Default
"c...c"	quoted string (see page 28)	any text characters enclosed in double quotes	no default

Group

This instruction is in the Configuration and Status Group.

Use

To add comments to HP-GL/2 instruction lists.

CP, Character Plot

Purpose

To move the pen the specified number of spaces and lines from the current pen location. Use CP to position a label for indenting, centering, and so on. It does *not* plot characters; that is normally done by the LB (Label) instruction.

Syntax

CP *spaces,lines[;]*
     or
CP *[;]*

Parameter	Format	Functional Range	Parameter Default
spaces	clamped real	–32 768 to 32 767	no default
lines	clamped real	–32 768 to 32 767	no default

Group

This instruction is in the Character Group.

Use

The CP (Character Plot) instruction includes an automatic pen up. When the instruction is completed, the original pen up/down status is restored.

CP moves the pen position in relation to the current position. CP is a movement instruction and does not affect the margin; to repeat the same movement for subsequent labels, you must issue new CP instructions. (For information about the carriage-return point, see *Moving to the Carriage Return Point* on page 66.) For more information on spaces, lines, and the character cell, refer to *Working with the Character Cell* on page 58.

- **No parameters:** Performs a Carriage Return and Line Feed (returns to the carriage-return point and moves one line down).

- **spaces:** Specifies the number of spaces the pen moves relative to the current pen location. Positive values specify the number of spaces the pen moves to the right of the current pen position; negative values specify the number of spaces the pen moves to the left. Right and left are relative to the current label direction. The space width is uniquely defined for each font; use the ES (Extra Space) instruction to adjust the width.

  Note: If you are using a proportionally-spaced font, the width of the Space (**SP**) control code is used.

- **lines:** Specifies the number of lines the pen moves relative to the current pen location. Positive values specify the number of lines the pen moves up from the current pen position; negative values specify the number of lines the pen moves down (a value of –1 is equivalent to a Line Feed). Up and down are relative to the current label direction. The Line Feed distance is uniquely defined for each font; use the ES (Extra Space) instruction to adjust the height.

When you move the pen up or down a specific number of lines, the carriage-return point shifts up or down accordingly.

The illustration below shows the interaction of label direction and the sign (+/–) of the parameters.

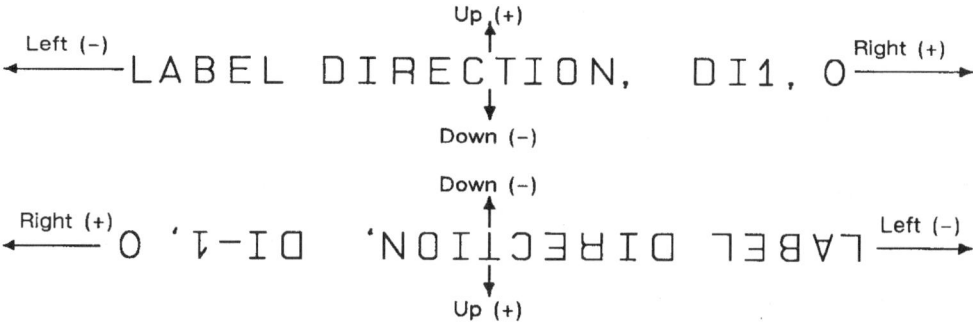

Figure 67. Interaction of Label Direction and Parameter Sign

The following illustration shows the direction of labeling with a vertical text path (set by "DV1" or "DV1,0"); refer to the DV (Define Variable Text Path) instruction for more information).

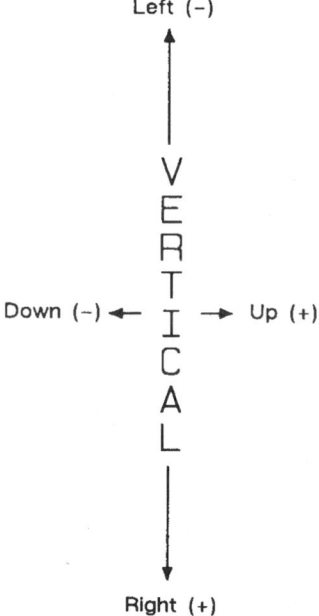

Figure 68. Labeling with a Vertical Text Path

HP-GL/2
INSTRUCTIONS

Related Instructions

DI   Absolute Direction
DR   Relative Direction
DV   Define Variable Text Path
ES   Extra Space
LB   Label
LO   Label Origin
SB   Scalable or Bitmap Fonts
SI   Absolute Character Size
SR   Relative Character Size

Example

The following example produces lettering along a line (but not directly on top of it), and aligns labels along a left margin. Movement of the carriage-return point is demonstrated, as well as different methods of placing the text. The text is placed using the CP instruction with parameters, then with a Carriage Return-Line Feed (**CR LF**) combination, and using a CP instruction without parameters to emulate a **CR LF**.

PA	5000,2500;	Specify absolute plotting and move to (5000,2500).
PD	1500,2500;	Set the pen down and draw a line to (1500,2500).
PU	;	Lift the pen.
CP	5,.35;	Move the pen 5 spaces to the right and 0.35 lines up so that the label is placed just above the line.
DT$,1;		Define a label terminator ($) and specify that it does not print.
SD	1,21,2,1,4,14,5,0,6,3,7,52;	Designate a 14-point Univers Bold font.
SS	;	Select it.
LBABOVE THE LINE$;		Print the first line of text. (Note that there are no spaces after "LB".)
PA	2500,2500;	Move the pen to (2500,2500).
WG	20,0,360;	Draw a dot marking the new carriage-return point (360° black-filled wedge with a diameter of 20 plotter-units).
CP	0,−.95	Move the pen down 0.95 lines, with no left or right movement.
LBBELOW THE LINE **CR LF** WITH A NEAT$;		Print the second line; Carriage Return-Line Feed; print the third line.
CP	;	The CP instruction without parameters functions as a **CR LF**.
LBMARGIN$;		Print the fourth line.

Figure 69. CP (Character Plot) Instruction

CR, Set Color Range for Relative Color Data

Purpose

To establish the range for specifying primary color data—for example, red/green/blue (RGB). This instruction maps current pen colors to a numeric range while leaving the current palette colors themselves unchanged. Pen plotters ignore (NOP) this instruction.

In an RGB color model, primary1 ("p1") is red, primary2 ("p2") is green, and primary3 ("p3") is blue.

Syntax

CR *black-ref_p1,white-ref_p1,black-ref_p2,white-ref_p2,black-ref_p3,white-ref_p3[;]*
or
CR *[;]*

Parameter	Format	Functional Range	Parameter Default
black-ref (p1, p2, p3)	clamped real	–32 768 to 32 767	0
white-ref (p1, p2, p3)	clamped real	–32 768 to 32 767	255

Group

This instruction is in the Palette Extension.

Use

The ***black-reference*** for a primary color denotes a value assigned to the absence of that color. The ***white-reference*** denotes the value given to a fully saturated primary color. When you have set the reference ranges, use the PC (Pen Color Assignment) instruction to define the colors of your pens.

- **No parameters:** Defaults the black color references to 0 and the white references to 255. Equivalent to "CR0,255,0,255,0,255;".

- **black-ref, white-ref (primary1, primary2, primary3):** Sets the color to a range for each primary color. The first two parameters set the black- and white-references (respectively) for primary1 (or red), the second pair for primary2 (or green), and the final pair for primary3 (or blue).

Using a black-reference of 0 and a white reference of 100 makes it easy to specify colors as percentages of their fully saturated levels. Use the instruction "CR 0,100,0,100,0,100;".

The reference values are reset to their defaults by the IN (Initialize) instruction.

In dual-context mode, CR can change the black- and white-references for palettes created by IN, BP, or **ESC*v#W**. The new references are remembered when the PCL or HP RTL context is entered. This instruction is ignored if the current palette was created by **ESC*r#U** or **ESCE**. The equivalent PCL and HP RTL command is Configure Image Data (bytes 6 through 17).

Related Instructions

NP   Number of Pens
PC   Pen Color Assignment
SV   Screened Vectors
TR   Transparency Mode

Example

CR   0,63,0,63,0,63;   This instruction sets the black references for each primary to 0, and the white references to 63. The value for a medium blue would be 0,0,31.

CR   4,63,0,127,0,31;   This instruction sets the black reference to 4,0,0 and the white reference to 63,127,31. In this case, medium blue would be 4,0,15.

Possible Error Conditions

Error Condition	Error Number	Printer or Plotter Response
One to five parameters	2	The instruction is ignored
Seven or more parameters	2	The extra parameters are ignored
The black reference value for any primary color is equal to its white reference value	3	The instruction is ignored

CT, Chord Tolerance Mode

Purpose

To specify whether the *chord_angle* parameter of the AA, AR, AT, CI, EW, RT, and WG instructions is interpreted as a chord angle in degrees or as a deviation distance in current units. This instruction changes the way the number of chords is determined. It is defaulted by DF or IN.

Syntax

CT *mode[;]*
     or
CT*[;]*

Parameter	Format	Functional Range	Parameter Default
mode	clamped integer	0 or 1	0

Group

This instruction is in the Technical Graphics Extension.

Use

A plotted circle or arc actually consists of a series of straight line segments (chords) that approximate to arc segments. Increasing the number of chords increases the smoothness of the circle or arc, but uses more of the device's disk space. Chord tolerance is the acceptable deviation from a smooth circle, and can be established as either a chord angle or a deviation distance.

- **No parameter**: equivalent to "CT0".

- **mode**: Specifies the type of chord tolerance, as follows:

  0   Sets the chord tolerance mode to ***chord angle***, which specifies, in degrees, the maximum angle created when lines from each end of the chord intersect the center point of the circle. When chord tolerance is specified as a chord angle, a circle or arc will have the same number of chords, regardless of its size. See the left-hand side of Figure 70.

  1   Sets the chord tolerance mode to ***deviation distance***, which specifies, in current units, the maximum distance between the chord and the arc segment it represents. When you specify a deviation distance, the number of chords in a circle will vary with its size. See the right-hand side of Figure 70.

Note that when you change from the default mode of chord angle to deviation distance, the chord angle parameter of the arc instructions (AA, AR, AT, and RT), the wedge instructions (EW and WG), and the circle instruction (CI) will be interpreted as current units, not degrees.

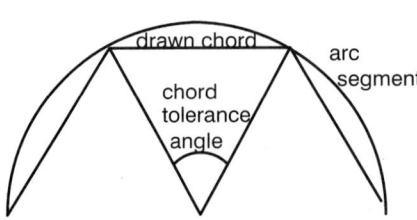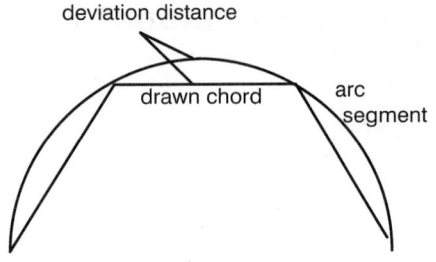

Figure 70. Chord Tolerance Mode

Related Instructions

AA   Arc Absolute
AR   Arc Relative
AT   Absolute Arc Three Point
CI   Circle
EW   Edge Wedge
RT   Relative Arc Three Point
WG   Fill Wedge

Possible Error Conditions

Error Condition	Error Number	Printer or Plotter Response
The mode is not 0 or 1	3	The instruction is ignored

DC, Digitize Clear

Purpose

To terminate digitize mode and reactivate automatic pen lift and storage. This instruction is only supported by pen plotters.

Syntax

DC *[;]*

Group

This instruction is in the Digitizing Extension.

Use

If you are using an interrupt routine in a digitizing program to branch to another plotting function, use DC to clear the digitize mode immediately after the branch.

When the device receives the DC instruction, it terminates digitize mode. It may also turn off any control-panel light (awaiting input of digitized point) and reactivate automatic pen lift.

Refer to *The Digitizing Extension* on page 89 and your device's documentation for more information.

Related Instructions

DP   Digitize Point
OD   Output Digitized Point and Pen Status
OS   Output Status

Possible Error Conditions

Error Condition	Error Number	Plotter Response
One or more parameters are specified	2	The parameters are ignored

DF, Default Values

Purpose

To return the device's HP-GL/2 settings to the factory default settings. Use the DF instruction to return the device to a known state while maintaining the current locations of P1 and P2, unlike the IN (Initialize) instruction. When you use DF at the beginning of a instruction sequence, graphics parameters such as character size, slant, or scaling are defaulted.

Syntax

DF *[;]*

Group

This instruction is in the Configuration and Status Group.

Use

The DF instruction resets the device to the following conditions:

Function	Equivalent Instruction	Default Condition
Anchor Corner	AC;	Anchor corner set to the origin of the hard-clip limits
Alternate Font Definition	AD;	Restore default (device-dependent) alternate font characteristics
Character Fill Mode	CF;	Solid fill, no edging, uses the current pen
Absolute Direction	DI;	Absolute character direction parallel to X-axis
Define Label Terminator	DT;	**ETX** and non-printing mode
Define Variable Text Path	DV;	Text printed in the +X-direction with Line Feed in the −Y-direction
Extra Space	ES;	No extra space
Fill Type	FT;	Solid bidirectional fill (all previously specified parameters for other fill types revert to their defaults)
Input Window	IW;	Hard-clip limits (printable area)
Line Attributes	LA;	Butt caps, mitered joins, and miter limit=5
Label Origin	LO1;	Standard labeling starting at current location
Line Type	LT;	Solid line, relative mode, pattern length=4% of diagonal distance from P1 to P2
Plotting Mode	PA;	Absolute plotting
Polygon Mode	PM0;PM2;	Polygon buffer cleared
Raster Fill	RF;	Solid raster fill in the current color for all patterns
Scale	SC;	User-unit scaling off

Function	Equivalent Instruction	Default Condition
Standard Font Definition	SD;	Restore default (device-dependent) standard font characteristics
Absolute Character Size	SI;	Turns off size transformation
Character Slant	SL;	No slant
Symbol Mode	SM;	Turns off symbol mode
Select Standard Font	SS;	Standard font selected
Transparent Data	TD;	Normal printing mode
User-Defined Line Type	UL;	Defaults all 8 line types

In addition, the device updates the carriage-return point for labeling to the current pen location. (See page 66 for more information on the carriage-return point.) DF defaults the PD and PU forms of the PA and PR instructions to be forms of PA; it clears the current pattern residue and terminates any sequence of continuous vectors (see the LA and LT instructions).

The DF instruction does not affect the following HP-GL/2 conditions:

- Locations of P1 and P2.

- Current pen, its selection, location, width, width unit selection, and up/down state.

- Plot size.

- HP-GL/2 drawing rotation.

- Generated errors are not cleared.

Using DF with the Technical Graphics Extension

The DF instruction also affects the following instructions:

Function	Equivalent Instruction	Default Condition
Chord Tolerance Mode	CT;	Sets the mode to chord angle
Merge Control	MC;	Sets merge control off
Media Type	MT;	Device-dependent—uses the control-panel setting
Quality Level	QL;	Device-dependent
Sort	ST;	Device-dependent
Velocity Select	VS;	Device-dependent speed for all pens

Using DF with the Palette Extension

The DF instruction also affects the following instructions:

Function	Equivalent Instruction	Default Condition
Set Color Range for Relative Color Data	CR 0,255, 0,255, 0,255;	Range 0 through 255 for each primary color (red, green, blue)
Number of Pens	NP;	Device-dependent
Pen Color Assignment	PC;	Determined by the number of pens
Screened Vectors	SV;	No screening (solid vectors); defaults other previously specified options
Transparency Mode	TR1;	Transparency mode on

Using DF in a Dual-Context Environment

The DF instruction also affects the following instructions:

Function	Equivalent Instruction	Default Condition
Anchor Corner	AC;	Places the anchor point at the origin of the current coordinate system
Input Window	IW;	Sets the user window equal to the hard-clip limits
Scalable or Bitmap Fonts	SB0;	Scalable fonts only

Using DF with the Advanced Text Extension

The DF instruction also affects the following instructions:

Function	Equivalent Instruction	Default Condition
Label Mode	LM;	8-bit mode, row-number 0
Scalable or Bitmap Fonts	SB0;	Scalable fonts only

Related Instructions

BP	Begin Plot
IN	Initialize
LM	Label Mode
MC	Merge Control
PP	Pixel Placement

DI, Absolute Direction

Purpose

To specify the slope or direction at which characters are drawn, independent of P1 and P2 settings. Use DI to change labeling direction when you are labeling curves in line charts, schematic drawings, blueprints, and survey boundaries.

Syntax

DI *run,rise[;]*
or
DI *[;]*

Parameter	Format	Functional Range	Parameter Default
run (or cos θ)	clamped real	−32 768 to 32 767	1
rise (or sin θ)	clamped real	−32 768 to 32 767	0

Group

This instruction is in the Character Group.

Use

The DI instruction updates the carriage-return point to the current location. While DI is in effect, with or without parameters, the label direction is not affected by changes in the locations of P1 and P2. However, the DV (Define Variable Text Path) instruction interacts with the DI instruction (and DR), as explained later in this section.

The DI instruction remains in effect until another DI or DR instruction is executed, or the device is initialized or set to default conditions.

- **No parameters:** Defaults the label direction to absolute and horizontal (parallel to X-axis). Equivalent to "DI1,0".

- **run or cos θ:** Specifies the X-component of the label direction.

- **rise or sin θ:** Specify the Y-component of the label direction.

Together, the parameters specify the slope and direction of the label.

You can express the parameters in measured units as *run* and *rise*, or using the trigonometric functions cosine and sine according to the following relationships:

where: *run* and *rise* = number of measured units
θ = the angle measured in degrees
$\sin\theta/\cos\theta$ = *rise/run*
$\theta = \tan^{-1}(rise/run)$
and $\tan\theta = \sin\theta/\cos\theta$

Note that the *run* and *rise* determine the slope or angle of an imaginary line under the base of each character in the label. See Figure 71.

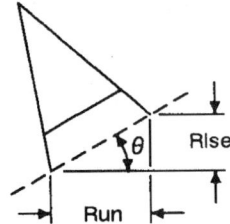

Figure 71. Character Slope Rise and Run

When plotting in horizontal mode (that is, you have not used the DV [Define Variable Text Path] instruction), the *run* and *rise* appear to determine the slope of the entire label. However, if you have used the DV instruction to label in a vertical path, the label appears to slant in the opposite direction, even though the base of each letter is plotted on the same slope. Figure 72 compares how labels plotted with the same *run* and *rise* parameters appear with horizontal "DV0" and vertical "DV1" text paths.

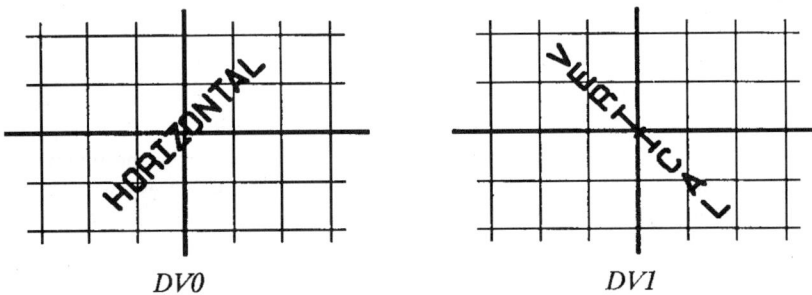

Figure 72. Effect of Horizontal and Vertical Text Paths

For devices that support the Dual-Context Extension, if an "SB1;" instruction has been sent, the device draws the label along the nearest perpendicular. In the case of bisection, the angle is rounded down (so 45° would be rounded to 0°). See Figure 73.

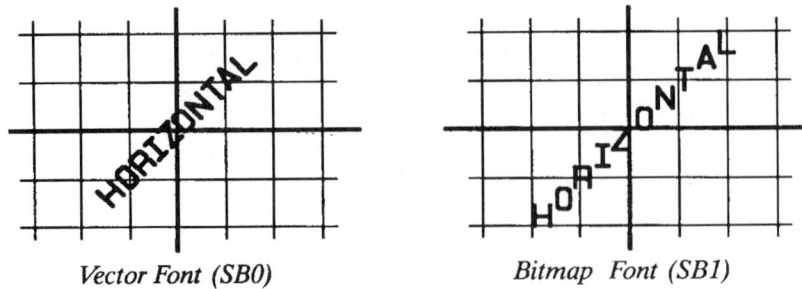

Figure 73. Scalable Versus Bitmap Variable Text Path Printing

Suppose you want your label plotted in the direction shown in Figure 74. You can do this in one of two ways: measure the *run* and *rise*, or measure the angle.

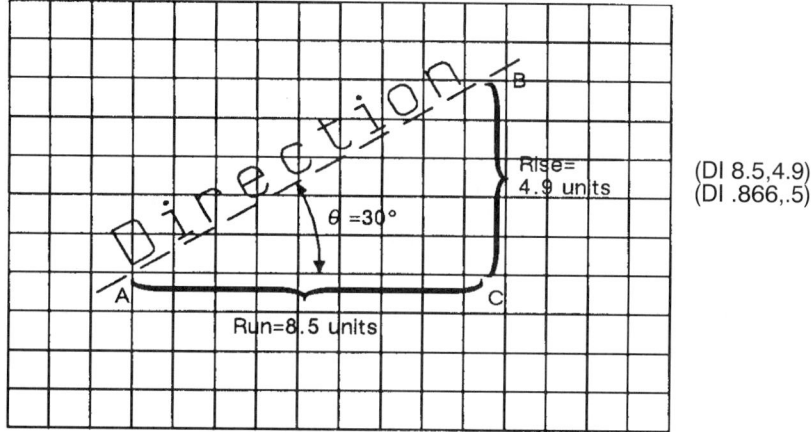

Figure 74. Label Print Direction Rise and Run

To measure the *run* and *rise*, first draw a grid with the lines parallel to the X- and Y-axis. The grid units should be the same size on all sides, but their actual size is irrelevant. Then, draw one line parallel to the label and one parallel to the X-axis. The lines should intersect to form an angle.

Select a point on the open end of your angle (where another line would create a triangle). On the line parallel to the X-axis, count the number of grid units from the intersection of the two lines to your selected point. This is the *run*; in Figure 74, the *run* is 8.5. Now, count the number of units from your selected point along a perpendicular line that intersects the line along the label. This is the *rise*; in Figure 74, the *rise* is 4.9.

Your DI instruction using the *run* and *rise* is "DI8.5,4.9;".

If you know the angle (θ), you can use the trigonometric functions sine (sin) and cosine (cos). In this example, $\theta = 30°$, cos $30° = 0.866$, and sin $30° = 0.5$.

Your DI instruction using the sine and cosine would be "DI.866,.5;".

Whichever set of parameters you use, the label is drawn in the same direction as shown in Figure 74.

When using either method, at least one parameter must not be zero. The ratio of one parameter to the other is more important than the actual numbers. The following table lists three common label angles produced by using 1's and 0's.

DI instruction	Label direction
DI 1,0;	horizontal
DI 0,1;	vertical
DI 1,1; (or any other equal non-zero values)	45°

The relative size and sign of the two parameters determine the amount of rotation. If you imagine the current pen location to be the origin of a coordinate system for the label, you can see that the signs of the parameters determine which quadrant the label is in.

Examples

PA 3500,2500;	Enter absolute plotting mode and move to (3500,2500).
DT*;	Define an asterisk (*) as the label terminator.
DI 1,1;	Select the first quadrant.
LBDIRECTION**CR***;	Print the word "DIRECTION" and send a Carriage Return to return the pen to the carriage-return point (3500,2500).
DI −1,1;	Select the second quadrant.
LBDIRECTION**CR***;	Print the word and Carriage Return.
DI −1,−1;	Select the third quadrant.
LBDIRECTION**CR***;	Print the same word and Carriage Return.
DI 1,−1;	Select the fourth quadrant.
LBDIRECTION**CR***;	Print the same word and Carriage Return.

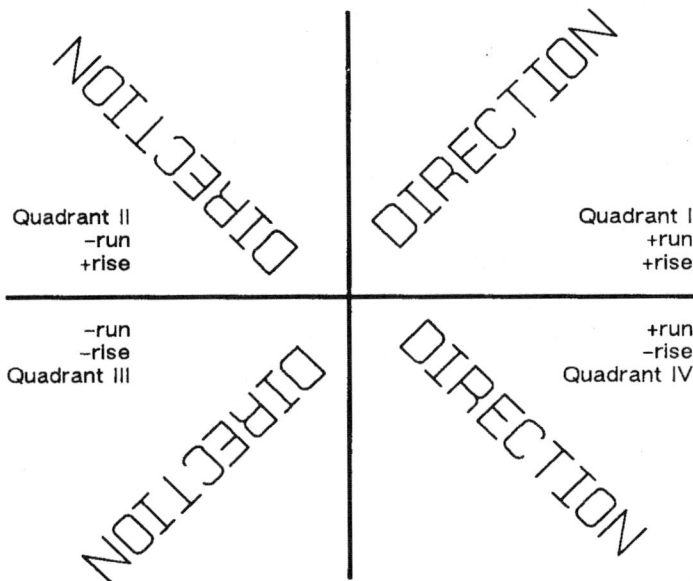

Quadrant II
−run
+rise

Quadrant I
+run
+rise

−run
−rise
Quadrant III

+run
−rise
Quadrant IV

Figure 75. Varying Print Direction with the DI Instruction

The following example illustrates the use of positive and negative parameters, the use of the cosine and sine, how the LB instruction updates the current pen location, and how DI updates the carriage-return point.

PA 3500,2500;	Specify absolute plotting and move to (3500,2500).
DT#,1;	Define the "#" character as the label terminator.
DI 0,1;	Set the label direction to print at 90°.
LB____1990#;	Print "____1990".
DI 1,1;	Set the label direction to 45°.
LB____1991#;	Print "____1991".
DI 1,0;	Set the label direction to 0°.
LB____1992#;	Print "____1992";
DI .71,−.71;	Change the label direction using the cosine and sine of 315°.
LB____1993#;	Print "____1993".
DI 0,−1;	Change the label direction using the cosine and sine of 270°.
LB____1994**CR**#;	Print "____1994"; Carriage Return.
DI −.71,−.71;	Set the label direction using the cosine and sine of 270°.

LB____1995**CR#**;	Print "____1995"; Carriage Return.
DI ,-1,0;	Set the label direction using the cosine and sine of -180°.
LB____1996**CR#**;	Print "____1996"; Carriage Return.

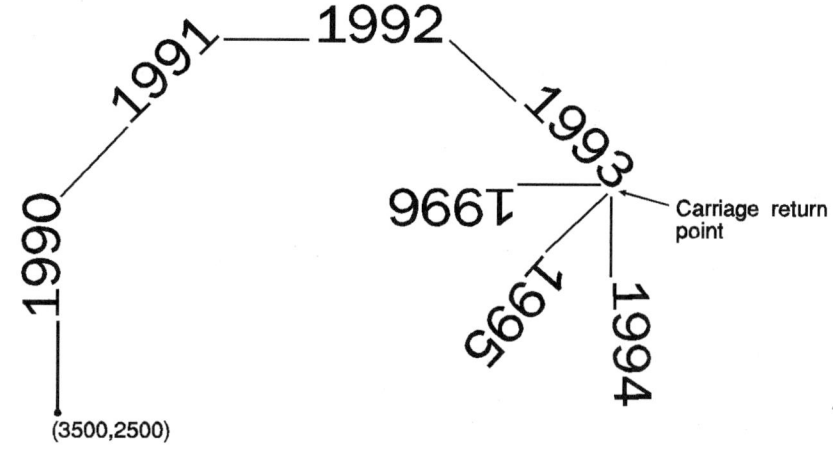

Figure 76. Using the DI (Absolute Direction) Instruction with Labels

Related Instructions

CF	Character Fill Mode
CP	Character Plot
DR	Relative Direction
DV	Define Variable Text Path
LB	Label
SB	Scalable or Bitmap Fonts
SI	Absolute Character Size
SL	Character Slant
SR	Relative Character Size

Possible Error Conditions

Error Condition	Error Number	Printer or Plotter Response
Both parameters = 0 or number out of range	3	Ignores instruction

DL, Download Character

Purpose

To design characters and load them into a buffer for repeated use. Use DL whenever you want to create characters or symbols that are not included in the device's character sets.

Syntax

DL *character_number[,up],X,Y...[[,up],X,Y][;]*

      or

DL *character_number[;]*

      or

DL *character_number1,character_number2[,up],X,Y...[[,up],X,Y][;]*

      or

DL *character_number1,character_number2[;]*

      or

DL *[;]*

Parameter	Format	Functional Range	Parameter Default
character_number, character_number1, character_number2*	clamped integers	0 through 255	no default
up	clamped integer	−128	no default
X,Y coordinates	clamped integers	−127 through 127	no default

*   A pair of character numbers (*character_number1,character_number2*) is only valid in 16-bit mode (see the LM [Label Mode] instruction on page 208).

Group

This instruction is in the Technical Graphics Extension.

Use

After you designate (SD or AD) and select (SS or SA) the HP-GL/2 downloadable 8-bit character set (character set 531, symbol set ID 16S), use the DL instruction to create characters vector by vector, one character per instruction. Once defined with DL, characters can be used in the LB instruction. They can also be used in symbol mode (SM), but will not be centered unless they have been defined that way in the character grid. All text attributes (size, slant, direction, and label origin) apply to downloadable characters. The characters you define in the downloadable set have fixed spacing and are upright. All text attributes (size, slant, direction, and label origin) apply to downloadable characters. They may be intermixed with other fonts. After LB prints the character, the character origin is advanced 48 grid units, unless modified by the ES (Extra Space) instruction.

- **No parameters**: Clears all characters in the downloadable character set from the buffer. All characters are then undefined.

- **character_number**: An integer in the range 33 to 126, specifying the decimal value of the character. If the *character_number* has been previously defined, the new definition overwrites the old one.

  In 8-bit mode, *character_number* specifies the character number of the character, and there should not be any subsequent *character_number2* specified. In 16-bit mode (see the LM instruction on page 208), the character number is specified by the pair of numbers, *character_number1,character_number2*.

  When it is not followed by additional coordinate parameters ("DL*character_number[;]*" or "DL*character_number1,character_number2[;]*"), this instruction clears the corresponding character from the downloadable set. Clearing a character makes it undefined, and referring to such a character in a label string results in a space.

- **up**: A clamped integer with the value −128. The *up*-flag indicates that the next pair of coordinates defines a move with the pen up; subsequent moves are made with the pen down. Pen up is the default for the first pair of coordinates.

- **X, Y coordinates**: Clamped integers in the range −127 to 127 primitive grid units. These coordinates are drawn on a 32-by-32-unit grid. After the first pair, which always defines a pen-up move, all coordinates define moves with the pen down, unless they are preceded by an *up*-flag.

  The number of characters following the *character_number* parameter is not restricted. Your device can download 94 characters with at least 20 points (coordinate pairs) in each character.

In symbol mode, the character drawn at the vector end-points uses the current downloaded definition, not the definition in effect when the SM was received. If a downloaded character defined at the time of SM becomes undefined before the execution of the symbol mode (by PA or PR), no symbol is drawn and error 3 is generated. The vectors specified by PA or PR are, however, drawn normally.

If any HP-GL/2 error is generated while processing DL, the partially defined character is not saved, and the old character is cleared.

Defining a Downloadable Character

The device allocates space in the downloadable character buffer as needed. The DL font uses a fixed overhead of 206 bytes (consumed when the first character is downloaded), plus two overhead bytes per defined character. The points in a DL character average 1½ bytes each.

1. Design the character in absolute units on a 32-by-32-unit grid in a 48-by-64-unit cell.

   Note that the origin (0,0) is in the lower-left corner of the grid. This is the same grid used for fixed-vector character sets in the device. The area occupied by a 32-by-32-unit grid is approximately the size of an uppercase A. The downloaded character may extend outside this grid to ±127 units on each axis. The point size of a downloadable set corresponds to 48 grid units.

2. Assign a character number (decimal code) to the downloadable character.

3. Designate the starting point with the first X,Y coordinate pair, which is always a pen-up move.

4. Specify the vectors of the character using absolute X,Y coordinates.

Related Instructions

AD	Alternate Font Definition
LB	Label
SA	Select Alternate Font
SD	Standard Font Definition
SS	Select Standard Font

Possible Error Conditions

Error Condition	Error Number	Printer or Plotter Response
Y-coordinate missing	2	Ignores instruction
Up-flag follows X-coordinate	2	Ignores instruction
Parameter out of range	3	Ignores instruction
X,Y data out of range	3	Ignores instruction
Buffer overflow	7	Ignores instruction

Example

This sequence of instructions uses a character that is downloaded:

AD   1,531,3,3   Alternate Font Definition: character set 531, pitch 3 characters per inch.

DL   65,   10,0,   10,30,   28,30,   28,24   Download Character number 65 ("A"), starting at (10,0), draw to (10,30), to (28,30), and finally to (28,24).

PU   Pen Up.

PA   300,300   Plot Absolute, moves the pen to (300,300).

LBThe symbol for gamma is **SOAETX**   Label, using the shift-out (**SO**) character, decimal code 14, to switch to the alternate font, and the end-of-text (**ETX**) character, decimal 3, to terminate the text.

(An alternative sequence, using the SA [Select Alternate Font] instruction, would be:

         LBThe symbol for gamma is **ETX**SALBA**ETX**

but is four bytes longer.)

This is the result:

The symbol for gamma is Γ

Figure 77 shows how the gamma symbol fits in its character grid.

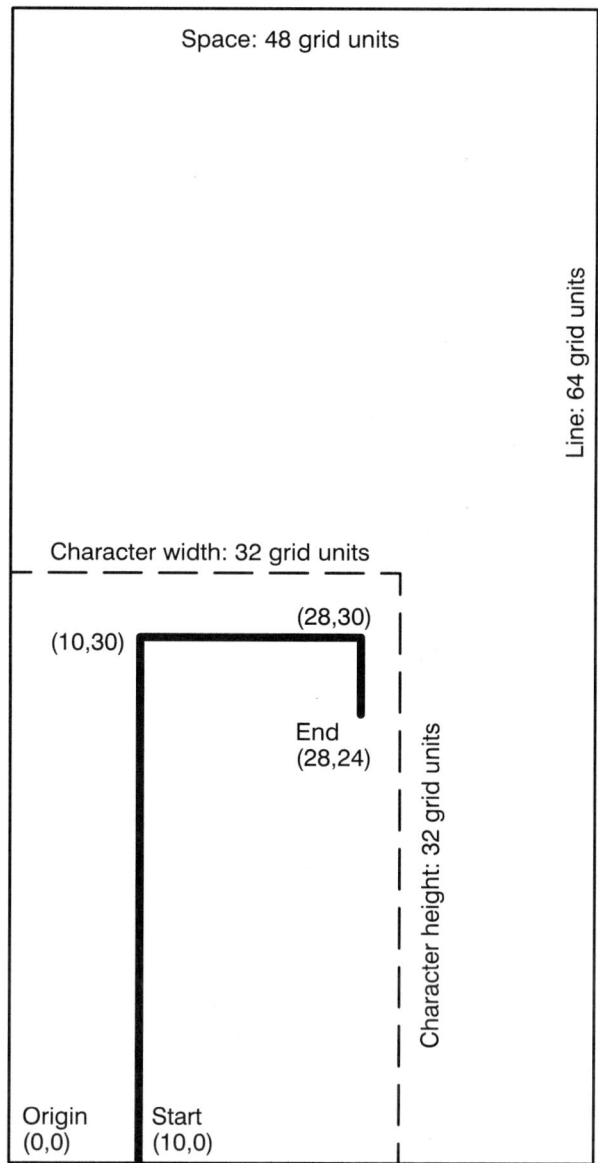

Figure 77. Creating a Downloaded Character

DP, Digitize Point

Purpose

To enable digitize mode and suppress automatic pen lift and storage. In digitize mode, you have full control of the pen holder. The device remains in digitize mode until a point is entered using a front-panel control, or digitize mode is terminated by the DC (Digitize Clear) instruction.

Syntax

DP [;]

Group

This instruction is in the Digitizing Extension.

Use

This instruction suppresses any automatic pen storage and lift that may be implemented in the plotter.

This instruction may turn on a control-panel light to indicate that it is waiting for you to enter a point. Use the control-panel cursor-buttons to move the digitizing sight to the appropriate location, lower the sight, and then press the appropriate control-panel button (usually the Enter button).

Entering a point sets bit position 2 of the OS instruction status byte to indicate that a digitized point is available for output when requested by the OD instruction. Use the OD instruction to retrieve the X,Y coordinates of the point and the pen state (up or down). Then you can display these coordinates on your computer screen or write them to a file.

See *The Digitizing Extension* on page 89 for more information.

Related Instructions

DC   Digitize Clear
OD   Output Digitized Point and Pen Status
OS   Output Status

Possible Error Conditions

Error Condition	Error Number	Plotter Response
One or more parameters are specified	2	The parameters are ignored

DR, Relative Direction

Purpose

To specify the direction in which labels are drawn, relative to the scaling points P1 and P2. Label direction is adjusted when P1 and P2 change so that labels maintain the same relationship to the scaled data. Use DR to change labeling direction when you are labeling curves.

Syntax

> DR *run,rise[;]*
>   or
> DR *[;]*

Parameter	Format	Functional Range	Parameter Default
run	clamped real	−32 768 to 32 767	1% of $P2_X$–$P1_X$
rise	clamped real	−32 768 to 32 767	0

Group

This instruction is in the Character Group.

Use

The DR instruction updates the carriage-return point to the current location. While DR is in effect, with or without parameters, the label direction is affected by changes in the location of P1 and P2. DR is also affected by the DV (Define Variable Text Path) instruction. Refer to the DI instruction for an explanation of this interaction.

A DR instruction remains in effect until another DR or a DI instruction is executed, or until the device is initialized or set to default conditions.

- **No parameters:** Defaults the label direction to relative and horizontal (parallel to the X-axis). Equivalent to "DR1,0".

- **run:** Specifies a percentage of the distance between $P1_X$ and $P2_X$.

- **rise:** Specifies a percentage of the distance between $P1_Y$ and $P2_Y$.

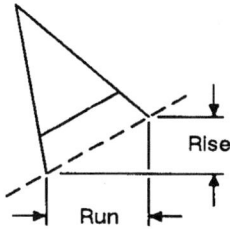

Figure 78. Rise and Run Parameters

You define the parameters of *run* and *rise* as shown in Figure 78.

With the DR instruction, the use of *run* and *rise* is somewhat different than with DI. *Run* is expressed as a percentage of the horizontal distance between P1 and P2; *rise* is expressed as a percentage of the vertical distance between P1 and P2.

$$\text{actual run} = run \text{ parameter} \div 100 \times (P2_X - P1_X)$$

$$\text{actual rise} = rise \text{ parameter} \div 100 \times (P2_Y - P1_Y)$$

Figure 79 shows the effects of using three different sets of *run* and *rise* parameters. Notice how the text baseline varies as the *run* percentage is greater than, equal to, and less than the value for the *rise*.

To calculate the angle of the label, use the *run* and *rise* parameters to form a fraction that is less than or equal to 1. It doesn't matter whether *run* or *rise* is the numerator. For example, if *run*=4 and *rise*=6, the fraction is 4/6; if *run*=6 and *rise*=4, the fraction is still 4/6.

The larger of the two terms determines whether the directional line intersects the top or side of the P1/P2 area, as follows:

- If *run*=*rise*, the fraction is 1, and the directional line runs from corner to corner of the P1/P2 area. (The exact corner is determined by the sign of the parameters.)

- If *run*>*rise*, the line intersects the side of the plotting area, a fraction of the way up towards the top scaling point. For example, if P1 is in the lower-left corner, *run*>*rise*, and the fraction is 1/2, the directional line intersects half-way up towards P2.

- If *run*<*rise*, the line intersects the top of the plotting area, a fraction of the way across towards the right scaling point. For example, if P1 is in the lower left corner, *run*<*rise*, and the fraction is 2/6, the directional line intersects the top one-third (2/6) of the way towards P2.

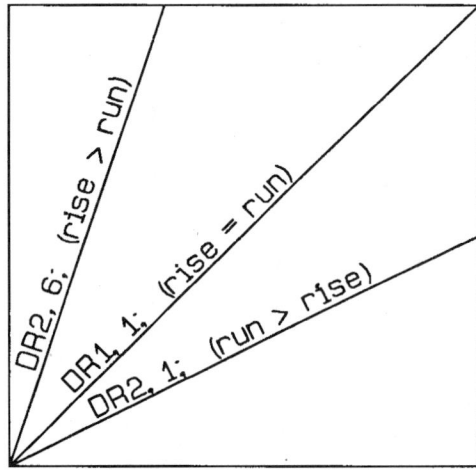

Figure 79. Effects of Different Rise/Run Parameters

If the P1/P2 rectangle is square, the DR and DI instructions have exactly the same effect. The advantage of using the DR instruction is that, as the locations of P1 and P2 change, the slope of the baseline changes to match the stretching or compressing of the P1/P2 rectangle.

For example, if the relative direction is set so that *rise=run*, the slope of the baseline is 45° as long as the P1/P2 rectangle is square. If the P1/P2 rectangle stretches so that it is twice as high as it is wide, the slope of the baseline remains parallel to an imaginary line running from P1 to P2 (see Figure 80).

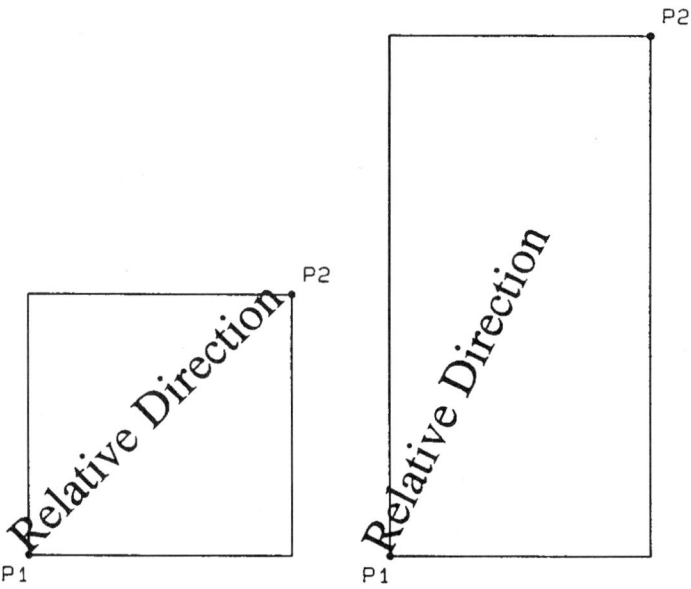

Figure 80. Effects of P1 and P2 on Label Direction with the DR Instruction

Labels begin at the current pen location and thus are drawn parallel to the directional line, not necessarily on it. Also, negative parameters have the same effect on direction as described for the DI instruction.

At least one parameter must not be zero. The ratio of the parameters to each other is more important than the actual numbers. The table below lists three common label angles produced by using ones and zeros.

DR instruction	Label direction
DR 1,0;	horizontal
DR 0,1;	vertical
DR 1,1; (or any other equal non-zero values)	diagonal from P1 to P2

The relative size and sign of the two parameters determine the amount of rotation. If you imagine the current pen location to be the origin of a coordinate system for the label, you can see that the signs of the parameters determine in which quadrant the label is in.

DR and DI Compared

DR acts like DI except that DR parameters are relative to the locations of P1 and P2. Therefore, as shown below, for some P1/P2 orientations, positive DR parameters produce the same effects as negative DI parameters.

If P1 = (0, 0) and P2 = (10 000, 5 000), DR 1,1 is equivalent to DI 2,1;

If P1 = (0, 5 000) and P2 = (10 000, 0), DR 1,1 is equivalent to DI 2,–1;

If P1 = (10 000, 0) and P2 = (0, 5 000), DR 1,1 is equivalent to DI –2,1;

If P1 = (10 000, 5 000) and P2 = (0, 0), DR 1,1 is equivalent to DI –2,–1;

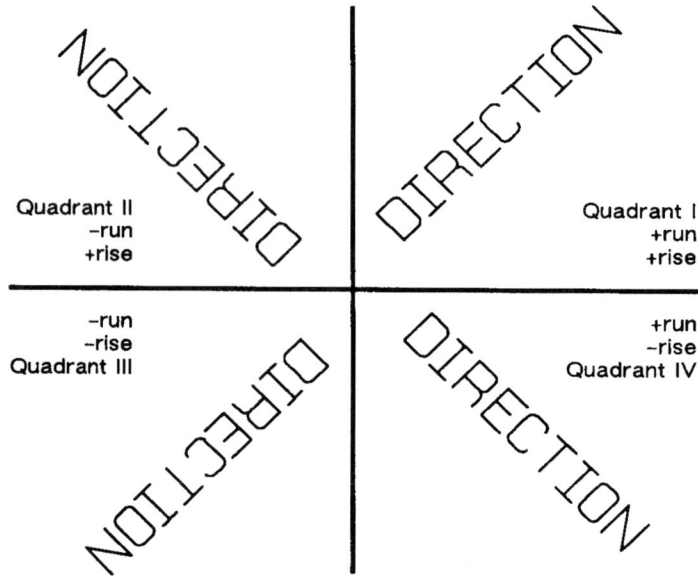

Figure 81. Varying Print Direction with the DR Instruction

Related Instructions

CF	Character Fill Mode
CP	Character Plot
DI	Absolute Direction
DV	Define Variable Text Path
IP	Input P1 and P2
IR	Input Relative P1 and P2
LB	Label
SB	Scalable or Bitmap Fonts
SI	Absolute Character Size
SL	Character Slant
SR	Relative Character Size

Example

This example illustrates the use of positive and negative parameters, how the LB instruction updates the current pen location, and how DR updates the carriage-return point.

Note that this is the same example shown with the DI instruction. The only changes are switching the DI to DR and using the 1:0 ratio instead of the sine and cosine. However, if you print them both and measure them, you'll discover that they are slightly different sizes. The size difference results from the DR instruction's use of the percentage of the P2/P1 distance.

Note; Labels begin at the current pen location and thus are drawn parallel to the directional line, not necessarily on it.

PA 3500,2500;	Specify absolute plotting and move to (3500,2500).
DT#,1;	Define the "#" character as the label terminator.
DR 0,1;	Set the label direction
LB____1990#;	Print "____1990".
DR 1,1;	Set the label direction
LB____1991#;	Print "____1991".
DR 1,0;	Set the label direction
LB____1992#;	Print "____1992".
DR 1,–1;	Change the label direction
LB____1993#;	Print "____1993".
DR 0,–1;	Set the label direction.
LB____1994**CR#**;	Print "____1994" and Carriage Return.
DR –1,–1;	Set the label direction.
LB____1995**CR#**;	Print "____1995" and Carriage Return.
DR –1,0;	Set the label direction.
LB____1996**CR#**;	Print "____1996" and Carriage Return.

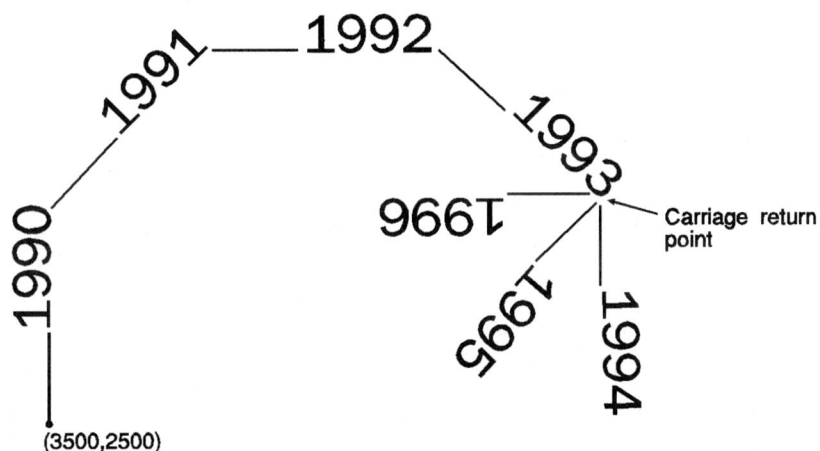

Figure 82. Using the DR (Relative Direction) Instruction with Labels

Possible Error Conditions

Error Condition	Error Number	Printer or Plotter Response
Both parameters = 0 or number out of range	3	Ignores instruction

DT, Define Label Terminator

Purpose

To specify the character to be used as the label terminator and whether it is printed. Use DT to define a new label terminator if you need a different one or if your computer cannot use the default (**ETX**, decimal code 3).

Syntax

> DT *label_terminator[,mode];*
> > or
> DT *;*

You must use a terminator (;) with this instruction.

Parameter	Format	Functional Range	Parameter Default
label_terminator	label	any character except **NULL**, **LF**, **ESC**, and **;** (decimal codes 0, 5, 27, and 59 respectively)*	**ETX** (decimal code 3)
mode	clamped integer	0 or 1	1 (non-printing)

* If you specify a *label_terminator* of decimal code 0, 5, or 27, the device ignores the instruction; the terminator remains unchanged.

Group

This instruction is in the Character Group.

Use

The character immediately following DT is interpreted to be the new label terminator. You must terminate all LB (Label) instructions following a DT instruction with the specified label terminator.

- **No parameters:** "DT;" defaults the label terminator to **ETX** (*not* a semicolon) and the mode to non-printing. Equivalent to "DT**ETX**,1;".

- **label_terminator:** Specifies the label terminator as the character immediately following the DT mnemonic. (If you use a space between the mnemonic and your intended *label_terminator* parameter, the space becomes the label terminator; that is why the examples of DT in this book show no space after the instruction mnemonic, unlike most other instructions.)

- **mode:** Specifies whether the label terminator is printed.

  0 The label terminator prints if it is a printable character and performs its function if it is a control code.

  1 The label terminator does not print if it is a printing character and does not perform its function if it is a control code. (This is the default.)

In 16-bit mode, the label terminator and all 8-bit control codes of an LB instruction must have a first byte set to 0. For example, an escape character (**ESC**, ASCII 27) would be sent as a 0 followed by a 27. The exception is **ESCE** in dual-context devices, which is parsed and executed regardless of byte boundaries with the LB and SM instructions.

If you are using LM to label a 16-bit character set, you need to switch back to 8-bit mode for the terminator. DT works with 8-bit terminators only; it does not work with 16-bit characters.

A DT instruction remains in effect until another DT instruction is executed, or the device is initialized or set to default conditions.

Related Instructions

LB   Label
TD   Transparent Data

Examples

The following instructions show how to define and print using a non-printing label terminator:

DT#;   Define "#" as the label terminator.
LBThe label terminator WILL NOT print.#;   This instruction would print as:

The label terminator WILL NOT print.

This example shows how to define and use a printable label terminator:

DT#,0;   Define "#" as the label terminator.
LBThe label terminator WILL print.#;   This instruction would print as:

The label terminator WILL print.#

DV, Define Variable Text Path

Purpose

To specify the text path for subsequent labels and the direction of Line Feeds as either right, left, up, or down. Use DV to "stack" characters in a column.

Syntax

DV *path[,line][;]*
or
DV *[;]*

Parameter	Format	Functional Range	Parameter Default
path	clamped integer	0, 1, 2, or 3	0 (horizontal)
line	clamped integer	0 or 1	0 (normal Line Feed)

Group

This instruction is in the Character Group.

Use

The DV instruction determines the ***text path***, the direction that the current location moves after each character is drawn and the direction that the carriage-return point moves when a Line Feed is included in the label string. It alters the relative positions of successive characters in a label, but does not change the orientation of individual characters. It updates the carriage-return point to the current pen location.

- **No parameters:** Defaults the text path to horizontal (not stacked) with normal Line Feed. Equivalent to "DV0,0".

- **path:** Specifies the location of each character with respect to the preceding character, relative to the labeling direction defined by the DI or DR instructions. The text path set by DV is not affected by changes in P1 and P2.

    0 0° (in the +X-direction). Within a label, each character begins to the right of the previous character. This is a horizontal text path (unless altered by DI or DR).

    1 –90° (in the –Y-direction). Within a label, each character begins below the previous character. This is a vertical text path (unless altered by DI or DR).

    2 –180° (in the –X-direction). Within a label, each character begins to the left of the previous character. This is a horizontal text path (unless altered by DI or DR).

    3 –270° (in the +Y-direction). Within a label, each character begins above the previous character. This is a vertical text path (unless altered by DI or DR).

    For PCL printers, the *path* values represent paths that are to the right (0), down (1), left (2), and up (3).

Figure 83 shows the four text paths. +X is to the right; +Y is up.

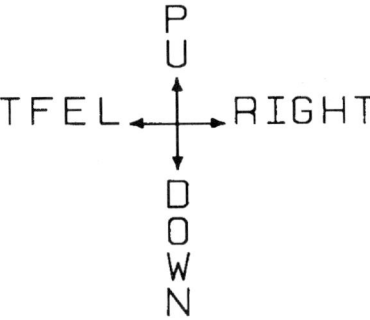

Figure 83. Four Text Paths

- **line:** Specifies the location of each character with respect to the preceding character, relative to the labeling direction defined by the DI or DR instructions.

  0 –90° (normal Line Feed). Sets the direction of Line Feeds –90° with respect to the text path.

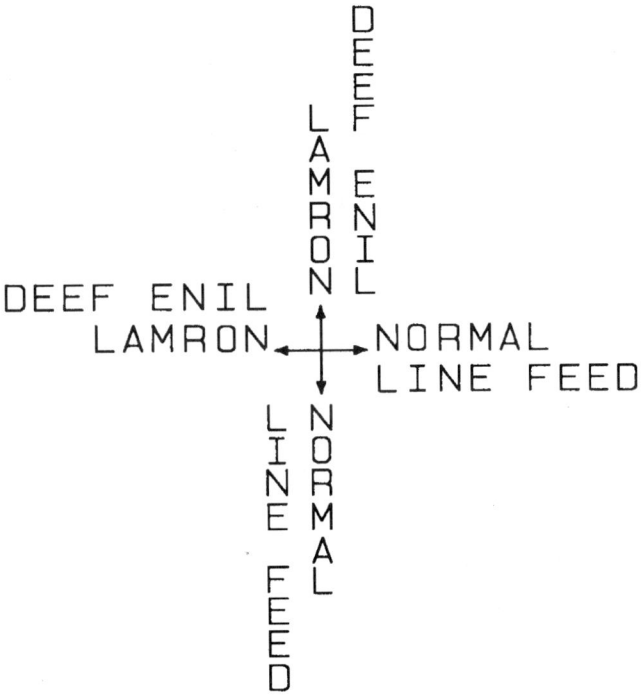

Figure 84. DV Instruction Character Position for Normal (0) Parameter (+X is to the right; +Y is up)

1   +90° (reversed Line Feed). Sets the direction of Line Feeds +90° with respect to the text path.

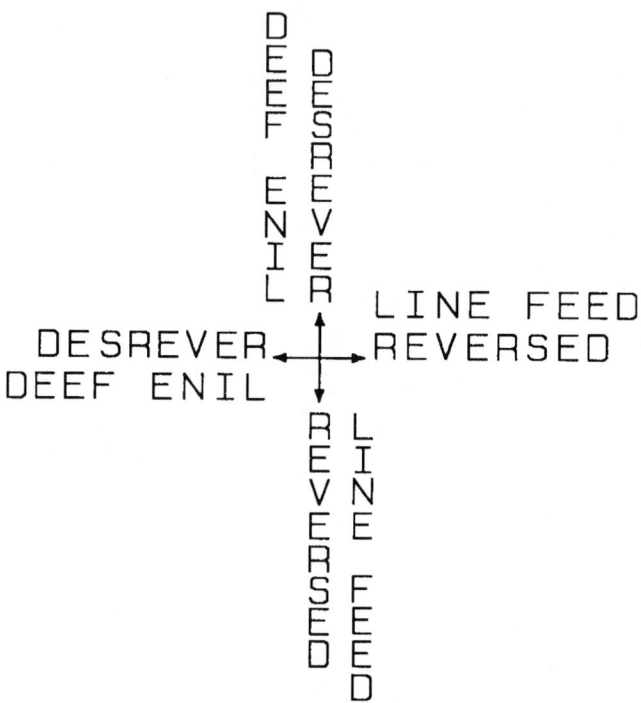

Figure 85. DV Instruction Character Position for Reverse (1) Parameter

Note: Used with specific LO (Label Origin) settings, labels can be concatenated (see the LO instruction on page 211).

Related Instructions

CP	Character Plot
DI	Absolute Direction
DR	Relative Direction
LB	Label
LO	Label Origin

Example

The following example illustrates how Line Feeds and Carriage Returns affect vertical labels. Horizontal labels are shown for comparison.

PA	2000,3000;	Specify absolute plotting and move to (2000,3000).
DV	1;	Define the text path so that each character begins below the previous character (vertical text path).
DT@;		Define the "@" character as the label terminator (non-printing).
LBABC**CR LF**@;		Print ABC, followed by a Carriage Return and Line Feed.
LBDEF**LF**@;		Print DEF, followed by a Line Feed.
LBGHI**LF**@;		Print GHI, followed by a Line Feed.
LO	3;	Change the label origin to 3 (the default LO1 was used prior to this).
LBJKL@		Print KJL.
LO	1;	Return to the default label origin.
PA	4000,3000;	Move to (4000,3000).
DV	0;	Define the text path so that each character begins to the right of the previous one (horizontal [default] text path).
LBABC**CR LF**@;		Print ABC, followed by a Carriage Return and Line Feed.
LBDEF**LF**@;		Print DEF, followed by Line Feed.
LBGHI@;		Print GHI (without a Carriage Return or Line Feed).

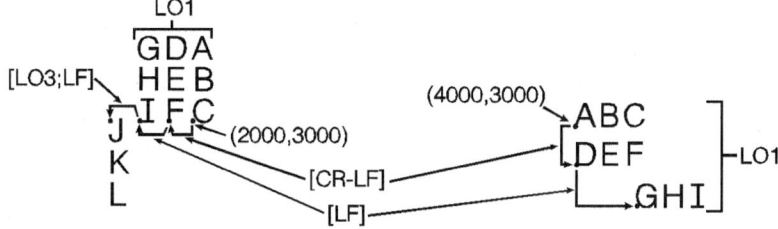

Figure 86. Using the Define Variable Text Path (DV) Instruction with Labels

EA, Edge Rectangle Absolute

Purpose

To define and outline a rectangle using absolute coordinates. Use EA when drawing charts or schematic diagrams that require rectangles.

Syntax

EA *X,Y[;]*

Parameter	Format	Functional Range	Parameter Default
X,Y coordinates	current units	*device-dependent* (at least -2^{23} to $2^{23} - 1$)	no default

Group

This instruction is in the Polygon Group.

Use

The EA instruction defines and edges a rectangle using absolute coordinates and the current pen, line type and line attributes. The EA instruction performs an automatic pen down. When the instruction execution is complete, the original pen location and up/down status are restored.

- **X,Y coordinates:** Specify the opposite corner of the rectangle from the current pen location. The current pen location is the starting point of the rectangle. Coordinates are interpreted in current units: as user-units when scaling is on; as plotter-units when scaling is off.

The following illustration shows the current pen location in the lower-left corner and the instruction's X,Y coordinates in the upper-right corner. Depending on the coordinate values, the points can be in any two diagonally opposite corners.

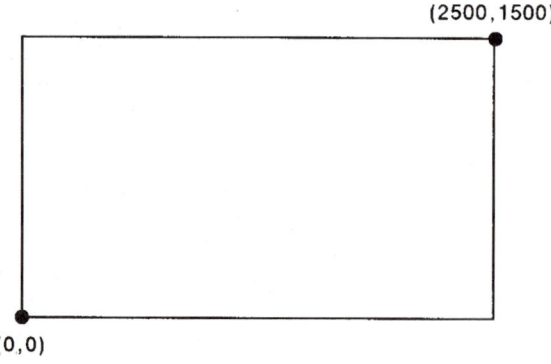

Figure 87. Simple Edged Rectangle

Note: Any line drawn along the border of the effective window causes the line to be clipped, producing a line width one-half of the defined pen width. For example, if the above rectangle is drawn at the window border, all the lines are half the width of any other lines that may be drawn since they are clipped at the window borders.

The only difference between the EA instruction and the RA (Fill Rectangle Absolute) instruction is that the EA instruction produces an outlined rectangle, and RA, a filled one.

The EA instruction clears the polygon buffer and then uses it to define the rectangle before drawing. Refer to *Drawing Polygons* on page 49 for more information.

A dot is drawn if the X,Y coordinates coincide with the current position. A line is drawn if one of the coordinates equals the corresponding coordinate of the current position.

Related Instructions

EP	Edge Polygon
ER	Edge Rectangle Relative
FP	Fill Polygon
LA	Line Attributes
LT	Line Type
PW	Pen Width
RA	Fill Rectangle Absolute
RR	Fill Rectangle Relative

Example

The following example uses absolute coordinates to draw some rectangles. The same image is drawn using the ER instruction instead in the example on page 167. Compare this EA example with the ER example to understand the differences between the coordinates used (relative as against absolute).

SC	0,150,0,150,1;	Set up user scaling, with P1 being (0,0) user-units and P2 being (150,150) user-units. Isotropic scaling is specified.
PA	75,105;	Specify absolute plotting mode and move to (75,105).
EA	115,130;	Use EA to outline the shape of a rectangle that begins at (75,105) and has an upper-right corner of (115,130) user-units.
PA	95,105;	
PD	95,95;	Draw a line from (95,105) to (95,95).
PD	65,95,65,90;	Draw a line from the current pen location (95,95) to (65,95), and another line from there to (65,90).
PU	45,90;	Lift the pen and move to (45,90).
EA	85,65;	Draw the outline of a rectangle with an upper-left corner of (45,90) and a lower-right corner of (85,65).
PU	95,95;	Lift the pen and move to (95,95).
PD	125,95,125,90;	Lower the pen and draw a line to (125,95), then to (125,90).
PU	145,90;	Lift the pen and move to (145,90).
EA	105,65;	Draw the outline of a rectangle, with the upper-right corner at (145,90) and the lower-left corner at (105,65).

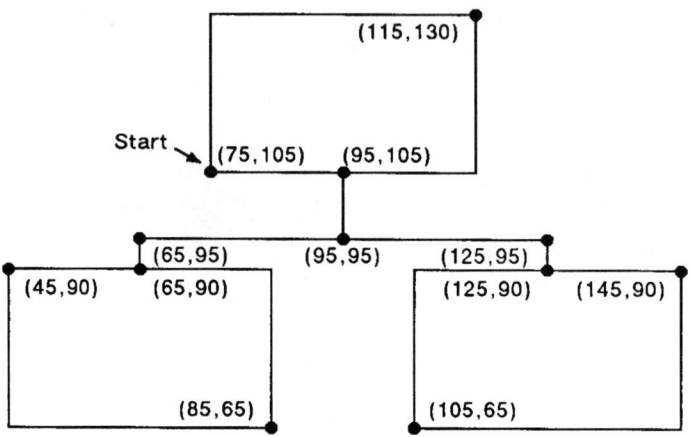

Figure 88. Using the EA (Edge Rectangle Absolute) Instruction

Possible Error Conditions

Error Condition	Error Number	Plotter Response
Parameter(s) would make the device enter "lost" mode	3	The instruction is ignored

EC, Enable Cutter

Purpose

To enable or disable the automatic cutter function on your device. Not all devices have an automatic cutter.

Syntax

EC *n[;]*
  or
EC *[;]*

Parameter	Format	Functional Range	Parameter Default
n	clamped integer	–32 768 to 32 767	no parameter (enabled)

Group

This instruction is in the Technical Graphics Extension.

Use

If the cutter is enabled, cutting is done after each PG and RP instruction. Roll-feed devices that do not have a cutter may draw a line where the media should be cut.

- **No parameter**: Enables the cutter function. This is the default condition.

- **n:** Disables the cutter function. This may be any number (a clamped integer) in the device's range.

EP, Edge Polygon

Purpose

To outline the polygon currently stored in the polygon buffer. Use EP to edge polygons that you defined in polygon mode and with the Fill Rectangle and Wedge instructions (RA, RR, and WG).

Syntax

EP *[;]*

Group

This instruction is in the Polygon Group.

Use

The EP instruction outlines any polygon that is currently in the polygon buffer. This includes wedges and rectangles defined using the EA, ER, EW, RA, RR, and WG instructions. EP accesses the data in the polygon buffer, but does not clear the buffer or change the data in any way.

The EP instruction only edges between points that were defined with the pen down, using the current pen, line type and attributes. When the instruction execution is complete, the original pen location and up/down status are restored.

EP is ignored in polygon mode (after "PM0" and before "PM2") or whenever the buffer is empty.

Related Instructions

EA	Edge Rectangle Absolute
ER	Edge Rectangle Relative
EW	Edge Wedge
LA	Line Attributes
LT	Line Type
PM	Polygon Mode
PW	Pen Width
RA	Fill Rectangle Absolute
RR	Fill Rectangle Relative
WG	Fill Wedge

Example

The following example creates a shape in polygon mode, then uses EP to outline it.

PA	2000,10;	Specify absolute plotting and move to position (2000,10).
PM	0;	Enter polygon mode.
PD	10,2000, 10,10, 2000,10;	Store a pen down instruction, and then store points (10,2000), (10,10), and (2000,10).
PM	1;	Close the polygon.
PU	610,610;	While still in polygon mode, lift the pen and move to (610,610).
CI	500;	Draw a circle with a diameter of 500 plotter-units.
PM	2;	Close the current subpolygon and exit polygon mode.
EP	;	Outline the polygon that was just stored in the polygon buffer.

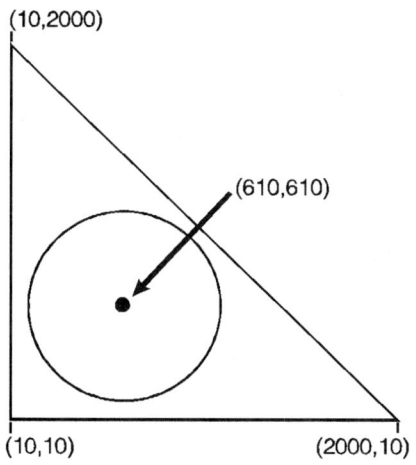

Figure 89. Using the EP (Edge Polygon) Instruction

ER, Edge Rectangle Relative

Purpose

To define and outline a rectangle using relative coordinates. Use ER when drawing charts or schematic diagrams that require rectangles.

Syntax

ER *X,Y[;]*

Parameter	Format	Functional Range	Parameter Default
X,Y increments	current units	*device-dependent* (at least -2^{23} to $2^{23} - 1$)	no default

Group

This instruction is in the Polygon Group.

Use

The ER instruction defines and edges a rectangle using relative coordinates and the current pen, line type, and line attributes. The ER instruction includes an automatic pen down. When the instruction operation is complete, the original pen location and up/down status are restored.

- **X,Y increments:** Specify the opposite corner of the rectangle from the current pen location. The current pen location is the starting point of the rectangle. Increments are interpreted in current units: as user-units when scaling is on; as plotter-units when scaling is off.

The following illustration shows the current pen location in the lower-left corner and the instruction's X,Y increment location in the upper-right corner. When you draw a rectangle, these points can be in any two diagonally opposite corners.

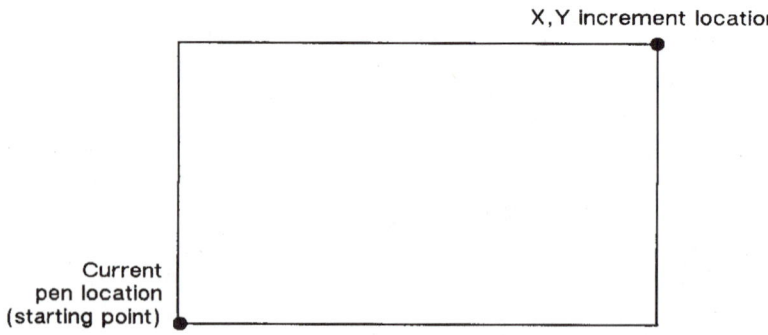

Figure 90. ER (Edge Rectangle Relative) Instruction

The only difference between the ER instruction and the RR (Fill Relative Rectangle) instruction is that the ER instruction produces an outlined rectangle, and RR a filled one.

The ER instruction clears the polygon buffer and then uses it to define the rectangle before drawing. Refer to *Using the Polygon Buffer* on page 45 for more information.

A dot is drawn if both X and Y coordinates are zero. A line is drawn if one of the coordinates is zero.

Related Instructions

EA	Edge Rectangle Absolute
EP	Edge Polygon
FP	Fill Polygon
LA	Line Attributes
LT	Line Type
PW	Pen Width
RA	Fill Rectangle Absolute
RR	Fill Rectangle Relative

Example

The following example uses relative coordinates to draw the same image shown in the EA instruction example. Compare this example with the EA example to understand the differences between the coordinates used.

SC	0,150,0,150,1;	Specify user scaling, with P1 being (0,0) and P2 (150,150); the "1" indicates isotropic scaling.
PA	75,105;	Enter absolute plotting mode and move to (75,105).
ER	40,25;	Draw a rectangle using the current pen location as the lower-left corner and a point (40,25) user-units away as the upper-right corner.
PR	20,0;	Specify relative plotting and move the pen 20 user-units to the right.
PD	0,–10;	Place the pen down and draw a line to a point 10 user-units down.
PD	–30,0,0,–5;	With the pen down, move 30 user-units to the left and 5 units down.
PU	–20,0;	Lift the pen and move 20 user-units to the left.
ER	40,–25;	Draw the outline of a rectangle with the current pen location as one corner and a point (40,–25) user-units away as the opposite corner.
PU	50,5;	Lift the pen and move 50 user-units to the right and 5 units up.
PD	30,0, 0,–5;	Place the pen down and draw a line 30 user-units to the right, then 5 units down.
PU	20,0;	Lift the pen and move 20 user-units to the right.
ER	–40,–25;	Draw a rectangle from that point, with the current pen location being one corner and the opposite corner being 40 user-units to the left and 25 units down.

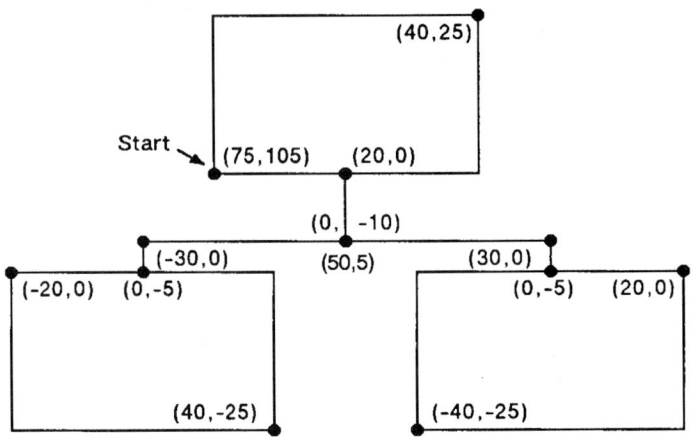

Figure 91. Using the ER (Edge Rectangle Relative) Instruction

Possible Error Conditions

Error Condition	Error Number	Plotter Response
Parameter(s) would make the device enter "lost" mode	3	The instruction is ignored

ES, Extra Space

Purpose

To adjust the space between characters and lines of labels without affecting the character size.

Syntax

ES *width[,height][;]*
or
ES *[;]*

Parameter	Format	Functional Range	Parameter Default
width	clamped real	−32 768 to 32 767	0
height	clamped real	−32 768 to 32 767	0

Group

This instruction is in the Character Group.

Use

The device interprets the parameters as follows:

- **No parameters:** Defaults the spaces and lines between characters to no extra space. Equivalent to "ES0,0".

- **width:** Specifies an increase (positive number) or decrease (negative number) in the space between characters. The *width* parameter is a fraction of the character plot cell width. For example, "ES.15" under default conditions causes the CP cell width to increase by 15% (1.15 × its current width). Character images are not distorted by ES. For maximum legibility, do not specify more than one extra space or subtract more than half a space.

- **height:** Specifies an increase (positive number) or decrease (negative number) in the space between lines. The *height* parameter is a fraction of the line-feed height of the character plot cell. For maximum legibility, do not specify more than two extra lines, or subtract more than half a line.

For proportionally spaced fonts, the ES percentage applies to each individual character cell; therefore cell size varies from character to character.

An ES instruction remains in effect until another ES instruction is executed, or until the device is initialized or set to default conditions.

Related Instructions

CP   Character Plot
LB   Label

Example

PA	2500,3200;	Specify absolute plotting and move to (2500,3200).
SI	.187,.269;	Specify a relative character size of .187 cm wide by .269 cm high.
DT#;		Define the "#" character as the label terminator.
ES	;	Set the extra space setting to default (no extra space).
LBES; CAUSES#;		Print "ES; CAUSES".
CP	;	Use a CP instruction to produce a **CR LF**
LBTHIS SPACING.#;		and print "THIS SPACING."
PA	2500,2500;	Move to (2500,2500).
ES	−.1,−.25;	Decrease the inter-character spacing by .1 and the inter-line spacing by 0.25.
LBES−.1,−.25; CAUSES#;		Print "ES−.1,−.25; CAUSES".
CP	;	Send CP to produce **CR LF**,
LBTHIS SPACING.#;		and print "THIS SPACING."
PA	2500,1800;	Move to (2500,1800).
ES	.2,.25;	Increase the inter-character spacing by .2 and the inter-line spacing by .25 of the Space control code.
LBES.2,.25; CAUSES#;		Print "ES.2,.25; CAUSES".
CP	;	Send CP to produce **CR LF**,
LBTHIS SPACING.#;		and print "THIS SPACING."

```
ES; CAUSES
THIS SPACING.


ES-.1, -.25; CAUSES
THIS SPACING.


ES.2, .25; CAUSES
THIS SPACING.
```

Figure 92. Adding Extra Space to Labels

EW, Edge Wedge

Purpose

To outline any wedge. Use EW to draw sections of pie charts.

Syntax

EW *radius,start_angle,sweep_angle,[,chord_angle][;]*

Parameter	Format	Functional Range	Parameter Default
radius	current units	*device-dependent* (at least -2^{23} to $2^{23} - 1$)	no default
start_angle	clamped real	$-32\,768$ to $32\,767$ (modulo 360)	no default
sweep_angle	clamped real	$-360°$ to $+360°$	no default
*chord_angle**	clamped real	$0.0°$ to $360°$	*device-dependent* (usually $5°$)

* If you have used the "CT1" instruction, the *chord_angle* is interpreted as a *deviation distance* in current units; see the CT instruction on page 133.

Group

This instruction is in the Polygon Group.

Use

The EW instruction defines and edges a wedge using the current pen, line type and attributes. The EW instruction includes an automatic pen down. When the instruction execution is complete, the original pen location and up/down status are restored.

EW deletes any stored polygon and stores the wedge in the polygon buffer with an implicit pen-down that overrides any explicit pen-up (PU); therefore the wedge may be subsequently filled by FP or re-edged by EP.

If the wedge has more points than will fit in the polygon buffer, the portion of the wedge that fits in the buffer is closed and edged, and the remainder of the wedge is discarded.

The only difference between the EW instruction and the WG (Fill Wedge) instruction is that the EW instruction produces an outlined wedge, and the WG instruction, a filled one.

Always use isotropic scaling in drawings that contain wedges unless you wish the wedges to "stretch" with changes in the aspect ratio of the drawing (causing elliptical wedges). For more information, refer to the discussion of scaling and the SC (Scale) instruction on page 290.

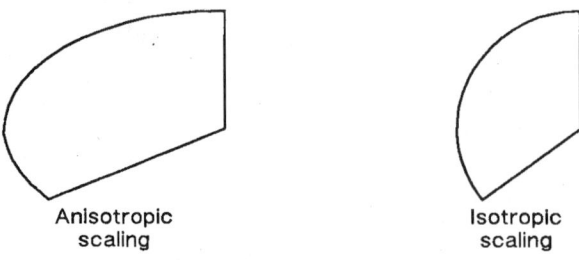

Figure 93. Anisotropic and Isotropic Scaling of Wedges

- **radius:** Specifies the distance from the current pen location to the start of the wedge's arc.
  Since the wedge is a portion of a circle, this parameter is the radius of the circle. It
  specifies the distance from the current pen location (which becomes the center of the
  circle), to any point on the circumference of the circle.

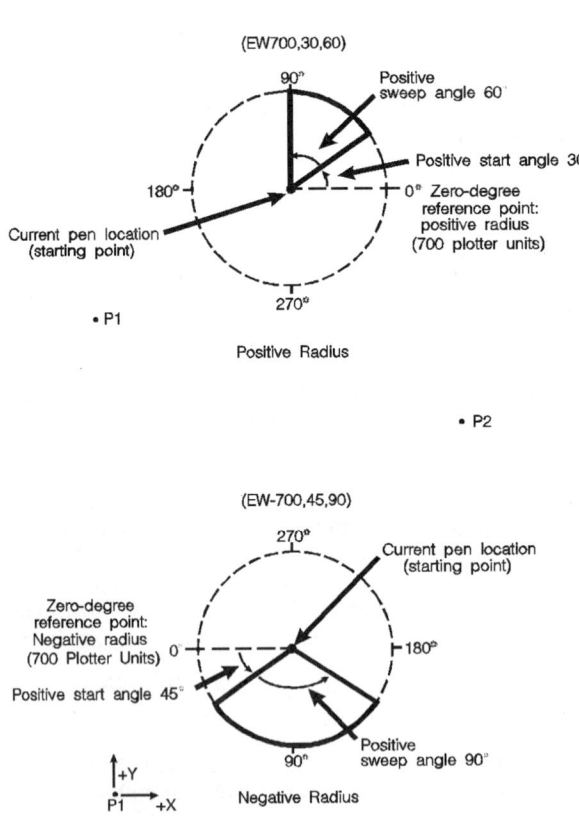

Figure 94. Wedges with Positive and Negative Radii

The radius is interpreted in current units: as user-units when scaling is on; as plotter-units
when scaling is off. The sign (positive or negative) of the radius determines the location of
the zero-degree reference point. Figure 94 shows the location of the zero-degree reference

point for a positive and negative radius. The X- and Y-axes are to the right and upwards respectively.

- **start_angle:** Specifies the beginning point for the arc as the number of degrees from the zero-degree reference point. A positive start angle positions the radius counter-clockwise from the zero-degree reference point. A negative start angle positions the radius clockwise from the zero-degree reference point. Counter-clockwise is considered the direction from the positive X-axis towards the positive Y-axis of the coordinate system. Changes to orientation, P1 and P2 locations, and scaling can each have an effect on the direction of rotation.

- **sweep_angle:** Specifies the number of degrees through which the arc is drawn. A positive sweep angle is in the direction of the +X-axis to the +Y-axis; a negative sweep angle is in the direction of the +X-axis to the −Y-axis. However, the relative position of the +X-axis to the +Y-axis can change as a result of scaling point or scaling factor changes, thus, changing the direction of the sweep angle. Angles with absolute values greater than 360° have their signs preserved, and they are bounded to 360°. If the sweep angle is ±360° after bounding, no radius is drawn.

- **chord_angle:** Specifies the chord angle used to draw the arc. Refer to the AA (Arc Absolute) instruction discussion on page 100 for further information on chords and chord angles.

A zero radius draws a dot at the current position; a zero sweep angle draws a line from the current position to the start of the wedge's arc.

Related Instructions

CI	Circle
CT	Chord Tolerance Mode
EP	Edge Polygon
FP	Fill Polygon
LA	Line Attributes
LT	Line Type
PW	Pen Width
SC	Scale
WG	Fill Wedge

Possible Error Conditions

Error Condition	Error Number	Printer or Plotter Response
Polygon buffer overflow	7	Edges contents of buffer

Example

SC	−3000,3000,−2000,2000,1;	Enter scaling mode, specifying P1 as (−3000,−2000) and P2 as (3000,2000). Use isotropic scaling.
PA	0,0;	Specify absolute plotting and move to user-unit location (0,0).
EW	−1000,90,180;	Draw a wedge section with a radius of 1000 user-units, a start angle of 90°, and a sweep angle of 180°. The minus sign before the radius (−1000) sets the zero-degree reference point to the left side of the drawing.
EW	−1000, 330,120;	Using the same center point and zero-degree reference point, draw a wedge section outline starting at 330° and sweeping 120°.
PR	−60,110;	Move the cursor 60 user-units to the left and 110 user-units up.
EW	−1000,270,60;	From the new center point location, draw a wedge using a negative zero-reference point, starting at 270° and sweeping for 60°.

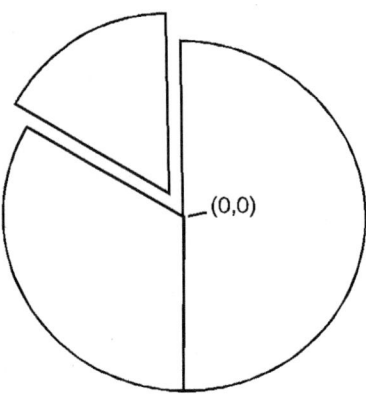

Figure 95. A Simple Pie Chart

FI, Primary Font Selection by ID

Purpose

To designate any font that has been assigned a font ID as the primary (standard) font. Font IDs are assigned in the PCL environment.

Syntax

FI *font_ID[;]*

Parameter	Format	Functional Range	Parameter Default
font_ID	integer	0 to 32767	no default

Group

This instruction is in the Dual-Context Extension for PCL-devices only. HP RTL does not have any support for fonts.

Use

- **font_ID:** A non-negative integer assigned in the PCL environment. If the designated font is present, the primary font attributes are set to those of the selected font. If the selected font is proportionally spaced, the pitch attribute is not changed. The instruction is ignored if no font exists with the specified ID.

This instruction allows any accessible font that has been assigned a *font_ID* number to be selected as the primary (standard) font (the font characteristics are assigned to the standard font). As mentioned, the font must be accessible to the device as either a resident font, a downloaded font, or a loaded cartridge font. To be selected, the font must have been previously assigned a font ID number in PCL mode. Also, for scalable fonts, the FI instruction must be preceded by an SD instruction specifying the font's point size or pitch (see the example below).

When the device receives this instruction and the requested font is present, the primary font characteristics are set to those of the requested font. If the selected font is proportionally spaced, the pitch characteristic is not changed.

- This instruction does not select the font for label printing if you are currently using the alternate font.

- The FI instruction implicitly changes the value of SB. For example, if "SB0;" is in effect and FI selects a bitmap font, SB is set to 1. This affects the performance of certain HP-GL/2 instructions. Refer to the SB instruction on page 288.

Related Instructions and Commands

AD	Alternate Font Definition
FN	Secondary Font Selection by ID
LB	Label
SA	Select Alternate Font
SB	Scalable or Bitmap Fonts
SD	Standard Font Definition

SS   Select Standard Font
ESC(#X   Select Primary Font by ID #
ESC)#X   Select Secondary Font by ID #
ESC*c#D   Font ID
ESC*c#F   Font Control

(The commands that begin with **ESC** are PCL commands.)

Example

The following example demonstrates assigning a font ID number from within PCL mode, entering HP-GL/2 mode, using the FI instruction to select that font, and printing a short line of text.

ESC*c15D	Specify a font ID number of 15.
ESC(s1p18v0s3b52T	Select an 18-point Univers Bold font as the primary font.
ESC*c6F	Assign the currently selected font as a temporary font with the current ID number (15).
ESC%0B	Enter HP-GL/2 mode.
IN ;	Initialize HP-GL/2 mode.
SP 1;	Select pen number 1.
PA 1500,1500;	Move to location (1500,1500).
DT#;	Define "#" as a label terminator (non-printing).
LBLaserJet Printers**CR LF**#;	Print "LaserJet Printers" in the currently selected font, which is the default stick font; Carriage Return/Line Feed. (Note, label text should not contain carriage-returns or any control codes unless specifically desired for plotting.)
SD 4,18;	Use the SD instruction to designate an 18-point font from within HP-GL/2 mode.
FI 15;	Then select the PCL font with font ID number of 15 as the primary font.
SS	Then select the primary font for printing.
LBLaserJet Printers#;	Print "LaserJet Printers" in the newly selected font.

LaserJet Printers
LaserJet Printers

Figure 96. Printing Labels Using the Primary Font

FN, Secondary Font Selection by ID

Purpose

To designate any font that has been assigned a font ID as the secondary (alternate) font. Font IDs are assigned in the PCL environment.

Syntax

FN *font_ID[;]*

Parameter	Format	Functional Range	Parameter Default
font_ID	integer	0 to 32767	no default

Group

This instruction is in the Dual-Context Extension for PCL-devices only. HP RTL does not have any support for fonts.

Use

- **font_ID:** A non-negative integer assigned in the PCL environment. If the designated font is present, the secondary font attributes are set to those of the selected font. If the selected font is proportionally spaced, the pitch attribute is not changed. The instruction is ignored if no font exists with the specified ID.

  This instruction allows any accessible font that has been assigned a *font_ID* number to be selected as the secondary (alternate) font (the font characteristics are assigned to the secondary font). The font must be accessible to the device as either a resident font, a downloaded font, or a loaded cartridge font. To be selected, the font must have been previously assigned a font ID number in PCL mode. Also, for scalable fonts, the FN instruction must be accompanied by an AD instruction specifying the font's point size (see the example below).

  When the device receives this instruction and the requested font is present, the secondary font characteristics are set to those of the requested font. If the selected font is proportionally spaced, the pitch characteristic is not changed.

- This instruction does not select the font for label printing if you are currently using the standard font.

- The FN instruction implicitly changes the value of SB. For example, if "SB0;" is in effect and FN selects a bitmap font, SB is set to 1. This affects the performance of certain HP-GL/2 instructions. Refer to the SB instruction on page 288.

Related Instructions

AD	Alternate Font Definition
FI	Primary Font Selection by ID
LB	Label
SA	Select Alternate Font
SB	Scalable or Bitmap Fonts
SD	Standard Font Definition

SS   Select Standard Font
ESC(#X Select Primary Font by ID #
ESC)#X Select Secondary Font by ID #
ESC*c#D   Font ID
ESC*c#F   Font Control

(The commands that begin with **ESC** are PCL commands.)

Example

The following example demonstrates assigning a font ID number from within PCL mode, entering HP-GL/2 mode, using the FN instruction to select that font, and printing a short line of text.

ESC*c28D	Specify a font ID number of 28.
ESC(s1p18v0s3b52T	Select an 18-point Univers Bold font as the primary font.
ESC*c6F	Assign the currently selected font as a temporary font with the current ID number (28).
ESC%0B	Enter HP-GL/2 mode.
IN ;	Initialize HP-GL/2 mode.
SP 1;	Select pen number 1.
PA 1500,1500;	Move to location (1500,1500).
DT#;	Define "#" as a label terminator (non-printing).
LBLaserJet Printers**CR LF**#;	Print "LaserJet Printers" in the currently selected font, which is the default stick font; Carriage Return/Line Feed.
AD 4,18;	Use the AD instruction to designate an 18-point font from within HP-GL/2 mode.
FN 28;	Assign the PCL font with font ID number of 28 as the secondary font.
SA ;	Then select the font.
LBLaserJet Printers#;	Print "LaserJet Printers" in the newly selected font.

LaserJet Printers
LaserJet Printers

Figure 97. Printing Labels Using the Secondary Font

FP, Fill Polygon

Purpose

To fill the polygon currently in the polygon buffer. Use FP to fill polygons defined in polygon mode or with the Edge Rectangle or Edge Wedge instructions (EA, ER, EW, RA, RR, or WG).

Syntax

FP *fill_method [;]*

　　　　or

FP *[;]*

Parameter	Format	Functional Range	Parameter Default
fill_method	clamped integer	0 or 1	0 (even/odd fill)

Group

This instruction is in the Polygon Group.

Use

The FP instruction fills any polygon that is currently in the polygon buffer. FP accesses the data in the polygon buffer, but does *not* clear the buffer or change the data in any way.

The FP instruction fills between points defined with either the pen down or the pen up. The polygon is filled using the current pen, fill type, line type and attributes (if the fill type is not raster). The FP instruction includes an automatic pen down. When the instruction execution is complete, the original pen location and up/down status are restored.

- **No parameter:** Uses the odd-even algorithm; same as "FP0".

- **fill_method:** Specifies the algorithm used to determine which portions of the polygon are "inside" the polygon and therefore are to be filled:

    0   Even/odd fill algorithm (default)

    1   Non-zero winding fill algorithm

Note: The **even/odd** (method 0) and **non-zero** (method 1) winding fill methods are described in detail under *Filling Polygons* on page 50.

Related Instructions

EA	Edge Rectangle Absolute
ER	Edge Rectangle Relative
EW	Edge Wedge
FT	Fill Type
LA	Line Attributes
LT	Line Type
PM	Polygon Mode
PW	Pen Width

RA	Fill Rectangle Absolute
RR	Fill Rectangle Relative
WG	Fill Wedge

Example

The example below creates a polygon composed of two subpolygons. In this case, the FP instruction fills alternating areas, beginning with the outside area.

PA	1500,1500;	Specify absolute plotting and move to (1500,1500).
PM	0;	Enter the polygon mode.
CI	1000,60;	Store a circle with radius of 1000 plotter-units and a 60° chord angle.
PA	1500,1500;	Store a pen move to (1500,1500),
CI	500;	and another circle with a 500 plotter-units radius and a 5° (default) chord angle.
PM	2;	Close the current polygon and exit polygon mode.
LT	4;	Select line type 4.
FT	3,50,45;	Select fill type 3. Specify a 50 plotter-units distance between the fill lines, and slant the lines at a 45° angle.
FP	;	Using even/odd fill method, fill the polygon currently in the polygon buffer with the line and fill types just specified.

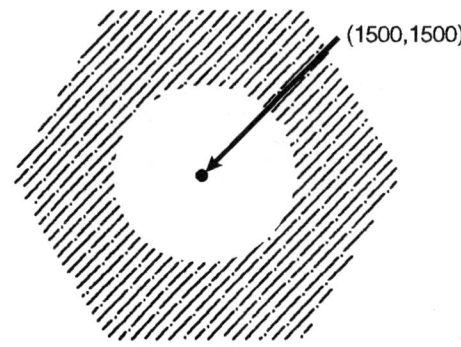

(1500,1500)

Figure 98. Filling a Polygon

FR, Frame Advance

Purpose

To advance the media to align adjacent frames, forming the equivalent of a long-axis plot. The device treats each frame as a separate window and plots only the data falling within that window. Using the PS (Plot Size) instruction for long-axis plotting is simpler and faster than using FR.

Syntax

FR [;]

Group

This instruction is in the Technical Graphics Extension.

Use

FR updates the current pen location to the new plotter-unit origin, leaves the pen in the up position, and clears the polygon buffer.

The *length* parameter of the PS (Plot Size) instruction determines the frame size. When *length*≥*width*, the orientation is reverse landscape and each FR instruction extends the plot in the direction of the positive X-axis. When *length*<*width*, the orientation is reverse portrait and each FR instruction extends the plot in the direction of the positive Y-axis.

The length advanced with an FR instruction is shorter than that of a PG instruction; the margins between the plotter areas are deleted so that the frames share a common edge.

After each frame advance, the plotter-unit origin moves to the lower-left corner of the new frame. The physical locations of P1 and P2 are retained, but the logical locations relative to the current origin change.

FR is ideal for use with roll-feed plotters. When using single-sheet devices, frames will share a common edge only when complete frames will fit on the current sheet. If multiple frames will not fit, the current page is printed and ejected. The next sheet loaded will contain the new frame. Any device that can store an entire multi-frame plot can print multiple copies using either the BP or RP instructions.

Note that a cut-sheet device which cannot store the entire plot can still produce multiple copies *when specified in the BP instruction*; however, the user must collate the copies. In this case, however, the RP instruction is equivalent to a PG.

Related Instructions

AC   Anchor Corner
IW   Input Window
PS   Plot Size

Example

In the following example, the P1/P2 values are input as

IP   0,0,20000,7200;

After sending FR, the logical values of P1 and P2 on the new frame become (−10 000,0) and (10 000,7200) respectively.

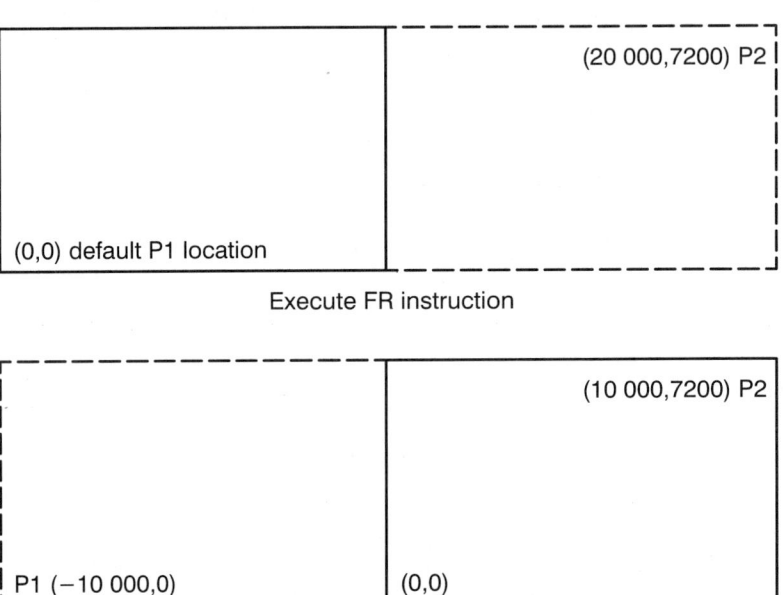

Figure 99. Using the FR (Frame Advance) Instruction

The anchor corner and window retain their coordinate values after each frame advance. If specified in user-units, they maintain their physical locations with respect to P1 and P2; if specified in plotter-units, they shift their physical locations with the plotter-unit origin. If you have not sent an AC or IW instruction, each frame advance defaults the anchor corner and window with respect to the hard-clip limits of the current frame.

FT, Fill Type

Purpose

To select the shading pattern used to fill polygons (FP), rectangles (RA or RR), characters (CF), or wedges (WG). Use FT to enhance plots with solid fill, parallel lines (hatching), cross-hatching, or patterned (raster) fill.

Syntax

FT *fill_type[,option1[,option2]][;]*

　　　or

FT *[;]*

Parameter	Format	Functional Range	Parameter Default
fill_type	clamped integer	1, 2, 3, 4, 10, 11, 21, 22	1
option1, *option2*	clamped real	*fill_type*-dependent*	*fill_type*-dependent*

*　　Refer to the table following the parameter descriptions.

Group

This instruction is in the Line and Fill Attributes Group.

Use

There are six base forms of fill type, and additional ones for devices that support the dual-context environment—see page 83. The *fill_type* parameter tells the device which form you are using.

- **No parameters**: equivalent to "FT1"—the fill type is solid.

- **fill_type**: selects the fill pattern. It is a clamped integer whose value is restricted to those given in the table below, which lists the *option* parameter values and the corresponding *fill_type*s.

- **option1** and **option2**: When the option parameters are omitted, the device uses the last specified parameters for that fill type. For example, if you specified *fill_type* 3 with line spacing and angle parameters, then switched to *fill_type* 4 without specifying any line parameters, the device would draw fill type 4 with default line spacing and angles because they have not yet been specified for that fill type. If you then switched back to fill type 3, you would not need to respecify the line spacing and angle parameters because the device would use the values previously specified for the fill type 3 instruction.

The ranges (clamped real values) and definitions of these optional parameters depends on the type of fill selected, as follows:

Fill_type	Description	Option1	Option2	Note
1	solid bidirectional	(ignored)	(ignored)	1
2	solid unidirectional	(ignored)	(ignored)	1
3	hatched (parallel lines)	spacing of lines	angle of lines	2
4	cross-hatched	spacing of lines	angle of lines	2
10	shading	shading level	(ignored)	3
11	user-defined pattern (using RF instruction)	raster-fill index	pen flag	4
21	predefined pattern imported from PCL or HP RTL	pattern type	(ignored)	5
22	user-defined pattern (using PCL or HP RTL command)	pattern ID	(ignored)	6

Notes:

1. Directionality is pertinent to pen plotters only. On raster devices, only primary colors are guaranteed to be truly solid. Other colors may be produced by a dither pattern, and will be as close to solid as the device can produce, or the device may choose the closest primary color. *Option1* and *option2* are both ignored.

2. For *fill_type*s 3 and 4, the *option1* parameter specifies the distance between the lines in the fill. This distance is specified in current units measured along the X-axis. The default spacing is 1% of the diagonal distance from P1 to P2. Subsequent changes in the P1/P2 locations affect this distance and therefore spacing. *Option1* must be a positive number up to 32 767 (if 0 is specified, 1% is used). Spacing is interpreted as a percentage only in its default state; otherwise, it is interpreted as current units.

    The *option2* parameter specifies an angle in degrees, of the lines in the fill. The range of valid values is −32 768 to 32 767, though the useful range is 0° to 360°. This angle is measured counter-clockwise from the positive plotter-unit X-axis, as shown in Figure 27 on page 44. 0 and 180 are horizontal, 90 and 270 are vertical. For *fill_type* 3, the pattern for each hatched line starts on a line through the anchor corner at a 90°-angle to the angle parameter, and every other hatch line is staggered one-half the pattern length. One set of lines for cross-hatched fill types is drawn at the specified angle, and the other set is drawn at that angle plus 90°.

    *Fill_type*s 3 and 4 use the current pen, line type, and attributes unless the spacing is such that the fill pattern is solid.

    If spacing is defined in plotter-units, turning scaling on or changing the locations of P1 and P2 has no effect. If, however, the spacing is defined in user units, the spacing fluctuates with changes to P1 and P2 or scaling. Turning off scaling causes the spacing to be frozen in the plotter-unit equivalent of its current user-unit value.

    When you fill with adaptive line types (those whose value is negative), the pattern length is adjusted to fit an integral number of complete patterns between polygon edge intersections, and there is no staggering of the pattern in every other hatch line; the anchor corner only affects the positioning of the hatch fill lines. The vector used in adjusting the pattern length is each line segment of the hatch fill, that is, each interior piece between two edges of the polygon.

The end-points of hatched fills are treated with the current line cap. Lines are not clipped to the polygon.

3. For *fill_type* 10, the *option1* value specifies the level of shading. The level is specified as a percentage. The device uses at least nine predefined levels of shading equally divided between 0 and 100%. The default is 50%. Each shading level is generated by adding white pixels to the current pen color raster pattern; these added pixels are the only white pixels in the pattern that are subject to transparency (see the TR instruction on page 318). The following illustration shows various levels of shading and the specified percentage:

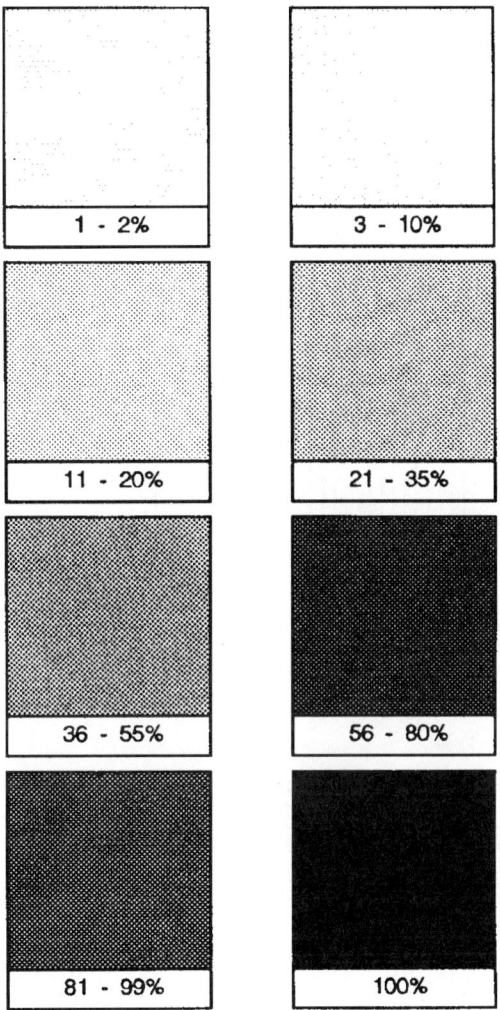

Figure 100. Shading Patterns

4. For *fill_type* 11, the *option1* parameter selects the corresponding user-defined raster fill. The range is the same as the *index* parameter of the RF (Raster Fill Definition) instruction; the default is 1. If the pattern was defined using only 1s and 0s (see the RF instruction), the pattern is printed in the current pen color; *option2* specifies whether or not the current color should be applied. If *option2* is "1" (true), the color of the currently selected pen is applied to the 1s pixels in the pattern. If *option2* is "0" or is not present, the pattern of the

1s pixels is printed in the color of pen number 1. If the pattern definition includes indexes other than 0 and 1, *option2* is ignored. If you have not used an RF instruction, the device uses solid fill.

Figure 101. User-Defined Fill Pattern

Using FT in a Dual-Context Environment

Additional fill types (21 and 22) are imported from PCL or HP RTL. *Fill_type* 21 selects a PCL or HP RTL predefined patterned fill. *Option1* specifies a pattern type from 1 to 6 (see Figure 102). *Option2* is ignored. *Fill_type* 22 uses the PCL or HP RTL user-defined fill specified by **ESC***c#W. *Option1* is the PCL or HP RTL ID of the user-defined fill. *Option2* is ignored. An invalid *option1* (for example, where the pattern has been deleted), prints a solid fill in the current color.

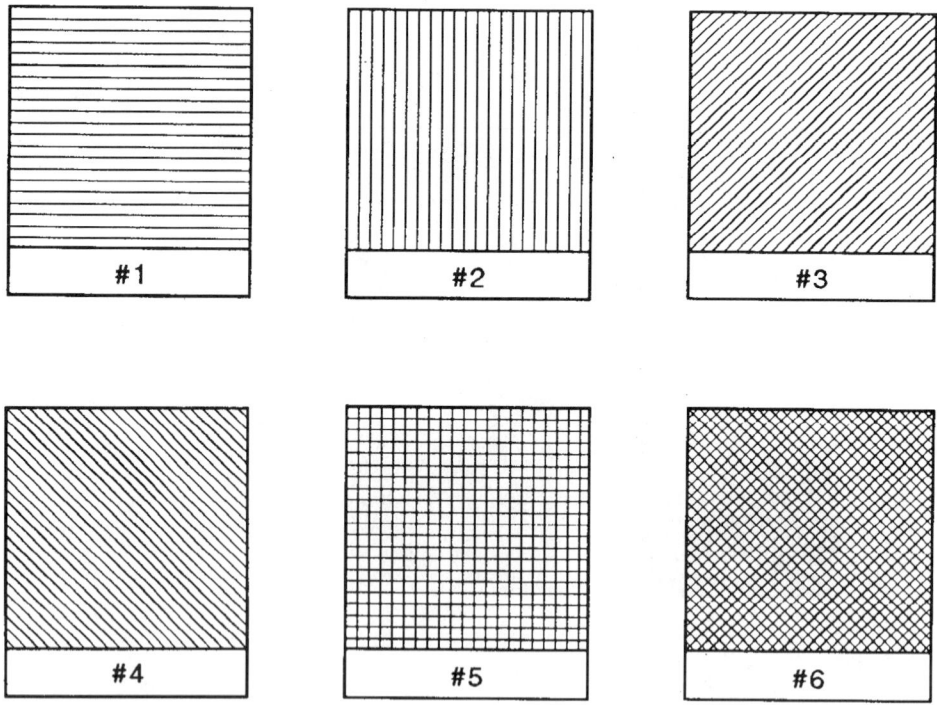

Figure 102. Patterns for Fill Type 21

5. For *fill_type* 21, which is only available with devices that support the dual-context extension, the predefined pattern fill is imported from PCL or HP RTL. *Option1* specifies the pattern type, using a value from 1 to 6 as shown in Figure 102.

1	horizontal lines
2	vertical lines
3	diagonal lines (lower left to upper right)
4	diagonal lines (lower right to upper left)
5	cross-hatching with horizontal and vertical lines
6	cross-hatching with diagonal lines.

6. For *fill_type* 22, which is also only available with devices that support the dual-context extension, the user-defined fill pattern is that specified using the **ESC***c#W PCL or HP RTL command. *Option1* specifies the PCL or HP RTL identification of the user-defined pattern fill. If option1 is invalid for any reason (for example, the pattern was deleted), the device uses a solid fill in the current color.

Note that PCL and HP RTL use the term "pattern" for fill-type.

Related Instructions

CF	Character Fill Mode
LA	Line Attributes
LT	Line Type
PW	Pen Width
RF	Raster Fill Definition
FP	Fill Polygon
RA	Fill Rectangle Absolute
RR	Fill Rectangle Relative
SV	Screened Vectors
WG	Fill Wedge

Example

This sequence of instructions:

PA	2000,2000;	Specify absolute plotting and move to location (2000,2000).
FT	;	Fill Type, default value 1 (solid bidirectional).
RR	2500,300;	Fill Rectangle Relative coordinates.
EP	;	Edge Polygon (outlines current polygon).
PR	0,300;	Plot Relative coordinates.
FT	3,80,30;	Fill Type, type 3 (hatching), spacing 80 user-units (X-direction), inclination 30°.
RR	2500,300;	Fill Rectangle Relative coordinates.
EP	;	Edge Polygon.
PR	0,300;	Plot Relative coordinates.
FT	10,36;	Fill Type 10 (shading), 36%.
RR	2500,300;	Fill Rectangle Relative coordinates.
EP	;	Edge Polygon.

produces this output:

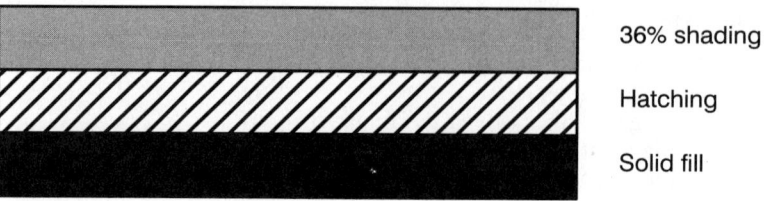

36% shading

Hatching

Solid fill

Figure 103. Rectangles with Different Fill Types

IN, Initialize

Purpose

To resets all programmable HP-GL/2 functions to their default settings. Use the IN instruction to return the device to a known HP-GL/2 state and to cancel settings that may have been changed by a previous instruction sequence. (The **ESCE** Reset command and the BP [Begin Plot] instruction issue an automatic IN instruction).

Syntax

IN *n[;]*

or

IN *[;]*

Parameter	Format	Functional Range	Parameter Default
n	clamped integer	1 (see below)	no parameter

Group

This instruction is in the Configuration and Status Group.

Use

- **No parameter:** Defaults to the feature settings specified using the device's control panel, and sets all other programmable HP-GL/2 features to their factory defaults.

- **n:** Defaults all programmable HP-GL/2 features to the factory-set conditions.

  If *n* is fractional, it is rounded to the nearest integer, so 0.6 is rounded to 1. Any number in the range -2^{23} to $2^{23}-1$ (other than 1 on some devices) is treated like "IN;" (no parameter).

  An "IN1" instruction is used in some devices, principally pen plotters, as a temporary override of control-panel defaults; a subsequent "IN" (with no parameter) will restore the control-panel defaults. *"IN1" is not recommended unless it is imperative that the program control the device.*

All instruction sequences should begin with IN to clear unwanted conditions from the previous instruction sequence, even though an **ESCE** command and a BP (Begin Plot) instruction automatically execute an IN instruction. All HP-GL/2 errors are cleared.

Once HP-GL/2 mode is entered and instructions are issued, the HP-GL/2 conditions are no longer initialized. To place HP-GL/2 into the default state, send the IN instruction.

IN does not default pen selection; the pen selected before IN remains selected afterwards, and is raised (up state) in the lower-left corner of the hard-clip limits.

The IN instruction sets the device to the same conditions as the DF (Default Values) instruction (see page 136), plus the following:

Function	Equivalent Instruction	Default Condition
Plot Absolute	PA0,0;	Returns the pen location to the lower-left corner of the hard-clip limits
Pen Up	PU;	Raises the pen
Pen Width	PW;	Sets the pen width to 0.35 mm
Rotate Coordinate System	RO0;	Cancels drawing rotation
Input P1 and P2	IP;	Sets P1 and P2 to the lower-left and upper-right corners, respectively, of the hard-clip limits
Pen Width Unit Selection	WU;	Sets pen width mode to metric; units are millimeters

Using IN in a Dual-Context Environment

The IN instruction interacts with PCL. In dual-context mode it will overwrite the PCL color configuration and replace it with the HP-GL/2 default. For this reason, the instruction should not be used in the middle of a job.

Using IN with the Palette Extension

The IN instruction also affects the following instruction:

Function	Equivalent Instruction	Default Condition
Number of Pens	NP;	Sets number of pens to 2 or 8 (see page 225)

Using IN with the Technical Graphics Extension

The IN instruction also affects the following instruction:

Function	Equivalent Instruction	Default Condition
Plot Size	PS;	Sets the plot length to the hard-clip limits

Related Instructions

BP   Begin Plot
DF   Default Values
OS   Output Status

IP, Input P1 and P2

Purpose

To establish new or default locations for the scaling points P1 and P2. P1 and P2 are used by the SC (Scale) instruction to establish user-unit scaling. You can also use IP in advanced techniques such as printing mirror-images (as explained on page 35), enlarging and reducing drawings (see page 33), and enlarging and reducing relative character size (see page 308), changing label direction (see page 149), changing pen widths (see pages 264 and 328), changing spacing for hatch-filled patterns (see page 183), or changing the line type pattern length (see page 215). IP does not affect the window limits (see page 197).

Syntax

IP $P1_X,P1_Y[,P2_X,P2_Y][;]$
  or
IP $[;]$

Parameter	Format	Functional Range	Parameter Default
$P1_X,P1_Y,P2_X,P2_Y$	integer	-2^{30} to $2^{30}-1$	(see below)

Group

This instruction is in the Configuration and Status Group.

Use

The default location of P1 for "printers" (that is, devices that do not support the Technical Graphics Extension) is the lower-left corner of the hard-clip limits; the default location of P2 is the upper-right corner, as shown in Figure 104. (The default picture frame extends from the top margin to the bottom margin, and from the left edge to the right edge of the logical page.) For "plotters" (that is, devices that do support the Technical Graphics Extension) the default position and orientation of the X- and Y-axes is different (see Figure 8 on page 9) but the positions of P1 and P2 relative to the axes is as in Figure 104.

- **No parameters:** Sets P1 and P2 to their default locations, adjusted by any current axis rotation.

  Note: If an IP instruction without parameters is executed after the axes are rotated with the RO instruction, P1 and P2 locations change to reflect the rotation. If the coordinate system orientation subsequently changes (for example, by sending an RO instruction), the plotter-unit position is maintained with respect to the new orientation.

- **X,Y coordinates:** Specify the location of P1 (and, optionally, P2) in plotter-units (see page 12). Specifying P2 is not required. If P2 is not specified, P2 tracks P1 and its coordinates change so that the X,Y distances between P2 and P1 stay the same. This tracking process can locate P2 outside the effective window. Used carefully, the tracking function can be useful for preparing more than one equal-sized drawing on a page. For an example, refer to *Drawing Equal-Sized Pictures on a Page* on page 34. Neither X,Y coordinate of P1 can equal the corresponding coordinate of P2. If either coordinate of P1 equals the corresponding coordinate of P2, the coordinate of P2 is incremented by 1 plotter-unit.

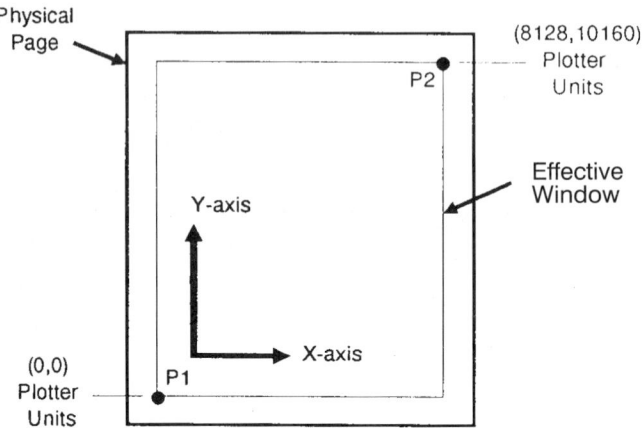

Figure 104. Default P1/P2 Locations for an 8-inch by 10-inch Page

The locations of P1 and P2 interact with the following instructions:

DR   Relative Direction
FT   Fill Type
IW   Input Window
LB   Label
LT   Line Type
PW   Pen Width
RO   Rotate Coordinate System
SC   Scale
SR   Relative Character Size
WU   Pen Width Unit Selection

An IP instruction remains in effect until another IP instruction is executed, an IR instruction is executed, the device is initialized, or a PS (Plot Size) instruction is issued on a "clean" (unplotted) page.

IP clears the current pattern residue and terminates any continuous vector sequence (see the LA and LT instructions).

Using IP in a Dual-Context Environment (PCL only)

"IP;" sets P1 to the lower-left corner of the PCL picture frame (viewed from the current HP-GL/2 orientation) and P2 to the opposite corner. Parameters are scaled by the picture frame scaling factor.

Related Instructions

IR   Input Relative P1 and P2
IW   Input Window
OP   Output P1 and P2
RO   Rotate Coordinate System
SC   Scale

Possible Error Conditions

Error Condition	Error Number	Printer or Plotter Response
One or three parameters	2	Ignores instruction

IR, Input Relative P1 and P2

Purpose

To establish new or default locations for the scaling points P1 and P2 relative to the hard-clip limits. P1 and P2 are used by the SC (Scale) instruction to establish user-unit scaling. IR can also be used in advanced techniques such as printing mirror-images (as explained on page 35), enlarging and reducing drawings (see page 33), and enlarging and reducing relative character size (see page 308), changing label direction (see page 149), changing pen widths (see pages 264 and 328), changing spacing for hatch-filled patterns (see page 183), or changing the line type pattern length (see page 215). IR does not affect the window limits (see page 197).

Syntax

IR $P1_X,P1_Y[,P2_X,P2_Y][;]$
   or
IR $[;]$

Parameter	Format	Functional Range	Parameter Default
$P1_X,P1_Y,P2_X,P2_Y$	clamped real	−32 768 to 32 767	0,0,100,100%

Group

This instruction is in the Configuration and Status Group.

Use

When P1 and P2 are set using IR, the scaled area is page size-independent. The P1/P2 rectangular area will occupy the same proportional space on any size media.

- **No parameters:** Defaults P1 and P2 to the lower-left and upper-right corners of the hard-clip limits, respectively.

- **X,Y coordinates:** Specify the location of P1 (and, optionally, P2) as percentages of the hard-clip limits (specifying P2 is not required). If P2 is not specified, P2 tracks P1; the P2 coordinates change so that the distances of X and Y between P1 and P2 remain the same. This tracking process can cause P2 to be located outside the effective window. Used carefully, the tracking function can be useful for preparing more than one equal-sized drawing on a page. For an example, refer to *Drawing Equal-Sized Pictures on a Page* on page 34.

Neither X,Y coordinate of P1 can equal the corresponding coordinate of P2. If either coordinate of P1 equals the corresponding coordinate of P2, the coordinate of P2 is incremented by 1 plotter-unit.

Sending the instruction "IR25,25,75,75" establishes new locations for P1 and P2 that create an area half as high and half as wide as the hard-clip limits, in the center of the page. Refer to Figure 105.

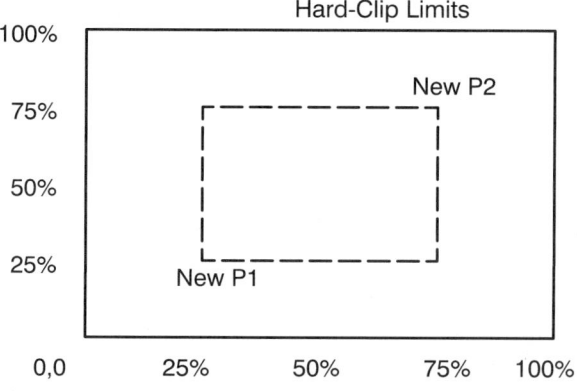

Figure 105. Example Using IR 25,25,75,75

P1 or P2 can also be set outside the hard-clip limits by specifying parameters less than zero or greater than 100. For example, sending "IR–50,0,200,100" would set P1 and P2 as shown in Figure 106.

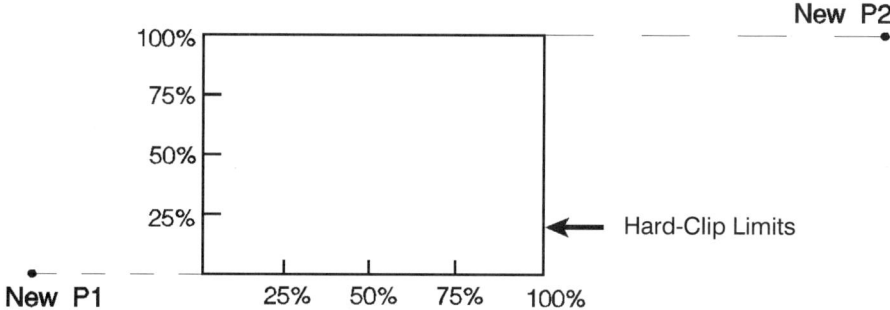

Figure 106. Example Using IR –50,0,200,100

If you specify P1 and P2 beyond the hard-clip limits, your drawing is scaled with respect to those locations; however, only the portion of the drawing fitting within the hard-clip limits is drawn.

Note: The specified P1/P2 percentages are converted to the equivalent plotter-unit coordinates. If the coordinate system orientation subsequently changes (for example, by sending an RO instruction), the plotter-unit position is maintained with respect to the new orientation. If an IP instruction without parameters is executed after the axes have been rotated with the RO instruction, P1 and P2 locations change to reflect the rotation.

The locations of P1 and P2 interact with the following instructions:

DR	Relative Direction
FT	Fill Type
IW	Input Window
LB	Label
LT	Line Type
PW	Pen Width
RO	Rotate Coordinate System
SC	Scale
SR	Relative Character Size
WU	Pen Width Unit Selection

An IR instruction remains in effect until another IR instruction is executed, an IP instruction is executed, or the device is initialized, or a PS (Plot Size) instruction is issued on a "clean" (unplotted) page.

IR clears the current pattern residue and terminates any continuous vector sequence (see the LA and LT instructions).

Using IR in a Dual-Context Environment (PCL only)

The references to the hard-clip limits are replaced by the PCL picture frame. The default positions for P1 and P2 are the lower-left and upper-right corners of the picture frame, as viewed from the current orientation.

Related Instructions

IP	Input P1 and P2
IW	Input Window
OP	Output P1 and P2
RO	Rotate Coordinate System
SC	Scale

Possible Error Conditions

Error Condition	Error Number	Printer or Plotter Response
One or three parameters	2	Ignores instruction
More than four parameters	2	Uses first four parameters

IW, Input Window

Purpose

To define a rectangular area, or window, that establishes soft-clip limits. Subsequent HP-GL/2 drawing is restricted to this area. Use IW to restrict printing to a specified area on the page.

Syntax

IW X_{LL},Y_{LL},X_{UR},Y_{UR}[;]
 or
IW [;]

Parameter	Format	Functional Range	Parameter Default
X_{LL},Y_{LL},X_{UR},Y_{UR}	current units	*device-dependent* (at least -2^{23} to $2^{23} - 1$)	hard-clip limits (the picture frame in PCL dual-context mode)

Group

This instruction is in the Configuration and Status Group.

Use

The device interprets the instruction parameters as follows.

- **No parameters:** Resets the soft-clip limits to the hard-clip limits.

- **X,Y coordinates:** Specify the opposite diagonal corners of the window area. For PCL printers, these are the lower-left (LL) and upper-right (UR) corners. Coordinates are interpreted in the current units: as user-units when scaling is on; as plotter-units when scaling is off.

  If the X or Y parameters of the lower-left corner are greater than the equivalent parameters of the upper-right corner, parameters are automatically exchanged. The window is a line if $X_{LL} = X_{UR}$ or $Y_{LL} = Y_{UR}$, and a dot if all parameters are equal.

  For plotters, the corners used depend on the orientation; see *Interactions between Different Coordinate Systems* on page 8.

When scaling is off, the window is defined in plotter-units and is static, that is, it is not affected by changes to P1 and P2. (However, in dual-context mode, parameters specified in plotter-units are scaled by the picture frame scaling factor.)

When scaling is on, subsequent changes to P1 and P2 move the window in relation to the physical page, but keep the same user coordinate locations. However, sending a subsequent SC instruction binds the window to its equivalent plotter-units. The window does not change with any subsequent IP or IR instructions.

When you turn on the device, the window is automatically set to the hard-clip limits. You can define a window that extends beyond these limits; however the device cannot print vector graphics beyond the effective window. All programmed pen motion is restricted to this area. For more information, refer to *Windowing: Setting Up Soft-Clip Limits* on page 39.

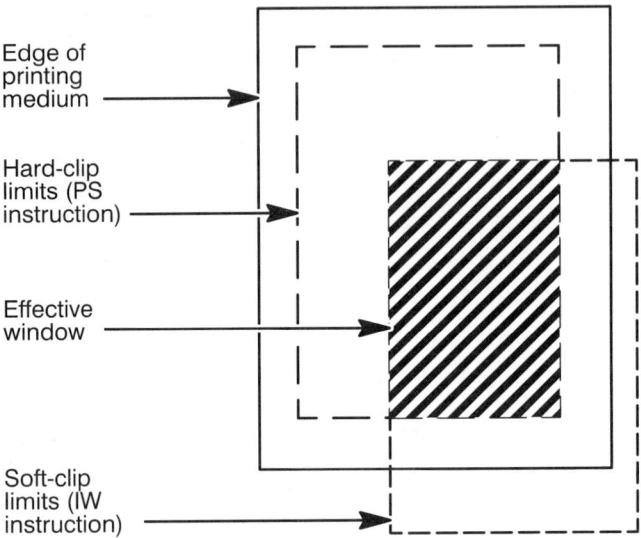

Edge of printing medium

Hard-clip limits (PS instruction)

Effective window

Soft-clip limits (IW instruction)

Figure 107. Effective Window

If the window falls entirely outside of the hard-clip limits, no image is drawn. This can happen when you define a window that is normally within the hard-clip limits and a subsequent RO (Rotate Coordinate System) instruction moves the window outside the hard-clip limits.

The IW instruction remains in effect until another IW instruction is executed, the device is initialized or set to default conditions, or a PS is issued on a clean page. Power-on, IN, or DF default the window to the hard-clip limits.

IW clears the current pattern residue and terminates any continuous vector sequence (see the LA and LT instructions).

Using IW in a Dual-Context Environment (PCL only)

"IW;" defaults the window to the PCL picture frame. The maximum printable area is the intersection of the user-defined window, PCL picture frame, the PCL logical page, and the hard-clip limits. Parameters specified in plotter-units are scaled by the picture frame scaling factor.

Related Instructions

FR	Frame Advance
IP	Input P1 and P2
IR	Input Relative P1 and P2
RO	Rotate Coordinate System
SC	Scale

Example

The following example draws a label, then establishes a window and again draws the label along with a line. Notice how the line and label are clipped after the window is established, but not before.

SI	.2,.35;	Set Absolute Character Size to 0.2 by 0.35 cm.
PA	2000,3200;	Specify absolute plotting and move to location (2000,3200) (plotter-units).
DT@,1;		Define label terminator to be the "@" character, without printing the character.
LBTHIS IS AN EXAMPLE OF IW@;		Print a label beginning at (2000,3200).
IW	3000,1300,4500,3700;	Specify a soft-clip window (in plotter-units).
PD	2000,1700	Pen Down; print a line from the current pen position to (2000,1700). Current pen position at start of instruction is at the letter W baseline.
LBTHIS IS AN EXAMPLE OF IW@;		Print the same label at (2000,1700).
PU	3000,1300;	Pen Up and move to position (3000,1300).
PD	4500,1300,4500,3700;	Pen Down and begin drawing box indicating the soft-clip window.
PD	3000,3700,3000,1300;	Finish drawing the soft-clip window box.
PU	;	Pen Up.

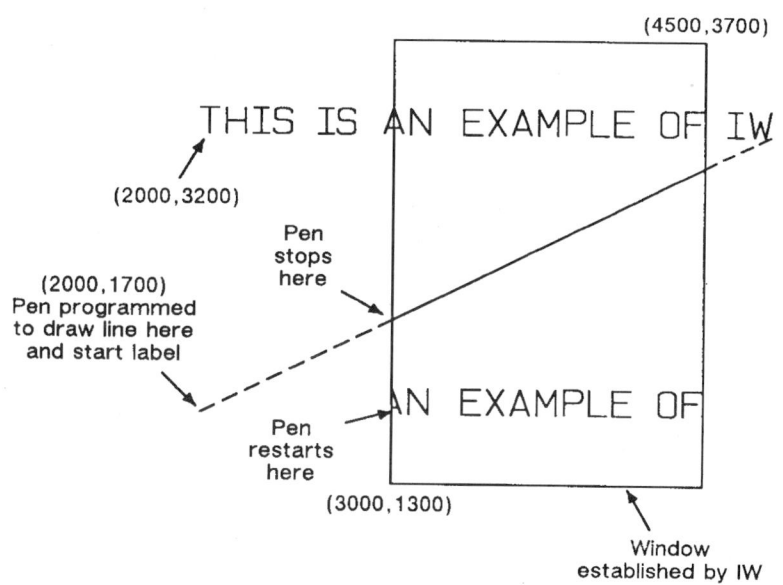

Figure 108. How the IW (Input Window) Instruction Clips

LA, Line Attributes

Purpose

To specify how line ends and line joins are physically shaped. Use this instruction when drawing lines thicker than 0.35 mm.

Syntax

LA *kind,value[,kind,value[,kind,value]][;]*
  or
LA *[;]*

Parameter	Format	Functional Range	Parameter Default
kind	clamped integer	1, 2, or 3	no default
value	clamped integer clamped integer clamped real	Kind 1: 1 through 4 Kind 2: 1 through 6 Kind 3: 1 through 32 767	1 (Butt) 1 (Mitered) 5

Group

This instruction is in the Line and Fill Attributes Group.

Use

There are three line attributes: *line ends*, *line joins*, and the *miter limit*. The LA instruction parameters are used in pairs: the first parameter, *kind*, selects a line attribute, and the second parameter, *value*, defines the appearance of that attribute. The device uses the current line attributes when the optional parameter pairs are omitted.

- **No parameters:** Defaults the line attributes to butt ends, mitered joins, and a miter limit of 5. Equivalent to "LA1,1,2,1,3,5".

- **kind:** Specifies the line attribute for which you are setting a value. Attributes and *kind* parameter values are listed in the following table.

- **value:** Defines the characteristics of the attribute specified by the *kind* parameter. The available values are listed in the following table and described under each attribute.

The current line attributes remain in effect when optional parameter pairs are omitted.

A continuous sequence of pen-down vectors uses the current line join and miter limit for coincident first and last points. A continuous vector sequence is interrupted when a vector's end point is not coincident with the next pen-down vector's starting point, or by the AC, DF, IN, IP, IR, IW, LA, LT, PG, PW, RF, RO, RP, SC, SP, TR, UL, or WU instruction.

Instructions that restore the current pen position (CI, EA, EP, ER, EW, FP, PM, RA, RR, and WG) save the last vector's end point upon completion. The pen-down sequence is continued when the current pen position is restored. The last vector's end point is also saved by CP or LB and before each SM symbol is drawn; the vector sequence is continued if the starting point of the next pen-down vector is coincident with the saved vector end point, that is, there can be any number of pen-up vectors between two consecutive pen-down vectors.

The clipping of a line end and line join is device-dependent.

The ends of each dash are treated with the current line cap; corners with a dash are treated with the current line join. Labels are always drawn with rounded ends and joins.

Attribute	Kind	Value	Description
Line Ends: (Lines with a width less than a device-dependent limit always have butt caps and no join, regardless of the current attribute setting)	1	1 2 3 4	Butt (default) Square Triangular Round
Line Joins: (Lines with a width less than that same device-dependent limit always have butt caps and no join, regardless of the current attribute setting)	2	1 2 3 4 5 6	Mitered (default) Mitered/beveled Triangular Round Beveled No join applied
Miter Limit: (Full range is 1 to 32 767, but values less than 1 are automatically set to 1)	3	Device-dependent	5 (default, refer to description under *Miter Limit* on page 203)

Line Ends

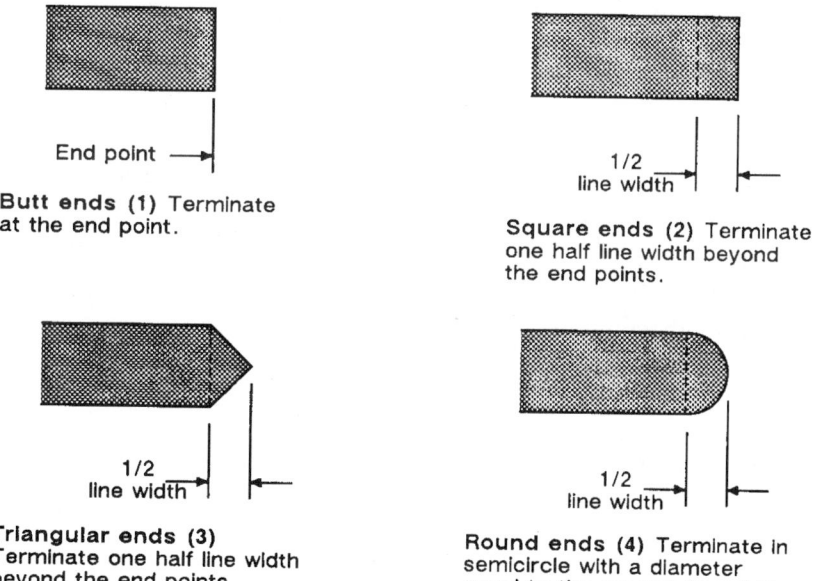

End point →

Butt ends (1) Terminate at the end point.

1/2 line width

Square ends (2) Terminate one half line width beyond the end points.

1/2 line width

Triangular ends (3) Terminate one half line width beyond the end points.

1/2 line width

Round ends (4) Terminate in semicircle with a diameter equal to the current line width.

Figure 109. Four Line Ends

The value you specify for line ends determines how the ends of line segments are shaped. Figure 109 describes the four types of line ends.

Line Joins

The value you specify for the line joins attribute determines how connecting line ends (corners) are shaped. The following illustration describes the five types of line joins. If the first and last points of a series of lines are the same, they join according to the current line join and miter limit.

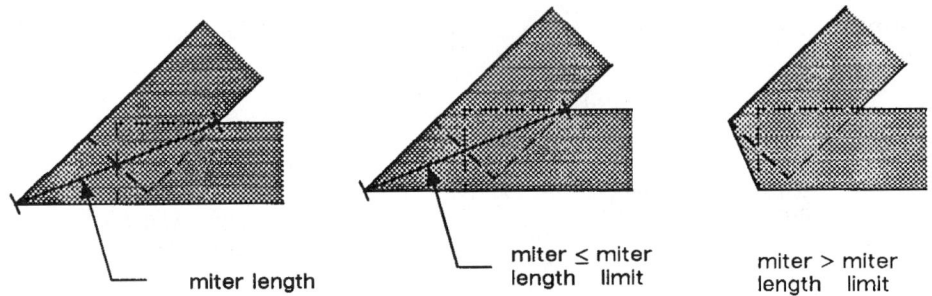

Mitered join (1)
Formed by two lines extending from the outer edge of each vector until they meet. The miter limit applies to this join.

Mitered/beveled join (2) Formed by two lines extending from the outer edge of each vector until they meet. If the miter length exceeds the miter limit, a beveled join is used.

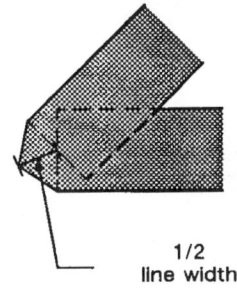

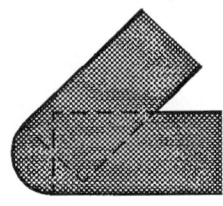

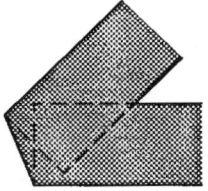

Triangular join (3) Formed by two lines extending from the outer edge of each vector to a point 1/2 line width beyond the end intersection of the vectors.

Rounded join (4) Formed by an arc with a diameter equal to the current line width

Beveled join (5)
Formed by a line connecting the outer edge of one vector to the outer edge of the other vector.

Figure 110. Five Line Joins

When you select "no join" ("LA2,6;"), the currently selected line ends for the two lines merely overlap. Refer to the following illustration.

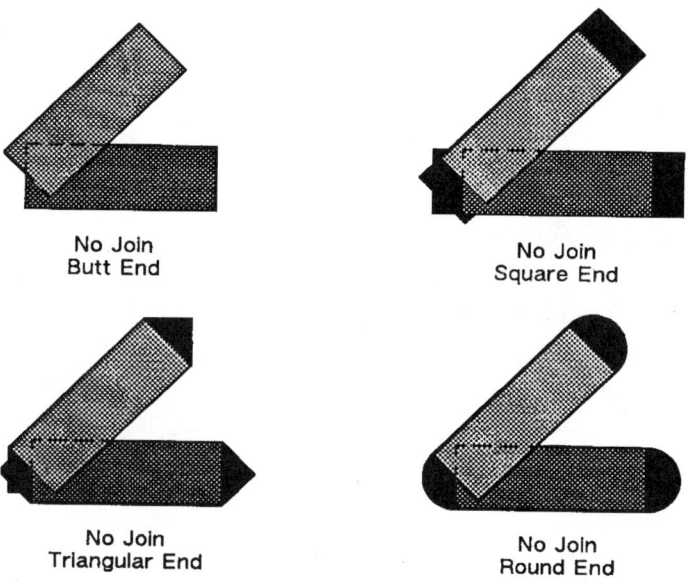

No Join
Butt End

No Join
Square End

No Join
Triangular End

No Join
Round End

Figure 111. Overlapping Line Ends without Line Join Selection

Miter Limit

The value you specify for miter limit determines the maximum "length" of a mitered join, as shown in the following illustration. The miter limit is the ratio of the miter length (the length of the diagonal line through the join of two connecting lines), to the line width. For example, with the default miter limit of 5, the miter length can be as long as 5 times the line width.

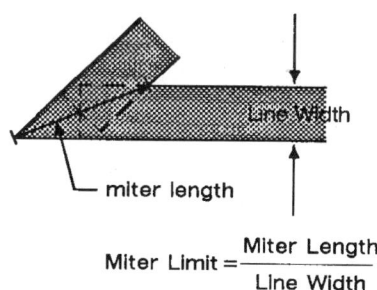

$$\text{Miter Limit} = \frac{\text{Miter Length}}{\text{Line Width}}$$

Figure 112. Miter Limit

When the miter length exceeds the miter limit, the point of the miter is clipped to the miter limit (the clipped miter is equivalent to a beveled join). The default miter limit is usually sufficient to prevent clipping except at very narrow join angles.

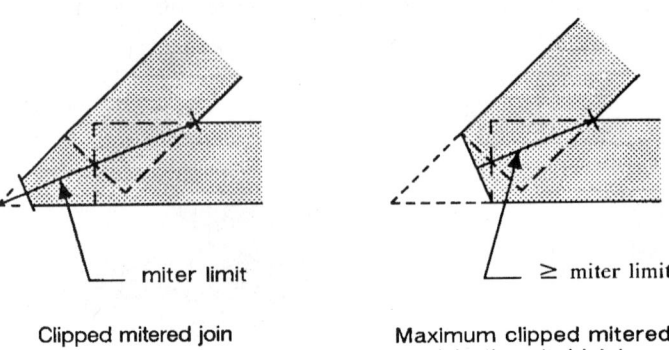

miter limit

≥ miter limit

Clipped mitered join

Maximum clipped mitered
join (beveled join)

Figure 113. Miter Limit Clipping

An LA instruction remains in effect until another LA instruction is executed, or the device is initialized or set to default conditions.

Related Instructions

AA	Arc Absolute
AR	Arc Relative
AT	Absolute Arc Three Point
BR	Bezier Relative
BZ	Bezier Absolute
CI	Circle
EA	Edge Rectangle Absolute
EP	Edge Polygon
ER	Edge Rectangle Relative
EW	Edge Wedge
FP	Fill Polygon
FT	Fill Type
LT	Line Type
PW	Pen Width
RA	Fill Rectangle Absolute
RR	Fill Rectangle Relative
RT	Relative Arc Three Point
UL	User-Defined Line Type
WG	Fill Wedge

Possible Error Conditions

Error Condition	Error Number	Printer or Plotter Response
Kind or *value* is within the data format limits, but outside the range defined by the instruction	0	The *kind,value* pair is ignored; all other *kind,value* pairs are executed

Example

The following example draws an electrical ground symbol using the LA instruction.

PA	4000,3000;	Specify absolute plotting and move the pen to (4000,3000).
PW	2;	Set the pen width to 2 mm.
LA	1,3;	Specify a triangular line end.
PD	3500,2500,4000,2000;	Place the pen down, and draw from the current location to (3500,2500), then to (4000,2000).
PU	3500,2500;	Lift the pen and move to (3500,2500).
LA	2,2,3,20;	Set the line join to mitered/beveled and the miter limit to 20.
PD	3000,2500,3000,2300;	Set the pen down and draw a line to (3000,2500), then to (3000,2300).
PU	2500,2300;	Lift the pen and move it to (2500,2300).
LA	1,4;	Specify round line ends.
PD	3500,2300;	Draw a line to (3500,2300).
PU	2700,2100;	Lift the pen and move to (2700,2100).
PD	3300,2100;	Then set the pen down and draw a line to (3300,2100).
PU	2900,1900;	Lift the pen and move to (2900,1900).
PD	3100,1900;	Then draw a line to (3100,1900).

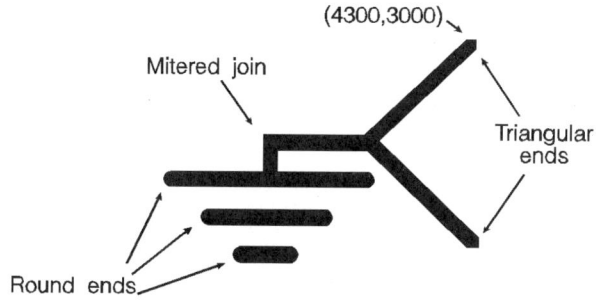

Figure 114. Line Attributes Example

LB, Label

Purpose

To print text using the currently defined font. Use LB to annotate drawings or create text-only charts.

Syntax

LB *text . . . text label_terminator*

Parameter	Format	Functional Range	Parameter Default
text . . . text	character	any character(s)	no default
label_terminator	character, as de-fined by DT	any character except **NULL**, **LF**, **ESC**, and **;** (decimal codes 0, 5, 27, and 59 respectively)	**ETX** (decimal code 3)

Group

This instruction is in the Character Group.

Use

The LB instruction includes an automatic pen-down function. When the instruction is completed, the original pen up/down status is restored.

- **text . . . text:** Up to 256 ASCII characters, drawn using the currently selected font. (Refer to the AD, SA, SD, and SS instructions for details on specifying and selecting fonts.)

  Don't leave any spaces between LB and its text (unless that is what you want).

  You can include control characters such as the Carriage Return (**CR**, decimal code 13) and Line Feed (**LF**, decimal code 10). These characters invoke the specified function or not, depending on the transparent data mode; see the TD instruction on page 316.

  The label begins at the current pen location, (unless altered by LO). After each character is drawn, the pen is moved to the next character origin. The pen location is not updated until LB is terminated. An embedded line feed moves both the pen and the carriage-return point one line in the current line direction; an embedded carriage return moves the pen to the carriage-return point. (Refer to *Working With the Character Cell* on page 58.)

- **label_terminator:** Terminates the LB instruction. You *must* use the special label terminator (refer to the DT instruction on page 154) to tell the device to exit the label mode. If you do not use the label terminator, everything following the LB mnemonic is printed in the label, including other instructions. The default *label_terminator* is the non-printing end-of-text character **ETX** (decimal code 3). You can define a different terminator using the DT instruction.

LB updates the current pen position, but not the carriage-return point. The AA, AR, AT, CP, DF, DI, DR, DV, IN, LO, PA, PE, PR, RO, and RT instructions, and PU or PD with parameters, or CP with a non-zero *lines* parameter all update the carriage-return point to the current pen position.

In 16-bit mode, the label terminator and all 8-bit control codes must have the first byte set to zero. For example, an escape character (**ESC**, ASCII 27) would be sent as a 0 followed by a 27. The exception is **ESCE** in dual-context devices, which is parsed and executed regardless of byte boundaries with the LB and SM instructions.

Related Instructions

AD	Alternate Font Definition
CP	Character Plot
DI	Absolute Direction
DR	Relative Direction
DT	Define Label Terminator
DV	Define Variable Text Path
ES	Extra Space
FI	Select Primary Font
FN	Select Secondary Font
LO	Label Origin
SA	Select Alternate Font
SB	Scalable or Bitmap Fonts
SD	Standard Font Definition
SI	Absolute Character Size
SL	Character Slant
SR	Relative Character Size
SS	Select Standard Font
TD	Transparent Data

Example

PA	2500,2500;	Move to absolute location (2500,2500).
DT*;		Specify the asterisk (*) as the label terminator.
SD	1,21,2,1,4,25,5,0,6,3,7,52;	Designate the 25-point Univers Bold font as the standard font.
SS	;	Select it.
LBThis is a Label.*;		Prints "This is a Label." in the currently selected font.

This is a Label.
(2500,2500)

LM, Label Mode

Purpose

To determine how the LB (Label) and SM (Symbol Mode) instructions interpret characters. It is mostly used with two-byte character sets such as Kanji.

Syntax

LM *mode,[row_number][;]*
    or
LM *[;]*

Parameter	Format	Functional Range	Parameter Default
mode	clamped integer	0 or 1	0 (8-bit)
row_number	clamped integer	0 through 255	0

Group

This instruction is in the Advanced Text Extension.

Use

- **No parameters:** Equivalent to "LM0,0".

- **mode:** Determines the interpretation mode as follows:

    0 (8-bit mode; the default). Interprets each byte as a character.

    1 (16-bit mode). Interprets every two bytes as a character.

- **row_number:** Used only in mode 0 (8-bit) when a 16-bit character set is selected. The *row_number* indicates the first byte, with an LB or SM instruction supplying the second byte.

Changing Label Mode turns Symbol Mode off (it executes "SM;"—see the SM instruction on page 303).

If *mode* specifies 8-bit, LB and SM interpret each byte as a character code. If *mode* specifies 16-bit, LB and SM interpret each pair of bytes as a character code. LM does not affect the DT (Define Label Terminator) and DL (Download Character) instructions.

In 16-bit mode, the label terminator and all 8-bit control codes must have the first byte set to zero. All other byte 1 values are treated as undefined characters. For example, an escape character (**ESC**, ASCII 27) would be sent as a 0 followed by a 27. The exception is **ESCE** in dual-context devices, which is parsed and executed regardless of byte boundaries with the LB and SM instructions.

A 16-bit character-set can be regarded as a two dimensional, 256 x 256 matrix. In 16-bit mode, the first parameter specifies the row and the second specifies the column.

The *row_number* parameter is used only if a 16-bit character-set is being interpreted in 8-bit mode; the first byte is then assumed to equal the *row_number*. For example, if you enter

"LM0,37" and select a 16-bit character set, the label string "LBAB**ETX**" will print characters (37,65) and (37,66)—characters A and B are ASCII characters 65 and 66.

In 8-bit mode the label buffer holds at least 256 characters, including control codes and the label terminator. In 16-bit mode, the label buffer holds at least 128 characters.

Printing Kanji and Other Two-Byte Characters

HP-GL/2 allows 8-bit character sets like ASCII with a maximum of 256 characters, and 16-bit character sets like Kanji with a possible 65 536 characters; however, LB assumes a default mode of 8-bit characters. Therefore, to print Kanji, change the mode with LM, select a Kanji font, and use LB to send a 16-bit label:

1.   Select 16-bit character mode via the LM instruction ("LM1;").

2.   Select a Kanji font using the SD or AD instructions (for example, "SD1,1611;SS;").

3.   Send the label with LB, specifying two bytes for each desired character.

If the Kanji symbol set is selected and an unrecognized character is seen, the undefined Kanji character (four dots defining the character cell area) are printed instead of a space.

When printing a Kanji typeface, the stroke weight may be automatically lightened to achieve satisfactory print quality for complex characters.

Figure 115 shows LB in normal data mode with either Kanji Set 16-bit symbol set invoked. Set 1611 is JIS Kanji Level 1. Set 1643 is JIS Kanji Levels 1 and 2. The result applies in either 8-bit mode with *row_number* set to the byte 1 value or the byte values used in 16-bit mode.

The black zone encompasses the defined area for either Kanji character set. In this zone, LB prints either a Kanji character or 4 dots.

In the blue-shaded zones, the action is as though byte 2 were from the US ASCII character set.

The white zones would print a space as for undefined character codes.

In the gray-shaded zones, the action is dependent on label mode, LM. In 8-bit mode, each byte is interpreted as in the US ASCII character set. This makes the *row_number* useful with the two Kanji character sets; in some implementations of 16-bit character sets, the use of *row_number* may be disallowed in 8-bit mode if those sets define characters in this region. In 16-bit mode, LM1, values in these zones are undefined character codes that print a space.

In 16-bit mode with an 8-bit character set invoked, all byte 1 values except zero become undefined character codes.

This concept is consistent with transparent data mode and can be extended for symbol mode. In transparent data mode, control codes and undefined characters print a space. In symbol mode, the character actually printed at the end of vectors is taken from the currently invoked character set. Thus, defining a symbol character in 16-bit mode and then invoking an 8-bit set would draw a space. Similarly, in 8-bit mode with a 16-bit set invoked, the character drawn would come from above using *row_number* for byte 1 and the symbol character value for byte 2. Note that changing from 8- to 16-bit mode or vice versa turns symbol mode off.

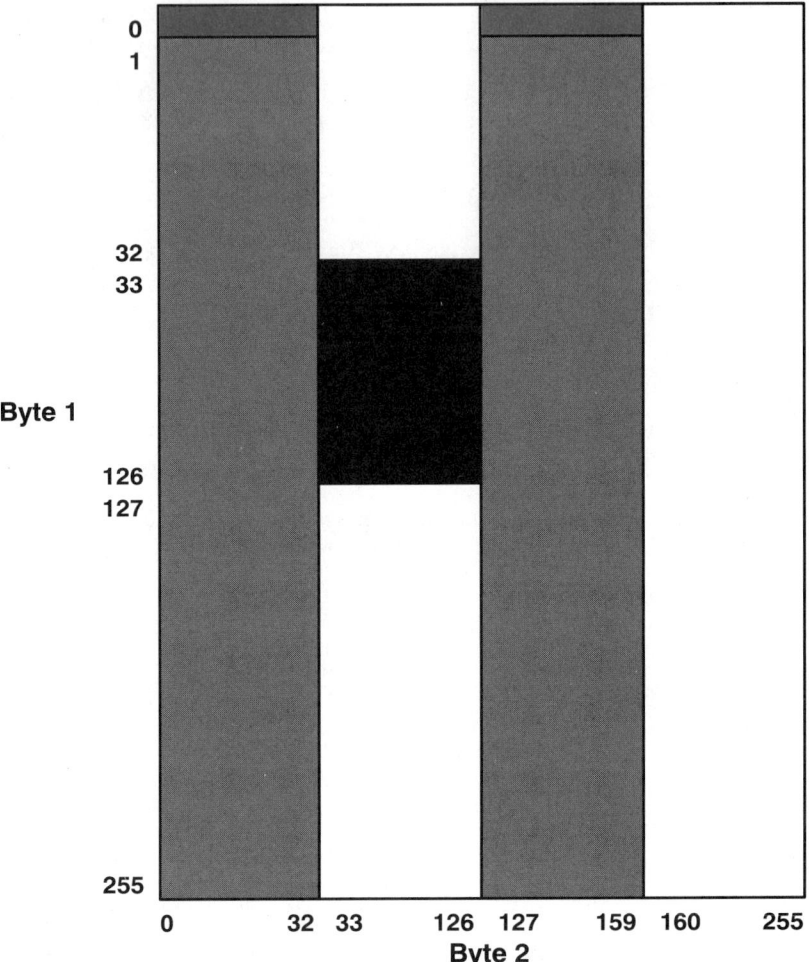

Figure 115. Printing Two-Byte Characters

Related Instructions

LB   Label
SM   Symbol Mode

Possible Error Conditions

Error Condition	Error Number	Printer or Plotter Response
Row_number is less than 0 or greater than 255	3	*Row_number* is set to zero and the instruction is executed

LO, Label Origin

Purpose

To position labels relative to the current pen location. Use the LO instruction to center, left justify, or right justify labels. The label can be drawn above or below the current pen location and can also be offset by an amount equal to .25 times the point size (or 16 grid units [0.33 times the point size] for the Stick font).

Syntax

LO *position[;]*
        or
LO *[;]*

Parameter	Format	Functional Range	Parameter Default
position	clamped integer	1 through 9, 11 through 19, or 21	1

Group

This instruction is in the Character Group.

Use

The device interprets the parameters as follows:

- **No parameter:** Defaults the label origin. Equivalent to "LO1".

- **position:** Specifies the label location relative to the current pen location. Values 1, 2, 3, 11, 12, or 13 left-justify the label; values 4, 5, 6, 14, 15, or 16 center the label; and values 7, 8, 9, 17, 18, or 19 right-justify the label. Values 11, 14, or 17 position the character cell above the current pen location; values 13, 16, or 19 position the label below the current pen position or at intermediate points. Values 1 to 9 position the character cell relative to the current pen position; values 11 to 14 and 16 to 19 offset the labels (the offset is one-quarter of the character's point size, or one-third of the point size [16 grid units] for stick fonts). Left and right are interpreted relative to the character baseline; above and below are relative to the character-up vector. The position numbers are graphically illustrated in Figure 116. Each dot represents the current pen location.

The values 11 to 14 and 16 to 19 differ from LO 1 to 4 and 6 to 9 only in that the labels are offset from the current pen location. Values 5 and 15 are the same.

The label position 21 provides a PCL-compatible label origin. The character(s) are printed at the same location as in PCL. (Label position 21 is not shown in Figure 116 because the exact location is dependent on the PCL position.)

Label origins do not change text path. To change the text path, use the DV (Define Variable Text Path) instruction.

Each time an LO instruction is sent, the carriage-return point is updated to the location the pen was in when the LO instruction was received. The current pen location (but not the carriage-return point) is updated after each character is drawn and the pen automatically moves to the next character origin. If you want to return a pen to its previous location prior to the next label instruction, you can send a Carriage Return after the label text but before the label terminator.

LO positions are applied to imaginary box drawn round the label on a line-by-line basis, regardless of the text path set by DV. Figure 116 shows LO positions for each of the possible text paths. Note the horizontal and vertical offsets for values 11 to 14 and 16 to 19.

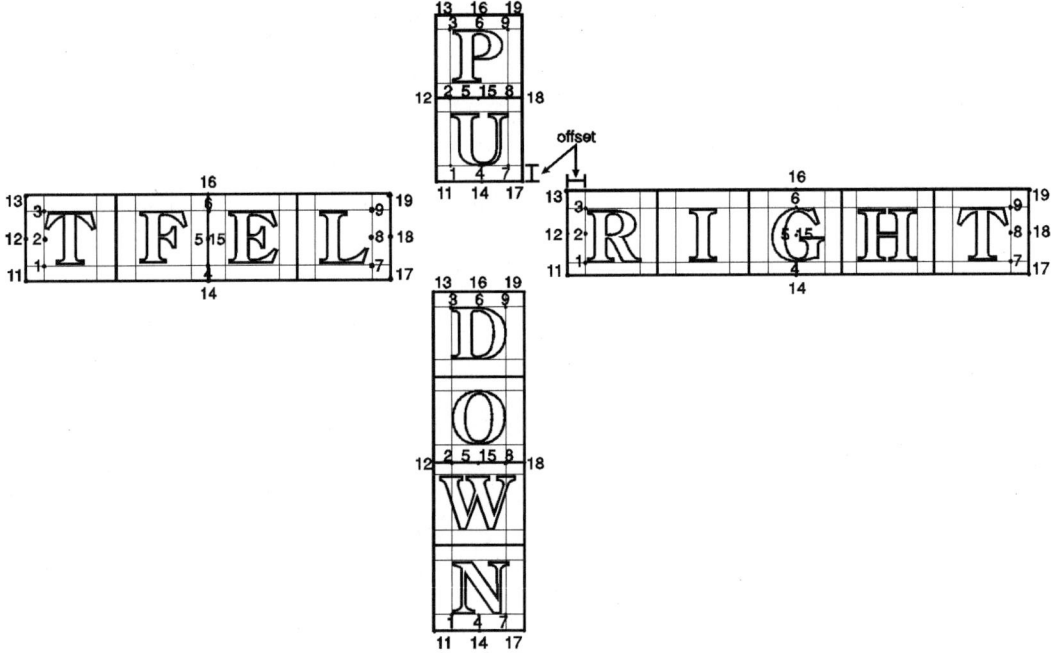

Figure 116. Label Origin Positioning

LO updates the carriage-return point to the current position. The current pen position (but not the carriage-return point) is updated after each character is printed, and the pen moves automatically to the next character origin. When you embed Carriage Return characters in a label, each portion of the label is positioned according to the label origin, just as if they were written as separate label instructions. A Carriage Return after the label, but before the label terminator, returns the pen to the current origin before the next LB.

Control characters such as spaces, horizontal tabs, or backspaces affect the label length for positioning purposes; however, a backspace at the beginning of a label is ignored.

An LO instruction remains in effect until another LO instruction is executed, or the device is initialized or set to default conditions.

The pen position at the end of the label string depends on whether two successive LB instructions concatenate together as though only one label was given. The DV/LO combinations which permit concatenation are:

Text Path	Label Origin
DV0 (right)	LO's 1, 2, 3, and 11, 12, 13, and 21
DV1 (down)	LO's 3, 6, 9, and 13, 16, 19
DV2 (left)	LO's 7, 8, 9, and 17, 18, 19
DV3 (up)	LO's 1, 4, 7, and 11, 14, 17, and 21

The DV and LO combination is applied on a line-by-line basis; a "line" is established by a carriage return, line feed, or the label terminator.

The following two rules determine where the pen is positioned after a label string is drawn. Rule 1 is for DV/LO combinations which permit concatenation; rule 2 clarifies other DV/LO combinations:

- If a concatenation combination is specified, the pen position is updated to give the normal delta X space between the last character of the first label, and the first character of the second label.

  Note: For proportional fonts that use a pair-wise spacing table, the pen position is updated using an average delta X space.

- If a non-concatenation combination is specified, the pen position that existed immediately prior to the LB instruction is restored.

Related Instructions

CP	Character Plot
DV	Define Variable Text Path
LB	Label

Example

SP	1;	Select pen number 1.
SC	–4000,4000,–5000,5000;	Specify scaling by assigning (–4000,–5000) to P1 and (4000,5000) to P2.
SI	.17,.26;	Set the absolute character size to 0.17 cm wide by 0.26 cm high.
PA	0,500;	Move to (0,500).
PD	–500,0, 0,–500, 500,0, 0,500;	Set the pen down and draw lines from (0,500) to (–500,0), to (0,–500), to (500,0), and then to (0,500).
DT#;		Define label terminator as "#" character.
CI	10;	Draw a small circle (radius 10 plotter-units) to represent the label origin point.
LO	4;	Specify a label origin of 4.
LBCentered on point#;		Print "Centered on point".
PU	–500,0;	Lift the pen and move to (–500,0).
CI	10;	Draw another small circle.
LO	18;	Specify a label origin of 18.
LBLeft center offset#;		Print "Left center offset".
PU	0,–500;	Lift the pen.
CI	10;	Draw another small circle.

LO	13;	Specify label origin number 13.
LBRight offset from point#;		Print "Right offset from point".
PA	500,0;	Move to (500,0).
CI	10;	Draw another small circle (dot).
LO	3;	Specify label origin number 3.
LBRight hang from point#;		Print the last label, "Right hang from point".

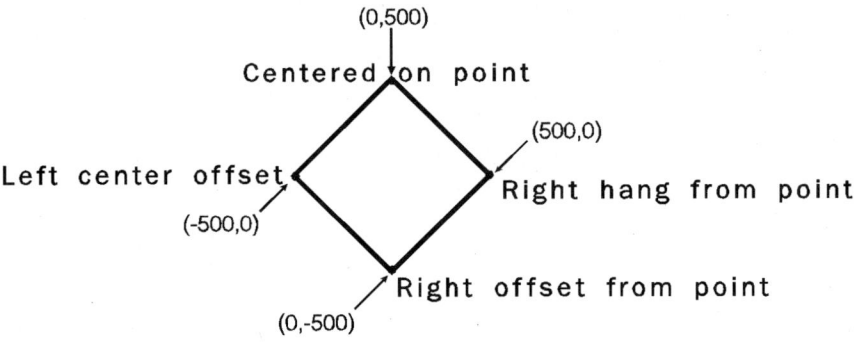

Figure 117. Hanging Labels from Various Points

LT, Line Type

Purpose

To specify the line pattern to be used when drawing lines. Use LT to vary lines and enhance your plot. Note that the ends of dashed line segments in a line pattern are affected by current line attributes (refer to the LA instruction on page 200).

Syntax

LT *line_type[,pattern_length[,mode]][;]*
        or
LT *[;]*
        or
LT 99 *[;]*

Parameter	Format	Functional Range	Parameter Default
line_type	clamped integer	−8 through 8, 99	solid line restores previous line type
pattern_length	clamped real	>0 through 32 767	4% of the distance between P1 and P2
mode	clamped integer	0 or 1	0 (relative)

Group

This instruction is in the Line and Fill Attributes Group.

Use

The LT instruction applies to lines drawn by the AA, AR, AT, CI, EA, EP, ER, EW, FP, PA, PD, PE, PR, RA, RR, RT, and WG instructions. Line types are drawn using the current line attributes set by the LA (Line Attribute) instruction. For example, if you have used LA to specify rounded ends, the device draws each dash in a dashed line pattern with rounded ends.

- **No parameters:** Defaults the line type to solid and saves the previous line type, pattern length, and any unused portion of the pattern (residue).

- **line_type:** Subsequent lines are drawn with the corresponding line pattern. Line patterns can be of fixed or adaptive type.

    Positive line types (1 to 8) are *fixed* line types and use the specified pattern length to draw lines. Any unused part of the pattern (the residue) is carried over into the next line to give the appearance of the pattern wrapping round corners. The residue is saved when any of the following instructions are received: CI, EA, EP, ER, EW, FP, PM, RA, RR, or WG. The residue is restored when the current pen position is restored upon completion of these HP-GL/2 instructions. You can redefine the eight line types using the UL instruction.

    The current residue and vector end point are also saved before each symbol is drawn, and on receipt of a CP, LB, or SM instruction. The current residue is restored if the starting point of the next pen-down vector coincides with the saved vector end point; there can be any number of pen-up vectors before the pen-down vector.

Line patterns are composed of alternate pen down and pen up moves which are percentages of the pattern length (the first percentage is always pen down). Figure 118 first shows the line type patterns, then gives the pattern percentages.

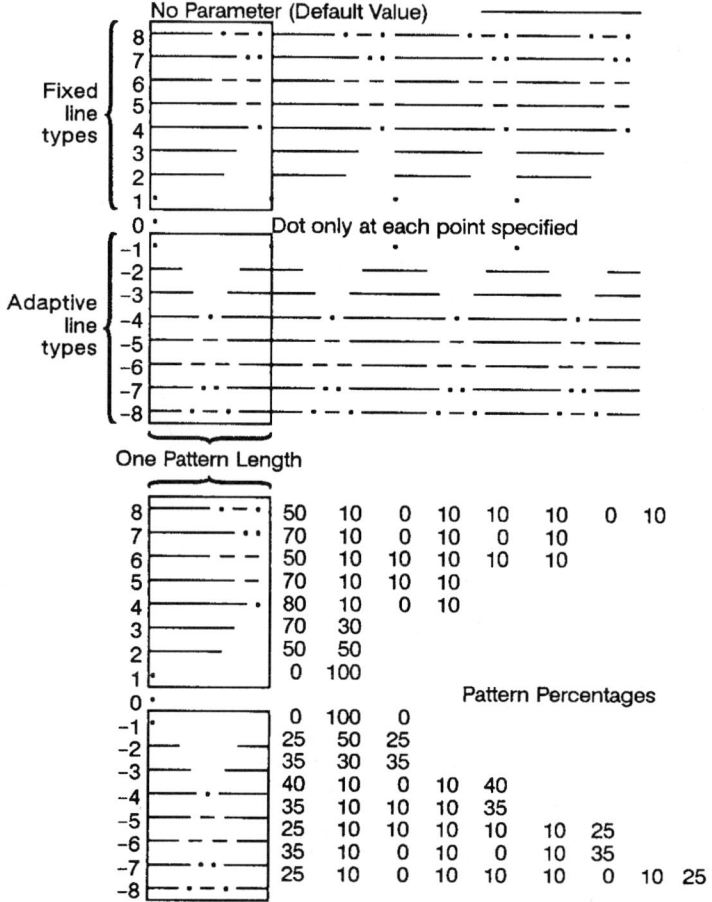

Figure 118. Line Type Patterns and Pattern Percentages

Instructions that Affect LT1 to LT8

The following instructions clear the current residue and vector end points:

AC	Anchor Corner
DF	Default Values
IN	Initialize
IP	Input P1 and P2
IR	Input Relative P1 and P2
IW	Input Window
LA	Line Attributes
LT	Line Type (except "LT;" and "LT99")
PG	Advance Full Page

PW	Pen Width
RF	Raster Fill Definition
RO	Rotate Coordinate System
RP	Replot
SC	Scale
SP	Select Pen
TR	Transparency Mode
UL	User-Defined Line Type
WU	Pen Width Unit Selection

A zero line type (0) draws only a dot at the X,Y coordinates for AA, AR, AT, BR, BZ, CI, PA, PD, PR, and RT instructions. Zero pen-down values and zero-length lines also produce dots. A dot is a vector that is one plotter-unit long; it is drawn using the current line end and pen width. (Dots within lines are drawn at the correct angle, but zero-length vectors are drawn along the user's current X-axis.)

Negative line types (–1 to –8) are *adaptive* line types, using the same patterns as line types 1 to 8. However the pattern length is automatically adjusted so that each line contains one or more complete patterns.

Adaptive line types are derived from the corresponding fixed line types; if the fixed line type ends in a "pen-up stretch", the first percentage is reduced by half and the amount that it is reduced is added as the last percentage. This ensures that the drawn vector end points are always visible when an adaptive line type is selected; the pattern is "on" (or had the pen down) at the beginning and end of the pattern repeat segment.

For redefined fixed line types (see the UL instruction) that end in a "pen-down stretch", the adaptive line type is derived by adding the first and last pen-down gap percentages and using half the sum for both the first and last gap percentages.

Note: Do not use an adaptive line type when you draw circles, arcs, wedges, or polygons. The device will attempt to draw the complete pattern in every chord; there are 72 chords in a circle using the default chord angle.

LT99 restores the previous line type (and residue if it is a fixed-line type).

Note: If a solid line type is selected ("LT;") when the LT99 instruction is issued, and the current pen position has not changed, the previously selected line type can be invoked using LT99. LT99 is ignored when a non-solid line type is in effect, or if the pen is in a different position from when the previous non-solid line ended. An example using this instruction is to print a line in a non-solid line type, followed by a rectangle in solid black; beginning at the end point of the previous line, use LT99 to print another line in the previous non-solid line type.

Instructions that Affect LT99

Sending any of the following instructions while plotting with a solid line type clears the previous line type and a subsequent "LT99" has no effect:

AC	Anchor Corner
BP	Begin Plot
DF	Default Values
IN	Initialize
IP	Input P1 and P2
IR	Input Relative P1 and P2
IW	Input Window
LA	Line Attributes
LT	Line Type (except "LT;" and "LT99")

PG	Advance Full Page
PW	Pen Width
RF	Raster Fill Definition
RO	Rotate Coordinate System
SC	Scale
SP	Select Pen
TR	Transparency Mode
UL	User-Defined Line Type
WU	Pen Width Unit Selection

- **pattern_length:** Specifies the length of one complete line pattern, either as a percentage of the diagonal distance between the scaling points P1 and P2 or in millimeters (see *mode* below). You must specify a length greater than zero (or use the default). If you do not specify a length, the device uses the last value specified.

- **mode:** Specifies how the values of the *pattern_length* parameter are interpreted. If you do not specify a *mode*, the device uses the last value specified.

  0   Relative mode: Interprets the *pattern_length* parameter as a percentage of the diagonal distance between P1 and P2.

  When specified as a percentage, the pattern length changes along with changes in P1 and P2.

  1   Absolute mode: Interprets the *pattern_length* parameter in millimeters.

  When specified in millimeters, fixed line-type patterns assume the specified length, but adaptive line-type pattern lengths are adjusted downward to fit an integral number of patterns per vector. (This is true for relative mode and absolute mode.)

If you do not specify the *pattern_length* and *mode* parameters, then the device uses their current values. When using relative mode and isotropic scaling, the *pattern_length* changes with changes to X_{min}, Y_{min} and X_{max}, Y_{max}.

An LT instruction remains in effect until another LT instruction is executed or the device is initialized or set to default conditions.

Related Instructions

AA	Arc Absolute
AR	Arc Relative
AT	Absolute Arc Three Point
CI	Circle
EA	Edge Rectangle Absolute
EP	Edge Polygon
ER	Edge Rectangle Relative
EW	Edge Wedge
FP	Fill Polygon
FT	Fill Type
PA	Plot Absolute
PD	Pen Down
PE	Polyline Encoded
PR	Plot Relative
PW	Pen Width
RA	Fill Rectangle Absolute

RR	Fill Rectangle Relative
RT	Relative Arc Three Point
UL	User-Defined Line Type
WG	Fill Wedge

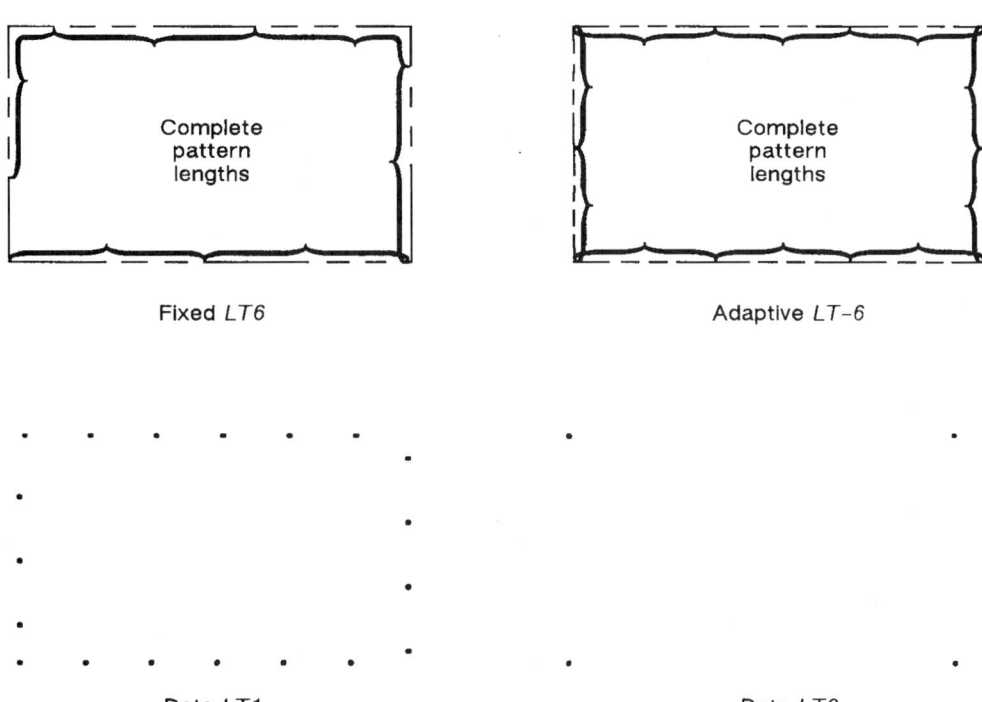

Figure 119. Rectangles Drawn with Fixed and Adaptive Line Types

Possible Error Conditions

Error Condition	Error Number	Printer or Plotter Response
Pattern_length is 0	3	Ignores the instruction
Mode is not 0 or 1	3	Ignores the instruction

MC, Merge Control

Purpose

To provide control over the color of those pixels where two or more graphics intersect on the page. This instruction is for raster devices only; it performs no function on pen plotters.

Syntax

MC *mode[,opcode][;]*
  or
MC *[;]*

Parameter	Format	Functional Range	Parameter Default
mode	clamped integer	0 or 1	0 (off)
opcode	clamped integer	0 to 255	252 (mode=0) 168 (mode=1)

Group

This instruction is in the Technical Graphics and the Advanced Drawing Extensions.

Use

The merged color is a result of a device-dependent table look-up algorithm in the device. The table look-up functions on a pixel-by-pixel basis and applied to all graphics done with HP-GL/2 instructions: vectors, text, and polygon fill (including raster patterns).

- **No parameters**: equivalent to "MC0". Defaults merge control to off.

- **mode:** A clamped integer which specifies one of the following modes:

  0 **Merge control off**: each graphic replaces the pixels at the destination location, and overwrites the pixels without merging. This is the default.

  1 **Merge control on**: the device creates a merge color at the intersection of the vectors.

- **opcode:** Specifies the logical operations that are to be performed on a source, destination, and patterned image before drawing the final image. These raster operations are defined in RGB space and are listed in the table on pages 473 and 474. This parameter is a clamped integer in the range 0 to 255. The default is 252 when *mode*=0, and 168 when *mode*=1.

The logical operations are defined in reverse polish notation (RPN) with the following definitions:

D: Destination (that is, the pixel that is already defined at the point)
S: Source (the new pixel to be applied to the point)
T: Texture (any fill pattern)

a: And   o: Or
n: Not   x: Exclusive or

For example, when the *mode* is 0, the *opcode* default is 252 (*TSo*), which is the logical operation
> Texture or Source.

When the *mode* is 1, the *opcode* default is 168 (*DTSoa*), which is the logical operation
> Destination and (Texture or Source).

Finally, a more complex example is the value 225 (*TDSoxn*), which is the logical operation
> not (Texture xor (Destination or Source)).

The MC (Merge Control) instruction is closely related to the Logical Operation (**ESC***l#O) of PCL and HP RTL (see page 422); the *opcode* values are the same as the numerical (#) parameter of that command. *Logical Operations* on page 367 contains more information that equally applies to the MC instruction.

The following table shows three common *opcodes*, constructed by reading the output values bottom-up.

Pixel Combinations			Desired Destination Values		
Texture Pixel	Source Pixel	Destination Pixel	Source Overwrite	Trans-parency	Source/ Destination XOR
0	0	0	0	0	0
0	0	1	0	1	1
0	1	0	1	1	1
0	1	1	1	1	0
1	0	0	0	0	0
1	0	1	0	1	1
1	1	0	1	1	1
1	1	1	1	1	0
		Resulting Opcode:	204 (0xCC)	238 (0xEE)	102 (0x66)

Using MC in a Dual-Context Environment

The MC instruction interacts with PCL and HP RTL. In dual-context mode the raster operation set by this instruction carries over to PCL or HP RTL; similarly any raster operation set in PCL or HP RTL using the Logical Operation command carries over to HP-GL/2.

Related Instructions and Commands

RF   Raster Fill Definition
ESC*l#O Logical Operation

MG, Message

Purpose

To write a message to the display on a device's control panel. If the device does not have a control panel with a display, this instruction is ignored (a NOP).

Syntax

MG *message[;]*
        or
MG *[;]*

Parameter	Format	Functional Range	Parameter Default
message	quoted string	any characters	no default

Group

This instruction is in the Technical Graphics Extension.

Use

Character codes in the message are interpreted in the character set enabled at power-up for display of control-panel menu commands and error messages. The character set selected for labeling does not affect the display of this instruction.

- **No parameter**: clears the display.

- **message:** Long text lines automatically wrap to the next line if one exists. Once the end of the display is reached, however, the message does not wrap and overwrite the beginning of the display.

   You can use the following control codes within your message: Backspace (**BS**), Line Feed (**LF**), Carriage Return (**CR**); all other control codes (see page 67) are ignored.

If your device uses one display for displaying messages and control-panel menus, the device switches between the MG message and the control-panel menu (for user responses). The device restores the MG message after the user responds to the control-panel prompt. The device retains the message until it is overwritten or cleared by another MG instruction or the device is initialized.

MT, Media Type

Purpose

To indicate the type of media loaded in the device. This instruction, when used, *must* appear in the picture header state; otherwise it is ignored.

Syntax

MT *type[;]*
          or
MT *[;]*

Parameter	Format	Functional Range	Parameter Default
type	clamped integer	0 to 6	*device-dependent*

Group

This instruction is in the Technical Graphics Extension.

Use

Your device uses this information according to its plotting or printing technology. The device might, for example, change the resolution, the ink-drop volume, the speed of plotting or printing, or change from unidirectional to bidirectional plotting, or respond in some other way as necessary. The actual changes made may take into account both the MT and QL (Quality Level) instructions, internal knowledge of the pen type, and any control-panel set-ups.

All devices recognize the types listed, though several of the types may be treated in the same way, for example, 1 and 3.

- **No parameter**: The device uses the control-panel setting.

- **type**: A clamped integer in the range 0 to 6, specifying the type of media, as follows:

   0   Paper

   1   Transparency film

   2   Vellum

   3   Polyester film, such as Mylar

   4   Translucent paper

   5   Special paper

   6   Glossy paper

Related Instruction

QL   Quality Level

HP-GL/2
INSTRUCTIONS

Possible Error Conditions

Error Condition	Error Number	Printer or Plotter Response
Instruction used outside picture header state (see page 78)	1	Ignores instruction

NP, Number of Pens

Purpose

To establish the size (the number of pens) of the HP-GL/2 palette.

Syntax

NP *n[;]*

    or

NP *[;]*

Parameter	Format	Functional Range	Parameter Default
n	clamped integer	*device-dependent**	*device-dependent***

*   Parameter must be a power of two.

**   The default palette size for monochrome raster devices is 2. The default palette size for color raster devices is 8.

Group

This instruction is in the Palette Extension.

Use

The palette is an array of logical pens, each having an associated color value and an associated width. Define pen colors through the PC (Pen Color Assignment) instruction, described on page 239. Establish pen widths through the PW (Pen Width) and WU (Pen Width Units Selection) instructions, described on pages 264 and 328 respectively.

- **No parameter:** Defaults the palette size for monochrome devices to 2 pens, and for color raster devices to 8 pens.

- **n:** Sets the size of the palette as a power of 2. If *n* is not a power of 2, the device uses the next larger power of 2. The maximum value of *n*, while device-dependent, is equal to or greater than the number of distinct colors the device can produce. If *n* is greater than the maximum, the device uses the maximum-size palette.

  For pen plotters, NP defines the number of pens and also pen number 0; thus "NP8" defines pens 1 through 8 plus no pen (pen 0).

  For raster devices, NP defines the palette size, for pens numbered 0 through *n–1*; thus "NP8" defines pens 0 through 7.

NP does not default pen colors or widths for existing pen values. For example, if the palette size is decreased from 8 to 4, the pen colors and widths of the first four pens of the old palette are retained. If the palette size is increased from 8 to 16, the colors and widths for the first eight pens remain the same, and those for the remainder are defaulted.

If the current pen is outside the range of the new palette size, the device applies a modulo function to select a pen number within the range of the new palette. The base of the modulo function is either *n* (for a pen plotter) or *n–1* (for a raster device), that is 8 or 7 in the examples above. See the SP instruction on page 306.

This instruction is usually defaulted by the IN (Initialize) and BP (Begin Plot) instructions.

In dual context environments, you should import the palettes created within PCL, rather than defining palettes with this instruction.

Possible Error Conditions

Error Condition	Error Number	Printer or Plotter Response
n<2	3	Ignores instruction

NR, Not Ready

Purpose

To take the device off-line for a specified amount of time. This can enable you to set control-panel conditions before starting to plot or print.

Syntax

NR *timeout[;]*

or

NR *[;]*

Parameter	Format	Functional Range	Parameter Default
timeout	clamped integer	0 to 7200	0

Group

This instruction is in the Technical Graphics Extension.

Use

Place this instruction at the beginning of a plot after the IN or BP instruction. The *timeout* feature of this instruction allows the user to set up pen groupings, media registration, pen force and acceleration, and so on. The device restores its online status and resumes plotting when either the *timeout* elapses or the user puts the device back online (whichever comes first).

- **No parameter**: Defaults the *timeout* to zero (no time-out); equivalent to "NR0".

- **timeout:** Specifies in seconds how long a user may need to perform any control-panel set-up operations or media loading. The maximum time-out is device-dependent and may be clamped without error.

On devices that cannot perform a page advance, the PG instruction places the device in a "not ready" state. The device remains off-line until new media is loaded or the necessary user interaction occurs.

The function performed by "NR;" may produce an indefinite time-out by enabling single-user mode in a device that can be logically configured to be either a shared or a single-user device, for example, a device that can accept plots from several ports at once, by interleaving plots in a queue, or from a single port with no interleaving. This change is device-dependent and is enabled using front-panel interaction or switches that can be set by the user.

OD, Output Digitized Point and Pen Status

Purpose

To output the X,Y coordinates and pen status (up or down) associated with the last digitized point. The ranges of the X,Y coordinates are the hard-clip limits of the device; the pen status is either 0 (up) or 1 (down).

Syntax

OD ;

You must use a terminator with output instructions.

Group

This instruction is in the Digitizing Extension.

Use

Use the following procedure for sending output instructions:

1. Send the OD instruction to the device as you do other HP-GL/2 instructions.

2. Read the device's output response immediately using an input statement appropriate to your programming language, keeping in mind the number and type of the variables.

Response	Format	Range
x,y,pen status *(followed by a terminator)*	x,y: current units	*device-dependent* (at least -2^{23} to $2^{23}-1$)
	pen status: integer	0 (up) or 1 (down)

Receipt of this instruction clears bit position 2 of the OS instruction status byte. The timing of output depends on the interface you are using.

The terminator is a carriage return (**CR**) for RS-232-C, IEEE-1284-compatible, and MIO interfaces and carriage return and line feed (**CR LF**) for HP-IB interfaces.

3. Output digitized points one at a time. Digitize the point, then output the point to the computer. Continue in this manner until all points on your plot are digitized.

Related Instructions

DC   Digitize Clear
DP   Digitize Point
OS   Output Status

Possible Error Conditions

Error Condition	Error Number	Printer or Plotter Response
One or more parameters are specified	2	The parameters are ignored

OE, Output Error

Purpose

To debug programs by retrieving a number that corresponds to the HP-GL/2 error received by the plotter since the most recent OE, BP, or IN instruction, or power-up. Do *not* use this instruction on networks or unidirectional interfaces.

Syntax

OE ;

You must use a terminator with output instructions.

Group

This instruction is in the Technical Graphics Extension.

Use

The OE instruction outputs an integer in the range 0 through 7, corresponding to the first HP-GL/2 error (if any) that has occurred. The plotter only outputs the first error. If you suspect more than one error, place the instruction in as many locations in your program as necessary. The following table defines the error numbers:

Error Number	Meaning
0	No error
1	Unrecognized instruction (or not recognized in current state)
2	Wrong number of parameters
3	Out-of-range or invalid parameter
4 and 5	Not used
6	Position overflow ("lost" mode; see page 23)
7	Buffer overflow, or out of memory

After returning the error number, the plotter sets its internal error number to zero, and clears bit 5 of the status byte (see the OS instruction), indicating that no error has occurred since the last OE instruction.

A posted error is not changed until it is cleared.

Multiple errors are set from left to right. For example, "LA 1,9,2;" causes an invalid parameter error (3) because of the "9", not a wrong number of parameters error (2).

An instruction is ignored for the following error conditions:

Unrecognized instruction
Missing required parameters
Parameter exceeds the defined limits.

If more parameters are supplied than are expected for an instruction, the extra parameters are ignored and the instruction is executed normally. An error 2 is posted.

If the polygon buffer is full and insertion of more data is attempted, only the portion of the polygon that fits in the buffer is edged and filled; then an error 7 is posted. The polygon buffer is large enough to store at least 512 vertices.

If a parameter in the AD, LA, PA, PD, PR, PU, or SD instructions exceeds the limits defined by the data format type, the out-of-range parameter and all subsequent parameters are ignored. However, if a *kind* or *value* parameter to the AD, BP, LA, or SD instruction is within the data format type limits, but outside the range defined by the instruction, that parameter pair is ignored; all preceding and subsequent valid pairs are executed. Integer parameter values are rounded before range checking is performed.

Example

This sequence of instructions contains two errors:

PA	1000,1000,20;	PA instruction should have an even number of parameters
ED	;	Non-existent instruction
OE	;	Output Error

This OE instruction returns 2 followed by a terminator. (The terminator is a carriage return [**CR**] for RS-232-C, IEEE-1284-compatible, and MIO interfaces and carriage return and line feed [**CR LF**] for HP-IB interfaces.) By referring to the table, you know that error 2 indicates the wrong number of parameters. Once the first error is corrected, run the program again to find the other HP-GL/2 error.

OH, Output Hard-Clip Limits

Purpose

To output the X,Y coordinates of the current hard-clip limits to the computer. Use OH to determine the plotter-unit dimensions of the area within which plotting can occur. Do *not* use this instruction on networks or on unidirectional interfaces.

Syntax

OH ;

You must use a terminator with output instructions.

Group

This instruction is in the Technical Graphics Extension.

Use

The OH instruction outputs four integer values, X_{LL}, Y_{LL}, X_{UR}, Y_{UR}, representing the hard-clip limits.

The coordinates are always expressed in plotter-units and represent the lower-left (X_{LL}, Y_{LL}) and upper-right (X_{UR}, Y_{UR}) corners of the hard-clip limits. After sending the OH instruction, have your computer program immediately read the device's output response.

Example

The following program outputs the plotter identification. Use whatever statements your computer language requires to perform the input and output operations.

Send to the device:	"**ESC**%−1BBPIN" Enter HP-GL/2 mode, begin a plot, and initialize HP-GL/2.
Send to the device:	"OH;" Output Hard-Clip Limits.
Read from the device:	A,B,Y,Z Read the values into four variables, A, B, Y, and Z.
Print:	A,B,Y,Z Print out the four variables, A, B, Y, and Z.

Typical output from the OH instruction might be:

```
0  0  21050  15000
```

followed by a terminator. (The terminator is a carriage return [**CR**] for RS-232-C, IEEE-1284-compatible, and MIO interfaces and carriage return and line feed [**CR LF**] for HP-IB interfaces.)

Related Instruction

PS   Plot Size

OI, Output Identification

Purpose

To output the plotter's identifying order number. This information is useful in a remote operating configuration (where several plotters are connected to the computer) to determine which plotter model is online, or when software needs the plotter's model number. Do *not* use this instruction on networks or on unidirectional interfaces.

Syntax

OI ;

You must use a terminator with output instructions.

Group

This instruction is in the Technical Graphics Extension.

Use

The OI instruction outputs the *plotter ID*, which is a character string of up to 30 characters, and represents the device's order number and letter.

Example

The following program outputs the plotter identification. Use whatever statements your computer language requires to perform the input and output operations.

Send to the device:	"**ESC**%–1BBPIN" Enter HP-GL/2 mode, begin a plot, and initialize HP-GL/2.
Send to the device:	"OI;" Output Identification.
Read from the device:	A$ Read the device's identification into the program.
Print:	A$ Print it out.

Typical output from this instruction might be:

C4699A

followed by a terminator. (The terminator is a carriage return [**CR**] for RS-232-C, IEEE-1284-compatible, and MIO interfaces and carriage return and line feed [**CR LF**] for HP-IB interfaces.)

OP, Output P1 and P2

Purpose

To output the X, Y coordinates (in plotter-units) of the current scaling points P1 and P2 to the computer. Use OP to help compute the number of plotter-units per user-unit when scaling is on. OP can also be used with the IW (Input Window) instruction to set the window to P1 and P2 from your program. Do *not* use this instruction on networks or on unidirectional interfaces.

Syntax

OP ;

You must use a terminator with output instructions.

Group

This instruction is in the Technical Graphics Extension.

Use

The OP instruction outputs four integer values, $P1_X$, $P1_Y$, $P2_X$, $P2_Y$, representing the values of the coordinates of P1 and P2. The range is device-dependent, but is at least -2^{23} to $2^{23}-1$.

Note that P2 tracks P1 and can be outside your plotter's range.

The P1 and P2 coordinates are output as plotter-units. After sending the OP instruction, have your program immediately read the plotter's response.

On completion of the output, bit position 1 of the status word is cleared; refer to the OS (Output Status) instruction.

Example

The following program outputs the plotter's P1 and P2 coordinates. Use whatever statements your computer language requires to perform the input and output operations.

Send to the device:	"**ESC**%–1BBPIN" Enter HP-GL/2 mode, begin a plot, and initialize HP-GL/2.
Send to the device:	"OP;" Output P1 and P2.
Read from the device:	A,B,X,Y Read the values of P1 and P2 into your program.
Print:	A,B,X,Y Print them out.

Typical output from this simple program might be:

```
0  0  21050  15000
```

followed by a terminator. (The terminator is a carriage return [**CR**] for RS-232-C, IEEE-1284-compatible, and MIO interfaces and carriage return and line feed [**CR LF**] for HP-IB interfaces.)

Related Instructions

IP	Input P1 and P2
IR	Input Relative P1 and P2
OS	Output Status
PS	Plot Size

OS, Output Status

Purpose

To output the decimal value of the status byte. Use OS to debug your program. Do *not* use this instruction on networks or on unidirectional interfaces.

Syntax

OS ;

You must use a terminator with output instructions.

Group

This instruction is in the Technical Graphics Extension.

Use

The OS instruction outputs an integer in the range 0 through 255, corresponding to the value of the status byte.

When this instruction is executed, the internal 8-bit status byte is converted into an ASCII integer between 0 and 255, followed by a terminator, and sent to your computer. (The terminator is a carriage return [**CR**] for RS-232-C, IEEE-1284-compatible, and MIO interfaces and carriage return and line feed [**CR LF**] for HP-IB interfaces.) Your computer program should read the response; refer to the following table to find the *largest decimal value* that can be subtracted from the output response; the condition corresponding to that value has been met.

Continue subtracting the largest possible decimal value from the remainder of the output response. Each time you subtract a value, the corresponding condition has been met. Continue this process until the remainder is 0.

Decimal value	Meaning	Bit number
1	Pen is down	0
2	P1 or P2 newly established; cleared by OP.	1
4	Digitized point entered; cleared by OD.	2
8	Initialized; cleared by OS.	3
16	Ready for data (bit always set to 1).	4
32	Error; cleared by OE.	5
64	Not used (reserved).	6
128	Not used (bit always set to 0).	7

On power-up, the status byte is 26, the sum of 16 (ready for data), 8 (initialized), and 2 (P1/P2 newly established). On execution of OS, bit number 3 is cleared and the status byte is 18.

See *Monitoring the Status Byte* on page 90 for further examples of how to use this instruction.

Related Instructions

IN Initialize
IP Input P1 and P2
IR Input Relative P1 and P2
OE Output Error
OP Output P1 and P2
PS Plot Size

Example

The following program outputs the numeric representation of the status byte. Use whatever statements your computer language requires to perform the input and output operations.

Send to the device:	"**ESC**%−1BBPIN" Enter HP-GL/2 mode, begin a plot, and initialize HP-GL/2.
Send to the device:	"OS;" Output Status.
Read from the device:	S.
Print:	S.

PA, Plot Absolute

Purpose

To establish absolute plotting and moves the pen to the specified absolute coordinates from the current pen position.

Syntax

PA *X,Y [,...][;]*
  or
PA *[;]*

Parameter	Format	Functional Range	Parameter Default
X,Y coordinates	current units	*device-dependent* (at least -2^{23} to $2^{23} - 1$)	no default

Group

This instruction is in the Vector Group.

Use

The device interprets the parameters as follows:

- **No parameters:** Establishes absolute plotting for subsequent instructions.

- **X,Y coordinates:** Specify the absolute location to which the pen moves. When you include more than one coordinate pair, the pen moves to each point in the order given, using the current pen up/down status. If the pen is up, PA moves the pen to the point; if the pen is down, PA draws a line to the point. Lines are drawn using the current line width, type, and attributes.

  Coordinates are interpreted in current units: as user-units when scaling is on; as plotter-units when scaling is off.

Note: If an odd number of coordinates is specified (in other words, an X coordinate without a corresponding Y coordinate), the device ignores the last unmatched coordinate.

When you use the SM (Symbol Mode) instruction, PA draws the specified symbol at each X,Y coordinate.

When you use the PM (Polygon Mode) instruction, the X,Y coordinates enter the polygon buffer for use when the polygon is edged or filled.

The carriage-return point (see page 66) is moved to the last X,Y.

Related Instructions

PE	Polyline Encoded
PR	Plot Relative
PD	Pen Down
PU	Pen Up
LA	Line Attributes
LT	Line Type
PW	Pen Width
SM	Symbol Mode

Possible Error Conditions

Error Condition	Error Number	Printer or Plotter Response
Odd number of parameters	2	Unmatched parameter is ignored

PC, Pen Color Assignment

Purpose

To assign colors to specific pens. This instruction is ignored by pen plotters.

Syntax

> PC *pen,primary1,primary2,primary3[;]*
> > or
> PC *pen[;]*
> > or
> PC *[;]*

Parameter	Format	Functional Range	Parameter Default
pen	integer	determined by NP	no default
primary1, primary2, primary3	clamped real	determined by CR	(see table below)

Group

This instruction is in the Palette Extension.

Use

With a red/green/blue (RGB) color model, *primary1* is red, *primary2* is green, and *primary3* is blue. RGB is the default color model for HP-GL/2 palettes. If your palette is imported from PCL in a dual-context environment, another color model may be in effect. See the *PCL 5 Color Technical Reference Manual* for details.

PC remains in effect until another PC instruction assigns new values for a specific pen or all pens in the palette, or until the device is initialized by the IN instruction. The first eight pens for color devices default to the colors in the table below, even when the palette is larger than eight pens. The remaining pen colors are device-dependent. For a monochrome device, 0 defaults to white; all remaining pen colors default to black.

- **No parameters:** Defaults the colors of all pens as in the table below.

- **pen:** Specifies the number of the pen being defined. When you specify only the *pen* number (and no RGB values), the pen assumes the color as specified in the table below for the color space of the palette (for example, "PC3;" defaults pen 3 to green). The range for the *pen* parameter is defined by the size of the palette; see the NP instruction on page 225.

- **primary1, primary2, primary3:** Specify the primary component values for the specified *pen*. Refer to the CR (Set Color Range for Relative Color Data) instruction on page 131 for a description of the range associated with the RGB values.

  If a *primary* parameter is outside the color range defined in the CR instruction, the value is clamped to the color range limits.

Number of Pens in Palette	Pen Number	Color	Monochrome
2 (NP2)	0	White	White
	1	Black	Black
4 (NP4)	0	White	White
	1	Black	Black
	2	Red	Black
	3	Green	Black
8 (NP8)	0	White	White
	1	Black	Black
	2	Red	Black
	3	Green	Black
	4	Yellow	Black
	5	Blue	Black
	6	Magenta	Black
	7	Cyan	Black

For a monochrome device that accepts color descriptions, pen 0 defaults to white; all remaining pen colors default to "equivalent gray levels". An equivalent gray level means that lighter colors (like yellow) are converted to light gray shades, and darker colors (like purple) are converted to dark gray shades. The mapping algorithm is device-dependent. However, equivalent gray levels are solid colors, and any white pixels in them are not subject to transparency mode (TR).

Example

The following instructions set pens 1, 2, and 3, using the default color range for an RGB color space:

PC   1,255,0,0;   Pen 1 is red.
PC   2,0,255,0;   Pen 2 is green.
PC   3,0,0,255;   Pen 3 is blue.

Possible Error Conditions

Error Condition	Error Number	Printer or Plotter Response
2 or 3 parameters	2	Ignores instruction
More than 4 parameters	2	Ignores extra parameters
Out-of-range parameter	3	Ignores instruction

PD, Pen Down

Purpose

To lower the device's logical pen and draw subsequent graphics instructions.

Syntax

PD *X,Y[,...][;]*
      or
PD *[;]*

Parameter	Format	Functional Range	Parameter Default
X,Y coordinates	current units	*device-dependent* (at least -2^{23} to $2^{23} - 1$)	no default

Group

This instruction is in the Vector Group.

Use

On pen plotters, this instruction lowers the pen to draw lines on the page. On other devices it emulates this lowering of the pen, and must be executed before lines can be drawn.

- **No parameters:** Prepares the device to draw subsequent graphics instructions.

- **X,Y coordinates** or **increments:** Draws (in current units) to the point specified. You can specify as many X,Y coordinate pairs as you want. When you include more than one coordinate pair, the device draws to each point in the order given. Coordinates are interpreted in current units: as user-units when scaling is on; as plotter-units when scaling is off.

  Whether the PD instruction uses coordinates or increments depends on the most recently executed PA or PR instruction. If no PA or PR instruction is issued, absolute plotting (PA) is used.

  The carriage-return point (see page 66) is moved to the last X,Y.

When you use the SM (Symbol Mode) instruction, PD draws the specified symbol at each X,Y coordinate.

When you use the PM (Polygon Mode) instruction, the X,Y coordinates enter the polygon buffer and are used when the polygon is edged or filled.

Note that "PD;PU;" leaves a dot.

Example

PA   10,10;   Begin absolute plotting from coordinate (10,10).
PD   2500,10,10,1500,10,10;   Set the Pen Down and draw lines between the specified points.

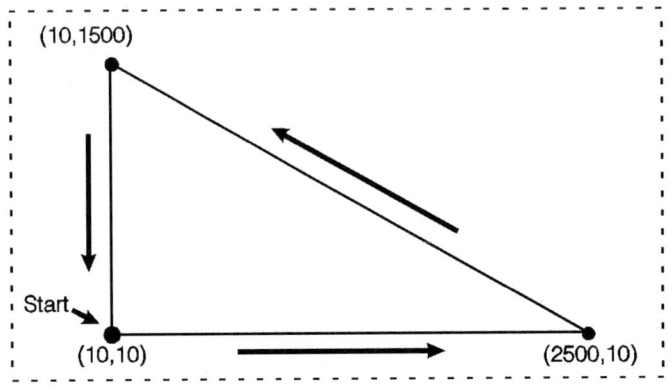

Figure 120. Using the PD (Pen Down) Instruction

Related Instructions

LA	Line Attributes
LT	Line Type
PA	Plot Absolute
PE	Polyline Encoded
PR	Plot Relative
PU	Pen Up
PW	Pen Width
SM	Symbol Mode

Possible Error Conditions

Error Condition	Error Number	Printer or Plotter Response
Odd number of parameters	2	Unmatched parameter is ignored

PE, Polyline Encoded

Purpose

To incorporate the PA, PR, PU, PD, and SP instructions into an encrypted format that substantially decreases the size of your file and the time required for data transmission. This instruction is especially useful when using an RS-232-C interface or when you need to minimize the file size.

Syntax

> PE *[flag[value]]coord_pair...[flag[value]]coord_pair;*
> > or
>
> PE *;*

Note: Parameter values are self-terminating; do not use commas with this instruction. Also, you *must* use a semicolon to terminate PE.

Parameter	Format	Functional Range	Parameter Default
flag	character	':', '<', '>', '=', or '7'	no default
value	character	*flag*-dependent*	see below
coord_pair	character	*device-dependent* (at least -2^{23} to $2^{23} - 1$)	no default

*   Refer to the table following the parameter description.

Group

This instruction is in the Vector Group.

Use

Lines are drawn using the current line type and current units. The device draws to all points with the pen down unless a pen-up *flag* precedes the X,Y coordinates. If the final move is made with the pen up, the pen remains in the up position; otherwise the pen is left in the down position.

The PE instruction causes the device to interpret coordinate pairs as relative coordinates unless they are preceded by an absolute-value *flag* ("="). Relative integer *coordinates* produce the most compact data stream. For best results, scale your drawings so you use only integer coordinates and use relative plotting mode. After PE is executed, the previous plotting mode (absolute or relative) is restored. The PE instruction represents vectors in base 64 (default) or base 32 (explained under *Encoding PE Flag Values and X,Y Coordinates*). In parameter *value* data, all spaces, delete characters, control characters, as well as ASCII characters 128 through 160 and 255 are ignored.

- **No parameters:** Updates the carriage-return point. The PE instruction without parameters does not affect the pen's current location or up/down status.

- **flag:** Indicates how the device interprets subsequent values. *Flags* are ASCII characters and are not encoded (unlike *values* and *coord_pairs*). The device disregards the eighth bit of a *flag* (for example, a character code of 61 and a character code of 189 both send "=" [the absolute flag]).

Flag	Meaning	Description
:	Select Pen	Indicates that the subsequent value is the desired pen number. A PE instruction without a select-pen flag defaults to the currently selected pen.*
<	Pen Up	Raises the pen and moves to the subsequent coordinate pair value. (All coordinate pair values not preceded by a pen-up flag are considered pen down moves.)**
>	Fraction-al Data	Indicates that the subsequent value specifies the number of fractional binary bits contained in the coordinate data. Default is zero.
=	Absolute	Indicates that the next point is defined by absolute coordinates.
7	7-bit Mode	Indicates that all subsequent coordinate pair values should be interpreted in 7-bit mode. Once you send a seven-bit flag, base 32 is used and eighth bits are ignored for the remainder of the instruction.

*   Because SP is not allowed in polygon mode, if you select a pen within PE while in polygon mode, the select-pen flag is ignored.

**   We recommend you always follow a pen-up flag with a relative move of (0,0). This ensures that the next plotting coordinates are drawn.

- **value:** Specifies data according to the preceding flag. For example, a *value* following a select-pen flag is a pen number. *Values* are encoded in the same manner as coordinate data. Instructions for encoding *values* follow the parameter descriptions.

  — *Pen Number*—Specifies the pen to be selected (the range is device-dependent). The pen number must be encoded into a base 64 or base 32 equivalent.

  — *Number of Fractional Binary Bits*—Specifies the number of fractional binary bits contained in the coordinate data. The number of fractional binary bits must be encoded into a base 64 or base 32 equivalent (see the explanation below).

Value	Format	Range
Pen number	integer	*device-dependent*
Number of fractional binary bits	integer	*device-dependent*

If the current pen position goes out of the supported range, the device ignores plotting instructions until it receives an absolute PA or PE coordinate within the range.

- **X,Y coordinates:** Specifies a coordinate pair encoded into a base 64 (default) or a base 32 equivalent. Use base 64 if your system can send 8 bits of data without parity. Use 7-bit mode and base 32 coordinate values if your system requires a parity bit.

When you are in symbol mode (refer to the SM instruction), PE draws the specified symbol at each X,Y coordinate. When you are in polygon mode (refer to the PM instruction), the X,Y coordinates enter the polygon buffer; they are used when the polygon is edged or filled.

This instruction updates the carriage-return point to the last X,Y position.

Encoding PE Flag Values and X,Y Coordinates

Flag values and X,Y coordinates are encoded into a base 64 (default) or base 32 equivalent (7-bit mode). The following steps give a generic algorithm for encoding a number. Assume x is the number to be encoded. Use steps 1 and 2 only if you are encoding fractional data; for integer data, begin with step 3. Note: When converting numbers to base 32 or 64 (step 4 in the following instructions), note that highest order digits are always in the high range, all other digits are in the low range. Therefore, if there is only one digit in a number, it is in the high range.

Steps	Example
1. Fraction adjustment. If you are using fractional data, this step converts the number of decimal places in your data to the number of binary fractional bits. Assume "n" is the number of fractional binary bits specified by the fractional data flag.	$x = 82.83$
a. Multiply the number of decimal places contained in the data by 3.33.	$2 \times 3.33 = 6.66$
b. Round that number up to the next integer to get integer n. $x = x \times 2^n$	$n = \text{round (decimal places} \times 3.33) = 7$ $x = 82.83 \times 2^7 = 10\,525.42$
2. Round to an integer. Round the results of step 1 to the nearest integer. $x = \text{round } (x)$	$x = \text{round } (10\,525.42) = 10\,525$

3. Set the sign bit. If x is positive, multiply it by two. If x is negative, multiply the absolute value of x by two and add one. This sets the sign bit.
    if $(x \geq 0)$
       $x = 2 \times x$
    else
       $x = 2 \times \text{abs}(x) + 1$
	$x = 2 \times 10\,525 = 21\,050$

4. Convert the number to base 64 or 32 and encode the data.

Convert x to a base 64 number if your system sends 8 bits without parity. Convert x to a base 32 number if your system sends 7 bits with parity (seven-bit flag is sent).

Encode each base 64 or 32 digit into the ASCII character range, as described below. Output each character as it is encoded, starting with the least significant digit. The most significant digit is used to terminate the number and is encoded into a different ASCII character range than the low-order digits.

Each number in a coordinate pair is represented as zero or more non-terminator characters, followed by a terminator character. A character is a non-terminator or terminator depending on the range it is in; refer to the following table. For example, in base 64 there are 64 non-terminator and 64 terminator characters. Either kind represents a "digit."

For 8-bit data (base 64), the non-terminators are in the range 63 through 126, and the terminators are in the range 191 through 254.
For 7-bit data (base 32), the non-terminators are in the range 63 through 94, and the terminators are in the range 95 through 126.

Note: *Values* following the fractional-data or select-pen flag also must be encoded.

Steps	Example

4. (continued)
 	
       while n $\geq$ base
           output CHR\$(63 + (n MOD base))
           n = n $\div$ base (discarding any remainder)
       end
       if base = 64 then n = 191 + n
       if base = 32 then n = 95 + n
       output CHR\$(n)	

a. Base 64. Encode all the low order digits into the ASCII range 63 to 126. For a digit with value i, use ASCII character CHR\$(63 + i). Encode the highest order digit (or the single digit in a one-digit number) into the range 191 to 254.	21 050$\div$4 096=5 rem 570
	570 $\div$ 64 = 8 remainder 58
	     5 in 4 096's place
	     8 in 64's place
	     58 in 1's place
	Low order digit: 1's place
	(range 63 to 126)
	     63 + 58 = 121
	  output CHR\$ (121)
	Next order digit: 64's place
	(range 63 to 126)
	     63 + 8 = 71
	  output CHR\$ (71)
	High order digit: 4 096's place
	(range 191 to 254)
	     191 + 5 = 196
	  output CHR\$ (196)

b. Base 32. Encode all the low order digits into the ASCII range 63 to 94. For a digit with value i, use ASCII character CHR\$(63 + i). Encode the highest order digit (or the single digit in a one-digit number) into the range 95 to 126.	21 050$\div$1 024=20 rem 570
	570 $\div$ 32 = 17 remainder 26
	     20 in 1024's place
	     17 in 32's place
	     26 in 1's place
	Low order digit: 1's place
	(range 63 to 94)
	     63 + 26 = 89
	  output CHR\$(89)
	Next order digit: 32's place
	(range 63 to 94)
	     63 + 17 = 80
	  output CHR\$ (80)
	High order digit: 1 024's place
	(range 95 to 126)
	     95 + 20 = 115
	  output CHR\$ (115)

Programming Considerations with the PE Instruction

When using PE (in the default relative mode), the application program does not know the current pen location after printing a label (normally, the current pen location is updated to the end of the label.) If this presents a problem in your program, follow these steps:

1. Create a flag called "lost" in your program.

    Note: At the beginning of your application program, set "lost" to "true". Then, specify the next coordinate in absolute mode (PA or PE=).

2. After labeling (or any instruction which updates the current pen location), set "lost" to "true".

3. If "lost" = "true" at the beginning of the PE instruction, use an Absolute flag for the first coordinate pair only (subsequent coordinates are interpreted as relative).

4. Set "lost" to "false".

When you are converting and encoding data, note the following:

- $n \div 64$. You can optimize your application by shifting six bits to the right, since shifting is normally faster than division.

- n MOD 64. The number can be logically AND'd with 63, also for improved performance.

Example

The following partial program converts three relative real coordinates to base 64:

Prompt user:	"Input number of fractional decimal places in data".
Read the response into:	F (in this example, 2 decimal places).

    Calculate Number of Fractional Binary Bits.

```
F = F * 3.33
F = INT(F)                INT is the integer function.
A = F
IF F ≥ 0 THEN F = 2*ABS(F) ELSE F = 2*ABS(F)+1
F = 191+F
Send to the device:       "PE>"+CHR$(F)   (using BASIC language notation)
    Convert coordinate data to base 64
FOR J = 1 to 6
  READ C
  C = C * (2^A)           (^ is the exponential function)
  C = INT(C)
  IF C ≥ 0 THEN C = 2*C ELSE C = 2*ABS(C)+1
  WHILE C ≥ 64
    Send to the device: CHR$(63+(C MOD 64))
    C = C ÷ 64
  End WHILE
  C = 191+C
  Send to the device:     CHR$(C)
NEXT J
Send to the device:       ";"
```

Typical data for this program might be: 10.58,0,–5.58,10.67,–5,–10.67

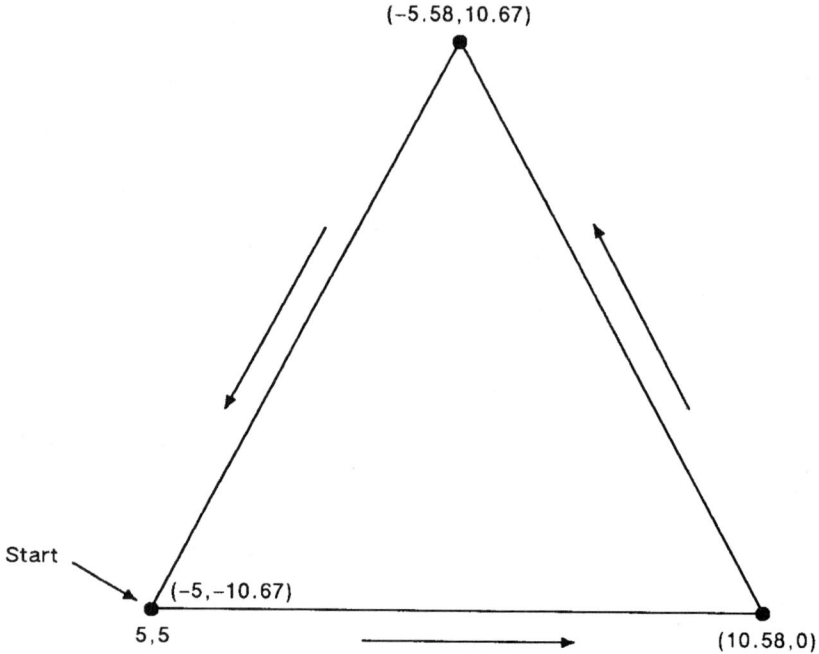

Figure 121. Triangle Drawn Using the PE (Polyline Encoded) Instruction

A PE instruction to draw this triangle, with numbers in brackets [] denoting ASCII characters, might be:

			Hexadecimal:
PE	: [197]	Select pen number 6 (191+6).	3A C5
	> [198]	7 fractional bits (2 decimal places, 191+7).	3E C6
	<	Pen up.	3C
	= [63][211][63][211]	Absolute move to (5,5).	3D 3F D3 3F D3
	[83][233][191]	Plot relative by (+10.58,+0).	53 E9 BF
	[84][213][107][233]	Plot relative by (−5.58,+10.67).	54 D5 6B E9
	[64][211][108][233]	Plot relative by (−5,−10.67).	40 D3 6C E9
	;	Terminate instruction.	3B

Related Instructions

LA	Line Attributes
LT	Line Type
PA	Plot Absolute
PD	Pen Down
PR	Plot Relative
PU	Pen Up
PW	Pen Width
SM	Symbol Mode

PG, Advance Full Page

Purpose

For devices with page advance capability: to terminate the plot being sent, to draw it, and to advance the page.

For devices without page advance capability: if the media has been plotted on, to perform the function of the NR (Not Ready) instruction (see page 227).

On PCL devices with HP-GL/2 capability, this instruction is ignored (see *Using PG in a PCL Dual-Context Environment* below).

Syntax

PG *n[;]*
           or
PG *[;]*

The PG instruction, with or without parameters, *must* be terminated with a semicolon unless it is immediately followed by the RP (Replot) instruction (see page 279).

Parameter	Format	Functional Range	Parameter Default
n	clamped integer	−32 768 to 32 767	no parameter

Group

This instruction is in the Configuration and Status Group.

Use

Some devices require an end-of-file marker to designate the end of incoming data. The PG instruction is a common marker for HP-GL/2 devices (the RP instruction is another). When the PG instruction is received, the plot is drawn and the page is ejected. If the plotter expects but does not receive the PG instruction, it will wait for user interaction through the control panel before it draws the plot.

PG moves the current pen location to the lower-left corner of the hard-clip limits on the next page, raises the pen, and retains the current plotting mode (relative or absolute). PG does not affect P1 and P2 values or plot rotation.

- **No parameter:** Advances the page only if you have plotted on the current page. This is the recommended method of using the PG instruction.

- **n:** Advances the page whether or not you have plotted on the media.

The current plot remains stored after a page eject until an instruction is received that marks the page or adds edges in the polygon buffer.

PG clears the current pattern residue and terminates any continuous vector sequence (see the LA and LT instructions).

Using PG in a Dual-Context Environment

PG is ignored in **PCL**. A page eject is possible but can only be accomplished by the form feed (**FF**) control character. A form feed causes an unconditional page eject and advances the current active position to the same horizontal position at the top of the next form (top margin). Note that the HP-GL/2 pen position is not affected by a form feed; it occupies the same position on the next page. A PCL reset, page length, page size, orientation, or input cassette control instruction causes a conditional page eject. When a page is ejected, the PCL cursor is set to the "home position" (at the left and top margin) on the new page. A page eject caused by a PCL command does not effect the HP-GL/2 cursor position.

This HP-GL/2 instruction is ignored by the device since it could cause undesirable results when importing plots. A page eject can be accomplished only from the PCL printer language mode.

In an **HP RTL** dual-context environment, an **ESCE** (Reset) command performs the PG function; a form feed (**FF**) character is ignored.

Related Instructions

BP	Begin Plot
PS	Plot Size
RP	Replot

PM, Polygon Mode

Purpose

To enter polygon mode for defining shapes, such as block letters or any unique area, and exits for subsequent filling or edging. Fill polygons using the FP (Fill Polygon) instruction or outline them using the EP (Edge Polygon) instruction.

Syntax

PM *polygon_definition [;]*
      or
PM *[;]*

Parameter	Format	Functional Range	Parameter Default
polygon_definition	clamped integer	0, 1, and 2	0

Group

This instruction is in the Polygon Group.

Use

In polygon mode, you define the area of the polygon(s) using graphics instructions. These instructions (and associated X,Y coordinates) are stored in the polygon buffer. The polygon is not drawn until you exit polygon mode and fill or outline the area.

- **No parameter:** Clears the polygon buffer and enters polygon mode. Equivalent to "PM0".

- **polygon_definition:** Defines polygon mode status as follows.

    0   Clears the polygon buffer and enters polygon mode.

    1   Closes the current polygon (or subpolygon) with a pen-up edge, and remains in polygon mode; all instructions sent following PM1 but before a PM2 (or the next PM1) are stored as one subpolygon.

    2   Closes current polygon (or subpolygon) and exits polygon mode.

The following paragraphs explain how to use each parameter. The order in which you use these instructions is very important. "PM1" and "PM2" are ignored if not preceded by "PM0".

"PM0" or "PM"

Use *"PM0"* to clear the polygon buffer and enter polygon mode. While in polygon mode, only certain instructions are allowed, as follows:

AA   Arc Absolute
AR   Arc Relative
AT   Absolute Arc Three Point

BP	Begin Plot (this instruction automatically closes polygon mode and initializes the device)
BR	Bezier Relative
BZ	Bezier Absolute
CI	Circle
CO	Comment
DF	Default Values (this instruction automatically closes polygon mode and applies defaults to the device)
IN	Initialize (this instruction automatically closes polygon mode and initializes the device)
PA	Plot Absolute
PD	Pen Down
PE	Polyline Encoded
PM1/PM2	Polygon Mode
PR	Plot Relative
PU	Pen Up
RT	Relative Arc Three Point

The polygon buffer stores the lines (vectors) that define your polygon. These vectors are accessed later when you exit polygon mode and fill or edge the polygon.

Note: While in polygon mode, the CI instruction is interpreted differently than other graphics instructions. Refer to *Drawing Circles in Polygon Mode* on page 52 for more details. When you use the PE instruction in polygon mode, you cannot change pens; any new pen selection is ignored.

When you define a polygon, the pen location before the "PM0" instruction is the first point (vertex) of the polygon, and the first point stored in the polygon buffer. For example, if you execute the instructions "PA0,1750;PM0", the absolute coordinates (0,1750) specify the first point of your polygon. Each subsequent pair of coordinates defines a point, or vertex, of the polygon.

You can define points with the pen up or down. However, the EP instruction only draws between points that are defined when the pen is down. On the other hand, the FP instruction fills the area(s) between all vertices, regardless of whether the pen is up or down when the vertices are defined.

It is good programming practice to "close" the polygon before exiting polygon mode. Closing a polygon means adding the final vertex that defines a continuous shape; the last coordinates or increments represent the same location as the first. If you have not closed the polygon, executing "PM1" or "PM2" forces closure by adding a point to close the polygon.

You can also use the IN (Initialize) or DF (Default Values) instructions while in polygon mode. Both instructions exit polygon mode, clear the polygon buffer, and begin executing subsequent instructions immediately. Output instructions can also be used; they are not stored in the polygon buffer, but are executed immediately. You must exit polygon mode to execute other HP-GL/2 graphics instructions.

"PM1"

Use "PM1" to close the current polygon (or subpolygon) and remain in polygon mode; the device adds a closure point if necessary. When you use "PM1", the point after "PM1" becomes the first point of the next subpolygon. This move is *not* used as a boundary when filling a polygon with FP. When drawing the polygon, the pen always moves to this point in the up position, regardless of the current pen status. Each subsequent coordinate pair after "PM1" defines a point of the subpolygon.

With the exception of the first chord in AA, AR, AT, and RT, this point is treated as a pen-up move regardless of the current pen state. All subsequent points become vertices of the subpolygon until "PM1" or "PM2". "PM1" adds a point to implicitly close a polygon that has not already been explicitly closed.

"PM2"

Use "PM2" to close the current polygon (or subpolygon) and exit polygon mode. Remember, if you have not closed your polygon, executing "PM2" adds a point to close the polygon. Refer to *"Lost" Mode* on page 23 for considerations that apply when the pen location becomes "lost".

After you exit polygon mode, the EP (Edge Polygon) or FP (Fill Polygon) instructions draw the polygon. Although points may be defined with the pen up or down, EP draws only between points defined with the pen down, while FP fills the areas between all defined points.

A polygon with fewer than three points is not drawn; it is not filled by FP nor edged by EP. This syntactical incompleteness is different from when a polygon is correctly specified but geometrically degenerate (for example, a polygon limited to coincident points is rendered as a dot, and one limited to collinear points is rendered as a line).

A point added by implicit closure counts as one of the three points. If a complex polygon contains a dot (a zero-dimension subpolygon), enough points must be specified (for example, by "PR0,0;") to have three upon closure.

Using PM in a Dual-Context Environment

ESCE is also recognized in polygon mode. It causes the device to exit polygon mode, clear the polygon buffer, exit HP-GL/2 mode, and eject a page. Sending an **ESCE** while in polygon mode is not recommended, but it performs an important function (allowing you to recover from a previous job that left the device in polygon mode).

Example

The following example draws the surface area of a 3-prong electrical receptacle as a series of subpolygons, then fills and edges it using the FP and EP instructions, respectively.

PA	2000,2000;	Specify absolute plotting and move to (2000,2000).
PM	0;	Enter polygon mode.
PD	3000,2000, 3000,3000;	Store a Pen Down instruction, and store locations (3000,2000) and (3000,3000).
PD	2000,3000, 2000,2000;	Store two more pen-down locations, (2000,3000) and (2000,2000).
PM	1;	Close the first polygon (the outer square).
PD	2080,2160, 2480,2160, 2480,2340, 2080,2340, 2080,2160;	Store 5 pen-down locations for a subpolygon.
PM	1;	Close the subpolygon (the lower rectangle).
PD	2080,2660, 2480,2660, 2480,2840, 2080,2840, 2080,2660;	Store pen-down locations for another subpolygon.
PM	1;	Close the second subpolygon (the upper rectangle).
PD	2920,2340, 2920,2660, 2720,2660;	Begin a third subpolygon that draws the ground plug portion of the receptacle.
AA	2720,2500,180;	Store a 180˚ arc that goes from (2720,2660) to (2720,2500).
PD	2920,2340;	Complete the ground-plug subpolygon.
PM	2;	Close the subpolygon and exit polygon mode.

FP	;	Fill (even/odd) the polygon.
EP	;	Then edge the polygon and subpolygons currently stored in the buffer.

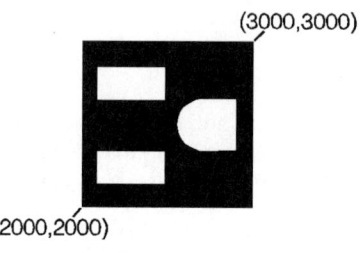

(3000,3000)

(2000,2000)

Figure 122. Example that Uses Polygon Mode

Related Instructions

EP	Edge Polygon
FP	Fill Polygon

Possible Error Conditions

Error Condition	Error Number	Printer or Plotter Response
Invalid instruction used in polygon mode	1	Ignores invalid instruction
Parameter out of range	3	Ignores instruction
Buffer overflow	7	Ignores overflowing points

PP, Pixel Placement

Purpose

To control how pixels are placed on a grid during polygon fills on raster devices.

Syntax

PP *mode[;]*
     or
PP *[;]*

Parameter	Format	Functional Range	Parameter Default
mode	clamped integer	0 or 1	0

Group

This instruction is in the Advanced Drawing Extension.

Use

- **No parameter**: Places pixels centered at grid intersections. Same as "PP0".

- **mode**: Specifies the placement mode.

    0   Grid intersection (the default). Places pixels centered at grid intersections.

    1   Grid centered. Places pixels inside the boxes created by grid intersections.

Microsoft© Windows™ fills polygons based on pixels placed between grid intersections. HP-GL/2 normally fills polygons with pixels placed at grid intersections (see below). Unwanted results occur when a polygon with a grid intersection-based fill is combined with ROPs (see the MC instruction on page 220). For example, two squares laid down side by side using an exclusive-OR logical operation will result in a blank line between them. Further details are in *Placing Pixels* on page 93.

Figure 123 shows the differences between filling a 2x2 rectangle with pixels placed at grid intersections (mode 0) and non-grid intersections (mode 1).

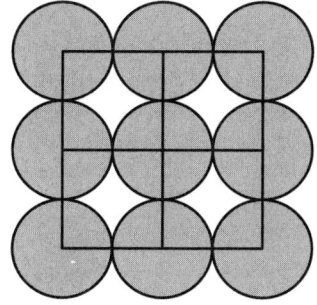
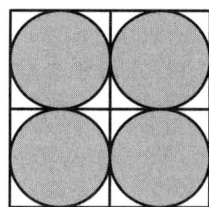

Figure 123. Pixel Placement

"PP1" decreases by one pixel the height and the width of the trapezoids formed by decomposition. "PP0" renders portions that are zero height or width as lines, and portions that are both zero length and width as dots. "PP1" does not render portions that are zero height or width.

Note that pixel placement is applied after the soft-clip window is established, so pixels may be subject to clipping.

Possible Error Conditions

Error Condition	Error Number	Printer or Plotter Response
Any *mode* value other than 0 or 1	3	Ignores instruction

PR, Plot Relative

Purpose

To establish relative plotting and move the pen to specified points, with each move relative to the current pen location.

Syntax

PR *X,Y[,...;]*
or
PR *[;]*

Parameter	Format	Functional Range	Parameter Default
X,Y increments	current units	*device-dependent* (at least -2^{23} to $2^{23} - 1$)	no default

Group

This instruction is in the Vector Group.

Use

The device interprets the parameters as follows:

- **No parameters:** Defaults to relative plotting mode for subsequent instructions.

- **X, Y increments:** Specify incremental moves relative to the current pen location. When you include more than one relative coordinate pair, the pen moves to each point in the order given (relative to the previous point), using the current pen up/down status.

  The carriage-return point (see page 66) is moved to the last X,Y.

If the pen is up, PR moves the pen to the point; if the pen is down, PR draws a line to the point. Lines are drawn using the current line width, type, and attributes.

When you use the SM (Symbol Mode) instruction, PR draws the specified symbol at each X,Y coordinate. When you use the PM (Polygon Mode) instruction, the X,Y coordinates enter the polygon buffer (and are used when the polygon is edged or filled).

Coordinates are interpreted in current units: as user-units when scaling is on; as plotter-units when scaling is off.

Related Instructions

LA	Line Attributes
LT	Line Type
PA	Plot Absolute
PD	Pen Down
PE	Polyline Encoded
PW	Pen Width
SM	Symbol Mode

Example

PA	10,10;	Move to absolute position (10,10).
PD	;	Put the pen down.
PR	2500,0, –2500,1500, 0,–1500;	Specify relative plotting and draw lines beginning at (10,10) and then moving the relative coordinate distances indicated.

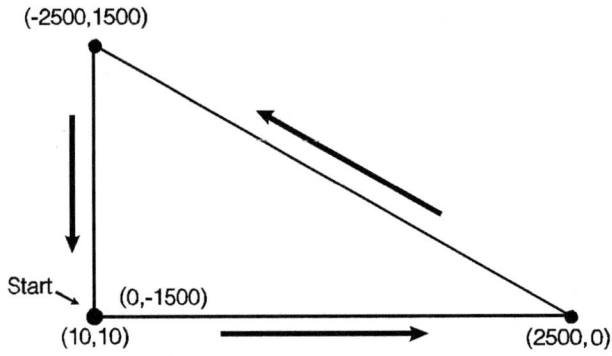

Figure 124. Plotting Using Relative Coordinates

Possible Error Conditions

Error Condition	Error Number	Printer or Plotter Response
An odd number of coordinates (an X coordinate without a corresponding Y coordinate)	2	Ignores the last unmatched coordinate

PS, Plot Size

Purpose

To set the hard-clip limits to a given size. Use PS to simplify long-axis plotting or to minimize paper waste when drawing small plots. This is especially useful for plotters with roll-feed media. When used, this instruction must appear in the picture header information (see page 78).

Syntax

PS *length[,width][;]*
     or
PS *[;]*

Parameter	Format	Functional Range	Parameter Default
length	integer	*device-dependent*	hard-clip limits*
width	integer	*device-dependent*	hard-clip limits*

*   The default *length* and *width* for single-sheet media is the hard-clip limits; for roll-feed media the default *length* is approximately 1.5 times the media width.

Group

This instruction is in the Technical Graphics Extension.

Use

Send PS immediately *after* the BP (Begin Plot) or IN (Initialize) instruction and *before* any drawing instructions. IN defaults PS if the device is in picture header state (see page 78), that is no marks have been made on the media; DF (Default Values) does not default PS. Note that the entire plot must be done within the scope of a single PS instruction; you cannot change the plot size in the middle of a plot.

- **No parameters:** Defaults the plot length and width to the hard-clip limits (the maximum printable area).

- **length:** Establishes a new length, in plotter-units, of the hard-clip limits. The *length* always corresponds to the direction of the plot frame advance. Refer to the documentation for your device or HP-GL/2 option for the maximum length of a single plot. If the *length* is less than or equal to 0, the device ignores the instruction.

- **width:** Establishes the new width, in plotter-units, of the hard-clip limits. The *width* is always the horizontal direction. If the *width* is less than or equal to 0, the device ignores the instruction.

If you specify a plot size larger than your media's maximum plotting area, your plot size is clamped to the hard-clip limits. Figure 125 indicates how PS orients the default coordinate system according to the *length* and *width* after clamping. The default origin defines the lower-left corner of the hard-clip limits and is always located on the side of the plot frame opposite the next plot frame.

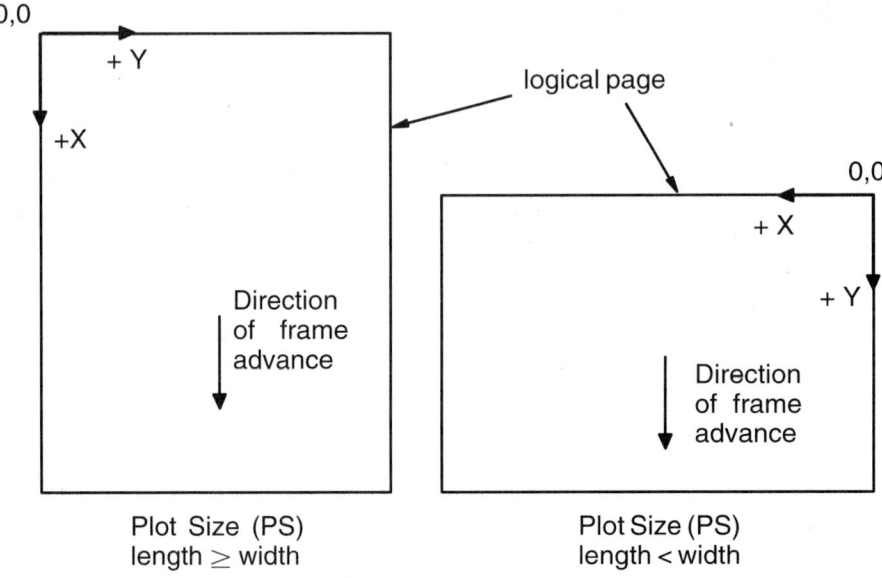

Figure 125. How Plot Size Affects the Coordinate System

PS defaults P1 and P2 to the lower-left and upper-right corners of the hard-clip limits, defaults the size of the user-defined window and the location of the anchor corner, and clears the polygon buffer. Any previous rotation (RO) is then added to the default X-axis orientation. Current scaling is applied to the new physical area. The device also updates the current pen location to the lower-left corner of the new plotting area.

If an RO (Rotate Coordinate System) instruction (see page 275) is sent after PS, the direction of the X-axis changes. The implementation of RO is relative to the autorotated position. PS sent after RO does not change the RO rotation, but does update the X-axis to the new longer side.

The PG (Advance Full Page) instruction will advance the media by the distance of the *length* parameter plus the necessary white space between plots. The following lists some standard paper sizes and equivalent PS parameters.

Measurement	Standard Paper Sizes	Equivalent PS Parameters*	
English	8.5 x 11 inches (A-size)	PS	8900,7350;
	11 x 17 inches (B-size)	PS	15000,9850;
	17 x 22 inches (C-size)	PS	21050,15000;
	22 x 34 inches (D-size)	PS	32300,21050;
Metric	210 x 297 mm. (A4-size)	PS	9600,7100;
	297 x 420 mm. (A3-size)	PS	14550,10600;
	420 x 594 mm. (A2-size)	PS	22450,14550;
	594 x 840 mm. (A1-size)	PS	31400,22450;

* These plot sizes are based on 16-mm margins on three sides of the media, the fourth margin being 40-mm. These values are also based on loading C-sized media horizontally in the device, with all other media being loaded vertically. Refer to the *User's Guide* for your device for instructions on loading media.

When combining the PS (Plot Size) and SC (Scale) instructions and accurate scaling is essential, note the following:

If you specify a plot size larger than your media's maximum plotting area, your plot size will be reduced to the hard-clip limits and your user-units will be smaller than you intended. To correct this, add an IP (Input P1 and P2) instruction so that the P1/P2 area is equal to the intended size of your PS instruction (IP0,0,*PSlength,PSwidth*). This moves P2 off the page, but guarantees accurate scaling. Place the IP instruction between the PS and SC instructions.

Note that devices that support the PS instruction have their origin as shown in Figure 125; other devices have their origin and orientation as shown in Figure 126.

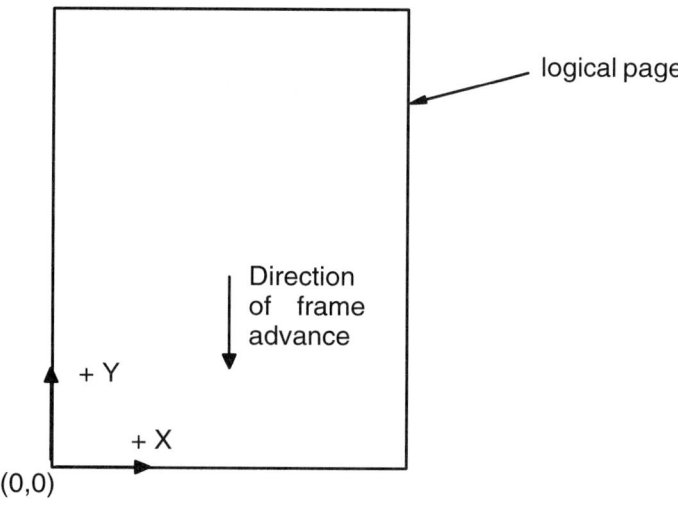

Figure 126. Origin and Orientation for Other Devices

Using PS in a PCL Dual-Context Environment

PS is ignored when HP-GL/2 is entered by **ESC**%#B with 0 or a positive value; the plot size is set by the PCL picture frame.

Related Instructions

FR   Frame Advance
OH   Output Hard-Clip Limits
PG   Advance Full Page

Possible Error Conditions

Error Condition	Error Number	Printer or Plotter Response
Length or *width* ≤ 0	3	Ignores instruction
Instruction used outside picture header state (see page 78)	1	Ignores instruction

PU, Pen Up

Purpose

To move to subsequent points without drawing. Use PU to move to another location without drawing a connecting line.

Syntax

PU *X,Y[,...;]*
    or
PU *[;]*

Parameter	Format	Functional Range	Parameter Default
X,Y coordinates or *increments*	current units	*device-dependent* (at least -2^{23} to $2^{23} - 1$)	no default

Group

This instruction is in the Vector Group.

Use

The PU instruction emulates a pen plotter which must raise the pen to prevent drawing stray lines on the page.

- **No parameters:** Prevents drawing subsequent graphics instructions (unless the instruction contains an automatic pen down).

- **X,Y coordinates** or **increments:** Move to the point(s) specified. You can specify as many X,Y coordinate pairs as you want. When you include more than one coordinate pair, the device moves to each point in the order given.

  The carriage-return point (see page 66) is moved to the last X,Y.

When you use the SM (Symbol Mode) instruction, PU draws the specified symbol at each X,Y coordinate.

When you use the PM (Polygon Mode) instruction, the X,Y coordinates enter the polygon buffer (for use when the polygon is edged or filled).

Coordinates are interpreted in current units: as user-units when scaling is on; as plotter-units when scaling is off. Whether the PU instruction uses absolute coordinates or relative coordinates (increments) depends on the most recently executed PA or PR instruction. If you have not issued a PA or PR instruction, absolute plotting (PA) is used.

Note that "PD;PU;" leaves a dot.

Related Instructions

PA   Plot Absolute
PD   Pen Down
PE   Polyline Encoded
PR   Plot Relative
SM   Symbol Mode

Possible Error Conditions

Error Condition	Error Number	Printer or Plotter Response
An odd number of coordinates (an X coordinate without a corresponding Y coordinate)	2	Ignores the last unmatched coordinate

HP-GL/2
INSTRUCTIONS

PW, Pen Width

Purpose

To specify a new width for the logical pen. Subsequent lines are drawn in this new width. Use PW to vary your lines and enhance your drawings. Pen width can be specified as a fixed value or relative to the distance between P1 and P2. The pen width units are selected using the WU instruction (the default is metric—millimeters).

Syntax

PW *width[,pen][;]*
　　　or
PW *[;]*

Parameter	Format	Functional Range	Parameter Default
width	clamped real	*device-dependent**	dependent**
pen	integer	*device-dependent*	all pens

*　Normally 0 to 32 767, but at least 16 384 plotter-units (409.6 mm).

**　Dependent on the mode set by the WU (Pen Width Unit Selection) instruction: if mode is metric, default width is 0.35 mm; if mode is relative, default width is 0.1% of the diagonal distance from P1 to P2.

Group

This instruction is in the Line and Fill Attributes Group.

Use

You may change the pen width as often as you like, without sending another SP instruction. If the pen is down when you change the width, the new width takes effect at the next line. *If you use WU to change the type of units used for the width parameter (metric or relative), send the WU instruction before PW.*

- **No parameters:** Defaults the pen line width according to the current units set by WU: 0.35 mm if metric; 0.1% of the diagonal distance from P1 to P2 if relative.

- **width:** Specifies the line width. When the parameter is zero or is thinner than the thinnest supported width, the device assumes the thinnest line width (1 dot wide). When it is greater than the device's maximum, the maximum is used.

- **pen:** Specifies the pen number to which the new width applies. If the pen parameter is not specified, the device applies the width to all pens. Specifying pen numbers less than 0 or greater than the number of pens available causes the device to ignore the instruction.

Note: Pen width does not set the width of lines for drawing labels (unless the stroke weight value is set to 9999 [Stick/Arc fonts only]). The width of character lines is determined by the stroke weight attribute of the AD (Alternate Font Definition) or SD (Standard Font Definition) instructions.

Vectors are drawn centered on coordinates, but any portion of a line width that extends beyond the window is clipped.

PW clears the current pattern residue and terminates any continuous vector sequence (see the LA and LT instructions).

A PW instruction remains in effect until another PW instruction or a WU instruction is executed. PW is not defaulted by the DF (Default Values) instruction.

Using PW in a PCL Dual-Context Environment

Metric widths are scaled by the ratio of the size of the PCL picture frame to the HP-GL/2 plot size. For example, if HP-GL/2 plot size is twice as large as the PCL picture frame, "WUPW.3" sets the vector width to 0.15 mm.

Example

PA	3500,2500;	Specify absolute plotting and move the pen to (3500,2500).
PW	1.5;	Select a pen width of 1.5 mm.
PD	4500,2800, 4500,1800, 3500,1500, 3500,2500;	Set the pen down and draw a line from the current position to (4500,2800), then (4500,1800), next to (3500,1500), and then to (3500,2500).
PW	.8;	Set the pen width to 0.8 mm.
PD	2300,2900, 2300,1900, 3500,1500;	Place the pen down and print a line to (2300,2900), then to (2300,1900), and finally to (3500,1500).
PW	.5;	Set the pen width to 0.5 mm.
PU	2300,2900;	Lift the pen, and move to (2300,2900).
PD	3300,3200, 4500,2800;	Set the pen down and draw a line to (3300,3200) and then another line to (4500,2800).
PW	.25;	Set the pen width to 0.25 mm.
PU	4500,1800;	Lift the pen, and move to (4500,1800).
PD	3500,2100;	Set the pen down and print a line to (3500,2100).

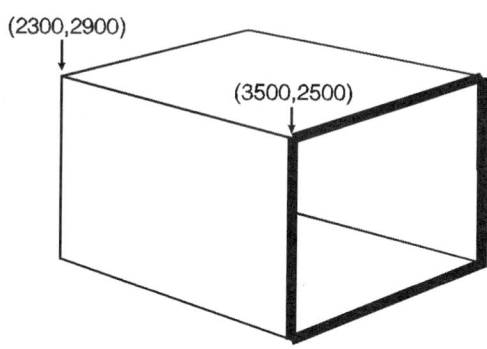

(2300,2900)

(3500,2500)

Figure 127. Pen Width

Related Instructions

SP   Select Pen
SV   Screened Vectors
WU   Pen Width Unit Selection

QL, Quality Level

Purpose

To set "best", "normal" or "draft" mode for your output. Use QL on raster devices to optimize your usage of toner or ink when draft quality is sufficient.

Syntax

QL *quality_level [;]*
> or

QL *[;]*

Parameter	Format	Functional Range	Parameter Default
quality_level	clamped integer	0 to 100	*device-dependent*

Group

This instruction is in the Technical Graphics Extension.

Use

The entire plot must be done with one quality level setting. You cannot change quality levels in the picture body state.

- **No parameter:** Device-dependent. Each device makes different use of this instruction depending on the hardware technology and firmware implementation. The result will be seen in different speed/quality trade-offs. For example, a pen plotter primarily varies pen speed, but may vary acceleration as well. An electrostatic plotter might vary paper speed, resolution, or rasterization algorithms. Refer to the manual for your product or HP-GL/2 option for the number of quality levels and the effects the various levels have on the output.

- **quality_level:** Specifies the level of quality for your plot from 0 (draft quality) to 100 (presentation, best, or final quality). The number of quality levels supported is device-dependent. When quality level is 0 (draft), a plotter might not implement MC (Merge Control) or might limit it to vectors only.

A device with only one quality level will ignore this instruction. A device with two or more levels will support at least 0 and 100 and will map any other value to one of the supported values. Mapping to another value may occur either through rounding to the nearest supported value (for example, a device with only two levels would treat "QL60;" the same as "QL100;"), or through applying a threshold (for example, anything over 80 is mapped to 100).

For a pen plotter, QL is primarily a speed control. The pen speed set by the VS (Velocity Select) instruction or from the device's control panel is the maximum speed, which corresponds to "QL0;". If the pen speed is not set by VS or from the control panel, the plotter determines the maximum speed based on its knowledge of the media type (from the MT instruction) and pen type (from the carousel). Minimum speed, corresponding to "QL100;", is linearly interpolated between the media and pen types. The default level for pen plotters is usually "QL0;" (maximum speed).

Possible Error Conditions

Error Condition	Error Number	Printer or Plotter Response
Instruction used outside picture header state (see page 78)	1	Ignores instruction

RA, Fill Rectangle Absolute

Purpose

To define and fill a rectangle using absolute coordinates. Use RA to fill rectangular shapes in drawings. (To outline a rectangle using absolute coordinates, use the EA instruction.)

Syntax

RA *X,Y[;]*

Parameter	Format	Functional Range	Parameter Default
X,Y coordinates	current units	*device-dependent* (at least -2^{23} to $2^{23} - 1$)	no default

Group

This instruction is in the Polygon Group.

Use

The RA instruction defines and fills a rectangle using the current pen, the current line and fill types, and absolute X,Y coordinates. The RA instruction includes an automatic pen down. When the instruction operation is complete, the original pen location and up/down status are restored.

- **X,Y coordinates:** Specify the corner of the rectangle that is diagonally opposite from the current pen location (the starting point of the rectangle). Coordinates are interpreted in current units: as user-units when scaling is on; as plotter-units when scaling is off.

Figure 128. Fill Rectangle Absolute

Note: Figure 128 shows the current pen location in the lower-left corner and the instruction's X,Y coordinates in the upper-right corner. Depending on the X,Y coordinates used, these points can be in any two diagonally opposite corners.

The only difference between the RA instruction and the EA (Edge Rectangle Absolute) instruction is that the RA instruction produces a filled rectangle, and EA, an outlined one.

The RA instruction clears the polygon buffer and then uses it to define the rectangle before drawing. Refer to *Using the Polygon Buffer* on page 45.

A dot is drawn if X,Y are coincident with the current position. A line is drawn if the X or Y coordinate equals the corresponding coordinate of the current position; for some hatch or raster-filled patterns, the line may fall in white spaces of the fill and not be drawn.

Related Instructions

EA	Edge Rectangle Absolute
EP	Edge Polygon
ER	Edge Rectangle Relative
FP	Fill Polygon
FT	Fill Type
LT	Line Type
RF	Raster Fill Definition
RR	Fill Rectangle Relative

Example

The following example uses RA with three different fill types to create rectangles such as those you might use in a bar chart. The rectangles in the right bar are edged using the EA instruction. (For more information about fill types, refer to the FT instruction description on page 183.)

PA	400,400;	Enter absolute plotting mode and move to (400,400).
RA	800,1200;	Draw a rectangle with (400,400) as the lower-left corner and (800,1200) as the upper-right corner.
PA	400,1200;	Move the pen to (400,1200).
FT	3,50;	Select fill type 3 (parallel lines) with a 50 plotter-units space between lines.
RA	800,1600;	Draw a rectangle with (400,1200) as the lower-left corner and (800,1600) as the upper-right corner.
PA	400,1600;	Move to (400,1600).
FT	4;	Specify fill type 4 (cross-hatching).
RA	800,2000;	Draw a rectangle with a lower-left corner of (400,1600) and an upper-right corner of (800,2000).
PA	1200,400;	Move to location (1200,400).
FT	;	Select the default fill type (solid black).
RA	1600,1200;	Fill and edge a rectangle using (1200,400) as the lower-left corner
EA	1600,1200;	and (1600,1200) as the upper-right corner.
PA	1200,1200;	Move to absolute position (1200,1200).
FT	3,50;	Select fill type 3, with a 50 plotter-units distance between each line.
RA	1600,1600;	Draw a rectangle with (1200,1200) as the lower-left corner and (1600,1600) as the upper-right.
EA	1600,1600;	Using the default line type, edge the rectangle just drawn.
PA	1200,1600;	Move to (1200,1600).
FT	4;	Select the cross-hatch pattern fill type.

| RA | 1600,2000; | Draw and edge a rectangle with the current pen location as one |
| EA | 1600,2000; | corner and (1600,2000) as the opposite corner. |

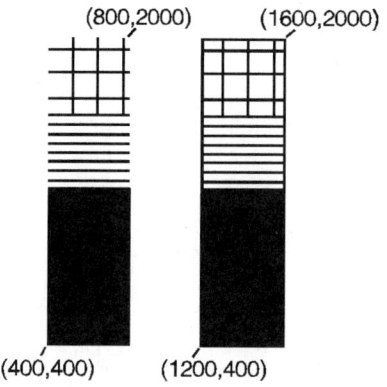

Figure 129. Filling a Rectangle Specified by Absolute Coordinates

Possible Error Conditions

Error Condition	Error Number	Plotter Response
Parameter(s) would make the device enter "lost" mode	3	The instruction is ignored

RF, Raster Fill Definition

Purpose

To define a rectangular pattern that may be used as area fill and for screened vectors (see the SV instruction). Use RF to create your own fill types and screen patterns.

Syntax

RF *index,width,height,pen_number[,...pen_number][;]*
    or
RF *index[;]*
    or
RF *[;]*

Parameter	Format	Functional Range	Parameter Default
index	clamped integer	*device-dependent*	1 (solid)
width	clamped integer	*device-dependent**	no default
height	clamped integer	*device-dependent**	no default
pen_number	integer	*device-dependent***	no default

*   The range is between 1 and a positive power of 2; at least the values 8, 16, 32, and 64 are supported.

**   See the NP (Number of Pens) instruction on page 225.

Group

This instruction is in the Line and Fill Attributes Group.

Use

The RF instruction does not *select* a fill type; use the FT (Fill Type) instruction with a type parameter of 11 and the corresponding raster fill *index* number for the second parameter (for example, "FT11,3" for an *index* number of 3).

- **No parameters:** Defaults all raster fill patterns to solid fill.

- **index:** Specifies the index number of the pattern being defined. At least eight patterns can exist concurrently.

  When you send RF with an index parameter only ("RF*index*;"), the corresponding pattern is defaulted to solid fill.

- **width, height:** Specify the width and height (in pixels) of the pattern being defined. A pixel is equal to the size of one dot at the current device resolution.

- **pen_number:** Represents a pixel in the pattern being defined and indicates its color.

The *pen_number* parameters define pixels left to right, top to bottom. Each pixel takes on the color of the specified pen (negative numbers are treated as zero). The total number of *pen_number* parameters should be equal to the *width* times the *height* parameters. For example, to define a pattern that is 8 x 16 pixels, you need 128 *pen_number* parameters. If you do not include enough *pen_number* parameters, the rest of the pixels are assumed to be white (zero). Patterns are printed in rows parallel to the plotter-unit X-axis.

The color palette current at the time of the fill, not at the time of the pattern definition, determines the pattern colors actually used (by FP, RA, RR, or WG). If a *pen_number* is larger than the palette in effect at the time of rendering, the modulo function is applied, as described for SP.

If the pattern associated with the particular *index* is defined multiple times during a single plot and all definitions are used to fill objects, the resulting patterns are device-dependent. (Devices using a direct bitmap may print the pattern defined when the object was filled, while devices using an intermediate data format may render all objects with the last pattern defined.)

A pattern defined only with the *pen_number* parameters 0 or 1 can be printed directly using the currently selected pen (see the FT instruction on page 183).

RF terminates the current vector path (see the LA instruction).

Related Instructions

AC	Anchor Corner
FT	Fill Type
SV	Screened Vectors

Example

PA	;	Specify absolute plotting.
PU	5,5;	Lift the pen and move to absolute position (5,5).
RF	2,8,4, 0,0,0,0,0,0,0,0, 0,0,0,1,1,0,0,0, 0,0,0,1,1,0,0,0, 0,0,0,0,0,0,0,0;	Define a raster fill pattern (index number 2) that is 8 dots wide by 4 dots high.
FT	11,2;	Select the user-defined pattern having an index number of 2.
RR	4000,800;	Fill a rectangle with the fill pattern just specified, with a lower-left corner of (5,5) and an upper-right corner 4000 plotter-units to the right and 800 plotter-units up.
EP	;	Edge the outline of the rectangle.

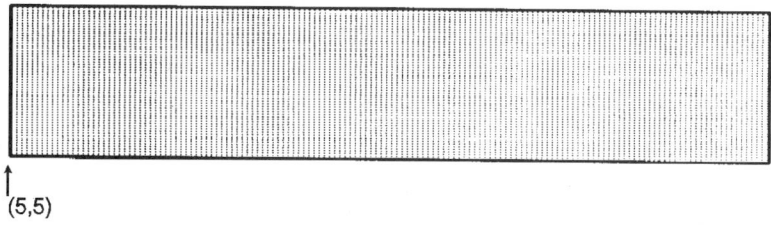

(5,5)

Figure 130. Raster Fill Definition

Possible Error Conditions

Error Condition	Error Number	Printer or Plotter Response
Index out of range	3	Ignores instruction

RO, Rotate Coordinate System

Purpose

To rotate the device's coordinate system relative to the default HP-GL/2 coordinate system, in the following increments of rotation: 90°, 180°, and 270°. Use RO to orient your drawing vertically or horizontally, or to reverse the orientation.

Syntax

RO *angle[;]*
    or
RO *[;]*

Parameter	Format	Functional Range	Parameter Default
angle	clamped integer	0°, 90°, 180°, or 270°	0°

Group

This instruction is in the Configuration and Status Group.

Use

The device interprets the instruction parameters as follows:

- **No parameter:** Defaults the orientation of the coordinate system to 0°. Equivalent to "RO0". This is the same as PCL's current orientation in PCL devices; for other devices, see the description of the PS (Plot Size) instruction on page 259.

- **angle:** Specifies the degree of rotation:

    0   Sets the orientation to horizontal (+X direction).

    90   Rotates and shifts the coordinate system 90° in a positive angle of rotation from the horizontal (+X direction).

    180 Rotates and shifts the coordinate system 180° in a positive angle of rotation from the horizontal (+X direction).

    270 Rotates and shifts the coordinate system 270° in a positive angle of rotation from the horizontal (+X direction).

The carriage-return point is updated to the current pen location.

A *positive angle* of rotation is in the direction of the +X-axis to the +Y-axis as shown in Figure 27 on page 44). (A *negative angle* of rotation is not allowed in the RO instruction.)

The relationship of the X-axis to Y-axis can change as a result of the scaling point or scaling factor changes, thus changing the direction of a positive angle of rotation.

The physical location of the pen does not change when you rotate the coordinate system. The device updates the pen's X,Y coordinate location to reflect the new orientation.

The scaling points P1 and P2 rotate with the coordinate system. However, they maintain the same X,Y coordinate values as before the rotation. This means that P1 and P2 can be located outside of the hard-clip limits. Follow the "RO90" or "RO270" instructions with "IP;" or "IR;" to relocate points P1 and P2 to their default locations for that orientation.

Rotation is not cumulative; "RO90RO90;" rotates 90°, not 180°.

The RO instruction remains in effect until the rotation is changed by another RO instruction, or the device is initialized. Figure 131 shows the default orientation for HP-GL/2 printers and the result of rotating the orientation for PCL devices, without relocating P1 and P2.

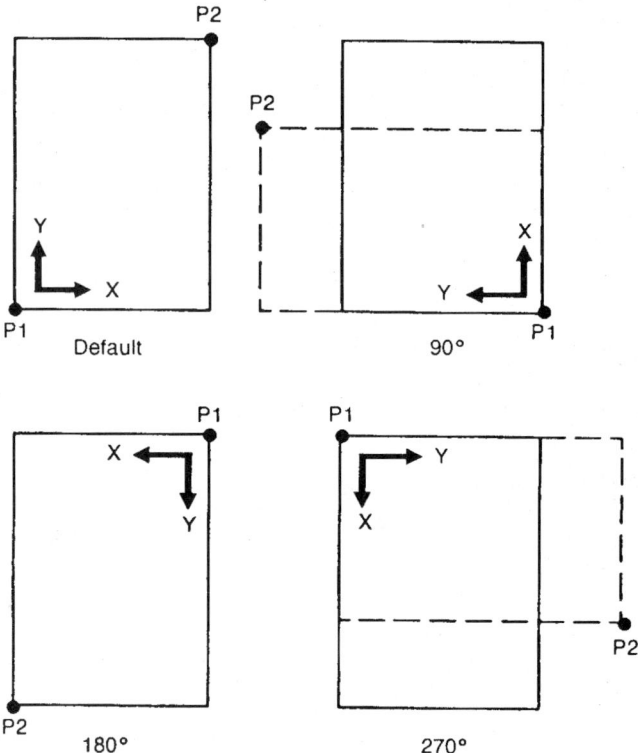

Figure 131. Using the RO Instruction without Using the IP Instruction

When the RO instruction is used, the soft-clip window, if defined, is also rotated, and any portion that is rotated outside of the picture frame is clipped to the picture frame boundaries. The soft-clip window can be set equal to the picture frame by issuing an "IW;" instruction (see Figure 132; the "PCL Picture Frame" is the hard-clip limits on non-PCL devices).

The RO instruction also rotates the contents of the polygon buffer, changes pen coordinates to reflect the new orientation (but does not affect the pen position), and terminates the current vector path (see the LA instruction).

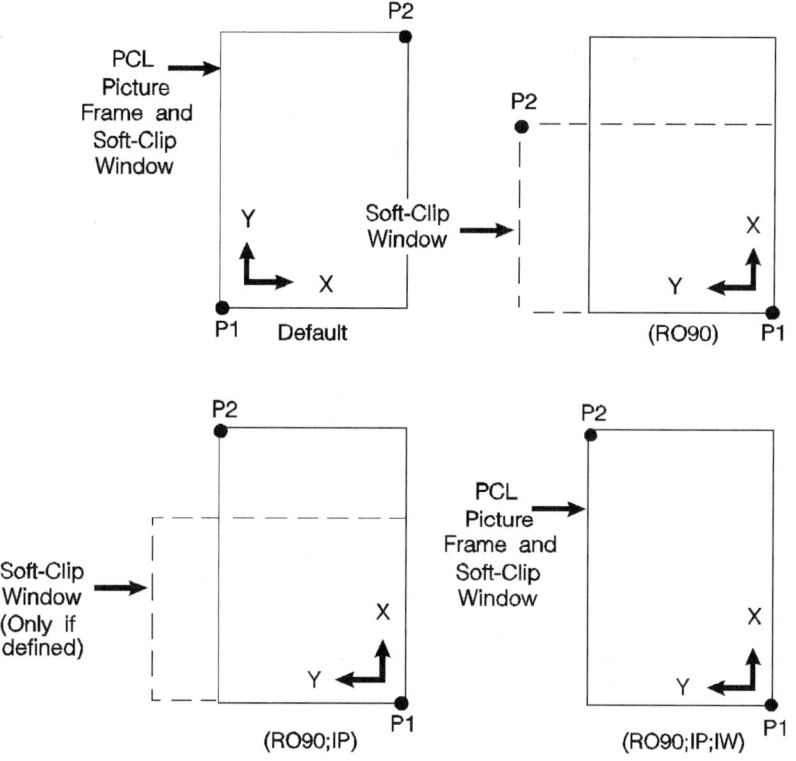

Figure 132. Using IP and IW after the RO Instruction

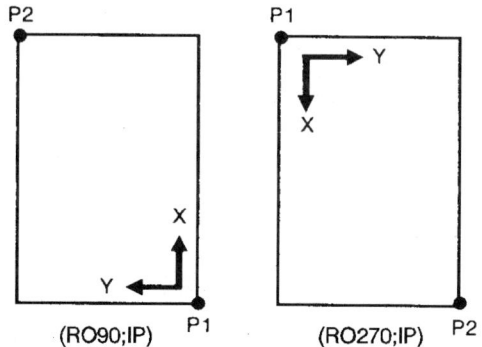

Figure 133. Using IP after the RO Instruction

Figure 133 shows the locations of P1 and P2 when you follow the rotation with the IP instruction.

When you set-up a soft-clip window (see the IW instruction), RO also rotates the window. If a portion of a window rotates outside the hard-clip limits, it is clipped. Note that "IP;" does not affect the window limits. Use "IW;" to reset the window to the size of the hard-clip limits.

Using RO in a PCL Dual-Context Environment

Rotations are relative to the default HP-GL/2 coordinate system, as defined for PCL. P1 or P2 may be rotated outside the current picture frame; they can be repositioned to the rotated lower-left and upper-right corners of the picture frame by issuing an "IP;" or an "IR;" instruction. The user-defined window is rotated, and any portion that is rotated outside the picture frame is clipped to the picture frame. The window can be set equal to the picture frame by an "IW;" instruction.

Related Instructions

IP	Input P1 and P2
IR	Input Relative P1 and P2
IW	Input Window

RP, Replot

Purpose

To draw multiple copies of plots. Your device must have an internal hard disk or designated buffer area to store the plot. This instruction is ignored on devices that cannot store the plot data.

Syntax

RP *n;*

   or

RP *;*

This instruction, with or without a parameter, must be terminated by a semicolon.

Parameter	Format	Functional Range	Parameter Default
n	clamped integer	−32 768 to 32 767	1

Group

This instruction is in the Configuration and Status Group.

Use

Use the RP instruction at the end of your plot, following the PG (Advance Full Page) instruction when you want more than one copy of a plot.

- **No parameter:** Assumes you want one additional copy.

- **n:** Specifies the number of additional copies required.

The device ignores the instruction when printing the current page would produce no marks on the media.

RP prints the page when the plot has not already been terminated by a PG instruction. If *n* is less than or equal to zero and there is no previous PG instruction, the device prints the page (it issues a "PG;" instruction) and otherwise ignores the instruction. If *n* is greater than the maximum value allowed for the device, the value is clamped to the maximum value.

RP clears the current pattern residue and terminates any continuous vector sequence (see the LA and LT instructions).

Using RP in a PCL Dual-Context Environment

This instruction is ignored in PCL; a page eject can only be accomplished from the PCL context by sending a form feed (**FF**) control character. To print more than one plot, use the NC (Number of Copies) instruction described on page 225.

Related Instructions

BP   Begin Plot
NC   Number of Copies
PG   Advance Full Page

RR, Fill Rectangle Relative

Purpose

To defines and fills a rectangle using relative coordinates. Use RR to fill rectangular shapes in drawings. (To outline a rectangle using relative coordinates, use the ER instruction.)

Syntax

RR *X,Y[;]*

Parameter	Format	Functional Range	Parameter Default
X,Y increments	current units	*device-dependent* (at least -2^{23} to $2^{23} - 1$)	no default

Group

This instruction is in the Polygon Group.

Use

The RR instruction defines and fills a rectangle using the current pen, the current line and fill types, and relative coordinates. The RR instruction includes an automatic pen down. After the instruction is executed, the original pen location and up/down status are restored.

- **X,Y increments:** Specify the corner of the rectangle that is diagonally opposite from the current pen location, which is the starting point of the rectangle. Coordinates are interpreted in current units: as user-units when scaling is on; as plotter-units when scaling is off.

Note: Figure 134 shows the current pen location in the lower-left corner and the instruction's X,Y increments in the upper-right corner. However, these points can be in any two opposite corners depending on the coordinates used.

Figure 134. Fill Rectangle Relative

The only difference between the RR instruction and the ER (Edge Relative Rectangle) instruction is that the RR instruction produces a filled rectangle, and ER, an outlined one.

The RR instruction clears the polygon buffer and then uses it to define the rectangle before drawing. A rectangle requires enough buffer space to hold five points.

A dot is drawn if both X and Y coordinates are zero. A line is drawn if one of the coordinates is zero.

Related Instructions

EA	Edge Rectangle Absolute
EP	Edge Polygon
ER	Edge Rectangle Relative
FP	Fill Polygon
RA	Fill Rectangle Absolute

Example

The following example uses RR with three different fill types (refer to the FT instruction description) to create rectangles such as those you might use in a bar chart. The rectangles in the right bar are edged using the ER instruction.

PA	400,400;	Specify absolute plotting and move to location (400,400).
RR	400,800;	Fill a rectangle with the default fill (black), with (400,400) as the lower-left corner and the upper-right corner 400 plotter-units to the right and 800 plotter-units up from there.
PR	0,800;	Enter the relative plotting mode and move 800 plotter-units in the Y direction.
FT	3,50;	Select fill type 3 (parallel lines).
RR	400,400;	Draw a rectangle using the current pen location as the lower-left corner; the upper-right corner is 400 plotter-units to the right and 400 plotter-units up from the lower-left corner.
PR	0,400;	Move 400 plotter-units up.
FT	4;	Select fill type 4 (cross-hatching).
RR	400,400;	Draw a rectangle using the current pen position as the lower-left corner and a point 400 plotter-units to the right and 400 plotter-units up as the upper-right corner.
PA	1200,400;	Move to absolute location (1200,400).
FT	;	Select the default fill type (solid black).
RR	400,800;	Draw and edge a rectangle that begins at the current pen position
ER	400,800;	and extends 400 plotter-units to the right, then 800 plotter-units up from there.
PR	0,800;	Move 800 plotter-units up from the current position.
FT	3,50;	Select fill type 3 (parallel lines), with 50 plotter-units between each line.
RR	400,400;	Draw and edge a rectangle using the current pen location as the
ER	400,400;	lower-left corner and a point 400 plotter-units up and 400 plotter-units to the right as the upper-right corner.
PR	0,400;	Move 400 plotter-units up from the current pen position.
FT	4;	Select fill type 4 (cross-hatching).
RR	400,400;	Draw and edge a rectangle using the current pen location as the
ER	400,400;	lower-left corner, the right corner being (400,400) relative plotter-units away.

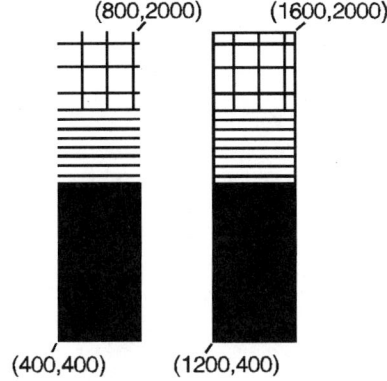

(800,2000)   (1600,2000)

(400,400)   (1200,400)

Figure 135. Filling Rectangles with Different Patterns Using Relative Coordinates

Possible Error Conditions

Error Condition	Error Number	Plotter Response
Parameter(s) would make the device enter "lost" mode	3	The instruction is ignored

RT, Relative Arc Three Point

Purpose

To draw an arc segment, using relative coordinates, from a starting point through an intermediate point to an end point. Use RT when you know these three points of an arc.

Syntax

RT $X_{incr\_inter}, Y_{incr\_inter}, X_{incr\_end}, Y_{incr\_end}[,chord\_angle][;]$

Parameter	Format	Functional Range	Parameter Default
X, Y increments (intermediate and end points)	current units	device-dependent (at least -2^{23} to $2^{23} - 1$)	no defaults
chord_angle*	clamped real	0° to 360°	device-dependent (usually 5°)

* If you have used the "CT1" instruction, the *chord_angle* is interpreted as a *deviation distance* in current units; see the CT instruction on page 133.

Group

This instruction is in the Vector Group.

Use

The RT instruction uses the current pen location and two specified points to calculate a circle and draw the appropriate arc segment of its circumference. The arc starts at the current pen location, using the current pen, line type, line attributes and pen up/down status. You specify the intermediate and end points. After drawing the arc, the pen location remains at the end of the arc; the carriage-return point (see page 66) is moved to the end of the arc.

- **$X_{incr\_inter}, Y_{incr\_inter}$:** Specify the location of an intermediate point of the arc in relative increments (relative to the current pen location). The arc is drawn in a negative or positive direction, as necessary, so that it passes through the intermediate point before the end point.

- **$X_{incr\_end}, Y_{incr\_end}$:** Specify the location of the end point of the arc in relative increments (relative to the current pen location).

- **chord_angle:** Specifies the chord angle used to draw the arc. The default is a device-dependent angle, normally 5°. The AA (Arc Absolute) instruction description on page 100 contains more information on chords and chord angles.

Intermediate and end point coordinates are interpreted in current units: as user-units when scaling is on; as plotter-units when scaling is off. If current scaling is not isotropic, the arc drawn is elliptical rather than circular. Note the following about intermediate and end points:

- If the intermediate point and end point are the same as the current pen location, the instruction draws a dot.

- If the intermediate point is the same as either the current pen location or the end point, a line is drawn between the current pen location and the end point.

- If the end point is the same as the current pen location, a circle is drawn, with its diameter being the distance between the current pen position and the intermediate point.

- If the current pen position, intermediate point, and end point are collinear, a straight line is drawn.

- If the intermediate point does not lie between the current pen location and the end point, and the three points are collinear, two lines are drawn, one from the current pen location and the other from the end point, leaving a gap between them. Refer to the following illustration. Both lines extend to the hard-clip limits or current window.

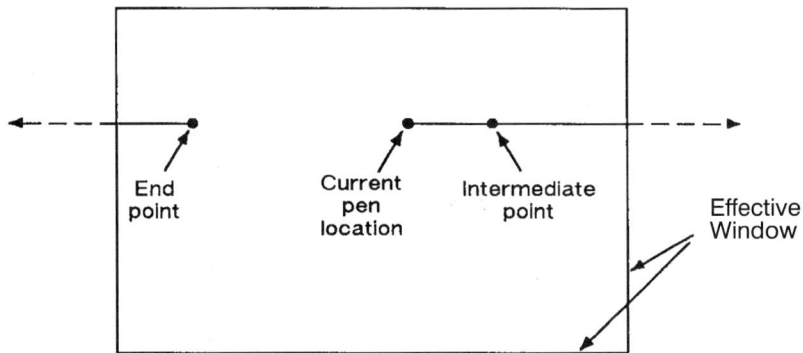

Figure 136. Relative Arc Three Point with Intermediate Point Outside End Points

Note that the CT (Chord Tolerance Mode) instruction in the Technical Graphics extension changes the computation.

Related Instructions

AA	Arc Absolute
AR	Arc Relative
AT	Absolute Arc Three Point
BR	Bezier Relative
BZ	Bezier Absolute
CI	Circle
LA	Line Attributes
LT	Line Type
PW	Pen Width

Example

PA	1000,100;	Specify the absolute point (1000,100) as the starting location.
PR	;	Specify relative plotting.
PD	1500,0;	Pen down, and draw to (1500,0) relative plotter-units from the current pen location (1000,100).
PU	−1850,1050;	Lift the pen and move (−1850,1050) relative coordinates.
PD	350,0;	Place the pen down, and draw a line 350 plotter-units in the X direction.
PU	−350,−700;	Lift the pen and move (−350,−700) plotter-units from the current location.
PD	350,0;	Place the pen down, and draw a line 350 plotter-units in the X direction.
PU	0,−350;	Lift the pen and move 350 plotter-units to the left.
PD	0,1500,1500,0;	Place the pen down, draw a line 1500 plotter-units up and then another line 1500 units to the right.
RT	700,−750,0,−1500;	Draw an arc from the current pen position through a point (700,−750) plotter-units away, with an ending point (0,−1500) plotter-units from the beginning of the arc.
PU	700,850;	Lift the pen and move it (700,850) plotter-units from the current pen position.
PD	;	Pen down.
RT	100,−100,0,−200;	Draw an arc from the current pen position, through a point (100,−100) plotter-units away, with an ending point (0,−200) from the starting point of the arc.
PU	100,100;	Lift the pen and move it (100,100) plotter-units from the current pen position.
PD	200,0;	Pen down, and draw a line 200 plotter-units in the X direction.

Figure 137. Example Using the RT Instruction

SA, Select Alternate Font

Purpose

To select the alternate font (already designated by the AD instruction) for subsequent labeling. Use the SA instruction to shift from the currently selected standard font to the designated alternate font.

Syntax

SA *[;]*

Group

This instruction is in the Character Group.

Use

The SA instruction tells the device to draw subsequent labeling instructions using characters from the alternate symbol set previously designated by the AD instruction. The SA instruction is equivalent to using the Shift Out control character (**SO**, decimal 14) within a label string.

The default designated alternate font uses symbol set 277 (Roman-8). The alternate font remains in effect until an SS instruction is executed, a Shift In control character (**SI**, decimal 15) is encountered, or the device is initialized or set to default conditions.

Related Instructions

AD	Alternate Font Definition
DT	Define Label Terminator
FI	Select Primary Font
FN	Select Secondary Font
LB	Label
SD	Standard Font Definition
SS	Select Standard Font

SB, Scalable or Bitmap Fonts

Purpose

To specify the type of font to be used in subsequent labeling. It allows you to restrict font selection to only scalable fonts and the stick and arc fonts, disregarding bitmap fonts.

Syntax

SB *n[;]*

or

SB *[;]*

Parameter	Format	Functional Range	Parameter Default
n	clamped integer	0 or 1	0

Group

This instruction is in the Dual-Context and Advanced Text Extensions.

Use

This instruction is defaulted by the DF (Default Values) and IN (Initialize) instructions. The SB instruction takes effect immediately, changing both the standard (primary) and alternate (secondary) fonts to be *scalable only* or *bitmap allowed*, as requested.

- **No parameter:** Defaults to scalable fonts. Equivalent to "SB0".

- **n:** Determines the type of font according to the following parameter values:

  0   Scalable fonts only.

  1   Bitmap fonts are allowed. All fonts will be subject to the same restrictions as bitmap fonts; that is, there is limited character fill, no slant, limited direction and size, and character-clipped rather than bit-clipped.

  SB1 (bitmap) changes the meanings of the following HP-GL/2 kernel instructions, and can affect their performance:

CF	Bitmap characters cannot be edged.
DI, DR	Bitmap characters can be printed only with orthogonal orientations (0°, 90°, 180°, or 270°). Refer to the DI instruction for an illustration of direction instructions with bitmap fonts.
SI, SR	Sizes for bitmap fonts are approximate only.
SL	Slant is ignored for bitmap fonts.

Scalable fonts respond more accurately to some HP-GL/2 instructions. The choice of scalable or bitmap fonts can affect the performance of the following HP-GL/2 instructions: AD, SD, CP, LB.

Note: The FI and FN instructions implicitly change the value of SB. For example, if SB = 0 and FI selects a bitmap font, SB is set to 1.

SB is ignored in devices that do not support both scalable and bitmap fonts.

Scalable fonts are computationally more complex than bitmap fonts, but they respond more accurately to some HP-GL/2 instructions. Bitmap fonts may offer a wider range of typefaces on some devices for plots that do not use the size, direction, slant, or character fill instructions.

SB takes place immediately, changing both the standard and alternate fonts to scalable or bit-map, as requested.

The DF and IN instructions default SB to 0.

Related Instructions

CF	Character Fill Mode
DI	Absolute Direction
DR	Relative Direction
SI	Absolute Character Size
SL	Character Slant
SR	Relative Character Size

SC, Scale

Purpose

To establish a user-unit coordinate system by mapping user-defined coordinate values onto the scaling points P1 and P2. For more information about the basic concept of scaling, refer to *Scaling* on page 24.

Syntax

SC $X_{MIN}, X_{MAX}, Y_{MIN}, Y_{MAX}[,type[,left,bottom]][;]$
    or
SC $X_{MIN}, X_{FACTOR}, Y_{MIN}, Y_{FACTOR}, type[;]$
    or
SC $[;]$

Parameter	Format	Functional Range	Parameter Default
X, Y coordinates	real	*device-dependent* (at least -2^{23} to $2^{23} - 1$)	no default
type	clamped integer	0, 1, or 2	0
left	clamped real	0 to 100%	50%
bottom	clamped real	0 to 100%	50%

Group

This instruction is in the Configuration and Status Group.

Use

There are three forms of scaling: anisotropic, isotropic, and point-factor. The *type* parameter tells the device which form you are using. Refer to the following table.

Scaling Form	Type	Description
Anisotropic	0	Establishes standard user-unit scaling allowing different unit size on X-axis and Y-axis.
Isotropic	1	Establishes standard user-unit scaling with same unit size on X-axis and Y-axis.
Point Factor	2	Establishes P1 user-unit location and a specific ratio of plotter-units to user-units.

An SC instruction remains in effect until another SC instruction is executed, or the device is initialized or set to default conditions.

- **No parameters:** Turns off scaling; subsequent coordinates are in plotter-units.

- **Parameters:** Turns on scaling as specified by the parameters; subsequent coordinates are in user-units.

Scaling Types 0 and 1

The following forms of scaling establish a user-unit coordinate system by mapping user-defined coordinate values onto the scaling points P1 and P2. The type parameter selects between anisotropic (type 0) and isotropic scaling (type 1).

Scaling Form	Type	Syntax
Anisotropic	0	$X_{MIN},X_{MAX},Y_{MIN},Y_{MAX}[,0];$
Isotropic	1	$X_{MIN},X_{MAX},Y_{MIN},Y_{MAX},1[,left,bottom]][;]$

- **$X_{MIN},X_{MAX},Y_{MIN},Y_{MAX}$:** These parameters represent the user-unit X- and Y-axis ranges, respectively.

  For example, "SC0,15,0,10" indicates 15 user-units along the X-axis and 10 user-units along the Y-axis. As a result, the first and third parameters (X_{MIN} and Y_{MIN}) are the coordinate pair that is mapped onto P1; the second and fourth parameters (X_{MAX} and Y_{MAX}) are the coordinate pair mapped onto P2. Using the same example, the coordinate location of P1 is (0,0) and P2 is (15,10). This is different from the IP instruction, where the parameters are expressed as X,Y coordinate pairs rather than as ranges.

  Note: X_{MIN} cannot be set equal to X_{MAX}, and Y_{MIN} cannot be set equal to Y_{MAX}.

  As their names suggest, you will normally want to specify X_{MIN} smaller than X_{MAX}, and Y_{MIN} smaller than Y_{MAX}. If you specify X_{MIN} larger than X_{MAX} and Y_{MIN} larger than Y_{MAX}, your illustration is drawn as a mirror-image, reversed and/or upside down, depending on the relative positions of P1 and P2.

  The parameters of the SC instruction are always mapped onto the current P1 and P2 locations. P1 and P2 retain these new values until scaling is turned off or another SC instruction redefines the user-unit values. Thus, the size of a user unit could change if any change is made in the relative position and distance between P1 and P2 *after* an SC instruction is executed.

  The new P1 and P2 points become the basis for all instructions that normally use P1 and P2 (DR, FT, SR, and so on); however, the new P1/P2 are temporary anchor points that are only in effect while the SC instruction that produced them is in effect; a new SC instruction uses the old P1/P2.

- **type:** Specifies anisotropic or isotropic scaling.

  0   Anisotropic scaling. Allows a user-unit along the X-axis to be a different size than user-units along the Y-axis. Printed shapes are distorted when you use anisotropic scaling. For example, a circle might be drawn as an ellipse—oval-shaped instead of round. (*Left* and *bottom* parameters are ignored for anisotropic scaling.)

  1   Isotropic scaling. Produces user-units that are the same size on both the X- and Y-axes. The following illustrations show how the device adjusts the location of (X_{MIN},Y_{MIN}) and (X_{MAX},Y_{MAX}) to create the largest possible isotropic area within the P1/P2 limits. (Remember, the user-units are always square regardless of the shape of the isotropic area.)

- **left, bottom:** Positions the isotropic area in the P1/P2 limits. (These parameters are always specified together and are valid for isotropic scaling only.) The *left* parameter indicates the percentage of the unused space on the left of the isotropic area; the *bottom* parameter indicates the percentage of unused space below.

The defaults for the *left* and *bottom* parameters are each 50%. This centers the isotropic area on the page with the unused space equally divided between left and right or top and bottom, as shown in the following illustrations.

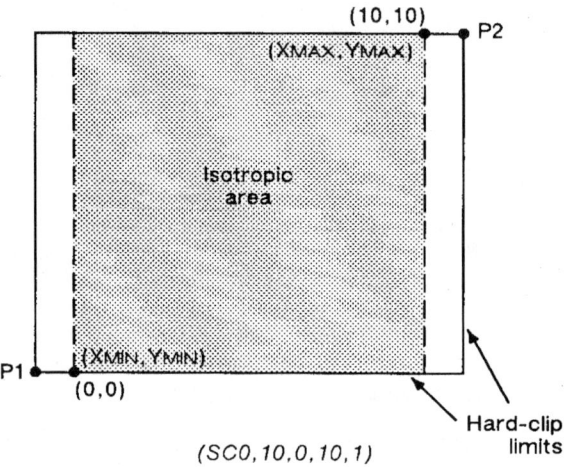

(SC0,10,0,10,1)

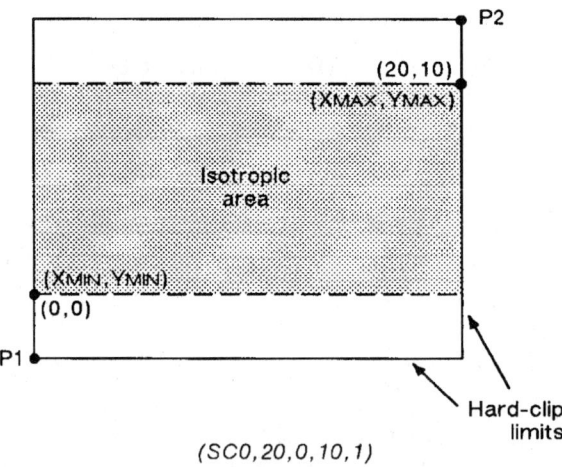

(SC0,20,0,10,1)

Figure 138. Isotropic Scaling

Although you *must* specify both parameters, the device applies only one: the *left* parameter applies when there is extra horizontal space; the *bottom* parameter applies when there is extra vertical space. The following examples illustrate *left* and *bottom* parameters of 0% and 100%.

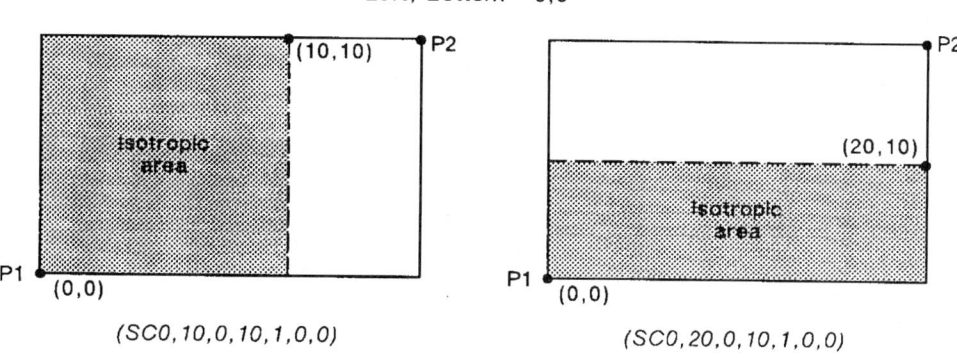

Left, Bottom = 0,0

(SC0,10,0,10,1,0,0)

(SC0,20,0,10,1,0,0)

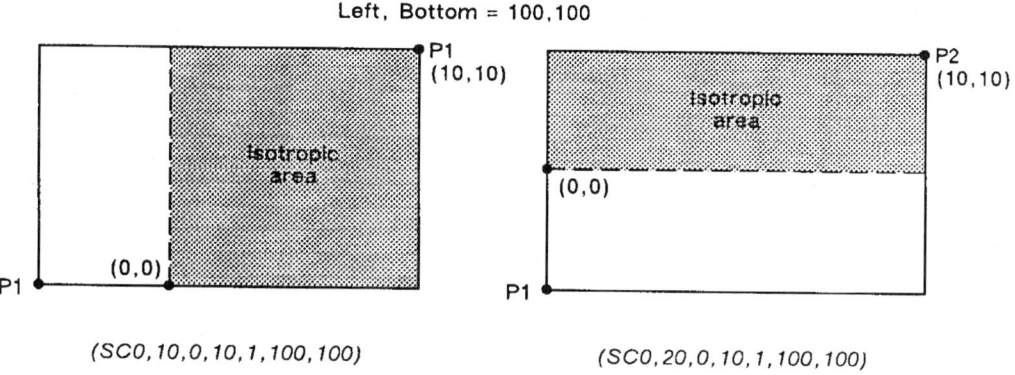

Left, Bottom = 100,100

(SC0,10,0,10,1,100,100)

(SC0,20,0,10,1,100,100)

Figure 139. Left and Bottom Parameters Set to 0 or 100%

Scaling Type 2

The third form of scaling, point-factor scaling, sets a specific ratio of plotter-units to user-units, and establishes the user-units coordinate of P1.

Scaling Form	Type	Syntax
Point Factor	2	$X_{MIN}, X_{FACTOR}, Y_{MIN}, Y_{FACTOR}, 2;$

- **$X_{MIN}, X_{FACTOR}, Y_{MIN}, Y_{FACTOR};$** Establish the user-unit coordinates of P1 and the ratio of plotter to user-units. X_{MIN} and Y_{MIN} are the user-unit coordinates of P1. X_{FACTOR} sets the number of plotter-units per user-unit on the X-axis; Y_{FACTOR} sets the number of plotter-units per user-unit on the Y-axis.

- **type:** Must be 2 for this type of scaling.

Using SC in a PCL Dual-Context Environment

When user-scaling mode is off, current units are:

(plotter-units * (PCL picture-frame-size ÷ HP-GL/2 plot-size))

Left and bottom parameters are relative to the PCL picture frame, viewed from the current orientation. The directional implications of left and bottom assume the default P1/P2 orientation.

Examples

The following examples explain the effect of several parameter selections.

SC	0,1,0,1,2;	Moves the origin to P1 and establishes a 1:1 ratio of user-units to plotter-units.
SC	0,40,0,40,2;	Allows scaling in millimeters since 1 millimeter = 40 plotter-units. Each user-unit is 1 millimeter.
SC	0,1.016,0,1.016,2;	Allows scaling in thousandths of an inch since 1 inch = 1016 plotter-units.

While scaling is on (after any form of the SC instruction has been executed), only those HP-GL/2 instructions that can be issued in "current units" are interpreted as user-units; the instructions that can be issued only in plotter-units are still interpreted as plotter-units. (The instruction syntax discussion pertaining to each instruction tells you which kind of units each parameter requires.)

The SC parameters are mapped onto the current locations of P1 and P2. P1 and P2 do *not* represent a graphic limit; therefore, the new user-unit coordinate system extends across the entire range of the plotter-unit coordinate system. Thus, you can print to a point beyond P1 or P2, as long as you are within the effective window. For example, you can print from the point (−1,3.5) to the point (5.5,1.5) as shown in the following illustration.

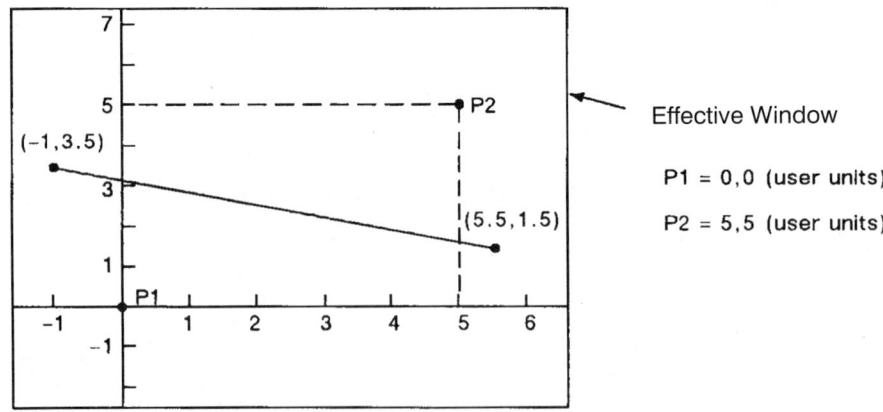

Figure 140. Example of Plotting beyond the P1/P2 Limits

Related Instructions

IP   Input P1 and P2
IR   Input Relative P1 and P2
IW   Input Window

Possible Error Conditions

Error Condition	Error Number	Printer or Plotter Response
More than 7 parameters	2	Executes first 7 parameters
For types 0 or 1: More than 6 or less than 4 parameters	2	Ignores instruction
For type 2: Other than 5 parameters	2	Ignores instruction
$X_{MIN}=X_{MAX}$ or $Y_{MIN}=Y_{MAX}$ or number out of range	3	Ignores instruction
$X_{FACTOR}=0$ or $Y_{FACTOR}=0$	3	Ignores instruction

HP-GL/2
INSTRUCTIONS

SD, Standard Font Definition

Purpose

To define the standard character set (font) and its characteristics: symbol set identification, font spacing, pitch, height, posture, stroke weight, and typeface. To define an alternate font, use the AD instruction.

Syntax

SD *kind,value...[,kind,value] [;]*
     or
SD *[;]*

Parameter	Format	Functional Range	Parameter Default
kind	clamped integer	1 to 7	no default
value	clamped real	*kind*-dependent*	*kind*-dependent*

*   Refer to the table following the parameter descriptions.

Group

This instruction is in the Character Group.

Use

This instruction is similar to the AD (Alternate Font Definition) instruction (see page 106) that defines a secondary HP-GL/2 font. The SD instruction defines the standard HP-GL/2 font and its characteristics: font spacing, pitch, height, posture, stroke weight, and typeface. It allows the font characteristics to be assigned to the primary font definition. Use SD to set up the standard font that you can easily access when labeling.

- **No parameters:** Defaults the standard font characteristics to that of the device-dependent default scalable font, not a bitmap font.

- **kind:** Specifies the characteristic for which you are setting a *value* (see the following table).

- **value:** Defines the properties of the characteristic specified by the *kind* parameter.

Note: When selecting fonts, the different characteristics (symbol set, spacing, pitch, etc.) are prioritized as shown in the table, with symbol set being the highest priority and typeface being the lowest. The font selection priority is the same for HP-GL/2 as for PCL font selection. For more information about the priority of font characteristics, see *How Your Device Selects Fonts* on page 63.

The tables in *Appendix C: Font Definitions* on page 475 list the *kind* parameters with their associated values (note that these tables are also valid for the AD [Alternate Font Definition] instruction). For kinds 1 and 7, your device may support values other than those listed there. Refer to your *User's Guide* or HP-GL/2 option manual for more information about the attributes and values supported.

Any combination of *kind, value* parameters is allowed; the last *value* specified for a given *kind* prevails.

Kind	Attribute	Range of Values	Default Value	Description
1	Character set	*device-dependent*	277	Roman-8
2	Font Spacing	0 (fixed), 1 (proportional)	*device-dependent*	fixed spacing
3	Pitch	>0 to 32 767 (valid to 2 decimal places)	*device-dependent*	characters per inch
4	Height	0 to 32 767	*device-dependent*	font point size
5	Posture	0 to 32 767	*device-dependent*	upright or italic
6	Stroke Weight	−7 to 7, 9999	0	normal
7	Typeface	*device-dependent*	*device-dependent*	scalable font

The IN (Initialize) and DF (Default Values) instructions restore default primary font attributes.

Related Instructions

AD	Alternate Font Definition
DT	Define Label Terminator
FI	Select Primary Font
FN	Select Secondary Font
LB	Label
SA	Select Alternate Font
SB	Scalable or Bitmap Fonts
SI	Absolute Character Size
SR	Relative Character Size
SS	Select Standard Font
TD	Transparent Data

Example

The instruction "SD1,21,2,1,4,25,5,0,6,3,7,51;" designates a 25-point *Gill Sans Bold* font in the ASCII symbol set (use the SS [Select Standard Font] instruction to select this font after it is designated):

SD	1,21	Symbol set—US ASCII
	2,1	Spacing—proportional
	4,25	Height—25-point
	5,0	Posture—upright
	6,3	Stroke weight—bold
	7,51;	Typeface—Gill Sans

Note that the *pitch* parameter is missing in the above instruction because the designated font is proportionally spaced.

SI, Absolute Character Size

Purpose

To specify the size of labeling characters in centimeters. Use SI to establish character size independent of P1 and P2.

Syntax

SI *width, height[;]*
or
SI *[;]*

Parameter	Format	Functional Range	Parameter Default
width	clamped real	–32 768 to 32 767	(see note)*
height	clamped real	–32 768 to 32 767	(see note)*

* Note: Dependent on the current pitch and font height set by the AD or SD instruction.

Group

This instruction is in the Character Group.

Use

While SI is in effect, with or without specifying parameter values, the size of characters in the currently selected font are not affected by changes in P1 and P2.

- **No parameters:** Character size is as specified by the SD (Standard Font Definition) and AD (Alternate Font Definition) instructions.

- **width:** Specifies the width of the nominal character in centimeters. A negative width parameter mirrors labels in the right-to-left direction. The nominal character width is 0.5 of the point size (0.67 for the stick font).

- **height:** Specifies the cap height in centimeters. A negative height parameter mirrors labels in the top-to-bottom direction.

If both the width and the height are negative, characters are rotated through 180°.

Changing character size also changes the width of line used to draw Stick font characters.

Note that in most languages the width of a letter is typically less than the height. If you set your characters to have a different "aspect ratio", they may look odd to your readers.

The maximum size of a character is device-dependent, but is larger than a page; for A-size devices, characters at least as large as 12 times the page width and height are possible; for roll–feed devices, characters up to the paper roll length are possible.

An SI instruction remains in effect until another SI instruction is executed, an SR instruction is executed, or the device is initialized or set to default conditions.

SI and SR functionality is the same, except that SR parameters are relative to P1 and P2. See the description of the SR instruction on page 308. When SI is in effect, moving P1 to the right of P2, or moving P1 above P2 does not cause character mirroring.

Bitmap Fonts

- If a bitmap font is selected, that is, the "SB1;" instruction is in effect, an SI instruction may not be executed accurately. Labels are rendered using the bitmap font that most closely approximates the character height or width specified by SI (character size is determined by height for proportional fonts and by width for fixed-spaced fonts).

- When "SB1;" is in effect, characters cannot be mirrored with negative SI parameters.

Using SI in a Dual-Context Environment

The *width* and *height* parameters, in centimeters, are adjusted by the picture frame scaling factor. The picture frame scaling factor is the ratio of the size of the PCL picture frame to the HP-GL/2 plot size. See the *PCL5 Printer Language Technical Reference* manual for more information.

Related Instructions

AD	Alternate Font Definition
CP	Character Plot
DI	Absolute Direction
DR	Relative Direction
LB	Label
SB	Scalable or Bitmap Fonts
SD	Standard Font Definition
SR	Relative Character Size

Examples

The following example demonstrates the SI instruction using both the default Stick typeface and the Univers typeface. The samples on the left were printed using the Stick font, first using the default (11.5-point) and then specifying an absolute character size of 1 cm wide by 1.5 cm high. On the right, a Univers font was used, first at 12-point and scaled to 1 cm by 1.5 cm using the SI instruction.

PA	700,3000;	Enter absolute plotting mode and move to (700,3000).
DT#;		Define the label terminator as the "#" character.
LBPrint#;		Print the word "Print" in the default font.
PA	700,2000;	Move to (700,2000).
SI	1,1.5;	Specify an absolute character size of 1cm wide by 1.5 cm high.
LBPrint#;		Print the word "Print".
SI	;	Send SI with no parameters to return to the default size.
SD	1,21,2,1,4,12,5,0,6,0,7,52;	Designate a 12-point Univers font.
SS	;	And select it.
PA	4000,3000;	Move to (4000,3000).
LBPrint#;		Print "Print" in 12-point Univers.
PA	4000,2000;	Move the pen to (4000,2000).
SI	1,1.5;	Specify a character size of 1 cm by 1.5 cm.
LBPrint#;		Then print "Print".

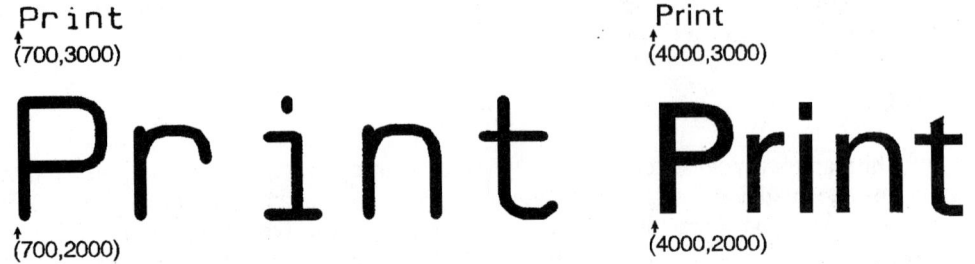

Print
(700,3000)

Print
(4000,3000)

Print Print

(700,2000)

(4000,2000)

Figure 141. Specifying Absolute Character Sizes

In each case the current pen location is at the end of the stem of the letter "P".

The following are examples of negative parameters producing mirror-images of labels. A negative width parameter mirrors labels in the right-to-left direction.

```
SI      −.6,.9;
LBPrint#;
```

Figure 142. SI Instruction with Negative *Width*

A negative height parameter mirrors labels in the top-to-bottom direction.

```
SI      .6,−.9;
LBPrint#;
```

Figure 143. SI Instruction with Negative *Height*

Negative width and height parameters together mirror labels in both directions, causing the label to appear to be rotated 180°.

```
SI      −.6,−.9;
LBPrint#;
```

Figure 144. SI Instruction with Negative *Width* and *Height*

SL, Character Slant

Purpose

To specify the slant at which labels are drawn using scalable or Stick fonts. Use SL to create slanted text for emphasis, or to re-establish upright labeling after an SL instruction with parameters has been in effect. (Note that the SL instruction has no effect when using bitmap fonts, that is, when an "SB1;" instruction is in effect.)

Syntax

SL *tangent_of_angle[;]*
      or
SL *[;]*

Parameter	Format	Functional Range	Parameter Default
tangent_of_angle	clamped real	−32 768 to 32 767	0

Group

This instruction is in the Character Group.

Use

The device interprets the parameters as follows:

- **No parameter:** Defaults the slant to zero (no slant). Equivalent to "SL0;".

- **tangent_of_angle:** Interpreted as an angle θ from the vertical. The base of the character always stays on the horizontal as shown in the following illustration.

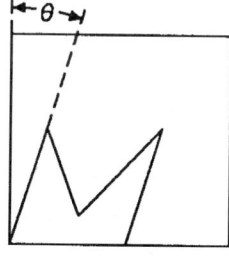
Positive Slant

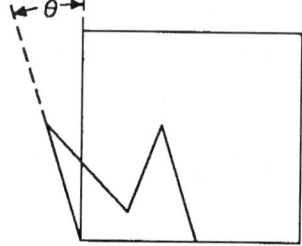
Negative Slant

Figure 145. Character Slant

The SL instruction only affects each character relative to an imaginary line beside the label. The direction or placement of the label on the drawing does not affect the SL instruction; neither do the settings of P1 and P2. The DI and DR instructions, however, do affect the slant direction, since the base of a character always stays on the baseline of the label.

You can specify the actual tangent value, or you can use the TAN function available in most computer languages. (Note: Many languages require that tangents be calculated in radians. Consult your programming language documentation if you are not familiar with your language's tangent function.)

An SL instruction remains in effect until another SL instruction is executed, or the device is initialized or set to default conditions.

Related Instructions

DI   Absolute Direction
DR   Relative Direction
LB   Label
SB   Scalable or Bitmap Fonts

Example

The following example illustrates the Slant instruction using an angle of 20° (tan 20° = 0.36).

SD   1,21,2,1,4,25,5,0,6,0,7,4101;   Designate the 25-point CG Times font as the standard (primary) font.
SI   .7,1;   Set the absolute character size to 0.7 cm wide by 1 cm high.
PA   1000,1000;   Establish absolute plotting and move to (1000,1000).
DT#,1;   Specify a label terminator (#).
SL   .36;   Set the slant angle for 20° from vertical (forward slant).
LBSlant#;   Print "Slant".
PA   1000,300;   Move to (1000,300).
SL   −.36;   Change the slant angle to −20° from upright.
LBSlant#;   And print "Slant".

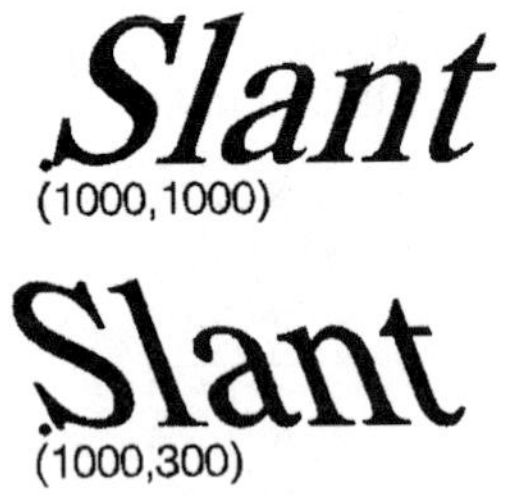

Slant
(1000,1000)

Slant
(1000,300)

Figure 146. Slanting to the Left and to the Right

SM, Symbol Mode

Purpose

To draw the specified symbol at each X,Y coordinate point using the PA, PD, PE, PR, and PU instructions. Use SM to create scatter-grams, indicate points on geometric drawings, and differentiate data points on multi-line graphs.

Syntax

SM *character[;]*
  or
SM *charactercharacter2[;]*
  or
SM *[;]*

Parameter	Format	Functional Range	Parameter Default
character *character2**	character	Decimal codes 1 to 255 (most printing characters except 0, 5, 27, and 59)**	no default

*   *Character2* is only valid in 16-bit mode (see the LM instruction on page 208). In 16-bit mode, both *character* and *character2* are needed to specify the character. In 8-bit mode, *character2* would be considered the start of a new instruction.

** Decimal code 59 (the semicolon) is an HP-GL/2 terminator and cannot be used as a symbol in any symbol set. Use it only to cancel symbol mode ("SM;").

Group

This instruction is in the Line and Fill Attributes Group.

Use

The SM instruction draws the specified symbol at each X,Y coordinate point for subsequent PA, PD, PE, PR, and PU instructions. The SM instruction includes an automatic pen down; after the symbol is drawn, the pen position and any dashed-line residue are restored.

- **No parameters:** Terminates symbol mode.

- **character, character2:** Draws the specified character centered at each subsequent X,Y coordinate. The symbol is drawn in addition to the usual function of each HP-GL/2 instruction.

The character is drawn in the font selected at the time the vectors are drawn. If you change to a new symbol set, the character changes to the corresponding character from the new symbol set. The character fill (CF), size (SI and SR), slant (SL), and direction (DI and DR) instructions affect how the character is drawn. Specifying a non-printing character cancels symbol mode. If downloadable characters have been defined (see DL) they can be used in symbol mode plotting.

An SM instruction remains in effect until another SM instruction is executed or the device is initialized or set to default conditions.

The character is centered at the coordinate point and printed after each vector intersection is drawn. The geographic middle of stick-font characters is the character center, but the middle is different for lowercase characters and characters with descenders. For all other fonts, the center of the rectangle formed by cap height and character width is the character center.

The pen is automatically lowered to draw the character at each point; however, this automatic pen-down does not affect the pen state used when drawing other entities.

Symbol mode only applies to the PA, PD, PE, PR, and PU instructions. The circle and rectangle instructions have symbols only for the PA instruction coordinate point.

Example

The following example shows several uses of symbol mode: with the pen down for a line graph, with the pen up for a scatter-gram, and with the pen down for geometric drawings.

Note: Symbol mode works only with the PA, PD, PE, PR, and PU instructions. Notice that the circle and rectangle have symbols only for the PA instruction coordinate point.

SM*;		Enter symbol mode, using the asterisk (*) as the symbol.
PA	200,1000;	Move to absolute location (200,1000).
PD	200,1230, 400,1560;	Set the pen down, and draw first to (200,1230), then to (400,1560).
PD	700,1670, 1300,1600, 1800,2000;	Place the pen down and draw from the current pen position (400,1560) to (700,1670), then to (1300,1600), then to (1800,2000).
PU	;	Lift the pen.
SM3;		Enter symbol mode again with "3" as the current symbol.
PA	700,500, 900,450, 1300,850;	Print a "3" in the following locations: (700,500), (900,450), and (1300,850).
PA	1750,1300, 2500,1350;	With the pen still up and "3" still the current symbol, print a "3" at (1750,1300) and (2500,1350).
PU	;	Lift the pen.
SM;		Exit symbol mode.
PA	3300,1100;	Move to (3300,1100).
PD	;	Set the pen down.
SMY;		Enter symbol mode with "Y" as the symbol.
PA	4400,1890;	Draw a line to (4400,1890) and print a "Y".
SMZ;		Re-enter symbol mode with "Z" as the current symbol.
PA	4600,1590;	Draw a line to (4600,1590) and print a "Z".
SMX;		Specify "X" as the next symbol.
PA	3300,1100;	Move to (3300,1100), and print an "X".
PU	;	Lift the pen.
SMA;		Specify "A" as the new symbol.
PA	4000,400;	Move to (4000,400).
CI	400;	Draw a circle with a radius of 400 plotter-units and print an "A" in the center.
SM*;		Specify "*" as the new symbol.
PA	2600,700;	Move to (2600,700).
EA	1500,200;	Edge the outline of a rectangle and print an "*" at the starting point.

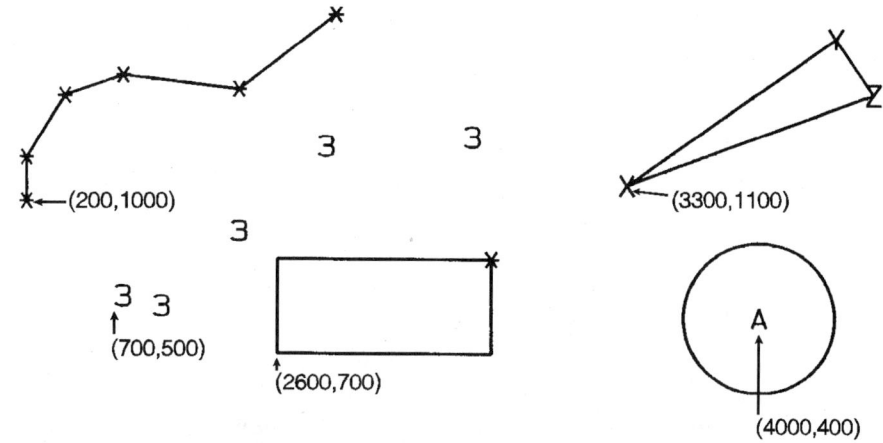

Figure 147. Drawing Symbols

Related Instructions

PA	Plot Absolute
PD	Pen Down
PE	Polyline Encoded
PR	Plot Relative
PU	Pen Up

SP, Select Pen

Purpose

To select the device's logical pen for subsequent plotting. An SP instruction must be included at the beginning of each instruction sequence to enable the device to draw.

Syntax

SP *pen_number[;]*
            or
SP *[;]*

Parameter	Format	Functional Range	Parameter Default
pen_number	integer	*device-dependent* (at least -2^{23} to $2^{23} - 1$)	0 (no pen)

Group

This instruction is in the Line and Fill Attributes Group.

Use

Although your device may not have physical pens, for the purpose of compatibility it has "logical" pens which you must select to print your drawing.

- **No parameters:** Equivalent to "SP0".

- **pen_number:** Selects the device's logical pen. The device will not draw unless an SP is sent.

    0 Selects pen 0 on raster devices. For pen plotters, stores the pen in the carousel and subsequent plotting commands are not drawn.

    >0 Selects the pen number. In raster devices, different pen numbers may represent pens of the same color but with different widths.

    The modulo function is applied if the pen number is greater than the current palette size or the maximum number of pens in the device:

    > for raster devices,
    >> pen_used = ((*pen_number* – 1) MOD (number_of_pens –1)) + 1

    > for pen plotters,
    >> pen_used = ((*pen_number* – 1) MOD (number_of_pens)) + 1

    For monochrome devices, if *pen_number*>0 a black pen is selected.

    Pen 0 defaults to white on black-and-white devices; other colors default to gray levels.

Use the PW (Pen Width) instruction to change the line width. You may change widths as often as you like, without sending an SP instruction again.

Note: If you are not using the TR (Transparency Mode) instruction, white is always transparent; a transparent pen is the same as no pen. For more information on the TR instruction see page 318.

The default black-and-white palette consists of two pens: black and white. The default color raster palette has eight pens defined below; pen 0 is selected at power-up.

Number of Pens in Device	Pen Number	Color
2	0	White
	1	Black
8	0	White
	1	Black
	2	Red
	3	Green
	4	Yellow
	5	Blue
	6	Magenta
	7	Cyan

SP clears the pattern residue and terminates any sequence of continuous vectors (see the LA and LT instructions).

Related Instructions

PW, Pen Width
TR, Transparency Mode
WU, Pen Width Unit Selection

SR, Relative Character Size

Purpose

To specify the size of characters as a percentage of the distance between P1 and P2. Use SR to establish relative character size so that if the P1/P2 distance changes, the character size adjusts to occupy the same relative amount of space.

Syntax

SR *width,height[;]*
    or
SR *[;]*

Parameter	Format	Functional Range	Parameter Default
width	clamped real	−32 768 to 32 767	0.75% of $P2_X$–$P1_X$
height	clamped real	−32 768 to 32 767	1.5% of $P2_Y$–$P1_Y$

Group

This instruction is in the Character Group.

Use

While the SR instruction is in effect (with or without parameters), changes in P1 and P2 affect the size of characters in the currently selected font.

- **No parameters:** Defaults the relative character width to 0.75% of the distance $(P2_X - P1_X)$ and the height to 1.5% of the distance $(P2_Y - P1_Y)$.

- **width:** Sets the character width to the specified percentage of the distance between the X-coordinates of P1 and P2. A negative width parameter mirrors labels in the right-to-left direction.

- **height:** Sets the character height to the specified percentage of the distance between the Y-coordinates of P1 and P2. A negative height parameter mirrors labels in the top-to-bottom direction.

If both the *width* and the *height* are negative, characters are rotated through 180°.

Note: Changing character size also changes the stroke weight of labels; the device adjusts characters relative to changes in P1/P2. As long as the aspect ratio remains the same with changes in P1/P2, characters will have the same appearance relative to the new P1/P2 rectangle.

The character size you specify with SR is a *percentage* of $(P2_X - P1_X)$ and $(P2_Y - P1_Y)$. The device calculates the actual character width and height from the specified parameters as follows:

actual width = (*width* parameter/100) x $(P2_X - P1_X)$

actual height = (*height* parameter/100) x $(P2_Y - P1_Y)$

For example, suppose P1 and P2 are located at (–6956,–4388) and (6956,4388), respectively. If you establish relative sizing and specify a width of 2 and a height of 3.5, the device determines the actual character size as follows:

width = (2/100) $\times$ (6956 – (– 6956)) = 278.24 plotter-units or 0.695 cm

height = (3.5/100) $\times$ (4388 – (– 4388)) = 307.16 plotter-units or 0.768 cm

If you changed P1 and P2 settings to (100,100) and (5000,5000), but did not change the SR parameters, the character size would change as follows:

width = (2/100) $\times$ (5000 – 100) = 98 plotter-units or 0.245 cm

height = (3.5/100) $\times$ (5000 – 100) = 171.5 plotter-units or 0.429 cm

Note that in most alphabets the width of a letter is typically less than the height. If you set your characters to have a different "aspect ratio", they may look odd to your readers.

Note: Either negative SR parameters or switching the relative position of P1 and P2 produces mirror-images of labels. When P1 is in the lower left and P2 is in the upper right, the SR instruction gives the same mirroring results as the SI instruction. However, if you move P1 to the right of P2, characters are mirrored right-to-left; when you move P1 above P2, characters are mirrored top-to-bottom. When *both* of these situations occur (using negative parameters in the SR instruction with an unusual P1/P2 position) double mirroring may result in either direction, in which case *the two inversions cancel*, and lettering appears normal.

An SR instruction remains in effect until another SR instruction is executed, an SI instruction is executed, or the device is initialized or set to default conditions.

If a bitmap font ("SB1;") is selected, SR may not accurately transform characters; labels are rendered in the font most closely approximating the height specified by SR. Negative parameters or unusual P1/P2 locations do not cause mirroring.

After SR is in effect, "SI;" must be sent to use the size specified by SD or AD.

Related Instructions

CP	Character Plot
DI	Absolute Direction
DR	Relative Direction
IP	Input P1 and P2
IR	Input Relative P1 and P2
SB	Scalable or Bitmap Fonts
SI	Absolute Character Size

Examples

The following example first shows a label with a character size relative to P1 and P2 (SR). Next, the locations of P1 and P2 are changed; then, the character size percentages are specified. Notice that the new character size has equal parameters of 2.5; because the P1/P2 area is square, the resulting characters are square.

IP	–6956,–4388,6956,4388;	Set P1 at (–6956,–4388) and P2 at (6956,4388).
DT@;		Specify "@" as the label terminator.
SR	;	Default the character size as a percentage of the P1/P2 rectangle.
PA	0,2700;	Move the pen to (0,2700).

LBRELATIVE LABEL SIZE@;   Print "RELATIVE LABEL SIZE".
IP   0,0,5500,5500;   Move P1 to (0,0) and P2 to (5500,5500).
PA   0,2000;   Then move the pen to (0,2000).
LBNEW P1 AND P2 CHANGE LABEL SIZE@;   Print "NEW P1 AND P2 CHANGE
                              LABEL SIZE".
PA   0,1000;   Move to (0,1000).
SR   2.5,2.5;   Set the character size to 2.5% by 2.5% of the P1/P2 rectangle.
LBNEW SR INSTRUCTION@;   Print "NEW SR INSTRUCTION".
CP   ;   Send CP for Carriage Return/Line Feed.
LBCHANGES LABEL SIZE@;   Print "CHANGES LABEL SIZE".

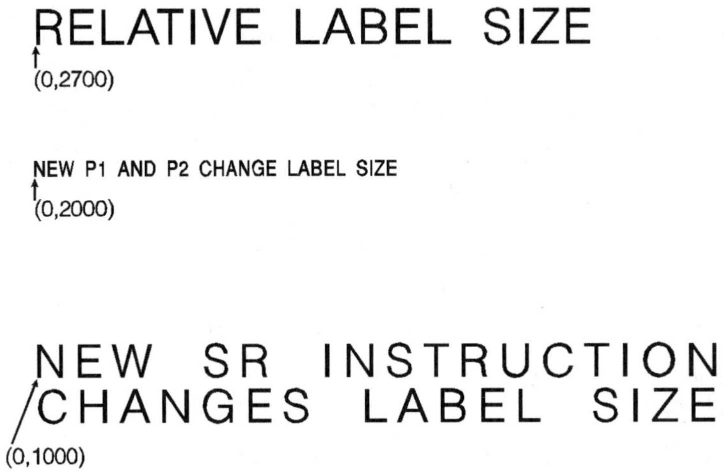

RELATIVE LABEL SIZE
↑
(0,2700)

NEW P1 AND P2 CHANGE LABEL SIZE
↑
(0,2000)

NEW SR INSTRUCTION
/CHANGES LABEL SIZE
/
(0,1000)

Figure 148. Using the SR Instruction

SR and SI functionality is the same, except that SR parameters are relative to P1 and P2.
Therefore, as shown in the following examples, some P1/P2 orientations cause positive SR
parameters to produce the same effect as negative SI parameters; corresponding mirror images
will be produced.

DI   1,0;   Horizontal labels
IP   0,0,10160,5080;   P1 = (0,0), P2 = (10160,5080)
SR   1,4;   Equivalent to "SI 0.25,0.5;"
IP   0,5080,10160,0;   P1 = (0,5080), P2 = (10160,0)
SR   1,4;   Equivalent to "SI 0.25,–0.5;"
IP   10160,0,0,5080;   P1 = (10160,0), P2 = (0,5080)
SR   1,4;   Equivalent to "SI –0.25,0.5;"
IP   10160,5080,0,0;   P1 = (10160,5080), P2 = (0,0)
SR   1,4;   Equivalent to "SI –0.25,–0.5;"

See the SI instruction on page 298 for further examples.

SS, Select Standard Font

Purpose

To select the standard font (already designated by the SD [Standard Font Definition] instruction) for subsequent labeling. Use the SS instruction to shift from the currently selected alternate font to the designated standard font.

Syntax

SS *[;]*

Group

This instruction is in the Character Group.

Use

The SS instruction tells the device to print subsequent labeling instructions using characters from the standard symbol set designated by the SD instruction. The SS instruction is equivalent to using the Shift In control character (**SI**, ASCII decimal code 15) within a label string.

The default-designated standard font is the Stick font, and uses symbol set 277 (Roman-8). This font is in effect when the device is initialized or set to default conditions. The SS instruction remains in effect until an SA instruction or a Shift Out control character (**SO**, ASCII decimal code 14) is executed.

Related Instructions

AD	Alternate Font Definition
DT	Define Label Terminator
FI	Select Primary Font
FN	Select Secondary Font
LB	Label
SA	Select Alternate Font
SD	Standard Font Definition

ST, Sort

Purpose

To specify how the device is to sort vectors for plotting. Raster devices ignore this instruction.

Syntax

ST *switches[;]*
      or
ST *[;]*

Parameter	Format	Functional Range	Parameter Default
switches	clamped integer	−1,0, and any sum of 1, 2, and 4 (1 through 7)	0

Group

This instruction is in the Technical Graphics Extension.

Use

The sorting switches are device-dependent and vary according to the hardware technology, buffer size, and plotting/CPU speed trade-offs.

- **No parameter:** Defaults the sorting to a device-dependent switch. Refer to the documentation for your device or HP-GL/2 option to determine what switches are supported and which is the default.

- **switches:** Determines sorting as follows:

  −1 Turns on all sorting (or optimal combination).

  0 Turns off all sorting; plots vectors in the order they are received.

  1 Pen sorting; vectors are sorted by pen color rather than in the order in which they were received.

  2 End-point swap (bidirectional plotting); swaps successive vector end points to minimize pen-up moves.

  4 Geographic sorting; sorts all vectors by their geographic area before moving to another area.

There are no out-of-range parameters (within the clamped integer constraint). The switches pertinent to the device are used, and others are ignored.

SV, Screened Vectors

Purpose

To select the type of screening (area fill) to be applied to vectors. Options include lines, hatching patterns (fill types 3 and 4), arcs, circles, edges of polygons, rectangles, wedges and PCL and HP RTL user-defined patterns. SV does not affect solid fill types, stroked characters, or edges of characters. Pen plotters ignore this instruction.

Syntax

SV *screen_type [,option1 [,option2]][;]*
      or
SV *[;]*

Parameter	Format	Functional Range	Parameter Default
screen_type	clamped integer	0, 1, 2, 21, 22	0: no screening (solid)
option1, option2	clamped integer	*screen_type*-dependent*	*screen_type*-dependent*

*   Refer to the table following the parameter descriptions.

Group

This instruction is in the Palette Extension.

Use

There are four types of screen fill: shaded fill, HP-GL/2 user-defined raster fill, predefined PCL and HP RTL cross-hatch patterns, and PCL and HP RTL user-defined patterns.

- **No parameters:** Defaults to no screening (solid fill—same as "SV0;").

- **screen_type:** Selects the types of screening as follows:

    0   No screening (options 1 and 2 are ignored)

    1   Shaded fill

    2   HP-GL/2 user-defined raster fill (RF instruction)

    21   Predefined PCL or HP RTL cross-hatch patterns

    22   PCL or HP RTL user-defined patterns

- **option1, option2:** The definition of these optional parameters depends on the *screen_type* selected.

Screen_Type	Description	Option1	Option2
1	Shaded Fill	% Shading (0 through 100) default is 50%	Ignored
2	HP-GL/2 User-Defined Raster Fill	Pattern Index (device-dependent: at least 1 to 8) default is 1	0—false (default) 1—true

- For *screen_type* 1, *option1* specifies the shading percentage using a number from 0 to 100. For example, to print vectors that are shaded 15%, specify "SV1,15;".

- For *screen_type* 2, *option1* specifies the index number of the fill pattern created using the RF (Raster Fill Definition) instruction.

  Option2 is a Boolean flag that is ignored unless the RF pattern is defined using only 0's and 1's. In such cases, if this parameter is 1, the current color is applied to the "1" pattern pixels, and white to the "0" pixels; if this parameter is 0, the "1" pattern pixels are printed in the color of pen number 1.

All parameters are optional. If all parameters are omitted, screening is turned off (the vectors are solid).

If *screen_type* is present, but option1 and/or option2 are omitted, values previously specified for the specified *screen_type* are used. If none have been specified since the last power-on, IN, DF, or **ESC**E Reset, the defaults are assumed.

All screening patterns use the current anchor corner (see the AC instruction description on page 103).

SV terminates the vector path (see the LA instruction).

Using SV in a Dual-Context Environment

Additional screen types (21 and 22) are imported from PCL or HP RTL.

Screen_Type	Description	Option1	Option2
21	PCL or HP RTL cross-hatch	1 through 6	Ignored
22	PCL or HP RTL user-defined pattern fill	Pattern ID	Ignored

- For *screen_type* 21, the *option1* parameter selects one of the six predefined cross-hatch patterns using a value between 1 and 6 (see Figure 149).

- For *screen_type* 22, the optional parameter selects the corresponding user-defined pattern specified by way of the **ESC***c#W instruction. *Option1* specifies the pattern associated with the user-defined fill pattern. An invalid *option1* (for example, a deleted pattern), prints a solid fill in the current color.

1	horizontal lines
2	vertical lines
3	diagonal lines (lower left to upper right)
4	diagonal lines (lower right to upper left)
5	cross-hatching with horizontal and vertical lines
6	cross-hatching with diagonal lines.

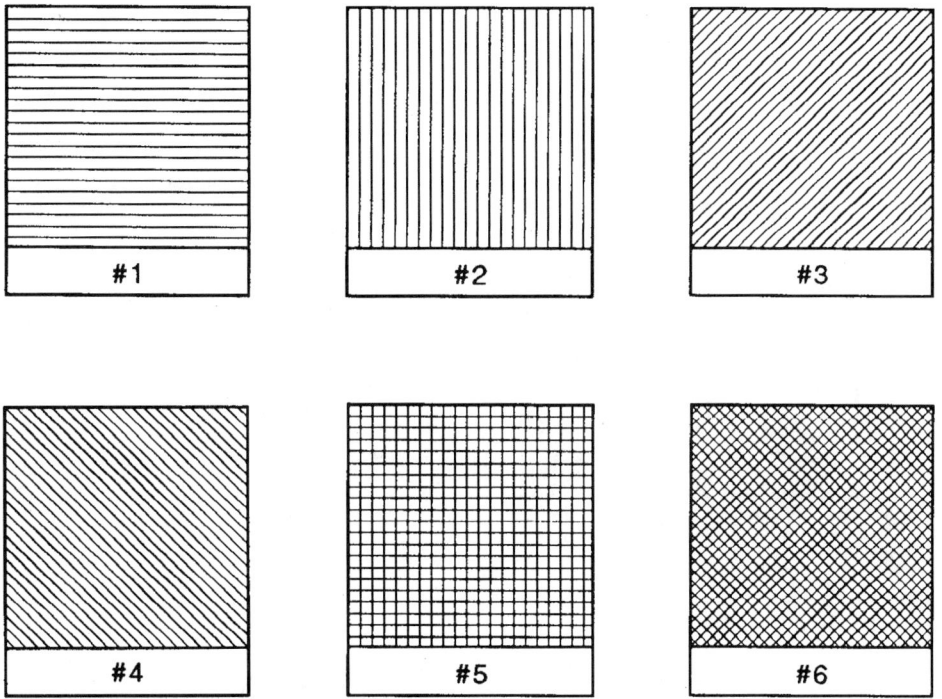

Figure 149. Patterns for Fill Type 21

Related Instructions

AC	Anchor Corner
FT	Fill Type
LT	Line Type
PW	Pen Width
RF	Raster Fill Definition
WU	Pen Width Unit Selection

TD, Transparent Data

Purpose

To specify whether control characters perform their associated control function or print as characters when labeling. Use the TD instruction to print characters that function only as control characters in normal mode.

Syntax

TD *mode[;]*
            or
TD *[;]*

Parameter	Format	Functional Range	Parameter Default
mode	clamped integer	0 or 1	0 (normal)

Group

This instruction is in the Character Group.

Use

The device interprets the parameters as follows:

- **No parameters:** Defaults the labeling mode to normal. Equivalent to "TD0".

- **mode:** Selects the normal or transparent data mode for labeling.

    0   Normal. Control codes with an associated functionality perform their function and do not print. Control characters with no defined function are ignored. Character codes that are undefined in the current font are printed as spaces. Refer to *Control Characters* on page 67.

    1   Transparent. All characters are printed and perform no other function (except the currently defined label terminator, which terminates the label). The device prints a space for non-printing or undefined characters.

Transparent data mode must be enabled to access printable characters which have character codes with an associated functionality in normal mode. For example, the left arrow in the PC-8 symbol set has a character code of 27. In normal mode, a character code of 27 is interpreted as an escape character (**ESC**); in transparent data mode, a character code of 27 prints a left arrow.

Using TD in a Dual-Context Environment

Note that in normal mode, **ESCE** within a label string causes a device reset and transition to the PCL or HP RTL environment. In transparent mode, **ESCE** within a label string is printed rather than performing a device reset.

Related Instructions

AD	Alternate Font Definition
DT	Define Label Terminator
LB	Label
SA	Select Alternate Font
SD	Standard Font Definition
SS	Select Standard Font

HP-GL/2
INSTRUCTIONS

TR, Transparency Mode

Purpose

To define how the white areas of the area-fill (or pattern) affect the destination graphics image.

Syntax

TR *n[;]*

      or

TR [;]

Parameter	Format	Functional Range	Parameter Default
n	clamped integer	0 or 1	1 (on)

Group

This instruction is in the Palette Extension.

Use

- **No parameters:** Defaults to transparency mode = on (equivalent to "TR1;").

- **n:** Specifies whether transparency mode is on or off:

    0   Transparency mode = off. Overlaying white areas are opaque.

    1   Transparency mode = on (default). Overlaying white areas are transparent.

When transparency mode is on (default), the portion of an area-fill (or pattern) which is defined by white pixels does not affect the destination; whatever was already written to the page "shows through" the white areas in the new image. "White" is defined as the white reference specified in the CR instruction.

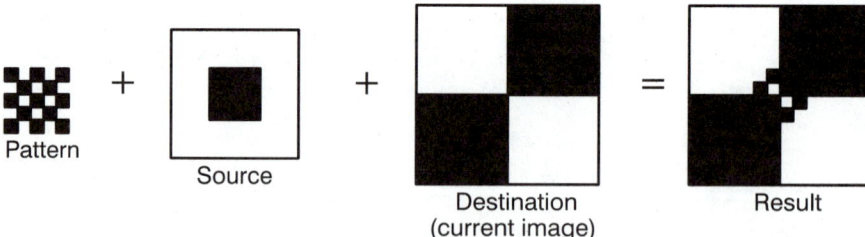

Figure 150. Transparency Mode On

When transparency mode is off, all source pixels are written to the destination, obscuring any underlying images.

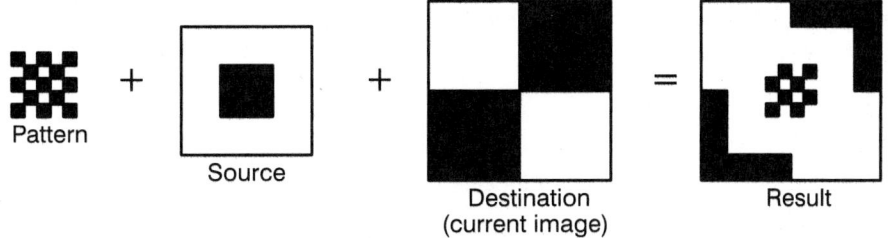

Figure 151. Transparency Mode Off

The transparency mode is defaulted by the **ESCE** (Reset) command, and the BP (Begin Plot), IN (Initialize) and DF (Default Values) instructions.

More information on the interactions between source data, texture, and destination data can be found in *Chapter 10: Interactions between Picture Elements* on page 365.

UL, User-Defined Line Type

Purpose

To create line types by specifying gap patterns, which define the lengths of spaces and lines that make up a line type.

Syntax

UL *index [,gap1,....,gapn][;]*
         or
UL *[;]*

Parameter	Format	Functional Range	Parameter Default
index	clamped integer	1 through 8 (or −1 through −8)	no default
gap1 to *gapn*	clamped real	0 to 32767	default line types

Group

This instruction is in the Line and Fill Attributes Group.

Use

The UL command allows you to define and store your own line types. The instruction does not itself select a line type. Use the LT instruction to select the line type once you have defined it with UL.

- **No parameters:** Defaults all line types (refer to the LT instruction).

- **index:** Identifies the number of the line type to be redefined. Specifying an *index* number without *gap* parameters sets the line type identified by the *index* to the default pattern for that number. The *index* number may not be 0.

  The *index* parameter uses absolute values, so "UL–n" is the same as "ULn". Redefining a standard fixed line type automatically redefines the corresponding adaptive line type.

- **gap1, ... gapn:** Specify alternate pen-down and pen-up stretches in the line type pattern; if gaps are numbered starting with 1, odd numbered gaps are pen-down moves, even numbered gaps are pen-up moves. The first gap is a pen-down move. Gap values are converted to percentages of the LT instruction's *pattern_length* parameter.

  A maximum of 20 gaps are allowed for each user-defined line type. *Gap* values must be non-negative; a *gap* value of zero produces a dot if specified for an odd numbered gap that is preceded or followed by a non-zero even-numbered gap. The sum of the gap parameters must be greater than zero.

The BP (Begin Plot), IN (Initialize) and DF (Default Values) instructions return user-defined line types to their default patterns.

UL clears the pattern residue and terminates any sequence of continuous vectors (see the LA and LT instructions).

Related Instructions

LA   Line Attributes
LT   Line Type

Example

The following example demonstrates redefining and printing a line type.

PA   4000,3000;   Specify absolute plotting and move to (4000,3000).

UL   8,0,15,0,15,0,15,40,15;   Redefine the user-defined line type with an index number of 8; specify the lines and spaces as follows, in percentages of the line distance: gap1 as a dot (0%), gap2 as a space (15%), gap3 as another dot (0%), gap4 as a space (15%), gap5 as another dot (0%), gap6 as a space (15%), gap7 as a line (40%), and gap8 as a space (15%).

LT   8,10;   Specify line type number 8 (just defined), with a pattern length of 10% of the distance between P1 and P2.

PU   2000,2500;   Lift the pen and move to (2000,2500).

PD   5000,2500;   Set the pen down and draw to (5000,2500).

Figure 152. Using a User-Defined Line Type

Possible Error Conditions

Error Condition	Error Number	Printer or Plotter Response
Sum of *gap* parameters equals zero	3	Ignores instruction
A *gap* is negative	3	Ignores instruction
Index out of range	3	Ignores instruction

VS, Velocity Select

Purpose

To specify the pen speed for pen plotters; other devices ignore this instruction. Use VS on pen plotters to optimize pen life and line quality for each pen and media combination. Increase line quality and create a slightly thicker line on any media by slowing the pen speed.

Syntax

VS *pen_velocity[,pen_number][;]*
      or
VS *[;]*

Parameter	Format	Functional Range	Parameter Default
pen_velocity	clamped integer	*device-dependent**	device-dependent
pen_number	clamped integer	*device-dependent***	all pens

*   Your plotter's fastest pen velocity may be greater or less than 60 cm/s. Refer to the manual for your plotter for more information.

**   Your plotter carousel may handle a different number of pens. Refer to the manual for your plotter or HP-GL/2 option for any additional information.

Group

This instruction is in the Technical Graphics Extension.

Use

Use the VS instruction to increase the pen life and line quality produced by your pens. Slowing the pen speed increases line quality.

The velocity set by this instruction (or the control panel) determines the maximum velocity corresponding to quality level 0 (see QL). As quality level is increased, the plotter will use a lower velocity, based on the maximum set by VS or the control panel. The default quality level (QL0) should be used when explicit control over velocity is required.

The VS instruction remains in effect until another VS instruction is received or the plotter is initialized or set to default conditions.

- **No parameters:** Sets the speed for all pens to the default value. Refer to the manual for your plotter or HP-GL/2 option for any additional information.

- **pen_velocity:** Specifies the pen speed in centimeters per second (cm/s). You can increment the pen speed by 1 cm/s. If the specified velocity is greater than the plotter's maximum speed, the maximum speed is used. The selected velocity applies only when the pen is down. The pen-up speed is device-dependent.

- **pen_number:** Applies the pen speed to a specific pen. When this parameter is omitted, the velocity applies to all pens.

The following table lists the velocity range and recommended speed for each pen type.

Pen Type	Recommended Velocity Range (cm/s)	Recommended Plotting Speed (cm/s)
Fiber-tip paper	5 to 80	40
Fiber-tip transparency	5 to 15	10
Disposable drafting	10 to 30	20
Refillable drafting	5 to 15	15

Note that your plotter may let you set pen speed from the control panel. However, the pen speed you specify using the control-panel buttons may apply to all pens. Refer to the manual for your plotter for any additional information.

Possible Error Conditions

Error Condition	Error Number	Printer or Plotter Response
More than 2 parameters	2	Ignores extra parameter
$Pen\_number \leq 0$	3	Ignores instruction
$Pen\_number >$ plotter's maximum	3	Ignores instruction

WG, Fill Wedge

Purpose

To define and fill any wedge. Use WG to draw filled sections of a pie chart.

Syntax

WG *radius,start_angle,sweep_angle[,chord_angle][;]*

Parameter	Format	Functional Range	Parameter Default
radius	current units	*device-dependent* (at least -2^{23} to $2^{23} - 1$)	no default
start_angle	clamped real	–32768 to 32767	no default
sweep_angle	clamped real	–360° to +360°	no default
*chord_ angle**	clamped real	0° to 360°	*device-dependent* (usually 5°)

* If you have used the "CT1" instruction, the *chord_angle* is interpreted as a *deviation distance* in current units; see the CT instruction on page 133.

Group

This instruction is in the Polygon Group.

Use

The WG instruction defines and fills a wedge using the current pen, fill type, and line types. The WG instruction includes an automatic pen down. When the instruction operation is complete, the original pen location and up/down status are restored.

The only difference between the WG instruction and the EW (Edge Wedge) instruction is that the WG instruction produces a filled wedge, and the EW, an outlined one.

WG deletes any stored polygon and stores the wedge in the polygon buffer with an implicit pen-down that overrides any explicit pen-up (PU); therefore the wedge may be subsequently re-filled by FP or edged by EP.

If the wedge has more points than will fit in the polygon buffer, the portion of the wedge that fits in the buffer is closed and filled, and the remainder of the wedge is discarded.

Always use isotropic scaling in any drawing that contains wedges (to avoid drawing an elliptical wedge). (Refer to *Scaling* on page 24 for more information.)

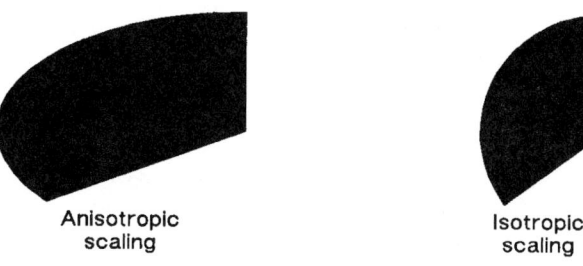

Anisotropic
scaling

Isotropic
scaling

Figure 153. Fill Wedge with Isotropic or Anisotropic Scaling

- **radius:** Specifies the distance from the current pen location to the start of the wedge's arc. Since the wedge is a portion of a circle, this parameter is the radius of the circle. It specifies the distance from the current pen location (which becomes the center of the circle), to any point on the circumference of the circle.

  The *radius* is interpreted in current units: as user-units when scaling is on; as plotter-units when scaling is off. The sign of the *radius* (+ or −) determines the location of the zero-degree reference point. Figures 154 and 155 show the location of the zero-degree reference point for a positive and negative radius.

- **start_angle:** Specifies the beginning point of the arc as the number of degrees from the zero-degree reference point. A positive start angle positions the radius in the positive direction (the direction from the +X-axis toward the +Y-axis) from the zero-degree reference point; a negative *start_angle* positions the radius in a negative direction from the zero-degree reference point. If you specify a start angle greater than 360°, a *start_angle* equal to the remainder of the *start_angle*/360° is used.

- **sweep_angle:** Specifies in degrees the angle through which the arc is drawn. A positive angle draws the angle in the positive direction (angle of rotation — +X-axis to the +Y-axis); a negative angle draws the angle in the negative direction (+X-axis to the −Y-axis). (Note, the relation of the +X-axis to the +Y-axis/−Y-axis can change as a result of scaling point or scaling factor changes.) Angles with absolute values greater than 360° have their signs preserved, and they are bounded to 360°. If the *sweep_angle* is ±360° after bounding, a radius is not drawn.

- **chord_angle:** Specifies the chord angle used to define the arc. Refer to the discussion of chord angles for the AA (Arc Absolute) instruction on page 100.

A zero *radius* draws a dot at the current position; a zero *sweep_angle* draws a line from the current position to the start of the wedge's arc.

Related Instructions

EP	Edge Polygon
EW	Edge Wedge
CI	Circle
FP	Fill Polygon
FT	Fill Type
SC	Scale

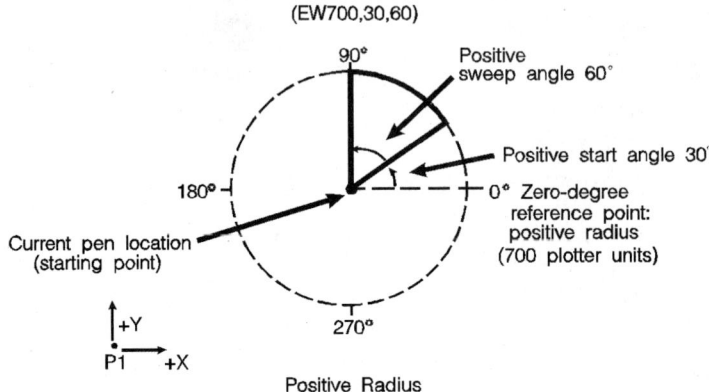

Figure 154. Terminology Used with Wedges

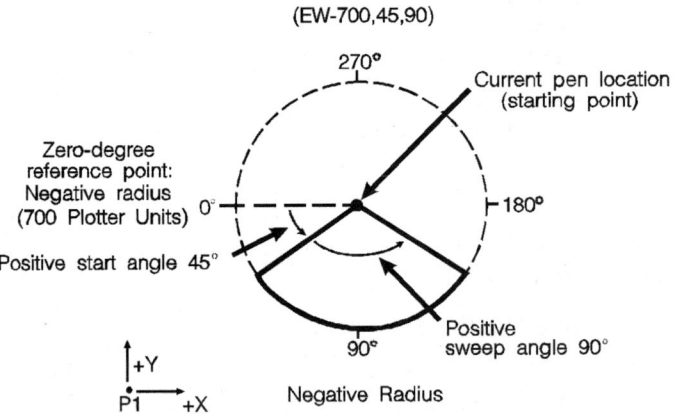

Figure 155. Wedge with a Negative Radius

Example of a Pie Chart

SC	−3000,3000,−2000,2000,1;	Set up user scaling, with P1 being (−3000,−2000) and P2 being (3000,2000). Specify isotropic scaling.
PA	0,0;	Enter absolute plotting mode and move to user-unit position (0,0).
FT	3,75,45;	Select fill type 3 (parallel lines), with 75 user-units between lines and the lines slanted 45°.
WG	−1000,90,180;	Fill a wedge with the current fill pattern; use a radius of 1000 user-units, a starting angle of 90° and a sweep angle of 180°. The zero-degree reference point is on the left side of the circle (indicated by the negative radius parameter [−1000]).
EW	−1000,90,180;	Draw an outline (edge) around the same wedge.
FT	4,60,45;	Select fill type 4 (cross-hatching), specifying 60 user-units between lines and with the lines tilted at 45°.
WG	−1000,330,120;	Fill a wedge that has the same radius and center point, but with a starting angle of 330° and a sweep angle of 120°.
EW	−1000,330,120;	Edge the same wedge.
PR	−60,110;	Specify relative plotting and move the pen 60 user-units to the left and 110 units up.
FT	1;	Select fill type 1 (solid black).
WG	−1000,270,60;	Fill a wedge with a radius of 1000 user-units, a start angle of 270°, and a sweep angle of 60°.
EW	−1000,270,60;	Edge the outline of the wedge that was just filled.

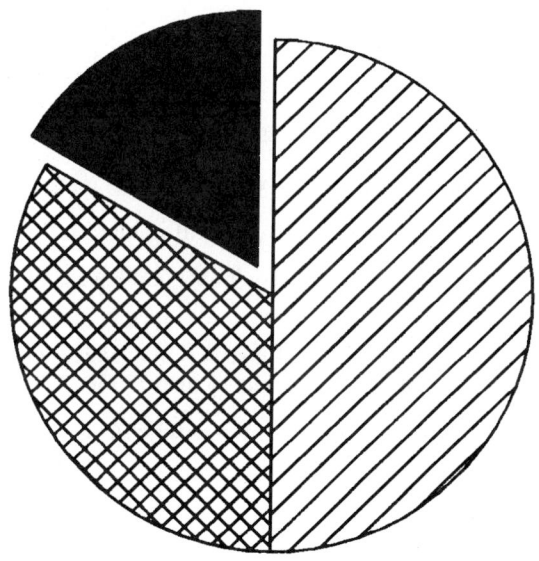

Figure 156. Pie Chart

The center point of the above circle is located at (0,0).

WU, Pen Width Unit Selection

Purpose

To specify how the width parameter of the PW (Pen Width) instruction is interpreted (whether metric or relative units).

Syntax

WU *type[;]*
     or
WU *[;]*

Parameter	Format	Functional Range	Parameter Default
type	clamped integer	0 or 1	0 (metric)

Group

This instruction is in the Line and Fill Attributes Group.

Use

Since using WU, with or without parameters, defaults all pen widths, send the WU instruction *before* a PW instruction (which sets a new pen width).

- **No parameter:** Defaults *type* parameter to 0 (metric) and all pen widths to 0.35 mm.

- **type:** Specifies how the *width* parameter of the PW (Pen Width) instruction is interpreted.

    0   Metric. Interprets the pen *width* parameter in millimeters.

    1   Relative. Interprets the pen *width* parameter as a percentage of the diagonal distance between P1 and P2.

A WU instruction remains in effect until another WU instruction is executed, or the device is initialized. WU is not defaulted by the DF (Default Values) instruction.

WU clears the current pattern residue and terminates any continuous vector sequence (see the LA and LT instructions).

Using WU in a PCL Dual-Context Environment

If an HP-GL/2 plot size is specified, metric units are adjusted by the current PCL picture frame scaling factor.

Related Instructions

SP   Select Pen
PW   Pen Width

Possible Error Conditions

Error Condition	Error Number	Printer or Plotter Response
Type parameter is not 0 or 1	3	Ignores instruction

Chapter 6: Summary of HP-GL/2 Device-Dependencies

The following HP-GL/2 attributes and parameters are device-dependent; check in the documentation for your device for the values and characteristics that it supports.

Functions Supported

- Which of the HP-GL/2 Extensions are supported—see *Chapter 4: The HP-GL/2 Extensions* on page 77.

- Whether the following instructions of the Technical Graphics Extension are supported:

  - DL (Download Character, page 144)

  - EC (Enable Cutter, page 163)

  - MG (Message, page 222)

  - NR (Not Ready, page 227)
      any clamping of the *timeout* parameter of NR
      the meaning of "NR;"

  - PS (Plot Size, page 259)

  - VS (Velocity Select, page 322)
      the range of supported pen velocities, including the pen-up speed, and the default velocity for VS.

- Whether the PG (Advance Full Page) instruction of the Configuration and Status Group is supported (see pages 30 and 249).

- Whether the RP (Replot) instruction of the Configuration and Status Group is supported (see pages 30 and 279).

  - The maximum number of replots supported (see page 279).

  - Whether the previous picture is replotted if a picture does not start with a BP (that is, it began after the last PG or RP), and an RP is issued while still in the picture header (see page 79).

- Function of the BP (Begin Plot) instruction of the Technical Graphics Extension (see pages 113—114).

  - In a dual-context environment,

  - Support of auto-rotation (see the *kind*=5 parameter of BP),

  - Picture name (the *kind*=1 parameter of BP).

Hardware and System Characteristics

- Whether the device is a "printer" or a "plotter" as defined on page 8.

- Timing of responses to output instructions (see pages 81 and 228).

- The default quality level and the range of levels supported for the QL (Quality Level) instruction (see page 267).

- The default type parameter of the MT (Media Type) instruction (see page 223).

- The range of supported sort algorithms for the ST (Sort) instruction (see page 312).

Coordinate Ranges

- The range of internally held coordinates (see page 23).

- X and Y parameter coordinate ranges in the following instructions:
  - AA   (Arc Absolute, page 100)
  - AC   (Anchor Corner, page 103)
  - AR   (Arc Relative, page 108)
  - AT   (Absolute Arc Three Point, page 110)
  - BR   (Bezier Relative, page 116)
  - BZ   (Bezier Absolute, page 118)
  - EA   (Edge Rectangle Absolute, page 160)
  - ER   (Edge Rectangle Relative, page 166)
  - IW   (Input Window, page 197)
  - PA   (Plot Absolute, page 237)
  - PD   (Pen Down, page 241)
  - PE   (Polyline Encoded, page 243)
  - PR   (Plot Relative, page 257)
  - PU   (Pen Up, page 262)
  - RA   (Fill Rectangle Absolute, page 269)
  - RR   (Fill Rectangle Relative, page 281)
  - RT   (Relative Arc Three Point, page 284)
  - SC   (Scale, page 290).

- The range of returned X and Y coordinates from the OD (Output Digitized Point and Pen Status) and OP (Output P1 and P2) instructions (see pages 228 and 233).

- The range of the number of fractional binary bits in the PE (Polyline Encoded) instruction (see page 243).

- Range of radii supported in the CI (Circle), EW (Edge Wedge), and WG (Fill Wedge) instructions (see pages 123, 171, and 324).

- The range of values of the *length* and *width* parameters of the PS (Plot Size) instruction (see page 259).

Chord Angles

- *Chord_angle* parameter default (usually 5°) in the following instructions:

AA	(Arc Absolute, page 100)
AR	(Arc Relative, page 108)
AT	(Absolute Arc Three Point, page 110)
CI	(Circle, page 123)
EW	(Edge Wedge, page 171)
RT	(Relative Arc Three Point, page 284)
WG	(Fill Wedge, page 324).

Fill Types and Line Properties

- The range of supported fill-types (see page 56).

- Edging width in the *edge_pen* parameter of the CF (Character Fill Mode) instruction (see page 120).

- The range of values of the *width* parameter of the PW (Pen Width) instruction (see page 264).

- The range of values of the miter limit attribute of the LA (Line Attributes) instruction (see page 200).

  - The clipping of a line end and line join (see page 200).

  - The lower limit below which line ends and line joins always have butt caps and no join.

- The supported *height*s and *width*s of raster fill patterns in the RF (Raster Fill Definition) instruction (see page 272).

Characters and Fonts

- Default label conditions for font spacing, pitch, height, posture, stroke weight, character width and height, and typeface (see pages 65, 106, and 296).

- Default scalable font (see page 106).

- Character sets and typefaces supported (*kinds* 1 and 7 of the AD and SD instructions—see pages 106, 296, and 475).

- The maximum size of a character (see page 298).

Pens and Colors

- The range of supported pens in the following instructions:

    CF   (Character Fill Mode *edge_pen* parameter, page 120)

    NP   (Number of Pens—the parameter must be a power of 2; the default palette size for monochrome raster devices is 2, and for color raster devices is 8—page 225)

    PE   (Polyline Encoded following a select-pen flag, page 243)

    PW   (Pen Width *pen* parameter, page 264)

    RF   (Raster Fill Definition *pen_number* parameters, page 272)

    SP   (Select Pen *pen_number* parameter, page 306)

    VS   (Velocity Select, page 322).

- In the PC (Pen Color Assignment) instruction, the colors assigned to any pens after the first eight for a color device, when no parameters are specified (see page 239).

- The table look-up algorithm in the device, to determine the merged color, using the MC (Merge Control) instruction (see page 220).

- The mapping from colors to gray levels in monochrome devices (see page 239).

Initial Conditions

- Language context when the device is powered on (see page 418).

- The default conditions set by the DF (Default Values) instruction (see page 136) for the following instruction defaults:

    AD   (Alternate Font Definition)

    MT   (Media Type)

    NP   (Number of Pens)

    QL   (Quality Level)

    SD   (Standard Font Definition)

    ST   (Sort)

    VS   (Velocity Select).

PART 3: HP RTL

This Part contains the following sections:

Chapter 7: HP RTL Concepts

HP RTL is Hewlett-Packard's Raster Transfer Language. It is a language that is understood by various plotters and printers, and is used to produce plotted or printed output from those devices. HP RTL is similar to Hewlett-Packard's PCL printer language; many of its commands are the same as those of PCL, though some are different, and you should be aware of these differences if you are already familiar with PCL.

This chapter makes some initial recommendations on writing HP RTL driver programs, and defines the syntax of HP RTL commands. Not all devices support all commands, or all parameter values of commands; check the product-specific documentation for details.

Writing HP RTL Drivers

Writing a raster driver is somewhat simpler than writing a vector driver, since raster drivers can assume that the data is already in raster format. HP RTL is made up of considerably fewer commands than its companion vector graphics language, HP-GL/2. On the other hand, since a raster-format image is closer to a raster device's native mode of operation than vector output, a raster language is by nature more device-dependent than a vector language.

Some users may choose to write a driver to support only one specific device. However, it is assumed that most driver authors will want to write their drivers in such a way that they can be easily adapted to different HP RTL devices, both present and future. This part of the book therefore attempts clearly to identify areas of the language that are device-dependent so that the programmer can define program variables and organize program procedures accordingly.

Printers and plotters with both HP-GL/2 and HP RTL share a consistent, verified command implementation across our product line. In addition, some plotters also include additional raster implementations.

When you are developing an HP RTL driver, consider the following aspects of the support you provide:

- Color and monochrome raster. Some monochrome devices convert color raster data to shades of gray.
- The resolution of your final output. For example, some devices support both 300 and 600 dots per inch (dpi) resolutions.
- Plotting "on-the-fly". Output begins immediately when the first row of raster data is received, unlimited raster print or plot sizes can be supported, though queueing and nesting are disabled.
- Image storing. Queueing and nesting of output may be supported if the data fits in memory (limited by the available memory on the device). When memory is full, the device may automatically switch to plotting on-the-fly.
- Raster data compression to improve throughput.

You should read *Appendix A: Writing Efficient Programs—Some Tips* on page 459.

HP RTL Command Syntax

HP RTL is based on Hewlett-Packard's PCL printer language, and uses the PCL language syntax. This section describes HP RTL syntax and explains how you can combine HP RTL commands. Note that although HP RTL is based on PCL and follows the PCL language syntax, HP RTL does not support the fonts and character commands that are part of PCL. HP RTL is used only to describe raster data. However HP RTL command definition is consistent with that of PCL, so the transition from one language to the other is quite simple, allowing a wide range of HP peripherals to be supported.

HP RTL language commands are compact escape sequence codes that are embedded in the job data stream. This approach minimizes both data transmission and command decoding overhead.

Notation for Parameter Formats

You must give parameters in the format required by each HP RTL command. The format of numeric parameters is usually as ASCII characters representing the number. Note that numeric ranges are minimums; your peripheral may support a larger range. Some values are described as *clamped*. This means that if the value is larger than the maximum allowed, the maximum is used; if it is less than the minimum allowed, the minimum is used. Note that the device does not recognize exponential format (for example, 6.03E8).

Where *binary numbers* must be entered into HP RTL commands, they are shown as a decimal value in parentheses. For example, the binary number **three** is denoted by (3), and is encoded in a byte as the binary sequence 00000011. These parentheses must not be encoded.

Other numbers are normally entered as ASCII characters.

Escape Sequences

HP RTL commands are also referred to as *escape sequences*. Escape sequence commands consist of two or more characters. The first character is always the ASCII escape character, identified by the **ESC** symbol. As the device monitors incoming data from a computer, it is "looking for" the **ESC** character. When the **ESC** character appears, the device reads it and its associated characters as a command to be performed and not as data to be printed. (An exception is when the **ESC** character appears in the middle of binary data of a specified length: it is interpreted as data, not as a command.)

There are two forms of HP RTL escape sequences: *two-character* escape sequences and *parameterized* escape sequences. The only two-character escape sequence used in HP RTL is **ESCE** for Reset.

Some escape sequences in this guide contain spaces for clarity. Do not include these spaces when using escape sequences (for example, do not leave a space between the **ESC** and the E of the Reset command). Note that raster commands are case-sensitive: an **ESCe**, for example, cannot be substituted for an **ESCE**.

Parameterized escape sequences normally contain a numeric parameter, which is shown in the syntax descriptions and in many examples by the # character. *In all cases, this must be replaced by a suitable value.*

Parameterized Escape Sequences

Parameterized escape sequences have the following form:

ESC X y # Z [data]

where y, #, and [data] may be optional, depending on the command. The following table summarizes the parameterized escape sequences:

HP RTL Syntax: ESC X y # Z[data]		
Parameter	**Parameter Type**	**Description**
X	Parameterized Character	A character indicating that the escape sequence is parameterized. Parameterized characters used in HP RTL are: % personality mode changes (ASCII code point 37), & device feature control commands (code point 38), * graphics control commands (code point 42).
y	Group Character	A character in the ASCII range 97–122 decimal (lower-case letters) which specifies the group type of control being performed. Group characters used in HP RTL are **a**, **b**, **c**, **l**, **p**, **r**, **t**, and **v**.
#	Value Field	A group of characters specifying a numeric value. The numeric value is represented as a string of ASCII characters within the range 48–57 decimal (**0** through **9**) which may be preceded by a **+** or **−** sign (ASCII code points 43 and 45) and may contain a fractional portion indicated by the digits after a decimal point (**.** −code point 46). The specific numeric ranges and defaults for each command are given in *Chapter 14: HP RTL Command Reference* starting on page 401.
Z	Termination Parameter Character	A character in the ASCII range 65–90 decimal (upper-case letters). This character terminates the escape sequence. See *Combining Commands* on page 340 for an explanation of the use of lowercase letters (those in the range 97–122).
[data]	Eight-bit binary data	The number of bytes of binary data is specified by the value field of the escape sequence. Binary data immediately follows the terminating character of the escape sequence. Where specific values for binary data are used in this book, they are described either in binary form or in decimal enclosed in parentheses. (Do not enclose the data in square brackets [ ] or parentheses (); these are included for clarity only.)

Note: For clarity in explaining how to use specific HP RTL commands, spaces have sometimes been inserted; *do not leave spaces* when you encode these commands.

Combining Commands

Following is an example of four HP RTL commands that have the effect of setting color index number 1 to be cyan (0% red, 100% green and blue, based on the default color range of 0 to 255):

ESC*v0A	Set Red Parameter to 0
ESC*v255B	Set Green Parameter to 255
ESC*v255C	Set Blue Parameter to 255
ESC*v1I	Assign Color Index 1.

In this example all the commands begin with the same parameterized character (*) and group character (v); the commands belong to the same group. When this is the case, the commands can be combined by making all termination parameter characters except the last one *lowercase*. The combined command series is:

ESC*v0a255b255c1I

The lowercase letters (a, b, and c) are ***termination parameter characters***, and can be any ASCII character in the range 97–122 decimal (a through z) only. The termination (final) parameter character (in this case I) must remain in uppercase.

Note the following about combining escape sequences:

- Parameter characters always apply to the value *preceding* the parameter character.

- Commands can only be combined when the first *two* characters after the **ESC**—the parameterized character and the group character—are identical.

- Combined commands are performed in the order that they are combined, from left to right. Each command is performed immediately; the device does not wait for the termination parameter character to begin executing the commands.

- Some commands do not allow a lowercase parameter character. These commands can only be used to *terminate* a combined command. *Chapter 14: HP RTL Command Reference* on page 401 shows which commands do and do not allow lowercase parameter characters. Commands that allow lowercase parameter characters are shown with both lowercase and uppercase letters separated by a vertical bar (|), for example, **ESC***v#a|A. Commands that require an uppercase parameter character are shown without the lowercase letter (for example, **ESC***rC).

Chapter 8: Defining an Image

This chapter describes how to set the size of your picture, how to control its resolution, and how to scale images. It also includes a description of the coordinate system and the current active position (CAP), and describes how to move about the page.

Setting Raster Boundaries

You can use HP-GL/2 instructions to define the logical page and window in which your HP RTL picture should appear. In addition, HP RTL supports its own raster height and width parameters, which can be used to save on data transmission time and for scaling.

Setting the Logical Page Size and Input Window in HP-GL/2

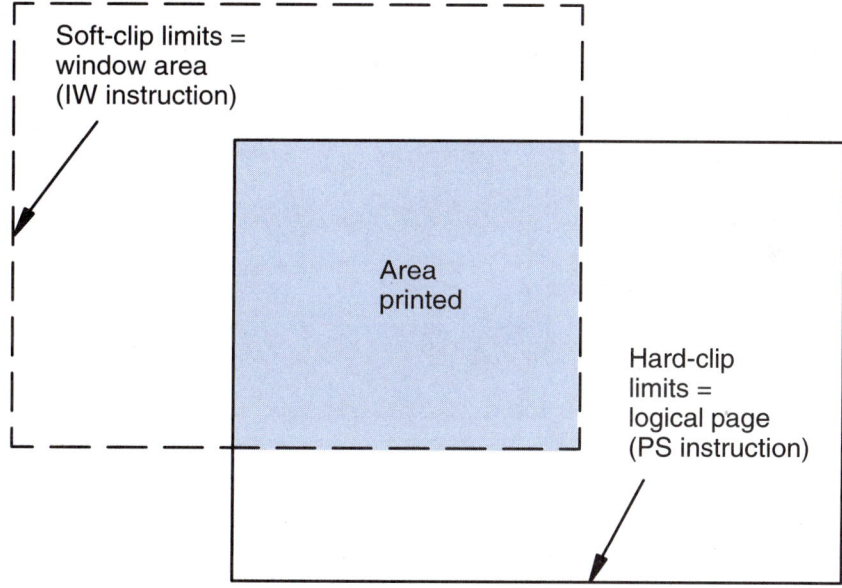

Figure 157. Using HP-GL/2 to Set Page Size and Window Size

Before entering HP RTL mode, you can define boundaries using the HP-GL/2 PS (Plot Size) and IW (Input Window) instructions. HP RTL respects these boundaries; no raster data will be printed outside them. If you fail to use the PS (Plot Size) instruction, the maximum length printable is 1.5 times the roll width (for roll-feed media).

The area defined by the PS instruction is referred to as the ***logical page***. Its borders are called the ***hard-clip limits***. The area defined by the IW instruction is called a ***window***; its borders form the ***soft-clip limits***. Full details of the PS and IW instructions are on pages 259 and 197 respectively. Note that HP-GL/2 scaling as defined using the SC (Scale) instruction is *not* carried over to HP RTL. HP RTL has its own scaling: see *Scaling Raster Images* on page 345.

HP-GL/2 and HP RTL do not automatically use the same units for defining resolution. HP RTL uses the device's native resolution; HP-GL/2 uses either device units or user units, which are defined with the instructions SC (Scale) and IP (Input P1 and P2). If you define the HP-GL/2 resolution to be the device's native resolution, you can thereby simplify coding your driver program. (There is more information in *Controlling Image Resolution* on page 344.)

Setting the Width and Height in HP RTL

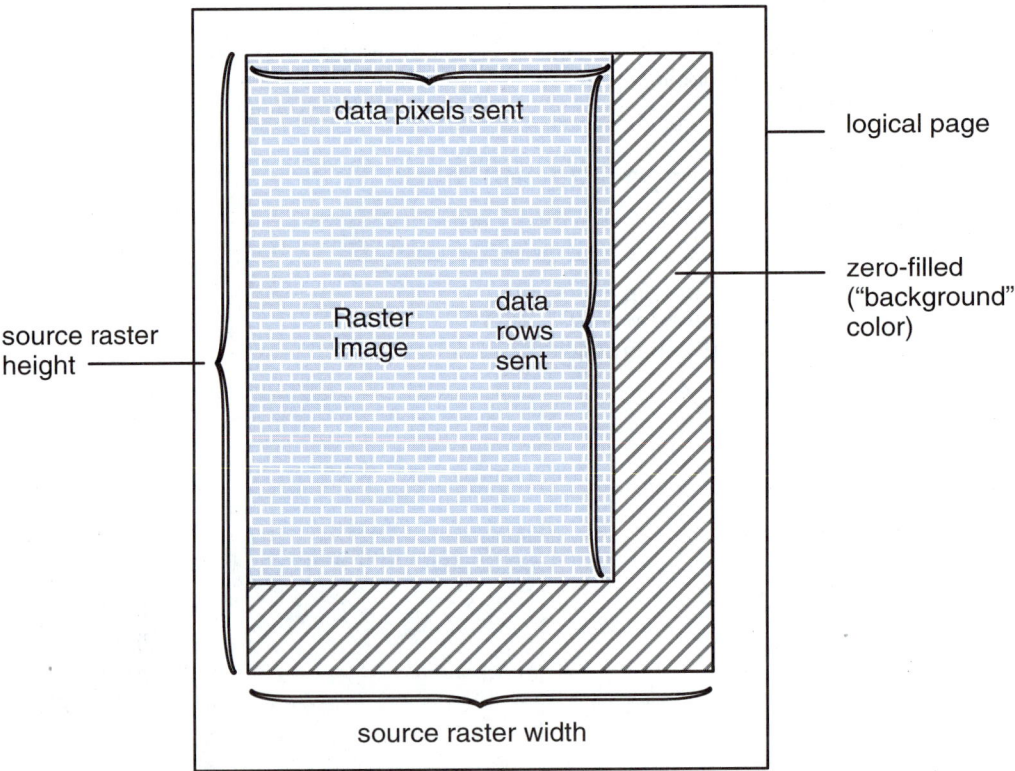

Figure 158. Setting the Width and Height in HP RTL

Besides setting boundaries in HP-GL/2, after entering HP RTL mode you can optionally set raster boundaries using the HP RTL commands Source Raster Width (**ESC***r#S) and Source Raster Height (**ESC***r#T). These commands define the boundaries of your output in terms of *pixel width* and *pixel height* respectively. (Pixel height is sometimes referred to as the number of *pixel rows*.)

The main advantage to setting source width and height is to avoid sending unnecessary data. When source width is specified and you send a row of data containing fewer pixels than the source width, the remaining pixels are filled with zeros by the device. (A zero-filled area is printed with the color defined for index 0. See *Using HP RTL Indexes* on page 358.) Similarly, when you send fewer rows of data than specified by source height, the empty rows are zero-filled by the device.

Figure 158 shows an example of zero-filling using source height and width.

When you send a row of pixels that is longer than the source width, the excess pixels are discarded; the data is clipped. When you send more rows than specified by source height, the excess rows are discarded.

It is also possible to set the Destination Raster Width (**ESC***t#H) and the Destination Raster Height (**ESC***t#V). When this is done, the source width and height are still used to determine zero-filling and clipping. *After* zero-filling and clipping, if scale mode is on (that is, the Start Raster Graphics command [**ESC***r#A] with a value of 2 or 3 has been used), the image is scaled to the destination width and height. (Note that source width and height *must* be specified for scaling to work. See *Scaling Raster Images* on page 345.) Finally, the image is clipped to the soft-clip and hard-clip limits defined by the HP-GL/2 instructions IW and PS.

The HP RTL raster system uses the concept of a bounded raster picture or raster area. Within this area, the device fills missing and incomplete rows with zeros and clips data that would fall outside. This is described more fully in *Using Index 0* on page 359.

The raster height extends vertically from the CAP to one of:

- The distance specified by Source Raster Height if raster scaling is off

- The distance specified by Destination Raster Height if raster scaling is on

- The row preceding an implicit or explicit End Raster Graphics command (**ESC***rC)

- The lower edge of the printable area.

The raster width extends from the left raster margin (the CAP or the left edge of the logical page), and is limited to one of:

- The distance specified by Source Raster Width if scaling is off

- The distance specified by Destination Raster Width if scaling is on

- The right edge of the logical page.

Source raster width and height refer to bits of "source" data. One bit of data may result in several physical pixels if the resolution is set to less than the physical device resolution. See *Controlling Image Resolution* on page 344.

Maximum Width and Height

Two factors govern the maximum raster image size:

- The device's physical limits: Physical limits include the maximum picture size (the maximum number of pixels for height and width), and the amount of data that a device can store in its memory or on its disk. See the device's documentation for information on how many pixels the device can handle, and how much memory and/or disk space is available for raster images.

- The HP RTL language limits: For all devices, the maximum source width is 65 535 pixels, and the maximum source height is 65 535 raster rows. Each limit applies only if the corresponding command (Source Raster Width or Source Raster Height) is issued.

Raster Graphics

A *dot* is the smallest mark a printer or plotter can make. Its size and spacing are device specific, and the size of a dot may vary in any device. A raster image is composed of *rows* of dots. These rows are organized from top to bottom of the image. A *pixel* is the smallest definable picture element in an image. A row of pixels is transferred to the printer or plotter as a string of *bytes* (a byte consists of eight bits). The *resolution* of an image is the number of dots per inch (dpi) in both dimensions of the image. At maximum device resolution, a pixel consists of one dot. At lower resolutions, or when you are scaling a picture, a pixel may consist of more than one dot.

Controlling Image Resolution

How you set the resolution determines how many physical dots are printed for each pixel of data you transfer. The maximum physical resolution varies from one device to another.

When you set the HP RTL resolution to the device's maximum physical resolution (the *machine resolution*), one dot is printed for each pixel of data you send. For instance, if the maximum physical resolution is 300 dots per inch (dpi) and you set the HP RTL resolution to 300 dpi, each pixel of data you send causes one dot to appear on the media. A resolution of 300 dpi means that the device can place dots of ink anywhere in a grid of 300-by-300 dots in every square inch of the printable area of the page.

Some devices allow different *native resolutions*, up to the machine resolution. In such cases, the native resolution can be set using the @PJL SET RESOLUTION=... command (see page 392). At lower native resolutions, each pixel consists of more than one dot, but dot spacing remains the same and the same number of dots per inch are printed.

When 150 dpi is requested in HP RTL in a machine whose native resolution is 300 dpi, printing is still at 300 dpi, but each pixel is now composed of four dots, and is twice as wide and tall as a pixel printed at 300 dpi. Your image data consists of 150 pixels for each linear inch, but 600 dots are actually printed (300 in each of two rows).

300 dpi   150 dpi   Machine resolution
in HP RTL   in HP RTL   is 300 dpi

Note that this means that the *same amount of data* produced at a lower resolution creates a larger image than the original; that is, the image is scaled up isotropically. For instance, if you set the resolution to half the original resolution, the same data produces an image that is twice as wide and twice as high as the original:

300 dpi   150 dpi

(Note that in both these diagrams, the positions and sizes of the dots are not intended to be an accurate representation.)

Requesting a lower resolution does not cause less detail to be printed. The device still prints at the native resolution, but it makes the image larger, for the same data. To keep the image the same size, you must send less data to the device, in this case one quarter.

If the native resolution is set to 300 dpi on a device that actually prints 600 dpi, and the requested resolution from HP RTL is, say, 200 dpi, the image is first approximated as close as it can by 300 dpi pixels, and then each 300 dpi pixel is printed as a 2x2 array of dots. If however, the native resolution on the same device is set to 600 dpi, each HP RTL pixel at 200 dpi will be printed as a 3x3 square of dots.

When the native resolution is smaller than the maximum physical resolution, the image is first scaled to the native resolution, and then scaled again to the physical resolution. The result is an image with lower resolution, but which occupies less memory.

If you set HP RTL resolution to be *greater* than the device's maximum physical resolution, more than one pixel of data is required to produce one physical dot on the device. This means that some detail is lost, and the image appears smaller than the original; it is scaled down isotropically. The device, as always, still prints at its maximum physical resolution, but it produces a smaller image.

The algorithm used for scaling down is device-dependent.

You use the HP RTL command Set Graphics Resolution (**ESC***t#R) to specify the resolution.

Note that the Set Graphics Resolution command does not affect the resolutions of fill patterns defined in HP-GL/2 using the RF (Raster Fill Definition) instruction. You may also be able to specify the device resolution through the device's control panel, or by using the @PJL SET RESOLUTION=... command (see page 392).

Continuous and Discrete Resolution

Continuous resolution means that you can specify any resolution within the allowable range; you are not restricted to specific values.

However, on devices that support only *discrete* resolutions, the device can only create pictures at certain well-defined resolutions. For instance, a device with a maximum physical resolution of 300 dpi may support only 75, 150, and 300 dpi. On these devices, if you request an unsupported resolution through HP RTL, the resolution value is mapped to the next higher supported resolution to ensure that the output is created without data loss. On the device just mentioned, if a you request a resolution of 200 dpi, it is printed at 300 dpi; if you request a resolution of 140 dpi, it is printed at 150 dpi.

Some devices support continuous resolutions within a certain range. Other devices only support incremental resolutions. Some devices support a discrete draft resolution for the fast production of prints; others allow a continuous range of resolutions for normal (final) or best (enhanced) quality output.

Scaling Raster Images

HP RTL does not follow HP-GL/2 scaling as defined with the HP-GL/2 SC (Scale) instruction. HP RTL does, however, support its own scaling using the Destination Raster Width, Destination Raster Height, and Start Raster Graphics commands. You can either enlarge or reduce an image using scaling. When scaling an image down, loss of detail always results. The algorithm used for scaling down is device-dependent.

The Start Raster Graphics command (**ESC***r#A) with a value of 2 or 3 turns on *scale mode*. In that case, the image is rendered in the specified size, independently of the resolution of the device.

The Source Raster Width (**ESC***r#S) and Source Raster Height (**ESC***r#T) commands define the size of the source, and the Destination Raster Width (**ESC***t#H) and Destination Raster Height (**ESC***t#V) commands define the size of the destination. (*Source data* is the data that is to be added to the page; *destination data* is the data after it has been placed on the page.) The scale factor is implicitly derived from the source and destination data sizes. However, scaling only occurs if both the width and the height of the source are explicitly specified.

If only one destination dimension is given, the other dimension is implicitly determined to maintain isotropic scaling (see page 13). If no destination dimensions are specified, the image is scaled so that it is the largest that will fit in the area between the current Y-position and the bottom edge of the current page, and the left graphics margin and the right edge of the page; isotropic scaling is maintained.

In order to use scaling, you must specify a *source* raster width and height. If one or the other is not specified, the device will not enter scale mode; the Start Raster Graphics command will default to scale mode off.

How to Scale an Image

Once you have set the page size using the HP-GL/2 PS (Plot Size) instruction, scaling occurs either *isotropically* (without distortion) or *anisotropically* (with distortion)—see page 13.

There are three options for scaling:

- You specify either a destination width *or* height, and Start Raster Graphics with scale mode on. In this case, the scale factor is determined by comparing the source and destination sizes for the dimension you specified (either width or height). Isotropic scaling is maintained; the image is not distorted.

- You specify both a destination width *and* height, and Start Raster Graphics with scale mode on. In this case, the scale factors are determined by comparing the source and destination sizes for both dimensions. The output is scaled anisotropically, that is, the image is "stretched" or "shrunk" to fit the destination dimensions. If the source-to-destination ratio is the same for both width and height, isotropic scaling results.

- You do not specify a destination width or height, and Start Raster Graphics with scale mode on. In this case, the image is scaled isotropically to render the largest image that fits on the part of the logical page that is below the CAP and to the right of the left graphics margin. (The left graphics margin is set either to the CAP's X-location or to the left side of the logical page when you Start Raster Graphics.) Note that since isotropic scaling is used, the image may not actually fill the logical page.

It is possible to set the destination width or height to be larger than the actual page size. In this case, the image is still scaled using the implicitly determined scale factor(s). After scaling, the image is clipped along the window and logical page boundaries set by the HP-GL/2 instructions IW and PS.

Figure 159 shows an example of isotropic and anisotropic scaling. It is assumed that no window is specified, and that the logical page is set to the same size as the destination dimensions. If the logical page were a different size, scaling would happen at the same ratio, but the image would be clipped to the logical page.

Zero-filling of pixels and rows based on source width and height is done *before* scaling. See *Setting the Width and Height in HP RTL* on page 342 for more information on zero-filling.

Scaling takes precedence over any resolution setting (from the HP RTL command Set Graphics Resolution). When scale mode is on, the resolution setting is ignored.

Scaling usually adds significantly to the processing time required to generate an image. As an alternative, you might consider scaling the image at the host computer before transmission. But if this increases the overall image size, the file will take longer to transmit, offsetting gains in printing speed.

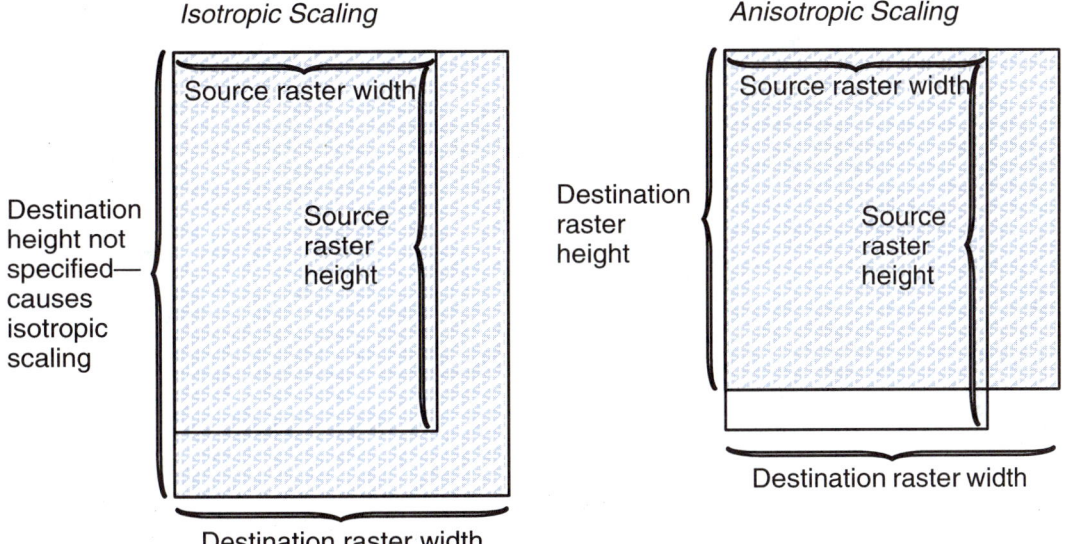

Figure 159. Specifying Scaling Parameters

The Current Active Position (CAP)

In the HP RTL coordinate system, the origin (0,0) is always the upper-left corner of the logical page. In the HP-GL/2 coordinate system, the origin (0,0) is the upper-left corner of the logical page when length ≥ width in the PS instruction, and the upper-right corner of the logical page when length < width in the PS instruction.

HP-GL/2 maintains the position of the pen on the paper as the "current pen location." In HP RTL terms, this is called the *current active position* (CAP). It can be thought of as the row and column location of the logical "cursor" within an image.

The device maintains HP-GL/2's pen location and HP RTL's CAP separately. It is possible, however, when switching from HP-GL/2 mode to HP RTL mode, to transfer the HP-GL/2 pen location so that it becomes the HP RTL CAP. Similarly, when switching from HP RTL mode to HP-GL/2 mode, you can choose to transfer the HP RTL CAP so that it becomes the HP-GL/2 pen location.

On some devices, the "auto-rotate" feature might cause HP-GL/2 objects to be rotated, but not HP RTL data. We therefore recommend that you disable this feature (using the HP-GL/2 Begin Plot instruction "BP5,1") to avoid problems when merged vector and raster data are used.

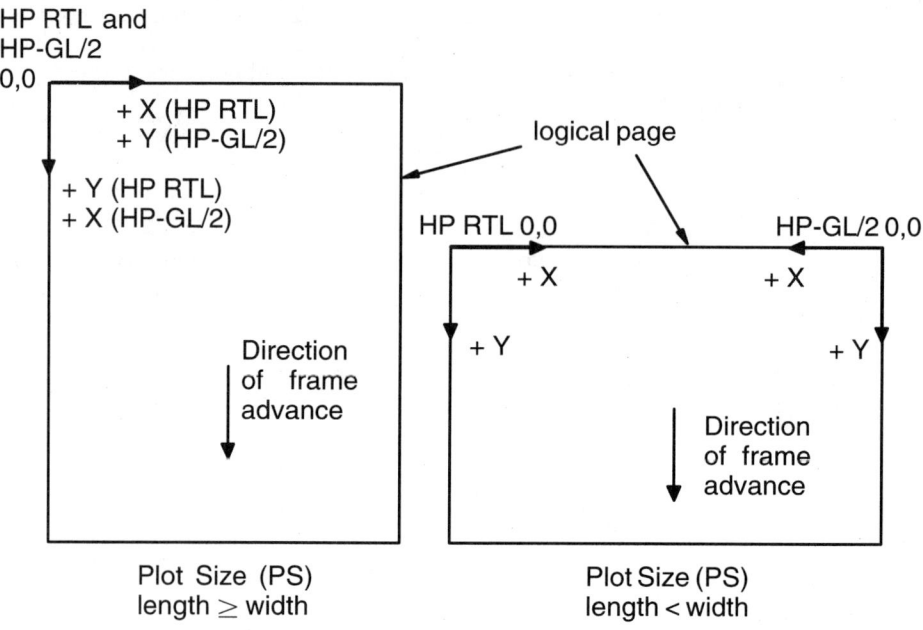

Figure 160. HP-GL/2 and HP RTL Page Orientations

Commands to Change the CAP

You use these HP RTL commands to move the Current Active Position (CAP):

Move CAP Horizontal (Decipoints), **ESC&a#H**, page 423
Move CAP Horizontal, **ESC*p#X**, page 424
Move CAP Vertical, **ESC*p#Y**, page 425
Y Offset, **ESC*b#Y**, page 451.

The Move CAP Horizontal and Move CAP Vertical commands use native resolution units, such as dots-per-inch.

Note that the Move CAP Horizontal (Decipoints) command and the Y Offset command in non-raster mode are to be made obsolete, so you should not use them in new application programs.

You can also use the Move CAP Horizontal (Decipoints) and Y Offset commands to move the HP RTL CAP. Both commands support *relative* positioning. Move CAP Horizontal (Decipoints) also allows you to position an *absolute* distance from the left boundary of the logical page. (A "decipoint" is 1/720 inch.)

The Reset command (**ESCE**) resets the CAP to the HP RTL origin (0,0). An HP-GL/2 PG (Advance Full Page) or BP (Begin Plot) instruction, or any instruction that results in a page advance, also resets the CAP to the HP RTL origin (0,0).

At the start of raster graphics, the CAP is at the current Y-position on the left graphics margin. After printing the raster image, the CAP moves to the left graphics margin at the dot row following the last row of raster data. If a Destination Raster Height command was issued, the final location of the CAP is on the left graphics margin, one dot row below the lowest part of the picture frame defined by that Destination Raster Height command.

Negative Motion

It can be important when you are printing or plotting an image for the device to know whether there might be any movement of the CAP in a direction opposite to the movement of paper. This is known as ***negative motion***. Negative motion is:

- Any HP-GL/2 drawing operation.
- Any operation that would print in the negative Y-axis direction with respect to previously printed data.
- Any Y Offset command in raster mode that moves the CAP in the negative Y-axis direction.

On devices that support it, you use this HP RTL command to tell the device whether to expect negative motion:

> Negative Motion, **ESC&a#N**, page 426.

You tell the device you are not using negative motion using the Negative Motion command with a value of 1 (**ESC&a1N**), the device may interleave parsing of data and printing, to reduce the printing time and to reduce the memory requirements. Printing on the device is not guaranteed if a command is later issued that might cause negative motion to take place.

HP RTL Native Resolution Units

CAP movement should normally be performed at HP RTL native resolution. The native resolution is usually a sub-multiple of the physical device resolution, which is the number of dots per inch that the device can print. HP RTL native resolutions are device-dependent. On devices that support several native resolutions, the native resolution may be selectable by the command:

> @PJL SET RESOLUTION=#, page 392.

The native resolution is used in HP RTL for two purposes:

- To select the resolution for CAP movements.

- To select the resolution to which the raster image is to be scaled. Selecting a smaller resolution than the device's maximum physical resolution uses less memory but does not exploit the detail that the device can provide. Lower resolutions are therefore recommended when you produce drafts, and not for final production runs.

Chapter 9: Defining Colors

This chapter describes how to define colors and how to select colors from a palette. It also describes halftoning and how to use patterns.

Primary Colors

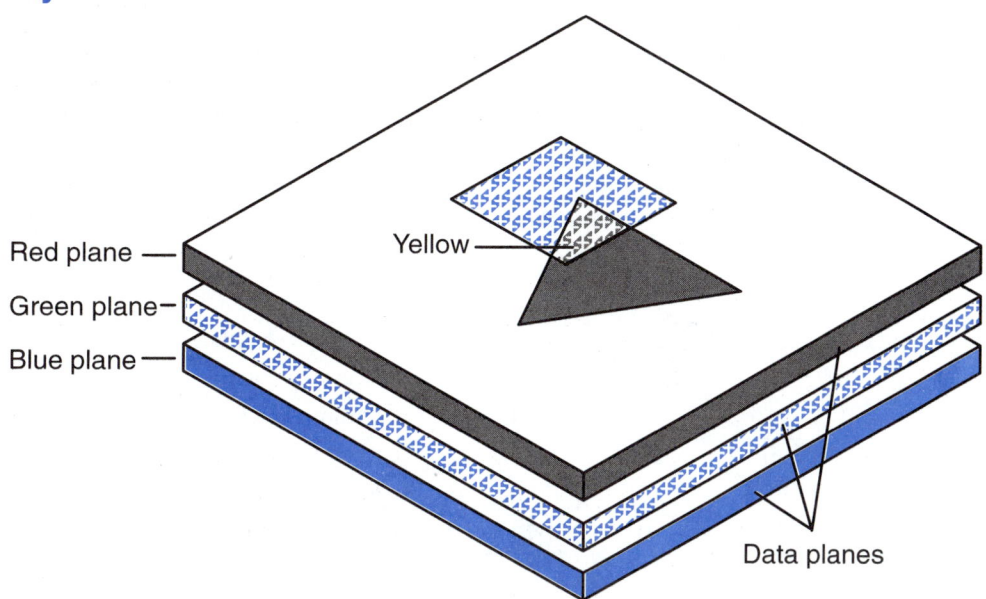

Figure 161. Planes of Primary Colors in a Red-Green-Blue Color Model

HP RTL is based on a "plane model" for defining images. You can think of one plane of data as a monochrome image, where "monochrome" doesn't necessarily mean black, but could be any single color. For devices that support multiple planes, by stacking planes on top of each other, different color combinations can be achieved. The more planes, the more color combinations are possible. If you use a red-green-blue (RGB) or a cyan-magenta-yellow (CMY) color model, you use three planes; with a black-cyan-magenta-yellow (KCMY) model there are four planes.

Two-tone monochrome devices support only one plane of data, which yields a two-tone image (normally black and white). Grayscale monochrome devices support multiple data planes but convert the planes to shades of gray for printing. Color devices support multiple data planes and actually print these multiple data planes in color. Color raster data may be interpreted as gray scales on monochrome devices or when monochrome/gray-scale is selected through the control panel of the device or through PJL.

Color specifications are based on a range of values for each primary component. The basis of these specifications is device-dependent. The end-points of the range for each component are called the **black** and **white references** for that component. Colors relative to these predefined limits are derived by specifying the amount of each component.

Assume, for instance, that you define one *plane* of data to be red, another green, and another blue. (These are, in fact, the recommended definitions for three-plane devices.) By laying these images on top of each other, up to eight colors can be achieved in any given pixel. All three together in one pixel gives white. Solid red and green together give yellow; green and blue together give cyan; and so on, following the standard red-green-blue (RGB) color model.

Palettes

A *palette* is a collection of colors, in which the color is selected by an index number. All HP RTL color modes have default palettes. Only one palette can be active at a time, though you can push palettes onto a stack and pop them from the stack. The active palette is overwritten whenever a new palette is created or a palette is popped from the stack. The active palette is always transferred between HP RTL and HP-GL/2 on devices that support palettes in HP RTL.

Figure 162 illustrates a palette. Each palette entry associates an index number with three primary color components; for HP-GL/2 only, a "pen width" is also associated with each entry.

	Primary 1 (e.g. red)	Primary 2 (green)	Primary 3 (blue)	HP-GL/2 pen width	
Index 0	255	255	255	0.10 mm	white
1	0	0	0	0.10 mm	black
2	255	0	0	0.40 mm	red
3	0	255	0	0.10 mm	green
4	255	255	0	0.20 mm	yellow
5	214	0	255	0.20 mm	light purple
6	233	233	233	0.15 mm	10% gray
n (maximum 255)	⋮			⋮	

Figure 162. A Palette

Specifying Colors

Colors can be specified by either **indexed** or **direct** selection. If you are using simple color mode or black-and-white mode (described below), only indexed selection is available. Otherwise, byte #1 of the Configure Image Data command (**ESC***v#W) determines the format in which raster data is to be transmitted and interpreted.

Raster colors—colors that are specified in raster transfer mode—can be selected directly or indirectly, depending on the meaning of the bits that are transferred; that is, the transmitted bit combinations for each pixel may form a palette index number or they may directly specify component proportions. Raster mode (see *Transferring Raster Data* on page 373) is normally entered by a Start Raster Graphics (**ESC***r#A) command and ended by an End Raster Graphics

(**ESC*rC**) command. In raster mode, the palette is only used for indexed color selection, and not for direct color selection.

Non-raster colors—for example, foreground colors or multi-colored patterns—cannot be selected directly. In non-raster mode, the palette is always used to select colors; the color of a pattern is specified using the Foreground Color (**ESC*v#S**) command.

Indexed Selection

Indexed selection specifies a color's index number in a palette. In non-raster mode, the Foreground Color command (**ESC*v#S**) selects a color by palette index. In raster mode, each data bit combination forms an index number. For example, three bits allow eight index numbers for eight colors.

Direct Selection

Direct selection specifies a color's proportions of the RGB primary colors. For example a 24-bit-per-pixel representation for the color *cyan* is (hexadecimal 00, FF, FF) for red, green, and blue primaries, and (FF, F0, 00) is a slightly red-tinted yellow.

Color Modes

There are four color modes in HP RTL: black-and-white, simple-color, HP RTL imaging, and HP-GL/2 imaging. All these modes create a palette; you cannot modify the palettes in simple color mode or in black-and-white mode.

Black-and-White Mode

This is the default color mode, and is the mode following power-up; the device reverts to this mode after a Reset (**ESCE**) command. The palette defines two colors: white at index 0 and black at index 1.

Simple Color Mode

This mode is entered using the Simple Color (**ESC*r#U**) command. It has a fixed size, fixed color, unmodifiable palette, which can be eight-color CMY, sixteen-color KCMY, two-color black and white, or eight-color RGB. It can only be used if the pixel encoding mode is indexed planar.

The Simple Color command should be used to specify CMY or KCMY data.

HP RTL Imaging Mode

This mode is entered using the Configure Image Data (**ESC*v#W**) command. It allows up to 24 bits per pixel for color specification. Using halftoning, you can specify more colors than with simple color mode. The pixel encoding mode, number of bits per pixel, number of bits per primary, black and white color references, and the color palette can all be programmed in this mode.

The Configure Image Data (**ESC*v#W**) command creates one of three different programmable palettes (see below).

The default HP RTL palettes are defined as follows:

Number of Planes	Index Number	Color
1 (bits per index=1)	0 1	White Black
2 (bits per index=2)	0 1 2 3	Black Red Green White
3–8 (bits per index=3 or greater)	0 1 2 3 4 5 6 7 > 7	Black Red Green Yellow Blue Magenta Cyan White Black

The black and white references specified by the Configure Image Data command have no effect on the default palettes; however if a palette entry is reprogrammed with a different color, the black and white references are used to specify the primary components of the new color.

HP-GL/2 Imaging Mode

In HP-GL/2, the IN (Initialize) and BP (Begin Plot) instructions start color imaging and also default the number of bits per index, and create a default programmable palette. This palette can be modified in HP RTL or in HP-GL/2. (The active palette can be transferred between HP RTL and HP-GL/2.)

As shown below, the default HP-GL/2 palettes are different from the default HP RTL palettes. These palettes can be modified in the same way as the default HP RTL palettes.

Number of Pens	Pen Number	Color
2	0 1	White Black
4	0 1 2 3	White Black Red Green
8	0 1 2 3 4 5 6 7 > 7	White Black Red Green Yellow Blue Magenta Cyan Black

Black and White References

For RGB color spaces, the ***black-reference*** for a primary color denotes a value assigned to the absence of that color, and the ***white-reference*** denotes the value given to a fully saturated primary color. Regardless of the number chosen, the white reference represents the maximum amount of output color that the device can produce, and the black reference is the minimum amount of that primary. For example, if you define the white reference for the color red to be 100, this number represents the reddest red that the device can produce. If instead you specified 10 as the white reference for red, 10 would still represent the same red.

For example, if the red, green, and blue white references are set to 64 and the black references are all 0, a 50% blue would be represented by the numbers 0, 0, 32, and a 50% yellow would be 32, 32, 0.

But if the white references are set to 64, 128, and 32 respectively, and the black references are set to 4, 0, 0, the 50% blue is 4, 0, 16 and the 50% yellow is 34, 64, 0.

However, for all practical purposes, the following values are recommended for each primary color: for an RGB color model use a white reference of 255 and a black reference of 0; for a CMY color model, use a white reference of 0 and a black reference of 255.

Color-Definition Commands

You use these commands to define how the device handles color data:

> Configure Image Data, **ESC***v#W[data], page 407
> Set Red Parameter, **ESC***v#A, page 440
> Set Green Parameter, **ESC***v#B, page 439
> Set Blue Parameter, **ESC***v#C, page 437
> Assign Color Index, **ESC***v#I, page 405
> Push/Pop Palette, **ESC***p#P, page 432
> Simple Color, **ESC***r#U, page 441.

If you are using the HP RTL command Configure Image Data to specify re-programmable palettes, for pixel encoding modes 0, 1, or 4, you use the Set Number of Bits per Index byte of this command to tell the device how many data planes to expect. This command also resets the HP RTL palette to its default—see *Defining the HP RTL Palette* on page 356.

You can combine different images with different numbers of planes on the same page. For instance, you could have a three-plane color image and one-plane monochrome image on the same page.

The Simple Color command should be used to specify CMY or KCMY data.

Encoding Colors

Several bits per pixel are required to produce multiple colors. The bits that define pixels may be encoded by ***plane***, by ***pixel***, or in ***plane-by-plane*** format. For HP RTL Imaging Mode, you use byte #1 of the Configure Image Data command (**ESC***v#W) to select the method.

Encoding by Plane

When colors are encoded by plane, each pixel in a row receives one bit (plane), then every pixel receives the next plane, until the pixels in a row are completely defined. That is, all the pixels in a row are partially defined by each plane until the last plane for that row is sent. The number of planes is the number of bits needed to define (color) a pixel by selecting a palette entry. For example, an 8-entry palette requires three planes ($2^3=8$). In the following example, the highlighted bits comprise the color index for the third pixel in the first row.

ESC*b#V	row 1	plane 1	b1 b1 **b1** b1 b1 b1 ...
ESC*b#V		plane 2	b2 b2 **b2** b2 b2 b2 ...
ESC*b#W		plane 3	b3 b3 **b3** b3 b3 b3 ...
ESC*b#V	row 2	plane 1	b1 b1 b1 b1 b1 b1 ...

Encoding by Pixel

When colors are encoded by pixel, all the bits for a pixel are sent as a group (for example, 24-bit RGB), then all the bits for the next pixel until the pixels in a row are defined. Each pixel receives all its bits before any bits are sent for the next pixel. Byte boundaries are ignored, with the bits for successive pixels following one another. For example, if four bits are needed to define a pixel, then every group of four bits in the data stream defines a pixel. The highlighted group below defines the second pixel in the first row.

| **ESC***b#W | row 1 | b4 b3 b2 b1 **c4 c3 c2 c1** ... |
| **ESC***b#W | row 2 | b4 b3 b2 b1 ... |

The HP RTL options for selecting colors and encoding raster data are:

	Planar Encoding	Pixel Encoding
Indexed Selection	Indexed planar	Indexed pixel
Direct Selection	Direct planar	Direct pixel

Encoding Plane-by-Plane

Another way of sending a color image to a device is by decomposing the entire image into separate color planes. This is typically done using the device's primary colors (for example, black, cyan, magenta, and yellow), and an entire image is sent for each primary color. The Y Offset command (**ESC***b#Y) is used to regain the starting position so that the planes can be overlaid as intended.

Defining the HP RTL Palette

HP RTL maintains an internal palette from which you can choose colors for each pixel of data.

For indexed selection, the size of the color palette depends on the number of planes being used: for one plane, there are two possible colors; for two planes, there are four possible colors; for three planes, there are eight possible colors; and so on. HP RTL allows for up to eight data planes or 256 possible colors. The maximum number of planes, and thus the maximum palette size, is device-dependent.

In indexed mode, data sent to the device uses the *index number* to choose a color for each pixel. See *Using HP RTL Indexes* on page 358.

In direct pixel encoding mode, the palette is not used.

Note that the HP RTL palette on some devices is independent of the HP-GL/2 palette. On these devices, palettes cannot be automatically transferred between HP-GL/2 and HP RTL. See the descriptions of the Enter RTL Mode and Enter HP-GL/2 Mode commands in *Chapter 14* for more information on transferring palettes.

Changing the Default Palette

Creating a new palette overwrites the old one. The Push/Pop Palette command (**ESC***p#P) can save (push) the current palette and then restore (pop) it. Palette entries can be modified in HP-GL/2 by the CR (Set Color Range for Relative Color Data), NP (Number of Pens), and PC (Pen Color Assignment) instructions, or by the HP RTL commands Set Red/Green/Blue Parameter (**ESC***v#A, **ESC***v#B, and **ESC***v#C) and Assign Color Index (**ESC***v#I).

When you switch from HP RTL to HP-GL/2 or vice versa, the palette is transferred. So any changes made in one environment are automatically transferred to the other. As a result, if you want to use separate palettes in the different environments, you must use the Push/Pop Palette command.

You can use a combination of commands to change the HP RTL palette defaults to any color. For instance, to set index 5 to a 50% blue, you use the following combined HP RTL command:

ESC*v0a0b127c5I

The commands combined here are Set Red Parameter, Set Green Parameter, Set Blue Parameter, and Assign Color Index. Note that 127 is halfway (50%) between 0 and 255, the default range for the Set Red/Green/Blue Parameter commands.

A "50%" blue may not appear the same on all devices. Differences in imaging technology, media, imaging agent (ink or toner, for example), and environmental conditions can cause color differences among devices. These differences are subject to program control, but their coverage is beyond the scope of this book.

You can assign any color supported by a device to an index. On some devices, non-primary colors are printed using a dithering technique. (Primary colors are those colors that a device can create by printing zero, one, or two ink or toner colors together, usually red, green, blue, magenta, cyan, yellow, black, and white.)

Changing the Black and White References

By default, the RGB value for black is 0,0,0, and the value for white is 255,255,255. You can change these white and black references using the HP RTL command Configure Image Data. For instance, if you work in percentages, you could use the following command to set the ranges to 0 to 100:

ESC*v18W (0) (0) (3) (8) (8) (8) (100) (100) (100) (0) (0) (0)

The last six numbers set the white references for red, green, and blue, and then the corresponding black references. (For clarity, numbers in the data string are shown in decimal, enclosed in parentheses. In practice, they must be transmitted as binary numbers, without parentheses; the first six are one-byte values, the second six are two bytes each. See page 407 for more information on the Configure Image Data command; the example on page 360 shows a similar command to that just described, but using different white reference values.)

Now, to set index 5 to 50% blue using the white and black references just defined, use the following combined command:

ESC*v0a0b50c5I

Using HP RTL Indexes

When you send raster data to the device, you send it one row at a time. Assuming you are sending single-plane data, you send all the data for the first row, then all the data for the second row, and so on.

For example, the loop in a sample program might look like this:

for n := 1 **to** number_of_rows **do**
    for m := 1 **to** width_in_pixels **do**
        send one pixel (one bit) of data;

You can think of the color palette as an array in a programming language. The color of each pixel is determined by "indexing into" the color palette using the bit value as the subscript. For a two-pen black-and-white palette, a "0" pixel accesses the color assigned to index 0 (by default, white); a "1" pixel accesses the color assigned to index 1 (by default, black).

For instance, assume you sent the following data to the device:

    0 1 0 1 1 1 1 1 0 0 0 0 1 1 1 1

Based on the HP RTL default palette, the first pixel would be white, the second black, the third white, and so on.

Multi-Plane Data

As with single-plane data, you send multi-plane data one row at a time. However, with multi-plane data, you send all the planes for each row together—all the planes for the first row, then all the planes for the second row, and so on. (Even in block transfers, the *order* of the data remains the same. Block transfers are explained under *Compressing Data* on page 378.)

For example, if you have three planes of data, the loop in a sample program might look like this:

for n := 1 **to** number_of_rows **do**
    begin
        send one row of data for first plane;
        send one row of data for second plane;
        send one row of data for third plane;
    end;

("Send one row of data" implies a loop to send each row a pixel at a time, as shown in the single-plane example above.)

Once the data for all planes in a row has been received, the bits that make up each pixel are combined to arrive at the index number. As with single-plane printing, this index number is used to index into the palette to determine which color to print each pixel.

For instance, assume you sent the following data to the device:

    Plane 1: 0 1 0 1 1 1 1 1 0 0 0 0 1 1 1 1
    Plane 2: 0 1 1 1 1 1 1 1 0 0 0 0 0 0 0 0
    Plane 3: 1 0 1 0 0 1 1 0 1 0 0 1 0 0 1 1

The color for each pixel is now defined by a three-digit binary number, which is the index number. Plane 1 is the *least* significant bit of the number; plane 3 is the *most* significant. To get the index number, turn the page clockwise so that the right edge is at the bottom. Read the binary numbers from left to right, top to bottom. The first pixel is 100, or decimal 4. The second (highlighted by the rectangle) is 011, or 3.

The index numbers for this row of pixels are: 4 3 6 3 3 7 7 3 4 0 0 4 1 1 5 5

If you are using the HP RTL default palette (see page 354), the first pixel of this row would map to index 4, which is blue. The second pixel maps to index 3, which is yellow. The third maps to index 6, which is cyan. And so on.

Note that when you are using three planes per row and the HP RTL default palette, you are effectively sending planes of red, green, and blue: plane 1 is red; plane 2 is green; and plane 3 is blue.

The same technique for determining index colors is used when there are only two data planes. In this case, the binary number is only two digits, so there are only four possible index numbers (0 to 3).

Using Index 0

Index 0 functions like any other index: you can assign a color to it, and you can send data such that any given pixel is printed with that color. The color of index 0 in the *default* palette is white for 1 plane per row and black for 2 or more planes per row.

When you use the HP RTL commands Source Raster Width (**ESC***r#S) and Source Raster Height (**ESC***r#T), 0 is also the default value for short or missing rows. This means, for instance, that you can use index 0 as a "background color" to form a border around an image. You must send the 0 for any border at the top and to the left of the image. But the device will automatically fill in the empty space to the right and below the image with zeros. Since there is less data to transmit, transmission time is reduced. See the illustration under *Setting the Width and Height in HP RTL* on page 342.

If you are in raster graphics mode (after a Start Raster Graphics command, **ESC***r#A) with scale mode off, you can use index 0 as a background color by using the Y Offset command (**ESC***b#Y) to skip over parts of the image that should be set to the color of index 0. Rows that you skip are filled with zeros and printed with the color of index 0. The Y Offset command is not allowed in raster graphics mode when scale mode is on (see page 377).

Another alternative is to create background or borders using HP-GL/2 commands before entering HP RTL mode.

Example: Programming the Color Palette

First the Configure Image Data command (**ESC***v18W[data]) is sent, where [data] is:

Byte #	Binary data	Decimal value	Effect
0	00000000	0	Color space device-dependent RGB
1	00000000	0	Pixel encoding mode is indexed by plane
2	00000011	3	3 bits per index
3	00001000	8	8 bits for red
4	00001000	8	8 bits for green
5	00001000	8	8 bits for blue
6, 7	0000000011111111	255	White reference for red is 255
8, 9	0000000011111111	255	White reference for green is 255
10, 11	0000000001111111	127	White reference for blue is 127
12, 13	0000000000000000	0	Black reference for red is 0
14, 15	0000000000000000	0	Black reference for green is 0
16, 17	0000000000000000	0	Black reference for blue is 0

Now program the palette to the desired values:

Set index 0 to white:

ESC*v255A	Set red parameter
ESC*v255B	Set green parameter
ESC*v127C	Set blue parameter
ESC*v0I	Assign to index 0

Set index 1 to green:

ESC*v0A	Set red parameter
ESC*v255B	Set green parameter
ESC*v0C	Set blue parameter
ESC*v1I	Assign to index 1

and so on until:

Set index 7 to black:

ESC*v0A	Set red parameter
ESC*v0B	Set green parameter
ESC*v0C	Set blue parameter
ESC*v7I	Assign to index 7

Halftoning

Halftoning is the process of placing pixels of primary or secondary colors adjacent to one another in a cell, to create the sensation of another color. Newspaper photographs are a typical example of halftoning, where, even in monochrome, continuous tones of gray are represented by clusters of black and white dots.

Color printers may use halftone algorithms to print a continuous-tone image using a set of pixels of the eight primary colors; in this way, the eye perceives a continuous range of colors. The Render Algorithm command (**ESC***t#J) provides a choice of various algorithms. A single page may use several Render Algorithm commands during page composition, but only one is in effect at any given time.

The Render Algorithm command allows for the following types of processing:

Pattern dither: Pixels are intensified by increasing the number of dots according to the desired density of color; the dots are scattered uniformly in a pattern. Normally this pattern uses a small matrix, and is therefore faster and requires fewer resources than other algorithms.

Clustered dither: This is similar to pattern dither, but the dots are placed so as to form "bigger" pixels instead of dispersing them. The result is a clustering of the intensified pixels. The result is similar to that often used in newspaper and magazine photographs.

Scatter dither: Pixels are intensified by increasing the number of dots according to the desired density of color; the dots are scattered in a random fashion. This method generally gives a better appearance than either pattern or clustered dither.

Device best: This is the render method that HP believes will provide the best output for a particular device in most cases. Note, however, that the recommended dither pattern varies with the image, the intended use of the image, and the subjective judgment of the user.

Patterns

A *pattern* is a rectangular area tile whose design is combined with the source data and the data already prepared for printing (the "destination" or "current image") at the place where the source is to be printed. It may be a single-plane monochrome mask or a multi-plane raster color pattern. The Current Pattern command (**ESC***v#T) designates an active pattern, which stays in effect until another is specified or the device is reset. A Reset command (**ESC**E) changes back to the default pattern, which is 100% black.

These are the commands that are used in conjunction with HP RTL patterns:

The Pattern ID command (**ESC***c#G) assigns a unique identification number to a user-defined or HP-defined pattern. User-defined patterns are downloaded with the Download Pattern command (**ESC***c#W). Such patterns should be no larger than the minimum needed to uniquely define the pattern. Colors in user-defined patterns are rendered as indexes into the current palette. HP-defined patterns do not have to be explicitly downloaded—they simply have to be selected for use. The supplied patterns are solid black (or Foreground Color, **ESC***v#S), solid white, shadings between 1% and 100%, and six hatched patterns (horizontal, vertical, and diagonal lines, and cross-hatching with horizontal and vertical lines or diagonal lines).

Patterns are selected for application to a raster image with the Current Pattern (**ESC***v#T) command. After use, a pattern should be deleted or reset to foreground color (using **ESC***v0T); otherwise all subsequent images will be filled with the pattern. Patterns can be deleted using the Pattern Control (**ESC***c#Q) command. A Reset (**ESC**E) defaults the pattern to 100% black.

Tiling is the means by which a pattern is applied to a source image. The pattern, whose upper-left pixel coincides with the ***pattern reference point***, is repeated horizontally and vertically across the page. The tiling of patterns is controlled by the Pattern Reference Point (**ESC***p#R) command. This command sets the pattern reference point at the CAP. The default pattern reference point is the upper left corner of the logical page (0,0); unless this command is sent, the pattern is tiled with respect to position (0,0).

To fill an area with a pattern, the base pattern is tiled (replicated) across the fill area. The pattern reference point is the starting point for tiling, where the upper left corner of the base pattern is positioned on the logical page.

When all tiles use the same pattern reference point, the pattern in adjoining or overlapping fragments is aligned. The Pattern Reference Point (**ESC***p#R) command sets the reference point to the CAP, allowing the pattern to be adjusted for different fill areas. The reference point may be shifted for as many fill areas as there are on a page; an area must be filled before the reference point is moved for the next area fill. This command can be used to start the pattern at a particular place in each adjoining or overlapping fragment of the fill area, regardless of alignment.

Two areas filled (tiled) when the Pattern
Reference Point is at the default (0,0) position

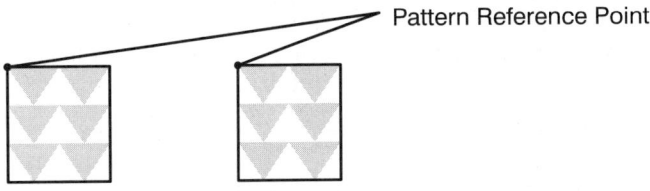

Pattern Reference Point

Two areas filled when the Pattern Reference
Point is placed at the upper left corner of
each area before tiling

Figure 163. Pattern Reference Point

Patterns, including user-defined patterns, are applied to images only when the pattern is selected by a Current Pattern (**ESC***v#T) command, which can occur any number of times per page.

Use the following general procedure to fill your images with a non-solid pattern. If you choose to use an HP-supplied pattern, you need only follow steps 2 and 4.

1. Define a binary raster image as the pattern.

2. Assign a pattern identification number (**ESC***c#G).

3. Download the pattern (**ESC***c#W).

4. Apply the pattern to subsequent images (**ESC***v#T).

Exporting Patterns to HP-GL/2

In HP-GL/2, patterns are downloaded by the RF (Raster Fill Definition) instruction and applied by the FT (Fill Type) or SV (Screened Vectors) instruction. The CF (Character Fill Mode) instruction specifies how outline fonts are to be rendered, including changing the fill pattern for bitmap and stick fonts. HP-GL/2 may use HP RTL patterns, but HP RTL cannot use HP-GL/2 patterns.

Pattern Orientation

Patterns are always rendered according to the coordinate system in use: in HP RTL, each row is generated along the X-axis and the rows are incremented along the Y-axis. Since HP RTL has a fixed orientation (the X-axis is horizontal and the Y-axis vertical), patterns are always produced with rows along the horizontal axis:

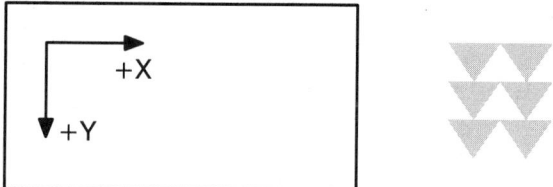

Figure 164. HP RTL Pattern Orientation

Patterns imported from HP RTL into HP-GL/2 inherit the current HP-GL/2 coordinate system, which defines the page orientation and the current rotation. Assuming a zero rotation ("RO0;"), HP RTL patterns obtain the following orientations for HP-GL/2 "plotters" (see page 8):

Page Portrait: Rows are produced along the vertical axis (X-axis from positive to negative) and rows increment along the horizontal axis (Y-axis from negative to positive). Thus patterns have an orientation of 270° with respect to HP RTL:

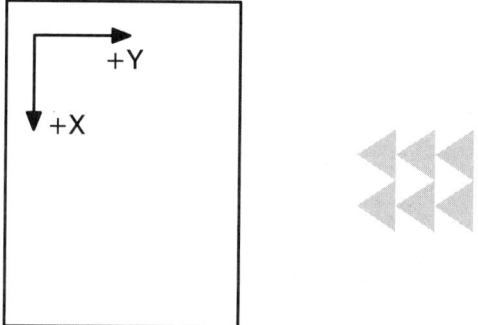

Figure 165. HP-GL/2 Pattern Orientation for Plotters with Portrait Layout

Page Landscape: Rows are produced along the horizontal axis (X-axis from positive to negative) and rows increment along the vertical axis (Y-axis from negative to positive). Thus patterns have an orientation of 180° with respect to HP RTL:

Figure 166. HP-GL/2 Pattern Orientation for Plotters with Landscape Layout

For HP-GL/2 "printers" (as defined on page 8), PCL, not HP RTL, is used for defining patterns. If an extra rotation is added with the RO command, this rotation also applies to the pattern.

Coincident Coordinate Systems: If you want the HP-GL/2 and HP RTL coordinate systems to coincide, use the technique described on page 38.

Chapter 10: Interactions between Picture Elements

Once an image has been placed on the logical page (for example, some vectors or text using HP-GL/2), and another image (for example, a scanned photograph) is to be added to it, you can specify how they are to be merged together, and how patterns, colors, and transparency filters will affect the final image. At the same time, using HP RTL, you can add color and patterns to your images. You can even change the appearance of data that has already been prepared and sent to the device. First, some terms.

The *destination image* or *current image* is whatever is currently defined on the page. This includes all images placed through previous operations, whether using HP-GL/2 or HP RTL.

Source data is the data that is about to be added to the page. There are two types of source data: mask and raster.

- *Mask source* is HP-GL/2 data. The source data acts like a stencil whose shape allows a pattern or the selected pen's color to pour through onto the page.

- *Raster source* is HP RTL data, and may be specified by either the indexed or direct method (see *Specifying Colors* on page 352). In the indexed method, each pixel identifies a palette index; in the direct method, each pixel is specified by its color components.

The meaning of *"white"* pixels depends on the type of image data: single-plane raster source, a white pixel is one whose value is a 0-bit; otherwise, for indexed raster source, a white pixel is one that selects a white palette entry, and for direct raster source, a white pixel is one for which all color primaries meet or exceed their *white reference* values. In HP-GL/2, source data is considered as a black mask, so there are no "white" pixels. Note that skipping over areas in raster mode automatically assigns index 0 (normally white) to empty areas; see *Using Index 0* on page 359 for more information.

There are two *transparency modes*, source transparency mode and pattern transparency mode. In both cases, the transparency mode affects only "white" pixels. When the mode is transparent, the "white" pixels, as defined above, have no effect on the destination (the current image); when the mode is opaque, the "white" pixels are applied to the destination. By default, white pixels are transparent for both HP RTL raster data and HP-GL/2 vector data.

- *Source transparency mode* is a flag that specifies whether the "white" pixels in the source image are transparent or opaque. In HP RTL, the source transparency is selected by the Source Transparency Mode command (**ESC***v#N); in HP-GL/2, there is no source transparency. Note that on devices that do not support the Source Transparency Mode command, the HP-GL/2 TR (Transparency Mode) instruction may apply to HP RTL data—see *The Product Comparison Guide for HP Languages on HP Plotters and Large-Format Printers* for further guidance.

- *Pattern transparency mode* is a flag that specifies whether the "white" pixels in the pattern are transparent or opaque. In HP RTL, the pattern transparency is selected by the Pattern

Transparency Mode command (**ESC***v#O); in HP-GL/2, it is selected by the TR (Transparency Mode) instruction.

- Transparency modes are defined before printable data is sent to the device. White dots that are introduced in the dithering process are not subject to transparency modes; they are always opaque.

Foreground color is the color selected by the Foreground Color command (**ESC***v#S) from the current palette. Foreground color affects everything except color patterns and HP-GL/2 primitives; HP-GL/2 uses the SP (Select Pen) instruction. Raster color interacts with foreground color. To avoid undesired interactions with color raster images, select a black foreground color.

For monochrome patterns, *texture* is the combination of a pattern and the foreground color. For user-defined color patterns, the term is synonymous with pattern.

Logical operations (or *raster operations*) are combinations of logical functions such as **and**, **or**, **xor**, and **not** applied to the source, texture, and destination (current image). Logical operations are applied using the Logical Operation command (**ESC***l#O—the character following the * is a lowercase letter L; that after the # is an uppercase letter O). Logical operations are also set by the HP-GL/2 MC (Merge Control) instruction; they are shared between HP RTL and HP-GL/2, the last one used prevailing in both environments. Logical operations and transparency modes are defined before the printable source data is sent to the device. The default source and pattern transparency modes are both transparent.

The transparency is specified first:

```
IF (source is transparent and source ≡ white)
       RETURN destination
IF (source is opaque and source ≡ white)
       RETURN logical operation (source, texture, destination)
IF (pattern is transparent and pattern ≡ white)
       RETURN destination
ELSE   RETURN logical operation (source, texture, destination)
```

These are the commands that are used in conjunction with transparency and logical operations:

Source Transparency Mode, **ESC***v#N, page 445
Pattern Transparency Mode, **ESC***v#O, page 431
Logical Operation, **ESC***l#O, page 422.

Texture

Texture is the result of a logical **and** operation on a downloaded monochrome pattern and the foreground color; or if the current downloaded pattern is multi-colored, synonymous with pattern (downloaded color patterns are not combined with the foreground color).

Texture is combined with the current image and a source image to produce a new image. The way in which they are combined is determined by a Logical Operation (**ESC***l#O). The logical operation performed is also affected by the source and pattern transparency modes.

Figure 167 shows how these components interact.

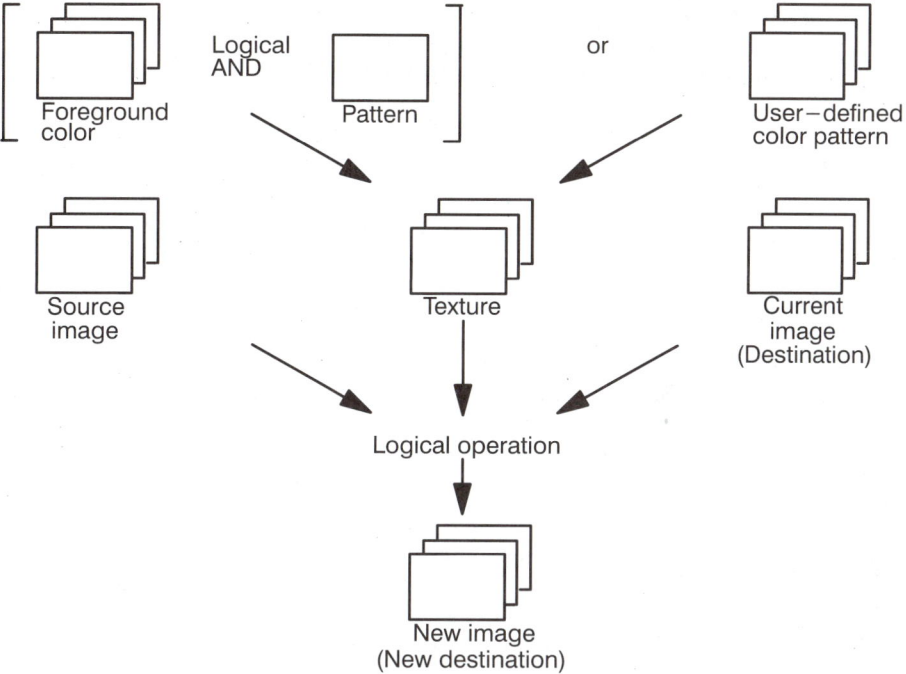

Figure 167. Forming a New Image Using Color, Pattern, and Source Image

Logical Operations

Logical operations are operations that are applied to three components: the destination (current image), the source data, and the texture. They are combinations of the logical operators **and**, **or**, **xor** and **not**. The numerical operand of the Logical Operation (**ESC***l#O) command or the MC (Merge Control) instruction defines what transformation is to be applied to these three operands. The table in the description of the command (see page 422) describes each transformation in reverse polish notation. Thus the default value (252) is TSo, which is (texture **or** source).

The operands and operators used are:

S = source	a = **and**	n = **not**
T = texture	o = **or**	x = **xor** (exclusive **or**)
D = destination (current image)		

The logical operations defined by HP RTL are specified in RGB-space, where white = 1 and black = 0. However, because the devices that support HP RTL normally operate in CMY-space where white = 0 and black = 1, the results may not be intuitive if you are used to thinking in CMY-terms. For example, **or**ing white with black in RGB-space yields white, which is the same as **and**ing in CMY-space. To convert from one color space to the other, write the operation code in binary, invert the bits (swap 0's and 1's), and reverse the order; thus TSo is 252, binary 11111100, which becomes 11000000, decimal 192 or TSa.

Which Logical Operation to Use?

To decide which numerical parameter to use in the Logical Operation command, you must first decide what logical combination of operations are to be applied to the three operands, T (texture), S (source image), and D (destination—current image). One way of doing this is to draw a matrix of the possible bit-values of the three operands, and of the desired result, like this:

	Bits							
	7	6	5	4	3	2	1	0
T: Texture (= color **and** pattern)	1	1	1	1	0	0	0	0
S: Source	1	1	0	0	1	1	0	0
D: Destination (current image)	1	0	1	0	1	0	1	0
Desired result: If S then D else T	1	0	1	1	1	0	0	0

The final row is the result you want to achieve for each setting of texture, source, and destination bits. Binary 10111000 is decimal 184, so the command to use would be ESC*l184O.

One bit is used to define each of the primary colors; the result of a logical operation is the Boolean transform applied to the operand bits. For example, consider what happens if a destination pixel is yellow (R=1, G=1, B=0), the texture color for that pixel is white (R=1, G=1, B=1), and the source is green (R=0, G=1, B=0), as shown in the following table:

	R	G	B
T: Texture	1	1	1
S: Source	0	1	0
D: Destination	1	1	0
Result:	1	0	1

Here, the result of operation 184 is shown; the pixel would appear magenta (R=1, G=0, B=1).

An Alternative Method

An alternative method is to describe the transformation as a Boolean expression; for example,
> (T **and** (**not** S)) **or** (S **and** D)   which is
> TSnaSDao   in reverse polish form;

if necessary, apply some simplifying transformations to get the result into one of the forms listed in the description of the Logical Operation command. In the above case, the formula can be transformed into TSDTxax, which, again, is operation 184.

[Some of the Boolean transformations that you might need to use are:

not (A **and** B) is equivalent to	(**not** A) **or** (**not** B)
not (A **or** B)	(**not** A) **and** (**not** B)
A **xor** B	(A **and** (**not** B)) **or** ((**not** A) **and** B)
A **and** (**not** A)	0
A **or** (**not** A)	1

Further treatment is beyond the scope of this guide—see any good textbook on Boolean algebra.]

A Choice of Operations

Some of the logical operations you might choose to use are:

184:	TSDTxax	If S then D, else T
240:	T	Use T only
102:	DSx	If S then invert D, else D
255:	1	White
226:	DSTDxax	If S then T, else D
204:	S	Use S only

The Default Print Model

The default print model is shown below.

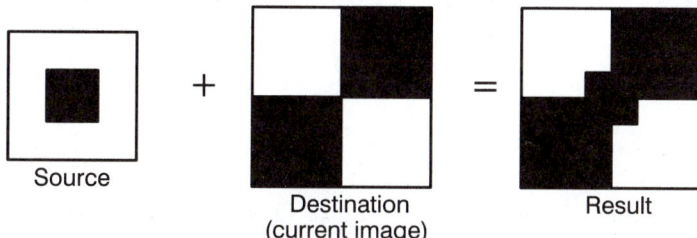

Source + Destination (current image) = Result

Figure 168. Creating an Image with Transparent "White" Source Pixels

The default source and pattern transparency modes, which are explained in the next section, are both transparent, and the default logical operation is **TSo** (Texture **or** Source, 252). (Note, however, that the MC (Merge Control) instruction can cause a default of **DTSoa** (168), depending on its *mode* parameter; for more information see the description of MC on page 220.)

In the case where a pattern is used, the result is:

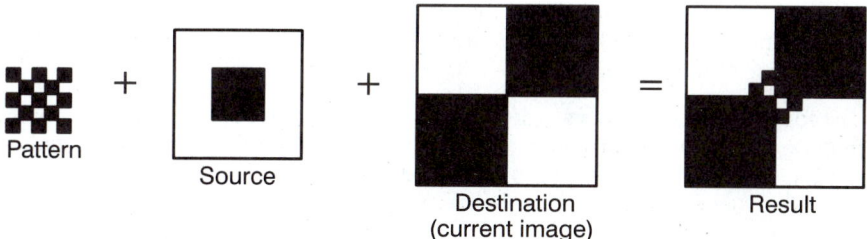

Pattern + Source + Destination (current image) = Result

Figure 169. Creating an Image with Transparent "White" Source and Pattern Pixels

Where a foreground color is defined, the result is:

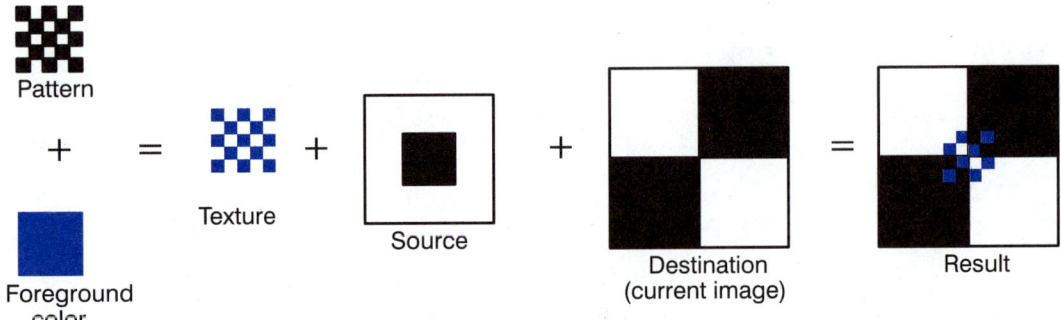

Figure 170. Creating an Image with Color and Transparent "White" Pixels

Transparency

There are two transparency modes, source transparency mode and pattern transparency mode.

Source transparency controls whether the white pixels in the source will affect the current image. If the mode is opaque, the white pixels affect the current image; when it is transparent, they don't. Pattern and foreground color do not affect white pixels.

Similarly, pattern transparency mode affects whether the white pixels in the pattern affect the current image.

Source transparency mode is set by the **ESC*v#N** command; pattern transparency mode is set by the **ESC*v#O** command. In both cases, #=0 is transparent and #=1 is opaque. These two commands do not apply to HP-GL/2 data.

Transparency modes and logical operations interact. Only in the case of both modes being opaque is the final transformation the same as the logical operation specified in the table of logical operations. In other cases, further transformations have to be applied to derive the final appearance of the image.

The four basic interactions are described below. For this discussion, *source_mask* and *pattern_mask* are the transparency masks, where transparent pixels are 0's and opaque pixels are 1's. These transparency masks are used to determine whether source pixels are to be applied to the destination.

Source and Pattern Both Opaque

texture   = color **and** pattern
result   = logical_operation (current_image, source_data, texture)

Source Opaque, Pattern Transparent

texture = color **and** pattern
temp_result = logical_operation (current_image, source_data, texture)
image_a = temp_result **and** (**not** source_mask)
image_b = temp_result **and** pattern_mask
image_c = (**not** pattern_mask) **and** source_mask **and** current_image
result = image_a **or** image_b **or** image_c

Source Transparent, Pattern Opaque

texture = color **and** pattern
temp_result = logical_operation (current_image, source_data, texture)
image_a = temp_result **and** source_mask
image_b = current_image **and** (**not** source_mask)
result = image_a **or** image_b

Source and Pattern Both Transparent

texture = color **and** pattern
temp_result = logical_operation (current_image, source_data, texture)
image_a = temp_result **and** source_mask **and** pattern_mask
image_b = current_image **and** (**not** source_mask)
image_c = current_image **and** (**not** pattern_mask)
result = image_a **or** image_b **or** image_c

The Effect of Transparency

The following illustrations show how texture and source are applied to a destination image, with various settings of the transparency modes. (In the case of a monochrome image, the texture is simply the pattern.)

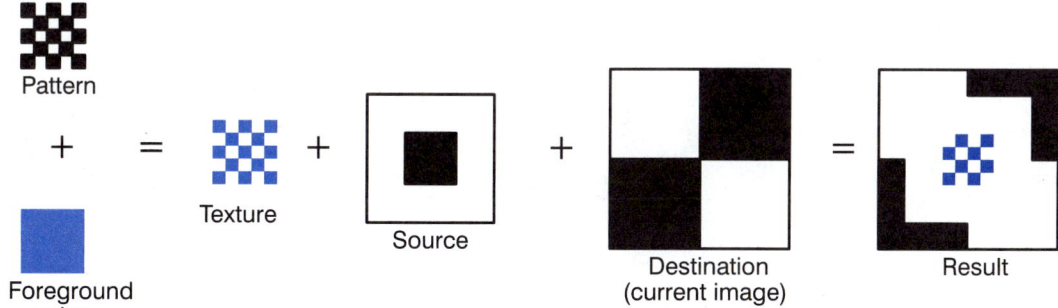

Figure 171. Creating an Image with Color Using Opaque Transparency Modes (Case 1)

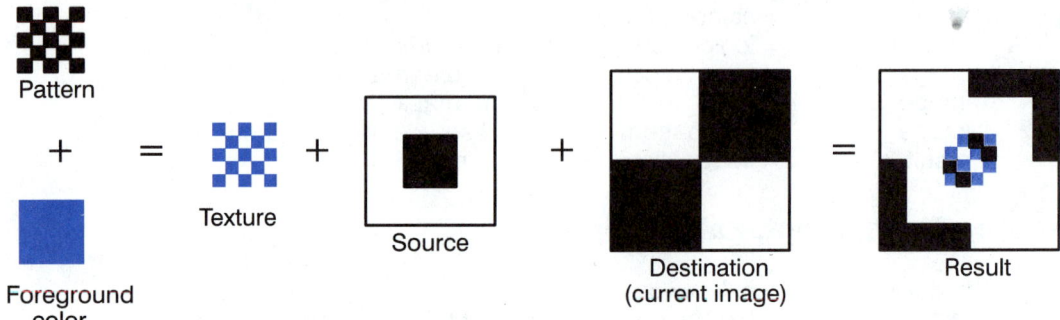

Figure 172. Creating a Color Image with Source Opaque and Pattern Transparent (Case 2)

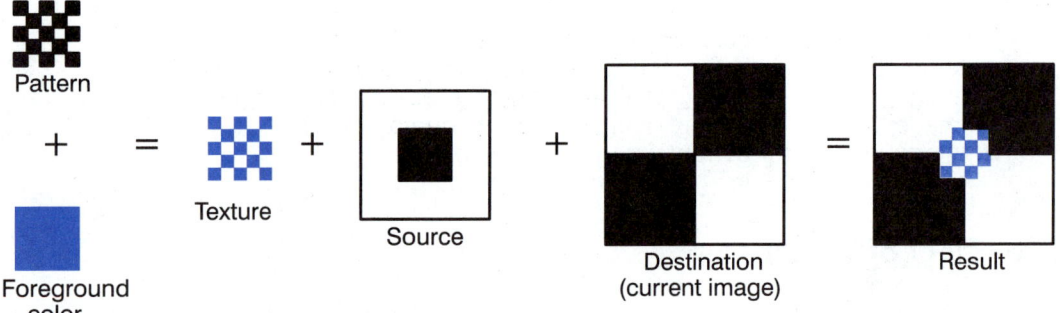

Figure 173. Creating a Color Image with Source Transparent and Pattern Opaque (Case 3)

Case 4 is shown in Figure 170 on page 370.

Chapter 11: Transmitting Data

So far we have looked at several concepts regarding raster data, as well as discussing some commands used for setting up the raster transfer. This section explains the basic commands used actually to transfer the data.

Transferring Raster Data

When all the setup is complete, you tell the device to expect raster data by sending the HP RTL command Start Raster Graphics (**ESC***r#A). The parameters in this command tell the device whether to start graphics at the left side of the logical page or at the CAP, and whether to start graphics with or without scaling. When the device is in *raster mode*, some commands are allowed and some are ignored—see the list of commands on page 401 for details.

The Raster Line Path command (**ESC***b#L) specifies the vertical direction in which the raster image will "grow". Because of problems that can occur if an image requires more memory than the device has available, you are recommended to use the "downwards" direction (**ESC***b0L) in this command. See *When Overflow Occurs* on page 374.

Once the device is in raster mode, you can send it data using two HP RTL commands: Transfer Raster Data by Plane (**ESC***b#V), and Transfer Raster Data by Row/Block (**ESC***b#W). The data sent with these commands must be formatted according to the current compression method—see *Compressing Data* on page 378.

The two Transfer commands are used to send raster data to the device in a row-by-row format. Transfer Raster Data by Plane (**ESC***b#V) increments the *plane counter* but not the *row pointer*; it is therefore used to send each plane in a multi-plane row except the last. Transfer Raster Data by Row/Block (**ESC***b#W) moves the CAP to the next raster row, and is therefore used to send the last plane of a multi-plane row.

When you have only one plane of data to print, you only need the second command, Transfer Raster Data by Row/Block. You send each row of raster data with this command. After the device renders this data internally, the row counter is incremented, and the device is ready to receive data for the next row. When you use a block-based compression method, you issue this command only once for each block.

When all the data for an image has been sent, you exit raster graphics mode with the HP RTL command End Raster Graphics.

Use these commands to enter and exit raster mode and to send raster data to the device:

Start Raster Graphics, **ESC***r#A, page 446
End Raster Graphics, **ESC***rC, page 417
Transfer Raster Data by Plane, **ESC***b#V[data], page 447
Transfer Raster Data by Row/Block, **ESC***b#W[data], page 449
Compression Method, **ESC***b#M, page 406
Y Offset, **ESC***b#Y, page 451
Raster Line Path, **ESC***b#L, page 433.

HP RTL
DATA TRANSMIT

Note that the Compression Method command, the two transfer commands, the Y Offset command, and the Raster Line Path command all begin with **ESC***b. You can combine these commands using the technique described on page 340. You must put the other commands *before* the transfer command in the combined command. Transfer commands (which must end in a capital letter, and are followed by data) can only *end* a combined command; they cannot begin one.

Implicit Start Raster Graphics

A Transfer Raster Data by Plane (**ESC***b#V[data]) or Transfer Raster Data by Row/Block (**ESC***b#W[data]) command is permitted with no preceding Start Raster Graphics (**ESC***r#A) command. Either transfer command implicitly puts the device into (unscaled) raster mode and uses the left edge of the logical page as the left graphics margin, corresponding to a Start Raster Graphics with parameter value 0. *It is strongly recommended, however, that you start raster graphics explicitly* using the Start Raster Graphics command.

Commands in Raster Mode

After an explicit or implicit Start Raster Graphics command, the device enters a restricted state called ***raster mode***. This mode "locks out" (ignores) commands that would affect rendering of the graphics image. These commands remain locked out until raster mode is terminated by an explicit or implicit End Raster Graphics command.

Some additional commands are ignored in scaled raster mode only. ***Scaled raster mode*** is in effect after a Start Raster Graphics command with a value of 2 or 3 is received (and Source Raster Width and Source Raster Height were specified), and until an implicit or explicit End Raster Graphics command.

Commands that are neither explicitly ignored or explicitly allowed when the device is in raster mode cause an implicit End Raster Graphics command to be executed, and are then executed as usual.

Implicit End Raster Graphics

Receipt of any data other than an HP RTL command listed on page 401 as explicitly allowed or explicitly ignored causes an implicit End Raster Graphics with all of its defined functionality. *It is strongly recommended, however, that you end raster graphics explicitly.*

When Overflow Occurs*

Your device uses internal random-access memory (RAM) to store vector and raster data. In normal operating mode, the device stores all data for an image before printing it in one pass.

It is possible, however, to send more data for one page than will fit in storage. This is more likely to occur with raster data, since this data is more voluminous than vector data. (In most cases, vector data is stored as endpoints, whereas raster data includes one bit of data for each color-plane of each pixel of the image.) Some very complex vector drawings may also overflow RAM.

If your images consistently overflow RAM and you have not expanded the RAM as much as

---

*   Note that this section does not apply to all HP RTL devices.

possible, you should consider adding more RAM for best performance.

A note on how images are stored in RAM:

- In most cases, vector data is converted to a special internal format that includes the endpoints and vector characteristics.

- Raster data is first decompressed (if one of the compression modes was used for transmission) and then recompressed using a special internal algorithm. The amount of RAM an image occupies depends on the density of the image. Very dense images like maps and scanned images occupy the most RAM.

There are two strategies that HP devices use to overcome problems associated with storage overflow: "on-the-fly" plotting and "superflow" mode.

On-the-Fly Plotting

Regardless of the amount of RAM installed in your device, when an image exceeds the available RAM, the device immediately enters on-the-fly plotting mode. The effect of this mode depends on whether the device was in the HP-GL/2 context or the HP RTL context when the overflow occurred.

If the device was in the HP-GL/2 (vector) context when the RAM overflow occurred, it switches to "flow mode" and discards the HP-GL/2 object. At this stage, nothing is printed, but a message such as Out of Memory/Data was lost may be displayed.

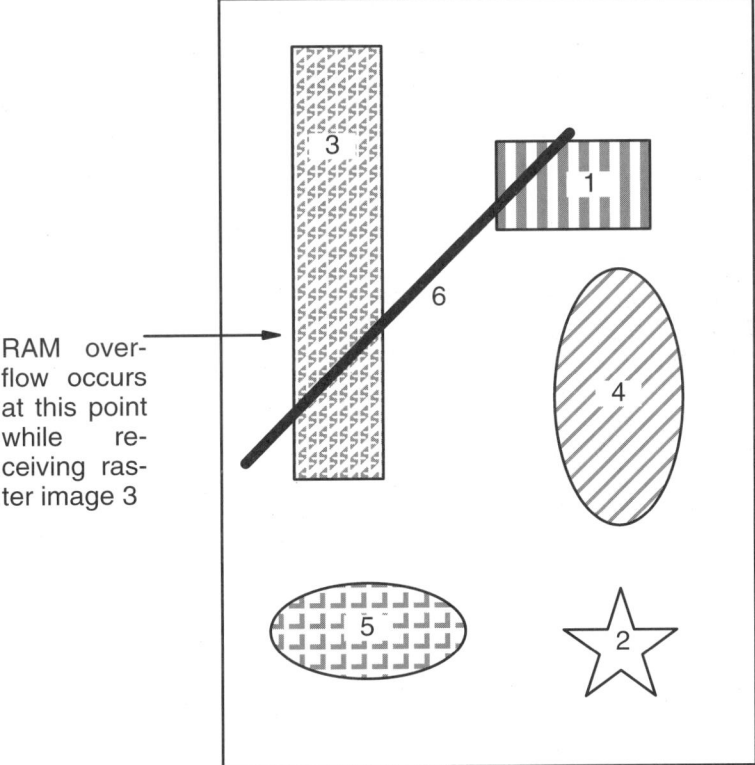

RAM overflow occurs at this point while receiving raster image 3

Figure 174. Page to be Printed

If the device was in HP RTL (raster) context when the RAM overflow occurred, it switches to "flow mode" and prints all vector and raster data it has received so far that are physically located above the one that caused the transition to "flow mode".

Once the device is in "flow mode", all HP-GL/2 objects that are subsequently received are discarded; all HP RTL objects are printed as they arrive, together with all objects already placed in the same area of the page, that arrived before "flow mode" was entered.

If a Y Offset command that would require reverse media movement is received during on-the-fly plotting, the Y Offset command is ignored and the remainder of the data is discarded.

The following example illustrates on-the-fly plotting.

Consider the page shown in Figure 174, consisting of vectors and several raster images. This is the file, as the final page is intended to look. The numbers represent the order in which the vectors and raster images are sent. Images 1, 3, 4, and 5, printed from the top to the bottom, are raster images. Images 2 and 6 are vector images.

If RAM overflows at the point shown while receiving raster image 3, the device enters on-the-fly plotting mode and finishes printing image 3. Part of image 4 is discarded because of negative motion; image 6 is discarded because it is an HP-GL/2 object. Image 2, however, which was completely received before image 3, *is* printed.

The actual page would appear as in Figure 175.

The implication of the on-the-fly memory-handling technique is that you should begin the data stream with the most important data to be certain it will print. In practical terms, this usually

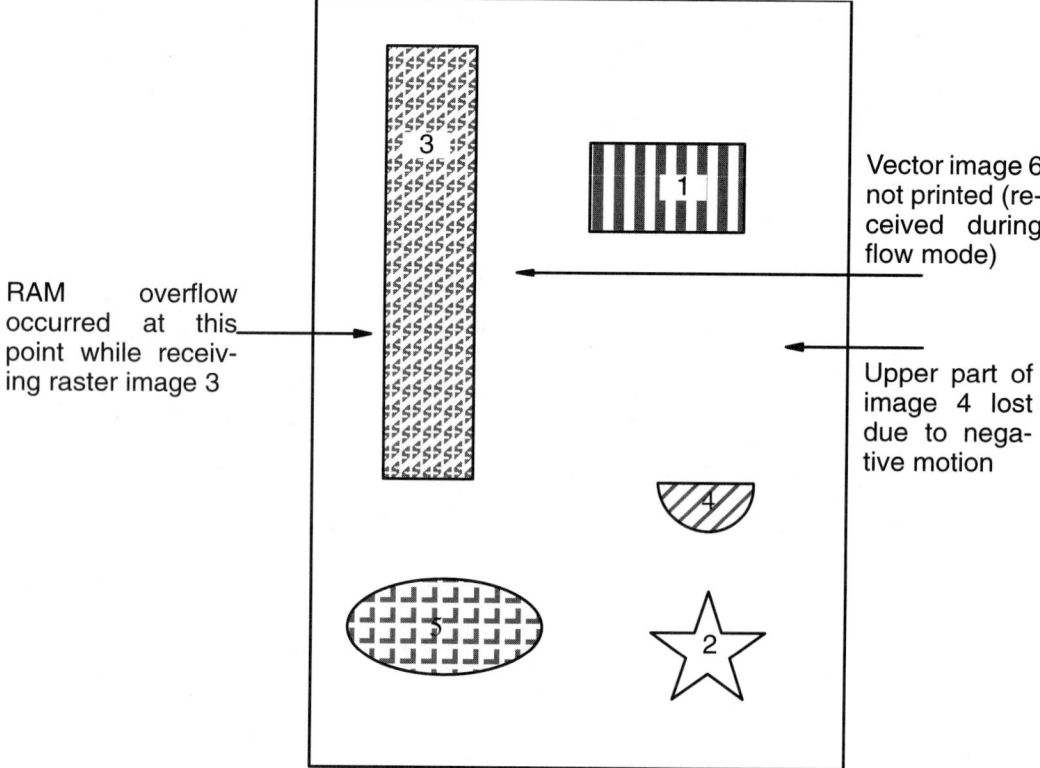

Figure 175. Output as it Appears on Media

means sending vectors before a large raster image, since the device can do on-the-fly plotting of the raster image.

"Superflow" Mode

An improved algorithm is used on some devices, compared with that just described. Again, when there is not enough memory to process a request, data so far accumulated is flushed, but only the minimum necessary to enable the processing of the new data.

Swaths (bands) of data are flushed each time an overflow occurs, the flushing continuing until there is sufficient memory to honor the request or until all swaths have been flushed.

Swaths are also flushed each time any type of object (vector or raster) is placed on the page at swath n and no negative motion is specified; in this case, all swaths up to and including swath $n-1$ are flushed. If any data is subsequently received for swaths up to $n-1$, it is lost and an error message is given.

The effect of this is that, provided pictures are properly ordered into bands, they are more likely to be printed successfully. Whenever possible, send to the device first those objects that occupy the top of the page, and afterwards those that come below.

In both vector and raster cases, memory overflow causes the device to print the uppermost part of the picture, and release the associated memory. It is then able to accept more data.

Plane-by-Plane Printing and Scaling

This section applies to devices, such as electrostatic plotters, that print one plane of a complete page, followed by the next plane, and so on until the entire page has been printed. Other devices, such as ink-jet plotters, can print all planes at once; this section does not apply to the latter type of device.

When scaling is on and you are using plane-by-plane printing, you cannot use the Y Offset command (**ESC***b#Y) to move the CAP. For this reason it is necessary to exit raster graphics mode before moving the CAP back to the top of the output between planes. Since exiting raster graphics also resets the compression method to the default (0), you must set the compression method again before going back into raster graphics mode.

Calculating the Y Offset value is more complicated for scaled printing than for unscaled printing. During unscaled printing, the device moves one physical row per row of data sent, so the Y Offset value is simply equal to the number of data rows sent. However, during scaled printing, the device generally prints more (or fewer) physical rows than the actual number of data rows sent, so the number of physical rows no longer equals the number of data rows. Since you must tell the Y Offset command the number of *physical* rows to move back the CAP, you must calculate the Y Offset based on how much the image was scaled.

The formula for calculating the Y Offset for scaled raster graphics is as follows:

$$offset = round \left(\frac{destination\ height}{720.0} \times resolution \right)$$

where

$round$ is a function that returns an integer after rounding.

destination height	is the value from the Destination Raster Height command, that is, the height of the destination image in decipoints.
720.0	is the number of decipoints per inch.
resolution	is the resolution in dots per inch (dpi) as specified in the Set Graphics Resolution command. If no resolution is set, use the device's default resolution. Note that although any resolution setting is ignored during scaled raster graphics, the Y Offset command is nonetheless sensitive to the current resolution setting. This is why the formula requires the resolution parameter.

In essence, the formula converts the destination raster height to inches, and multiplies it by the current dots-per-inch setting to get the number of dots to move. Multiply this offset value by −1 (to cause the page to move backwards), and use this as the value (#) in the Y Offset command, as in the *Summary of Normal Execution Sequence* on page 464.

If you specified destination raster width and not destination raster height, you can calculate the destination height as follows:

$$destination\ height = trunc\left(\frac{destination\ width}{source\ width} \times source\ height\right)$$

where

trunc	is a function that returns an integer after truncation.

Due to the potential for rounding error, it is more accurate to specify explicitly destination height in HP RTL than to calculate it using this formula.

Compressing Data

Raster images normally require that you send a bit (1/8 byte) of data for each pixel; if the image is in color, at least three bits are required per pixel, often much more. For this reason, raster image files are generally much larger than vector image files, in which only the endpoints are sent.

In order to cut down on the amount of data that must be sent for raster images, HP RTL offers several data compression methods. These methods use different "tricks" to reduce the quantity of data that must be transmitted. Most of the tricks involve having the device replicate identical data instead of sending it explicitly.

You use the HP RTL command Compression Method (**ESC***b#M) to select a compression method.

Note that data compression applies only to data transmission. As soon as the data is received by the device, it is decompressed, and then interpreted according to the pixel encoding mode.

Depending on the image and the compression method, a compressed image can be much smaller than an uncompressed one, with corresponding savings in data transmission time. For this reason, we recommend using data compression whenever possible. There is, of course, a trade-off between the host compression time plus device decompression time and the saving in transmission time.

For ease of explanation, the examples in this section are very small and therefore do not show any significant reduction in the size of the data.

Another way of reducing the amount of data sent to the device is to use the Y Offset command (**ESC*b#Y**). This allows you to send partial rows of data. The Transfer Raster Data by Plane (**ESC*b#V**) and Transfer Raster Data by Row/Block (**ESC*b#W**) commands also let you specify empty rows or planes, by using a zero parameter.

HP RTL supports seven data compression methods:

- Run-length encoding (row-based) – method 1, page 381

- Tagged Image File Format (TIFF) revision 4.0 "Packbits" encoding (row-based) – method 2, page 381

- Seed-row encoding (row-based) – method 3, page 382

- Adaptive encoding (block-based) – method 5, page 385

- Three CCITT methods for monochrome data – methods 6, 7, and 8, page 388.

In addition, there are two unencoded (uncompressed) methods:

- Row-based unencoded transmission – method 0, page 379

- Block-based unencoded transmission – method 4, page 379.

It is possible to mix compression methods on the same page. This allows you to use the most efficient method for each row, or, for block-based methods, for each block. You can also mix row-based and block-based methods in one image.

The following sections explain each data compression method. The method numbers refer to the respective values of the Compression Method parameter (#).

Row-Based Unencoded (Compression Method 0)

This is the default method; there is no compression of data. The number of bits required for each pixel is determined by the Configure Image Data (**ESC*v#W**) or Simple Color (**ESC*r#U**) command. For one bit per pixel, the most significant bit (bit 7) of the first byte corresponds to the first pixel in the row; the least significant bit (bit 0) corresponds to the eighth pixel in the row; the most significant bit of the second byte corresponds to the ninth bit in the row, and so on.

Data for each row must end on a byte boundary. If the number of bits per row is not evenly divisible by 8, you must still send a complete byte. For instance, if there are 2500 bits per row, you must send 313 bytes; the last four bits of the last byte can contain anything. You can use the Source Raster Width command (**ESC*r#S**) to clip off the unwanted data. You could also fill the trailing bits with data that will index to a non-printing color, usually white.

For example, to send the string of characters "UUUUATT" to the device, you would use the command sequence: **ESC*r1AESC*b0m7WUUUUATTESC*rC**.

Block-Based Unencoded (Compression Method 4)

This is basically the same as row-based unencoded, except that only one command is needed to transfer data for an entire block of data (Transfer Raster Data by Row/Block—**ESC*b#W**).

The first four bytes of the block make up a 32-bit number specifying the number of pixels of data to expect for each row. The device uses this value to determine when to increment the plane and row pointers. Note that this number is sent only at the beginning of the block, not at the beginning of each row. Also, this number is a true 32-bit unsigned binary integer, not a string of ASCII digits that make up a number as is the case with many other HP RTL parameters. Each pixel may be defined by more than one bit of data.

As with the row-based unencoded method, each row must start and end on a byte boundary. If the number of pixels per row specified in the first four bytes of the block is not evenly divisible by 8, it is rounded up to the next multiple of 8. For instance, if the first four bytes contain the number 2500, it is rounded up to 2504. Data is not clipped based on this four-byte number. Instead, the row is padded to or clipped at the Source Raster Width (**ESC***r#S). Similarly, the Source Raster Height (**ESC***r#T) command allows padding or clipping to the height of the image.

When the row is completely defined, the row-pointer is incremented, and plane pointer is reset to 1, and the CAP is set to the left graphics margin. If the last row of data specifies an incomplete row, or if all the planes have not been defined, the unspecified data is assumed to be 0.

With block-based transfers, data is still sent by row and by plane. For instance, with three planes per row, data for a block is transmitted as follows:

ESC*b#W	Transfer Raster Data by Row/Block
[number of pixels per row]	32-bit integer value
row 1 plane 1	Data organized by row and plane
row 1 plane 2	.
row 1 plane 3	.
row 2 plane 1	.
row 2 plane 2	
row 2 plane 3	
.	
.	
row *n* plane 1	
row *n* plane 2	
row *n* plane 3	

If there is only one plane per row, the data for each plane is transmitted as follows:

ESC *b#W	Transfer Raster Data by Row/Block
[number of pixels per row]	32-bit integer value
row 1	Data organized by row
row 2	.
.	.
.	.
row *n*	

The parameter value (#) in the Transfer Raster Data by Row/Block command (**ESC***b#W) refers to the size of the entire block, including the four-byte prefix; the value (#) is equal to

$$4 + \left(\left\lceil \frac{number\ of\ pixels\ per\ row}{8} \right\rceil \times number\ of\ rows \times number\ of\ planes \right)$$

The "number of pixels per row/8" expression, rounded up to the next integer, yields the number of bytes per row. (The angular brackets in the formula represent the "ceiling function," indicating that the result should be rounded up.)

Run-Length Encoding (Compression Method 1)

With run-length encoding, the raster data consists of byte pairs: the first byte is a repetition count, and the second byte is a data byte. The repetition count can range from 0 to 255, and tells how many times the following byte is to be repeated. A count of 0 means the following byte occurs only once and is not repeated. A count of 255 means the byte is repeated 255 times for a total of 256 occurrences.

Run-length encoding is a row-based encoding method; a separate Transfer Raster Data command is required for each plane and row.

Run-length encoding relies on byte pairs. If the parameter value (#) in the Transfer Raster Data command is odd, the entire transfer sequence is ignored.

Assume you want to send the following data to the device. The data is shown as binary numbers and as ASCII characters:

01010101	01010101	01010101	01010101	01000001	01010100	01010100
U	U	U	U	A	T	T

Using run-length encoding, you would use the following combined command to send the row. The numbers in parentheses must be sent as binary bytes. For instance, (3) is binary 00000011. The entire escape sequence is:

00011011	00101010	01100010	00110001	01101101	00110110	01010111	...
ESC	*	b	1	m	6	W	

...	00000011	01010101	00000000	01000001	00000001	01010100
	(3)	U	(0)	A	(1)	T

where

1 m	means compression method 1 (run-length encoding).
6 W	means there are six bytes of data following. Note that this is the length of the *compressed* data, not the uncompressed data.
(3) U	means repeat the "U" pattern 3 times for a total of four bytes.
(0) A	means do not repeat the "A" pattern.
(1) T	means repeat the "T" pattern once for a total of two bytes.

The data transfer sequence would be: **ESC***r1A**ESC***b1m6W(3)U(0)A(1)T**ESC***rC using the notation for binary numbers described above.

TIFF Packbits Encoding (Compression Method 2)

Tagged Image File Format (TIFF) "packbits" encoding is a combination of row-based unencoded and run-length encoding (methods 0 and 1). You can mix unencoded, or *literal*, bytes with repeated bytes.

TIFF Packbits encoding is a row-based encoding method. A separate Transfer Raster Data command is required for each plane and row.

With TIFF Packbits encoding, raster data is always preceded by a *control byte*. The control byte can fall into three ranges:

0 to 127   There are from 1 to 128 literal data bytes following the control byte. 0 means 1 literal byte; 127 means 128 literal bytes, and so on.

–1 to –127   The data byte following the control byte is repeated the number of times represented by the absolute value of the control byte. (Negative numbers are represented by their two's complement, that is, the number of identical bytes is equal to –(control byte) + 1.)

–128   This control byte is ignored, and the next byte is treated as a control byte.

Assume you want to send the same data as shown with run-length encoding to the device:

01010101	01010101	01010101	01010101	01000001	01010100	01010100
U	U	U	U	A	T	T

Using TIFF Packbits encoding, you could use the following combined command to send the row. As with run-length encoding, the numbers in parentheses must be sent as binary bytes. For instance, (–3), the two's complement of (3), is binary 11111101, decimal 253. Spaces are added for clarity.

        ESC * b 2m 6W (–3)U (0)A (–1)T

where   **2 m**   means compression method 2 (TIFF Packbits encoding).

            6 W   means there are six bytes of data following. Note that this is the length of the *compressed* data, not the uncompressed data.

            (–3) U   means repeat the "U" pattern 3 times for a total of four bytes.

            (0) A   means the "A" pattern is a 1-byte literal.

            (–1) T   means repeat the "T" pattern once for a total of two bytes.

Another valid way to code this data is with the following combined command:

        ESC * b 2m 6W (–3)U (2)ATT

Here, the last three bytes are sent as a literal, (2)ATT.

Again, the entire data transfer sequence would be:

        ESC*r1A**ESC***b2m6W(–3)U(0)A(–1)T**ESC***rC

or   **ESC***r1A**ESC***b2m6W(–3)U(2)ATT**ESC***rC

using the notation for binary numbers described above for run-length encoding.

When using TIFF Packbits encoding, it is more efficient to code two consecutive identical bytes as a repeated byte than as a literal. However, if the repeated bytes are preceded *and* followed by literal bytes, it is more efficient to code the entire group as literal bytes. It is always most efficient to code three identical bytes as a repeated byte.

Seed-Row or Delta-Row Encoding (Compression Method 3)

Seed-row encoding describes a raster row by recording only the changes from the previous row (the *seed row*). Seed-row encoding is sometimes called *delta row compression* because it identifies the *delta*, or change, between one row and the next. Unreplaced bytes are replicated from the seed row.

Seed-row encoding is a row-based encoding method. A separate Transfer Raster Data command is required for each plane and row.

With seed-row encoding, the device takes the previous row of data and makes the changes indicated by the delta data to create a new row. The new row is rendered, and becomes the new seed row.

The format of a single *delta* is:

<command byte> [<optional offset bytes>] <1 to 8 replacement bytes>

The command byte contains both an offset and the number of bytes to replace:

Number of bytes   Relative offset from last untreated byte
to replace

The three higher-order bits indicate the number of consecutive bytes to replace (000=1 to 111=8). The five lower-order bits contain the offset relative to the current byte of the byte to be replaced. The values of the offset have the following definitions:

0–30   Relative offset of 0–30 bytes from the first *untreated* byte (either the first byte in a row, or the first byte following the most recent replacement byte). The first offset in a raster row is relative to the left graphics margin. One to eight replacement bytes follow this command byte.

       For example, assume that the current byte is the first byte in the row. If the offset is 7, bytes 0 through 6 are unchanged; and if there are five replacement bytes, bytes 7 through 11 are replaced. The new current byte is 12. A second offset of 3 means that bytes 12, 13, and 14 are unchanged and byte 15 is the next to be replaced.

31   Indicates that an additional *offset byte* follows the command byte. The value of the offset byte is added to the command byte offset (31) to get the actual offset. If the offset byte is 0, the offset is 31. If the offset byte value is 255, yet another offset byte follows. The last offset byte is indicated by a value less than 255. All the offset bytes are added to the offset in the command byte to get the actual offset value.

       For example, if there are two offset bytes and the last contains 175, the total offset would be 31+255+175=461.

Consider the following data stream using seed-row encoding. The data is shown as binary numbers:

000 11111   11111111   10000000   10010111

where: 000   means replace one byte.
               11111   means add 31 to offset, and that the next byte is an offset byte.
               11111111 means add 255 to offset, and that the next byte is an offset byte.
               10000000 means add 128 to the offset; since this is less than 255, the next byte is the data byte.
               10010111 replaces the byte at an offset of 31 + 255 + 128 = 414 bytes.

The seed row is initialized to 0 whenever raster mode is entered. Every raster transfer affects the seed row, regardless of the compression method; this allows seed-row encoding to be combined with other methods to achieve better compression performance.

A vertical offset also affects the seed row. The Y Offset command (**ESC***b#Y) skips rows, leaving them blank, and sets the seed row to zero. **ESC***b0Y moves down zero rows (or up, if the Raster Line Path command specified upward movement) and sets the seed row to zero.

Seed-Row Encoding and Raster Width

The width of the seed row is equal to the Source Raster Width (**ESC***r#S).

The Transfer Raster Data commands (**ESC***b#V and **ESC***b#W) both contain a number (#) of bytes of data to expect for the entire command. If this byte count is reached before the literal replacement count is met, the byte count has precedence, and no further bytes are replaced in that row. Data beyond the byte count is parsed as ASCII commands and not as binary data.

Seed-Row Encoding and Multi-Plane Data

When you are using more than one plane of data per row, the device maintains a seed row for each plane. This allows seed-row compression to operate on each plane of graphics independently. However, a Y Offset affects all planes and seed rows simultaneously.

Programming with Seed-Row Encoding

With seed-row encoding, if only one bit in a row is different from the preceding row, then only one replacement byte must be sent (with its location specified in one or more command bytes). Here, seed-row encoding is very efficient. However, if a row is completely different from the preceding row, then the entire row must be transmitted. In this case, another compression method might be more efficient. For this reason, seed-row encoding is often mixed with other compression methods for greatest efficiency.

In order to mix compression methods, it is important to understand how the seed row is affected by various HP RTL commands.

Effect of Other Commands on the Seed Row

The seed row is updated by all row-based graphics transfers. This means that data sent with any row-based compression method is available as a seed row. (In multi-plane images, a separate seed row is updated for each plane.)

The seed row is zeroed by the Start Raster Graphics, End Raster Graphics, and Y Offset commands. If there is more than one plane of data, all seed rows are zeroed. In addition, the seed row is zeroed at the completion of any block-based transfer.

Note the effect of the following commands when the device is in raster mode (after a Start Raster Graphics command) and seed-row encoding is active:

ESC*b0W	Transfer Raster Data by Row/Block. Repeats the previous row. The seed row is unchanged.
ESC*b1Y	Move down one raster row. The seed row is set to zeros.
ESC*b0Y	Move down zero raster rows (that is, do not move the CAP). The seed row is set to zeros.

Horizontal CAP moves have no effect on the seed row.

Example of Seed-Row Encoding

The following data is to be compressed using seed-row encoding. It is assumed there is only one plane of data. All graphics data is given in binary. The italicized bytes are the ones replaced using seed-row encoding:

Byte #:	1	2	3	4	5
Row 1:	00000000	*11111111*	00000000	00000000	00000000
Row 2:	00000000	11111111	*11110000*	00000000	00000000
Row 3:	*00001111*	11111111	11110000	*10101010*	*10101010*

The following HP RTL commands generate the data shown above:

ESC*r1A

> Start Raster Graphics initializes the seed row to all zeros.

ESC*b3m2W   000 00001   11111111   [data is shown in binary]

> Compression Method to 3 (seed-row encoding) and Transfer Raster Data by Row/Block for row 1. One byte is replaced. The command byte signifies a single byte replacement (top three bits are 0) and the replacement occurs with an offset of 1 byte from the current position (lower five bits contain a relative offset of 1). The replacement byte follows and contains 11111111.

ESC*b2W   000 00010   11110000   [data is shown in binary]

> Transfer Raster Data by Row/Block for row 2. One byte is replaced. The command byte signifies a single byte replacement (top three bits are 0) and the replacement occurs with an offset of 2 bytes from the current position (lower five bits contain a relative offset of 2). The replacement byte follows and contains 11110000.

ESC*b5W   000 00000   00001111   001 00010   10101010   10101010
[data is shown in binary]

> Transfer Raster Data by Row/Block for row 3. Three bytes are replaced using two commands. The first command byte signifies a single byte replacement (top three bits are 0) and the replacement occurs with an offset of 0 bytes from the current position (lower five bits contain a relative offset of 0). The replacement byte follows and contains 00001111. The second command calls for the replacement of two bytes (top three bits are 001) and the replacement occurs with an offset of 2 bytes from the current untreated position (lower five bits contain a relative offset of 2). The two replacement bytes follow the command byte.

Adaptive Encoding (Compression Method 5)

Adaptive compression uses compression methods 0 to 3 to compress optimally an entire *block* of data. When the row data within a block is no longer optimally compressed by one method, the compression method can be changed to adapt to the data. Adaptive compression also allows the specification of empty or duplicate rows to skip white space or replicate identical rows within a block.

In adaptive compression, a raster image is interpreted as a block of data, rather than as individual rows. The Transfer Raster Data by Row/Block command (**ESC*b#W**) is sent only once at the beginning of a raster transfer; its value field specifies the number of bytes in the block. The block size of the compressed data is limited to 32 767 bytes. To transfer more bytes, more blocks can be sent.

Adaptive compression uses three control bytes at the beginning of each row within the block. The first of these bytes, the command byte, identifies the type of compression for that row. The following two bytes specify either the number of bytes within the row or the number of duplicate or empty rows. The following shows the format of an adaptive compression raster row:

```
<command byte><# of bytes or rows><# of bytes or rows><raster data>
```

The *command byte* designates the compression method, an empty row, or a duplicate row. The following shows the command byte values, which are sent in binary format:

Byte = 0   Unencoded
       1   Run-Length Encoding
       2   Tagged Image File Format (TIFF) revision 4.0
       3   Delta Row
       4   Empty Row
       5   Duplicate Row

If an out-of-range command byte is encountered on a row, the remainder of the block is skipped, the CAP is not updated, and the seed row is cleared.

For cases 0 to 3, the two-byte binary field (*# of bytes or rows*) specifies the row length (that is, the total number of bytes to be transferred for that row within the raster block). For cases 4 and 5, this field defines the number of empty or duplicate rows to be encountered after the current row, including the current row. The most significant byte (high byte) of this field is sent first, followed by the least significant byte (low byte).

The maximum value for *# of bytes or rows* is 65 535; however, the image is clipped to the logical page. The value does not include the three control bytes (the command byte and itself). Values 0 to 3 indicate the identical compression methods described previously. Values 4 and 5 are explained below.

Empty Row   A command byte of 4 causes a row of zeros to be printed. The number of rows printed is contained in *# of bytes or rows*, following the command byte. An empty-row operation resets the seed row to 0 and updates CAP.

Duplicate Row   A command byte of 5 causes the previous row to be printed again the number of times contained in *# of bytes or rows*, following the command byte. A duplicate-row operation updates CAP, but does not change the seed row.

Adaptive Compression Guidelines

- Compression methods cannot be mixed within one row.

- Within a block, the seed row is updated by every raster compression method or type of row. For example, a row compressed with method 2 updates the seed row, while the effect of an empty row initializes the seed row to zeros. Maintaining the seed row allows method 3 to be mixed with other methods in order to achieve optimal compression performance.

- CAP is updated with each row of the raster block.

- The Y Offset command moves the entire block of raster data and also initializes the seed row to zeros. The seed row is set to 0 even if the Y Offset is 0.

- Block size takes precedence over row length. If the row length of any line exceeds the block size, the row size is truncated to the block size.

- For method 1, a row length of 0 increments the CAP and zero-fills the seed row. If the row length is odd, the CAP is incremented and the row data is skipped (thrown away), but the seed row is unchanged.

- For method 2, if the row length is 1, then one byte is consumed from the I/O, and the CAP is incremented. The data is ignored and the seed row is zeroed.

- For methods 2 and 3, if the row length terminates the data before the control byte value is satisfied (for example, the literal byte count is greater than the row length), the data following the control byte (if any) is discarded. The CAP is incremented.

- Since method 3 requires that the seed row be available when entering raster mode, the seed row is initialized to 0s on raster graphics mode entry (**ESC***r#A). The seed row is also initialized on receipt and completion of each raster block.

- For method 3, if the row length is 0, the current row is duplicated and the CAP is incremented.

- For method 3, if the row length is 1, then one byte is consumed from the I/O, the current row is duplicated and CAP is incremented. The data is ignored.

- For duplicate and empty rows a row length of 0 does not update CAP; however, the seed row is initialized to 0.

Example of Adaptive Encoding

The following example demonstrates adaptive compression:

ESC*t300R	Sets the graphics resolution to 300 dpi.
ESC*r1A	Start Raster Graphics initializes the seed row to all zeros.
ESC*b5M	Set Compression method to 5, Adaptive Compression.
ESC*b84W	Transfer a raster block of data containing 84 bytes as detailed below.

As you see in the example data below, the first three rows are compressed using method 3 compression. The next row is compressed by compression method 1. The following three rows of data are specified as duplicate rows of the previous row. Finally, the last three rows are compressed using method 3. The CAP is updated after each raster row within the block is processed. (The row number is *not* part of the data.) All data shown is in hexadecimal format.

Row	Command Byte	Bytes or Rows	Raster Data (hexadecimal)
1	03	00 09	E0 FF F0 00 FF FF 00 0F FF
2	03	00 09	E0 00 00 FF F0 0F FF 00 00
3	03	00 09	E0 FF F0 00 FF FF 00 0F FF
4	01	00 06	00 FF 05 00 00 FF
5	05	00 03	
6	03	00 09	E0 FF F0 00 FF FF 00 0F FF
7	03	00 09	E0 00 00 FF F0 0F FF 00 00
8	03	00 09	E0 FF F0 00 FF FF 00 0F FF

ESC*rC End Raster Graphics.

CCITT Encoding Methods

The first four bytes of the Transfer Raster Data by Row/Block (**ESC***b#W) command are a 32-bit unsigned binary integer that specifies the number of pixels in a row. After decoding, any data exceeding the specified Source Raster Width (**ESC***r#S) is clipped, and any incompletely specified rows are appended with 0s. If Source Raster Height (**ESC***r#T) is specified, undefined rows are zero-filled and excess rows are clipped.

CCITT Groups 3 and 4 encoding methods are by current definition monochrome compression methods, that is, data is sent for one plane only. The colors defined for indexes 0 and 1 are always used for printing, regardless of how many planes were defined with the Set Number of Bits per Index byte of the HP RTL command Configure Image Data. When index 0 is set to a color other than white, a two-color image results: index 0's color appears wherever a "0" bit is sent, and index 1's color appears wherever a "1" bit is sent. The CCITT methods are particularly useful for text data.

A transfer command with a count of 4 is analogous to sending **ESC***b0W in compression method 0; nothing is transferred but the seed row is zeroed.

Since methods 6, 7, and 8 are defined only for monochrome devices, selecting any of these methods causes the device to assume that all data planes except the first are zeroed; that is, the data is interpreted as 0s and 1s that are to be rendered in the colors currently defined as index 0 and 1, respectively. The number of bits per index as set by the Configure Image Data (**ESC***v#W) command and the palette are unchanged.

CCITT Group 3 One-Dimensional Encoding (Compression Method 6)

CCITT Group 3 one-dimensional encoding is a block-based compression method that uses a statistical encoding similar to Huffman encoding. The length of alternating white and black (0- and 1-bit) runs are calculated, and then a table lookup is employed to output the corresponding binary codes. Refer to CCITT Fascicle VII.3 Recommendation T.4 for details.

CCITT Group 3 Two-Dimensional Encoding (Compression Method 7)

CCITT Group 3 two-dimensional encoding is similar to CCITT Group 3 one-dimensional encoding; row 1 uses one-dimensional encoding, and rows 2 through K–1 are sent using two-dimensional encoding, where K is the K-factor used when the data was encoded. Refer to CCITT Fascicle VII.3 Recommendation T.4 for details.

CCITT Group 4 Encoding (Compression Method 8)

CCITT Group 4 encoding is a block-based compression method similar to the CCITT Group 3 encoding methods, except that all encoding is two-dimensional; it does not include end-of-line delimiters, and does not allow padding to byte boundaries. Refer to CCITT Fascicle VII.3 Recommendation T.6 for details.

Chapter 12: Interactions between HP RTL and Other Systems

Interactions with Physical Device Settings

Potentially, the settings of the control panel of a plotter or printer may affect the resolution of printing, whether color or monochrome output is to be produced, and other parameters concerning the overall rendering of data. See the documentation associated with the device for more details.

Interactions with HP-GL/2

Subject to some constraints, you can combine, on the same page, images defined by HP RTL and vector graphics produced by HP-GL/2. HP RTL interacts with HP-GL/2 in several ways. When HP-GL/2 vector data and HP RTL raster data are combined, their temporal order is maintained, and each source component is combined with the destination bitmap according to the print model state variable settings in effect when that component was issued. By default, white is transparent in both environments. The following table summarizes these interactions and tells you where to turn for more information. Section names in italics refer to section titles; command names refer to command descriptions in *Chapter 14*. You can find a full description of all HP-GL/2 instructions in *Part 2* of this book.

Summary of HP-GL/2 Interactions

Interaction	Description
Transferring the HP-GL/2 pen position to the HP RTL Current Active Position (CAP) and conversely	See *Changing Language Contexts and Modes* on page 391, the Enter RTL Mode command on page 420, and the Enter HP-GL/2 Mode command on page 418.
Transferring the HP-GL/2 palette to the HP RTL palette and conversely	See *Changing Language Contexts and Modes* on page 391, the Enter RTL Mode command on page 420, and the Enter HP-GL/2 Mode command on page 418. The IN (Initialize), BP (Begin Plot), and NP (Number of Pens) instructions change the unified palette to the configuration defined in HP-GL/2.

Interaction	Description
Setting boundaries (hard-clip and soft-clip limits) using the HP-GL/2 PS (Plot Size) and IW (Input Window) instructions; beware of unexpected interactions due to the different coordinate systems used, and on rotation.	See *Setting Raster Boundaries* on page 341. The PS (Plot Size) instruction is automatically imported into HP RTL mode, and sets the logical page size to the hard-clip limits. Similarly, the IW (Input Window) instruction sets the soft-clip limits. Clipping may occur unexpectedly if you fail to use these instructions.
Resetting the HP RTL CAP to its origin with HP-GL/2 instructions that cause a page advance	See *The Current Active Position (CAP)* on page 347. Any command that results in a page advance, such as PG (Advance Full Page), BP (Begin Plot), or RP (Replot), results in resetting the HP RTL CAP to (0,0).
Exiting the HP-GL/2 picture header state due to raster transfer commands	See *Changing Language Contexts and Modes* on page 391.
Using HP RTL patterns in HP-GL/2	See *Exporting Patterns to HP-GL/2* on page 362 and *Pattern Orientation* on page 363. HP RTL cannot use patterns defined using HP-GL/2; HP-GL/2 can use HP RTL patterns to fill areas. However, the Set Graphics Resolution (**ESC***t#R) command does not affect the resolution of raster fill patterns defined with the RF (Raster Fill Definition) instruction.
MC (Merge Control) instruction and the Logical Operation command	The Logical Operation (**ESC***l#O) command and the MC (Merge Control) instruction are shared between languages—the last one sent is applied to subsequent images and vectors. Whether the TR (Transparency Mode) instruction is transferred to HP RTL is device-dependent.

On devices that support it, the currently specified Media Type (MT instruction) may apply to the overall rendering of vector and raster data. Potentially, front panel features may also affect the overall rendering of both vector and raster data. See *The Product Comparison Guide for HP Languages on HP Plotters and Large-Format Printers* for more information.

The Reset (**ESCE**) command is recognized in both the HP-GL/2 and HP RTL contexts, with the exception of two cases: in HP-GL/2 label mode with "TD1;" in effect, and in an HP RTL binary data transfer.

Commands and instructions that set the color reference values for palette definitions are separate and non-interacting. (These are Configure Image Data—**ESC***v#W and Set Color Range for Relative Color Data—CR.) When a palette is imported from one context to another, the colors are remapped to achieve visibly identical colors using the current color reference in the target context. In other words, the colors that are imported are already normalized to physical device colors, which are not affected by the current color references in the context just entered.

Changing Language Contexts and Modes

You use these commands to switch between HP-GL/2 and HP RTL, and to reset the device:

> Enter HP-GL/2 Mode **ESC%#B** page 418
> Enter RTL Mode **ESC%#A** page 420
> Reset **ESCE** page 435.

See the command descriptions, starting on page 401, for further details.

In order to process HP RTL commands, the device must first be put into the HP RTL context or "mode." If the device is in the HP-GL/2 context, you use the context-switching command Enter RTL Mode to tell the device to begin processing HP RTL commands. (Enter RTL Mode is the same as the Enter PCL Mode command used to enter the PCL context on PCL devices.) If the device is in a language context other than HP-GL/2, you may have to return to HP-GL/2 mode before changing to HP RTL mode.

Sending raster data exits the HP-GL/2 "picture header state," so HP-GL/2 instructions like PS (Plot Size) must be sent *before* sending any raster data.

When you first enter the HP RTL context, you are in the HP RTL command mode. You can set boundaries, colors, resolution, and other parameters in this mode.

From the HP RTL command mode, you must enter the HP RTL raster mode in order to transfer raster data to the device (see *Transferring Raster Data* on page 373). You can think of the raster mode as a subset of the command mode. Some parameter-setting commands are ignored during the raster mode. You use the HP RTL commands Start Raster Graphics and End Raster Graphics to enter and leave raster mode.

A further distinction is made as to whether the device is in *scaled* or *unscaled* raster mode. The parameter in the Start Raster Graphics command tells the device whether to enter scaled or unscaled raster mode.

When you are finished with an HP RTL command set, you use the HP RTL command Enter HP-GL/2 Mode to return to processing HP-GL/2 vectors. A plotter that does not allow mixing HP-GL/2 and HP RTL on the same page is called a ***stand-alone plotter***, set by **ESC%−1B**; one that does allow such mixing is a ***dual-context*** plotter, set by **ESC%#B** with #≥0. If HP-GL/2 is entered with a −1 parameter (**ESC%−1B**), all HP RTL state variables, including "negative motion disabled", are ignored. Switching back into HP RTL mode causes a Reset (**ESCE**) to be performed.

Transferring Pen Position and Palettes

The Enter RTL Mode (**ESC%#A**) and Enter HP-GL/2 Mode (**ESC%#B**) commands both have parameters that allow you to transfer the pen position between the two contexts. On devices that support unified palettes, the palette is always transferred when you switch modes.

When a palette is transferred, both its size and the colors of its entries are imported, and the device remaps the colors as necessary to achieve visibly identical colors in the target context. That is, the color of the HP-GL/2 pen 0 matches the color of the HP RTL palette at index 0, pen 1 matches index 1, and so on. The default palette in the target context is not affected. (Indexes are explained in *Using HP RTL Indexes* on page 358.)

Some devices do not support transferring palettes between the HP-GL/2 and HP RTL contexts. *The Product Comparison Guide for HP Languages on HP Plotters and Large-Format Printers* gives more information.

Merging Vector and Raster Data

HP RTL devices allow you to mix HP-GL/2 vector data and HP RTL raster data on the same page.

You can send HP-GL/2 vector data and HP RTL raster data in any order. You can even send multiple vector and raster images for the same page. The only limitation is disk or memory space.

Vector and raster images are rendered in the order they are received. (*Rendering* refers to when the image is created in the device's internal bitmap.) The image is not normally drawn until the device receives an HP-GL/2 end plot instruction, usually a PG (Advance Full Page).

When vectors are rendered on top of raster images, the result is dependent on the HP-GL/2 instructions TR (Transparency Mode) and MC (Merge Control), though a later Logical Operation (**ESC***l#O) command overrides a Merge Control instruction.

When raster images are rendered on top of other raster images or on top of vectors, the result depends on the current Source Transparency Mode (**ESC***v#N) and Logical Operation (**ESC***l#O) commands that are in effect, though a later HP-GL/2 MC (Merge Control) instruction overrides a Logical Operation.

Some devices that support nesting allow pictures to be rotated automatically, using the "auto-rotate" feature. When you are merging vector and raster data, you are recommended to disable this feature, using the HP-GL/2 "BP5,1" instruction.

Some devices may have to start printing before receiving the entire image in order to free up memory. When this is the case, subsequent vector instructions in the data stream may be ignored; only the current raster image is completed. For this reason, it is recommended that on devices supporting "on-the-fly" plotting, vectors be sent before raster data whenever possible. This way, no vector data will be lost, and as long as only one raster image follows the vector data, the raster image will print to completion. On devices that support "superflow" mode, vector and raster data should be sent sorted in bands. See *When Overflow Occurs* on page 375 for more about this.

Handling of merged vector and raster data in plane-by-plane mode (where the Set Pixel Encoding Mode byte of the Configure Image Data command is set to 4, indexed plane-by-plane) is device-dependent.

Printer Job Language (PJL)

Access to printer and plotter languages other than HP-GL/2 and HP RTL is supported through the Printer Job Language (PJL). PJL is available from the HP RTL or HP-GL/2 context through the Universal Exit Language/Start of PJL command (**ESC**%−12345X).

Which languages a device supports is device-dependent.

PJL Commands Supported on HP RTL Devices

Here is a summary of the PJL commands used by devices that support HP RTL. Note that not all devices recognize all PJL commands or all operands of PJL commands. All these commands are preceded by @PJL and followed by a carriage return/line feed pair, as shown in the example that follows the summary. White space (tabs or blanks) around equals-signs is optional, as is trailing white space following the command, before carriage return (**CR**) and line feed (**LF**). See the *Printer Job Language Technical Reference Manual* for full details, and *The Product Comparison Guide for HP Languages on HP Plotters and Large-Format Printers* for information relating to specific devices.

```
@PJL COMMENT

@PJL ECHO

@PJL ENTER LANGUAGE =   HPGL
                        HPGL2
                        POSTSCRIPT

@PJL EOJ [NAME = "..."]

@PJL JOB  [NAME = "..."]

@PJL RESET

@PJL SET   MARGINS = NORMAL|SMALLER
           MIRROR = ON|OFF
           ORIENTATION = PORTRAIT|LANDSCAPE
           PALETTESOURCE = DEVICE|SOFTWARE
           PAPERLENGTH = value in decipoints (1/720-inch)
           PAPERWIDTH = value in decipoints (1/720-inch)
           RENDERMODE = COLOR|GRAYSCALE
           RESOLUTION = 300|600
           RET = ON|OFF

ESC%-12345X (universal exit language)
```

Example Showing the Structure of a PJL Job

```
ESC%-12345X@PJL JOB NAME = "..." CR LF
@PJL COMMENT HP DESIGNJET 750C PLOTTER USING CR LF
@PJL COMMENT ...  HP-GL/2, MONOCHROME, 600dpi CR LF
@PJL SET RESOLUTION = 600 CR LF
@PJL SET RENDERMODE = GRAYSCALE CR LF
@PJL SET MIRROR = OFF CR LF
@PJL SET MARGINS = NORMAL CR LF
@PJL SET PALETTESOURCE = SOFTWARE CR LF
@PJL SET PAPERLENGTH = 8423 CR LF
@PJL SET PAPERWIDTH = 5958 CR LF
@PJL SET ORIENTATION = PORTRAIT CR LF
@PJL SET RET = ON CR LF
@PJL ENTER LANGUAGE = HPGL2 CR LF
...  (HP-GL/2 instructions and HP RTL commands) ...
ESC%-12345X@PJL EOJ NAME = "..." CR LF
```

Note that the @PJL SET command overrides the control-panel settings, allowing drivers to define their own requirements without interference from the control panel.

AppleTalk

If your printer or plotter is connected to an Apple computer network, you can use the AppleTalk Configuration command (**ESC&b#W**) to communicate with an AppleTalk driver. See page 404 for information about this command.

Chapter 13: HP RTL
Raster Programming Examples

HP RTL supports several methods for sending raster data to devices. You set the method using the pixel encoding mode byte of the Configure Image Data command.

Some devices do not support plane-by-plane mode. All devices support row-by-row mode within the limits of memory and disk space.

This section shows three examples of raster programs:

- 3-bit RGB color or 1-bit monochrome data with merged HP-GL/2 and no scaling

- CMY or KCMY data without scaling

- 24-bit RGB data with scaling.

The program examples show you the commands required for general raster programs, and the order in which they must be sent to the raster device. You may need to adapt these examples to your specific application. Use of the Source and Pattern Transparency Mode commands, and the Negative Motion command depend on the requirements of your application program.

Spaces, brackets [ ], and parentheses () are only included in the commands for clarity; do not include them in your programs. (However, spaces in PJL commands *are* significant.)

For a note on *Using HP RTL with Programming Languages*, see page 462.

Example of RGB Color or Monochrome Data with Merged HP-GL/2 and No Scaling

Here we show how to print some raster data as part of a driver that also does vector plotting. We assume that half-toning is done by the driver. All parameter fields are ASCII character data unless otherwise specified.

ESC%–12345X	(Enter PJL) This is a universal exit language/start of PJL. Immediately afterwards send the following commands to assign a job name, and to switch the device out of PJL and into HP-GL/2 language:
@PJL JOB NAME=``...``**CR LF**	Insert any further PJL commands, such as @PJL SET RESOLUTION=600**CR LF** to further control the image, before entering HP-GL/2.
@PJL ENTER LANGUAGE=HPGL2**CR LF**	
ESCE	(Reset) Reset HP RTL and HP-GL/2 defaults.
ESC%0B	(Enter HP-GL/2 Mode). This command is required when combining vector and raster data. If this sequence is not used, or the parameter is –1 as required by an HP-GL/2-only driver, any

		vectors sent before raster will be plotted and ejected before raster data is rendered.
BP	5,1;	(Begin Plot) Turn off auto rotation to prevent the possible crossing of raster and auto-rotated vector data due to possible image nesting.
IN	;	(Initialize) Include this for devices that do not recognize the BP instruction.
PS	*length, width*;	(Plot Size) Set the logical HP-GL/2 and HP RTL page size. Parameters are in device units (1016 per inch, 40 per millimeter).
TR	0;	Turn off Transparency mode (if applicable).
`<vector data>`		When merging HP-GL/2 data, send all vector (HP-GL/2) data that is to be rendered before the raster image. If you are using devices that operate most efficiently when pictures are organized into swaths, you may want to switch back and forth between vector mode and raster mode, so as to organize the data into appropriate bands; send first the data that is to appear at the top of the page, and so on. In this case there is a trade-off between the number of switchings and the need to order the data into bands.
PU	;	(Pen Up) Raise the pen.
PA	*x,y*;	(Plot Absolute) Move to an absolute location to begin the raster image. Parameters X,Y are in HP-GL/2 plotter units.
ESC%1A		(Enter RTL) Enter HP RTL mode using the current HP-GL/2 pen position as Current Active Position (CAP).
ESC*v1N		Turn off Source Transparency mode to cover vector images that are overlapped by HP RTL raster data.
ESC*v1O		Turn off Pattern Transparency mode also.
ESC&a1N		(Negative Motion) The value 1 specifies that no negative motion will be used. Only raster data will be received from now to the end of the page. This causes printing to begin immediately rather than waiting for memory to fill or all the raster data to be sent to the device. This setting is recommended if you organize your data so that "on-the-fly" plotting is done (see page 375); do not use it if you organize your data into bands for devices that use "superflow" mode (see page 377).
ESC*r#S		(Source Raster Width) Width (#) is specified in pixels. Source raster height is not required; the height of the image is defined by the number of rows transmitted.
ESC*t#R		(Set Graphics Resolution) The default is 300 dpi. The value must be consistent with that used in the @PJL SET RESOLUTION command. (The PJL command specifies how the device is to operate; the **ESC*t#R** command sets the resolution of the data.)

Color Raster

If you are using color raster data, continue as follows:

ESC*v6W[0][0][3][8][8][8]   Configure Image Data – configures the raster mode. Note: The parameter values in brackets are in binary not ASCII.
Color space = 0
Pixel encoding mode =0 (Indexed by *plane*)
Bits per index =3 (3 bits per *index*)
Bits per Red primary =8 (8 bits per *red*)
Bits per Green primary =8 (8 bits per *green*)
Bits per Blue primary =8 (8 bits per *blue*)

ESC*r1A   Start raster graphics at the CAP.

Repeat for each raster row:

ESC*b#M   (Compression Method)   Raster data compression is highly recommended to improve throughput. Test each row for the most efficient method.

ESC*b#V<data>   Send *red* data

ESC*b#V<data>   Send *green* data

ESC*b#W<data>   Send *blue* data and increment row.
The # parameter specifies the number of bytes of <data> following the V and W specifiers.

ESC*rC   End raster graphics.

ESC%0B   Return to HP-GL/2 mode.

PG   ;   End and print the current page.

ESCE   (Reset)   Reset HP RTL and HP-GL/2 defaults.

ESC%–12345X@PJL EOJ NAME=" . . . "**CR LF**
Exit the current language context and start PJL.

Monochrome Raster

If you are using monochrome raster data, continue as follows:

ESC*r1A   Start raster graphics at the CAP.

Repeat for each raster row:

ESC*b#M   (Compression Method)   Raster data compression is highly recommended to improve throughput. Test each row for the most efficient method.

ESC*b#W<data>   Send raster data and increment row.
The # parameter specifies the number of bytes of <data> following the W specifier.

ESC*rC   End raster graphics.

ESC%0B   Return to HP-GL/2 mode.

PG   ;   End and print the current page.

ESCE   (Reset)   Reset HP RTL and HP-GL/2 defaults.

ESC%–12345X@PJL EOJ NAME=" . . . "**CR LF**
Exit the current language context and start PJL.

Example of CMY or KCMY Data without Scaling

The following sequence is recommended for sending row-by-row raster data to the device. All parameter fields are ASCII decimal data unless otherwise specified.

ESC%–12345X	(Enter PJL) This is a universal exit language/start of PJL. Immediately afterwards send the following commands to assign a job name, and to switch the device out of PJL and into HP-GL/2 language:
@PJL JOB NAME="..."**CR LF**	Insert any further PJL commands, such as
	@PJL SET RESOLUTION=300**CR LF**
	to further control the image, before entering HP-GL/2.
@PJL ENTER LANGUAGE=HPGL2**CR LF**	
ESCE	(Reset) Reset HP RTL and HP-GL/2 defaults.
ESC%0B	(Enter HP-GL/2 Mode). This command is required when combining vector and raster data. If this sequence is not used, or the parameter is a –1 as required by an HP-GL/2- only driver, any vectors sent before raster will be plotted and ejected before raster data is rendered.
BP 5,1;	(Begin Plot) Turn off auto rotation to prevent the possible crossing of raster and auto-rotated vector data due to possible image nesting.
IN ;	(Initialize) Include this for devices that do not recognize the BP instruction.
PS *length, width*;	(Plot Size) Set the logical HP-GL/2 and HP RTL page size. Parameters are in device units (1016 per inch, 40 per millimeter).
ESC%#A	(Enter RTL) Enter HP RTL mode using the current active position (CAP).
	# = 0, use the previous HP RTL CAP
	# = 1, use the current HP-GL/2 pen position as CAP
ESC*v1N	Turn off Source Transparency mode, where appropriate.
ESC*v1O	Turn off Pattern Transparency mode, where appropriate.
ESC&a1N	(Negative Motion) The value 1 specifies that no negative motion will be used, plot on the fly. Only raster data will be received from now to the end of the page. This causes printing to begin immediately rather than waiting for memory to fill or all the raster data to be sent to the device. This setting is required for simple-color mode using a KCMY palette.
ESC*r#S	(Source Raster Width) Width (#) is specified in pixels. Source raster height is not required; the height of the image is defined by the number of rows transmitted.
ESC*t#R	(Set Graphics Resolution) The default is 300 dpi. The value must be consistent with that used in the @PJL SET RESOLUTION command. (The PJL command specifies how the device is to operate; the **ESC***t#R command sets the resolution of the data.)
ESC*r#U	(Simple Color) Color selection from a CMY or KCMY palette. Value (#) = –4 KCMY palette, 4 planes
	–3 CMY palette, 3 planes
ESC*r1A	Start raster graphics at the CAP.

398

Repeat for each raster row:

ESC*b#M	(Compression Method) Raster data compression is highly recommended to improve throughput. Test each row for the most efficient method.
ESC*b#V<data>	Send *Black* data (send this plane if KCMY) is selected
ESC*b#V<data>	Send *Cyan* data
ESC*b#V<data>	Send *Magenta* data
ESC*b#W<data>	Send *Yellow* data and increment row.
	The "#" parameter specifies the number of bytes of <data> following the V and W specifiers.
ESC*rC	End raster graphics.
ESC%0B	Return to HP-GL/2 mode.
PG ;	End and print the current page.
ESCE	(Reset) Reset HP RTL and HP-GL/2 defaults.
ESC%−12345X@PJL EOJ NAME="..."**CR LF**	
	Exit the current language context and start PJL.

Example of 24-bit RGB Data with Scaling

In this example 24-bit/pixel data is sent to the device, to be halftoned and scaled by the device before printing. This is a good solution where the driver does not want to do the halftoning. All parameter fields are ASCII decimal data unless otherwise specified.

The driver may need to perform gamma and color corrections to the image prior to printing. A typical gamma correction factor for an HP DesignJet 650C model B printing on HP Special Paper is around 2.5. Each pixel needs to be modified by the equation:

$$\text{new\_pixel\_value} = ((\text{pixel\_value}/255)^{1/gamma}) * 255 + 0.5$$
$$\text{where } gamma=2.5$$

The function is usually implemented by a lookup table for the 256 possible pixel values.

Some PCL devices are capable of performing gamma correction using the Gamma Correction (**ESC***t#I) command; in such cases the driver should not perform gamma corrections, or a double correction will occur; the original unmodified data should be sent.

ESC%−12345X@PJL JOB NAME="..."**CR LF**	Insert any further PJL commands, such as
	@PJL SET RESOLUTION=300**CR LF**
	to further control the image, before entering HP-GL/2.
@PJL ENTER LANGUAGE=HPGL2**CR LF**	Enter PJL (Printer Job Language) and switch into HP-GL/2 language.
ESCE	Reset HP RTL and HP-GL/2 defaults.
ESC%0B	Enter HP-GL/2 mode.
BP 5,1;	Initialize, and turn off auto-rotation.
PS x,y;	Set the logical HP RTL page size hard-clip limits. Specify x,y in device units (1016 per inch, 40 per millimeter) to set new page size—it will allow printing of greater than default page length.
TR 0;	Turn off Transparency mode.
ESC%0A	Enter HP RTL mode using the current active position (CAP).
ESC*v1N	Turn off Source transparency mode.
ESC*v1O	Turn off Pattern transparency mode.

ESC&a1N	No negative motion, printing to begin immediately rather than waiting for memory to fill or all the raster data to be sent to the device, if applicable.
ESC*r#S	Set source raster width (in pixels).
ESC*r#T	Set source raster height (in pixels).
ESC*t#H	Set raster destination width (in decipoints—1/720–inch).
ESC*t#V	Set raster destination height (in decipoints—1/720–inch). The ratio of source to destination sets the amount of up-scaling or down-scaling. Note that the Set Graphics Resolution (**ESC***t#R) command is not used in scaling mode.
ESC*v6W[0][3][3][8][8][8]	Configure Image Data – configures the raster mode. Note: The parameter values in brackets are in binary not ASCII.
	Color space = 0
	Pixel encoding mode =3 (direct by *pixel*)
	Bits per index =3 (3 bits per *index*)
	Bits per Red primary =8 (8 bits per *red*)
	Bits per Green primary =8 (8 bits per *green*)
	Bits per Blue primary =8 (8 bits per *blue*)
ESC*r3A	Turn on scaling mode and start raster graphics at the CAP.

Repeat for each raster row:

ESC*b#M	Compression method. Raster data compression is highly recommended to improve throughput (data transmission). Test each row for the most efficient method.
ESC*b#W\<data>	Send data. Each 24-bit pixel is sent as a sequence of three bytes. The data format is RGBRGBRGB... The number of RGB triplets is the width defined by Raster Source Width above. The # is the total number of bytes in \<data> and, if not compressed, would be three times the width.
ESC*rC	End raster graphics.
ESC%0B	Return to HP-GL/2 mode.
PG ;	End of page terminator.
ESCE	(Reset) Reset HP RTL and HP-GL/2 defaults.
ESC%–12345X@PJL EOJ NAME=" . . . "**CR LF**	
	Exit the current language context and start PJL.

Chapter 14:
HP RTL Command Reference

The following table lists the commands of HP RTL in the order of their escape sequences, with their parameterized characters in the order:

%   Personality mode changes

&   Device feature control commands

*   Graphics control commands.

It also shows the pages on which you can find more information about them; the notes are on page 403. (The table on page 402 gives the same information, organized by function.) All commands are described in detail on pages 404 through 451 in the order of their command names.

Command name	Escape sequence	Page	Notes
Enter RTL Mode	ESC%#A	420	4
Enter HP-GL/2 Mode	ESC%#B	418	4
Universal Exit Language/Start of PJL	ESC%–12345X	450	4
Move CAP Horizontal (decipoints)	ESC&a#h|H	423	4, 5
Negative Motion	ESC&a#n|N	426	4
AppleTalk Configuration	ESC&b#W[binary data]	404	3
Raster Line Path	ESC*b#l|L	433	1
Compression Method	ESC*b#m|M	406	3
Transfer Raster Data by Plane	ESC*b#V[data]	447	3
Transfer Raster Data by Row/Block	ESC*b#W[data]	449	3
Y Offset	ESC*b#y|Y	451	2, 6
Pattern ID	ESC*c#g|G	429	3
Pattern Control	ESC*c#q|Q	428	3
Download Pattern	ESC*c#W[pattern data]	415	3
Logical Operation	ESC*l#o|O	422	1
Push/Pop Palette	ESC*p#p|P	432	1
Pattern Reference Point	ESC*p#r|R	430	3
Move CAP Horizontal (RTL units)	ESC*p#x|X	424	4
Move CAP Vertical (RTL units)	ESC*p#y|Y	425	4
Start Raster Graphics	ESC*r#a|A	446	1
Source Raster Width	ESC*r#s|S	444	1
Source Raster Height	ESC*r#t|T	443	2

Command name	Escape sequence	Page	Notes
Simple Color	**ESC***r#u|U	441	1
End Raster Graphics	**ESC***rC	417	3
Destination Raster Width	**ESC***t#h|H	414	2
Render Algorithm	**ESC***t#j|J	434	1
Set Graphics Resolution	**ESC***t#r|R	438	1
Destination Raster Height	**ESC***t#v|V	413	2
Set Red Parameter	**ESC***v#a|A	440	1
Set Green Parameter	**ESC***v#b|B	439	1
Set Blue Parameter	**ESC***v#c|C	437	1
Assign Color Index	**ESC***v#i|I	405	1
Source Transparency Mode	**ESC***v#n|N	445	3
Pattern Transparency Mode	**ESC***v#o|O	431	3
Foreground Color	**ESC***v#s|S	421	1
Current Pattern	**ESC***v#t|T	412	3
Configure Image Data	**ESC***v#W[data]	407	1
Reset	**ESC**E	435	4

Here is the same information organized by function:

Command name	Escape sequence	Page	Notes
Context Switching:			
AppleTalk Configuration	**ESC**&b#W[binary data]	404	3
Enter HP-GL/2 Mode	**ESC**%#B	418	4
Enter RTL Mode	**ESC**%#A	420	4
Universal Exit Language/Start of PJL	**ESC**%−12345X	450	4
Reset	**ESC**E	435	4
Defining an Image:			
Destination Raster Height	**ESC***t#v|V	413	2
Destination Raster Width	**ESC***t#h|H	414	2
Move CAP Horizontal (decipoints)	**ESC**&a#h|H	423	4, 5
Move CAP Horizontal (RTL units)	**ESC***p#x|X	424	4
Move CAP Vertical (RTL units)	**ESC***p#y|Y	425	4
Negative Motion	**ESC**&a#n|N	426	4
Raster Line Path	**ESC***b#l|L	433	1
Set Graphics Resolution	**ESC***t#r|R	438	1
Source Raster Height	**ESC***r#t|T	443	2
Source Raster Width	**ESC***r#s|S	444	1
Y Offset	**ESC***b#y|Y	451	2, 6

Command name	Escape sequence	Page	Notes
Defining Colors:			
Assign Color Index	**ESC***v#i**l**	405	1
Configure Image Data	**ESC***v#W[data]	407	1
Foreground Color	**ESC***v#s**l**S	421	1
Push/Pop Palette	**ESC***p#p**l**P	432	1
Render Algorithm	**ESC***t#j**l**J	434	1
Set Blue Parameter	**ESC***v#c**l**C	437	1
Set Green Parameter	**ESC***v#b**l**B	439	1
Set Red Parameter	**ESC***v#a**l**A	440	1
Simple Color	**ESC***r#u**l**U	441	1
Defining Patterns:			
Current Pattern	**ESC***v#t**l**T	412	3
Download Pattern	**ESC***c#W[pattern data]	415	3
Pattern Control	**ESC***c#q**l**Q	428	3
Pattern ID	**ESC***c#g**l**G	429	3
Pattern Reference Point	**ESC***p#r**l**R	430	3
Interactions between Picture Elements:			
Logical Operation	**ESC***l#o**l**O	422	1
Pattern Transparency Mode	**ESC***v#o**l**O	431	3
Source Transparency Mode	**ESC***v#n**l**N	445	3
Transmitting Data:			
Compression Method	**ESC***b#m**l**M	406	3
End Raster Graphics	**ESC***rC	417	3
Start Raster Graphics	**ESC***r#a**l**A	446	1
Transfer Raster Data by Plane	**ESC***b#V[data]	447	3
Transfer Raster Data by Row/Block	**ESC***b#W[data]	449	3

Notes:

1. Command is ignored in raster mode, without ending raster mode implicitly.

2. Command is allowed in non-scaled raster mode, but is ignored in scaled raster mode without ending raster mode implicitly.

3. Command is always allowed in raster mode.

4. Command is allowed in raster mode, and ends raster mode implicitly.

5. Command is to be made obsolete—use **ESC***p#X instead.

6. Command is to be made obsolete outside of raster mode—use **ESC***p#Y instead.

AppleTalk Configuration

ESC&b#W[data]

Purpose

This command provides communication with an AppleTalk driver. It is not used in DOS.

Parameter and Termination Character

Number of bytes of ASCII character data. The default is 0.

    Range: 0 through 32 767. Other values cause the command to be ignored.

This command cannot be combined with others that follow. The uppercase "W" terminator must be used with this command.

Use

This command can be used to provide a job name, to rename the printer for identification on the AppleTalk network, or to provide a printer type, such as HP-GL/2 or PostScript. The data field consists of a keyword (JOB, RENAME, or TYPE), a space, and a value; the value is terminated either by a null (**NUL**) character or by the expiration of the count of data bytes. The following binary sequences are recognized:

JOB <job name>

   This renames the current job; up to 127 characters can be specified; there is no default job name.

RENAME <new name>

   This changes the name field of the device's AppleTalk Network Identifier (Name Binding Protocol name field); between 1 and 31 characters can be specified; all characters are valid except a null (**NUL**) which terminates the device name, "@", ":", "*", "=", "≈" (hexadecimal C5) and hexadecimal FF. (If an invalid character appears, the command is ignored.)

TYPE <type name>

   This changes the type field of the device's AppleTalk Network Identifier (Name Binding Protocol type field); between 1 and 31 characters can be specified; all characters are valid except a null (**NUL**) which terminates the device type, "@", ":", "*", "=", "≈" (hexadecimal C5) and hexadecimal FF. (If an invalid character appears, the command is ignored.) Type changes occur only after the present job is completed.

Assign Color Index

ESC*v#iI

Purpose

This command assigns the currently specified red, green, and blue (RGB) parameters to the designated index number. RGB parameters are specified by the Set Red Parameter (**ESC***v#A), Set Green Parameter (**ESC***v#B), and Set Blue Parameter (**ESC***v#C) commands.

Parameter

Index number. The default is 0.

   Range: 0 to $(2^n - 1)$ where n is the number of bits per index (planes per row) specified in the Set Number of Bits per Index byte of the Configure Image Data command. (Assign Color Index with an out-of-range value resets the RGB parameters to 0, but is otherwise ignored.)

Use

The parameters set by Set Red/Green/Blue Parameter are reset to 0 after executing this command.

This command is ignored during raster mode.

Compression Method

ESC*b#m|M

Purpose

This command determines how raster data is interpreted in the Transfer Raster Data by Plane and Transfer Raster Data by Row/Block (**ESC***b#V or **ESC***b#W) commands. The compression method stays in effect until explicitly changed by another Compression Method command or until defaulted by an explicit or implicit End Raster Graphics (**ESC***rC) or a machine Reset (**ESC**E).

Parameter

The following values are allowed. The default is 0.

0   unencoded (row-based)

1   run-length encoding (row-based)

2   Tagged Image File Format (TIFF) revision 4.0 "Packbits" encoding (row-based)

3   seed-row or delta–row encoding (row-based)

4   unencoded (block-based)

5   adaptive encoding (block-based)

6   CCITT Group 3 one-dimensional encoding (block-based)

7   CCITT Group 3 two-dimensional encoding (block-based)

8   CCITT Group 4 encoding (block-based)

Range: 0 through 8 (out-of-range or unimplemented values default to 0).

Use

See *Compressing Data* on page 378 for a description of the data compression methods. The following is a summary of the format of data used in methods 1, 2, 3, and 5:

1   { <repetition-count> <literal data-byte to be repeated> }...

2   { { <0 to 127> <1 to 128 literal data-bytes> } |
{ <−1 to −127> <data-byte to be repeated 1 to 127 times> } |
{ −128 (ignored)} }...

3   { <no. of replacement bytes (000 to 111 = 1 to 8; 3 bits)
    + offset from current byte (5 bits)>
[<additional offset byte(s)>] <1 to 8 replacement bytes> } ...

5   { <command byte> <no. of bytes/row (2-byte field)><raster data> } ...
    Command byte = 0 Unencoded
                  1 Run-Length Encoding
                  2 Tagged Image File Format (TIFF)
                  3 Delta Row
                  4 Empty Row
                  5 Duplicate Row

Configure Image Data

ESC*v#W[data]

Purpose

This command configures the device for color imaging by performing the following actions:

- Specifies the number of bits per index and defaults the color palette accordingly.

- Sets the color space.

- Sets the pixel encoding mode.

- Sets the number of bits per primary for red, green, and blue.

- Sets the white- and black-reference values for red, green, and blue.

Parameter and Termination Character

There is no default. The parameter is defined as follows:

6 Perform the actions listed above. Set the white- and black-reference values based on the number of bits per primary red, green, and blue. In this case, the black reference is always set to 0, and the white reference is set to $2^{\text{number of bits per primary}} - 1$. Use 8 bits per primary to retain the default color range of 0 through 255 ($2^8 - 1 = 255$).

18 Perform the actions listed above. Set the white and black reference values to the explicit settings in the last 12 bytes of the data.

Range: 6, 18. (Other values less than 18 cause the command to be ignored. Values greater than 18 are valid, but only the first 18 bytes are used.)

This command cannot be combined with others that follow. The uppercase "W" terminator must be used with this command.

Use

This command is ignored in raster mode.

The data field is interpreted as shown in the table on the next page. Bytes 0 through 5 are interpreted as six 1-byte unsigned binary integers; bytes 6 through 17 are interpreted as six 2-byte signed binary integers.

The sections *Encoding Colors* on page 355 and *Defining the HP RTL Palette* on page 356 describe the concepts behind the Configure Image Data command. Refer to this section for more information on data planes, the color palette, indexes, and raster modes.

Byte	Bit Number 15	8	7	0	Byte
0	Color Space		Pixel Encoding Mode		1
2	Number of Bits per Index		Number of Bits per Primary Red		3
4	Number of Bits per Primary Green		Number of Bits per Primary Blue		5
6	White Reference for Red				7
8	White Reference for Green				9
10	White Reference for Blue				11
12	Black Reference for Red				13
14	Black Reference for Green				15
16	Black Reference for Blue				17

The following sections describe each Configure Image Data parameter as a subcommand.

Byte 0: Set Color Space

Sets the color space.

Byte 0 value: The following value is allowed:

> **0**   (The default)   Device-dependent red/green/blue.

> **Range:** 0 (out-of-range values default to 0). Other values are reserved for future color spaces.

Byte 1: Set Pixel Encoding Mode

Defines how the device is to render planes of raster data.

Byte 1 value: The following values are allowed:

> **0**   (The default)   Indexed by plane (indexed color selection; encoded by plane). Also called row-by-row raster mode.

> **1**   Indexed by pixel (indexed color selection; encoded by pixel).

> **2**   Direct by plane (direct color selection; encoded by plane).

> **3**   Direct by pixel (direct color selection; encoded by pixel).

> **4**   Indexed plane-by-plane (encoded plane-by-plane).

> **Range:** 0 through 4 (out-of-range values cause the entire Configure Image Data command to be ignored).

Note: Plane-by-plane mode (parameter value 4) is only supported on a limited number of color devices. Also, some raster devices render color data in gray-scales when set to monochrome mode.

See also *Merging Vector and Raster Data* on page 392 for information on how raster and vector data are overlaid.

Indexed by Plane (mode 0)

In mode 0, one bit (plane) is sent for each pixel in a row; then the next plane is sent, until the pixels are completely defined. The planes define a pixel by forming a palette index number. Assuming three bits per pixel, the highlighted bits below are the palette entry for pixel 4 (i1 is the least significant bit).

row 1	plane 1 (red)	i1 i1 i1 *i1* i1 ...
	plane 2 (green)	i2 i2 i2 *i2* i2 ...
	plane 3 (blue)	i3 i3 i3 *i3* i3 ...
row 2	plane 1 (red)	i1 i1 i1 i1 i1 ...

In row-by-row raster mode, images with more than one plane per row are specified by sending all the planes for each raster row before proceeding to the next row. Depending on the compression mode, row-by-row raster mode allows both the Transfer Raster Data by Plane and Transfer Raster Data by Row/Block commands. For more information, see *Transferring Raster Data* on page 373.

In this mode, the picture may switch back and forth between HP-GL/2 data and HP RTL raster data, and the objects are overlaid in temporal order.

Indexed by Pixel (mode 1)

In mode 1, each pixel in a row receives all its bits, then the next pixel receives all its bit, and so on. The bits of each pixel form a palette index number. Byte boundaries are ignored, with the bits for successive pixels following one another. Assuming four bits per pixel, the highlighted bits below define the index for pixel 2 of row 1. Again, i1 is the least significant bit.

row 1	i4 i3 i2 i1 *i4 i3 i2 i1* ...
row 2	i4 i3 i2 i1 i4 i3 i2 i1 ...
row 3	i4 i3 i2 i1 i4 i3 i2 i1 ...

Direct by Plane (mode 2)

In mode 2, the data for each row is downloaded by sequential planes, and directly specifies each color component. Byte boundaries are ignored, with the bits for successive pixels following one another. The highlighted block below defines the actual primaries for pixel 4 of row 1.

row 1	plane 1 (red)	r r r *r* r r r ...
	plane 2 (green)	g g g *g* g g g ...
	plane 3 (blue)	b b b *b* b b b ...
row 2	plane 1 (red)	r r r r r r ...

Direct by Pixel (mode 3)

In mode 3, the color raster data is downloaded pixel by pixel, and directly specifies each color component. Byte boundaries are ignored, with the bits for successive pixels following one another. Assuming eight bits per primary, the highlighted block below defines the actual primaries for pixel 1 of row 2.

row 1	r7–r0 g7–g0 b7–b0 ...
row 2	*r7–r0 g7–g0 b7–b0* ...
row 3	r7–r0 g7–g0 b7–b0 ...

Indexed Plane-by-Plane (mode 4)

In mode 4, you can obtain large color pictures that would otherwise exceed the device's memory limits. When used in this way, device specific restrictions may affect temporal ordering or the ability to switch between vector and raster data. Mode 4 uses this procedure:

- Separate the color image into four bilevel bitmaps representing the cyan, magenta, yellow, and black planes.

- Set the number of bits per index to 1.

- In between planes, redefine palette index #1 for each plane.

- In between planes, use the Y Offset command (**ESC***b#Y) to reposition the CAP so that the planes will line up as intended.

- Send the planes in order, one at a time, using the Transfer Raster Data by Row/Block command (**ESC***b#W). While in plane-by-plane mode, if data is sent using the Transfer Raster Data by Plane command (**ESC***b#V) the command and the associated data are parsed and ignored.

In plane-by-plane mode, index 0 is always treated as *transparent*, and setting index 0 to another color has no visible effect until row-by-row raster mode is resumed. In plane-by-plane mode, index 1 is interpreted as the primary nearest to the color assigned to index 1.

Byte 2: Set Number of Bits per Index

Sets the number of bits required for indexing into the relative color palette when the Pixel Encoding Mode is 0, 1, or 4; it is ignored for modes 2 and 3. It creates a default palette of the size 2^n where n is the number of bits per index.

Byte 2 value: Number of bits to access a palette entry (that is, number of planes per row). The default is 1.

> **Range:** 1 through 8 (0 is interpreted as 1).

Note: The maximum number of bits per index (and thus the maximum palette size) is device-dependent. Values greater than those supported by a device are clamped to the highest supported value.)

The default HP RTL palettes are described under *Defining the HP RTL Palette* on page 356.

Bytes 3 through 5: Set Number of Bits per Primary

Sets the number of bits per primary for red (byte 3), green (byte 4), and blue (byte 5).

Bytes 3–5 value: Number of bits of data. There is no default.

> **Range:** 0 to 255.

Note: The maximum number of bits per primary is device-dependent and also depends on the mode. Values greater than those supported by a device are either clamped to the highest supported value or cause the command to be ignored.

If the Configure Image Data parameter value (#) is 6, these bytes determine the white- and black-reference values for the color range. In this case, the black reference is always set to 0, and the white reference is set to $2^{\text{number of bits per primary}} - 1$. Use 8 to retain the default color range of 0 through 255 ($2^8 - 1 = 255$).

The following table shows sample values for the number of bits per primary, and the resulting color ranges:

Color	If the number of bits per primary is...	...the black and white references can be...
Red (Byte 3)	8	0 through 255
Green (Byte 4)	6	0 through 63
Blue (Byte 5)	8	0 through 255

Bytes 6 through 17: Set Color Range White/Black Reference

Set the limits for RGB parameters by setting white and black references for each primary color. You can only include these bytes in the data when the Configure Image Data value (#) is 18.

Bytes 6–17 values: White and black references, as shown in the table at the beginning of the Configure Image Data command.

The defaults are: 0 for the black references,
$2^{\text{number of bits per primary}} - 1$ for the white references.

Range: –32 768 through 32 767 for each reference.

Use these bytes to explicitly set the black and white references. These are the limits defined for the primaries of a color, and are used to specify colors directly in pixel encoding modes 2 and 3. They are also used to specify colors when modifying the palette, but have no effect on the default palette colors. White and black references for each color primary can be set in two ways:

- Implicitly, using the short form of the Configure Image Data command, with a value field of 6. Bytes 6 through 17 are not sent, and the white and black references for each primary are set implicitly: black references are set to red=0, green=0, blue=0; white references are set to

$$
\begin{aligned}
\text{red} &= 2^{(\text{\# bits per red primary})} - 1, \\
\text{green} &= 2^{(\text{\# bits per green primary})} - 1, \\
\text{blue} &= 2^{(\text{\# bits per blue primary})} - 1.
\end{aligned}
$$

- Explicitly, using the long form of the Configure Image Data command, with a value field of 18.

The default black reference is red=0, green=0, blue=0; the default white reference is red=255, green=255, blue=255.

Setting the black reference greater than the white reference for any of the three RGB components produces an inverse mapping for that color component. For example, if the black and white references for red are set to 255 and 0 respectively, a value of 50 would represent a fairly intense red.

White and black reference changes affect the palette only following palette reprogramming commands (**ESC***v#A, **ESC***v#B, **ESC***v#C, and **ESC***v#I).

Note: The equivalent HP-GL/2 instruction is CR (Set Color Range for Relative Color Data).

Current Pattern

ESC*v#t|T

Purpose

This command selects the current pattern type for raster images.

Parameter

The following values are allowed. The default is 0.

       0   Solid black or foreground color.

       1   Solid white.

       2   HP-defined shading pattern.

       3   HP-defined hatched pattern.

       4   User-defined pattern.

       Range: 0 to 4.

Use

Values of 2, 3, and 4 activate the "current pattern", which is the one defined by Pattern ID (**ESC*c#G**), see page 429. The current pattern remains active even if Pattern ID is subsequently changed, that is, until a new Current Pattern command is issued.

This command is ignored during raster mode.

Destination Raster Height

ESC*t#v|V

Purpose

This command defines the height in decipoints (1/720 inch) of the destination raster image denoted by subsequent Start Raster Graphics (**ESC***r#A) commands with the scale mode on (parameter value 2 or 3).

Parameter

Height in decipoints. There is no default.

        Range: 0 through 65 535 (out-of-range values are clamped).

Zero or absent values default destination raster height to a value in which isotropic scaling is maintained.

Use

If the specified destination height exceeds the logical page size, the scale factor is maintained and the image is clipped at the top or bottom boundary of the logical page, depending on the Raster Line Path (**ESC***b#L).

This command is ignored during raster scaling mode.

See also *Scaling Raster Images* on page 345.

Destination Raster Width

ESC*t#hlH

Purpose

This command defines the width in decipoints (1/720 inch) of the destination raster image denoted by subsequent Start Raster Graphics (**ESC***r#A) commands with scale mode on (parameter value 2 or 3).

Parameter

\#   Width in decipoints. There is no default.

Range: 0 through 65 535 (out-of-range values are clamped).

Zero or absent values default destination raster width to a value in which isotropic scaling is maintained.

Use

If the specified destination width exceeds the logical page size, the scale factor is maintained and the image is clipped at the right boundary of the logical page.

This command is ignored during raster scaling mode.

See also *Scaling Raster Images* on page 24.

Download Pattern

ESC*c#W[pattern data]

Purpose

This command loads user-defined pattern data.

Parameter and Termination Character

The number of bytes of pattern data. The default is 0.

Range: 0 to $2\,147\,483\,647$ ($2^{31} - 1$).

This command cannot be combined with others that follow. The uppercase "W" terminator must be used with this command.

Use

Loaded patterns may be loaded by their ID number, deleted, and made temporary or permanent. The pattern being loaded is assigned the current value of the Pattern ID (**ESC*c#G**). Any pattern that already has this ID is deleted before the new pattern is loaded. If the current pattern, specified by the last Pattern ID command, is deleted, the current pattern reverts to solid black or foreground color.

Colors in user-defined patterns are rendered as indexes into the current palette. A color pattern that uses non-primary colors (colors other than black, white, red, green, blue, cyan, magenta, or yellow) may interact with dithering, producing unpredictable results.

For efficient use of memory, the defined pattern size should be no larger than the minimum necessary to make the pattern unique.

The byte-aligned binary data field is shown on the next page. Missing data is assumed to be zero; excess or invalid data is discarded. Four formats are available: 0, 1, 20, and 21.

Format byte: The following pattern formats are supported:

0   1 bit per pixel: black and white, or foreground color and white.
These patterns have one bit per pixel; a 1-bit indicates black or the foreground color; a 0-bit indicates white or transparent (depending on the source and pattern transparency modes). A 0-bit cannot be colored.

1   1 or 8 bits per pixel. These patterns use the current palette; data is sent pixel by pixel, and the pixel encoding byte determines the number of bits defining a pixel.

20   Resolution-specified pattern; 1 bit per pixel, as for Format 0; the pixel-encoding byte must be 1.

21   Resolution-specified pattern; 1 or 8 bits per pixel, as for Format 1; the pixel-encoding byte must be 1 or 8.

Formats 0 and 1

Byte	Bit Number 15 ... 8 7 ... 0		Byte
0	Format (0 or 1; see above)	Reserved (0)	1
2	Pixel encoding (see below)	Reserved (0)	3
4	Height in pixels—the number of raster rows in the pattern, interpreted at the pattern resolution; if the height is 0, the data is ignored and no pattern is defined.		5
6	Width in pixels—the number of raster dots in the pattern, interpreted at the pattern resolution; if the width is 0, the data is ignored and no pattern is defined.		7
8 . . .	Pattern image—the raster image describing the pattern; rows must be word-aligned.		9 . . .

Pixel encoding byte: The value is either 1 or 8.

1   The color of each pattern dot is specified by a single bit, supporting a palette of two colors (which need not be black and white).

8   The color of each pattern dot is specified by one byte of data, allowing 256 colors. If the value of any byte is greater than the current palette size, the modulo function is applied to the value.

The default resolution for formats 0 and 1 is 300 dpi.

Formats 20 and 21

Byte	Bit Number 15 ... 8 7 ... 0		Byte
0	Format (20 or 21; see above)	Reserved (0)	1
2	Pixel encoding (1 or 8; as for formats 0 and 1 above)	Reserved (0)	3
4	Height in pixels (as for formats 0 and 1 above).		5
6	Width in pixels (as for formats 0 and 1 above).		7
8	X resolution—for printers that operate in either 300 dpi or 600 dpi mode. Any 300 dpi image requested while the device is in 600 dpi mode is scaled to the correct size. Any 600 dpi image requested while the device is in 300 dpi mode is discarded.		9
10	Y resolution—as X resolution. The X and Y resolutions must be the same.		11
12 . . .	Pattern image—the raster image describing the pattern; rows must be word-aligned.		13 . . .

End Raster Graphics

ESC*rC

Purpose

This command ends raster mode. It signifies the end of the transfer of a raster graphics image and ends the current raster row.

Parameter and Termination Character

There is no value parameter. If a value field (between the "r" and the "C") is received, it is ignored and the command is still executed.

This command cannot be combined with others that follow. The uppercase "C" terminator must be used with this command.

Use

Receipt of this command causes the following operations, in order:

1. Resets the seed row used by compression method 3 to zeros.

2. If a source raster height was specified, moves the CAP vertically, in the direction specified by Raster Line Path (**ESC***b#L), to the raster row immediately following the end of the raster area. If no source raster height was specified, the CAP is positioned in the direction of Raster Line Path to the row following the last completed row.

3. Fills the area through which the CAP moves with zeros.

4. Moves the CAP horizontally to the left graphics margin. If raster graphics started at the current CAP (Start Raster Graphics 1 or 3), the CAP after the End Raster Graphics is at the same X-coordinate as the starting CAP. If raster graphics started at the left edge of the logical page (Start Raster Graphics 0 or 2), the CAP after the End Raster Graphics is at the left edge of the logical page.

5. Defaults the compression method to 0.

6. Enables commands that were ignored by Start Raster Graphics (**ESC***r#A).

7. Resets the plane pointer to the first plane of the next row.

Note: When this command is received before a row is completed, it is device-dependent whether or not the incomplete row is rendered. If rendered, the incomplete row is zero-filled, the row is incremented, and the plane pointer is set to the first plane of the next row. If not rendered, the row is not incremented as the result of the incomplete row.

See also *Implicit End Raster Graphics* on page 374.

Enter HP-GL/2 Mode

ESC%#B

Purpose

This command causes the device to begin interpreting incoming data as HP-GL/2 instructions instead of HP RTL commands. It is ignored if received when the device is in HP-GL/2 mode.

Parameter and Termination Character

The following values are allowed:

−1 Context switch from HP RTL to "stand-alone plotter" (see below).

0 The HP-GL/2 pen position is set to the previous HP-GL/2 pen position.

1 The HP-GL/2 pen position is set to the current HP RTL CAP.

Range: −1, 0, or 1. A missing value is interpreted as 0 and negative values become −1. Positive values set the functions according to the last bit position.

This command cannot be combined with others that follow. The uppercase "B" terminator must be used with this command.

Use

The HP-GL/2 palette is set to the HP RTL palette. HP-GL/2 and HP RTL have a unified palette, that is, the HP-GL/2 palette is set to the HP RTL palette when entering HP-GL/2 mode.

Note: Some devices do not support transferring the palette from HP RTL to HP-GL/2.

For parameter values 0 and 1, the usual HP-GL/2 environment is modified. For parameter value −1, the HP-GL/2 context behaves as a stand-alone plotter, except that the Reset (**ESC**E) and Enter RTL Mode commands (**ESC**%#A) are recognized.

HP-GL/2 mode remains in effect until **ESC**%#A, **ESC**E, power-on, or a PJL context switch (**ESC**%−12345X). The language context at power on is device-dependent.

Except for the CAP, palette, and the current MC (Merge Control) setting—which comes from the Logical Operation setting—HP-GL/2 state variables are not affected by HP RTL mode and retain their previous HP-GL/2 values upon receipt of this command. However, state variables *are* reset by the BP (Begin Plot) instruction, which is executed for a parameter value of −1.

Stand-Alone Plotter Mode

Execution as a single-context, stand-alone plotter involves the following sequence:

1. Enter HP-GL/2 mode using a −1 parameter (**ESC**%−1B).

2. Transmit one or more HP-GL/2 plots.

3. Exit HP-GL/2 mode (**ESC**%#A, **ESC**E, or **ESC**%−12345X)

Upon entering HP-GL/2 with a –1 parameter ("stand-alone plotter" mode), the following actions occur:

1. A conditional page advance is performed. That is, if any data was received for the current page, a page advance is performed. This causes the page to plot.

2. The HP-GL/2 BP (Begin Plot) instruction is executed. This performs an HP-GL/2 initialization. Thus the HP-GL/2 output begins on a new page. Note that stand-alone plotter mode does not allow plotting vector (HP-GL/2) and raster (HP RTL) data on the same page.

3. No HP RTL commands except Reset (**ESCE**), Enter RTL Mode (**ESC%#A**), and Universal Exit Language/Start of PJL (**ESC%–12345X**) are recognized.

When you switch back from stand-alone plotter mode to HP RTL mode (with the Enter RTL Mode command), the current page is closed and printed and a conditional page advance is performed; a Reset is also performed.

Dual-Context Mode

When the value field is non-negative, the HP-GL/2 and HP RTL contexts can be merged. Both types of data can be used on the same page, with HP-GL/2 graphics integrated directly with HP RTL images. HP RTL patterns can be used in HP-GL/2. The CAP, the palette, and the logical operation are also transferred between HP-GL/2 and HP RTL.

If HP-GL/2 is entered with a value of 1, the carriage-return point is also updated to the new current position, that is, the current HP RTL CAP.

The HP RTL palette redefinition commands (Configure Image Data—**ESC*v#W**, Set Red/Green/Blue Parameter—**ESC*v#A**, **ESC*v#B**, **ESC*v#C**, and Assign Color Index—**ESC*v#I**) change the colors selected by the SP (Select Pen) instruction.

If a Reset (**ESCE**) command is issued in dual-context mode, it affects the HP-GL/2 state as follows:

*   A BP (Begin Plot) instruction is executed in the Technical Graphics Extension.

*   The HP-GL/2 plot size and orientation revert to their defaults.

*   The pen colors selected by the SP (Select Pen) instruction revert to their defaults.

The HP RTL palette is transferred to HP-GL/2 and the following occurs:

1. The widths associated with entries in the imported HP RTL palette are defaulted according to the current setting of the WU (Pen Width Unit Selection) instruction.

2. The palette becomes the HP-GL/2 default palette for the BP (Begin Plot) and IN (Initialize) instructions until an "IN 1;", Reset (**ESCE**) or Enter RTL Mode (**ESC%#A**) command is executed.

3. If the current pen number is larger than the imported HP RTL palette size, the modulo function (as defined in the SP [Select Pen] instruction) is applied to obtain a pen number that can index into the HP-GL/2 palette.

Enter RTL Mode

ESC%#A

Purpose

This command, also known as Enter PCL Mode, causes the device to begin interpreting incoming data as HP RTL commands. It exits HP-GL/2 mode.

Parameter and Termination Character

The following values are allowed:

0   (The default) The HP RTL CAP is set to the previous HP RTL CAP.

1   The HP RTL CAP is set to the HP-GL/2 pen position.

Range: 0, 1. A missing or negative value is interpreted as 0. All other values set the functions according to the last bit position.

This command cannot be combined with others that follow. The uppercase "A" terminator must be used with this command.

Use

The HP RTL palette is set to the HP-GL/2 palette. HP-GL/2 and HP RTL have a unified palette, that is, the HP RTL palette is set to the HP-GL/2 palette when entering HP RTL mode.

Note: Some devices do not support transferring the palette from HP-GL/2 to HP RTL.

No HP RTL state variables except the CAP, palette, and the current MC (Merge Control) setting—which becomes the Logical Operation setting—are explicitly affected by exiting HP-GL/2 mode. The HP RTL *default* palette is unaffected; only the *user-defined* palette is updated. Also the current setting of the number of bits per index is modified to the smallest value which will accommodate all entries in the new palette. (Number of bits per index is normally set via the Configure Image Data command, **ESC*v#W**.)

The PS (Plot Size) and IW (Input Window) currently specified for HP-GL/2 mode are automatically imported into HP RTL mode. The logical page size is set to the hard-clip limits, the HP RTL CAP is updated to retain its logical position, and any subsequent raster image is clipped to the IW window.

If the current HP-GL/2 position is outside the bounds of the HP RTL logical page and the value field is 1, the CAP is set to the nearest point on the logical page boundary.

This command is ignored if it is received when the device is already in HP RTL mode, except that it implicitly performs an End Raster Graphics command (**ESC*rC**) if the device is in raster mode.

Foreground Color

ESC*v#sIS

Purpose

This command sets the foreground color to the specified index of the current palette.

Parameter

Index number. The default is 0.

Range: 0 through 2^n-1, where n is the number of bits per index.

Out-of-range values are mapped into a new index using the modulo(palette-size) function. For example, if the current palette size is 8 and the parameter specified is 10, the index is mapped as 10 modulo 8, that is, 2. If the current palette was created in HP-GL/2, the mapping used by HP-GL/2 is used, as described for the SP (Select Pen) instruction on page 306.

Use

Foreground Color affects monochrome patterns defined in HP RTL. It has no effect on HP-GL/2 data; HP-GL/2 uses the selected pen and ignores the foreground color.

To avoid unwanted interactions with color raster images, you are advised to select a black foreground color.

After you have defined a foreground color, changing any of the following will not change the foreground color until a new Foreground Color command is issued:

- Active palette
- Configure Image Data command (**ESC*v#W**)
- Render Algorithm command (**ESC*t#J**).

This command is ignored during raster mode.

Logical Operation

ESC*l#olO

Purpose

This command specifies the logical (raster) operation (ROP) to be performed in RGB-space on the destination (D), source (S), and texture (T) data to produce new destination data. (The "texture" is explained on page 366; the "destination" is the current image on the composed page.)

Parameter

Logical operation value, as defined on page 473.

        Range: 0 to 255. The default is 252 (TSo, Texture or Source).

Use

This command provides 256 logical operations that map directly to their Microsoft® ROP3 counterparts. For full details of the behavior of this command, and its use, see page 367.

Note: The equivalent HP-GL/2 instruction is MC (Merge Control), see page 220.

The Logical Operation command interacts with HP-GL/2. In dual-context mode the raster operation set by this command carries over to HP-GL/2; similarly any raster operation set in HP-GL/2 using the MC (Merge Control) instruction carries over to HP RTL.

Move CAP Horizontal (Decipoints)

ESC&a#hlH

Purpose

This command moves the CAP horizontally by the specified number of decipoints (1 decipoint = 1/720 inch). Horizontal movement is independent of the device's resolution. Devices that do not have an integral number of decipoints to dots implement fractional decipoints for dot addressing.

Note: This command is to be made obsolete; do not use it in new applications—use Move CAP Horizontal (HP RTL Native Resolution Units) instead (**ESC***p#X)—see page 424.

Parameter

Number of decipoints. A missing parameter is interpreted as 0.

Range: −32 767 through 32 767 (out-of-range values are clamped).

Use

Use a plus sign (+) before the number to move to the right *relative* to the CAP, a minus sign (−) to move to the left *relative* to the CAP, and no sign to move an *absolute* distance from the logical page left bound.

This command can move the CAP anywhere along the horizontal axis. Requests for movement outside the logical page are allowed.

Note: The physical distance covered by a byte depends on each device's physical resolution. For instance, at 300 dpi, there are 300/8 = 37.5 bytes per inch, so each byte is 1/37.5 = .027 inches wide.

Move CAP Horizontal (HP RTL Native Resolution Units)

ESC*p#x|X

Purpose

This command moves the CAP horizontally by the specified number of HP RTL Native Resolution Units. Thus if the native resolution is 300 dots-per-inch, a horizontal move of two inches requires a parameter value of 600.

Parameter

Number of HP RTL Native Resolution Units. There is no default.

Range: −32 767 through 32 767 (out-of-range values are clamped).

Use

Use a plus sign (+) before the number to move to the right *relative* to the CAP, a minus sign (−) to move to the left *relative* to the CAP, and no sign to move an *absolute* distance from the logical page left bound.

This command can move the CAP anywhere along the horizontal axis. Requests for movement outside the logical page are allowed. The movement is independent of the raster resolution, as set by the Set Graphics Resolution (**ESC***t#R) command.

Some devices support several native resolutions, which can be selected with the command:
@PJL SET RESOLUTION=... (see page 392).

Move CAP Vertical (HP RTL Native Resolution Units)

ESC*p#ylY

Purpose

This command moves the CAP vertically by the specified number of HP RTL Native Resolution Units. Thus if the native resolution is 300 dots-per-inch, a vertical move of two inches requires a parameter value of 600.

Parameter

Number of HP RTL Native Resolution Units. There is no default.

        Range: −32 767 through 32 767 (out-of-range values are clamped).

Use

Use a plus sign (+) before the number to move down *relative* to the CAP, a minus sign (−) to move up *relative* to the CAP, and no sign to move an *absolute* distance from the logical page top bound.

This command can move the CAP anywhere along the vertical axis. Requests for movement outside the logical page are allowed. The movement is independent of the raster resolution, as set by the Set Graphics Resolution (**ESC*t#R**) command.

Some devices support several native resolutions, which can be selected with the command:
        @PJL SET RESOLUTION=... (see page 392).

Negative Motion

ESC&a#nlN

Purpose

This command specifies whether negative motion will be used. *Negative motion* is defined as:

- Any HP-GL/2 drawing operation

- Any operation that would print in the negative Y-axis direction with respect to previously printed data

- Any Y Offset in raster mode that moves the CAP in the negative Y-axis direction.

For further information about negative motion, see the description of the CAP on page 347, and the explanation of "on-the-fly" plotting on page 375.

Parameter

The following values are allowed. The default is 0.

0   Image may contain negative motion.

1   Image contains no negative motion.

Range: 0, 1 (a missing value is interpreted as 0, and other values cause the command to be ignored).

Use

Negative motion is any command that would potentially require the CAP to move in a negative Y direction. In particular, when Raster Line Path (**ESC***b#L) = 0, any negative Y Offset (**ESC***b#Y) command; when raster line path = 1, any positive Y Offset command, or any data transfer command; or any HP-GL/2 drawing operation.

A value of 0 enables negative motion. Multiple raster images and merged raster and vector images may be composed on a page before printing begins.

A value of 1 disables negative motion. A device may interleave parsing and printing to reduce page printing time and memory requirements. A value of 1 guarantees the printing of parsed data while data printing advances in the positive Y-axis direction.

Devices normally compose an entire page in memory or on a hard disk before printing. This command, with a parameter value of 0, allows for multiple raster images on a page, or for merged raster and vector images on the page.

However, if there is only one raster image remaining to put on the page, and that image does not use negative motion, it is advantageous on some devices to issue this command with a 1 parameter. These devices can begin printing immediately, without waiting for the entire image to be stored in memory or on disk.

Note: Some devices cannot simultaneously receive and print raster images. On these devices, this command has no effect.

If negative motion is set to 1 and the image nonetheless contains negative motion (as defined above), the effect is device-dependent.

Note: If HP-GL/2 is entered with a −1 parameter (**ESC%−1B**), all HP RTL state variables are ignored, including "negative motion disabled". Switching back to HP RTL causes a Reset (**ESCE**) to be performed.

Pattern Control

ESC*c#qIQ

Purpose

This command manipulates user-defined patterns. See *Patterns* on page 361.

Parameter

\#   The following values are allowed. The default is 0.

0   Delete all patterns (temporary and permanent)

1   Delete all temporary patterns

2   Delete the pattern specified by the last Pattern ID command.

Range: 0, 1, 2. The command is ignored for other values.

Use

Temporary patterns are deleted by a Reset (**ESCE**).

If a pattern used on the current page is deleted, it is retained internally and not disposed of until the page is printed.

If the current pattern, specified by the last Pattern ID command, is deleted, subsequent raster images will be rendered in black or the foreground color.

Note: Support of permanent patterns is device-dependent.

Pattern ID

ESC*c#glG

Purpose

This command designates a unique identification number for user-defined and HP-defined patterns. See *Patterns* on page 361.

Parameter

Pattern ID. The default is 0.

         Range: 0 to 32 767.

Use

This command must be sent before loading a user-defined pattern; when a new pattern is downloaded, any pattern that is already loaded and has the same pattern ID is deleted.

The "current pattern" is the one associated with the last specified ID when the Current Pattern (**ESC***v#T) command was executed. If no ID existed, raster images are rendered in black or the foreground color.

For HP-defined shading patterns, IDs 1 to 100 determine the shading (on a nonlinear mapping of 1% to 100%). For HP-defined hatched patterns, IDs 1 to 6 select the type of hatched pattern:

     1   Horizontal lines
     2   Vertical lines
     3   Diagonal lines (lower left to upper right)
     4   Diagonal lines (lower right to upper left)
     5   Cross-hatching with horizontal and vertical lines
     6   Cross-hatching with diagonal lines.

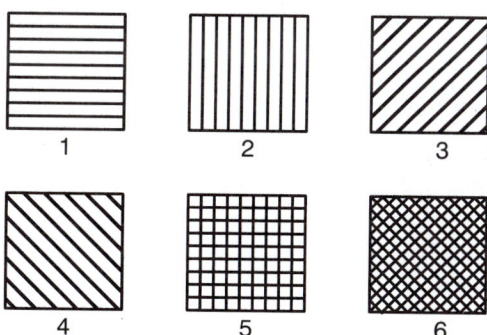

Figure 176. Shading Patterns

For raster images, an HP- or user-defined pattern is activated by specifying Pattern ID and Current Pattern (**ESC***v#T)—see page 412.

Pattern Reference Point

ESC*p#rlR

Purpose

This command sets the "tiling" (replication) of patterns with respect to the Current Active Position (CAP) rather than position (0,0). See *Patterns* on page 361.

Parameter

\#   Only the value 0 is allowed.

     Range: 0. The command is ignored for other values.

Use

Note: A similar, though not identical HP-GL/2 instruction is AC (Anchor Corner).

Pattern Transparency Mode

ESC*v#olO

Purpose

This command sets the pattern transparency mode. See *Patterns* on page 361.

Parameter

The following values are allowed. The default is 0.

0   Transparent; the pattern's white pixels are not applied to the destination; the destination image shows through the pattern.

1   Opaque; the pattern's white pixels are applied to the destination; the corresponding parts of the destination image are blocked out by the pattern.

Range: 0, 1. Other values cause the command to be ignored.

Use

A value of 0 makes the pattern's white areas transparent, allowing the corresponding parts of the destination image to show through. With a transparency mode of 1, the white pixels in the pattern are applied directly to the destination.

This command is ignored during raster mode.

Push/Pop Palette

ESC*p#plP

Purpose

This command saves (pushes) or restores (pops) the palette from the palette stack.

Parameter and Termination Character

#
The following values are allowed. The default is 0.

0 Pushes (saves) the palette.

1 Pops (restores) the palette.

Range: 0 or 1. This command is ignored for other values. A value of 0 pushes the current palette, which is unaffected. A value of 1 pops the most recently pushed palette, which overwrites the current palette and becomes the new current palette. As with any stack, the last item pushed is the first item popped.

Use

Pushing a palette saves the following parameters to allow for palette restoration:

- Color definitions for each palette entry.

- Pen widths (the palette is also used in HP-GL/2).

- Black and white references.

- Number of bits per index expected for raster transfers.

- Pixel encoding mode.

- Number of bits per primary expected for raster transfers.

Stack size is limited by the device's available memory. Pushes past the stack limit or attempts to pop an empty stack are ignored. **ESCE** empties the palette stack and overwrites the current palette with the default black and white palette. Entering PJL, which causes an **ESCE**, has the same effect. The HP-GL/2 instructions IN and BP overwrite the current palette with the default HP-GL/2 palette, but have no effect on the palette stack.

Raster Line Path

ESC*b#IIL

Purpose

This command specifies the following:

- The vertical direction that a Transfer Raster Data by Row/Block (**ESC*b#W**) command increments the raster row within an image.

- The vertical direction that the Y Offset (**ESC*b#Y**) command moves the CAP.

- The vertical direction in which an explicit or implicit End Raster Graphics (**ESC*rC**) command moves the CAP if a Source Raster Height (**ESC*r#T**) command has been specified.

The handling of line feeds in HP-GL/2 labels is not affected.

Parameter

The following values are allowed. The default is 0.

0   Increment raster row in the +Y direction of the HP RTL coordinate system.

1   Increment raster row in the –Y direction of the HP RTL coordinate system.

Range: 0, 1 (a missing value is interpreted as 0, and other values cause the command to be ignored).

Use

This command is ignored after the Start Raster Graphics (**ESC*r#A**) or Transfer Raster Data (**ESC*b#V** or **ESC*b#W**) commands until the next explicit or implicit End Raster Graphics (**ESC*rC**) command. Since the raster image will "grow" in the specified direction, it is the user's responsibility to position the CAP to avoid unwanted overlaying of the image with vector or other raster graphics.

Render Algorithm

ESC*t#jlJ

Purpose

This command selects the algorithm to be used for rendering page marking entities on a given page. See *Halftoning* on page 360.

Parameter

The following values are allowed. The default is 0; note that the PCL default for this command is 3.

0   Device best.

3   Pattern dither (to be made obsolete; use 11 instead).

5   Device best (monochrome).

7   Cluster-ordered dither.

8   Cluster-ordered dither (monochrome).

11 Pattern dither.

12 Pattern dither (monochrome).

13 Scatter dither.

14 Scatter dither (monochrome).

Range: 0, 3, 5, 7, 8, 11, 12, 13, 14. The command is ignored for other values of the parameter.

Use

The device-best halftone algorithm is device-dependent.

Monochrome Rendering: A gray value is generated from the three primary colors; this value is computed according to the NTSC standard, which for device RGB color space is
$$\text{Gray} = 0.3 \times \text{Red} + 0.59 \times \text{Green} + 0.11 \times \text{Blue.}$$

Cluster-Ordered Dither: A pixel is intensified at a point (x,y) depending on the desired intensity, $I(x,y)$, and on an n-by-n dither matrix, D, where
$$i = x \text{ modulo } n$$
$$j = y \text{ modulo } n.$$
For RGB color spaces, if $I(x,y) < D(i,j)$, the point corresponding to (x,y) is intensified; otherwise it is not. The intensity of each primary color is determined according to this scheme. The relationship between I and D depends on the specified color space.

Reset

ESCE

Purpose

This command causes the following actions:

- Prints any partial pages of data which may have been received. Reset does not cause a page eject if the page does not contain an image (raster graphics or HP-GL/2 graphics).

- Executes the HP-GL/2 instructions BP (Begin Plot) and IN (Initialize).

- Resets all programmable features to their default values. Programmable features whose defaults can be set from the front panel are set to those defaults. Values reset are:

  Graphics resolution

  Compression method

  Seed row

  Source width to logical page width

  Bits per index

  Pixel encoding mode

  Number of bits of red, green, and blue

  Scaling off

  Render algorithm to device-best

  Foreground color

  Logical operation

  Source and pattern transparency to transparent

  Current pattern to solid

  Pattern reference point to (0,0)

  Palette HP RTL black-and-white.

- Returns and fixes the HP RTL CAP to (0,0).

- Deletes temporary patterns.

- Returns the device to HP RTL parsing mode.

- Implicitly ends raster mode, if necessary.

Parameter and Termination Character

There is no value parameter.

This command cannot be combined with others that follow. The uppercase "E" terminator must be used with this command.

Use

Both the HP-GL/2 and HP RTL contexts recognize the Reset command.

After the Reset command, the device remains online, no subsequent data is lost, and there is no effect on I/O or host-to-peripheral communication.

ESCE is a valid HP-GL/2 terminator, and incorporates all the functionality of the BP (Begin Plot) and IN (Initialize) instructions, as well as defaulting the HP RTL and HP-GL/2 palettes.

Within an HP-GL/2 label, when transparent data mode is on ("TD1;"), **ESC**E is interpreted as data and does not reset the device. When "TD0;" is in effect, the command causes a reset.

When the device is expecting HP RTL data, **ESC**E is interpreted as data and does not reset the device. The device expects HP RTL data following the HP RTL commands Configure Image Data (**ESC***v#W), Transfer Raster Data by Plane (**ESC***b#V), and Transfer Raster Data by Row/Block (**ESC***b#W). The length of the data the device expects varies and is specified in each command.

Set Blue Parameter

ESC*v#clC

Purpose

This command specifies the blue component of any new color entry of the color palette.

Parameter

Blue parameter. The default is 0.

    Range: Black reference to white reference for blue (as defined in the Configure Image Data command, **ESC***v#W). Out-of-range values are clamped. (The absolute limits are –32 768 to 32 767.)

Use

The parameter is applied and then initialized to 0 after each Assign Color Index command (**ESC***v#l).

Set Graphics Resolution

ESC*t#rlR

Purpose

This command defines the resolution at which graphics data is to be plotted or printed.

Parameter

Resolution in dots per inch (dpi). The default resolution is device-dependent.

Range: 0 through 32 767 (out-of-range values are clamped). The 0 through 32 767 range represents HP RTL limits; device limits may be more restrictive. The actual physical (or native) resolution is device-dependent. Support of *continuous* or *incremental* resolution is device-dependent.

Use

If the requested resolution is not supported, the resolution value is mapped to the next higher supported resolution to ensure that the picture is printed without data loss. For example, if a device supports both 180 dpi and 90 dpi and the requested resolution is greater than 90 dpi, 180 dpi is selected; otherwise 90 dpi is selected. If the resolution value is greater than the maximum for the device, that maximum is used.

The graphics resolution is ignored in raster scaling mode. The supplied source and destination widths and heights are used instead; see page 346.

This command is ignored during raster mode.

On devices that support several native resolutions, the image is first scaled up or down to the native resolution selected by the @PJL SET RESOLUTION command. Selecting a low native resolution uses less memory but has more granularity; it is more appropriate for draft quality. A high native resolution uses more memory but has better quality. For example, if the resolution is set to 300 dpi through PJL and the Set Graphics Resolution command specifies a larger value (such as 600), the image is scaled down to 300 dpi, with loss of detail. If the device's machine resolution is 600 dpi, pixels are then replicated.

See also *Controlling Image Resolution* on page 344.

Set Green Parameter

ESC*v#blB

Purpose

This command specifies the green component of any new color entry of the color palette.

Parameter

Green parameter. The default is 0.

Range: Black reference to white reference for green (as defined in the Configure Image Data command, **ESC***v#W). Out-of-range values are clamped. (The absolute limits are −32 768 to 32 767.)

Use

The parameter is applied and then initialized to 0 after each Assign Color Index command (**ESC***v#l).

Set Red Parameter

ESC*v#alA

Purpose

This command specifies the red component of any new color entry of the color palette.

Parameter

Red parameter. The default is 0.

Range: Black reference to white reference for red (as defined in the Configure Image Data command, **ESC***v#W). Out-of-range values are clamped. (The absolute limits are −32 768 to 32 767.)

Use

The parameter is applied and then initialized to 0 after each Assign Color Index command (**ESC***v#I).

Simple Color

ESC*r#ulU

Purpose

This command creates a fixed-size palette whose color specification cannot be modified. The pixel encoding mode is always indexed planar.

Parameter and Termination Character

The following values are allowed. The default is to use the current palette, which may be the HP-GL/2 palette.

      –4 Four planes, device black/cyan/magenta/yellow (KCMY) palette.

      –3 Three planes, device cyan/magenta/yellow (CMY) palette.

      1 One plane, black.

      3 Three planes, device red/green/blue (RGB) palette.

      Range: –4, –3, 1, 3.

Use

This command creates a new palette and overwrites the current palette. HP RTL commands and HP-GL/2 instructions that modify the palette (NP, PC, **ESC*v#A**, **ESC*v#B**, **ESC*v#C**, and **ESC*v#I**) are ignored. When a Simple Color palette is popped from the stack (using **ESC*p#P**), it cannot be modified; pixel encoding then reverts to indexed planar.

RGB, CMY, or KCMY raster data must be sent by plane (using **ESC*b#V**) and by row (using **ESC*b#W**). The last plane in each row is sent with the **ESC*b#W** command; all other planes are sent with the **ESC*b#V** command.

When KCMY mode is selected:

—   HP RTL devices lock out the Color Model and HP-GL/2 objects, so KCMY raster objects cannot be mixed with any other object on the same page.

—   Raster scaling is also ignored in this mode.

—   Gray-scaling in KCMY mode is rendered as black and white, but the gray-scale algorithm is device-dependent.

—   Transparencies and logical operations are not supported.

When CMY mode is selected using the Simple Color command, it is device-dependent whether you can use scaling.

Planes must be sent in order; for example, for CMY, cyan, magenta, yellow.

The Simple Color palettes are listed on the next page.

4-plane KCMY (value = –4)

Index	Black pen	Color pen(s)
0	White	White
1	Black	White
2	White	Cyan
3	Black	Cyan
4	White	Magenta
5	Black	Magenta
6	White	Blue
7	Black	Blue
8	White	Yellow
9	Black	Yellow
10	White	Green
11	Black	Green
12	White	Red
13	Black	Red
14	White	Black
15	Black	Black

3-plane CMY (value = –3)

Index	Color
0	White
1	Cyan
2	Magenta
3	Blue
4	Yellow
5	Green
6	Red
7	Black

Single-plane K (value = 1)

Index	Color
0	White
1	Black

3-plane RGB (value = 3)

Index	Color
0	Black
1	Red
2	Green
3	Yellow
4	Blue
5	Magenta
6	Cyan
7	White

Source Raster Height

ESC*r#tlT

Purpose

This command specifies the height in pixel rows of the source raster image denoted by subsequent Start Raster Graphics (**ESC***r#A) commands. Height is perpendicular to the pixel rows and is measured in the direction specified by the Raster Line Path command (**ESC***r#L).

Parameter

Height in pixel rows. There is no default.

Range: 0 through 65 535 (out-of-range values are clamped). A missing parameter is interpreted as 0.

Note: The 65 535 limit is the HP RTL limit. Actual limits are device-dependent. Values exceeding the device limits are clamped.

Use

The Source Raster Width (**ESC***r#S) and Source Raster Height commands must precede a Start Raster Graphics (**ESC***r#A) command where scale mode is set to "on" (parameter value 2 or 3). Without the Source Raster Width and Source Raster Height commands, raster graphics will begin with the scale mode off, that is, as if a parameter value of 0 or 1 were sent.

A Reset command causes an explicitly set source raster height to become undefined.

Plane or row data that is not specified for the full source raster height is filled out with zeros. Zero-filled data is printed in the color specified for index 0 in the palette.

When a Transfer Raster Data (**ESC***b#V or **ESC***b#W) command is received that causes any pixel row to extend beyond the row boundary set by the Source Raster Height command, the row outside the boundary is clipped. This includes the case where the CAP is moved beyond the height boundary or above the starting position with a Y Offset (**ESC***b#Y) command and the printing of raster data is attempted.

If the user has specified a source raster height of 0 and a Start Raster Graphics (or Transfer Raster Data) command is received, then the entire raster graphic is clipped.

If the user has not set the source raster height, then raster height is not used; that is, there is no default value.

Upon receiving an explicit or implicit End Raster Graphics command, the CAP is set to the left graphics margin of the next pixel row after the raster height boundary. The location of the "next" pixel row depends on the direction specified by the Raster Line Path command.

See also *Setting the Width and Height in HP RTL* on page 342.

HP RTL
REFERENCE

Source Raster Width

ESC*r#slS

Purpose

This command specifies the width in pixels of the source raster image denoted by subsequent Start Raster Graphics (**ESC***r#A) commands. Width is in the direction of (parallel to) the raster rows.

Parameter

Width in pixels. The default is the logical page width for unscaled graphics (from the left graphics margin), undefined for scaled graphics.

Range: 0 through 65 535 (out-of-range values are clamped). A missing parameter is assumed to be 0.

Note: The 65 535 limit is the HP RTL limit. Actual limits are device-dependent. Values exceeding the device limits are clamped.

Use

The Source Raster Width and Source Raster Height (**ESC***r#T) commands must precede a Start Raster Graphics (**ESC***r#A) command where scale mode is set to "on" (parameter value 2 or 3). Without the Source Raster Width and Source Raster Height commands, raster graphics will begin with the scale mode off, that is, as if a parameter value of 0 or 1 were sent.

The default source raster width is also affected by changes in the left graphics margin; that is, if a Start Raster Graphics command is sent with a parameter value of 1 or 3 (which sets the left graphics margin to the CAP), the default source raster width is interpreted as extending from the left graphics margin to the right edge of the logical page. This "tracking" behavior terminates when the source raster width is set explicitly, and resumes after a Reset (**ESCE**) command.

Plane or row data that is not specified for the full source raster width is filled out with zeros; data exceeding the source raster width is clipped. (Zero-filled data is printed in the color specified for index 0 in the palette.)

If the user specified a source raster width of 0 and a Start Raster Graphics (or Transfer Raster Data) command is received, the entire raster graphic is clipped.

This command is ignored during raster mode.

See also *Setting the Width and Height in HP RTL* on page 342.

Source Transparency Mode

ESC*v#nlN

Purpose

This command sets the source image's transparency mode to transparent or opaque.

Parameter

The following values are allowed. The default is 0.

0   Transparent; the source's white pixels are not applied to the destination; the destination image shows through the source.

1   Opaque; the source's white pixels are applied to the destination; the corresponding parts of the destination image are blocked out by the source.

Range: 0, 1. Other values cause the command to be ignored.

Use

A value of 0 makes the source's white areas transparent, allowing the corresponding parts of the destination image to show through. With a transparency mode of 1, the white pixels in the source are applied directly to the destination.

This command is ignored during raster mode.

Note: Some devices do not support this command; consider using the HP-GL/2 TR (Transparency Mode) instruction instead.

Start Raster Graphics

ESC*r#alA

Purpose

This command places the device in raster mode with scale mode on or off, fixes the starting position of the graphics image, and sets the left graphics margin.

Parameter

The following values are allowed. The default value is 0.

0   Start raster graphics at logical page left bound.

1   Start raster graphics at the current active position (CAP).

2   Turn on scale mode and start graphics at logical page left boundary.

3   Turn on scale mode and start graphics at the CAP.

Range: 0 through 3 (out-of-range values default to 0).

Use

Both Source Raster Width (**ESC***r#S) and the Source Raster Height (**ESC***r#T) must be specified before starting raster graphics in scale mode. If neither is specified, or if only one is specified, a Start Raster Graphics command with a parameter value of 2 or 3 will function as if the parameter value were 0 or 1, respectively; that is, raster graphics will start with scale mode off.

A value of 0 or 2 starts the image at the current vertical position on the left boundary of the logical page; that is, the left graphics margin is set to 0. A value of 1 or 3 starts the image at the current position; that is, the left graphics margin is set to the current horizontal position.

For a Raster Line Path (**ESC***b#L) of 0 (the default), the starting corner becomes the upper-left corner of the image. For a Raster Line Path of 1, the starting corner becomes the lower-left corner of the picture.

Values of 2 or 3 turn scale mode on. Scaled images are rendered in the specified size independent of device resolution.

On devices that support several native resolutions, the image is first scaled up or down to the native resolution selected by the @PJL SET RESOLUTION command. Selecting a low native resolution uses less memory but has more granularity; it is more appropriate for draft quality. A high native resolution uses more memory but has better quality.

Note: When you scale an image down, loss of detail always results. The algorithm used for scaling down is device-dependent.

See also *Implicit Start Raster Graphics* on page 374.

Transfer Raster Data by Plane

ESC*b#V[data]

Purpose

This command transfers the number of bytes specified in the value field to the device, but does not move the CAP to the next raster row. The plane pointer is incremented, but not the row pointer. This command is used when the raster data is encoded by plane, as specified by the Simple Color (ESC*r#U) command or the Configure Image Data (ESC*v#W) command; it is used to send each plane in the row except the last; the Transfer Raster Data by Row/Block (ESC*b#W) command is used for the last row and to update the row pointer to the beginning of the next row.

Parameter and Termination Character

Number of bytes in the data field. If data is compressed, this refers to the length of the *compressed* data. There is no default.

         Range: 0 through 32 767. Out-of-range values are clamped.

If the number of bytes specified in the value field (#) is greater than 32 767, the first 32 767 bytes following the command are interpreted as data, and byte 32 768 is interpreted as the beginning of the next HP RTL command.

This command cannot be combined with others that follow. The uppercase "V" terminator must be used with this command.

Use

Use this command to send each plane except the last in a multi-plane raster row. It is not used for single-plane rows, or for the last plane in a multi-plane row, since row position is not affected by this command. To transfer raster data and increment the row pointer, the Transfer Raster Data by Row/Block (ESC*b#W) command must be sent. The least significant planes are sent first (see *Multi-Plane Data* on page 358).

The number of data bytes is independent of source raster width and can vary from plane to plane. If the image width can accommodate more data than is sent, the undefined data is assumed to be all zeros. For information on how to use this feature, see *Setting the Width and Height in HP RTL* on page 342.

Empty planes can be sent using Transfer Raster Data by Plane with a value of 0 (ESC*b0V). A row can be ended "early" with a Transfer Raster Data by Row/Block with a value of 0 (ESC*b0W). Absent data is assumed to be zeros: in row-by-row raster mode, when the combined planes yield an index of 0, those pixels are rendered with whatever color has been assigned to index number 0 in the color palette. (This command is not used in plane-by-plane raster mode.) This can be used as a method of data compression.

Extra planes are ignored. For example, if three planes have been assigned to each row with the Set Number of Bits per Index byte of the Configure Image Data (ESC*v#W) command, but four planes are sent for a given row, the fourth plane is ignored. If a Transfer Raster Data by Row/Block command is used for one of the extra color planes, the data is ignored, but the row is incremented and subsequent planes are again interpreted as valid data (for the next row).

The data in the data field is interpreted according to the current compression method. This command is used only for row-based compression methods. The Transfer Raster Data by Plane command and its associated data are parsed and ignored if sent when a block-based compression method is in effect. See the Compression Method (**ESC***b#M) command for a listing of row-based and block-based compression methods.

This command is only allowed in row-by-row raster mode. (Plane-by-plane raster mode requires only one plane of data at a time, so this command is not needed.) If this command is received when the device is in plane-by-plane raster mode, the command and its associated data are parsed and ignored.

Note: When an explicit or implicit End Raster Graphics (**ESC***rC) command is received before the row is completed with a Transfer Data by Row/Block command, it is device-dependent whether or not the incomplete row is rendered. See the note under the End Raster Graphics command.

Note: If a block of data is transferred using a block-based compression mode before the previous row is completely defined, the plane pointer is set to the first plane of the next row at the beginning of the block transfer. As with End Raster Graphics, it is device-dependent whether or not the incomplete row is rendered.

Transfer Raster Data by Row/Block

ESC*b#W[data]

Purpose

This command transfers the number of bytes specified in the value field to the device in a row-by-row or block format depending on the current compression method (**ESC***b#M). This command is used when the raster data is encoded by pixel, as specified by the Configure Image Data (**ESC***v#W) command, and for the last plane of a multi-plane row; the Transfer Raster Data by Plane (**ESC***b#V) command is used for the planes of multi-plane data before the last.

Parameter and Termination Character

Number of bytes in the data field. If data is compressed, this refers to the length of the *compressed* data. There is no default.

Range: 0 through 2 147 483 647 ($2^{31} - 1$) (out-of-range values are clamped).

This command cannot be combined with others that follow. The uppercase "W" terminator must be used with this command.

Use

For row-based formats, this command is used for single-plane rows (including those sent in plane-by-plane mode) or for the last plane in a multi-plane row. After execution, the row pointer is incremented, the plane pointer in a multi-plane row is reset to 1, and the CAP is set to the left graphics margin at the start of the next row.

For block-based formats, this command is used for block transfer of single- or multi-plane rows with implied or explicit row and plane divisions. Row and plane divisions depend on the number of planes and the current compression method. At the end of the block transfer, the row pointer is incremented, the plane pointer is set to the first plane of the next row, and the CAP is set to the left graphics margin.

Empty or incomplete rows may be sent. See Transfer Raster Data by Plane (**ESC***b#V).

Universal Exit Language/Start of PJL

ESC%–12345X

Purpose

This command causes the current context processor to shut down in an orderly fashion and exit into the Printer Job Language (PJL). See page 392 for more information about PJL.

Parameter and Termination Character

**–12345** Exit the current language context and start PJL.

Range: –12345. Only the exact nine-character sequence (**ESC**%–12345X) is guaranteed to cause exit from the current language context. Note that the value (–12345) is a *string of characters* and not an integer value.

This command cannot be combined with others that follow. The uppercase "X" terminator must be used with this command.

Use

This command performs the following actions:

- Performs all the actions associated with the Reset command (**ESC**E).

- Turns control over to PJL.

The command is always recognized in both the HP-GL/2 and HP RTL contexts, except in the following cases:

- In the HP-GL/2 context, within an HP-GL/2 label, when transparent data mode is on ("TD1").

- In the HP RTL context, when in an HP RTL binary data transfer.

Note: Devices that support only HP-GL/2 and HP RTL may ignore this command. On devices that support additional language contexts, the command may or may not be recognized in those contexts.

Y Offset

ESC*b#ylY

Purpose

This command moves the CAP vertically the number of pixel rows specified in the value field.

Parameter

Number of pixel rows of vertical movement. There is no default.

Range: −32 767 through 32 767 (out-of-range values are clamped; a missing value is interpreted as 0).

Use

Use a plus sign (+) before the value, or an unsigned value, to move the CAP in the direction specified by the Raster Line Path (**ESC***b#L) command. Use a minus sign (–) before the value to move the CAP in the direction opposite to the raster line path. The CAP is allowed to move outside the logical page. Unlike the Move CAP commands (**ESC***p#X, **ESC***p#Y, and **ESC**&a#H), there is no absolute move possible with this command.

This command is to be made obsolete outside of raster mode.

When Y Offset is used in raster mode, skipped rows are zero-filled up to the offset requested, or the current source raster height, whichever comes first. If a negative Y Offset value places the CAP above the position at which raster graphics was started (or below in the case of Raster Line Path = 1), no zero-filling is done for rows that lie outside the raster area.

The physical distance that this command moves the CAP varies according to the current resolution.

Executing this command causes the seed row to be zeroed, even if the command has a 0 or missing parameter value (#).

This command is ignored during raster scaling mode. Use the Move CAP Vertical (**ESC***p#Y) command instead.

Note: When this command is received before a row is completed, it is device-dependent whether or not the incomplete row is rendered. If it is rendered, the incomplete row is zero filled, the row pointer is incremented, and the plane pointer is reset to 1. If it is not rendered, the row pointer is not incremented as a result of the incomplete row.

Chapter 15: Summary of HP RTL Device-Dependencies

The following table lists the HP RTL characteristics that can vary among devices.

Dependency	Description
Resolution, Rendering, and Scaling	
Size and spacing of dots	See *Raster Graphics* on page 344.
Native device resolution	The actual number of dots per inch (dpi) a device can plot. "Native" resolutions are usually a multiple of physical device resolution. Native resolutions can be set by the @PJL SET RESOLUTION command. See *Controlling Image Resolution* on page 344, the Set Graphics Resolution (**ESC***t#R) command on page 438, the Move CAP (**ESC***p#X and **ESC***p#Y) commands on pages 424 and 425, and *Printer Job Language (PJL)* on page 392.
Resolution type	Options are continuous or incremental resolution. Only devices that support continuous resolution can accurately plot a specific resolution. See *Continuous and Incremental Resolution* on page 345 and the Set Graphics Resolution (**ESC***t#R) command on page 438.
Resolution Range and Default	Allowable range and default for the Set Graphics Resolution (**ESC***t#R) command. The resolution setting is independent of the physical device resolution. Images are scaled to the requested resolution. If explicit scaling is requested in the Start Raster Graphics (**ESC***r#A) command, the resolution setting is ignored. See *Controlling Image Resolution* on page 344, *Draft and Final Resolution* on page 345, and the Set Graphics Resolution command on page 438.
Scaled-Down Rendering	When scaling an image down, loss of detail always results. The algorithm used for scaling down is device-dependent. See *Controlling Image Resolution* on page 344 and *Scaling Raster Images* on page 345.
Source Raster Height (**ESC***r#T) and Source Raster Width (**ESC***r#S) Ranges	These ranges are determined by a device's physical limits. See *Setting the Width and Height in RTL* on page 342, and the command descriptions on pages 444 and 443.

Dependency	Description
Plot Management	
Large Plots	What happens if a plot is too large to fit into the memory of the device is device-dependent. See *When Overflow Occurs* on page 375.
Negative Motion Command Implementation	Some devices cannot simultaneously receive and plot raster images. On these devices, the Negative Motion (**ESC&a#N**) command has no effect. When the command promises no negative motion and the image nonetheless contains negative motion, the effect is device-dependent. See *Negative Motion* on page 349 and the description of the Negative Motion command on page 426.
Color Palette Management	
Color Support	Options are full color, grayscale monochrome (color maps to gray), and two-tone monochrome (no color support). Two-tone monochrome devices may not support certain HP RTL commands. See *Primary Colors* on page 351, *Specifying Colors* on page 352. The actual color printed is also device-dependent.
Maximum Palette Size	The larger the palette, the more colors can be explicitly defined. Palette size is set using the Number of Bits per Index byte of the Configure Image Data (**ESC*v#W**) command. The maximum value corresponds to the number of data planes the device supports. See *Defining the RTL Palette* on page 356 and the Configure Image Data command on page 407.
Number of Bits per Primary	This byte of the Configure Image Data (**ESC*v#W**) command determines the ranges for defining custom palette colors. See page 407.
Palette Transferability	Some devices allow you to transfer the color palette between RTL and HP-GL/2. See *Defining the RTL Palette* on page 356, *Transferring Pen Position and Palettes* on page 391, and the descriptions of the Enter HP-GL/2 Mode (**ESC%#B**) command on page 418 and the Enter RTL Mode (**ESC%#A**) command on page 420.
Pixel Encoding Mode	Some devices support a special pixel encoding mode called plane-by-plane raster. Pixel encoding mode is set in the Configure Image Data (**ESC*v#W**) command. Future devices may support other pixel encoding modes. See the description of the Configure Image Data command on page 407. Merging vector and raster data is also device-dependent; see page 392.
Non-primary Colors	Some devices plot non-primary colors using a dithering technique. See *Defining the RTL Palette* on page 356, *Halftoning* on page 360, and the interaction with patterns in the description of the Download Pattern (**ESC*c#W**) command on page 415.

Dependency	Description

Miscellaneous Dependencies

Rendering of Incomplete Rows

When the CAP is moved with a Y Offset (**ESC***b#Y) command, or when raster graphics mode ends, some devices plot rows that are incomplete; other devices discard data received so far for that row. See the descriptions of the Y Offset command on page 451, the End Raster Graphics (**ESC***rC) command on page 417, the Transfer Raster Data by Plane (**ESC***b#V) command on page 447, and the Transfer Raster Data by Row/Block (**ESC***b#W) command on page 449.

Language Contexts

The language context at power-on is device-dependent.

Some devices require the Enter RTL Mode (**ESC**%#A) command to be issued in the HP-GL/2 context. See *Changing Language Contexts and Modes* on page 391.

Some devices support language contexts other than HP-GL/2 and HP RTL using the Universal Exit Language / Start of PJL (**ESC**%–12345X) command. This command may or may not be recognized from within the additional contexts. See *Changing Language Contexts and Modes* on page 391, Printer Job Language (PJL) on page 392, and the command description on page 450.

Control Panel

Settings from the control (front) panel of the device may affect plots. See *Interactions with Physical Device Settings* on page 389.

PART 4: Appendixes

This Part contains the following sections:

Appendix A: Writing Efficient Programs–Some Tips

Before you can write graphics programs for your plotter or printer, you must be familiar with your computer and a programming language the computer understands. You can use any computer system and programming language that outputs ASCII literal strings and uses input and output statements to transfer information to and from a peripheral device. This book assumes that you already have experience in the programming language you select.

This appendix discusses the following fundamental programming concepts:

- Using a programming language.

- How to structure a complete graphics program.

- Using HP-GL/2 instructions and HP RTL commands.

- Making efficient use of your system.

- Page layout and positioning.

- Preparing your data.

- Using color.

- User operations.

If you are an inexperienced HP-GL/2 or HP RTL programmer, use the following guidelines to ensure success:

- Know your equipment; this includes the computer and the device. Know how to write, edit, save, and run a program. Determine how your computer sends (outputs) information to and reads (inputs) information from peripheral devices.

- Know your programming language. Get a good programming manual for the language you are using, that is specific to your computer system. Always use the syntax your language requires. Common mistakes are substituting the letter O for the number *zero*, or a lowercase letter L for the number *one*. Also, substituting a semicolon for a comma or omitting a quotation mark can make the difference between failure and success.

- Enter HP-GL/2 instructions as they appear in the text. You may omit spaces and, for most instructions, the terminating semicolon.

- Enter HP RTL commands exactly as they appear in the text. Normally every letter, symbol, and number is significant. In some cases extra spaces have been inserted in the examples to improve their clarity; these can safely be omitted from your programs. In all cases, the "#" character in the command definition must be replaced by a numeric value as defined for the command.

Using a Programming Language

How you send an instruction or command to your device depends on the programming language you are using. Some languages include some graphics statements, but these are primarily for the computer's monitor. Some common languages used for printing and plotting are BASIC, FORTRAN, Pascal, and C.

BASIC (Beginner's All-purpose Symbolic Instruction Code) is one of the most common languages used for printing and plotting. It uses statements resembling English to perform many complex operations. Note that any graphics statements included in your version of BASIC are probably designed for your computer monitor, not your printer or plotter.

FORTRAN (FORmula TRANslator) is a problem-oriented language. Programmers can think in terms of the problem and write programs as algebraic expressions and arithmetic statements.

Pascal is a block-structured language requiring structured programming, but still allowing many operator and control statements.

C is a general-purpose programming language at a fairly low level, with economy of expression and modern control flow and data structures as its primary attributes.

Follow these steps to send an instruction in your language:

1. Use whatever opening statements are required to define the computer's output port and establish the device as the recipient of an output string. These are called configuration statements and usually must be the first statements in your program.

2. Send the string to the device using an output statement.

Note: Before sending any instructions or commands to your device, you must be certain that your computer and device are communicating properly. Refer to your peripheral's documentation for interconnection instructions.

Using HP-GL/2 With Programming Languages

Upon entry into HP-GL/2 mode, a good programming practice is to select a pen and issue a pen-up move to the initial starting position. This ensures that a pen is selected and is in the proper position to begin drawing.

The HP-GL/2 examples included in this book are given in a "generic" format (they show the instructions required to perform a specific function but do not use a specific programming language). In most cases, the instructions are accompanied by a brief description of the instruction being used.

To specify a point when programming an application, you must always give a complete X,Y coordinate pair; the X coordinate is first and the Y coordinate second. This book shows coordinate pairs in parentheses (X,Y) for clarity. **Do not use parentheses in your instruction sequence**.

To see how HP-GL/2 instructions are used in BASIC and the C programming language, see the following examples.

Example: BASIC Language

This example uses the BASIC language to print three lines forming a simple triangle (shown in Figure 177); note that "CHR$(27)" is the escape character, denoted in this book by the symbol **ESC**.

```
10 LPRINT CHR$(27);"E";              :REM Reset the device
20 LPRINT CHR$(27);"%0B";            :REM Enter HP-GL/2 Mode
30 LPRINT "IN";                      :REM Initialize HP-GL/2 Mode
40 LPRINT "SP1PA10,10";              :REM Select Pen and move to (10,10)
50 LPRINT "PD2500,10,10,1500,10,10;";:REM Pen down and draw the triangle
60 LPRINT CHR$(27);"%0A";            :REM Enter PCL or HP RTL Mode
70 LPRINT CHR$(27);"E";              :REM Reset to end job/eject page
```

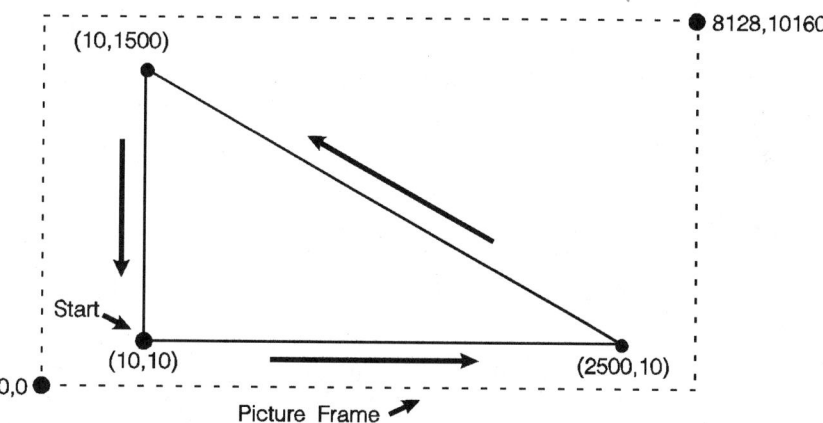

Figure 177. Using a Programming Language (BASIC or C) to Draw a Triangle

Example: C Programming Language

This example uses the C programming language to print the same three lines shown in Figure 177; "\033" is the octal character for ASCII code point 27, the escape character, denoted in this book by the symbol **ESC**.

```
#include <stdio.h>
main()
{
FILE *prn;
prn = fopen("PRN","wb");                    /* Open the device */
fprintf(prn,"\033E");                       /* ESCE to reset device */
fprintf(prn,"\033%0B");                     /* Enter HP-GL/2 */
fprintf(prn,"IN");                          /* Initialize HP-GL/2 Mode */
fprintf(prn,"SP1PA10,10");                  /* Select pen 1 and move to (10,10) */
fprintf(prn,"PD2500,10,10,1500,10,10;");    /* Pen down and draw the triangle */
fprintf(prn,"\033%0A");                     /* Enter PCL/HP RTL at previous CAP */
fprintf(prn,"\033E");                       /* Reset to end job/eject page */
}
```

Using HP RTL with Programming Languages

Most of the HP RTL examples in this book show simply the strings of characters that have to be sent to the device to achieve a particular result. In each case you will need to place these strings in suitable output statements of the programming language you are using. All HP RTL commands start with the ASCII escape character, decimal 27. If you are programming in BASIC, this will normally be encoded as CHR$(27). Thus to send a sequence of commands represented in this book as:

> **ESC***v1N
> **ESC**&a1N

you might code this in BASIC as

```
PRINT #1, CHR$(27)+"*v1N"
PRINT #1, CHR$(27)+"&a1N"
```

A Complete Graphics Program

This section describes the structure of a program that uses HP-GL/2 and HP RTL to plot data.

Initialization and Termination—Device Reset

Hewlett-Packard strongly recommends the use of both the **ESC**E command and the **ESC**%−12345X command (Universal Exit Language/Start of PJL—also referred to as the "UEL Command") at the beginning and end of each job. (The order of these commands is critical; refer to the following example.) This allows the next job to start with the default settings as a known base. Starting with the default environment at the beginning of each print job eliminates the need to set every feature each time a job is run.

ESC%−12345X	UEL command (exit language)
PJL preamble	Job control commands such as @PJL JOB NAME="..."
ESCE	Reset command
Page 1 header	Page control commands
Page 1 body	
...	
Page n header and body	Page control commands (if a number of consecutive pages within a job have the same format, the associated page control commands only need to be sent once for that group of pages)
ESCE	Reset command
ESC%−12345X @ PJL EOJ NAME="..."	UEL command (exit language) and end job

Note that the UEL command has the same effect as the Reset command, and also enters PJL mode for printers and plotters that support PJL. The Reset command should be included to ensure backward compatibility with devices that do not support PJL.

Do not perform a Reset within a job, except between pages to reestablish all default values for HP-GL/2 and HP RTL.

Starting a Program

Whatever programming language you use, you should start it with the following sequence of commands and instructions:

ESC%–12345X (Enter PJL) This is a universal exit language/start of PJL. Immediately afterwards, without an intervening **CR LF**, send the following commands to assign a job name, and to switch the device out of PJL and into HP-GL/2 language:

`@PJL JOB NAME="..."`**CR LF** Insert any further PJL commands, such as
　　　　　　`@PJL SET RESOLUTION=600`**CR LF**
to further control the image, before entering HP-GL/2.

`@PJL ENTER LANGUAGE=HPGL2`**CR LF**

ESCE (Reset) Reset HP-GL/2 and other defaults.

ESC%#B (Enter HP-GL/2 Mode). The parameter (#) may be –1, 0, or 1, and depends on whether or not you are mixing HP-GL/2 vector data with HP RTL raster images or PCL5 font characters. This command is described on page 418.

The Body of a Program

`BP   5,1;` (Begin Plot) Tells the device that a new picture is coming. BP ensures that output is written to a clean page. It also ensures that devices with HP-GL/2 and HP-GL emulation are switched to the HP-GL/2 mode. A recommended pair of parameters is 5, 1 to set auto-rotation off.

`IN   ;` (Initialize) Initializes the device to specific defaults.

`PS   `*length, width*`;` (Plot Size) Sets the hard-clip limits using the specified length and width, including long-axis plots. It is important for devices with nesting capability to be able to determine the plot size with the PS instruction. It is also important for roll-feed plotters as the media will then advance only the size of the page specified. Parameters are in device units (1016 per inch, 40 per millimeter).

`TR   0;` Turn off Transparency mode to improve throughput (if applicable).

`<vector data>` When merging HP-GL/2 data with HP RTL or PCL data, send all vector (HP-GL/2) data that is to be rendered before the raster image. However, if you are using devices that operate most efficiently when pictures are organized into swaths, you may want to switch back and forth between vector mode and raster mode, so as to organize the data into appropriate bands; send first the data that is to appear at the top of the page, and so on. In this case there is a trade-off between the number of switchings and the need to order the data into bands.

Switching Modes

ESC%#A (Enter RTL Mode) Once the HP-GL/2 setup is complete, transfer to HP RTL. Use the **ESC%#B** (Enter HP-GL/2 Mode) command to switch back to HP-GL/2.

Summary of Normal Execution Sequence for HP RTL

The normal execution sequence for raster commands, without color, is as follows:

Set Graphics Resolution	**ESC***t#R	
Source Raster Height	**ESC***r#T	
Source Raster Width	**ESC***r#S	
Destination Raster Height	**ESC***t#V	(if you are using scaling)
Destination Raster Width	**ESC***t#H	(if you are using scaling)
Configure Image Data	**ESC***v#W[data]	
Start Raster Graphics	**ESC***r#A	
Compression Method	**ESC***b#M	
Transfer Raster Data	**ESC***b#W[raster data] or **ESC***b#V[raster data]	
...		
Y Offset	**ESC***b#Y	
Compression Method	**ESC***b#M	
Transfer Raster Data	**ESC***b#W[raster data] or **ESC***b#V[raster data]	
...		
Compression Method	**ESC***b#M	
Transfer Raster Data	**ESC***b#W[raster data]	
...		
End Raster Graphics	**ESC***rC	

Note that the resolution, width, and height are all set outside the *start...data...end* sequence. The picture should be sent, using the most efficient compression method for each row, during the *start...data...end* sequence.

Ending a Program

Your program should finish (in HP-GL/2) with:

PG ;	End and print the current page. Don't forget the semicolon.
ESCE	(Reset) Reset defaults.
ESC%−12345X@PJL EOJ NAME=" . . . "**CR LF**	
	Exit the current language context and start PJL.

Summary of recommended initialization and termination sequence

---

Enter PJL, start a new job, and switch to HP-GL/2	**ESC**%−12345X@PJL JOB NAME="..."**CR LF** @PJL ENTER LANGUAGE=HPGL2**CR LF**
Initialize (merged vector and raster)	**ESCEESC**%0BBPINPS10160,8116;
Print or plot data	. . .
Terminate, advance page	PUSP0PG;
On closing a job: Reset, universal exit language/start PJL, and end job	**ESCEESC**%−12345X@PJL EOJ NAME="..." **CR LF**

Using HP-GL/2 Instructions and HP RTL Commands

Not all devices interpret all commands and instructions in the same way. See *The Product Comparison Guide for HP Languages on HP Plotters and Large-Format Printers* for device-dependencies.

NOP'd Instructions and Commands

Be aware of any instructions and commands that are ignored by your target devices.

Combined Commands

In HP RTL, combined commands are shorter than commands spelled out separately; the shorter commands require less data transmission time. See *Combining Commands* on page 340.

Output Instructions

Do not use HP-GL/2 output instructions to interrogate the device for information. Network and Centronics interface support becomes difficult, if not impossible, when information is requested from the device.

Making Efficient Use of Your System

Here are some suggestions that may help you to create efficient graphics programs, including device drivers.

Getting to Know HP-GL/2

Firstly, you should read through *Chapters 2*, *3*, and *4* of this book. They explain the concepts used by HP-GL/2. Try to get familiar with some of the simpler instructions in the Kernel. Look up their descriptions in the reference section of the book (*Chapter 5*). These descriptions contain many examples of partial programs that use the instructions being defined.

If you see unfamiliar instructions, find the instruction description in the reference part of the book and read about the instruction; instructions are listed alphabetically by their two-character mnemonics. Think of an application that you would like to program and then look for an example that uses some of the elements you desire. After trying some examples and seeing how the instructions interact, you should be well on your way to learning the HP-GL/2 language.

HP-GL/2 Vector Graphics

There are different approaches (instructions) and techniques that can be used to create an HP-GL/2 picture. To assist in determining the most efficient approach to creating an image, several points are identified below:

- When you use line caps and joins:
    - Most efficient—round join with butt cap
    - Least efficient—round join with triangular cap.

- When you use text, if you want the character to be printed at the same location as it would in PCL, use label origin position 21.

- Default pen widths (5 dots wide or less) produce the highest speed.

- Hewlett-Packard recommends using polygon mode when the number of points in a polygon is 1000 or less.

- The Polyline Encoded instruction can reduce data by 60% to 70%.

- When drawing shapes, use a instruction that was designed to draw that shape. For example, to draw a rectangle, use the ER instruction to produce it, instead of stroking the shape line by line.

- When drawing arcs or circles, use the Bezier instructions to eliminate the need to compute the chord angle, thus resulting in better quality and efficiency.

- To Scale text, use the IIP-GL/2 font selection commands, such as SD or AD, that usc Intellifont or TrueType to scale the text. Scaling text in HP-GL/2, using the SR or SI instructions, is much less efficient.

- Font transformations in HP-GL/2, such as mirroring, scaling, slanting, rotating, and outlining are very processing intensive. An ERROR 21 (print overrun) may occur. The error can be controlled by using the HP LaserJet Page Protection feature, if available.

Automatic Pen Down

The following instructions include an automatic pen down as part of their function. After completing their function, they restore the pen to its previous state (up or down). For more information, see page 23.

CI, EA, EP, ER, EW, FP, LB, RA, RR, SM, WG.

"Lost" Mode

The pen position may sometimes become unknown to the device. This can happen as a result of scaling. It is known as "lost" mode. See page 23 for more information.

Current Location

The following instructions update the current location. See page 66 for more information.

AA, AR, AT, BR, BZ, DF, DI, DR, DV, IN, LO, PA, PD, PE, PR, PU, RO, and RT.

Appearance of Characters

To obtain the most typographically correct characters, use "SI;" to disable graphic transformations, so that characters will be as close as possible to what the font designer intended. Size will be based solely on parameters last specified by AD or SD. If special graphic effects are desired, such as distorting or mirroring of characters, enable graphic transformations with SI and SR.

Performance

The printing speed will vary with the performance of the sending computer and the complexity of the picture being sent. In general the objective is to get the total processing and transmission times below the print time. Care should be taken when selecting:

- The type and performance of the driving computer.

- Choice of I/O system (Centronics, IEEE-1284-compatible, RS-232, Networking, and so on).

- HP RTL raster mode: 24-bit/pixel RGB, 1-bit/pixel Mono, 3-bit/pixel RGB or CMY or 4-bit/pixel KCMY.

- In HP RTL, the scaling factor.

- In HP RTL, the data compression technique used.

- Transparency modes. In HP RTL, set both the source and pattern transparency modes to opaque where possible.

Host Computer Resources

Consider scaling images at the host computer instead of in the device. Which method is best depends on available host resources, page size, image complexity, and the scale factor. Comparative testing should look at host processing time, data transmission time, and device processing time.

Memory Size

In normal operation graphical objects sent to the device are stored in memory until the complete image has been sent. The amount of memory needed for an image will depend on the number and type of the objects and how well the device can compress them internally. Pictures containing a lot of images or detailed drawings will use more memory. Printing will automatically begin when the memory is full.

When printing images it is often useful to disable this feature by sending the HP RTL command to prevent Negative Motion (**ESC&a1N**). This saves memory, and printing will start as soon as the first rows of data have been received. Only images that do not move the current active position (CAP) up the page can use this mode.

Configure Image Data Command

The Configure Image Data command has implications on the kind of data generated in the device, and although it is device-dependent, there are some general guidelines on memory requirements. The fastest method is direct selection using three planes; monochrome is next efficient, followed by direct selection by pixel with default black and white reference values; Simple Color mode is also efficient; all other methods are generally less efficient.

PCL Commands

Since PCL printers are command-driven devices and each command takes a finite amount of time to process, pages composed of a large number of commands may not print at maximum speed. Most commands can be used frequently on a page without adversely affecting the printer's performance; however, certain commands take more time to process and therefore, if used frequently on a page, may decrease printer performance. An excessive number of font selections per page (selection using font characteristic commands or selection by ID number) may decrease printer performance.

Print Data

There is a limit on the amount of data, as well as the number of commands, that the printer can process per page at maximum speed.

Print Overrun

As data is received by the printer, it is processed and stored in an intermediate format. The intermediate data is later processed and printed. During the physical printing of a page, the page moves through the printer at a constant speed. Thus, some pages cannot be printed because the page's intermediate data cannot be processed fast enough to keep up with the physical speed of the page as it moves through the printer. When this condition occurs, an error number "21" ("ERROR 21" – print overrun) is displayed on the printer's control panel. A page causing this error can be printed by setting the printer's page protection feature to ON (see next section).

Page Protection

If enabled, page protection reserves an amount of memory for the page image process, allowing the printer to create the entire page image (in memory) before physically moving the paper through the printer.

Note: The page protection feature is available only with additional optional memory on many HP LaserJet printers. (One exception is the LaserJet 4 printer, which supports page protection for letter-size paper *in 300 dpi mode* with the standard 2 Mbytes memory.) Refer to the appropriate *User's Manual* for specific memory requirements.

The Page Protection feature can be used to prevent possible "ERROR 21" conditions. "ERROR 21" is reported when data is too complex for the device to process concurrent with actual physical printing. A frequent cause of "ERROR 21" when printing graphics is that the program sends commands to print a single point many times during the page run.

Page protection can be set for letter, A4, or legal sized pages. Set page protection for the page size most often used.

Input/Output

The *throughput* of your device is the time it takes to complete a page. To take full advantage of your peripheral's speed, use a parallel interface, such as Centronics or HP-IB. For the best throughput with an RS-232-C interface, use the highest baud rate the device supports.

Parallel and network communications interfaces provide the fastest data transmission times. This is particularly important when transmitting raster data. However, if you use the RS-232-C serial interface, turn parity checking off at the device. If parity checking is on, the eighth bit of each byte is used as a check bit, which is inconsistent with raster data.

The parallel (Centronics) interface has higher throughput than the RS-232-C serial I/O. Raster graphics processing will usually benefit from increased I/O throughput.

Page Layout and Positioning

How you present information on the page may have a bearing on the programming techniques used.

Page Orientation and Size

HP RTL orientation is portrait; HP-GL/2 has the X-axis along the larger axis, and the Y-axis along the shorter axis. See *The Coordinate System* on page 7.

If the user specifies page size in inches, the driver multiplies the size by 1016; if specified in millimeters, by 40. Then use the PS instruction to specify the page size.

Area of the Output

Some devices have a built-in default for the size of their output. This can be set smaller by changing options on the control panel of the device. To make pictures longer than these sizes it is necessary to set the plot size using the HP-GL/2 PS (Plot Size) instruction.

The PS (Plot Size) instruction currently specified for HP-GL/2 mode is automatically imported into HP RTL mode; the logical page size is set to the hard-clip limits. The IW (Input Window) specified for HP-GL/2 mode is also imported into HP RTL mode. Vector and raster images are clipped to the window area.

Zero Filling

By using source raster width and height, you can avoid sending unnecessary "blank" data for borders. You can also use the Y Offset command to skip over rows that should be left zero, thus creating a background. See *Using Index 0* on page 359.

Moving the Current Active Position

There are four commands that set the CAP position in HP RTL (the current active position):

- Move CAP Horizontal (native HP RTL units)   **ESC*p#X**

- Move CAP Vertical (native HP RTL units)   **ESC*p#Y**

- Move CAP Horizontal (decipoints)   **ESC&a#H**

- Y Offset (pixels)   **ESC*b#Y**

The Y Offset command (when in non-raster mode) and Move CAP Horizontal (Decipoints) command are to be made obsolete, so you should not use them in new application programs.

Preparing Your Data

How you send data to the device has a significant effect on the overall performance of your plotting or printing system.

Raster Graphics

To minimize I/O transmission time and conserve memory, avoid sending to the device unnecessary raster data that represents white space. This is accomplished using the raster compression modes and raster reduction techniques available.

Set the resolution before the Start Raster Graphics command. Once this command is received, the resolution cannot be changed until after an End Raster Graphics command is issued.

Some applications and I/O drivers insert Carriage Returns and Line Feeds into the data stream sent to the printer. This modification of data must be suppressed for correct operation with HP RTL.

The most efficient way to draw lines (horizontal, vertical, and diagonal) and polygons is using HP-GL/2 vector graphics.

Data Compression

Mix compression methods to get the most efficient transmission. See *Compressing Data* on page 378. If you are using TIFF Packbits encoding, see the note in that section on when to encode data and when to send literal data.

There are seven compression methods available that will considerably improve throughput, and two methods of sending uncompressed raster data. The amount of compression that can be achieved varies considerably with the type of data being sent. Large areas of color compress well whereas images with a lot of detail do not. We recommend your driver should try each compression mode on each row of data and send the one that turns out to be smallest. (Note: Compression modes 6, 7 and 8 are for monochrome only.)

Sending Raster Data

Raster data is printed a row at a time. Avoid using the negative Y Offset command (**ESC***b#Y) as this requires a significant amount of additional memory for the device to handle the move. If you do not use negative motion and you are not sending any vector data, you can indicate this using **ESC**&a1N and printing begins immediately (on-the-fly) with the first row of raster data the device receives.

Merged Vector and Raster Data

When you use both HP RTL and HP-GL/2 in an application program, you should try to minimize the number of switches of context between these two environments. Note that the palette is transferred when you switch environments.

Vectors could be given first priority in occupying memory space with whatever is left over for raster data. Vector and raster data are treated on a first-in-first-out basis. The bottom portion of raster data sent could be lost if the combined vectors and raster exceed the memory space. If multiple raster images are sent to the same page and the memory space is exceeded, printing begins and all subsequent vector and raster images are ignored. The image that hit the limit will be printed in its entirety.

You can merge vector and raster data as long as your vector and raster data take up less than the available memory. Although the vector data can be sent at any time, we strongly recommend you send all the vector data first in case you run out of memory and so that raster printing can begin on-the-fly. In situations where the device runs out of memory during HP RTL, the image data will be printed as long as the CAP position does not move backwards with respect to the motion of the paper. An alternative strategy is to arrange data into bands, for devices that use superflow mode (see *"Superflow" Mode* on page 377).

The interaction between the vector and raster data is determined in HP-GL/2 by the TR (Transparency Mode) instruction and in HP RTL by the Source Transparency (**ESC***v#N) command, and in both environments by the latest MC (Merge Control) instruction or Logical Operation command issued.

Merging HP-GL/2 and HP RTL data is *not supported* for KCMY data using the Simple Color (**ESC***r–4U) command.

Scaling Raster Images

HP RTL images can be enlarged or reduced by the device. To scale the image:

- Set the Source Raster Width (**ESC***r#S) and Source Raster Height (**ESC***r#T) to the source image size.

- Set the Destination Raster Width (**ESC***t#H) and Destination Raster Height (**ESC***t#V) to the new size.

- Send the Start Raster Graphics (**ESC***r#A) command with parameter 2 or 3 (to enable scaling.) The scale factor is implied by the relationship between source and destination sizes. Scaling is achieved by pixel replication.

Note that the HP-GL/2 scaling defined by the SC (Scale) command has no effect on HP RTL images.

Transparency

In HP RTL, it is usually more efficient to explicitly set the transparency modes off initially, and then to switch them on and off as required.

Using Color

Consider the following aspects of the use of color in your output.

KCMY Operation

When sending 4-bit/pixel KCMY output, it is possible to place up to 4 dots of ink per pixel on the paper (it is normally limited to 2 dots). With some media types this may result in excessive wetting of the media and care should be taken when writing drivers to avoid these conditions.

Color Palette Operations

HP-GL/2 and HP RTL can share one common (unified) palette. Palette entries can be modified in either HP-GL/2 (NP, CR, PC) or HP RTL (**ESC***v#A, **ESC***v#B, **ESC***v#C, **ESC***v#l) commands. IN and BP always establish a default HP-GL/2 palette whose size is device-dependent.

The palette is copied from one context to another via the context-switch commands (**ESC**%#A and **ESC**%#B). When a palette is imported, both its size and the colors of its entries are imported.

User Operations

Users can affect the way the device operates, by selecting options on the front control panel. However, a driver can override control-panel settings by using appropriate PJL commands (see page 392).

Troubleshooting

Sometimes you may find that your printer or plotter produces results that you did not expect. First check in the device's *User's Guide* to see that the feature you want is supported. Other software that you are using may also have documentation that you should check.

Appendix B: Logical Operations

These logical operations are used with the HP-GL/2 MC (Merge Control) instruction (see page 220) and the HP RTL Logical Operation (**ESC***l#O) command (see page 422).

Input Value	Boolean Function	Input Value	Boolean Function	Input Value	Boolean Function
0	0	38	SDTSaox	76	SDTana
1	DTSoon	39	SDTSxnox	77	SSTxDSxoxn
2	DTSona	40	DTSxa	78	TDSTxox
3	TSon	41	TSDTSaoxxn	79	TDSnoan
4	SDTona	42	DTSana	80	TDna
5	DTon	43	SSTxTDxaxn	81	DSTnaon
6	TDSxnon	44	STDSoax	82	DTSDaox
7	TDSaon	45	TSDnox	83	STDSxaxn
8	SDTnaa	46	TSDTxox	84	DTSonon
9	TDSxon	47	TSDnoan	85	Dn
10	DTna	48	TSna	86	DTSox
11	TSDnaon	49	SDTnaon	87	DTSoan
12	STna	50	SDTSoox	88	TDSToax
13	TDSnaon	51	Sn	89	DTSnox
14	TDSonon	52	STDSaox	90	DTx
15	Tn	53	STDSxnox	91	DTSDonox
16	TDSona	54	SDTox	92	DTSDxox
17	DSon	55	SDToan	93	DTSnoan
18	SDTxnon	56	TSDToax	94	DTSDnaox
19	SDTaon	57	STDnox	95	DTan
20	DTSxnon	58	STDSxox	96	TDSxa
21	DTSaon	59	STDnoan	97	DSTDSaoxxn
22	TSDTSanaxx	60	TSx	98	DSTDoax
23	SSTxDSxaxn	61	STDSonox	99	SDTnox
24	STxTDxa	62	STDSnaox	100	SDTSoax
25	SDTSanaxn	63	TSan	101	DSTnox
26	TDSTaox	64	TSDnaa	102	DSx
27	SDTSxaxn	65	DTSxon	103	SDTSonox
28	TSDTaox	66	SDxTDxa	104	DSTDS-onoxxn
29	DSTDxaxn	67	STDSanaxn	105	TDSxxn
30	TDSox	68	SDna	106	DTSax
31	TDSoan	69	DTSnaon	107	TSDTSoaxxn
32	DTSnaa	70	DSTDaox	108	SDTax
33	SDTxon	71	TSDTxaxn	109	TDSTDoaxxn
34	DSna	72	SDTxa	110	SDTSnoax
35	STDnaon	73	TDSTDaoxxn	111	TDSxnan
36	STxDSxa	74	DTSDoax	112	TDSana
37	TDSTanaxn	75	TDSnox		

Input Value	Boolean Function	Input Value	Boolean Function	Input Value	Boolean Function
113	SSDxTDxaxn	161	TDSTnaoxn	209	TSDTxoxn
114	SDTSxox	162	DTSnoa	210	TDSnax
115	SDTnoan	163	DTSDxoxn	211	STDSoaxn
116	DSTDxox	164	TDSTonoxn	212	SSTxTDxax
117	DSTnoan	165	TDxn	213	DTSanan
118	SDTSnaox	166	DSTnax	214	TSDTSaoxx
119	DSan	167	TDSToaxn	215	DTSxan
120	TDSax	168	DTSoa	216	TDSTxax
121	DSTDSoaxxn	169	DTSoxn	217	SDTSaoxn
122	DTSDnoax	170	D	218	DTSDanax
123	SDTxnan	171	DTSono	219	STxDSxan
124	STDSnoax	172	STDSxax	220	STDnao
125	DTSxnan	173	DTSDaoxn	221	SDno
126	STxDSxo	174	DSTnao	222	SDTxo
127	DTSaan	175	DTno	223	SDTano
128	DTSaa	176	TDSnoa	224	TDSoa
129	STxDSxon	177	TDSTxoxn	225	TDSoxn
130	DTSxna	178	SSTxDSxox	226	DSTDxax
131	STDSnoaxn	179	SDTanan	227	TSDTaoxn
132	SDTxna	180	TSDnax	228	SDTSxax
133	TDSTnoaxn	181	DTSDoaxn	229	TDSTaoxn
134	DSTDSoaxx	182	DTSDTaoxx	230	SDTSanax
135	TDSaxn	183	SDTxan	231	STxTDxan
136	DSa	184	TSDTxax	232	SSTxDSxax
137	SDTSnaoxn	185	DSTDaoxn	233	DSTDS-anaxxn
138	DSTnoa	186	DTSnao	234	DTSao
139	DSTDxoxn	187	DSno	235	DTSxno
140	SDTnoa	188	STDSanax	236	SDTao
141	SDTSxoxn	189	SDxTDxan	237	SDTxno
142	SSDxTDxax	190	DTSxo	238	DSo
143	TDSanan	191	DTSano	239	SDTnoo
144	TDSxna	192	TSa	240	T
145	SDTSnoaxn	193	STDSnaoxn	241	TDSono
146	DTSDToaxx	194	STDSonoxn	242	TDSnao
147	STDaxn	195	TSxn	243	TSno
148	TSDTSoaxx	196	STDnoa	244	TSDnao
149	DTSaxn	197	STDSxoxn	245	TDno
150	DTSxx	198	SDTnax	246	TDSxo
151	TSDTSonoxx	199	TSDToaxn	247	TDSano
152	SDTSonoxn	200	SDToa	248	TDSao
153	DSxn	201	STDoxn	249	TDSxno
154	DTSnax	202	DTSDxax	250	DTo
155	SDTSoaxn	203	STDSaoxn	251	DTSnoo
156	STDnax	204	S	252	TSo
157	DSTDoaxn	205	SDTono	253	TSDnoo
158	DSTDSaoxx	206	SDTnao	254	DTSoo
159	TDSxan	207	STno	255	1
160	DTa	208	TSDnoa		

Appendix C: Font Definitions

The font definitions in this Appendix apply to the *kind* and *value* parameters of the AD (Alternate Font Definition) and SD (Standard Font Definition) instructions of HP-GL/2. See pages 106 and 296 respectively.

Kind 1: Symbol Set

The symbol set characteristic defines the set of characters to be used in the standard (SD) or alternate (AD) font. These values are listed in order of the PCL identification; they are also listed by symbol-set name on page 477.

Note: Stick font is available only in ASCII, Roman-8, and Roman Extension symbol sets.

Value	Description and Symbol Set ID
0 (and 277)	Roman-8 (default set) [8U]
1	Math-7* [0A]
2	Line Draw-7* [0B]
3	HP Large Characters (264x Terminals)* [0C]
4	Danish/Norwegian version 1 (ISO 60) [0D]
5	Roman Extensions* [0E]
6	French (ISO 25)* [0F]
8	Hebrew-7 [0H]
9	Italian (ISO 15) [0I]
11	JIS ASCII* (ISO 14) [0K]
12	Line Draw-7 [0L]
13	Math-7 [0M]
14	ECMA-94 Latin 1 (8-bit version; ISO 8859/1) [0N]
15	OCR-A [0O]
16	APL (typewriter-paired) [0P]
18	Cyrillic ASCII (ECMA-113/86; ISO 8859/5) [0R]
19	Swedish for names (ISO 11) [0S]
20	Thai-8 [0T]
21	ANSI US ASCII (ISO 6) [0U]

Value	Description and Symbol Set ID
22	Arabic (McKay's version)* [0V]
25	3 of 9 Barcode [0Y]
26	Not used [0Z]
36	Norwegian Version 2 [1D]
37	United Kingdom (ISO 4) [1E]
38	French (ISO 69) [1F]
39	German (ISO 21) [1G]
43	Katakana* (ISO 13) [1K]
44	HP Block Characters [1L]
45	Tech-7 (DEC) [1M]
47	OCR-B [1O]
48	APL (bit-paired) [1P]
50	Cyrillic [1R]
53	Legal [1U]
57	Industrial 2 of 5 Barcode [1Y]
76	Tax Line Draw [2L]
78	ECMA-94 Latin 2 (ISO 8859/2) [2N]
79	OCR-M [2O]
83	Spanish (ISO 17)* [2S]
85	International Reference Version (ISO 2)* [2U]
89	Matrix 2 of 5 Barcode [2Y]

Kind 1: Symbol Set (continued)

Value	Description and Symbol Set ID	Value	Description and Symbol Set ID
114	PC Cyrillic [3R]	299	Korean-8 [9K]
115	Swedish (ISO 10)* [3S]	300	Ventura ITC Zapf Dingbats [9L]
145	PC Line [4O]	309	Windows [9U]
147	Portuguese (ISO 16)* [4S]	330	PS Text [10J]
153	Interleaved 2 of 5 Barcode [4Y]	332	PS ITC Zapf Dingbats [10L]
173	PS Math [5M]	334	ECMA-113/88 Latin/ Cyrillic (ISO 8859/5.2) [10N]
174	ECMA-128 Latin 5 (ISO 8859/9) [5N]	341	PC-8 (Code Page 437) [10U]
181	HPL Language Set [5U]	364	ITC Zapf Dingbats Series 100 [11L]
185	CODABAR Barcode [5Y]	373	PC-8 Danish/Norwegian [11U]
202	Microsoft Publishing [6J]	396	ITC Zapf Dingbats Series 200 [12L]
205	Ventura Math [6M]	405	PC-850 Multilingual [12U]
217	MSI/Plessey Barcode [6Y]	426	Ventura International [13J]
234	DeskTop [7J]	428	ITC Zapf Dingbats Series 300 [13L]
243	HP European Spanish [7S]	458	Ventura US [14J]
245	OEM-1 (DEC Set) [7U]	501	Pi Font [15U]
249	Code 11 Barcode [7Y]	505	USPS Zip [15Y]
263	Greek-8 [8G]	531	HP-GL Download [16S]
264	Hebrew-8 [8H]	563	HP-GL Drafting [17S]
267	Kana-8 [8K]	565	PC-852 (Latin 2) [17U]
268	Line Draw-8 [8L]	595	HP-GL Special Symbols [18S]
269	Math-8 [8M]	1611	JIS Kanji-1 [50K]
275	HP Latin Spanish [8S]	1643	JIS Kanji-2 [51K]
276	Turkish-8 [8T]		
277 (and 0)	Roman-8 (default set) [8U]		
278	Arabic-8 [8V]		
281	UPC/EAN Barcode [8Y]		

*　Not recommended for future use. This symbol set is of limited usage and is being discontinued.

Here is the same information ordered by symbol-set name:

Kind 1: Symbol Set

Value	Description and Symbol Set ID	Value	Description and Symbol Set ID
21	ANSI US ASCII (ISO 6) [0U]	57	Industrial 2 of 5 Barcode [1Y]
48	APL (bit-paired) [1P]	153	Interleaved 2 of 5 Barcode [4Y]
16	APL (typewriter-paired) [0P]	85	International Reference Version (ISO 2)* [2U]
22	Arabic (McKay's version)* [0V]	9	Italian (ISO 15) [0I]
278	Arabic-8 [8V]	364	ITC Zapf Dingbats Series 100 [11L]
185	CODABAR Barcode [5Y]	396	ITC Zapf Dingbats Series 200 [12L]
249	Code 11 Barcode [7Y]	428	ITC Zapf Dingbats Series 300 [13L]
18	Cyrillic ASCII (ECMA-113/86; ISO 8859/5) [0R]	11	JIS ASCII* (ISO 14) [0K]
50	Cyrillic [1R]	1611	JIS Kanji-1 [50K]
4	Danish/Norwegian version 1 (ISO 60) [0D]	1643	JIS Kanji-2 [51K]
234	DeskTop [7J]	267	Kana-8 [8K]
14	ECMA-94 Latin 1 (8-bit version; ISO 8859/1) [0N]	43	Katakana* (ISO 13) [1K]
		299	Korean-8 [9K]
78	ECMA-94 Latin 2 (ISO 8859/2) [2N]	53	Legal [1U]
		2	Line Draw-7* [0B]
334	ECMA-113/88 Latin/ Cyrillic (ISO 8859/5.2) [10N]	12	Line Draw-7 [0L]
		268	Line Draw-8 [8L]
		1	Math-7* [0A]
174	ECMA-128 Latin 5 (ISO 8859/9) [5N]	13	Math-7 [0M]
		269	Math-8 [8M]
6	French (ISO 25)* [0F]	89	Matrix 2 of 5 Barcode [2Y]
38	French (ISO 69) [1F]	202	Microsoft Publishing [6J]
39	German (ISO 21) [1G]	217	MSI/Plessey Barcode [6Y]
263	Greek-8 [8G]	36	Norwegian Version 2 [1D]
8	Hebrew-7 [0H]	15	OCR-A [0O]
264	Hebrew-8 [8H]	47	OCR-B [1O]
44	HP Block Characters [1L]	79	OCR-M [2O]
243	HP European Spanish [7S]	245	OEM-1 (DEC Set) [7U]
531	HP-GL Download [16S]	114	PC Cyrillic [3R]
563	HP-GL Drafting [17S]	145	PC Line [4O]
595	HP-GL Special Symbols [18S]	341	PC-8 (Code Page 437) [10U]
3	HP Large Characters (264x Terminals)* [0C]	373	PC-8 Danish/Norwegian [11U]
275	HP Latin Spanish [8S]	405	PC-850 Multilingual [12U]
181	HPL Language Set [5U]		

Kind 1: Symbol Set (continued)

Value	Description and Symbol Set ID	Value	Description and Symbol Set ID
565	PC-852 (Latin 2) [17U]	45	Tech-7 (DEC) [1M]
501	Pi Font [15U]	20	Thai-8 [0T]
147	Portuguese (ISO 16)* [4S]	276	Turkish-8 [8T]
332	PS ITC Zapf Dingbats [10L]	37	United Kingdom (ISO 4) [1E]
173	PS Math [5M]	281	UPC/EAN Barcode [8Y]
330	PS Text [10J]	505	USPS Zip [15Y]
0 and 277	Roman-8 (default set) [8U]	426	Ventura International [13J]
5	Roman Extensions* [0E]	300	Ventura ITC Zapf Dingbats [9L]
83	Spanish (ISO 17)* [2S]	205	Ventura Math [6M]
115	Swedish (ISO 10)* [3S]	458	Ventura US [14J]
19	Swedish for names (ISO 11) [0S]	309	Windows [9U]
76	Tax Line Draw [2L]	25	3 of 9 Barcode [0Y]
		26	Not used [0Z]

* Not recommended for future use. This symbol set is of limited usage and is being discontinued.

Kind 2: Font Spacing

The font spacing characteristic defines whether the spacing is fixed (all characters occupying an equal horizontal space) or proportional (each character occupying a space proportional to its size). Refer to *Types of Fonts* on page 59.

Value	Description
0	Fixed spacing (default)
1	Proportional spacing

Kind 3: Pitch

The pitch characteristic is a horizontal measurement defining the number of characters-per-inch for fixed-spaced fonts. Note: When selecting proportional fonts, do not include pitch in the font definition instruction (SD or AD).

Value	Description
0 to 32 767.999 9	Characters per inch (default: device-dependent)

Fixed-spaced fonts depend on *pitch* to determine character size. Proportional fonts ignore *pitch*. Note that with the SD and AD instruction you cannot create tall, skinny characters or short, wide characters; the character aspect ratio is preserved unless an SI or SR instruction overrides it.

Kind 4: Height

For proportional fonts, the height characteristic defines the font point size (the height of the character cell). (Fixed-spaced fonts ignore height; the point size is calculated using the font pitch.) There are approximately 72 points in an inch. Note that with the font definition instruction (SD or AD), you cannot create tall, skinny characters or short, wide characters; the character aspect ratio is preserved.

Value	Description
0 to 32 767.999 9	Font point size (default: device-dependent)

Kind 5: Posture

Posture defines the character's vertical posture. The default posture is upright.

Value	Description
0	Upright (default)
1	Italic
2	Alternate Italic

Kind 6: Stroke Weight

The stroke weight characteristic defines the line thickness used in the font's design.

Value	Description	Value	Description
−7	Ultra Thin	1	Semi Bold
−6	Extra Thin	2	Demi Bold
−5	Thin	3	Bold
−4	Extra Light	4	Extra Bold
−3	Light	5	Black
−2	Demi Light	6	Extra Black
−1	Semi Light	7	Ultra Black
0	Medium, Book or Text	9999	Stick font only

The default stroke weight is medium. When relative sizing is in effect, changes in P1 and P2 cause the relative stroke weight to change in relation to the change in P1/P2. If the aspect ratio of the P1/P2 rectangle is maintained as P1 and P2 are moved, a medium stroke weight font still looks "medium" after it is enlarged or reduced.

Note: Available stroke weights are the same as those available within PCL.

When the Stick font (typeface 48) is selected, the value 9999 renders it using the current pen width.

Kind 7: Typeface

The typeface characteristic selects the font's design style, which gives the font its distinctiveness. Typefaces can only be printed if the device has access to them; if they are internal fonts, are soft fonts that are downloaded to the device, or if they reside in a font cartridge or single inline memory module (SIMM) that is plugged into the device. All HP-GL/2 devices support the stick fonts (48, 49, and 50).

These typeface names may be registered trademarks of a third party. Use of these fonts may be conditional upon a license grant from the owners of the fonts. Hewlett-Packard makes no representation as to the quality or performance of the fonts, and any reference to the fonts does not grant any license or right to use the fonts.

The same information is ordered by typeface-name on page 481.

Value	Description	Value	Description
0	Line Printer or Line Draw	42	Goudy Old Style
1	Pica	43	ITC Zapf Chancery
2	Elite	44	Clarendon
3	Courier	45	ITC Zapf Dingbats
4	Helvetica	46	Cooper
5	Times Roman	47	ITC Bookman
6	Letter Gothic	48	Stick (default)
7	Script	49	HP-GL drafting
8	Prestige	50	HP-GL fixed arc
9	Caslon	51	Gill Sans
10	Orator	52	Univers
11	Presentation	53	Bodoni
13	Serifa	54	Rockwell
14	Futura	55	Melior
15	Palatino	56	ITC Tiffany
16	ITC Souvenir	57	ITC Clearface
17	Optima	58	Amelia
18	ITC Garamond	59	Park Avenue
20	Coronet	60	Handel Gothic
21	Broadway	61	Dom Casual
23	Century Schoolbook	62	ITC Benguiat
24	University Roman	63	ITC Cheltenham
27	ITC Korinna	64	Century Expanded
28	Naskh (generic Arabic typeface)	65	Franklin Gothic
29	Cloister Black	68	Plantin
30	ITC Galliard	69	Trump Mediaeval
31	ITC Avant Garde Gothic	70	Futura Black
32	Brush	71	ITC American Typewriter
33	Blippo	72	Antique Olive
34	Hobo	73	Uncial
35	Windsor	74	ITC Bauhaus
38	Peignot	75	Century Oldstyle
39	Baskerville	76	ITC Eras
41	Trade Gothic	77	ITC Friz Quadrata
		78	ITC Lubalin Graph

Kind 7: Typeface (continued)

Value	Description	Value	Description
79	Eurostile	103	ITC Ronda
80	Mincho	104	OCR-A
81	ITC Serif Gothic	105	ITC Century
82	Signet Roundhand	106	Englische Schreibschrift
83	Souvenir Gothic	107	Flash
84	Stymie	108	Gothic Outline (URW)
87	Bernhard Modern	109	Stensil (ATF)
89	Excelsior	110	OCR-B
90	Grand Ronde Script	111	Akzidenz-Grotesk
91	Ondine	112	TD Logos
92	P.T.Barnum	113	Shannon
93	Kaufman	114	ITC Century
94	ITC Bolt Bold	152	Maru Gosikku
96	Helv Monospaced	153	Gosikku (Kaku)
97	Revue	154	Socho
101	Garamond (Stempel)	155	Kyokasho
102	Garth Graphic	156	Kaisho

Here is the same information ordered by typeface name:

Kind 7: Typeface

Value	Description	Value	Description
111	Akzidenz-Grotesk	65	Franklin Gothic
58	Amelia	14	Futura
72	Antique Olive	70	Futura Black
39	Baskerville	101	Garamond (Stempel)
87	Bernhard Modern	102	Garth Graphic
33	Blippo	51	Gill Sans
53	Bodoni	153	Gosikku (Kaku)
21	Broadway	108	Gothic Outline (URW)
32	Brush	42	Goudy Old Style
9	Caslon	90	Grand Ronde Script
64	Century Expanded	60	Handel Gothic
75	Century Oldstyle	4	Helvetica
23	Century Schoolbook	96	Helv Monospaced
44	Clarendon	34	Hobo
29	Cloister Black	49	HP-GL drafting
46	Cooper	50	HP-GL fixed arc
20	Coronet	71	ITC American Typewriter
3	Courier	31	ITC Avant Garde Gothic
61	Dom Casual	74	ITC Bauhaus
2	Elite	62	ITC Benguiat
106	Englische Schreibschrift	94	ITC Bolt Bold
79	Eurostile	47	ITC Bookman
89	Excelsior	105	ITC Century
107	Flash	114	ITC Century

Kind 7: Typeface (continued)

Value	Description	Value	Description
63	ITC Cheltenham	10	Orator
57	ITC Clearface	15	Palatino
76	ITC Eras	59	Park Avenue
77	ITC Friz Quadrata	38	Peignot
30	ITC Galliard	1	Pica
18	ITC Garamond	68	Plantin
27	ITC Korinna	11	Presentation
78	ITC Lubalin Graph	8	Prestige
103	ITC Ronda	92	P.T.Barnum
81	ITC Serif Gothic	97	Revue
16	ITC Souvenir	54	Rockwell
56	ITC Tiffany	7	Script
43	ITC Zapf Chancery	13	Serifa
45	ITC Zapf Dingbats	113	Shannon
156	Kaisho	82	Signet Roundhand
93	Kaufman	154	Socho
155	Kyokasho	83	Souvenir Gothic
6	Letter Gothic	109	Stensil (ATF)
0	Line Printer or Line Draw	48	Stick (default)
152	Maru Gosikku	84	Stymie
55	Melior	112	TD Logos
80	Mincho	5	Times Roman
28	Naskh (generic Arabic typeface)	41	Trade Gothic
		69	Trump Mediaeval
104	OCR-A	73	Uncial
110	OCR-B	52	Univers
91	Ondine	24	University Roman
17	Optima	35	Windsor

Glossary of Terms and Abbreviations

Symbols

The representation of a numerical parameter in a parameterized escape sequence or HP RTL command. See the **Value Field** in the table on page 339.

| The vertical bar, when shown in a command, indicates that one or other of the options either side may be chosen, but not both. For example, in the command "**ESC***v#a|A", either the "a" or the "A" may be coded, resulting in the command "**ESC***v#a" or "**ESC***v#A". See *Combining Commands* on page 340.

A

absolute movement: Moving to a point, the location of which is specified with respect to the origin of the coordinate system. See page 10.

adaptive compression: In HP RTL, a method of compressing data in which an entire block of data is processed. The method varies according to the data, using a combination of unencoded, *run-length encoding*, *TIFF encoding*, and *seed-row encoding*. See page 385.

adaptive line type: In HP-GL/2, when the length of the pattern forming a line is adjusted automatically so that one or more complete patterns are used to form the line. Contrast with *fixed line type*. See the LT (Line Type) instruction on page 215.

anchor corner: In HP-GL/2, the starting point of a fill pattern. See page 57 and the AC (Anchor Corner) instruction on page 103.

angle of rotation: See *rotation* and Figure 27 on page 44.

anisotropic scaling: Scaling of an image in which the width and height are scaled by different proportions, turning circles into ellipses and squares into rectangles. See page 13.

AppleTalk: A networking system for use with Apple computers.

arc font: A font whose characters are drawn as a series of vectors. The font is proportionally spaced. See *Types of Fonts* on page 59.

ASCII: American Standard Code for Information Interchange.

aspect ratio: The ratio of the width to the height of an image.

B

background color: In HP RTL, the color selected by index 0; in black-and-white mode, this is white by default.

backspace (BS): A control character, ASCII 8, that causes the pen location to move backwards in a label. See page 67.

baseline: The imaginary line on which a line of text rests. A character's descender (such as the bottom of a lowercase "g") extends below the baseline. See page 58.

baud rate: The rate at which data is transmitted on a serial channel, such as RS-232-C, between a computer and a peripheral device. To communicate properly, the computer and the peripheral device must be configured to the same baud rate.

best print quality: Multiple passes, unidirectional, interlaced print quality.

bit: The binary ones and zeros in computer data. In monochrome printers, a single bit defines a pixel: a 1-bit prints a black pixel and a 0-bit prints a white pixel.

Bits	Pixel rows
11111111	● ● ● ● ● ● ● ●
10101010	● ● ● ●

A color pixel may require more bits per pixel; for example, two bits for four colors, three bits for eight, and so on.

bitmap: A region of memory treated as a rectangular array of pixels. Bitmap graphics is the same as *raster graphics*.

bitmap font: A font whose characters are defined as an array of dots in a raster pattern. Bitmap characters are always placed in an orthogonal direction to the page. See *Types of Fonts* on page 59.

black-and-white mode: In HP RTL, the default color mode following a Reset command. White is at index 0, black at 1. See page 353.

black reference: For RGB color spaces, the minimum amount of a primary color that a device can produce, normally none. (Contrast with *white reference*.) See pages 131 and 355.

buffer: A part or parts of computer or device memory where data is held until it can be processed. The term is usually applied to a memory area reserved for I/O operations.

C

CAD: Computer-Aided Design.

CAP: Current Active Position.

cap height: The distance from the baseline to the top of a capital letter. For most fonts, the cap height is approximately 0.7 times the point size (0.67 times the point size for the stick font). See page 58.

carriage axis: In HP RTL, the Y-axis. The direction across the paper, perpendicular to the direction of movement of the paper.

carriage return (CR): A control character, ASCII 13, that causes the pen location to move to the *carriage-return point* in a label. See page 67.

carriage-return point: The location to which a **CR** control character returns the pen, the beginning of a line of text. See page 66.

CCITT: The International Telegraph and Telephone Consultative Committee of the International Telecommunication Union, which sets international standards for hardware and communications protocols.

(The acronym is from the French name of the organization.)

CCITT compression methods: Data compression methods specified by CCITT recommendations. See page 388.

Centronics I/O: An industry standard unidirectional parallel input/output interface. (See also *parallel interface*.)

character: A letter, digit or other symbol that is represented by one byte (or, for Asian characters, two bytes).

character height: The vertical area allocated for character rendering. See page 58.

character origin: The point at which the baseline meets the left edge of the character cell. See page 58.

character plot cell: A rectangular area with the height of a linefeed and a width extending from the beginning of one character to the beginning of the next (delta-X). See page 58.

character plot cell width: The distance from the left edge of one character to the beginning of the next character. See page 58.

character set: Same as *font*.

character width: The lateral area allocated for character rendering. See page 58.

chord angle: See *chord tolerance*.

chord tolerance: In HP-GL/2, the amount by which a chord deviates from a true circle or arc, expressed either as a *chord angle* or a *deviation distance*. See page 79 and the CT (Chord Tolerance Mode) instruction on page 133.

clamped integer: An integer value that is constrained within certain limits. If the value supplied is greater than the maximum, the maximum value is used; if it is less than the minimum, the minimum value is used. See pages 27 and 338.

clipping limit: See *hard-clip limit* and *soft-clip limit*.

clustered dither: A type of dither that grows a big dot by adding neighboring dots to it. See *dither*.

CMY: Cyan–magenta–yellow; CMYK is the same as KCMY (black–cyan–magenta–yellow).

color palette: See *palette*.

color selection: See *direct color selection, indexed color selection*.

command: An order to a device to perform some function. The term used in this book to refer to the interface with HP RTL. HP RTL commands are all *escape sequences*. Contrast with *instruction*.

compression: The compacting of data so that more efficient use is made of the means of transmission between a computer and a peripheral device. HP RTL supports several methods of data compression. The Set Compression Method command (**ESC***b#M) allows you to code raster data in any of several formats. See pages 378 and 406.

configuration: The process of changing the settings of a device. This is normally done using the control panel or PJL.

context: The environment in which a command or instruction is executed; in *dual-context* mode, either HP-GL/2 vector data or HP RTL images are accepted by the device; in *single-context* mode, only HP-GL/2 instructions are valid.

continuous tone: Halftoning in which the variations are rendered as a continuous series of tones without using a dither pattern. See page 360.

control code: A non-printable ASCII character that indicates a printer or plotter function, for example, carriage return (**CR**) or line feed (**LF**). See page 67.

control panel: The combination of keys, LEDs, and a display that allows an operator to communicate with a device and allows the device to communicate with an operator.

coordinate system: The grid of X and Y values that define a point on a page. See page 7.

Current Active Position: In HP RTL, the position on the logical page where the next graphics dot will be printed. Compare with the *pen location* in HP-GL/2. See page 347.

current image: Whatever is currently defined on the page. This includes all images placed through previous operations. Also called the *destination*.

D

data compression: See *compression*.

decipoint: A unit of measurement equal to 1/720-inch.

default: A value used instead of one explicitly specified. A factory default is a value programmed into a device at the factory. A user default is one that can be changed by the user, either from the control panel or through programming.

delta-row encoding: Same as *seed-row encoding*.

delta-X: The implied pen movement that occurs after a character is printed, including the space taken up by the character as well as the white space between the characters set by the ES (Extra Space) instruction. See page 58.

destination: Same as *current image*.

deviation distance: See *chord tolerance*.

device: A printer or plotter attached to a computer.

device best: In HP RTL, half-toning in which the rendering is what HP considers will provide the best output for a particular device in most cases. See page 360.

direct by pixel: In HP RTL, a color selected *directly*, with the data for each row being downloaded pixel by pixel. See the description of the Configure Image Data (**ESC***v#W) command on page 407.

direct by plane: In HP RTL, a color selected *directly*, with the data for each row being downloaded plane by plane. See the description of the Configure Image Data (**ESC***v#W) command on page 407.

direct color selection: In HP RTL, a color selected by specifying the proportions of its primary components. For example, a 24-bit-per-pixel representation of a reddish yellow might be 0xfff000, where 0xff is the red component, 0xf0 is the green part, and 0x00 is the blue. (Contrast with *indexed color selection*.) See page 352.

dither: A pixel is intensified at a point (x,y) depending on the desired intensity, I(x,y), and on an n x n dither matrix, D, where

$$i = x \text{ modulo } n$$
$$j = y \text{ modulo } n$$

For RGB color spaces, if $I(x,y) < D(i,j)$, the point at (x,y) is intensified; otherwise it is not. This applies to each primary color. (Also called *ordered dither* or *clustered dither*.) See page 360.

dot: The smallest mark a printer or plotter can make; its size and placing are device-specific. The number of dots printed per inch is the device's native resolution.

downloading: Transmitting data from a computer to a peripheral device, such as a plotter or a printer.

dpi: Dots per inch; the device's addressable resolution of raster images.

drafting font: A font in which the characters are designed to provide reliable character recognition in situations where photo reduction may cause image degradation and loss of resolution. See *Types of Fonts* on page 59.

driver: Software used to control input and output between a computer and a peripheral device, such as a printer or a plotter.

dual-context plotter: A plotter mode that allows the mixing of HP-GL/2 and HP RTL images on the same page. Contrast with *stand-alone plotter*. See the description of the Enter HP-GL/2 Mode (**ESC%#B**) command on page 418 and *The Dual-Context Extension* of HP-GL/2 on page 83.

E

effective window: The area where the *hard-clip limits* and *soft-clip limits* overlap.

encoding by pixel: In HP RTL, when all the bits for a pixel are sent as a group (for example, 24-bit RGB), then all the bits for the next pixel until the pixels in a row are defined. Each pixel receives all its bits before any bits are sent for the next pixel. See *indexed by pixel* and the description of the Configure Image Data (**ESC*v#W**) command on page 407.

encoding by plane: In HP RTL, when each pixel in a row receives one bit (plane), then every pixel receives the next plane, until the pixels in a row are completely defined. That is, all the pixels in a row are partially defined by each plane until the last plane for that row is sent. The number of planes is the number of bits needed to define (color) a pixel. See *indexed by plane* and the description of the Configure Image Data (**ESC*v#W**) command on page 407.

encoding plane-by-plane: In HP RTL, a method of encoding color images in which the colors are separated into cyan, magenta, yellow, and black planes. These planes are then transferred to the device one at a time and aligned using the Y Offset command. See *indexed plane-by-plane* and the description of the Configure Image Data (**ESC*v#W**) command on page 407.

end-of-text (ETX): A control character, ASCII 3, that is used to terminate HP-GL/2 labels. See page 67.

escape character: The ASCII character whose decimal value is 27, used at the start of all HP RTL commands. It is denoted by the symbol **ESC** in this book. As the printer or plotter monitors incoming data from a computer, it is "looking for" this character. When this character appears, the device reads it and its associated characters as a command to be performed, not as data to be printed or plotted.

escape sequence: A sequence of characters, starting with an *escape character*. HP RTL commands are escape sequences.

even/odd fill method: In HP-GL/2, a method of determining which parts of a polygon should be filled. See page 51.

extension: The device-specific sets of instructions in HP-GL/2. See page 20.

F

factory default: Settings that are programmed into a device at the factory. They are used unless you override them using the control panel of the device or by sending appropriate commands to the device.

fast or draft print quality: Typically, single-pass, bidirectional print quality.

fill type: The HP-GL/2 term for a *pattern*.

final or normal print quality: The recommended print quality, with a good balance between quality and performance.

fixed-arc font: A font in which the horizontal space for all characters is the same. Characters are drawn using arcs for greater smoothness. See *Types of Fonts* on page 59.

fixed line type: In HP-GL/2, when the pattern forming a line is drawn at the specified length; any unused part of the pattern (the *residue*) is used on the next line of a continuous vector sequence. Contrast with *adaptive line type*. See the LT (Line Type) instruction on page 215.

fixed-spaced font: A font whose *delta-X* is the same for every character. See page 58.

fixed-vector font: A font in which the horizontal space for all characters is the same, and each character is always drawn using a fixed number of vectors, regardless of its size or direction. See *Types of Fonts* on page 59.

font: A set of characters that uses each code-point for a specific purpose, such as the alphabet and associated characters for a national language, or a set of graphics. Also called *character set*.

foreground color: In HP RTL, the color selected by the Foreground Color command (**ESC***v#S) from the current palette. Foreground color affects everything except color patterns and HP-GL/2 primitives. Raster color interacts with foreground color. See page 421.

front panel: See *control panel*.

G

gamma correction: A correction that is applied to the intensity of a color to improve its perceived correctness.

gray scale: Same as *gray shade*.

gray shades: On a monochrome device, the various densities of black that produce shades of gray on the paper. Images that are created in color may map the colors to gray shades when they are printed on a monochrome device.

H

halftoning: In HP RTL, the reduction of a colored image from, say, 256 colors to 8; or the conversion of a colored image to monochrome. The Render Algorithm command (**ESC***t#J) provides a choice of algorithms. See pages 360 and 434. See also *dither*.

hard-clip limit: A boundary of a printing area beyond which a device cannot print or plot. See page 5.

hard-clip limit origin: The point with coordinates (0,0) in the coordinate system; this varies depending on whether the device is a printer or a plotter, whether it supports PCL or HP RTL, and whether the orientation is portrait or landscape. See *Interactions between Different Coordinate Systems* on page 8.

HP-GL/2: Hewlett-Packard's Graphics Language/2, that is understood by many plotters and printers. For various types of images (many types of technical drawings and business graphics, for example), it is advantageous to use vector graphics instead of raster graphics. Advantages include faster I/O transfer of large pictures and smaller storage requirements.

HP RTL: Hewlett-Packard's Raster Transfer Language, that is understood by many plotters and printers. For various types of images, it is advantageous to use raster graphics.

I

IEEE-1284 interface: An industry standard bidirectional parallel input/output interface. (See also *parallel interface*.)

image: A picture composed of rows of dots; same as *raster graphics*.

indexed by pixel: In HP RTL, a color selected by *index*, with the data for each row being downloaded pixel by pixel. See *encoding by pixel* and the description of the Configure Image Data (**ESC***v#W) command on page 407.

indexed by plane: In HP RTL, a color selected by *index*, with the data for each row being downloaded plane by plane. See *encoding by plane* and the description of the Configure Image Data (**ESC***v#W) command on page 407.

indexed color selection: In HP RTL, a color selected by its index number in the palette. In an eight-color palette, three bits are sufficient to define the palette. (Contrast with *direct color selection*.) See page 352.

indexed plane-by-plane: In HP RTL, a color selected by *index*, with the data for the entire image being downloaded plane by plane. See *encoding plane-by-plane* and the description of the Configure Image Data (**ESC***v#W) command on page 407.

initialize: To set a peripheral device, such as a plotter, to known defaults. See *reset*.

instruction: The term used in this book to refer to the interface with HP-GL/2. Contrast with *command*.

I/O: Input/Output.

I/O buffer: The random access memory (RAM) within a printer or plotter where commands and data are stored.

isotropic scaling: Scaling of an image in which the width and height are scaled by the same proportions, keeping circles circular and squares square. See page 13.

J

job boundary: The beginning or end of a print job, indicated using the @PJL JOB or @PJL EOJ command.

K

KCMY: Black–cyan–magenta–yellow.

kernel: The principal set of instructions in HP-GL/2. See page 17.

L

label: In HP-GL/2, any printed text. See *The Character Group* on page 57.

label mode: In HP-GL/2, whether characters consist of one or two bytes. See the LM (Label Mode) instruction on page 208.

landscape: Picture orientation where the width is greater than the height, typical of landscape paintings.

line feed (LF): The distance from the baseline of a line of text to the baseline of the next character line above or below. A control character, ASCII 10, that causes the pen location to move downwards one character in a label. See pages 58 and 67.

logical operations: Combinations of logical functions such as AND, OR, XOR, and NOT applied to the source, texture, and current image. Logical operations are applied using the MC (Merge Control) instruction and the Logical Operation command (**ESC***l#O). See pages 220, 367 and 422.

logical page: That part of the physical page on which an image can be drawn, as defined by the HP-GL/2 PS (Plot Size) instruction. See *hard-clip limit*.

"lost" mode: When the HP-GL/2 current *pen location* is outside the range of coordinates of the device. See page 23.

M

machine resolution: See *resolution*.

mask source: See *source data*.

media: The paper or other substance on which a picture is printed or plotted.

media axis: X-axis.

mnemonic: The two-character name of an HP-GL/2 instruction. See page 25.

mode: The environment within which commands and instructions are recognized and executed. For example, HP RTL, HP-GL/2, or PJL. (Also called *context*.)

monochrome: Black and white images. A device that prints or plots monochrome images may be able to produce shades of gray (see *gray shades*).

N

native resolution: The physical *resolution* of the device. A device may support more than one native resolution, which can be selected using the command @PJL SET RESOLUTION=# (see page 392).

negative motion: Any of the following:

- An HP-GL/2 drawing operation

- An operation that would print in the negative Y-axis direction with respect to previously printed data

- A Y Offset in raster mode that moves the CAP in the negative Y-axis direction.

See pages 349 and 426.

noise dither: Same as *scatter halftone dither.*

non-raster color: A color selected in non-raster mode, for example, a foreground color or a colored pattern; the *palette* is always used to select such colors.

non-raster mode: A state in which the device can handle commands that affect rendering. (See also *raster mode.*)

non-zero winding fill method: In HP-GL/2, a method of determining which parts of a polygon should be filled. See page 51.

normal print quality: Single-pass, non-depleted print quality.

O

on-the-fly plotting: When the buffer memory in a device becomes full, some devices plot everything that is currently held in the buffer. As a result, they can continue with the current plot, provided that it does not require negative motion of the medium. See page 375.

ordered dither: See *dither.*

orientation: The presentation of graphics on a page. See *landscape* and *portrait* and also *Interactions between Different Coordinate Systems* on page 8. In HP-GL/2, the amount by which characters in a label are rotated.

origin: See *hard-clip limit origin.*

overflow: To exceed the capacity of the storage space in a buffer. When buffer overflow occurs, the excess data may be lost.

P

P1, P2: See *scaling points* and page 31.

packbits encoding: See *TIFF packbits encoding.*

page dirty: A page to which vector or raster data has been sent.

palette: A collection of colors that are selected by index numbers. Only one palette can be active at a time. See page 356.

paper axis: In HP RTL, the X-axis. The direction in which the paper moves.

parallel interface: An input/output (I/O) interface that transmits more than one bit of information simultaneously. Centronics and IEEE-1284 are industry-wide parallel interface standards.

pattern: A rectangular area tile whose design is applied to the current image through the source. It may be a single-plane monochrome mask or a multi-plane raster color pattern. In HP RTL, the Current Pattern command (**ESC***v#T) designates an active pattern, which stays in effect until another is specified or the device is reset. A reset changes back to the default pattern, which is 100% black. Foreground color is not applied to a color pattern. See page 361. (HP-GL/2 uses the term *fill type.*)

pattern dither: Halftoning in which pixels are intensified by increasing the number of dots according to the desired density of color; the dots are scattered in a pattern.

pattern transparency mode: In HP RTL, a flag that specifies whether the "white" pixels in the pattern are transparent or opaque. When the mode is transparent, the "white" pixels have no effect on the current image; when the mode is opaque, the "white" pixels are applied to the current image. See page 370.

PCL: Printer Control Language. For more information see *PCL 5 Printer Language Technical Reference Manual.*

pen: In HP-GL/2, a pen has an associated color and width and is used to draw primitives.

pen location: In HP-GL/2, the X and Y coordinates of the point where the logical pen would next mark the media. Compare with the *Current Active Position* in HP RTL. See page 23.

pen status: In HP-GL/2, whether the logical pen is up (and therefore not marking the media) or down (drawing). See page 22.

peripheral device: A device separate from, but used with, a computer; for example, a printer or a plotter.

physical page: The size of the sheet or roll of media installed on the device.

physical resolution: See *resolution.*

picture body: In HP-GL/2, the state when marks have been made on the media. Contrast with *picture header.* See page 78.

picture frame: The destination rectangle when transferring an HP-GL/2 plot to the PCL logical page. PCL picture frame size commands specify its size.

picture frame anchor point: The upper left corner of the picture frame, which is set to the current active position (CAP) in the PCL environment when the picture frame anchor point command is executed.

picture frame scaling factor: The ratio of the size of the picture frame to the size of the HP-GL/2 plot. There may be two scaling factors for the X and Y directions.

picture header: The state when no marks have yet been made on the media. Contrast with *picture body.* See page 78.

picture presentation directives: PCL commands that enter and leave the HP-GL/2 context, define a delimiting rectangle (the picture frame) for the HP-GL/2 plot, and specify a scaling factor.

pie chart: A circle divided up into sections, each representing a part of some statistical data. See page 47.

pitch: The number of characters per inch. It is the inverse of delta-X. A pitch of 10 means that the delta-X is one-tenth of an inch; ten characters will fit into a one-inch space. Pitch is only used to measure fixed-space fonts, because proportionally-spaced fonts include characters with different delta-X values. See page 58.

pixel: The smallest definable picture element in an image. At maximum machine resolution, a pixel consists of one *dot.* When scaling up, or at lower resolutions, a pixel may consist of more than one dot.

pixel height: The height of an image, in terms of number of pixels.

pixel rows: Same as *pixel height.*

pixel width: The width of an image, in terms of number of pixels.

PJL: Printer Job Language. PJL commands provide job-level control, such as the ability to switch between plotter languages between jobs, to change the printer's control panel settings, and modify the message displayed on the control panel. See the *Printer Job Language Technical Reference Manual.*

plane: In HP RTL, a separation of a color image into monochrome parts, each consisting of one primary color. When the planes are laid upon one another, the full color image results. See page 351.

plane counter: In HP RTL, an internal counter that records which color plane is being processed in the device.

plotter: A device that produces output from a computer on paper or other media. The output is primarily graphics and images, but can also include text. In HP-GL/2, the term should strictly be used only for devices that support the PS (Plot Size) instruction of the Technical Graphics Extension (contrast with *printer*).

plotter-unit: The default unit of measure for HP-GL/2 devices, 0.025 millimeters. See page 12.

point size: A character measure roughly equivalent to the height of a capital letter M plus the depth of a descender, usually measured in units of 1/72-inch. See page 58.

polygon: A closed sequence of line segments.

polygon mode: In HP-GL/2, when the device is storing information about polygons and other objects into the *polygon buffer*, before drawing or filling the item. See page 49.

polygon buffer: In HP-GL/2, a temporary storage area in which information about polygons is stored. See page 45.

portrait: Picture orientation where the width is less than the height, typical of portrait paintings.

posture: An attribute of a font that indicates whether characters are upright or italic. See the SD (Standard Font Definition) instruction on page 296.

predefined palette: A palette that is built in to the device.

primitive: Any graphic item that marks the page (characters, vectors, polygons, and so on).

print cartridge: A cartridge containing ink which is directed through a series of tiny nozzles in its end. They can provide a wide range of pen attributes, removing the need to select and load pens into a carousel. Print cartridges have replaced pens and thereby provide a more versatile means of printing images.

print quality: This can be *best* (or *enhanced*) *print quality*, *fast* (or *draft*) *print quality*, or *normal* (or *final*) *print quality*.

printable area: The area of a physical page in which the printer or plotter is able to place ink. See *hard-clip limit*.

printer: A device that produces output from a computer on paper or other media. The output is primarily text, but can also include graphics and images. In HP-GL/2, the term should strictly be used only for devices that do not support the PS (Plot Size) instruction of the Technical Graphics Extension (contrast with *plotter*).

proportionally-spaced font: A font whose *delta-X* varies from one character to another. See page 58.

Q

quality of printing: This can be *best* (or *enhanced*) *print quality*, *fast* (or *draft*) *print quality*, or *normal* (or *final*) *print quality*.

R

raster area: In HP RTL, the bounds of a raster picture. Within this area, the printer or plotter fills missing or incomplete rows with zeros, and clips data that would fall outside. See also *raster height*, *raster width* and page 342.

raster clean: In HP RTL, a page to which no raster data has been sent.

raster color: In HP RTL, a color specified in raster mode; the *palette* is used for *indexed* color selection, but not for *direct* color selection.

raster graphics: Images composed of rows of dots. (Contrast with *vector graphics*.) See pages 4 and 344.

raster height: In HP RTL, the vertical distance between the Current Active Position (CAP) and one of:

- the distance specified by Source Raster Height (**ESC***r#T) if scaling is off,

or:

- the row preceding an End Raster command (**ESC***rC),

or:

- the lower edge of the logical page.

See page 343.

raster mode: In HP RTL, the Start Raster (**ESC***r#A) command begins a restricted state called raster mode, where raster data is sent to the device. Raster mode continues until an End Raster (**ESC***rC) command is executed. See page 374.

raster operations: See *logical operations*.

raster scaling: In HP RTL, if scaling is on, the size of the raster picture is determined by Destination Raster Width (**ESC***t#H) and Destination Raster Height (**ESC***t#V). To enable raster scaling, Source Raster Height (**ESC***r#S) and Source Raster Width (**ESC***r#T) must be specified, but destination sizes are optional, defaulting to logical page boundary. See page 345.

raster source: See *source data*.

raster width: In HP RTL, the distance between the left raster margin (the Current Active Position [CAP] or the left edge of the logical page) and:

- the distance specified by Source Raster Width (**ESC***r#S) if scaling is off,

or:

- the right edge of the logical page.

See page 343.

relative movement: Moving to a point, the location of which is specified with respect to the current location of the pen. See page 10.

rendering: In HP RTL, the process of interpreting data as a raster image when the image is created in the device's internal bitmap at native resolution.

reset: A state in which the plotter or printer is in a known condition. A device can be reset by sending the Reset command (**ESCE**). See page 435.

residue: See *fixed line type*.

resolution: Image sharpness. *Physical or machine resolution* is the number of dots per inch (dpi) that a device is capable of printing. A resolution of 300 dpi means that the printer or plotter can place dots of ink anywhere in a grid of 300-by-300 dots in every square inch of the printable area of the page. Some devices allow different *native* resolutions, up to the machine resolution. See page 344.

reverse polish notation: A notation for Boolean (logical) expressions in which the operands are placed before the operators. For example, "**T S and**" denotes the expression "**T and S**"; "**AB or not**" denotes "**not (A or B)**".

RGB: Red–green–blue.

ROP2, ROP3: Microsoft's version of *logical operations*; see the Microsoft document *Binary and Ternary Raster Operation Codes*.

rotation: Turning the axes of coordinates through a multiple of 90°. See page 44.

row: In HP RTL, a line of dots that extends across the page.

row-by-row raster mode: In HP RTL, the encoding mode in which data is *indexed by plane*. See also *encoding by plane* and *indexed by plane*, and the description of the Configure Image Data (**ESC*v#W**) command on page 407.

row pointer: In HP RTL, an internal pointer to the row of data that is being processed by the device.

RS-232-C interface: A serial interface standardized by the Electronic Industries Association.

run-length encoding: A method of compressing data in which each byte of data is preceded by a count of the number of times it is to be repeated. See page 381.

S

scalable outline font: A font whose characters can be displayed at any size. See *Types of Fonts* on page 59.

scale: To divide the printing area into units convenient for your application.

scale mode: In HP-GL/2, whether user-units are being used; scale mode is "on" following an SC (Scale) instruction with parameters. In HP RTL, the same as *scaled raster mode*. See pages 24 and 345.

scaled raster mode: In HP RTL, a mode in which the size of the raster picture is determined by the Destination Raster Width (**ESC*t#H**) and Destination Raster Height (**ESC*t#V**) commands. See page 345.

scaling points: In HP-GL/2, the opposite points, P1 and P2, that are used to specify user-unit coordinates for scaling drawings. See page 31.

scatter halftone dither: A dithering method whereby dither thresholds are randomly distributed within a large cell.

seed-row encoding: A method of compressing data in which only those bytes in the row that are different from those in the previous row are transmitted. (Also known as *delta-row encoding*.) See page 382.

serial interface: An input/output (I/O) interface that transmits information bit-by-bit. RS-232 is an industry-wide standard form of serial interface.

setup sheet: A sheet of paper used to show the current configuration settings of a plotter. On some devices, by marking new choices on a setup sheet and loading it into the plotter, the configuration of the plotter can be changed.

shift in (SI): A control character, ASCII 15, that changes from the alternate to the standard font in a label. See page 67.

shift out (SO): A control character, ASCII 14, that changes from the standard to the alternate font in a label. See page 67.

simple color mode: In HP RTL, a mode, entered by the Simple Color command (**ESC*r#U**), that creates a fixed color, unmodifiable palette. The palette can be an 8-pen CMY palette or a 4-pen KCMY palette. The pixel encoding mode is indexed planar. See pages 353 and 441.

single-context plotter: Same as *stand-alone plotter.*

soft-clip limit: A user-defined limit beyond which the device will not print or plot. Also referred to as a *window.* See page 5.

source data: The data that is to be added to the page. There are two types of source data—*mask* and *raster.* In both cases, the transparency mode affects only "white" pixels. See page 365.

Mask source is HP-GL/2 data. The data acts like a stencil whose 1-bits allow the pattern or selected pen color to pour through onto the page.

Raster source is HP RTL data, and may be specified by either the indexed or direct method (see *direct color selection* and *indexed color selection*). In the indexed method, each pixel identifies a palette index; in the direct method, each pixel is specified by its color components.

source transparency mode: A flag that specifies whether the "white" pixels in the source image are transparent or opaque. When the mode is transparent, the "white" pixels have no effect on the current image; when the mode is opaque, the "white" pixels are applied to the current image. See page 370 and the TR (Transparency Mode) instruction on page 318.

space (SP): A control character, ASCII 32, that causes the pen position to move one character to the right so that a blank space appears in a label. See page 67.

stand-alone plotter: A plotter that does not allow mixing HP-GL/2 and HP RTL on the same page. See the description of the Enter HP-GL/2 Mode (**ESC**%#B) command on page 418.

state variables: The values held internally by a device that indicate how it should handle data, commands, and instructions; for example, whether negative motion is allowed.

stick font: A font whose characters are drawn as a series of vectors. The font is fixed-spaced. All HP-GL/2 devices support stick fonts. See *Types of Fonts* on page 59.

stroke weight: An attribute of a font that indicates the thickness of its characters, such as thin, medium, or bold. See the SD (Standard Font Definition) instruction on page 296.

subpolygon: A part of a polygon; for example, the letter "D" is two subpolygons—the outline and the "hole". See page 49.

switching: Changing a plotter or printer from one mode to another, for example, from HP-GL/2 mode to HP RTL mode. See page 391.

symbol mode: In HP-GL/2, when a character is drawn at the end of each vector. See the SM (Symbol Mode) instruction on page 303.

T

tab: See *horizontal tab.*

Tagged Image File Format encoding: See *TIFF packbits encoding.*

text path: The direction that the current pen location moves after a character is drawn. See the DV (Define Variable Text Path) instruction on page 156.

texture: The result of a logical **and** operation on a downloaded monochrome pattern and the foreground color; or if the current downloaded pattern is multi-colored, synonymous with pattern (downloaded color patterns are not combined with the foreground color). See page 366.

TIFF packbits encoding: A method of compressing data in which allows for sequences of repeated bytes and sequences of unrepeated bytes of data. See page 381.

tiling: The means by which a pattern is applied to a source image. The pattern, whose upper-left pixel coincides with the *fill reference point*, is repeated horizontally and vertically across the page. See page 361.

transparency mode: How the pattern's white pixels affect the destination. In transparent mode, white pixels have no effect on the destination. In opaque mode, white pixels block out corresponding destination areas. See pages 73 and 370, the TR (Transparency Mode) instruction on page 318, and the Source Transparency Mode and Pattern

Transparency Mode commands on pages 445 and 431 respectively.

transparent data mode: In HP-GL/2, when the function of a control character is ignored and its graphic image or a space is printed. See page 67.

typeface: An attribute of a font that describes the design style of its characters. See the SD (Standard Font Definition) instruction on page 296.

U

UEL command: See *Universal Exit Language command*.

Universal Exit Language command: The command that switches to PJL mode. It consists of an escape character (**ESC,** decimal 27) followed by the eight characters "%–12345X". The UEL command causes the device to leave HP RTL or HP-GL/2 mode and return to PJL. See page 450.

user default: A default that is selectable through the device's control panel. For example, the number of copies, manual feed mode, color or monochrome, and so on.

user-defined shading pattern: In addition to the patterns that are built into HP RTL, users can define their own patterns. These are downloaded using the Download Pattern (**ESC***c#W) command, and can be used in both HP RTL and HP-GL/2 contexts. See pages 361 and 415.

user-unit: The size of units defined for a device's X and Y coordinates in HP-GL/2. See page 12.

V

variable-arc font: A font in which the characters are proportionally spaced. Characters are drawn using arcs, so that they have smoother contours. See *Types of Fonts* on page 59.

vector graphics: A method of drawing lines, area fills, and other objects. (Contrast with *raster graphics* and see also *HP-GL/2*.) See page 4.

W

wedge: A section of a circle, commonly used to draw *pie charts*. See page 47.

"white" pixels: In HP RTL, for indexed raster source, a white pixel is one that selects a white palette entry. For direct raster source, a white pixel is one for which all color primaries meet or exceed their *white reference* values. See page 365.

white reference: For RGB color spaces, the value given to a fully saturated primary color, the maximum amount of a primary color that a device can produce (in a red–green–blue model, the reddest red, greenest green, or bluest blue). (Contrast with *black reference*.) See pages 131 and 355.

window: See *soft-clip limit*.

X

X-axis: In HP RTL, the paper axis. In HP-GL/2, the direction of the X-axis depends on the orientation of the media and whether the device is a "printer" or a "plotter"; this may be changed by a RO (Rotate Coordinate System) instruction. See page 8.

Y

Y-axis: In HP RTL, the carriage axis. In HP-GL/2, the direction of the Y-axis depends on the orientation of the media and whether the device is a "printer" or a "plotter"; this may be changed by a RO (Rotate Coordinate System) instruction. See page 8.

Y offset: In HP RTL, a movement in the Y-axis. See the description of the Y Offset command on page 451.

Z

zero-degree reference point: A point that determines the orientation of a wedge. See page 324.

zero-filling: In HP RTL, within a raster area, the device fills missing or incomplete rows of data with zeros.

Index

Symbols

character, meaning of in command syntax, 483

| character, meaning of in command syntax, 483

A

AA (Arc Absolute) instruction, 100
  example of use, 102
    with PM, 253
  how to use, 43

abbreviations, 483

Absolute Arc Three Point (AT) instruction. *See* AT (Absolute Arc Three Point) instruction

Absolute Character Size (SI) instruction. *See* SI (Absolute Character Size) instruction

absolute coordinates, 10, 483
  example of use, 161

Absolute Direction (DI) instruction. *See* DI (Absolute Direction) instruction

AC (Anchor Corner) instruction, 103
  example of use, 104
  how to use, 57
  in dual-context mode, 87

AD (Alternate Font Definition) instruction, 106
  accessing special characters, 73
  example of use, 107
    with DL, 146
    with FN, 178
  how to use, 72

adaptive, line type, 217, 483

adaptive data compression, 385, 483
  example, 387

Advance Full Page (PG) instruction. *See* PG (Advance Full Page) instruction

advanced drawing extension, 92
  summary of instructions, 21

advanced text extension, 92, 94
  summary of instructions, 22

advancing the media, 181

alternate font, 177, 287

Alternate Font Definition (AD) instruction. *See* AD (Alternate Font Definition) instruction

anchor corner, 57, 483
  AC instruction, 103
  FR instruction, 182
  picture frame, 84, 490

Anchor Corner (AC) instruction. *See* AC (Anchor Corner) instruction

angle of rotation, 44

angles, measuring, 141

anisotropic scaling, 13, 483
  raster images, 346
  SC instruction, 290

AppleTalk, 393, 483

AppleTalk Configuration command, 393, 404

AR (Arc Relative) instruction, 108
  example of use, 109
  how to use, 43

Arc Absolute (AA) instruction. *See* AA (Arc Absolute) instruction

arc font, 60, 483

Arc Relative (AR) instruction. *See* AR (Arc Relative) instruction

arcs
  accuracy of drawing, 133
  counting points, 53
  drawing, 43
    example, 43

ASCII, meaning of, 483

aspect ratio, 483

Assign Color Index command, 405
  use of, 357

AT (Absolute Arc Three Point) instruction, 110
  example of use, 112
  how to use, 43

auto-rotate feature, 347, 392

B

background color, 359, 483

backspace (**BS**) control character, 67, 483

baseline, 58, 483

BASIC, use of, 460

baud rate, 483

Begin Plot (BP) instruction. *See* BP (Begin Plot) instruction

bell (**BEL**) control character, 67

best print quality, 483

Bezier Absolute (BZ) instruction. *See* BZ (Bezier Absolute) instruction

Bezier curves, drawing, 92

Bezier Relative (BR) instruction. *See* BR (Bezier Relative) instruction

binary data, in RTL commands, 339

bit, definition of, 483

bitmap, 484

bitmap font, 59, 484
SB instruction, 288

black reference, 355, 484
changing, 357
CR instruction, 131
primary colors, 352

black-and-white color mode, 353, 484

block-based unencoded data compression, 379–380

borders, creating, 359

boundaries of an image, 341

BP (Begin Plot) instruction, 113
auto-rotate feature, 347, 392
dual-context mode, 87, 419
HP-GL/2 imaging mode, 354
Reset command in dual-context mode, 419, 435
resetting HP RTL state variables, 348, 418
stand-alone plotter mode, 419

BR (Bezier Relative) instruction, 116
example of use, 117

BS (backspace) control character, 67, 483

buffer, 484
polygon, 44, 52

BZ (Bezier Absolute) instruction, 118
example of use, 92, 119

C

C language, use of, 460

CAP. *See* current active position

cap height, 59, 484

carriage axis, 484

carriage return (**CR**) control character, 68, 484
adding to a label, 68

carriage-return point, 139, 484
CP instruction, 130
DR instruction, 149
moving to, 66

CCITT, 484
Group 3 encoding data compression, 388
Group 4 encoding data compression, 388

cell
character, 58, 59
width of character, 59

Centronics interface, 80
and raster graphics, 468, 484

CF (Character Fill Mode) instruction, 120
example of use, 122
in HP-GL/2, 362
use with SB, 288

character
adjusting space, 169
bitmap fonts, 60
cap height, 59, 484
cell, 58, 59
width, 59
definition of, 484
height, 484
default, 65, 66
lines, 70
origin, 59, 484
pitch, 58, 490
default, 65
plot cell, 484
width, 484
posture, default, 65
scalable, 60
set. *See* font
size, 298, 308
slant, 69, 301
slope, 139
spacing, 70
default, 65

INDEX

INDEX

INDEX

text
  angle, 70
  character positioning, 211
  path, 156, 493
  printing, 206
  printing or plotting at an angle, 141
texture, 493
  HP RTL, 366
  HP-GL/2, 73
  logical operations, 366
TIFF Packbits encoding data compression, 381, 493
  example, 382
tiling, 361, 493
TR (Transparency Mode) instruction, 318
  example of use, with filling and edging, 45
  for HP-GL/2 patterns, 366
  interaction with HP RTL, 392
  use if Source Transparency Mode command unavailable, 365
Transfer Raster Data by Plane command, 447
  use of, 373
Transfer Raster Data by Row/Block command, 449
  adaptive data compression, 385
  block-based unencoded compression, 379, 380
  CCITT data compression methods, 388
  seed-row compression, 384, 385
  transferring raster data, 373
  use of, 385
transferring raster data, 373
translucent paper, specifying media type, 223
transmission time, 470
transparency, 370
  effect on logical operations, 366, 371
  efficient programming, 471
  pattern transparency mode, 365, 489
  source transparency mode, 365
transparency film, specifying media type, 223
transparency mode, 73, 493, 494
Transparency Mode (TR) instruction. *See* TR (Transparency Mode) instruction
transparent data, 67
Transparent Data (TD) instruction. *See* TD (Transparent Data) instruction

typeface, 480, 494
  default, 66
  of selected font, 64

U

UL (User-Defined Line Type) instruction, 320
  example of use, 321
unidirectional interface, 80
units
  device internal, 12
  PCL and HP RTL coordinate system, 12
Universal Exit Language/Start of PJL command, 450, 494
  use of, 392
upright. *See* posture
user default, 494
user-defined fill types, 56
User-Defined Line Type (UL) instruction. *See* UL (User-Defined Line Type) instruction
user-defined shading pattern, 494
  Download Pattern command, 415
  FT instruction, 183
user-unit, 12, 494
  in scaling, 291

V

value field, in RTL commands, 339
values allowed for parameters, 27
variable-arc font, 61, 494
vector data, 4
  merging with raster data, 392, 470
vector fill, 313
vector graphics, 494
vector group, 41
  summary of instructions, 18
vellum, specifying media type, 223
Velocity Select (VS) instruction. *See* VS (Velocity Select) instruction
vertical tab (**VT**) control character, 68
vertical text path, 129
VS (Velocity Select) instruction, 322
VT (vertical tab) control character, 68

W

wedges, 494
  drawing, 47
    example, 48
  filling, 324
    example, 48
weight of font, 479
WG (Fill Wedge) instruction, 324
  compared with EW (Edge Wedge), 171
  example of use, 47, 327
    with CP, 130
white pixels, 365, 494
white reference, 355, 494
  changing, 357
  CR instruction, 131
  primary colors, 352
  transparency mode, 365
white space, 470
width of an image, 342
  maximum, 343
width of lines, 57, 298
window. *See* soft-clip limits
WU (Pen Width Unit Selection) instruction, 328
  in dual-context mode, 89, 419

X

X-axis, 494
  PCL and HP RTL coordinate system, 12

Y

Y Offset, definition of, 494
Y Offset command, 451
  and Negative Motion command, 426
  current active position (CAP), 348
  efficient programming, 469
  index 0, 359
  memory considerations, 470
  moving the CAP, 469
  plane-by-plane encoding, 356
  plane-by-plane plotting and scaling, 377
  seed-row compression, 384
Y-axis, 494
  PCL and HP RTL coordinate system, 12

Z

zero filling, 494
  and scaling, 346
  index 0, 359
  using source width and height, 343
  Y Offset command, 469
zero-degree reference point, 494

Please give us your feedback on the quality of this documentation

You can fill out this sheet and mail it to the address overleaf.

Or you can reach us by e-mail at:
devkit@bpo.hp.com
Attn: Learning Products Dept.

Alternatively, you can fax this sheet to:
Spain (+34) 3 582 1400
Attn: Learning Products Dept.

Name:

Job Title:

Organization:

Address:

Phone:

Circle the appropriate score	*Poor*	▶	▶	▶	*Excellent*
Overall ease of use of this manual	1	2	3	4	5
Use of language in the document	1	2	3	4	5
Use of graphics in the document	1	2	3	4	5

Please explain any low score:

Any other comments on this book:

Thank you

◀ ◀ ◀ **Any comments?**

AFFIX
STAMP
HERE

Hewlett-Packard Company
Barcelona Division
Attn: Learning Products Dept.
Avda. Graells, 501
08190 Sant Cugat del Vallès
Spain